Special Edition
USING
Lotus Notes 4

que®

Special Edition

USING
Lotus Notes 4

Written by Cate Richards

with

Mark Williams
David Hatter
David Medinets
Robert Weberg

Mick Baitinger
Frank T. Paolino, Jr.
Karl Wapst

que®

Special Edition Using Lotus Notes 4

Copyright© 1996 by Que® Corporation

Library of Congress Catalog No.: 95-72584

ISBN: 0-7897-0368-8

98 97   6 5 4 3

Interpretation of the printing code: the rightmost double-digit number is the year of the book's printing; the rightmost single-digit number, the number of the book's printing. For example, a printing code of 96-1 shows that the first printing of the book occurred in 1996.

Screen reproductions in this book were created using Collage Plus from Inner Media, Inc., Hollis, NH.

Composed in *Stone Serif* and *MCPdigital* by Que Corporation

To my parents, Ann and Bill Collins, for their continuing support and faith in me over the years. And to my son, Robert Richards, who is my inspiration in all that I do.

About the Authors

Cate Richards is a Senior Workgroup Consultant for U.S. Technologies, a Premium Lotus Business Partner, in Orlando, Florida. Her primary responsibility is to work with her clients to help automate and maintain their business systems using Lotus Notes as the platform. She also spends a great deal of her time training her clients in the use of Notes, assisting them with reengineering their business procedures, and working with them to document their policies, procedures, and systems. She has worked with Lotus Notes for over five years, and has been a beta test participant since version 2.0 of Notes. Cate holds a Masters in Business Administration degree from the Roy E. Crummer Graduate School of Business at Rollins College in Winter Park, Florida and a Bachelor of Arts degree in Marketing from the University of South Florida in Tampa, Florida. This is Cate's fourth writing endeavor on Lotus Notes books for Que.

Mark Williams is a technical writer specializing in Windows help systems. He is currently developing help systems for SAFECO Insurance Company, and has written help manuals and computer-based training for a variety of software and aerospace companies. In his "other life," Mark operates a sheep farm and weaving business with his wife and two children.

David Hatter holds a B.S. in Information Systems from Northern Kentucky University, and has been programming for more than four years. He is a senior developer for one of the largest Lotus Notes shops in the Cincinnati, Ohio area and has been very fortunate to work with several other very talented Notes developers. He occasionally dabbles in both through work and through a local community education program. He lives in Ft. Wright, Kentucky with his wife Leslee.

David Medinets has been programming since 1980, when he starting with a Radio Shack Model 1. He still fondly remembers the days when he could cross-wire the keyboard to create funny-looking characters on the display. Since those days, he has spent time debugging Emacs on UNIX machines, working on VAXen, and messing about with DOS microcomputers. David is married to Kathryn, works at Prudential Insurance in Roseland, New Jersey, and can be reached at **medined@planet.net**. He has also co-authored *Special Edition Using Turbo C++ 4.5 for Windows* (Que), *Microsoft Office Unleashed* (SAMS), and *Visual Basic Unleashed* (SAMS).

Robert L. Weberg is a Senior Systems Analyst for Continental Bank in Chicago. He develops applications and business systems in Ami Pro, Lotus 1-2-3, Paradox, and Lotus Notes. Robert resides with his wife in the Bartlett, Illinois area.

Mick Baitnger lives and works in Washington, D.C. where he is a consultant for NEXGEN Solutions, a consulting and services company and a Lotus Business Partner. As part of NEXGEN's workgroup computing division, he provides consulting services to large and small commercial clients throughout the country. His expertise is in Lotus Notes, which he has been working with for the past three years, particularly with application development and deployment. In addition to a B.S. in Electrical Engineering from Penn State University, he holds several Lotus Notes certifications. He can be reached via Notes Net at **Mick Baitinger @ NGSINC @ NOTES NET**.

Frank T. Paolino, Jr. founded the Mayflower Consulting Group in 1983, providing systems planning, design, and consulting services to a wide range of clients in the insurance, banking, retail, and manufacturing community. He and his firm have successfully designed and marketed products to the computer industry. Currently, he is developing sophisticated data integration tools for Notes designers and developers. Frank holds an MBA degree from the University of Massachusetts at Amherst and a B.S. degree in Chemistry from the University of Lowell. He is married, with three children.

Karl Wabst is a Sr. Computer Analyst with NEXGEN Solutions, Inc., based in Washington D.C. He has been administering servers and developing Lotus Notes applications for five years. Karl worked with AT&T on the implementation of Network Notes, one of the largest single site Notes installations in the world today. Prior to that, Mr. Wabst worked at Reuters Information Services Downtown District in New York City, as a Lotus Notes and Novell Network Administrator. Karl holds a B.A. in Psychology from SUNY at Stony Brook. He currently resides in St. Louis, Missouri.

Acknowledgments

Mark Williams, one of my cohorts at U.S. Technologies, deserves a big thank you for not only pitching in and writing the LotusScript chapters in this book—as well as the appendixes—but also for helping me with my daily work load. Mark was my sounding board for many ideas during the course of writing this book, and helped me greatly in gathering the files you will find on the CD-ROM included with this book. He is truly a great worker, and a true friend. Thanks also go to his wife, Vicki, who has put up with the constant disruption of Mark's life with a wonderful sense of humor.

Thanks to Master Hyun Park, my Tae Kwon Do instructor, for getting rid of the neck and back pain from sitting so long at the computer—and for making sure I stayed physically fit during the course of writing this book! Thanks also to all of my partners at Master Park's Tae Kwon Do World school in Altamonte, Florida for cheering me on and providing a great outlet for all of the stress built up while working towards the deadline (sorry if I kicked anyone too hard)!

Special thanks go to all of the guys that pitched in at the last minute and wrote chapters of this book to meet the deadline. David Hatter, Robert Weberg, Frank Paolino, David Medinets, Mick Baitinger, Karl Wapst, and again, Mark Williams all stepped in and assisted in making this book happen when we lost the original co-author of the book. Thanks also to Paul Greenberg, Henry Newberry, and Steve Osborne for all of the information they provided for the book. Without their assistance, this book would not have made it to press! Thanks also to all of the contributors of information in this book, and on the CD-ROM. Your assistance is greatly appreciated!

Heartfelt thanks go out to the folks at Lotus who have helped throughout the course of the development of this book—Kathy White and Dick Alme, for always taking the time to answer questions, provide contact information, and help facilitate the collection of material for this book. Thanks also to Jeff Blaney, who has been so responsive on getting each test build of the beta software to me as quickly as possible—and to Judith Tracy, Peter Cohen, Susan Ryan, and the rest of the folks at Lotus who have helped so much!

I would be remiss if I did not thank all of the folks at U.S. Technologies (who are too many to name individually), who are a great bunch of people to work with! They were a great source of information and inspiration during the course of writing this book. Thanks to my boss, Peter Steele, for making sure I received all of the information and software I needed to get the book done!

Thanks to all of the folks at Que who helped make this book happen—Fred, Al, Robin, Maureen, and all of the other editors who helped mold this work into a book (and helped keep me on time!). Thanks also to the tech editor, Andy Shafran, whose insight and detailed review of the information in this book is greatly appreciated! The folks at Que are the best around—even if they do require a turn around time that keeps you working all night and through the weekend! Salute!

Last, but not by any means least, my most special thanks to my family who understood when I was too busy for months to do anything but work. Mom and Dad, you are the greatest! Without you I couldn't have gotten through this! And to my wonderful son, Robert—you are a very special boy for being so understanding about Mommy having to work on "that book" all the time. Now we will have some time to play! I love you all!

We'd Like to Hear from You!

As part of our continuing effort to produce books of the highest possible quality, Que would like to hear your comments. To stay competitive, we *really* want you, as a computer book reader and user, to let us know what you like or dislike most about this book or other Que products.

You can mail comments, ideas, or suggestions for improving future editions to the address below, or send us a fax at (317) 581-4663. For the online inclined, Macmillan Computer Publishing has a forum on CompuServe (type **GO QUEBOOKS** at any prompt) through which our staff and authors are available for questions and comments. The address of our Internet site is **http://www.mcp.com** (World Wide Web).

In addition to exploring our forum, please feel free to contact me personally to discuss your opinions of this book: I'm **75230,1556** on CompuServe, and I'm **bgambrel@que.mcp.com** on the Internet.

Thanks in advance—your comments will help us to continue publishing the best books available on computer topics in today's market.

Bryan Gambrel
Product Development Specialist
Que Corporation
201 W. 103rd Street
Indianapolis, Indiana 46290
USA

Contents at a Glance

Notes Basics

Going Mobile

Designing Applications

Advanced Notes Topics

Contents

7 Working with Text   235

8 Working with Documents   269

II Designing Applications 323

9 Creating New Databases 325

10 Designing Forms 357

15 Buttons and Agents   557

16 LotusScript: A Whole New Programming Language   589

22 Notes: Under the Hood   791

V Working with the World of Notes   823

VI Achieving Success with Business Partners 891

26 U.S. Technologies   893

27 Synergistics, Inc.   911

FOREWORD

On December 6, 1989, Lotus Development Corp. began a journey. On this date, Lotus introduced Lotus Notes, a product that has drastically changed the way companies worldwide communicate, collaborate, and coordinate among themselves, with other companies, and with their customers. Based on a distributed, replicated document database, an enterprise scalable messaging infrastructure, and a robust cross-platform client/server application development environment, Notes erased the traditional boundaries to storing, managing, and distributing business information, as well as automating critical business processes.

As the product has matured, Notes has defied definition by expanding its reach from a product, to an environment that business people can work and live in. Notes is a true client/server system that not only supports all of the major operating systems and network architectures, but also masks the underlying complexities and incompatibilities among systems.

But perhaps Notes' greatest advantage is its ability to support a rich set of applications. Through support of standards such as DDE and OLE, coupled with the development of Notes Companion products such as Phone Notes, Video Notes, and, most recently, the InterNotes product line, Notes provides a repository for any type of object, from text and images, to audio and video.

A burgeoning industry has developed from Notes ability to support such a rich set of applications. To date, the Lotus Business Partner Program comprises more than 12,000 partners who offer products and services based on Notes and other Lotus technologies. Through a symbiotic relationship, Lotus provides its Partners with software information, tools, support, and marketing programs to assist them in developing and marketing their products and services; these Partners in turn provide invaluable feedback and perspective on how Lotus can continue to advance Notes. This brings us to Release 4.

With feedback from these Partners, as well as customers, Notes Release 4 has taken an immense leap forward. With more than 3.3 million customers and more than 7,000 companies, Notes has become for companies the central access point to find and share information, whether it's located in e-mail, relational databases and host-based systems, or in any desktop application or the World Wide Web. As you will read in more detail in the pages to follow, we categorize the most exciting Notes R4 enhancements in six main areas, though the full list of enhancements is in the hundreds:

- **Integrated Client/Server Messaging**—Notes Release 4.0 includes world-class, robust client/server e-mail and messaging, including a greatly enhanced user interface based on the award-winning cc:Mail UI.
- **Ease of Use**—In addition to user interface enhancements, Notes Release 4.0 adds intuitive new tools, such as intelligent agents, to make it easier for users to store and navigate information.

- **Mobility**—Mobile users have always benefited from Notes' unique replication capabilities. Notes Release 4.0 adds additional usability enhancements and tools to greater exploit and manage information remotely.

- **Application Development and Programmability**—Notes Release 4.0 includes LotusScript 3.0, a cross-platform, BASIC compatible, object oriented programming language, in addition to advanced Notes programming tools.

- **Enterprise Management**—For administrators, Notes Release 4.0 offers enhanced administration and management, increased server performance, and greater scalability for more efficient management of mission-critical, enterprise-wide Notes applications.

- **Internet Integration**—New features in Notes Release 4.0, such as the InterNotes Web Navigator and the bundling of the InterNotes Web Publisher, give users access to the Internet and allows them to integrate Internet resources into their Notes environment. Also, by mid-year 1996, the Release 4 server will include native support for HTTP, HTML, and Java, providing customers with full Web server functionality within a Notes server.

All of this combines, we believe, to make Notes Release 4 the premier groupware platform in the industry. With Notes Release 4, Lotus presents a tightly integrated, fully interactive, secure groupware platform with more than six years and four major releases behind it. Once again, the bar is raised.

So welcome to Notes Release 4, the most significant milestone in the Notes journey to date, but far from the final destination.

Regards,
Steve Sayre
Vice President of Lotus Notes Marketing
Lotus Development Corp.

Introduction

In our daily work, many of us have been caught up in the eternal—and often infernal—chase of paper around the organizations in which we work and communicate. Coworkers send flyers reminding everyone of the company picnic. The Human Resource department modifies several policies in the HR manual and then reprints and ships the 3"-thick manual to all employees. You must order supplies, so you fill out a purchase request and forward it to your manager to approve, who forwards it to Accounting to approve, who forwards it to Purchasing to order, who then forwards the form back to you to let you know it has been ordered. Does any of this seem familiar? It is this chase after paper that companies have struggled with that has created the perfect environment for Lotus Notes to take hold, and quickly become the market leader in groupware technology.

Groupware is software designed to be used by groups of people sharing information and working together. It lets a group of people use the same information—but oftentimes in different ways depending on their particular needs. Lotus Notes lets you perform many of the common activities you currently partake in during the workday: exchanging mail, sharing ideas, accessing information, and planning for the future. Notes endeavors to literally replace paper documents with electronic documents, but with a twist. You can create sophisticated workflow applications that automate—and often streamline—your business processes. Notes does not simply create a copy of a paper form; it "moves" it through the business process through the use of electronic signatures, status conditions, and other indicators. Notes lets you automate your workflow, recreating the path your document takes, often times improving it as unnecessary steps are made more visible for inspection or elimination.

What Is Lotus Notes?

If you ask anyone who works with Lotus Notes to define what it is, you are most likely going to get a different answer from each person you talk to. Lotus Development Corporation representatives themselves often struggle with defining Notes—because it can mean different things to each organization that uses it. Some refer to Lotus Notes as a *document database*—but don't let that simple definition fool you. Notes is more than a receptacle for storing documents, like many of the more traditional types of databases.

It's perhaps better to think of Notes as a way of organizing documents and making them available to groups of people. However, the word *document* can often be misleading, as many think only of text when they think of documents. With the rich text field capability of Lotus Notes, a document can contain just about any electronic object, which is why many refer to Lotus Notes as a *storage container*. You can embed or import graphics into documents, incorporate spreadsheets, insert video files that can be viewed straight from the document, insert voice messages that can be played with the click of a button, and attach any file in any format to a document for distribution to others.

With Notes' open, nonproprietary format, it can also serve as the "glue" that helps your other applications talk to each other. You can use Notes to gather and workflow information around your organization as a front-end, user-friendly GUI (graphical user interface), and then schedule the information to download into your more traditional legacy mainframe applications. You can also develop sophisticated applications in languages like Visual Basic and C, and then pass the information collected in those applications to Notes to be stored or workflowed around an organization. With Notes' new ability to work with information on the Internet through the InterNotes family of products and the built-in Web browser, Notes now combines the rich text and security capabilities of its package with the vast frontier of information on the Internet—providing you with the best of both worlds.

Benefits of Notes

Notes' unique database structure lets you keep track of complex, relatively unstructured information (which is how you typically receive most information) and makes that information available to groups of users on a network—whether they are connected directly to the network, or are dialing in from remote locations. Notes helps eliminate much of the redundant paperwork and steps in your business processes by moving the flow of documents from paper format—where typically one person reviews the information at a time—to an electronically organized workflow in which many can review, approve, and communicate the information with the click of a button. In a world where companies must cut costs while increasing the speed in which people must communicate with each other to maintain a competitive presence, Lotus Notes can provide the companies using it a definite edge.

Who Should Use This Book?

This book is written for the "power user" of Lotus Notes—someone who wants to use Notes for more than accessing e-mail and a few databases that have already been designed. It is also a great resource for existing Notes users who need to get up and running on a much-enhanced, but significantly different version of Lotus Notes. The user will, of course, receive guidance in all of the activities to get started using Notes R4—sending e-mail, composing documents, changing the way you view information, and so on—so the new user for Lotus Notes will benefit from this book too!

Readers of this book will also gain insight into many of the ways Notes is applied in organizations by reading the chapters in Part VI, "Achieving Success with Business Partners," which exposes three of Lotus' successful Business Partners and how they apply Notes in their own organization, as well as how they work to satisfy their clients' needs. These chapters provide you with a lot of ideas in how to apply Notes (and its companion products) in your own organizations—or if you are also a Notes Consultant, perhaps provide a few tips for successfully meeting your client needs.

This book is also for the reader who wants to learn more about the products and services offered by Lotus Development Corporation, and other third-party vendors, to enhance his or her use of Notes. You will read about Lotus' companion products, support programs, Business Partner programs, and education and certification programs. You will also get a peek into just a few of the thousands of applications and adjunct products that are available on the market to run with Notes.

The CD-ROM that accompanies this book contains applications, demos, screencams, and white papers (research studies) provided by Lotus Development and many of the third-party vendors to give you a feeling for many of the products and services available in the market, as well as to give you ideas on how you might want to use Notes in your organization. Also available on the CD-ROM is the WorldCom Setup and Help databases; so if you decide you want to access any of the services you read about from WorldCom, you have the applications that will help speed up the process.

Finally, for those of you who would like to view this book on your computer, rather than always from the printed version, you can access the entire book in Adobe Acrobat file format on the CD-ROM. There is an added bonus on the CD-ROM as well—all of the new LotusScript 3 Notes classes are also available to you in a single document. So if you don't want to have to open each individual help document describing a Notes class you need to use while programming in Notes R4's new programming language, you can access the Notes Classes file.

How To Use This Book

This book is divided into six parts. The earlier parts are intended for a general audience, and the later parts depend on an understanding of the previous parts. You will also find a wealth of information in the appendixes and on the CD-ROM to help you further understand Notes. Even if you are an "old hat" to Notes, check out the beginning chapters to review many of the changes incorporated in Notes R4.

Part I—Notes Basics

Part I discusses the basic nature of Lotus Notes, and presents an overview of its capabilities. In this part of the book, you find out what has changed between Lotus Notes R3.x and Lotus Notes R4. This is light reading, but recommended for all readers, both new users and veterans of Lotus Notes.

In Chapter 1, "Getting Started with Lotus Notes," you are introduced to the concepts of working with groupware, understanding the Notes interface, and starting and exiting Lotus Notes. This chapter also highlights many of the new features available with Notes R4.

In Chapter 2, "Customizing Notes," you learn how to personalize your Notes setup, create custom SmartIcons, and work with your DESKTOP.DSK file.

Chapter 3, "Using Databases," provides the foundation for working with any database. You learn about the basic components of a Notes database and how to use them.

Chapter 4, "Getting Started with Electronic Mail," walks you through working with Lotus Notes' e-mail package.

To gain insight into how the Name & Address Book acts as the heart of the Lotus Notes system, read Chapter 5, "Using the Address Books." It provides instructions for using the Name & Address Book when addressing e-mail, as well as creating group lists, person documents, and other functions available to you in working with the Name & Address Book.

Chapter 6, "Advanced Mail," continues the discussion of working with e-mail, covering such advanced topics as working with attachments, forwarding documents via mail, and many other tips for getting the most out of mail.

Chapter 7, "Working with Text," walks you through all of the commands and features available to enhance text in your documents. You learn how to change font attributes, control margin settings, use the Clipboard, and work with bullets and numbering.

In Chapter 8, "Working with Documents," you explore features available in Notes that add pizzazz to your documents. You learn how to create tables, hotspots, collapsible sections, links, and more. You also learn how to use the Lotus Notes spell checking feature.

Part II—Designing Applications

In Part II, you learn the basic building blocks used in creating or redesigning a Notes database application. This part of the book also explores design, @function, and LotusScript terminology. If you are already an experienced Lotus Notes programmer, you may still want to skim through these sections as so much has changed from Lotus Notes R3.x to Lotus Notes R4.

In Chapter 9, "Creating New Databases," you are introduced to the basic building blocks of application design, including learning how to create applications from templates, work with the design menus, and develop graphical navigators.

To take a deeper look into developing database forms, see Chapter 10, "Designing Forms." In this chapter, you learn how to create a form from scratch. This chapter provides a basic understanding of form design—as well as some tips on using some of the more advanced features available to you when creating forms.

Chapter 11, "Designing Views," delves further into application design by looking at how you design the views that report information. This chapter walks you through creating a view from scratch. You will learn the basics of view design and many of the advanced features as well.

Chapter 12, "Integrating Notes 4.0 with Other Applications," provides the basics for working with OLE2, FX (field exchange), and other methods that let you incorporate information from other applications into Notes databases.

Chapters 13 and 14, "Working with Formulas" and "Formula Functions," provide you with a foundation for using Lotus Notes formula function programming. These chapters supplement the chapters on creating databases, forms, views, and other programmable objects by providing you the rules and explanations for writing formulas using Notes' functions.

Chapter 15, "Buttons and Agents," looks at designing and incorporating buttons and agents into your Notes application to enhance the design and user-friendliness of the application and to perform routine "housekeeping" features within an application.

Finally, Chapters 16 and 17, "LotusScript: A Whole New Programming Language" and "Writing Scripts with LotusScript," delve into the basics of working with Lotus Notes' new programming language.

Part III—Going Mobile

In Part III, you will learn how to work with Notes remotely—not connected to a network. Remote users must set up their systems to prepare for working disconnected from the server, and then initiate communication with the server each time they are ready to send and received information. This section provides users with the instructions to prepare and work off of the network with Notes. Even if you are not a Notes user, you may benefit from scanning these chapters as you may be communicating with remote users—and would therefore benefit from seeing Notes from their point of view.

In Chapter 18, "Setting Up To Go Remote," you learn what you will need to work with Notes away from a network. You also learn how to set up Notes to go on the road.

Chapter 19, "Working Remote," walks you through the process of working remote, which is calling the servers and replicating (exchanging) information with the servers. You will also learn tips on keeping the size of your remote databases manageable.

Part IV—Advanced Notes Topics

As you and your business become more experienced with Lotus Notes, you will undoubtedly want to really take advantage of the special features of the program. This part of the book delves further into these more advanced topics of Lotus Notes.

Chapter 20, "Security and Encryption," takes a look at the security features in Notes. Understanding your Notes ID and certificates, managing database access control, and working with encryption are just a few of the important topics in this chapter.

Chapter 21, "Taking Advantage of Notes Release 4 Features," introduces you to some more advanced application design techniques discussed in previous chapters, and takes a peek at the new Web browser included with Notes R4.

Chapter 22, "Notes: Under the Hood," explains the behind-the-scenes happenings of Lotus Notes from a high level. You gain an understanding into the role servers play, the platforms they work on, the new centralized Notes Administration interface, and other features that Notes uses to keep the people on your system communicating. This chapter is geared toward the user who needs to understand what is going on in the background so that applications are developed correctly, or to answer some of the "why is this happening?" questions that frequently occur when users work with Notes.

Part V—Working with the World of Notes

Part V takes a different look at Lotus Notes by looking at what is going on outside of your organization in regard to Notes, and provides you with information on the various services available to you and your organization from Lotus Development Corporation.

Chapter 23, "Extending Your Enterprise," looks at how you can use Notes to communicate with organizations outside of your own network, and the benefits that can be gained by doing so. You read about two of the network providers, AT&T Network Notes and WorldCom, that provide networking services that assist you in communicating your applications outside of your organization. You also read about many of the applications running on these networks already.

Chapter 24, "Inside Lotus Development Corporation," looks at the support services, education and certification, and Business Partner programs offered by Lotus Development Corporation.

Chapter 25, "Add-On and Third-Party Products," provides you with detailed descriptions of Lotus' companion products (products that work with Notes to enhance its functionality). Also in this chapter is information about a few of the many third-party applications that have been built to run with Lotus Notes.

Part VI—Achieving Success with Business Partners

When you work with Notes, you often need the assistance of a third-party consultant. Lotus Development Corporation hosts a network of consultant companies called Business Partners that is available to assist you with application development, training, system installation and administration, and any other need that you may have in successfully implementing Lotus Notes. This section highlights three of the Business Partners—U.S. Technologies (Chapter 26), Synergistics, Inc. (Chapter 27), and NEXGEN Solutions (Chapter 28).

In these chapters, you learn not only about the services companies like these can provide you, but you also get a glimpse into how they do business. Included are many of the Notes applications and companion products they use in-house to meet their own needs. You will walk away from these chapters with many ideas that you can use in your organization to further your success in using Notes.

Appendixes

You will also find a wealth of information in the appendixes and on the enclosed CD-ROM to further facilitate your understanding of Lotus Notes. The appendixes provides additional reference information that supports many of the chapters in this book.

Appendix A, "SmartIcons," provides you with a listing of all of the SmartIcons and their descriptions for quick reference.

Appendix B, "Database Templates," gives a brief description of the templates shipping with Lotus Notes R4. Use this appendix to quickly get an idea of what is available for your use.

Appendix C, "Command Reference," provides a detailed list of the Notes R4 menu commands—and their corresponding hot keys. Use this as a quick reference for finding those elusive commands while learning your way around Notes.

Appendix D, "Special Characters," details the list of special characters available when working with Notes. Use this table as a quick reference when working with special characters (like the registered trademark).

Appendix E, "Migrating from Notes Release 3 to Release 4," is a collection of tips and ideas to help the project manager put together a migration project plan. While creating a migration plan is typically unique to each company implementing Notes R4, this appendix provides you with a list of possible questions to consider before implementation.

Appendix F, "Remote Troubleshooting," provides a list of problems and solutions for many of the most common problems experienced when working remote. Use this appendix in conjunction with the Mobile Survival Kit and Smartform Modem Doctor databases located on the CD-ROM to help resolve remote troubles.

Appendix G, "Using the CD-ROM," provides you with a brief insight into the contents of the enclosed CD, and provides you with the instructions on how to access the information.

The CD-ROM provides screencams of add-on and third-party products, application demos, sample Notes databases, and additional technical and reference information. Also included is an electronic version of this book for your use. Refer to the detailed index at the back of this book to facilitate your location of information.

Conventions Used in This Book

Que has over a decade of experience writing and developing the most successful computer books available. With that experience, we've learned what special features help readers the most. Look for these special features throughout the book to enhance your learning experience.

Several type and font conventions are used in this book to help make reading it easier:

- *Italic type* is used to emphasize the author's points or to introduce new terms.
- Screen messages, code listings, and command samples appear in `monospace typeface`.
- Anything you are asked to type appears in **boldface**.

Tip

Tips present short advice on a quick or often overlooked procedure. These include shortcuts that can save you time.

Note

A note provides additional information that may help you avoid problems, or offers advice that relates to the topic.

Caution

Cautions warn you about potential problems that a procedure may cause, unexpected results, and mistakes to avoid.

    ▶▶ See these cross-references for more information on a particular topic.

Sidebar

Longer discussions not integral to the flow of the chapter are set aside as sidebars. Look for these sidebars to find out even more information.

Troubleshooting

What is a troubleshooting section?

Troubleshooting sections anticipate common problems in the form of a question. The response provides you with practical suggestions for solving these problems.

Part I

Notes Basics

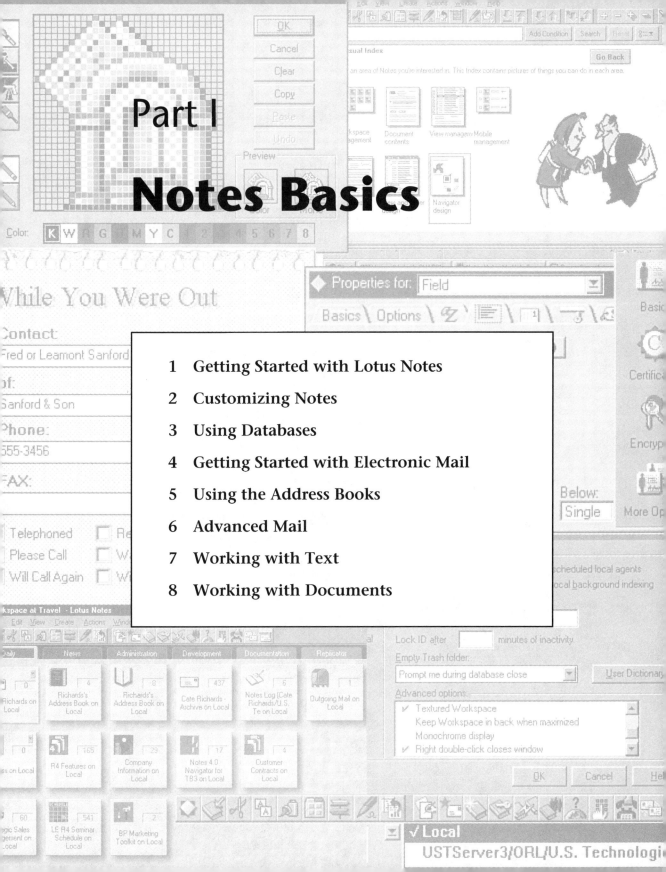

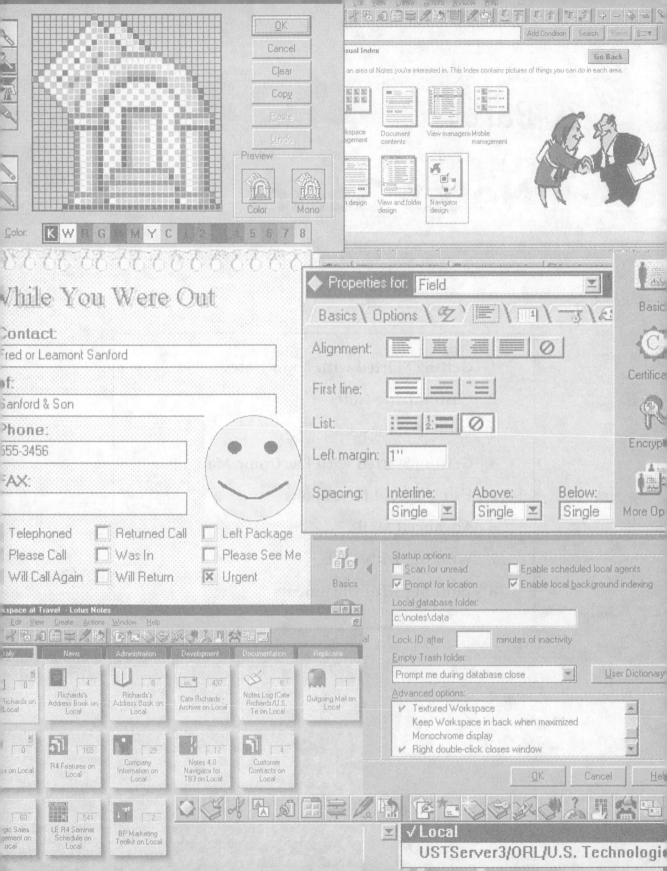

CHAPTER 1

Getting Started with Lotus Notes

In this chapter, you learn about the important concepts that form a foundation for everything you do with Notes. You will come to understand the basics of how Notes works and get started on working with Notes. This chapter covers the following topics:

- Understanding Notes capabilities
- New features in Release 4
- Getting started
- Understanding the Notes workspace
- Adding and opening databases
- Working with views, panes, and folders
- Creating and editing documents
- Exiting and saving documents
- Getting help

Welcome to Lotus Notes R4

Often, the most difficult part of working with Lotus Notes is trying to explain just what it is! The new user may simply think of Lotus Notes as electronic mail (e-mail)— because that is often where you begin your introduction to Notes. Others may call it a database software package, a workflow product, a document library, groupware, communication software, and so on. In truth, Notes is all of these things, and more. If you are looking for a single sentence that can best define Lotus Notes, consider the following quote taken from the Notes Beta Program Introduction Letter in describing the reason for the changes found in Notes R4:

> "Among other things, this release substantially advances the definition of Notes as an integrated messaging system and rapid groupware application development environment."

It is true, Notes can be used simply as an e-mail package that allows you to send e-mail to other Notes users on your network. Or, with the inclusion of some special software and gateways that can be installed by your Notes Administrator, your e-mail capabilities can be extended to let you send and receive faxes, communicate with Notes users outside of your network, and even send mail over the Internet to non-Notes users. In essence, if your network is set up to use the adjunct products available with Notes, it becomes the user-friendly, single source of access to multiple e-mail and other communication services.

Businesses benefit greatly not only from Notes' powerful e-mail capability, but from the ability to redefine and automate their business processes. For example, businesses using Notes have successfully automated either the hiring process in their companies or the purchase approval process—to include signature authorizations at each phase. Some companies run their entire business communications on Notes, often using Notes as a front-end data gathering tool for information that will eventually end up stored on a mainframe. Likewise, many companies build reporting applications in Notes that import data from mainframe computers to report across a wide range of users in a corporation.

There are not many business applications that cannot find a home in Notes 4. Many applications are simple, easy-to-develop databases that allow you to better communicate with a group of users, while other applications may be sophisticated business process "programs" developed with a combination of Lotus Notes and other programming languages and software tools. These applications can be designed by someone in your organization, or by outside consultants. As you use this book, you will learn a great deal about the tools, consultants, applications, and methods for successfully working with Notes 4. Throughout this book, you will find many examples of companies using Lotus Notes—along with descriptions of the applications they have built. Hopefully, these examples will further aid your understanding of how Notes can benefit you in your business.

Note

While this book focuses on what Lotus Notes is, it would be prudent to briefly discuss what it isn't. Lotus Notes is not a relational database system, in which changes made to one record will automatically update all instances of that entry throughout the system.

For example, in the banking industry, an application may exist that tracks all of the information about a banking customer for each account held at the bank. If the customer changes his or her phone number, a relational system would update that change throughout every record in the system related to that customer. In Lotus Notes, if the phone number changed in a customer record, an agent would have to be created to update all instances of that phone number in subsequent documents related to that client—or the records would have to be individually edited to make the change. Careful layout of the design of a database can overcome some of these limitations, but keeping this limitation in mind is warranted when deciding upon which system you need to resolve your business problems.

> Lotus Notes is also not meant to be a high volume transactional based system where thousands of documents are accessed and created each day. While Notes can handle high-volume tasks with some careful planning and development, the responsiveness and capacity of the system may suffer. Consider the transaction volume level when selecting what type of system will best meet your business needs.

What's New in Notes R4?

For those of you who have worked with Lotus Notes in the past, you will find changes that will further enhance your use of Notes. These changes have been brought about by the wealth of information provided by end users, Business Partners, and Lotus support desk information collected over the past few years.

In January of 1995, Lotus Development Corporation hosted the second Lotusphere—a week-long convention held annually in Orlando, Florida. This sold-out convention was used to launch the first sneak peek into what was being planned for Notes R4. The response by the attendees at the demonstration was overwhelming—often erupting into cheers and applause for the new features being demonstrated. The initial response of many users to using Notes R4 has been equally promising.

With so much acclaim, it is helpful to briefly describe some of the major changes and features that have been made in Notes R4. You will quickly see that the list is long. Hopefully, you will find some features that were on your wish list as well!

Install/User Setup Profile. Lotus Notes R4 provides users the capability of defining multiple Location documents that let them define user Location profiles which include the user's home server, passthru server and its phone number, additional dial-in servers and their phone numbers, and Location name. These Location documents are used to indicate how Notes will work with the network and e-mail.

 ▶▶ See "Setting Up Locations," p. 658

Workstation/Setup. Lotus Notes R4 provides many new features that let users work smarter from their Workstation. Notes 4 makes it easier for users to configure and work with their Notes environment by putting more of the configuration options settings at your fingertips. You can easily customize your environment without being an advanced Notes user or programmer. Just a few of the features added in Notes R4 for workstations enable you to do the following:

- Change your Notes Preferences for User, Ports, Mail, and International settings in one dialog box.
- Create locations so you can store different communication settings for each place you work with Notes—for example, your home or a hotel room.
- Start the Agent Manager so you can run agents in the background. (*Agents* is the new term for macros in Notes R4.)

- Add extra tabs to the workspace.
- Start background indexing so you can create full text indexes in the background.
- A toggle switch to keep all Notes windows within the main Notes window, or to display each Notes window individually, without reference to the size or location of the main Notes window.
- Keep the main Notes workspace behind other windows you open automatically while you work.
- Mark documents as being "read" without opening them, when you read them in the preview pane. When you mark a document as having read it, you remove the unread document marker that appears in the view next to the new document.
- Check spelling in more languages with additional dictionaries.
- Tell Notes to ask you whether to save mail that you send.
- Tell Notes to notify you when you have new mail.
- Reorder ports so that Notes uses selected ports first when you try to make a connection.
- Trace a network connection so that you can find out if, and where, a network problem is occurring.
- Compact your workspace file.

Document Features. Notes R4 provides many new features that make working with documents easier, and more robust. Like all of the other new features discussed in this chapter, Lotus has added many that affect how you work with documents—reading, creating, and editing them. This section provides you with a glimpse into just a few of the new features available to you when working with documents. With Lotus Notes R4, you can do the following:

- Read or edit a document in the preview pane without opening the full document window.
- Save multiple versions of a document with different names.
- Switch to edit mode by double-clicking the left mouse button anywhere within the document.
- Create links to views and databases as well as to other documents.
- Create hotspots from text and/or pictures that display pop-up text, link to a document, view a database, or run a formula, action, or script.
- Use the permanent pen to add comments to existing text in a different style.
- Add bullets to paragraphs automatically.
- Create numbered lists automatically.
- Collapse one or more paragraphs into a single line of text, called a *section*, that readers can expand when they want to read its contents.

- Assign named paragraphs styles to a key and cycle through them by pressing the key when you format paragraphs.

- Include a selected font in a named paragraph style.

- Use an enhanced ruler to format paragraphs.

- Select from an expanded color palette of 240 colors for such design features as form backgrounds, navigators fill, and so forth.

- Format one or more columns or rows in a table by selecting them individually.

- Specify zero as the minimum spacing in tables between columns and rows.

- Hide the horizontal scroll bar so you can see more of a document.

- Display hidden characters such as tabs and carriage returns.

Application Design. Notes R4 also provides more functionality for designing Notes applications. With the incorporation of a new scripting language and the use of such features as graphical navigators, the new features in Notes R4 let you take Notes database design much further than prior releases of Notes. Notes R4 provides you with the capability of creating very sophisticated applications. You can also do the following:

- Control when the About Database document is displayed.

- Launch an attachment or link in the About Database document the first time your database opens.

- Display a default navigator when your database opens.

- Access other databases using the ODBC database driver.

- Provide actions that simplify editing or workflow tasks and display them in a button bar and menu.

- Tie actions to OLE objects to move information between applications.

- Generate keyword, reader, and author lists from Address Books, the Access Control List, and views without writing formulas.

- Create reusable groups of fields (called *subforms*).

- Merge replication conflicts in one document.

- Test forms that contain objects or actions.

- Create forms that allow authors to be anonymous.

- Create forms that inherit the contents of a linked or parent document.

- Always open documents in edit mode.

- Add a collapsed section to a form (and control access to it).

- Hide or display text or buttons on a form using a formula

- Place objects at a fixed location by creating a layout region.

- Use LotusScript, Lotus' object-oriented scripting language, to write advanced programs associated with forms/fields.

- Create view selections and column views without writing formulas.

■ Provide actions that simplify document or workflow tasks and display them in a button bar and menu.

■ Give users an icon to click to display keywords.

■ Create graphical navigators with hotspots to help new users find information.

■ Show hundreds of new icons in columns.

■ Design a view that jumps to the top or the bottom row when it is opened.

■ Create multiple-line or double-spaced rows.

■ Show views without margins or column headers.

■ Use @AllChildren and @AllDescendants to write view selection formulas that select a set of documents and their responses (instead of all responses).

■ Use LotusScript to write advanced programs associated with view actions and agents.

Agent (Macro) Features. Notes R4 uses agents to automatically perform sequences of tasks for you. In Notes R3, these agents were referred to as macros. Notes R4 lets you perform a much wider range of tasks with agents, as you will see described here. The following list provides you with just a sampling of the new capabilities of Notes R4 agents. With agents, you can do the following:

■ Create an agent without writing a formula.

■ Create more than one mail-activated or paste-activated agent for a database.

■ Create agents that maintain the Access Control List.

■ Use an Agent Builder to manage agents.

■ Test agents.

■ Log an agent's progress.

Mobile Features. As you will learn in Chapter 18, "Setting Up To Work Remote," and Chapter 19, "Working Remote," you can use Lotus Notes when you are not connected to a network, and then have Notes exchange information in the databases you have stored on your hard drive, with copies of those databases on the server. Notes R4 makes working remote much easier than previous versions of Notes and provides many new advanced features as well. With the new features available for remote Notes, you can do the following:

■ Use the Replicator to call servers and replicate databases more easily.

■ Choose a mobile location from the status bar to use the communication settings that apply to where you're working.

■ Call a passthru server and access multiple servers through a single phone connection.

■ Display replicas of a database as a single stacked icon.

■ Replicate selected folders and views without having to write a formula.

- Change the modem file directory and use consolidated modem files.
- Use Help Lite to get help while you travel and save disk space.

Printing. If you are connected to a printer, you can check out some of the new features Notes R4 has to offer for printing Notes documents and views. As you will see, Notes has included features that let you print attachments while reading them from the new Universal Viewer. Notes has also improved your ability to print graphics and supply other information that is included when Notes prints information from the database. With the new printing features of Notes R4, you can do the following:

- Specify a printer from the File Print dialog box.
- Print file attachments when reading the attachment with a viewer.
- Automatically scale graphics fully for printing.
- Specify multiple-line headers and footers.
- Print a list of documents in a folder.

Information Sharing. If you want to share information, you can use Notes R4 to do the following:

- Use enhanced OLE 2.0 features, such as in-place editing and drag-and-drop (available for Windows 3.1, 3.11, Windows for Workgroups 3.11, and Windows 95—and to OS/2 and UNIX to a lessor extent).
- Include an object's text in a full text index.
- Use the Attachment Viewer (which is built into Notes R4) to view an attached file directly in Notes—even if you don't own the application in which the file was created.

Notes Administration. Notes R4 also provides Notes administrators new tools to help manage the Notes environment. Notes administrators will find the new QuickAdmin feature, centralized administration panel, and other enhancements make their management of the Notes network much easier. The major new features provide administrators more control over their Notes environment and enable them to do the following:

- Use a centralized Server administration interface called QuickAdmin.
- Run QuickAdmin on a Notes workstation, or run as a standalone non-modal administration program on the server or a workstation by entering a command.
- Use new server commands, such as SHOWSESSIONS, on the server console.
- Run new server programs, such as the Admin Proxy Agent.
- Use new and updated NOTES.INI variables, such as UPDATERS.
- Update the NOTES.INI file while the server is running (Server Configuration document in the Public Name & Address Book).
- Rename, re-certify, and delete user and servers from a central location.
- Easily change user and server IDs from non-hierarchical to hierarchical.

- Upgrade Desktop and Express licenses to Notes client licenses.

- Support multiple licenses types on Notes servers.

- Support multiple Notes servers on one system.

- Provide password filtering, multiple passwords, and admin prompting, which supports SmartCards and AT&T Common Login.

- Connect servers running different protocols via a third server, called a *passthru server*, that runs both protocols.

- Trace the network connections among servers for mail, replication, and passthru.

- Allow workstations and servers running different network protocols to send mail and to connect, access, and replicate Notes databases via a passthru server.

- Enable single copy object store for mail to store single copies of mail messages on a server in a central database where all recipients share them.

- Determine the fastest way to send mail between servers using mail trace.

- Use mail trace to locate and debug mail routing problems.

- Use only two databases to monitor statistics and events on servers.

- Generate analysis reports to help you analyze reported statistics on servers.

- Use wildcards with the SHOW STATS command to display a subset of statistics on servers.

Name and Address Book Template. The Name & Address Books in Notes R4 have changed substantially. Even if you have previously worked in other versions of Notes, you will want to make sure you review the new features in this section, as well as read more about these features in Chapter 5, "Using the Address Books," and Chapter 18, "Setting Up To Go Remote." The highlights added to the Name & Address Books—the heart of the Notes system—enable you to do the following:

- Provide two templates for the Name & Address Books—one for the Server copy of the Name & Address Book, and a second for your personal Name & Address Book.

- Assign new Admin roles (create, modify, delete) to handle Users, Groups, Servers, and Networks.

- Allow admin roles to provide horizontal (multiple domains) or vertical (single domains) administration.

- Provides a cleanup agent (Admin Agent) that reconciles all the Public Name & Address Book documents and access control lists (ACLs) after a user or server is renamed, recertified, or deleted.

Database Management/Replication. Notes R4 provides many new features that help you manage and replicate your Notes databases. These features provide further reporting capabilities for Notes databases, limit the size a database can grow to, and further assist you in managing applications across your organization—as well as those you may use just for yourself! With the new features available to you for managing your databases and database replication schedules, you can do the following:

- Run a database analysis on a database and its replicas to collect information from a variety of sources and post it in one centralized database designed to track information on servers and workstations.

- Limit the size a database can attain and send a warning when a database approaches its size limit on servers and workstations.

- Use multiple replicators concurrently on a server.

- Specify replication type(s) in the NOTES.INI file for server and workstation.

- Provide enhanced replication history in the log file for server and workstation.

- Provide additional replication settings for databases on servers or local workstations.

Network Features—Network Port Configuration. Notes R4 makes it easier for you to manage your port configuration. You can see at a glance what your port settings are, reorder the port listings with the click of the mouse, and further enhance your port setups with the new features added in Notes R4. You can do the following with the major new enhancements made to assist in configuring your ports to connect to the network:

- Access port configuration through the Notes Preferences dialog box.

- Reorder ports in the port selection list.

- Get additional setup options on ports specific to the port type.

- Get information on trace connections for each active port.

- See at a glance whether or not a port is installed.

Network Protocol Support. Notes R4 supports additional network protocols than were available in previous versions. Notes is built to run on most of the major platforms available in the industry today. As new releases of these platforms become available, Notes is updated to support them. With the new network protocols supported by Notes R4, you can do the following:

- Run Notes on AppleTalk on the Windows NT platform.

- Run Notes on Banyan VINES on the Windows NT platform.

- Run Notes on Banyan VINES and the Windows 95 platform.

- Run Notes on SPX and the Windows 3.x, NT, and 95 platforms.

- Run Notes on FTP TCP on OS/2 platform.

Living and Working in a Notes Culture

As mentioned previously, some companies use Lotus Notes to run all of their business communications, while others use it to automate specific tasks or processes in their organization. Some companies simply use the e-mail capabilities, and perhaps a few discussion databases. Regardless of the way a company uses Notes—at least initially—Notes is *change management*. In other words, it changes the way users communicate and work within an organization. Individuals at lower levels of a company may now have rapid access to information never before available, as well as the ability to funnel communication directly to management when necessary.

End users have more control over the look and feel of the databases they are using. Notes R4 provides users the capability of easily displaying information in a format that makes sense to them—rather than being "stuck" with the format developed by a programmer who does not use the information.

Applications are typically built and modified much faster than in traditional database packages, making it easier for organizations to match their communication structures to the ever-changing business processes caused by the pressures of the industries they are operating in. The ease and speed with which applications can be built—often referred to as Rapid Application Development, or RAD, in the industry—and altered lends itself toward reduced development costs.

Fewer programmers are required for application development in Notes, which often leads to radical changes in the way information systems departments are organized and staffed. Because Lotus Notes is built to run on a wide variety of platforms within a company, information systems departments are finding it easier to network various departments and locations with one communications package—where before this task was tedious, if not impossible. With the easy remote capabilities of Lotus Notes, many companies have moved more and more towards creating *virtual offices*—where the employee works from home.

Recent trends show that companies are building more and more applications that link them with their clients and vendors, making Notes a means of commerce and revenue generation to their businesses.

▶▶ See "Why Extend Your Enterprise?," p. 825

In short, Notes changes the way a company communicates. Managing this communication, and the applications that support it, provides a significant challenge. In this book, you will not only learn how to use Notes and begin developing applications, but you will also gain insight into managing your own communications needs.

Getting Started

Lotus Notes R4 will run with Windows, OS/2, and Macintosh. Notes runs best if used with the following hardware and software setup. Use the recommended equipment, if possible, rather than minimum requirements to improve the performance and minimize maintenance requirements.

> **Note**
>
> Lotus Notes is also designed to run under UNIX. However, the documentation for using the UNIX version of Notes was not available at the time this book was written. The instructions in this book will also apply to the UNIX version of Lotus Notes, but you will have to contact your Notes Administrator for any special requirements for installation.

Windows

Running Lotus Notes with Windows works best if you have at least the following configurations:

- A PC with an Intel 80486 or Pentium processor
- 6 MB of RAM for Windows 3.1 or 3.11 and Windows for Workgroups 3.11
- 12 MB of RAM for Win 95
- 14 MB of total RAM (for example, 8 MB of RAM and 6 MB of virtual memory)
- 120 MB hard-disk capacity minimum (though 200 MB is recommended to ensure that appropriate disk space is available for all versions of Windows, Notes, DOS, and all of the Notes databases you will be using)
- A Microsoft Windows supported display (i.e., EGA, VGA, mono VGA, SVGA, IBM 8414A, CGA, or Hercules)
- A mouse
- A printer
- Modem, X.PC protocol (supplied with Lotus Notes), and X.25 if you plan to work remote

> **Note**
>
> Lotus Notes is designed to run under Windows 3.1, 3.11, Windows for Workgroups 3.11, and Windows 95. You will also need MS-DOS or PC-DOS version 3.331 or later for Windows 3.1, 3.11, or Windows for Workgroups 3.11.

OS/2

Running Lotus Notes with OS/2 works best if you have at least the following configurations:

- A PC with Intel 80386, 80486, or Pentium processor (80486 or higher is recommended)
- 8 MB of RAM minimum (12 MB recommended)
- 120 MB of hard-disk capacity minimum (300 MB or larger recommended)
- A display supported by OS/2 3.0, OS/2 2.x, or Warp (i.e., EGA, VGA, XGA, IBM 8514)

- A mouse
- Any printer supported by OS/2 3.0 or OS/2 2.x
- OS/2 Version 3.0, Version 2.x, or Warp
- Modem, X.PC protocol (supplied with Lotus Notes), and X.25 if you plan to work remote

Macintosh

Running Lotus Notes with Macintosh works best if you have at least the following configurations:

- A Macintosh II-based, Performa, Macintosh Quadra, or PowerBook (except Model 100) model supporting a 68030 (or higher) processor.
- 12 MB RAM (8 MB reserved for Notes and 2.5 MB–3 MB available system memory)
- A high-capacity hard disk with 40 MB or more virtual memory available
- A Macintosh-compatible display adapter and monitor
- A mouse
- Apple-compatible printer
- System 7.0 (or higher)
- Apple Shared Library Manager
- Modem, X.PC protocol (supplied with Lotus Notes), and X.25 if you plan to work remote

The Windows, OS/2, and Macintosh versions of Lotus Notes work almost identically. When reading the instructions in this book, you don't need to worry about which version you have unless specifically instructed.

Note

You may want to check with your Notes administrator if you are unsure of your PC setup, and to make sure your Notes Network does not require any other special setups.

Starting Notes

 To start Notes, locate the Lotus Notes icon on your Windows or OS/2 desktop. The placement of this icon depends on how your company installed Notes on your PC.

The person who installs Notes on your desktop can determine where the icon appears on your desktop. You may have a group, or menu option, called Lotus Notes that includes the Lotus Notes program. You may want to copy the icon automatically to your Windows or OS/2 Startup folder so that Notes starts automatically each time you start Windows or OS/2.

Start Notes as you would any other program. Put the mouse pointer on the Notes icon and double-click. As Notes starts, it briefly presents a start-up logo. Eventually, you will see a screen similar to that shown in figure 1.1.

Notes Basics

> **Note**
>
> For those of you that are new to Win 95, the start procedure for Notes may appear a little different that what you are typically used to. Simply select Start, Programs. Find the menu option where your Notes program is located (usually Lotus Applications). Click the Notes menu item. Notes will start.

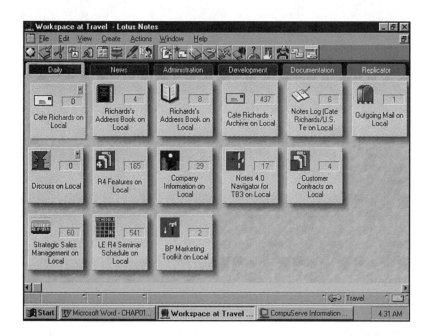

Fig. 1.1

You begin your work in Notes from the main Lotus Notes workspace.

> **Note**
>
> The exact configuration you see when you start Notes depends on the options you have selected. You learn more about selecting personal preferences in Chapter 2, "Customizing Notes."

Understanding the Notes Workspace

As with any Windows or OS/2 program, learning the various parts of the screen is the key to learning how to use Notes. In this section, you learn about the different parts of the Notes screen and how to control them using the mouse and keyboard. Figure 1.2 shows a typical Notes screen and some of the many features of the program that you'll come to know.

Fig. 1.2

Look at the changes Lotus has made to the workspace in Notes R4.

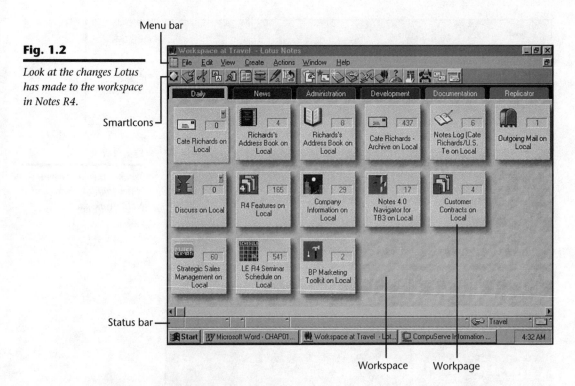

The Menu Bar

Near the very top of the Notes screen you see the menu bar, which contains words such as File, Edit, View, Create, Actions, Window, and Help when you first start Notes. Each word represents a menu of operations. Table 1.1 briefly summarizes the operations available through each menu on the menu bar. (You can view all of the menu and submenu commands in Appendix C, "Command Reference.")

Tip

Not all menu commands that will be available to you are displayed in the menu bar when you first start Notes. Some commands are available only when you are performing particular functions.

Table 1.1 **Menu Operations**	
Menu	**Operations Accessed**
<u>F</u>ile	Enables you to perform database operations, print, configure your environment, work remote (not connected to a network), manipulate attachments, bring information from word processors and other programs into Notes, and save information from Notes to other programs.
<u>E</u>dit	Contains functions for moving, copying, and making other changes to documents; checking spelling; linking; working with unread marks; searching for text; and undoing the last command you performed.
<u>V</u>iew	Enables you to determine what information you see on-screen.
<u>C</u>reate	Formerly the Compose menu command in Release 3 of Notes, <u>C</u>reate enables you to create messages, documents, folders, views, agents, database designs, sections, tables, objects, hotspots, and page breaks.
<u>A</u>ctions	Enables you to perform functions on a document, text, or database. You can move documents to folders; categorize documents; enter, change, or delete field values; edit, send, and forward documents; and perform advanced features like truncating, untruncating, and resaving documents.
<u>T</u>ext	Enables you to alter the size, color, and font style of text within your message, and to set tabs and margins.
<u>W</u>indow	Provides you with a list of open Notes windows and enables you to switch from one window to another. You can also elect to tile, cascade, minimize, and maximize windows through this menu item.
<u>H</u>elp	Provides you with online help to all Lotus Notes functions and enables you to determine the version of Notes you are using.
<u>D</u>esign	Provides you with menu selections available only when you are designing views, forms, subforms, navigators, fields, or agents. This menu command is only present when you are in design mode.

Databases and Workpages

You have already learned that Notes stores information in databases. Even if you use Notes only for sending and receiving electronic mail, you still need to learn how to manage databases, because your mailbox is a database. However, if you use Notes to its fullest, you and your co-workers will store and share many different kinds of information: status reports, customer records, sales prospects, various kinds of "paperwork," budgets, and so on. You may want to access dozens of different databases at different times. Organizing this information is the key to using Notes effectively.

Each database you work with is represented by an icon located on a *workpage*. When you first start up Notes R4, just below the SmartIcons you see what looks like a set of six file folder tabs, each representing a workpage. You can think of workpages as categories of data. Just as you may use different drawers in a file cabinet to contain related files, workpages enable you to organize your databases into as many as six sections. You decide what to call each workpage and which databases should be placed on each workpage.

In Notes R4, you can add or delete workspace tabs as you need them. You will learn more about how to do this in the section "Customizing Your Workspace" in Chapter 2, "Customizing Notes."

> **Note**
>
> There is a seventh tab titled Replicator. This tab is predefined by Notes to let you set up Notes to replicate database information between your remote PC and a Notes server, run agents, and send and receive mail when working remote. You will be learning more about this tab in the section, "Setting Up the Replicator" in Chapter 19, "Working Remote."

You can display any workpage by clicking the tab associated with that workpage. Each database appears as a box containing a name and a small icon. The icon is usually a picture that you can associate easily with the topic of the database. A database of un-solved problems may have an icon of a question mark, for example, or perhaps a frowning face. Sometimes each box displays other information about each database, depending on how you set up your preferences

 ▶▶ See "Customizing Information Displayed on Database Icons," p. 56

You decide what to call each workpage tab. Many users label the first workpage *Mail* and use it to contain the databases they need to send and receive e-mail, such as their mailbox and an address book that lists the users in your company. If you use Notes exclusively for mail, this workpage may be the only one you use. Together, the six workpages are known as your *workspace*.

Each Notes user can arrange his or her workpages in any convenient manner, and can place any database on any workpage. Notes does not require that everyone who uses a particular database put that database on the same page. The organization of your workspaces is completely up to you.

The SmartStatus Strip

The SmartStatus strip appears at the bottom of the screen. The SmartStatus is a strip of icons and messages that displays information about network and hard disk activity, mail, database access levels, text attributes, and various status messages (see fig. 1.3). The strip is divided into segments, which contain indicators. Table 1.2 describes the indicators in each segment.

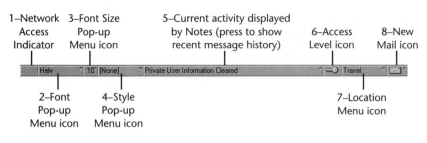

1–Network Access Indicator 3–Font Size Pop-up Menu icon 5–Current activity displayed by Notes (press to show recent message history) 6–Access Level icon 8–New Mail icon

Helv   10 [None]   ^ Private User Information Cleared   Travel

2–Font Pop-up Menu icon   4–Style Pop-up Menu icon   7–Location Menu icon

Fig. 1.3

The Status Bar displays current activities performed by Notes, and lets you quickly access some of the most used features in Notes through pop-up menu selection lists.

Notes Basics

Table 1.2 Understanding The Status Bar Icons	
Status Bar Icon	**Description**
1	The first segment indicates disk or network activity. If a lightning bolt appears, Notes is accessing data across the network. The segment is blank when Notes isn't performing network access.
2	The second segment shows the current font typeface you are using. This segment is used only when you're editing a document or designing a new form and your cursor is located in a Rich Text field (see Chapter 7, "Working With Text"). If you click this segment, Notes displays a list of available fonts and enables you to select a font.
3	The third segment—the Font size segment—like the typeface segment is available only during editing, and displays the current text point size. Clicking this segment displays a list of the available point sizes. You can select a new point size by clicking one of the sizes in the list.
4	The fourth segment—the Style segment—lets you select from a predefined style.
5	The fifth segment displays status and error messages.
6	The sixth segment—the Access Level segment—indicates your permission level for the database you now are accessing. In Chapter 20, "Security and Encryption," you learn about the various access levels and how to interpret the icon in this segment. If you click this segment, Notes displays a message explaining the meaning of the symbol.
7	The seventh segment—the Location segment—indicates how your machine is set up for working. For example, if your computer is connected permanently to a network, you will see Office (Network) appear in the section. Other settings, such as Travel (Remote), Island (Disconnected), and Edit Current will be discussed in Chapter 2, "Customizing Notes," and in Part III of this book, "Going Mobile."
8	The eighth segment displays an envelope when new mail has arrived for you (it is blank otherwise). Clicking this segment opens your mailbox.

Context-Sensitive Menus

You can access *context menus* by clicking once with your right mouse button anywhere in the Notes workspace. A context-sensitive menu of available commands appears next to your cursor providing you easy access to the most commonly-used functions performed in your current situation. The selections in this menu change as you perform different tasks in Notes. The context-sensitive menu in figure 1.4 shows the commands available while you are entering text in a mail message.

Fig. 1.4

Context-sensitive menus help speed your work with Lotus Notes by placing some of the most common features you need at the click of a mouse button.

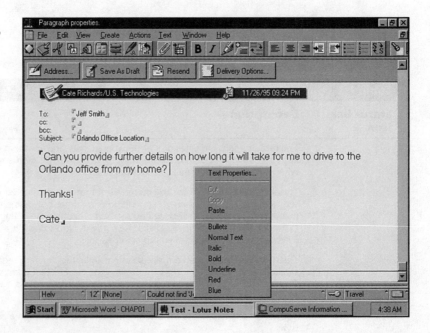

Working with SmartIcons

Notes provides yet another way to perform common functions. Arranged along one edge of the screen (usually the top) is a row of icons, known as *SmartIcons*, that represent common functions (see fig. 1.5). SmartIcons represent the same operations that you can access with the pull-down menus, but enable you to invoke these functions with a single click. For example, you can display the Notes ruler (explained in Chapter 7, "Working With Text") by clicking the SmartIcon that looks like a ruler, instead of choosing View, Ruler.

Notes provides a SmartIcon for almost every operation, but the entire collection of icons would fill the screen. After deciding which operations you perform most often, you can tell Notes which SmartIcons you want displayed.

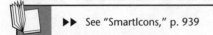

▶▶   See "SmartIcons," p. 939

I

Fig. 1.5

SmartIcons provide shortcuts to performing menu commands.

Notes Basics

New to Notes R4 is the ability for Lotus Notes to display context-sensitive SmartIcons—in other words, the icons displayed in the icon bar change according to where you are working at any given time.

Notes provides one set of SmartIcons—universal for you to choose from by default. You can, however, add additional icons to the list. You can also select the Context Icons option to have Notes automatically display different icons—based on the current tasks you are performing.

If you want to hide the SmartIcons from your workspace, choose File, Tools, SmartIcons and then deselect the Show Icon Bar option in the dialog box. Likewise, if you want to hide only those SmartIcons from the workspace that are context-sensitive, deselect Context Icons. Finally, if you want to hide the icon descriptions that are displayed as "bubble-help" when you point to an icon, you can deselect Descriptions. If you later change your mind, and want to display any of these features, return to this dialog box and reselect these options.

Note

You can also change the SmartIcon set by opening the SmartIcons dialog box and selecting the set you want to use from the drop-down list box. You will learn more about this dialog box in the next section.

Changing the Position of SmartIcons. You can change the position in which your SmartIcon palette is located. To do so, perform the following:

Tip

If you are new to Win 95, you can also reposition your Start menu by clicking anywhere within the bar and dragging it to a new position. This may make your workspace appear less cluttered at the bottom of your Notes windows.

---

1. Select File, Tools, SmartIcons. The SmartIcons dialog box appears (see fig. 1.6).

2. Click the down arrow in the Position list box.

3. Select the location in which you want the SmartIcons to be displayed: Left, Right, Top, Bottom, or Floating.

4. If you do not want to customize your SmartIcons further, select OK to save your settings and return to your workspace.

Fig. 1.6

Use the SmartIcons dialog box to add new icons to your SmartIcons bar, create custom SmartIcons, and change the position of the SmartIcons box.

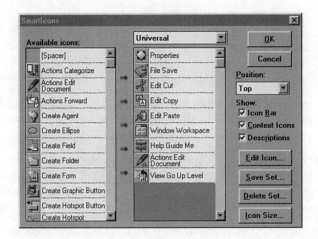

Selecting Floating from the list of positions lets you display the SmartIcons in a box that can be repositioned in the window by dragging it (see fig. 1.7). You can resize the floating SmartIcons box by clicking any of the corners of the box and dragging its borders until the box is the length or height you want. Figure 1.8 illustrates the same set of Mail SmartIcons floating after resizing.

Fig. 1.7

You can elect to have your SmartIcons floating on the workspace so that you can position them near the section of the page in which you are working.

Fig. 1.8

You can resize your floating SmartIcons box so that it is not in the way of the work you are performing and is the shape you want.

If you want to close the floating SmartIcons set, click the Close box in the upper left corner of the window. To redisplay the window, select the SmartIcon indicator on the status bar and select a SmartIcons set.

Tip

If you select Left or Right as the position for the SmartIcons, keep in mind that the height of your screen will not allow as many SmartIcons to be displayed as the width of your screen does. If you find that one of these settings frequently results in some of your SmartIcons being truncated from the set, you may want to select Top, Bottom, or Floating from the list, or customize the SmartIcon set you are using to display fewer icons.

Customizing SmartIcon Sets. Although Lotus constructed sets of icons that they thought would be useful, you are not locked into Lotus' choices. Within each set, you can add icons, remove icons, rearrange icons, or even create new sets.

To customize the SmartIcons, display the SmartIcons dialog box by choosing File, Tools, SmartIcons Setup (see fig. 1.9). The list box on the left displays all of the available SmartIcons that you can put on a SmartIcon bar. Next to each icon, Notes displays the menu selections you can make to perform the equivalent operation. (All these icons are described further in Appendix A.)

Click an icon and drag it to the desired
position in the current SmartIcon set

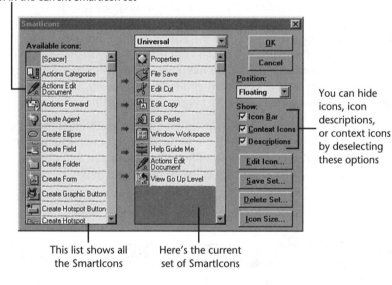

This list shows all   Here's the current
the SmartIcons   set of SmartIcons

Fig. 1.9

In addition to selecting and positioning the desired SmartIcon set, you can use this dialog box to modify any set of SmartIcons.

You can hide icons, icon descriptions, or context icons by deselecting these options

The list box in the center of the dialog box shows the icons that now make up one of the available SmartIcons set. (This section refers to this list box as the *current set*). Select the set of icons you want to customize.

To add a new icon to an existing set, find the icon in the list of available icons and drag it to the current set. Notes inserts it into the set. You can add the same icon to as many SmartIcon sets as you want. When you have added all of the SmartIcons you want to the current list, select OK to save your changes and return to the workspace.

> **Note**
>
> At the top of the list of available icons is a special item called Spacer. If you insert this item in an icon set, Notes inserts a small gap between icons.

To remove an icon from the current set, drag an icon from the current set off to one side, out of the current set list box. (It doesn't matter where you drag it, as long as it's out of the current set list box.) When you have removed all of the SmartIcons you want from current list, select OK to save your changes and return to the workspace.

You can also add and remove icons from the universal set of SmartIcons. While the universal set of icons was defined with those icons Lotus thought you might find valuable—regardless of where you were working in Notes—you may find, however, that you want other icons to display throughout your work in Notes. Notes displays the icons in the universal set in conjunction with the context-sensitive icons wherever you are working in Notes. Context-sensitive SmartIcons do not display in the list of current SmartIcons in the dialog box, but will appear to the right of them in the workspace when the situation calls for them to be active. When you are adding icons to this icon set, keep in mind that if you add too many icons, you will most likely run out of display room. If you want to add many more icons to the set, you will most likely need to display the set as floating to be able to view them all.

To create a new set of SmartIcons, first display an existing set and choose Save Set. Notes displays the Save Set of SmartIcons dialog box that enables you to assign a name to the new set. You also must provide a filename with an SMI extension. Then you can customize the new set as needed by adding and removing icons.

To delete an existing set, choose Delete Set. Notes lists all the existing sets. Select one or more sets and then choose OK. Notes deletes the sets you selected.

> **Caution**
>
> You cannot delete the Universal set of SmartIcons from the Delete Sets dialog box, but it can be deleted using a File Manager program or your system operating commands if you are not careful. This SmartIcon set's filename is UNIVERSE.SMI, and it must be present in your SmartIcon subdirectory as defined in your NOTES.INI file—even if you do not use it—or you will not be able to use SmartIcons in Lotus Notes. If this file is not present, you will be prompted by Notes for the Icon subdirectory the next time you start Notes. You will need to select Cancel multiple times to continue the start up. You won't have access to SmartIcons if this file is not present—even if you have other SmartIcon files defined.

Make sure you do not accidentally delete this file when you are cleaning up your files on your hard drive. If you should accidentally delete it, you can either reinstall Notes, use your operating system or File Manager to rename another SMI file you have created UNIVERSE.SMI, or create a blank text file using any text editor and save the file with the name UNIVERSE.SMI. This will allow Notes to start up without error messages, and will provide you with the capability of using SmartIcons.

Changing the Size of SmartIcons. There may be times where you need to change the size of the SmartIcons displayed. For example, you may want to increase the size of your SmartIcons when giving a presentation so that the audience can see which SmartIcons you are selecting. With the SmartIcons dialog box open, select the Icon Size button. The Icon Size dialog box appears as shown in figure 1.10.

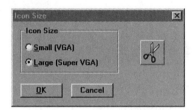

Fig. 1.10

You can increase the size of SmartIcons so that they are easier to see by selecting Large in the Icon Size dialog box.

Select Small (the default) if you want to display the SmartIcons in their usual size. Select Large if you want to display large SmartIcons—of course, you will not be able to display as many icons when you select Large. Large icons, however, are ideal if you are using Notes to make a presentation, or are working on a small screen.

Editing and Creating SmartIcons. You can edit and create new SmartIcons—with limitations. The existing, defined SmartIcons that perform commands—such as File, Print—cannot be edited. However, Notes provides several custom SmartIcons that you can use to create your own special SmartIcons to run macros easily. (Editing and creating a SmartIcon is easy, but you will need to understand formulas to do so. See Chapters 13, "Working With Formulas," and 14, "Formula Functions," for more information on writing formulas.)

Custom SmartIcons can be a real timesaver for commands frequently run or complicated tasks in which a macro is used. For example, if you frequently like to switch to the Calculator in Windows while you are working in Lotus Notes, you may want to add a custom icon to your SmartIcon set to automatically open the it. To do so, follow these steps:

1. Select the Edit Icon button in the SmartIcon dialog box. The Edit SmartIcons dialog box appears.

2. Scroll through the list of Custom Icons available for you to edit. Highlight the icon you want to use.

3. Edit the icon's name in the Description text box to describe the function it will perform. In this example, type **Calculator**. This is the name Notes will display in the bubble help that appears when you point to a SmartIcon on the workspace.

4. Select Formula to open the SmartIcons Formula dialog box as shown in figure 1.11.

Fig. 1.11

You can enter formulas to customize the functions of SmartIcons.

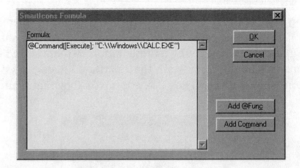

5. Type the formula you want to apply to the Custom Icon. In this example, you would enter the formula as it is displayed in figure 1.11. Note that the formula contains double backslashes between the drive and subdirectory names. When you write a directory path in Notes formulas, you must use double backslashes. You will learn more about writing formulas like this one in Chapter 13, "Working with Formulas."

6. Select OK, and then OK again to save the formula.

7. Add the newly created SmartIcon to your SmartIcon palette as described in the previous section, "Customizing SmartIcon Sets."

You can now use the edited SmartIcon to run the command to open File Manager whenever it is selected. When you exit File Manager, you will return to Notes exactly where you left it.

Opening and Viewing Databases

It is quite easy to open a database. Simply double-click a database icon corresponding to the database you want to use. Database icons appear as squares on your workspace, with the name and location of the database printed on it. Notes opens the database to display navigators, views, panes, and folders, as illustrated in figure 1.12. This section briefly describes how you move around a database to find the information you are looking for. If you have used a previous release of Lotus Notes before, you may still want to read this section as Notes has added many new features.

> **Note**
>
> If this is the first time you have opened the database, you will first see the *About This Database* document; which usually provides you with a summary of the purpose of the database, along with any rules for using it, and a contact name in case of problems. Take a moment to read the document, and then press the Esc key to exit the document. You will only see this document in subsequent uses of the database if you select Help, About This Database, or if the designer of the databases elects to have the document display upon each opening.

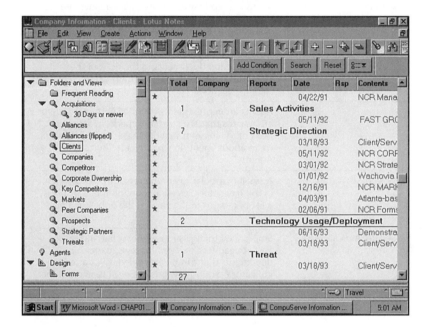

Fig. 1.12

Databases open to display navigators, views, panes, and folders, similar to those shown in your Public Name & Address Book.

Working with Panes

When you first open a database in Notes R4, you will notice that the window is split into two *panes*. The left pane displays the default database Navigator (usually the Folder Navigator) which provides a graphical way to navigate through the documents in the database. A database designer can also build other navigators, and assign one of them as the default navigator to be displayed when you open the database. Figure 1.12 displays the default folder navigator for Richard's address book.

The navigator contains symbols and text that guide you through working in the opened database. The symbols in Table 1.3 are present in most Folder Navigators. Database designers can incorporate additional symbols and graphics in navigators, as discussed in Part II of this book, "Designing Applications."

Table 1.3 Common Symbols Found in Most Database Navigators

Symbol	Represents	Description
📁	Folders	Folders are used to store related documents, or groupings of documents. Folders can contain documents, views, and other folders. You can drag documents from the view to the right of the navigator pane, and drop them in folders to store related topics. You will learn more about working with folders in Chapter 3, "Using Databases."
🔍	Views	Views are represented by a small magnifying glass. Views contain listings of documents that are sorted according to criteria defined by you or the database designer. For example, Figure 1.12 shows the Locations view highlighted—which displays the list of location documents to the right of the navigator pane. You will learn more about views in the next section.
💡	Agents	Agents are represented by a small lightbulb. Agents are macros that are created to perform assigned tasks on documents in a database. You will learn more about agents in Chapter 15, "Buttons and Agents."
📐	Design	A small triangular ruler represents the design menu in the navigator. Selecting a design menu displays a list of designs in the view to the right (see fig. 1.13).
▼	Section Indicators	Small, solid triangles represent section indicators and appear next to items in views, panes, or documents that can be expanded. Click a section indicator pointing towards the right to expand the section. Click the section indicators going down to collapse the section.

Selecting the symbols next to the identifying text will display the corresponding information in the views to the right of the pane.

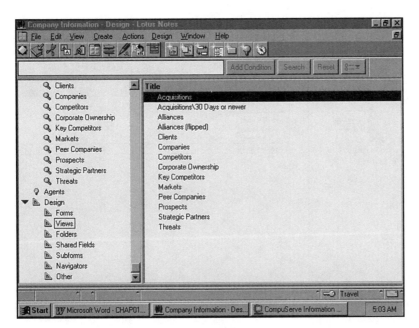

Notes Basics

Fig. 1.13

Selecting the design menu displays a list of designs in the view to the right.

Working with Views

The person who designs the database decides how the documents are ordered and categorized, and what information is displayed about each document. The way in which the list is presented is called a *view*; when the right side of a database is open, it displays the *view pane*. Figure 1.14 shows a sample view for the Richard's Address Book database. This view shows the Location documents used for network and remote connections with the server. (You'll learn more about server connections in Part III, "Going Mobile.")

The database designer may have determined that the list can be presented in several useful ways, and may have created several views. Consider a database that contains sales orders. A view called By Customer may present the documents (sales orders) strictly in alphabetical order by customer last name; another view, perhaps called By Sales Rep, may categorize documents by sales representative. By selecting a view, you can determine how Notes presents the list of documents.

Fig. 1.14

Views list all, or a subset, of the documents displayed in a database.

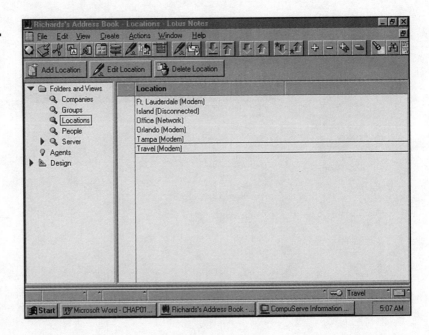

Different views may display the documents in the same order, but show different information about each document. A view called Revenue, for example, may show each document's customer name, gross sales amount, profit, and commission. Another view, called Customer, may list the same documents, but show customer address and phone number as well.

A view may not list all the documents in a database. A view called Delinquent Accounts, for example, may list only documents that represent unpaid sales orders at least 90 days late.

The designer of a database selects one of the views in the database as the *default view*, which Notes uses when you open the database for the first time. You can select another view at any time, as explained in the next section.

Selecting a View

When you open a database, Notes displays a view. If you are accessing this database for the first time, you see the default view—the view the designer thought most people would find most useful. Otherwise, Notes displays the last view you selected. (After you select a different view, Notes always remembers the view you last selected—even when you exit Notes.) In some databases, the database designer may have created only a single view, so your choice is limited to that view, unless you create a new view for yourself (discussed in Chapter 9, "Creating New Databases"). In most databases, however, you can choose from among several views.

You can select views from the navigator pane by clicking the text displaying a small magnifying glass next to it. You can also select a view by selecting View, and then choosing the title of the view you want to use (see fig. 1.15). Notice that the available views are listed in the drop-down menu and in the navigator. The active view has a checkmark next to it in the View menu and has a box surrounding the view title in the navigator.

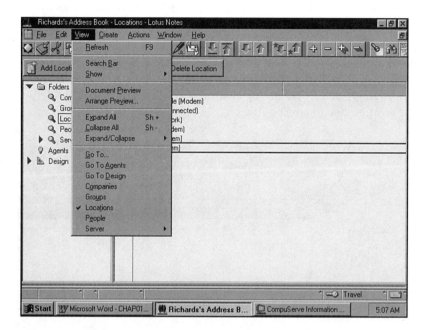

Fig. 1.15

Available views in a database appear at the bottom of the View menu command list.

Expanding Categories in Views

Categories in views are represented by small triangles, plus signs, or other graphics chosen by the designer of a database to indicate that there are collapsible categories in the view. These category indicators appear to the left of a category title. For example: if you select the text marked by a category indicator that is pointing to the right, you will expand the category to view more documents or categories. If you select text marked by a category indicator that is pointing down, you will collapse the category. You can also expand and collapse views by using SmartIcons, as shown in Table 1.4. You will learn more about working with views in Chapter 3, "Using Databases."

Table 1.4   SmartIcons That Help you Collapse and Expand View Categories

Icon	Contents	Action
+	Single plus sign	Expands one category level
−	Single minus sign	Collapses one category level
✛	Multi-plus sign	Expands all categories
⬒	Multi-minus sign	Collapses all categories

Working with Folders

Folders are similar to views, but can store other folders as well as documents. Folders are a great tool to use when you want to sort related documents in a database according to criteria that you set. You will learn more about creating and using folders in Chapter 3, "Working With Databases."

When you select a folder icon in the navigator, documents stored in the folder will be displayed in the view to the right. If the folder is marked with a category indicator, selecting the indicator will display additional folders stored within the folder. See figure 1.16 for an example of a folder storing all location documents, and subfolders sorting the same location documents by city.

Fig. 1.16

You can store folders within folders to further organize your documents.

Primary folder for a group of documents

Secondary folders that store a subset of documents in the primary folder

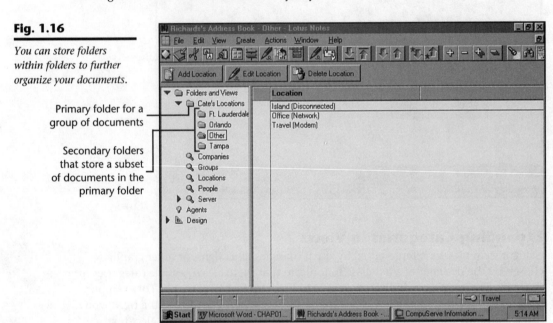

Understanding Documents

The building blocks for all databases are forms. A *form* is simply a template designed and stored in the database that users select to create a document that stores information. When you create a document in a database, you select from one of the forms created by the database designer. This form serves as a template for you to enter your information. When you save the information you have entered in the form, Notes displays it as a document in the database. This section will quickly walk you through understanding documents. You will learn, in detail, how to work with documents throughout all of Part I of this book.

Opening Documents

Lotus Notes provides several ways to open a document, once you have located the one you want to read in the view:

- Double-click the document's title
- Highlight the document and press the Enter key
- Highlight the document and select File, Open

When the document opens, you may scroll through its contents using the scroll bars to the right and bottom of the document window.

Creating Documents

Each database design can be different, providing a wealth of forms to be created. You may have forms to complete to enter time into a time-tracking database, or forms that order supplies from your purchasing department. Regardless, the method to create a document is typically the same. Select Create from the menu commands while you are in the database (see fig. 1.17). Select the form name that represents the document you want to create. The document will appear in edit form ready for you to enter information.

Note

Some designers may create databases in which you are prompted to create a new document by clicking a button, rather than selecting the form name from the Create menu. You will learn more about creating new documents in Chapter 3, "Using Databases."

Fig. 1.17

To create a document in a Notes database, you may pick from the available list of documents displayed in the Create submenu.

To enter text in a document, the document must be in edit mode—in other words, the brackets surrounding the fields must be open as displayed in figure 1.18. If you open an existing document and do not see the open brackets, double-click anywhere in the document, or select Actions, Edit Document—it will be placed in edit mode. Now you can enter or edit text as desired.

Fig. 1.18

A document in edit mode will display open brackets around the fields indicating that you can enter information into the fields.

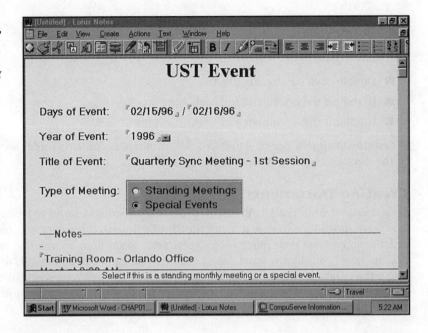

Exiting a Document

When you are ready to close a document, perform one of the following:

- Double-click the right mouse button (if you have this option selected in your preferences. Refer to Chapter 2, "Customizing Notes").
- Select File, Close.
- Press the Esc key.

Notes will close the document you are reading. If you entered or edited any information in the document, you will be prompted to save the document. Select Yes if you want to save the information, No if you want to discard your entries and exit anyway, and Cancel if you want to return to the document before saving.

Caution

If you select No when prompted to save your changes, Lotus Notes closes the document without saving any information you have added. You will lose all entries made. Select Cancel if you want to go back and add or remove information before saving.

Getting Help

Notes includes an extensive online help system using many of the new Notes R4 features. The help system contains hundreds of documents, each of which describes a

Notes topic. You can access the help system at any time by pressing F1. Notes will take you to the Guide Me help panel that relates to your current tasks. You can follow through the various linked documents to learn about the task you are trying to perform, or you can select the Help Topics button to exit the Guide Me panel and open the Help view. You can also access help directly by selecting Help, Help Topics or double-clicking the Notes Help database icon (see fig. 1.19).

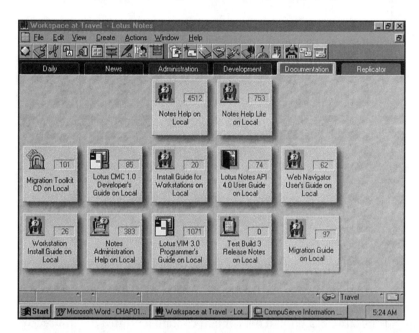

Fig. 1.19

Notes ships with two Help databases: the full Notes Help database and the remote Notes Help Lite database.

Notes Basics

Tip

For those who will be designing databases, and would like to see examples on the use of many of the new features of Lotus Notes, the Notes Help database utilizes many of those features in its design. If the database is stored on your hard drive, then you will be able to access the design of the database to see how it is put together. Pay a visit to the design of the navigators in the database to get an idea for how Lotus Notes panels and other navigators are put together—just don't change any of the design or your next help session may exhibit problems.

Lotus Notes provides what is known as *context-sensitive help*—whenever you press F1, Notes looks at what you're doing and tries to select the panel from its help database which will offer you the most useful information. For example, if you are in the middle of sending a mail message, pressing F1 displays a document that offers you information on sending mail messages. You can also press the Help Topics SmartIcon, if available, to open the Notes Help database.

Figure 1.20 shows a typical Notes help document. For help messages longer than can fit in the window, you can press the Page Up and Page Down keys to move through the text of the help document.

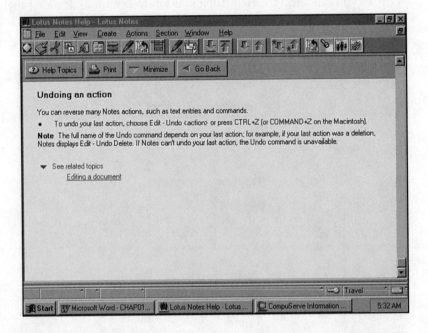

In a book you often find cross-references, in which one section of text makes references to another. For example, a printed book might contain a printed notation such as "See page 423 for more information." Lotus Notes includes the electronic equivalent, known as *hotspots*, which enable you to access related information in another help document.

In figure 1.20 notice that the words *Editing a document* are underlined (on-screen, they're also displayed in green text)—these are hotspots. The presence of this text attribute tells you that you can get more information about this term. If you double-click the text, Notes displays a different document that contains information about ways to change how paragraphs look. This document, in turn, might contain other hotspot links that can guide you to other related sections. You will learn more about hotspots in Chapter 8, "Working With Documents."

Some of the help articles also contain pop-up boxes, indicated by light green outline boxes, which provide quick definitions for important terms. For example, the words *edit mode* in figure 1.21 indicate the presence of a pop-up box. By pointing at the word in the box and holding the left mouse button, a box appears with a definition of the phrase within the box (see fig. 1.21).

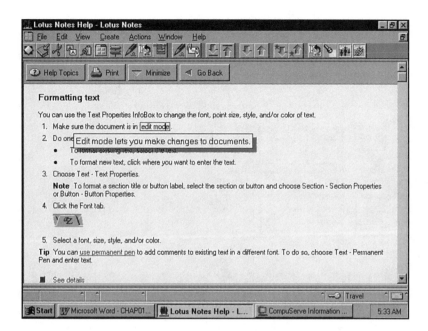

Fig. 1.21

*Pop-ups in Help documents
indicate additional
information about a word
or phrase. Click anywhere
in the pop-up box to view
the information.*

Notes Basics

At the top of the Help window, you will find a series of buttons that enable you to use Help to your best advantage. These buttons include the following:

- The Help Topics button opens the Help Index view, displaying a list of all documents in the database. The document you were viewing is still open, and can be accessed by closing the current window or selecting the document from the Window menu. This provides you with a fast way to look up another document without having to close the current one.
- The Print button lets you quickly print the current help document.
- The Minimize button lets you minimize the Help window.
- The Go Back button lets you go back one window (it is the same as pressing the Esc key).

If you are reading an article that you accessed through a *doclink*—a link icon resembling a document that opens another document related to the topic when you double-click it—or hotspot, you can press either the Esc key or click the Go Back button (if showing) to return to the Help document you were reading. If you are reading a document that you invoked by pressing F1, pressing Esc closes the help system and returns you to your previous activity.

Using the Visual Index

New to the Help database is the *Visual Index*, which takes advantage of new Notes features—hotspots and graphical navigators. You can open the Visual Index by clicking the Visual Index icon in the Navigator of the Notes Help database. The Visual Index, as shown in figure 1.22, shows graphical representations of subjects covered in the Help database.

Fig. 1.22

The Visual Help Index displays graphical representations of the types of visual Help documents available in the database. Just click any picture to open a visual help document about that subject.

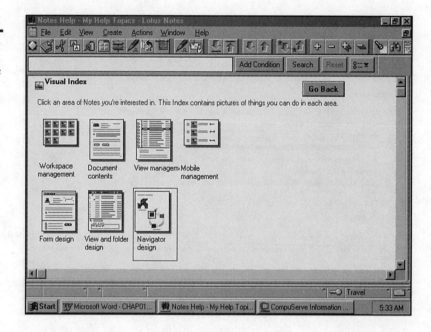

When you double-click one these graphics, a visual picture of a subject will appear (see fig. 1.23). You will notice several yellow bubbles with question marks on them. When you double-click one of these bubbles, you will learn how to perform the feature marked by the bubble. For example, double-clicking the yellow bubble positioned over the bullets in figure 1.24 will show text indicating that the feature is a bullet, and then will lead you to the steps for creating the bullets. You will learn even more about hotspots and graphical navigators in Chapter 8, "Working With Documents."

You can search for a particular help subject by using the Search Bar. To display the Search Bar, select View, Search Bar. The Search Bar will appear directly above the Help view. You can type words in the text entry box and then click the Search button. Notes will search through all of the documents in the database and display checkmarks next to the documents that meet your search criteria. You will learn more about using the Search features of Notes in Chapter 8, "Working With Documents."

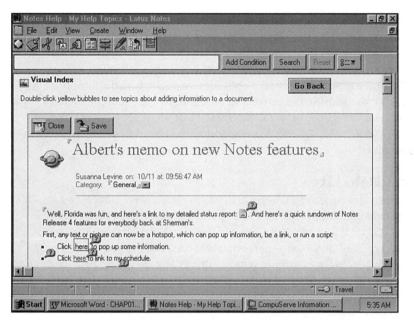

Fig. 1.23

Visual Index documents in the Help database provide quick, easy ways to learn about many of the features in Notes—just click any of the question mark indicators to display additional information about a topic.

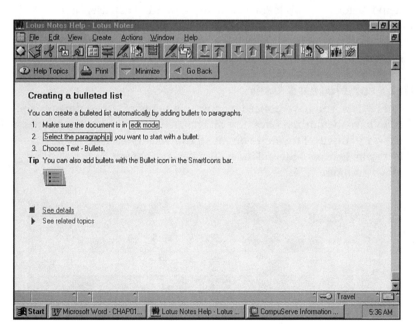

Fig. 1.24

After you click a question mark indicator, Notes will open a document describing how to use the corresponding feature.

Storing Help Topics for Quick Reference

While you are viewing the Help database navigator pane, you will notice a pink box surrounding the text, "To store topics for quick access later, drag them into this folder." Beside this text, you will see a small folder. As you read through Help documents, you may find a few that you will want to reference frequently. Simply highlight the document you want to reference and drag it onto the small folder. To view those topics that you have stored for quick access, select View, Navigators, Folders. Double-click the folder titled My Help Topics, and then choose from the list of documents in the view.

Using Notes Help Lite

Lotus Notes R4 provides an abridged version of Notes Help called *Notes Help Lite*. This database was installed on your hard drive when you installed Lotus Notes R4. The purpose of the database is to provide mobile users with a Help database that minimizes the amount of hard drive space needed, while continuing to supply valuable help information while you are working remote. Essentially, Help Lite provides help on the features you use in working with Lotus Notes remote—and excludes topics on design, administration, and LotusScript. The Visual Index is also excluded as the graphics take up more space.

If you look in Help Lite for topics that are not common to every day use, Notes will prompt you to access the network copy of the full Help database. If you elected to install both versions of Help during the installation of Notes R4, you can safely delete the Help Lite database as the documents are duplicates of the full Help database.

Getting Help for Notes 3 Users

If you were a Notes 3 user, you have noticed by now that many of the commands and actions you used to have memorized have now all changed! Lotus Notes R4 provides you with a quick way to discover the new command equivalents for Lotus Notes 3 commands. Select Help, Release 3 Menu Finder. The Release 3 Menu Finder window will appear as shown in figure 1.25.

Fig. 1.25

You can find the equivalent Notes R4 menu commands for tasks you used to perform in Notes R3 by selecting the R3 command you would use.

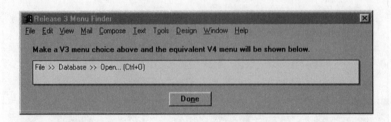

Select the menu command sequence you used to perform in Release 3 of Lotus Notes. The equivalent Release 4 commands will appear in the window. Perform the commands listed in the window to perform the same task as you used to perform in Release 3.

Exiting Notes

Because Notes provides many ways to perform most operations, you can find several ways to exit Notes. You can exit Notes by performing any of the following:

- Press Alt+F4.
- Choose File, Exit.
- Click the Control-menu box in the upper left corner of the Notes screen. The Control menu appears. Choose Close to quit Notes.
- Double-click the Control-menu box.

From Here...

This chapter showed you the basic terms that you will encounter throughout the book and when talking with other Notes users. You learned about the terms *database* and *document* and have learned something about the way Notes works. You have learned to start and exit Notes, open and close documents, and access Notes help.

For more information on the topics discussed in this chapter, refer to the following:

- Chapter 3, "Using Databases," teaches you how to work with Lotus Notes documents, views, and other features of a Notes database.
- Chapter 8, "Working With Documents," explains how to work with hotspots, doclinks, and other features that provide impact to your documents.
- Chapter 13, "Working With Formulas," shows how to create formulas that you can use to customize your SmartIcons.

Notes Basics

CHAPTER 2

Customizing Notes

Many people who use Notes spend most of their day working with it. If your job involves a great deal of contact with other people, much of that interaction may involve exchanging messages through Notes. If you're going to work frequently with Notes, you will be pleased that you can customize most aspects of the program.

This chapter provides tips and techniques that will let you customize the Notes environment in which you are working. In this chapter, you learn about arranging your workspace pages and icons, configuring Notes, and setting up your printer. You will also learn a little bit about a special Notes file—DESKTOP.DSK—and the importance it plays in working with Notes.

In this chapter, you learn about the following configuration options:

- Arranging your workspace
- Setting up your printer
- Changing your password
- Specifying your Notes preferences
- Working with your DESKTOP.DSK file

Customizing Your Workspace

Your workspace is the starting point for your Notes work each day. Even though organizing your workspace may not be as important to you as organizing the databases in which you work, it can help you quickly locate and work with the databases you need. A well-organized workspace appeals to people who think that a well-organized desk is important.

Note

As you work in Notes, you may be prompted for your Notes password. This usually happens when you first begin your session in Notes, or when you first try to access a database that is located on a server. You may also be prompted for your password—even if you already entered it during the working session—if you try to access a database that is encrypted on your hard drive, encrypted documents, or if you try to change your password or call a server from a remote location.

When you are prompted for your Notes password, type it in the Password dialog box displayed exactly as your password was given to you by your Notes Administrator. Keep in mind that Notes passwords are case-sensitive—you must enter the password in exactly the same case it was created in. For more information on Notes passwords, read Chapter 20, "Security and Encryption."

Arranging Workspace Pages

You already know that your Notes workspace is divided into six workspace pages and that each database you access appears as a box with an icon on one of the pages. When you add databases to your workspace and create your own databases, the first step is to select the page on which you want the database to appear.

When you start using Notes, you probably work with only a few databases: your mailbox, the Name & Address database, and perhaps one or two information databases your department uses. Because the number of databases with which you work is small, you probably put all your databases on a single workspace page.

As your familiarity with Notes increases and your use of Notes expands, you will work with more and more databases. Eventually, you may want to use more databases than can fit on a single workspace page—you can fit 95 database icons on a single workpage. Long before that happens, however, you will probably get the feeling that your page is cluttered and you will want to organize it.

Adding New Workpages

Notes R4 lets you add additional workpage tabs to better organize your workspace. You can have up to 32 workspace pages in addition to the workpage titled Replicator. Notes will automatically adjust the size of the tabs to accommodate the addition of extra tabs, and the size of the words you are entering as tab titles. However, if you enter more text/tab combinations than Notes has room to display, you will notice that the tabs on the right side of the workspace begin to disappear. If this happens, the only way you can move to those workpages is to highlight any workpage, and then press your right arrow key to view the contents of the hidden workpages. To add a new workpage, follow these steps:

1. Click a workspace tab. Notes inserts the workspace page to the left of the selected workspace page.

2. Choose Create, Workspace Page. If you haven't added a workspace page before, Notes asks if you want to upgrade your desktop file.

3. Click Yes to add the workspace page and upgrade your desktop file, or click No to cancel adding the page.

> **Caution**
>
> When you add additional workpages to your workspace, you modify your DESKTOP.DSK file—which stores your personal preferences and setup information. Once you modify this file in Notes R4, you cannot use the file with previous releases of Notes.

Deleting Workpages from Your Workspace

Just as you can add workpages to your workspace, you can also remove them. When you remove a workpage, however, you also remove any database icons you have positioned on the page. If you do not want to remove the icons from your workspace, you need to move them to another tab before following these procedures. To remove a workpage from your workspace, follow these steps:

1. Click the workspace page's tab.

2. Choose Edit, Clear or press Delete.

3. Click Yes to confirm the deletion or No to cancel it.

Naming Workpage Tabs

When you begin to feel that your workspace is getting cluttered, you may want to use the other workpages. To name a workpage, follow these steps:

1. Double-click the workspace tab that you want to name. The Properties InfoBox for the selected tab will appear (see fig. 2.1).

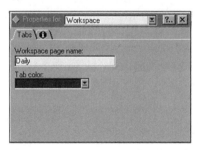

Fig. 2.1

You can name your workpages by opening the Workspace Properties InfoBox.

2. Type in the new name for the tab in the Workspace page name text entry box.

3. Select a color for the tab by choosing a color from the Tab color list box.

4. Double-click the Control-menu box (in this example, it's the X in the upper right corner of the box) to close the InfoBox and accept your edits.

Moving Databases on the Workspace

You can move databases from one page to another at any time. Click the workspace page on which the database now resides, and then drag the database from that page to the tab belonging to the page where you want to move the database. The Workpage tab will display a box around the title when the cursor is positioned correctly. Notes moves the database to that page. You can move multiple databases by holding down the Shift key, clicking each of the databases you want to move, and then dragging the icons to the new page.

As you move icons from one workspace page to another, you may find that the icons on the pages become rather disorganized. You can tell Notes to "straighten up" a workspace page by selecting the page and then choosing View, Arrange Icons. Notes arranges all the database icons on the current page at the top, with no gaps.

You can also move the icons on your Notes workspace without a mouse. To do so, follow these steps:

1. Select the icon you want to move.
2. Hold down the Shift and Ctrl keys at the same time.
3. Use the cursor arrows to reposition your icon.
4. Release the Shift and Ctrl keys.
5. Press Enter when you have completed the move.

The icons will now appear on the newly designated workpage.

Working with Stacked Icons

There are times when you may want to keep more than one database icon on your workspace for the same database. Perhaps you have access to the same database that is stored on more than one server on your network; or you may be working remote and keeping a replica copy of a database that is stored on your hard drive as well as the icon pointing to the main database stored on your network. Regardless, after awhile, your workspace may get too cluttered with all of the copies of the database icons displayed. You can set your workspace to show all database *replicas*—identical copies—as *stacked icons*. Stacked icons take up less room on your workspace and make it easier to work with all of the databases at once. When you stack icons, the topmost, leftmost icon appears at the top of the stack. Stacked icons appear with a stacked icon indicator in the upper right corner of the icon as shown in figure 2.2.

Stacking Database Icons. If your icons do not appear to be stacked, even though you are sure they are replicas, select View, Stack Replica Icons. A checkmark will appear to indicate that the selection is active. Notes will remember this setting until you turn it off.

Notes Basics

Fig. 2.2

You can stack replica copies of icons so that they take up less space on your workpage.

When you stack icons, Notes checks your location and displays either a server replica (if you are connected to the network in an office) or a local replica (if you are not connected to a network) at the top of the stack. The icons will automatically display the server name or "Local" in the title of the icon as they are brought to the top of the stack. This lets you quickly know which copy of the database you are using: a server (a network copy), or Local (a copy stored on your hard drive). For example, in figure 2.2, you see Cate Richards' database located on the Local hard drive.

If a database has replicas on multiple servers, and all are added to your workspace, the top left icon on the workpage will appear at the top of the stack when you elect to stack your icons.

Using Stacked Icons. Typically, you store replica copies of databases on your hard drive when you are working away from a network (refer to Chapter 18, "Setting Up To Go Remote," for more information on creating replica copies of databases). You may also keep replica copies of databases on your hard drive if you are making design modifications to a database, and don't want to do so directly in the production server copy.

Regardless of the reason for having multiple replicas of a database on your workspace, you may often find the need to switch between the replica copies during your work session. Because the replica that is at the top of the stack is the database that Notes works on, you simply need to select a new replica to be placed on the top of the stack. To do so, follow these steps:

1. Click the database indicator (down arrow) in the upper right corner of the database icon. The database icon menu drops down (see fig. 2.3).

Fig. 2.3

Select the database indicator to choose between replica databases when their icons are stacked.

2. Select the copy of the replica that you want to work in. For example, in figure 2.3, the Local copy of the database is currently at the top of the stack—the checkmark is displayed next to that location. To bring the network copy of the icon to the top of the stack, choose the server name in which the replica is stored. In this example, you would select USTServer3/ORL/U.S. Technologies.

> **Note**
>
> The Replicate option in the database location menu list is discussed in Chapter 18, "Setting Up To Go Remote."

If you decide you do not want to stack your replica icons anymore, select View, Stack Replica Icons to remove the checkmark. Your icons will automatically unstack and arrange themselves on the workspace.

Customizing Information Displayed on Database Icons

In addition to arranging the workspace pages on which your databases reside, you can customize the appearance of the database information displayed. The simplest database icon—and the default—consists of a picture (related to the content of the database) and the title of the database. Figure 2.4 shows a sample workspace page with three databases.

Fig. 2.4

These three databases show the default database information.

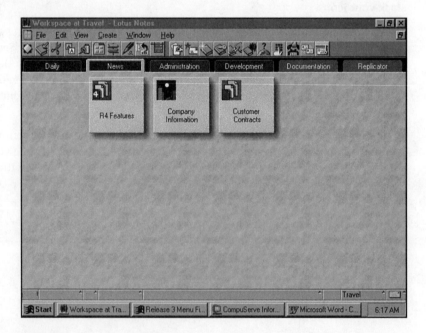

You can customize the icons, however, to display additional information about each database. The View menu contains two options that cause Notes to tell you more about each database on your workspace:

- **Unread Count**—This tells Notes to display a tiny window next to each icon, showing the number of unread documents in the database. This number tells you if you need to allocate time to read the contents of the database. Be aware, however, that Notes doesn't update this number every time someone enters a new document into the database. The Unread Count window shows only the number of documents that were in the database the last time you had the database open. If you want Notes to update the number of unread documents for each database, exit all of your databases and then press F9 or choose <u>V</u>iew, Re<u>f</u>resh Unread Count. Notes will also update the unread document counter the next time you start up Notes. The Unread count for the database you are working in will update when you exit the database.

> **Note**
>
> You can scan databases for unread documents in Notes which lets you quickly review new information stored in your databases. Read the section "Scanning Databases for Unread Documents" in Chapter 9, "Creating New Databases," for more information on this feature.

- **Server names**—This tells Notes to display the server name of each database under the database title. This information can be helpful if you need to know which server the database is located on.

> **Tip**
>
> If you hold the Shift key as you select <u>V</u>iew, Show <u>S</u>erver Names, Notes also displays the filename for each database. Notes will not display the filenames without also displaying the server names on the icons.

Figure 2.5 shows the same workspace page shown in figure 2.4, but with the unread document counter, server name, and filename showing.

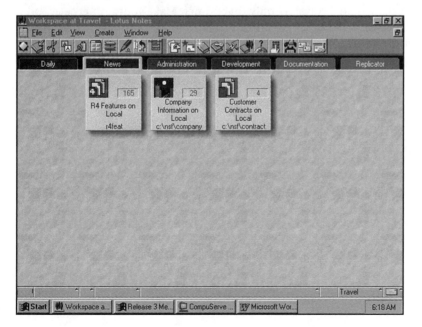

Fig. 2.5

If the full server name, or file path/name is too long to display on the database icon, you can find the same information by selecting File, Database, Properties.

You can also elect to enlarge the size of the database icon through the Notes Preferences settings as described in the next section. This enlarges the entire database icon—including the text size of the titles—which is great if you have difficulty reading the database titles. Keep in mind though that you will be able to see only a few icons in the workspace at a time, and long database title names will be truncated.

Note

For OS/2 3.1.5 Notes users, the VGA fonts may appear too small when using IBM's S3, 32-bit, and 64-bit graphic chips. If you have this difficulty, then you may want to increase the font size using File, Tools, User Preferences. You should also add this parameter to your NOTES.INI file:

        DISPLAY_FONT_INCREASE=1

The display font options are 1, 2, and 3. 1 works best for the video chips mentioned above.

You will read more about modifying the NOTES.INI file later in this chapter.

Setting Up Your Printer

You use your operating system software to tell your computer what kinds of printers are available. For example, in Win 95, you use the Printer's Properties InfoBox. The only information Notes needs is the printer(s) you want to use.

Choose File, Print to open the File Print dialog box displayed in figure 2.6. Select the Printer button located in the upper left portion of the dialog box. Notes will display a list of available printers in the Print Setup dialog box (see fig. 2.7). If you have only a single printer available, Notes displays only that printer. Make your printer selection and then select OK. After you select a printer, Notes routes all printouts to that printer until you change your selection.

Fig. 2.6

Select the Printer button to switch printers, or make changes to your printer setup in the File Print dialog box.

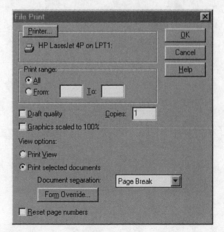

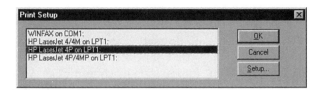

Fig. 2.7

Select the printer you want to use, or for which you want to make setup changes, from the list of printers you have available to you.

The Print Setup dialog box also enables you to configure various options about how the printer works by selecting the Setup button; you should not have to modify any of these options.

Perhaps the change most often made when changing printer setups is to switch between landscape and portrait printing. This change in paper orientation is made through your operating system printer setup, but can be reached by selecting File, Print, Printer, Setup. The Setup printer dialog box opens as shown in figure 2.8.

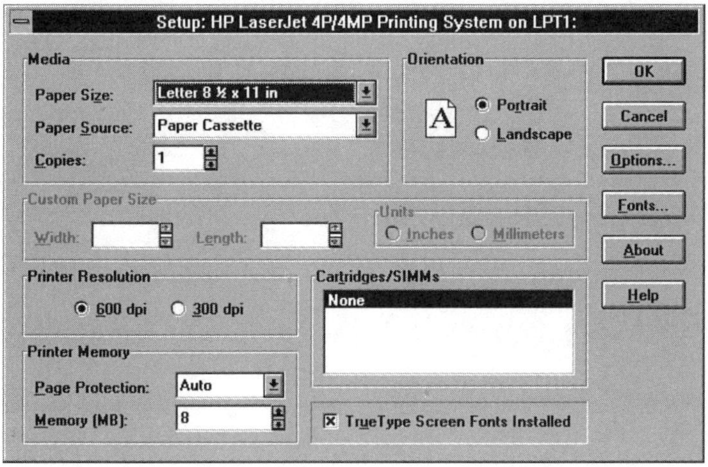

Fig. 2.8

You can switch between landscape and portrait printing in the Print Setup dialog box—if your printer supports landscape printing.

Figure 2.7 shows the Print Setup dialog box displayed when printing to the HP LaserJet 4P printer. This setup box, and the options available in it, is dependent upon the type of printer you have selected—so you may see a slightly different setup printer dialog box for your printer. In the Orientation combo box, select the paper orientation that you want to use, select OK, and then select OK again to save your settings. Typically, the page orientation settings will remain in effect until the next time you change them. However, some networks are set up and administered to always shift print settings back to their default—depending on how your PC is installed, and what operating system you are using.

If you have additional questions about the options available for your printer that are displayed in this dialog box, refer to your printer manual.

Changing Your Password

Notes maintains several important pieces of information about you. Some of this information—such as your user ID number—isn't of personal concern to you, but is vital to Notes. You can display some of the information by choosing File, Tools, User ID. Notes will prompt you for your Notes password. Type your password and click OK. When you choose this command, the User ID Information dialog box appears (see fig. 2.9).

Fig. 2.9

The User ID dialog box provides you a summary of your personal ID information. You can select the Set Password button to change your Notes password.

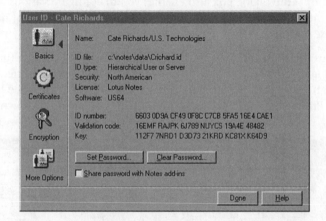

This dialog box provides the following information about your ID file:

- User name
- ID filename and location
- ID type
- Security (North American or International)
- License type
- ID number
- Software number
- Validation code
- Key

You also open this dialog box to do the following:

- Change your user name
- Work with certificates
- Configure for encryption
- Work with advanced options concerning your Notes ID

You will learn more about managing your Notes ID in Chapter 20, "Security and Encryption." For now, we will only look at changing your password.

Caution

Changing your user name removes *all* the certificates from your ID—you will have to acquire new certificates before you can use any shared databases (databases not on your local drive). Contact your Notes Administrator before performing this function!

Perhaps the most important selection on the User ID dialog box enables you to change your password. Security experts say that you should change your password on a regular basis, but most people change their passwords only when they have a pressing need for a new password—for example, if a trusted friend who knows the old password turns out to be a snoop!

To change your password, choose File, Tools, User ID. Enter your current Notes password when prompted. Select the Set Password button. The Enter Password dialog box appears, prompting you for your old password (see fig. 2.10). Enter your old password, and then select OK.

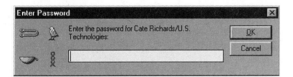

Fig. 2.10

You must first enter your old Notes password in the Enter Password dialog box, and then type your new password when prompted.

Notes will then prompt you with the Set Password dialog box shown in figure 2.11. Type in your new password and then select OK. As is always true when you enter a password, your new password doesn't appear on-screen as you type. To ensure your security, avoid creating passwords that can easily be guessed by those who know you—like your child's or pet's name. Also, as passwords are case-sensitive, you can decrease the chance of someone guessing your password by varying the case of the letters that make up your password. For example, if you want to enter **pluto3** as your password, trying entering **plutO3**—capitalizing the O (or any other letter). Adding numbers to the password also helps discourage people from discovering your password.

Note

The minimum number of characters you need to type to enter a new password may vary— depending on the minimum character limit your Notes Administrator may have set when your Notes ID was issued. Typically, the minimum character limit is set at eight, as suggested by Notes, but could be as low as zero—and anywhere in between. If you try to type a new password and Notes does not accept it, try typing a password with more characters.

Finally, Notes prompts you for your new password again—a safety feature that enables you to be sure that you typed the password correctly. Notes signals an error if you didn't type the same new password both times; otherwise, Notes accepts the new password, which you must use the next time you start Notes or clear your logon. Select D̲one to exit the User ID dialog box.

Fig. 2.11

You can enter a new password in the Set Password dialog box—but take note of the minimum number of characters your Notes ID requires for a password.

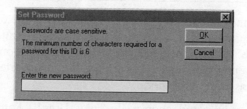

> **Caution**
>
> In the User ID dialog box, there is a Clear password button that removes your password. If you value the security of your mailbox, do not use this option. With your password cleared, anyone who has access to your laptop or PC can access your Notes mailbox and even send mail under your name.

Specifying Your Notes Preferences

Through Notes Preferences, you can customize various aspects of Notes. Choosing F̲ile, T̲ools, U̲ser Preferences gives you the Preferences dialog box which provides a single location for customizing all of your global preference settings.

The Preferences dialog box is divided into the following four sections:

- **Basics**—Displays a panel that enables you to control startup options, the location of your Notes data directory, colors, and your User Dictionary.
- **International**—Displays settings that let you customize the way Notes translates particular international symbols, casing, and collation. You can also select which international dictionary you want to use.
- **Mail**—Displays settings that let you specify how you want your mail treated. You also define the location of your mail database, and which mail program you are using.
- **Ports**—Enables you to control the serial or network port that Notes uses to connect with the Notes server. Your system administrator will be able to assist you with any changes you may want to make in this pane if you are unsure of the settings you need to make. If you are planning to work remote, read Chapter 18, "Setting Up To Go Remote," for more information on the Port settings you need to make.

Basic Settings

The Preferences dialog box always opens to the Basics settings as the default, as shown in figure 2.12. Most of the settings you make in this section will not take effect until you restart Lotus Notes.

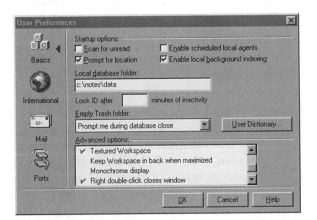

I

Notes Basics

Fig. 2.12

The Basics settings pane lets you change many of the default startup settings in Notes.

The largest portion of the dialog box is devoted to the Startup options, which consist of checkboxes and text entry boxes that govern the actions Notes takes each time you start Notes. The following sections describe the options.

Scanning Unread Documents. If you choose the Scan for unread option, Notes scans some or all of your databases for unread documents each time you start Notes. You can determine which databases Notes scans in the Scan Unread dialog box (for more information, see Chapter 8, "Working With Documents").

Prompting for Location. The Prompt for location option causes Notes to display the Choose Location dialog box every time you start Notes. You might find this feature handy if you travel frequently with your laptop, because you can select from any of the locations you have defined in your Name & Address book. The locations you define tell Notes whether it is on a network or is working remotely. It also lets you tell Notes what phone numbers to call if working remote, and what time zone you are working in. You can also change the date and time entries when prompted for your location. You will learn more about this setting in Part III of this book, "Going Mobile."

Starting the Agent Manager. If you want to automatically start the Agent Manager when you start Notes, select the Enable scheduled local agents option in the Preferences dialog box. With the Agent Manager, you can run agents (macros) in the background. This way, you can have Notes automatically perform tasks that you set up, such as filing documents, finding particular topics, or sending mail at particular times. You learn about working with agents in more detail in Chapter 15, "Buttons and Agents."

Indexing in the Background. The Enable local background indexing option lets you create full text indexes in the background—letting you continue to work while full text indexes are being created. A *full text index* is a collection of files that indexes the text in a database to let you search for text anywhere in the database through queries. You will learn more about full text indexes in Chapter 8, "Working With Documents."

Changing the Default Data Directory. The local database folder in the Preferences dialog box enables you to specify where Notes' data files are kept. C:\NOTES\DATA is the default. You can use this field to specify an alternate directory in which your local databases reside.

If you are upgrading from Notes 3 and did not store your databases in a sub-directory other than C:\NOTES (the default data directory for Notes 3), or you have otherwise specified C:\NOTES as your data directory, you can, and should, store your local databases in a directory other than C:\NOTES if possible. By storing the files in a subdirectory other than C:\NOTES, you can get easier access to them and protect your-self against accidentally deleting important system files when you are "house clean-ing" your data files. If you leave the data directory as C:\NOTES, then your database files will be stored along with all of the program files. Not only is this inefficient, but it can be dangerous as well. It takes longer for you to hunt through several filenames to find your database files when they are not stored separately; and you may acciden-tally select a program file by mistake when copying, moving, or deleting files, which may cause problems in running Notes. Keep in mind that if you move your data files to a different directory, some Notes functions may be affected, such as the use of in-dexes created in R3, or any formulas you have in a database that reference a particular database by the filename and its path.

> **Note**
>
> Release 4 of Notes uses C:\NOTES\DATA as the default data directory when the software is installed; this is a change from Notes 3, which used C:\NOTES as the data directory. Unless you change your data directory, this is where Notes will look for all of your data files. You will find a list of the data files that should be stored in your data directory later in this section.

You can easily create a new data directory and move your data files to it. Usually, this subdirectory is within the Notes subdirectory, but it doesn't have to be! In fact, there are some circumstances in which you may want to specify a different drive name as well as subdirectory name—usually when you are working in a situation in which your hard drive space is limited, but you have plenty of file storage space on a net-work drive.

> **Note**
>
> If you work remote frequently, then you will want to keep your data directory on your local hard drive as you will not always be connected to a LAN. This does not mean that you can't store databases on a network file server; it simply means that they will not be available to you when you are working remote.

To create a data directory other than C:\NOTES, follow these steps:

1. Change the data directory setup by selecting File, Tools, User Preferences and typing the new local database directory name in the text box. For example, type **C:\NOTES\DATA** (or substitute your new directory name for D:\NOTES\DATA).

> **Tip**
>
> Write the new data directory down, exactly as it was entered in this step. You may want to reference the full path and directory name in step 5.

2. Select OK to save the entry.

3. Close Notes and open File Manager or Explorer in Windows. If you are running a different operating system, follow your operating system's procedures for making subdirectories and moving files into them. You will need to close Notes to move the DESKTOP.DSK file as it will be in use otherwise.

   If you already have a C:\NOTES\DATA directory created, and just need to move your data files, skip to step 6.

4. Highlight the drive or directory folder where you want to locate the new data directory. For example, if you want the new data directory to be located within the Notes directory, highlight the Notes directory folder.

5. Select File, Create Directory. In the Create Directory dialog box, type the name of the new data directory. The name can contain up to eight characters (in our example, create a data directory in the C:\NOTES subdirectory named DATA).

6. Select File, Search. Type ***.NSF** in the Search For text box (make sure you include the asterisk in this entry). Type **C:** in the Start From text box if you want to copy all databases on your hard drive to your new data directory, and then choose OK. Once you have located all of your .NSF files, select all of them by pressing the Shift key and clicking the first filename in the list, and then the last filename in the list. All of the database files will be selected, and ready to move into the new data directory (DATA, in this example).

> **Note**
>
> If you have several subdirectories in which you store Notes databases and you only want to move the files in C:\NOTES, then you may want to enter **C:\NOTES** in the Start From text box to move only the databases stored in the existing C:\NOTES subdirectory.
>
> If your previous data directory was stored elsewhere, and you want to move your files, type that subdirectory's path in the Start From text box.

7. Select File, Move (not Copy, as that would leave a copy of the database files in the old directory—taking up unnecessary hard drive space). Enter the entire path name in the To text box. For this example, type **C:\NOTES\DATA** as the path.

   You must also move the following files to your new data directory following the same procedures in steps 4 and 5, substituting the appropriate file extensions as needed:

   - Any Version 2 databases stored with the .NS2 extension.
   - Your DESKTOP.DSK file. You will learn more about this file later in this chapter.
   - Any character and language files that you have installed. These files end in the .CLS file extension.
   - Your locally stored template files (.NTF files).
   - Your personal dictionary file (where you have defined words in the spell checker) titled USER.DIC.
   - If you work with OS/2, your NOTES.INI file.

8. Select OK to move the files.

9. Exit File Manager or Explorer and restart Notes.

You will now have a new data directory in which your existing Notes databases are located. You may experience a slight delay the first time you open a database that has been moved into the new data directory—this is because Notes is updating its location information.

If you receive a prompt from Notes indicating that it cannot find a database in the new data directory, check to make sure that the file was moved, and that you correctly updated the Local database directory name in the Preferences dialog box.

If you experience any problems—for example, Notes will not start after you make these changes, or you discover that your desktop is blank when Notes starts—check to make sure you correctly moved your DESKTOP.DSK file, NOTES.INI file (if you use OS/2), and the other files listed above into your new data directory.

Setting the Automatic Log-off Point. The Lock ID after minutes of inactivity option lets you specify the number of minutes you want Notes to keep your password active before logging you off when you haven't touched your keyboard or mouse.

> **Tip**
>
> Don't make this setting so short that you do not have a chance to review a complex document, embedded chart, or spreadsheet. A setting between 15–30 minutes is usually sufficient to protect your Notes security, while minimizing the number of times you spend typing your password during a Notes session.

Selecting Advanced Options. You can select from many advanced options that let you further control many of Notes options when it starts up. The list of options is summarized in the following sections.

Selecting a Font. Notes normally uses *proportional fonts*, where letters require varying amounts of screen space—a capital *M,* for example, takes up much more space than a lowercase *i.* The Typewriter fonts option tells Notes to display all information (including database titles, views, and documents) in *monospace fonts*, in which all letters take up the same amount of space. You may find this option useful for checking the width of columns. If a column is wide enough in a monospace font to display the entire contents of the column, it will probably be wide enough when you switch back to a proportional (non-monospace) font.

The Large fonts option tells Notes to display text in large letters. This will increase the font size displayed in the database icons (as well as the size of the database icon). It will also increase the font in the views and forms as it is displayed on your workstation. It will not change the size that the font prints, or the size in which it is displayed by other users—unless they have also selected Large fonts. You may find this option handy if the regular characters are too small to read comfortably on-screen, if you need to view the screen from a distance, or if you give a presentation in which many people need to see the screen.

> **Caution**
>
> Selecting this option may cut off text in your database titles. This happens because the text becomes too large to fit in the small areas.

Using Monochrome Settings. The Monochrome display option tells Notes to display everything in black and white (monochrome), even on a color monitor if you are using Windows-based operating systems, OS/2, or UNIX. You may find this option handy occasionally if you design databases and want to see how they would look on a monochrome monitor.

Keeping the Maximized Workspace in Back. The Keep Workspace in back when maximized option lets you keep the Notes workspace behind other open windows automatically when you have the Notes window maximized. This way, each time you close a window, Notes returns to the last window that was current instead of to the workspace.

Closing Windows with Right Double-Click. The Right double-click closes window option lets you use your right mouse button to close any open window by double-clicking it while your cursor is anywhere within the window. If you were a former Notes 3 user, you will probably want to select this option immediately!

Marking Previewed Documents as Read. Choose the Mark read when opened in preview pane option if you want Notes to mark a document as being read when you preview it using the preview pane. You will learn more about the preview pane in Chapter 3, "Using Databases."

Changing the Texture of Your Workspace. You can select to have Notes display the workspace with a 3D, marbled look by selecting Textured workspace. When you click a database icon with this selection, it appears to flatten against the workspace to indicate that it is selected.

Keeping All Notes Windows Within the Main Notes Window. You can select the Keep all Notes windows within the Main Notes Window (MDI) option to have Notes windows maximize only as large as the main workspace window. This option is selected as the default option. If you deselect this option, Notes windows opened within the main Notes window can be maximized to fill the entire screen—even if the main Notes window does not.

Make Internet URLs into Hotspots. You can select the Make Internet URLs into hotspots option to have Notes automatically convert Internet addresses into hotspots if you are set up to have Notes interface with the Internet through the new Web browser feature of Notes R4. URL stands for Uniform Resource Locator, which is the World Wide Web name for a document, file, or other resource. It describes the protocol required to access the resource, the host where it can be found, and a path to the resource on that host.

Emptying Your Mail Trash. Your mail database contains a trash folder that contains all of the mail you have marked for deletion during a session. You can tell Notes how to empty the trash folder. You have three options:

- Choose Prompt me during database close to have Notes ask you whether you want to clear the mail in the trash folder each time you close your mail database. This is the default selection.

- Choose Always during database close to have Notes automatically clear the mail in the trash folder each time you close your mail database.

> **Caution**
>
> Once you empty your trash folder, you can not undo your deletion selection. You will not be able to get the mail back!

■ Choose Manually to cancel automatic clearing of the trash folder. If you select this option, you will have to select Actions, Empty Trash to clear the mail in the trash folder.

Changing the User Dictionary. Selecting the Underline{U}ser Dictionary button causes Notes to display the User Spell Dictionary dialog box (see fig. 2.13). Through this dialog box, you can add, update, and delete words that you have defined in your personal data dictionary.

Fig. 2.13

Your User Spell Dictionary is used in conjunction with the Notes Spell Dictionary when you spell-check documents.

To add new words to your dictionary, type the new word in the text entry box at the bottom of the dialog box, and then click Add. To delete a word, select the word from the scrolling list box, and then press the Delete button. To edit an existing word, select the word from the scrolling list box, edit the text in the text entry box, and then select Update. Select OK to exit the dialog box and save your changes, or Cancel to exit without saving your changes.

Caution

Do not press Esc to exit this (or any) Notes dialog box. Doing so will cause you to lose any setting changes you have made—it is the same as clicking the Cancel button.

International Settings

To display the options for International settings, click the International icon in the Preferences dialog box. Notes displays the International settings panel shown in figure 2.14. Through this dialog box, you can control characteristics that tend to vary from one country to another. These characteristics are described in the following sections.

Note

The International settings here do not change the currency denomination indicator, nor the date format used in many countries outside of North America. You make these changes in your operating system.

(continues)

(continued)

For example, if you want to use British pounds Sterling, or the date format dd\mm\yy, you could open up the Control Panel in Windows and select the International icon. Change the Country setting to United Kingdom. The currency indicator and date format default would then be changed to reflect the common format used in the United Kingdom.

Check your operating system information for additional information on changing the international default settings.

Fig. 2.14

You can change your dictionary, Import/Export character translation sets, and other settings that typically change based upon your international location.

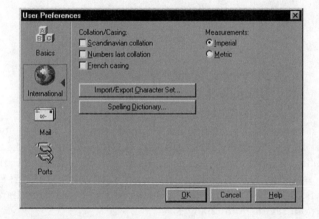

Controlling Collation and Casing. In Lotus Notes, database designers can specify that items listed in a view display in a particular sort order—ascending or descending. The Collation/Casing options let you tell Notes how to treat some of the characters when sorting. You can choose any or all of the options. If you choose Scandinavian collation, Notes puts accented characters at the end of the alphabet (which is where the Scandinavians put them). If you choose Numbers last collation, Notes considers numbers to come after letters (thus, part number 6X032 would appear after ZY512). If you choose French casing, Notes discards accent marks when you change lowercase letters to uppercase.

Notes uses Country Language Services files (.CLS files) to translate international currency symbols such as the pound (£) and the yen (¥) symbols, and accented letters when you import or export data from Notes. Notes also uses .CLS files to determine the order in which characters are sorted.

Tip

To resort the documents in an existing database with the selections made in this section, restart Notes and then press Shift+F9 after you open the database you want to view. If you want to re-index all databases, press Shift+F9 while viewing the main workspace—this may take awhile if you have a lot of databases on your workspace, or if the databases you are indexing have a large number of documents.

The collation and casing options are turned off by default. If you choose these options, they don't take effect until the next time you start Notes. If you can't safely assume that every user will set up the collation and casing options the way you want them to appear in a particular database, be sure to incorporate the necessary sort settings into your design.

Changing the Unit of Measurement. The Measurements radio buttons enable you to specify Imperial units of measurement (inches, the default) or Metric units (centimeters). Your choice determines whether you must specify margins and tabs in inches or in centimeters. If you have the ruler displayed, this option changes the unit of measurement to inches or centimeters.

Translating Files. The Import/Export Character Set button enables you to specify a file for translating foreign characters and symbols from a non-Notes file into Notes. When you press this button, you are greeted with the Choose Translation Table dialog box (see fig. 2.15).

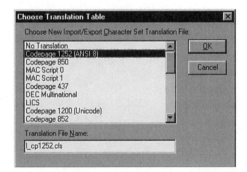

Fig. 2.15

The selection you make in the Choose Translation Table dialog box determines how Notes will translate characters when you import or export documents.

You can either select an existing translation (.CLS) file from the Choose New Import/ Export Character Set Translation File list box, or type the path and filename of a .CLS file that you want to use that is not stored in your data directory. See Chapter 12, "Integrating Notes 4.0 with Other Applications," for more information about importing and exporting data.

Selecting a Dictionary. The Spelling Dictionary button enables you to tell Notes which dictionary (such as French or British) to use, instead of the American dictionary. The following list shows the available dictionaries:

> British (ise) English
>
> British (ize) English
>
> British Medical (ise)
>
> British Medical (ize)
>
> Brazilian
>
> Canadian French
>
> Catalan

Czech

Danish

Finnish

French

Greek

Italian

Norwegian

Nynorsk

Polish

Portuguese

Russian

Russian Jo

Spanish

Swedish

Swiss German

American English

American Medical

Australian

German

Dutch German

Dutch Preferred

French (capital letters accented)

French (capital letters not accented)

The dictionary files selected here are not the same as your User Dictionary, in which you add terms when you select Define while using the spell checker. These files are located in your Notes program directories. The default file is English, denoted by the file name ENGLISH.DIC.

Tip

If you write documents that must be sent from your home office to an office in a different country, change the dictionary before running the spell checker. This is particularly helpful when sending/receiving documents between countries that vary in the use of British (ise) English and British (ize) English spellings.

Mail Settings

You can control how Notes accesses and processes your mailbox by selecting File, Tools, User Preferences, and then selecting the Mail icon in the left hand side of the dialog box. Notes displays the Mail setup options in the Preferences dialog box (see fig. 2.16).

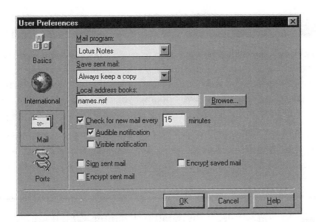

Fig. 2.16

You can customize the way Notes treats mail in the User Preferences Mail pane.

Notes Basics

Specifying the Mail Program and Mail File. The Mail program field identifies the mail system you are using, and should be set to Lotus Notes, the default, unless otherwise specified by your Notes administrator.

You specify where your mail file is located in the Location documents stored in your Personal Name & Address Book. Typically, your mail file is located in the C:\NOTES\MAIL subdirectory; and is typically named using the first letter of your first name, and the first seven letters of your last name—followed by the NSF file extension, for example, C:\NOTES\MAIL\DDERHAMM.NSF. If your mail file is located in a subdirectory other than C:\NOTES\MAIL, then you may need to edit your Location document accordingly. You can read more about working with Location documents in Chapter 18, "Setting Up To Go Remote."

> **Note**
>
> You can forward any mail document from any Notes database—if you are set up as the user of the workstation you are using. This means that in addition to switching to your user ID, and adding your mail database to the workspace, you must edit your Locations document to point to the correct mail file location and name. Click the Locations indicator in the status bar at the bottom of the Notes window, and select Edit, Current to open the current Location document in edit mode. Edit the mail file to indicate your mail filename. The entry usually looks something like mail\crichard. Press Esc to exit the document, and select Yes to save your setting. If you need to edit all of your Location settings, open your Personal Name & Address Book, and then select the Locations view from the Navigator. Edit each document as described previously. You will learn more about the Location document in Chapter 18, "Setting Up To Go Remote."

Saving Sent Mail. The Save sent mail option tells Notes how you want to treat mail when you select the Send button (or select Actions, Send Document). If you want to Always keep a copy of a memo that you send, select this option. If you do not want to save a copy when you send a memo, select Don't keep a copy. If you want Notes to prompt you to save every time you send a message, select Always prompt.

Caution

If you select Don't keep a copy, you will not be prompted to save a document when you select the Send button to send the message. Notes will simply send the document and close it. If you later need to reference the document, you will not be able to unless the recipient forwards it back to you. It is safer to select one of the other two options if you think you will need to review any of the messages you send.

However, if you right double-click, or press Esc to exit and send the document, rather than clicking the Send button, your default selection for saving sent mail will be highlighted in the checkbox, but you will be able to deselect the option for that instance before you select Yes to send the mail message.

Checking for New Mail. As you will learn in detail in Chapter 4, Mail notifies you when new mail arrives. By changing the number of minutes in the Check for new mail every minutes setting, you can control how often Notes checks the server to see whether new mail arrived in your mailbox. If you need to quickly know when new mail has arrived, enter a small number (perhaps 3 or 4). If you receive mail rarely, or if you do not need to be notified immediately, entering a larger number (15 or 20) saves your computer the work of frequent checking. If you uncheck the associated checkbox, Notes won't automatically inform you when new mail has arrived—you've got to check for yourself periodically.

Signing and Encrypting Sent Mail. If you select the Sign sent mail checkbox, Notes checks the Sign box when you mail a document. Chapter 4, "Getting Started with Electronic Mail," describes in more detail the Sign checkbox, which serves much the same purpose as a signature on a paper message.

Selecting the Encrypt sent mail option automatically checks the Encrypt box when you close a mail document. See Chapter 20, "Security and Encryption," for more information about encrypting messages.

Encrypting Saved Mail. If you check the Encrypt saved mail option, Notes encrypts mail stored in your mailbox on the server, and in your hard drive if you work remote and have a copy of your mail database there. While you can generally assume that your mailbox is private and secure, a few people, such as your system administrator(s), can access your mailbox without your permission. You can use this option if you are particularly concerned about keeping the messages in your mailbox secure.

Ports Settings

The Ports panel in the Preferences dialog box provides options and buttons that enable you or your system administrator to configure how your computer communicates with your server, and what kind of network or modem your computer has. After your computer is set up, you normally do not have to adjust any of these options if you are working on the network. If you are not experienced with the requirements of your network, consult with your system administrator if you need to change your Ports setup.

If you are working remote, then you will find that you may use the Ports preferences quite frequently. If you want to learn more about this preference panel, read Chapter 18, "Setting Up To Go Remote."

Configuring Options Under Windows and OS/2

Many of the most important preference choices you can make are controlled not by Notes, but by Windows, Macintosh, UNIX, or OS/2. For example, through the Windows Control Panel or the OS/2 System Setup, you can specify the following parameters:

- Some screen colors (for example, the colors of borders and title bars)
- Available fonts and font sizes
- International settings (such as country name, currency symbol, and time and date formats)
- Types and configurations of printers

Consult your Windows or OS/2 manual for more information about these parameters.

The *DESKTOP.DSK* File

When working with Notes, it is often helpful to understand a little something about the key files that are accessed in your daily use of the program. The DESKTOP.DSK file is one of the files that you should be familiar with. Information about your workspace is stored in your local data directory in a file named DESKTOP.DSK. This file stores the following information:

- The database icons you've added to your workspace
- The workpage tabs and names you've added to your workspace
- Settings made in the File Page Setup dialog box, such as headers and footers
- Design information about any private views or folders you may have
- The number of documents still unread in a database

Your DESKTOP.DSK tells Notes where it should display all of your database icons when you start up Notes. It also stores all of your private view definitions for all databases you have access to. *Private views* are ones that you have designed for yourself, that are not available to other users of a database. You will learn how to design them in Chapter 11, "Designing Views."

Caution

If you delete the DESKTOP.DSK file, or it becomes corrupted for any reason, you will lose all of the desktop settings (i.e., database icons, tab names, etc.), and you will lose all of your private views! Keep this in mind when working with this file. You should back up the DESKTOP.DSK file regularly, using your operating system—perhaps once a month, depending on how you'd feel if you experienced a problem that caused the loss of this file.

The DESKTOP.DSK file can grow as large as 50 MB—a big file! The larger your DESKTOP.DSK file, the slower your response time can become—not to mention the amount of space it takes up on your hard drive. As you add private views and databases to your desktop, this file grows.

Note

You can compact the DESKTOP.DSK file, just as you would any other database. Compacting databases is discussed in Chapter 3, "Using Databases."

When you delete database icons from your desktop, or private views from databases, the space that was taken up will be freed—but the size of the file will not be reduced. When you add new database icons to the workspace, or private views to databases, they will first take up the freed space—before the file size grows more.

Changing the Location of *DESKTOP.DSK*

By default, Notes will look for the DESKTOP.DSK file in the data directory (defined in the User Setup dialog box). The data directory is identified in the NOTES.INI file with the following parameter:

```
Directory=[drive]:\[directory]
```

If you want to locate the DESKTOP.DSK in a directory other than the data directory, you can add the following line to the NOTES.INI file:

```
Desktop=[drive]:\[directory]\DESKTOP.DSK
```

While it is recommended that you keep your DESKTOP.DSK file in your data directory under normal circumstances, you may find the need to locate an alternate DESKTOP.DSK file for when you perform demonstrations—in which you don't want your normal desktop settings displayed.

For example, if you wanted to store a second copy of your DESKTOP.DSK file to be used when teaching a class, you could enter the following in the NOTES.INI file:

```
Desktop=C:\CLASS\DESKTOP.DSK
```

When you start Notes, Notes will look in the CLASS subdirectory for the DESKTOP.DSK file. When you no longer want to use the special DESKTOP.DSK file, you will need to modify this line again to change where Notes looks for your DESKTOP.DSK file.

You will also need to store your DESKTOP.DSK file in a separate directory if you are sharing your workstation with someone else. In this circumstance, consult with your Notes Administrator for assistance, because special settings will need to be made to your workstation, in addition to locating your DESKTOP.DSK file in a separate directory.

Compacting Your *DESKTOP.DSK* File

As you work in Lotus Notes, you add database icons, workpages, private views, and other features whose definitions are stored in your DESKTOP.DSK file. As you remove some of these features, Notes leaves some "white space" in the database where the definition used to be stored. Over time, this white space builds up, and takes up valuable disk drive space. You can, however, remove the white space by compacting your DESKTOP.DSK file. This recovers unused disk space by removing references to databases you no longer have on your workspace. To compact your DESKTOP.DSK file, follow these steps:

1. Double-click any workspace tab. The Workspace Properties InfoBox will open.

2. Click the Information tab. (The tab is marked with a bold, lowercased *i*.) The Information tab will be displayed (see fig. 2.17).

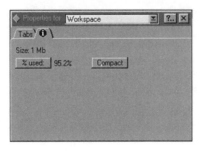

Fig. 2.17

The Information tab allows you to compact your DESKTOP.DSK *file.*

3. Click the % used button.

4. If the percentage is under 85 percent, click the Compact button. (If the percentage is over 85 percent, there's no need to compact yet.)

You will now be working with a cleaner DESKTOP.DSK file that takes up less space on your hard drive. You should periodically check the size of your DESKTOP.DSK file for "housekeeping"—particularly if you are short on hard drive space.

Notes Basics

Handling a Corrupted *DESKTOP.DSK* File

If your DESKTOP.DSK file becomes corrupted, you will need to close Notes and delete the DESKTOP.DSK file through your operating system commands. When you start Notes again, a new DESKTOP.DSK file will be created—of course, you lose all of your workspace customization and private view information.

> **Tip**
>
> By having a backup copy of your DESKTOP.DSK file, you can quickly restore your workspace and private views—without having to re-create the views from scratch. Simply copy the backup copy of the DESKTOP.DSK file over the corrupted file in your data directory.

From Here...

In this chapter, you learned how to customize some of the characteristics of Notes to your tastes. This customization should make your work with Notes more pleasing. For more information on the topics discussed in this chapter, refer to the following:

- Chapter 4, "Getting Started with Electronic Mail," teaches you how to work with Lotus NotesMail and the Name & Address Books.

- Chapter 11, "Designing Views," explains how to create private views, which enable you to list documents in a database according to your own needs.

- Chapter 18, "Setting Up To Go Remote," shows how to configure your laptop for remote access to Notes.

CHAPTER 3

Using Databases

Some of the thousands of companies that use Lotus Notes only use it for its e-mail capability. Most companies, however, find that Notes can provide additional flexibility and value through the unique database capabilities it provides. Lotus Notes databases can store, organize, and retrieve any type of information (text, graphics, sound, and so on), are easy to use, allow local and remote users to share information in a timely fashion, and can be developed very quickly.

This chapter discusses the following:

- Parts and types of databases
- How an access control list (ACL) works
- Changing database settings
- Opening, saving, closing, and deleting documents and databases
- Using the universal viewer
- Working with file folders
- Printing documents and views

Understanding Databases

Once you understand how databases are used and designed, you can begin to harness the power of Notes. Notes databases are very flexible and can be used for almost any application because they support *semi-structured* and *unstructured data* (this means that the type and amount of data can vary from record to record), support importing data from external applications, can create links to external applications to provide dynamic data updating, and can even have information e-mailed in. In addition, Notes provides very tight database security to hide your data from prying eyes.

Notes databases generally are grouped loosely into the following categories:

- System databases
- Mail databases
- Help databases
- Discussion databases
- Document libraries
- Tracking databases
- Workflow databases

These categories are presented only to describe the most common ways that Notes databases are used. This list is by no means inclusive of all the possible applications for Notes applications; in fact, many of the best Notes solutions are a mixture of different types of Notes applications.

> **Note**
>
> In Notes jargon, the terms *application* and *database* are used interchangeably because Notes databases contain the design elements that comprise an application.

Internally, Notes does not classify or categorize databases in any way. You use the same methods and commands to access and navigate through all Notes databases.

The following sections describe each type of database.

Databases

System databases provide important information to Notes. The system databases are especially important, as they contain information that is required for Notes to function correctly—well-maintained system databases can make your Notes sessions much more productive and enjoyable. The following short sections describe the system databases.

Address Books. Your *Public Address Book* and *Private Address Book* contain information about all Notes users in your company, as well as server connections, locations, groups, and many other types of Notes control documents. Chapter 5, "Using the Address Books," describes the address books in vivid detail—they are absolutely essential for Notes to operate correctly, as they are used to find other system users, to verify database access, and to do other important jobs. Figure 3.1 shows some typical address book icons.

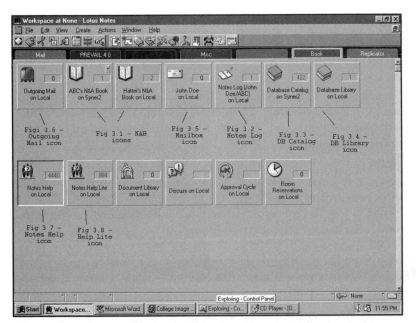

Fig. 3.1

The Public and Personal Name & Address Book icons—along with the other icons—have new R4 graphics.

Notes Log. Your personal *Notes Log* database records information about system activity that takes place while you are using Notes. Some of the many things that are tracked in the Notes Log are replication events, phone calls (if you are working remotely), database usage, and many other miscellaneous events. Each Notes server also has a Notes Log database that tracks server activity. The Notes Log database is an invaluable tool for troubleshooting problems

Database Catalog. The *database catalog* provides information regarding databases that are available to you in your Notes network, including information such as where each database is located, and the policy for using each database. The database catalog is a database that is automatically created when Notes is installed, and that normally is updated each night automatically by a server task on the Notes server.

Database Libraries. *Database libraries* are designed to make it easy for users to find databases that are of particular interest to them. Database libraries can be public (when they reside on a server) or private (when they reside on a workstation). When the Notes R4 client software is installed, it automatically creates a database library for your machine that keeps track of the databases on your machine. In addition, database libraries can be created on the server that pertain only to a specific type of database. For instance, all the databases regarding sales might be "published" in the Sales Library database so that other users can find them easily.

Mail Databases

Mail databases are databases that the Notes mail system uses to store and route e-mail messages. (These databases are covered in detail in Chapter 4, "Getting Started with Electronic Mail," and Chapter 6, "Advanced Mail.")

Mailbox. Your *mailbox* is the database in which Notes stores your incoming mail and your outgoing mail if you elect to save it. Chapter 4, "Getting Started with Electronic Mail," describes the basics of using your mailbox; Chapter 6, "Advanced Mail," contains more advanced information.

Outgoing Mailbox. The *outgoing mailbox* (this will automatically appear on your workspace when you are configured to use workstation-based mail) is used to store all outgoing mail until you connect with the server, and the router transfers the mail to the server. This database can be very helpful when troubleshooting mail problems for a workstation configured to use workstation-based mail.

> **Tip**
>
> If you are set up to use workstation-based mail, you can open the Outgoing Mail database and select the Pending Mail view to examine mail that is waiting to be sent. If you decide, for instance, that you would rather not send that mail to your boss stating that you quit, you can delete it from Outgoing Mail, and she'll never know the message was written.

Help Databases

In Notes R4, most, if not all, of the documentation is online in Notes databases. This is particularly useful because you can install these databases on your machine and take them with you wherever you go (at the cost of considerable disk space); and even better, you can Full Text Index the Help databases so that finding help on a given topic can be done very quickly and easily. Notes R4 ships with several Help databases, but the two that most users will find most useful are the Notes Help and Notes Help Lite databases.

Notes Help. The *Notes Help database* (HELP4.NSF) contains the full end user online documentation for Notes R4. Although this database can be very useful, it is also very large (4600+ documents for a total on-disk size of approximately 21 megabytes) and may be too much for users whose hard disk space is at a premium. If you have the space on your local workstation, it is highly recommended that you install this database and create a Full Text Index (which, using the default settings, will consume another 6 megabytes of disk space) on the database for easy searching.

Notes Help Lite. The *Notes Help Lite database* (HELPLITE.NSF) is a much smaller subset (it is approximately 6 megabytes) of the full Help database designed primarily with the mobile user in mind.

Other Help Databases. Notes also includes many other useful online help databases that you may or may not be able to access (if you cannot find the following databases, see your administrator):

- **Notes Administration Help** (HELPADMN.NSF)—This database contains detailed information geared towards Notes administrators.
- **Install Guide for Workstations** (WRKINST.NSF)—This database contains detailed information for people responsible for Notes R4 workstation installations.
- **Install Guide for Servers** (SRVINST.NSF)—Much like the Install Guide for Workstations, this database is geared towards Notes server installations.
- **Migration Guide** (MIGRATE.NSF)—This database contains detailed information for users migrating from older versions of Notes to Notes R4.
- **R4 Features** (R4FEAT.NSF)—This database serves to highlight many of the new features that can be found in Notes R4.

Sample Databases

Sample databases are databases that Lotus has developed and included for you to use as learning tools when building your own database applications. In addition, you can use these databases as foundations from which to build your own database applications. If your workstation was set up with the default installation, these databases are located in the C:\NOTES\DATA directory. These databases are known as *templates* and end in the extension NTF (Notes Template Facility)—you learn more about templates in later chapters. For example, you can examine MEETTRAK.NTF, a sample meeting-tracking database, to learn how the various components of a Notes database are assembled when building applications.

Discussion Databases

Discussion databases are one of the most common uses for Notes databases. These databases are designed to facilitate communication and collaboration among groups of people. Normally a discussion database has very little structure, so users are free to use it as they see fit. Many companies "cut their teeth" in database development and deployment with discussion databases because they usually are very simple, and can quickly provide a high return on investment. An example of a discussion database is a database that provides technical information and tips for users of Lotus Notes. Lotus includes a discussion database template, titled Discussion (R4) (DISCUSS.NTF is the actual filename) for you to use as a basis for designing discussion databases.

Document Libraries

Document library databases provide an electronic repository for documents that remain relatively static but must be distributed to a large or geographically-dispersed group of users in a timely fashion. A good example of this type of database is a marketing encyclopedia database that contains product information brochures, sales literature, and electronic presentations for salespeople to share and use while on the road. Lotus was kind enough to include the Document Library template, Document Library (R4) (DOCLIB4.NTF), that can be used when you want to create simple document library databases.

Tracking Databases

Tracking databases are usually highly interactive, and have many users contributing data to the database. An example of this would be a complaint-tracking database used by the customer service group to track complaints and progress toward resolution of the complaints. Another example would be a help desk database in which trouble tickets were entered. After each problem was resolved, the solution would be available for other technicians to use. Lotus has included the Room Reservations (R4) template (RESERVE4.NTF) that can be useful when creating a tracking application.

Workflow Databases

Workflow databases are used generally to automate routine tasks in order to compress cycle time and increase efficiency. A common application of this concept is an expense reports database that electronically routes expense reports to the proper managers for approval, and then to payroll for the payout. Lotus has included a workflow database template, Approval Cycle (R4) (APPROVE4.NTF is the actual filename) that can be very useful as the foundation for a workflow database.

Template Overview

Notes R4 ships with many other useful templates summarized in Table 3.1. For more information regarding the use of these templates, please see the document titled "About Notes Application Templates" in the Help Database, which provides a description of the usage of each template; or choose a template and click the About button in the New Database dialog box.

▶▶ See "Using Templates," p. 326

In addition to these templates, there are many advanced system templates that can be used, but these fall outside the scope of this chapter. For more information regarding these advanced templates, see the document titled "About Notes System Templates" in the Notes Help database.

Table 3.1 Useful Database Templates Included with Notes R4		
Template Title	**Template Name**	**Filename**
Approval Cycle	StdR4Approval	APPROVE4.NTF
Discussion (R4)	StdR4Disc	DISCUSS4.NTF
Document Library (R4)	StdR4DocLib	DOCLIB4.NTF
Lotus Smart Suite Library (R4)	StdR4DocLibLS	DOCLIBL4.NTF
Microsoft Office Library (R4)	StdR4DocLibMS	DOCLIBM4.NTF
Personal Journal (R4)	StdR4Journal	JOURNAL4.NTF
Room Reservations (R4)	StdR4Room	RESERVE.NTF

Accessing a Database

Before you can access the data contained in a Notes database, you must have a database icon that represents that database on your workspace. You can add an icon for any database to which you have been granted access rights (you learn more about access rights later in this chapter in the section "Understanding Access Control Lists") to your workspace.

Adding a new database icon to your workspace is quite simple. Figure 3.2 shows you the menu options you use to do so. Just choose File, Database, Open (or press Ctrl+0).

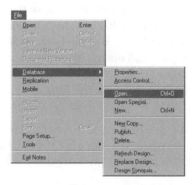

Fig. 3.2

The File menu options are used to add a database icon to your workspace.

You then are presented with a dialog box like the one shown in figure 3.3, giving you a list of the Notes servers available from your machine, and a list of all Notes databases on that server.

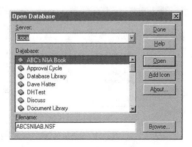

Fig. 3.3

The Open Database dialog box.

You can use the Server list box to choose the server on which the database of interest resides. Once you have chosen a server, the Database list box shows the title of each database on the server. If the server you have selected is not a local server (for instance, you are working remote) you can use the Call button to dial in to the server and see which databases are available.

Note

The list of databases you see might not include every database on the server, because the database designer or database manager may elect to hide certain databases from the Open Database dialog box, and/or some databases may reside in other Notes Named Networks. In addition, you do not necessarily have access rights to every database in the list. If you do not see a database listed, but you know the actual filename of the database, you can type it into the Filename field and open the database if you have sufficient access rights. If you cannot find a database that you think should be listed, or cannot access a listed database, see your administrator.

When you select a database from the list, the actual filename of the database is displayed in the Filename box below the Database list box. At this point, if you want to add a database icon to your workspace and open the database, click the Open button, which places the icon on your workspace and opens the database. If you only want to add the database icon to your workspace, click the Add Icon button (if you are going to add several icons, this is the best way to go, since opening each database would be an unnecessary waste of time).

The About button can be used to help you identify the use of a particular database. When you click the About button, the About document of the database (if one exists) is displayed—this should provide information on the intended use of a database.

As in all Windows applications, clicking the Help button at this location displays help about using the Open Database dialog. If you cannot find a database by its title, you can click the Browse button to display the standard File dialog box to allow you to search for a database by its filename (see fig. 3.4).

Fig. 3.4

The Choose a Notes database or template file dialog box.

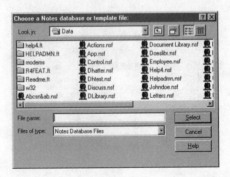

Once you have created an icon for the database you want to access, you are ready to begin working with the database. Before you do so, you need to understand what the different parts of a database are, and how those parts interact.

Parts of a Database

Each Notes database is a distinct, on-disk structure with a filename that must meet the operating system conventions and must be unique. For example, if you are using the Notes Windows 3.11 client, you are limited to the DOS naming standard, which is eight characters for the filename and three characters for the file extension. If you have questions about valid filename, consult the documentation for your operating system. By default, all Notes databases have the extension NSF.

Note

While Notes databases normally end with the NSF extension, a Notes database is not required to have an NSF extension. If you use an extension other than NSF, the database will not appear automatically in the Open Database dialog box in the list of database files.

Besides its filename, each database has a *database title* that is displayed on the database icon. Each database title can contain a maximum of 32 characters, allowing much more descriptive naming of the database. For example, you might have a Notes database that contains information about your competitors—its filename could be `COMPET.NSF` but the database title could be `ABC's Competitors' Information`. Unless you create your own databases, the filename and database title for each database you access already will have been defined by someone else.

If multiple users need access to a database, it must reside on the Notes server. If you are the only user, you may store it on the Notes server or keep it locally on your hard disk. In fact, one of the nicest features of Notes is that in most instances, you do not need to know where the database physically resides. Notes keeps track of database locations, and all you need to do is double-click the database icon to access whatever data the database contains.

Once you have accessed a database, it is important to understand how information is structured and organized by Notes. The internal architecture of a Notes database is unique. Like any database, a Notes database is a collection of related information, but unlike traditional relational databases, any type of information can be stored in a Notes database. In fact, Notes is particularly well suited at storing semi-structured information and unstructured information.

Lotus describes a Notes database as an object store—it can store, organize, and retrieve any type of data object. It might be helpful to visualize a Notes database as an open box. Just as you can put any real world object into an open box (if you have enough room in the box to accommodate the object), you can put any type of data object in a Notes database. Each database is comprised of several building blocks:

- Documents
- Forms
- Views
- Folders
- Fields
- Access control lists

Understanding Documents

The fundamental data storage units in a Notes database are *documents* (these correspond loosely to *records* in a relational database—see the following note). Each document contains one or more items that may store a variety of data types: text, numbers, dates, images, sound, and so on. All the information that pertains to one specific entry in the database is stored within a document. For example, if you are using a contact management database, one document in the database might contain information such as the company name, contact name, customer address, customer phone, and how many times you have contacted the customer. Each individual customer would have their own document.

Each document can contain any amount of information, from a single character to several pages of text and graphics—the size is limited only by the amount of available disk space. This lack of size limitations is in direct contrast to relational databases, where field and record sizes are strictly defined in the database structure.

> **Note**
>
> Relational databases store information by breaking it down into individual data elements and maintaining it in tabular fashion (think of a spreadsheet). Related data elements (fields) are grouped as rows in the table, and related rows (records) are stored in the same table (database). Because of this data-centered view, relational databases are *transaction-oriented* meaning they reflect only the most current state of the data. For data in a relational database to be useful, the end user must be able to sort and query the data in various ways.

The database designer developer's forms, in conventional terms, can be thought of as a data entry screen to provide the structure of a document. For more information on documents, see Chapter 8, "Working with Documents."

Forms

Forms essentially are templates that provide the format and layout when entering data into new documents, or when displaying and editing data from existing documents. Each database must contain at least one form, and the form that the designer decides will be the most used form is designated as the default form. Each form is created by the database designer, and can contain static text, fields, graphics, and buttons.

> **Note**
>
> It might be easier for you to understand Notes forms by thinking about pre-printed paper forms. Each year, for example, the IRS needs to collect certain information from you to guarantee that when April 15th rolls around, you have remitted the correct amount of income tax. In order to make it as easy as possible for you to give them the information they seek, and to ensure that they get the information they need, they provide the 1040 form. This form contains instructions to guide you as you fill out the form, special areas (fields) where you fill in the information they need, and sections that group logically related information. If the IRS did not provide these structured forms, they would face total chaos as there would be no consistency between the information from one taxpayer to the next. Notes forms work exactly the same way.

When you choose the Create menu to create a new document, Notes presents a list of forms that are available in the selected database (see fig. 3.5). You must choose a form from that list before you can enter data. Once a form has been selected, the form is displayed and you can begin to enter data into the fields present on the form.

Fig. 3.5

The Create menu in the Employee database.

When you elect to save the document, Notes stores the name of the form in use in a special field named "Form" in the document. The next time the document is accessed, Notes examines the contents of the Form field to determine which form should be used to display the document. If no form name is found, the document is displayed using the default form.

> **Note**
>
> Documents can be displayed using any form in the database; however, this can cause a great deal of confusion, as fields in the form might not align with items in the document. Data that the user expects to see might not be displayed, and data the user is not expecting might be displayed.

Views. In order for the individual data elements contained in Notes documents to become useful information, it must be organized in ways that are meaningful to the user, and it must be easily accessible. *Views* and *folders* provide the ability to easily organize the data, and to navigate through it. (Folders are discussed in the following section.)

Each database must have a minimum of one view. The database designer designates as the *default view* whichever view is most likely to be used, and this is displayed the first time each new database is opened. The ability to build and use several views and folders gives the end user a tremendous amount of flexibility when working with Notes documents.

> **Note**
>
> Notes keeps track of the last view opened, and displays this view each time the database is opened unless you use the View menu to choose a different view before opening the database.

If you have not yet opened the database, you can use the <u>V</u>iew menu to select any view that has been created for the database you are using (see fig. 3.6). If you have opened the database, you can use the <u>V</u>iew menu or the Navigator to select a view.

Fig. 3.6

The View menu for the
Employee database before
it has been opened.

Once you have opened a view, it is displayed in the view pane, and the name of the view has a checkmark next to it in the <u>V</u>iew menu to indicate that it is in use. (In the Navigator, the view in use is indicated by a blue magnifying glass.)

> **Note**
>
> Be aware that as the database grows in the number and size of documents stored within it, the views take more time to open.

Each view has a *selection formula* (created by the database designer) that tells the view which documents to display. Some views have a selection formula that will select and display all the documents in the database, while other views have selection formulas that only select a subset of the documents based on some criteria. For instance, a view in a sales tracking database might only select orders where the total sale price is greater than $50,000. View selection formulas allow the database designer to create highly customized views.

Generally, each row in a view represents a document; however, with the enhanced features of Notes R4 views, documents can span multiple rows so that more information can be displayed. Each column in the view can either display data from a field in the document, or can use a formula to compute a value to display.

As you can see in the view pane of figure 3.7, there are several columns that display data from each employee document in the database. The leftmost column in the view is a special feature in Notes views and folders called the *marker column*; it displays a variety of system information, and is separated from the other columns in the view by a thin gray line that extends the length of the view. If you delete a document, for instance, you see a small blue trash can icon in this column. If you have not opened a document, a star is displayed in this column.

Ascending and descending sort arrows

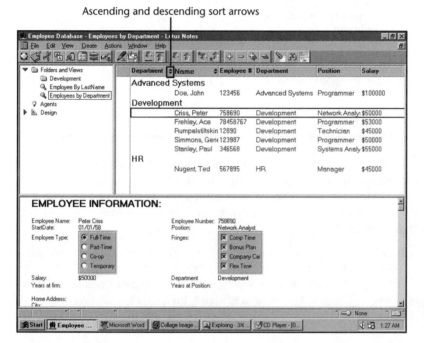

Fig. 3.7

The Employees by Department view.

Notes Basics

Note

The database designer is responsible for choosing the icons that are displayed in columns in the views and folders, as well as the colors that indicate different aspects of a view or folder, such as unread documents. The icons that appear in the view marker column cannot be changed in this version of Notes.

Table 3.2 summarizes the contents of the Employees by Department view.

Table 3.2   Summary of the Employees by Department View in the Employee Database

Column	Description	Sorted By	Categorized
Department	Displays the contents of the field Department.	Department	Yes
Name	Contains a formula that puts the last name before the first name so that this column can be sorted by last name.	Last name	No
Employee #	Displays the contents of the field EmployeeNumber.	No	No
Position	Displays the contents of the field position.	No	No
Salary	Displays the contents of the field salary.	No	No

An outstanding new feature of Notes R4 views and folders is the ability to dynamically resize columns, unless this feature has been explicitly disabled by the database designer. In order to resize columns in any view or folder, simply click the line separating any two columns, drag it sideways until the column reaches the width you desire, then release the mouse button.

This is all very nice, but what can a view really do for you? A view allows you to find and manipulate documents. Upon opening a view, a document is automatically selected—this is either the first document in the view, or the document you last selected when using the view. The selected document is highlighted by a bar known as the *selection bar*.

Note

The selection bar is usually, but not always, black. The database designer chooses the colors used for various aspects of the view or folder such as the view or folder background, the text of each column, and unread documents. In order to make the information displayed in the view or folder easy to read, Notes automatically chooses a contrasting color for the selection bar.

There are several methods that can be used to select a document in a view or folder. You can use the mouse and scroll bars to navigate through the documents, then click the document you are interested in using. You can also use the cursor keys to move the selection bar to the document you want.

> **Tip**
>
> If the first column of a view or folder is sorted, then you can just type in the first few characters of the item you want to find—Notes moves to the first document that matches whatever characters you have typed in. For Instance, if you are using a view that displays all your customers' names sorted alphabetically by last name, and you are looking for Philip Krezewicz, typing "Krez" should be enough to move you directly to the correct document.

Once you have selected the document of interest, you can open the document (to read or edit), print the document, or delete the document. The next few sections cover each of these topics in detail.

The database designer, in conjunction with the system users, decides which data elements from the underlying documents should be displayed, and how they should be organized. In most databases, many views are created so that users can easily navigate through the database using whatever information that they find most useful. For instance, in the contact management example you might have the following three views:

- **Contacts by Company**—Displays all the customer documents in the database, sorted and categorized by company name and contact name.
- **Contacts by State**—Displays all the customer documents in the database, sorted and categorized by state and then by company name.
- **Complaints by Customer**—Displays all the complaint documents in the database, sorted by customer.

By selecting different views, the user can examine different "snapshots" of the data; in fact, a view need not display all the documents in the database. A view named Calls This Week might only display a subset of customers that you spoke to this week, while a view named Calls Next Week might display all your calls scheduled for next week.

After using a database for some time, you might find that additional views and folders that are not currently part of the database design would aid in database navigation and manipulation. If other users might also benefit from the use of these new views, you can have the database designer create these views for you in the server copy of the database. If these are views that others are unlikely to use, you can build *private views*. Private views can sort and display the exact information that you want to see, but these views are inaccessible by other users.

> **Note**
>
> Shared and Shared Private on First Use views are stored as part of the database design, and can be replicated with other database design elements and data. Private views, on the other hand, are not stored as part of the database—they are stored in an individual user's DESKTOP.DSK file. See Chapter 2, "Customizing Notes," for more details on DESKTOP.DSK.

Folders. *Folders* are a cool new feature of Notes R4 and are very similar to views. The primary difference between folders and views are that folders do not require selection formulas and you must move documents into and out of folders. Folders can provide an easy way to organize documents by subject matter (or any other criteria that your little heart desires), and allow you to maintain a much smaller subset of documents than you could in a categorized view.

For example, you are the manager of the Technical Services department and you frequently use a view that selects all 2,200 documents in an employee database and is categorized based on the department field. Even though you are only interested in the Technical Services employees in most instances, you still have to deal with other documents in the view. You could create a folder called Tech Services and then select your employees in a view and drag them into the Tech Services folder, which would be a much smaller, faster, more manageable subset of data to work with.

Categories. In the view shown in figure 3.8, the departments within a company are organized into three categories: Advanced Systems, Development, and Human Resources (HR). The three categories are not documents, and you cannot open them as you could open documents. You can, however, perform operations on them.

Fig. 3.8

The Employees By Department view categorized on Department.

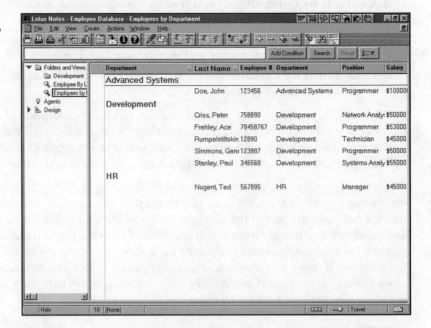

> **Note**
>
> In most views, category titles stand out from document titles by appearing in boldface. However, it is up to the database designer to set up this font option in the design of the view.

In figure 3.8, you can see documents listed under each category—such categories are said to be *expanded*.

Note

In Notes R3, most developers made the first column in a view display a plus sign (+) when the category is *collapsed* (when there are documents beneath the category that are not displayed) and a minus sign (–) when the category is *expandable*. In Notes R4, a twisty (small down arrow) display indicates an expandable category. You can click the twisty to expand and collapse the category. A twisty that points right rather than down indicates an expanded category.

To help reduce information overload, you can temporarily limit the amount of information displayed in a view by *collapsing* a category. When you double-click the name of the category, all of the documents in that category disappear. Alternatively, you can select the category and press the minus key (–); select the category and choose View, Expand/Collapse, Collapse Selected Level; or use the View Collapse SmartIcon. The documents themselves aren't deleted from the database, but Notes stops displaying them while the category is collapsed.

Note

Categories are not documents—they act only as headings so that documents can be logically grouped together. If you double-click any of the categories in a view, you expand or collapse that category. Categorization is a feature that the database designer builds into views and folders.

If you are only interested in employees in the Development department, for example, you can collapse the HR and Advanced Systems categories so that only employees in the Development department are displayed. You can later expand the other categories—that is, make the employees in other departments reappear—by double-clicking the other category names. Alternatively, you can expand the other categories by selecting them and pressing the plus key (+); selecting them and choosing View, Expand/Collapse, Expand Selected Level; or using the View Expand SmartIcon.

If you are working with a database that has dozens of categories, and you're interested in only one, you should collapse all categories by choosing View, Collapse All; by pressing the Shift and minus (–) keys simultaneously; or by using the View Collapse All SmartIcon. Then double-click (or use any of the previously mentioned methods) the one category you want to expand.

Similarly, you can expand all categories by choosing View, Expand All; by pressing the Shift and plus (+) keys simultaneously; or by using the View Expand All SmartIcon.

The ability to quickly expand and collapse categories in views and folders makes data much easier to work with.

Viewing the Database: Views, Folders, and Categories

As discussed briefly in Chapter 1, "Getting Started with Lotus Notes," the way you interact with Notes databases in Release 4 has been significantly overhauled. In Notes 3.x, when a database was opened, it immediately displayed a view window that showed either the most recently used view or the default view for the database if that was the first time the database was opened. The new user interface provides panes which are a series of smaller windows that work together to provide easy navigation through views and folders (views and folders are discussed in more detail in the following sections).

Figure 3.9 displays information from the Employee database. You can see that rather than one large view window, the screen is split into three distinct window panes separated by gray lines. Each of these panes has a very distinct and useful function:

- The leftmost pane on the top displays the *navigator pane* (a hierarchical structure of graphic objects that represent parts of the database), a feature that is totally new to Lotus Notes 4.0.

- To the right of the navigator pane you can see the *view pane*, which is not new but has been significantly redesigned. The view pane displays data from documents in the database which are selected by folders and views (folder and views are covered in detail in the following sections).

- Below the navigator pane and the view pane, you can see the *preview pane*, another new feature of Notes R4. The preview pane allows you to view the contents of a document without actually opening it, which can save significant time and effort.

Fig. 3.9

The various panes of the Notes R4 database interface.

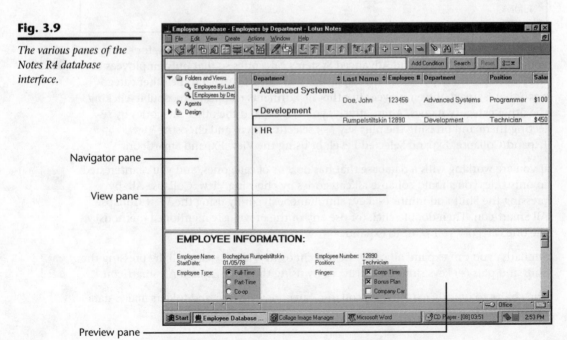

Navigator pane

View pane

Preview pane

Each of these panes can be resized to suit your taste, and the navigator and preview panes can be hidden if you don't find them useful or want to utilize the screen real estate in other ways.

Using the Navigator Pane. Because the navigator uses graphical icons and presents your choices in a hierarchical structure that can be expanded or collapsed to meet your needs, it is very easy to use. The folder at the top of the tree represents folders and views—you click this icon to expand a diagram of the folders and views available in the database. Each folder or subfolder is represented by a folder icon, and each view is represented by a magnifying glass. The currently selected icon turns blue; all other icons remain yellow.

 ◀◀ See "Working with Panes," p. 35

Previewing Documents with the Preview Pane. The preview pane is another completely new feature of Notes. It allows you to select a document in a view or folder, and to save time by viewing the contents of the document without actually opening the document. You can scan through a database very quickly using this tool.

The preview pane is flexible, and not only can be resized, but can be placed in a variety of on-screen locations. In order to change the placement of the preview pane, choose <u>V</u>iew, Arrange Pre<u>v</u>iew. You then click the button that corresponds to the placement you want.

> **Note**
>
> You can disable the preview pane if you don't find it useful. The <u>V</u>iew, Document <u>P</u>review menu option works like a toggle switch to enable and disable the preview pane. If a checkmark is visible next to this menu option, the preview pane is enabled.

Fields

After you select a form using <u>C</u>reate, Notes displays an empty document. Throughout the document you see fields in which you can enter data. Most documents contain several fields, which you can think of as the blanks on a paper form.

> **Note**
>
> The number, data type, and placement of fields within a form is determined by the database designer.

On Notes forms, editable field boundaries are delineated by small, gray, square brackets. Normally, each field has a label that explains what data should be entered into the field.

Tip

If the database designer has included field help (a useful feature to help guide users when entering data), additional information regarding the data expected in the field and the field's usage might be found by choosing View, Show, Field Help.

You can move the cursor from field to field using the directional arrows or the Tab key, or by clicking in whichever field you want the cursor located. If you are working in a rich text field, you cannot use the Tab key to move to the next field. See the later section "Rich Text Fields" for details on working in rich text fields.

Like most databases, Notes supports a variety of data types for fields. You might encounter a mixture of different data types when working with fields inside a Notes form. Figure 3.10 shows a sample form named Employee Information. This form contains many of the different supported data types.

Fig. 3.10

Fields on the Employee form.

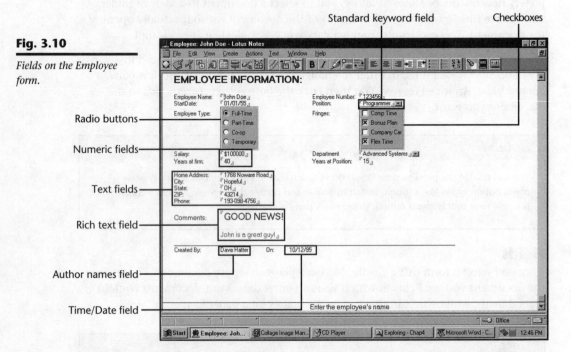

The supported field types are described in the following sections.

Text Fields. The *text* data type can be used to store alphanumeric data (essentially any character) that will not be used mathematically. Text fields, the most common type you will encounter, can hold a large amount of information (up to 15 KB). In the document in figure 3.10, Employee Name, Employee Number, Home Address, City, State, ZIP, and Phone are all text fields.

Tip

Numeric fields are needed only when the data values will be used in mathematical calculations. Data such as ZIP codes and phone numbers need not be stored in number fields since they normally are not used in calculations. Additionally, Notes provides developers with the ability to easily convert between data types.

Rich Text Fields. The *rich text field* (*RTF*) data type is similar to the text data type in that it stores alphanumeric data that will not be used mathematically. However, RTF is substantially more flexible, because it allows you to format the data. For instance, you can change font features such as style, size, or color, format text, insert objects from other applications, insert file attachments, and display graphics. In figure 3.10, Comments is a rich text field. Notice that the phrase "Good News" is larger than the surrounding text. Rich text fields, because of their ability to display any type of information, cannot be displayed in views, and in most cases cannot be used in formulas. Chapter 10, "Designing Forms," discusses rich text fields in more detail.

Tip

According to the Lotus Notes Application Developer's Reference, you should use rich text fields when your data meets any of the following conditions: "includes pictures or graphs, pop-ups, buttons, or embedded objects; or if you want users to use text attributes such as bold, italic, underlining, or color."

Keyword Fields. The *keyword* data type stores text, but allows you to choose a value from a list of predefined choices. Generally, designers use a keyword field when they want to ensure that the data entered in a field is from an acceptable list of values, or when they want to speed data entry. Although keyword fields store the data as text, the items in the list do not have to consist of only text characters. For example, a list of possible household salary ranges could be defined as: <$10,000, $10,001-$20,000, $20,001-$40,000, $40,001-$60,000, >$60,000.

There are three ways to display the list of keywords: standard keywords, checkboxes, or radio buttons. The following short sections describe each method.

Tip

Checkboxes are square; radio buttons are round. You can select as many checkboxes as you want, but you can select only one button in a group of radio buttons.

Standard Keywords. In figure 3.10, the Position and Department fields are standard keyword fields—you can choose only one of the positions defined in the list. When the cursor is positioned on such a field, repeatedly pressing the space bar causes Notes to display each possible value in turn. You also can press the first letter of the item you want—such as **P** for Programmer—and Notes fills in the rest of the word. If you want to see a list of all possible selections in a keyword field, place the cursor in the field and press Enter; or if the designer has enabled it (which is the default setting), you can click the Entry Helper button (the small, gray down-arrow button next to the field). Notes displays the Select Keywords dialog box (see fig. 3.11).

Fig. 3.11

A standard keyword dialog box for the Position field.

If you want to change the field to one of the values listed in the dialog box, you can select an item from the list, and then press Enter (or choose <u>O</u>K).

Note

Most keyword fields are designed to present you with a fixed set of values, and you are expected to choose one value from the list. The database designer can, however, allow you to enter something other than one of the predefined selections, or can allow you to select multiple items from the list. If a keyword field has been designed to allow new values, the Keywords dialog box contains an input box into which you can enter new text. If the keyword field supports multiple values, you can use the mouse to select several items from the list, and each is displayed in the field when the dialog box is closed.

Checkboxes. If the database designer has enabled the Checkbox option on a keyword field, you are presented with a vertical list of *checkboxes*. Each box represents one entry in the predefined list; by default, checkboxes are not mutually exclusive, so you can select one, several, or all of the boxes if you want them to apply. For example, the Fringes field in figure 3.10 lists four fringe benefits that the company provides; you can select whichever particular services the client uses. An X appears in each box you select, indicating that the client uses that service. An empty checkbox indicates that the selection does not apply.

Radio Buttons. If the database designer has enabled the Radio Buttons option, you are presented with a vertical list of *radio buttons*, so named because they function like the channel selector buttons on early car radios. Each button represents one item in the list, and you must choose one of several mutually exclusive items. In the Employee Type field in figure 3.10, for example, you can specify the type of employee. Selecting a button causes a black dot to appear in the button, and whichever button was previously selected is automatically deselected (the black dot disappears).

Time/Date Fields. The *time/date type* enables you to enter a time or date in a field. If the value you enter is not a valid time or date value, Notes prompts you to enter a valid one. In figure 3.10, the On field contains the date that the document was created.

Numeric Fields. The *number* data type expects a numeric value (0–9) such as the number of employees in a company, or the number of calls made to a customer. If a value entered in a number field is not a number, Notes prompts you to enter a valid value. The form in figure 3.10 contains three number fields: Salary, Years at Firm, and Years at Position. (The field containing a phone number cannot be a number field because it contains non-numeric characters such as parentheses, spaces, and dashes.)

Names Fields. There are three types of *names* data types: author names, reader names, and names. Each one provides special functionality when used on a Notes form, as explained in the following sections.

Note

Author names and reader names fields do not override the access control list for a database. They can only refine it. For instance, if your name is in a ReaderNames field in a document, but the ACL grants you "No Access," you will not be able to read the document. Additionally, if you are in the Group "Testers" and have Editor access to a database, but are not in the ReaderNames field in a document, you will not be able to read it.

Author Names. The *author names* data type contains a text list of Notes names (user names, group names, and access roles) that determine who can edit a document. When an author names field is used in a document, it creates a special field in the document named $UpdatedBy. If your user name appears in the author names field in a document, then you are able to edit that document; otherwise you are able to read but not edit the document. Author names fields work in conjunction with other Notes security features such as access control lists and reader names fields (discussed next) to provide additional database security. In figure 3.10, the document's Created By field is an example of an author names field.

Tip

You can click and hold an author names field in read or edit mode of any document to determine who has Editor access to the document.

Reader Names. The *reader names* type expects a text list of Notes names (user names, group names, server names, and access roles) that determine who can read a document. If your user name appears in the reader names field in a document, then you are able to read that document; otherwise you are not able to read the document, though it may still appear in views. Reader names fields work in conjunction with other Notes security features such as access control lists and author names fields to provide additional database security.

Names. The *names* data type can contain a text list of Notes names (user names, group names, server names, and access roles). A names field is useful when you want to display a list of user names, but are not trying to assign any type of access rights to a document.

Sections. The *section* data type defines an area on a form. A section can be used to limit who can read and or edit the document. This advanced field type is covered in the "Editable Field Formulas" section in Chapter 10, "Designing Forms."

Field Types. When defining a field, you not only define the type of data it can contain, you also have the following choices for each field: *editable, computed, non-editable, computed for display*, and *computed when composed*. The following sections examine the benefits and drawbacks of each of these options.

Editable Fields. An *editable field* can be any data type, and is stored in the document when the document is saved. The user enters the value for an editable field from the keyboard, or the database designer develops formulas (you learn more about formulas in Chapter 13, "Working with Formulas") that provide a default value that the user can change. When an editable field is displayed on a form, it is delineated with small, gray brackets, unless the data type is set to RTF, in which case the brackets are red. An example of an editable field would be a field named Phone Number where the user enters a phone number from the keyboard.

Computed Fields. The value of a *computed field* is calculated by formulas that the database designer develops. The user cannot change the value of a computed field (unless the formulas in the field are based on user input data), but this value is recalculated each time a document is edited, refreshed, or saved. Computed fields (including computed when composed and computed for display fields) can be used with all data types except RTF, and no brackets will be shown around these fields because the user cannot directly change the value. When the user elects to save the document, the value of the computed fields will be saved.

An example of the use of a computed field would be a field that reads the user name from your Notes ID and stores it in a field named Modified By each time the document is saved so that the person who last modified the document is tracked. Another example would be a field named Modified Date that reads the current system date and time the document was last modified and stores it upon saving the document.

Computed for Display Fields. The value of a *computed for display field* is calculated by formulas that the database designer develops. The user cannot change the value of such a field, and its value is recalculated each time a document is edited or refreshed.

The primary difference between computed and computed for display fields are that the values in a computed for display field are *not* saved in the document (which means they cannot be displayed in views). The main reason to use a computed for display field would be to display data to the user that can be easily computed, changes frequently, and does not need to be displayed in a view. If all of the aforementioned conditions are true, there is no reason to save values, thus saving precious disk space.

Computed When Composed Fields. The value of a *computed when composed field* is calculated by formulas that the database designer develops. The user cannot change the value of such a field, and its value is calculated only when the document is composed—this value is never recalculated. When the document is saved, all computed when composed fields are also saved.

An example of a use for this type of field might be for a field named Created By that reads the user name from the Notes ID in use when a document is composed and then stores that field when the document is saved.

Understanding Access Control Lists

When working with a database, you might discover that Notes does not allow you to perform all possible operations. Each database has a manager who is responsible for that database, and one of the manager's responsibilities is setting an *access control list* (*ACL*) so that data security and integrity is maintained.

The ACL performs three main functions related to database access:

- Defines who has access to a given database (the list may contain user names, server names, group lists, and database roles)
- Defines what the users can do to the database
- Defines groups for refined access to specific forms and views

Only the database manager (or any user with Manager access) may manipulate the ACL. Within the list, the manager arranges all users into one of the seven access levels shown in Table 3.3. Users at each level can perform only certain tasks. The list can include group names so that the manager can assign the same access privileges to an entire department or workgroup with just one entry.

Note

Throughout this book, whenever you read instructions for performing operations, you should keep in mind that Notes may not allow you to proceed if the database manager hasn't placed you at the required access level for that operation.

Notes Basics

Table 3.3   Notes Access Levels

Category	Tasks Allowed
No Access	Cannot access the database
Depositor	Can create new documents, but cannot edit or read existing documents, even those you created
Reader	Can read documents, but cannot edit documents
Author	Can create, read, and modify your own documents; can read documents created by other users
Editor	Can compose, edit, read, and possibly delete documents (this is a sub-option that can be toggled off or on a per user basis), including those created by other users
Designer	Has same access rights as the Editor level, and can also create, edit, or delete design elements such as forms and views
Manager	Has complete access to all facets of the database, including the ability to delete it from the hard disk and change the ACL

Your assigned access level can (and probably will) vary from one database to another, because the manager for each database decides what level you should have. Consider the following examples:

- For a database containing sales reports, you have Author access. This allows you to create new sales reports and to change them later. In addition, you can read sales reports entered by other users, but cannot edit other people's sales reports.

- For a database handling suggestions, comments and complaints, you have Depositor access, so you can add new suggestions to the database, but cannot read or edit them once they have been saved, much like an anonymous comments box hanging on the wall.

- For a database containing technical support material, you have Editor access. This allows you to add new documents, edit documents that you have created, and also edit documents that others have created.

- For a strategic plans database, unless you are an executive, you might be assigned No Access. At this level, you basically cannot do anything with the database.

Tip

To find out what access level you have been granted to a specific database, select the database icon and look at the third block from the right on your status bar. It displays an icon representing your access level. You can click that area of the status bar for a textual description of your access level.

Changing the Database Settings

Notes allows you to fine-tune a database by manipulating the many "database" settings that you can access through the database property sheet of each database. For instance, you can compact the database and make it smaller, or you can create a full-text index so that searching the database will be easier. By examining and learning the various options available to you, you can exert a tremendous amount of control over each database.

To access the database settings for a database, choose File, Database, Properties; select a database by clicking it; click the Properties SmartIcon; or right-click and choose Database Properties. This displays the Database Properties InfoBox (see fig. 3.12).

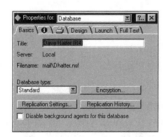

Fig. 3.12

The Basics tab of the Database Properties InfoBox enables you to edit particular database information.

In Notes R4, this InfoBox allows you to use the tabs at the top of the box to select which settings you are interested in. The following sections describe the settings on each tab.

Basics Settings

The first tab, Basics, allows you to view and edit some primary database information, including the following:

- **D Title**—This is the title that is displayed on the database icon and in the File Open dialog box. If necessary, you can change the title.

- **D Filename**—This is the actual name associated with the database file at the operating system level.

- **Server**—This is the name of the server on which the database resides. This is basically an FYI.

- **Replication History**—Click the replication History button to view or clear the replication history for the database. Each time a database replicates, this log is updated (this is covered in Chapter 22, "Notes: Under the Hood").

- **Replication Settings**—Click this button to view or edit the replication settings for the database (this is covered in Chapter 22, "Notes: Under the Hood").

- **Encryption**—Click the Encryption button to encrypt the local copy of this database, and thereby enforce local security. Encryption provides very tight security, but you will incur a modest performance hit. Encryption is covered in more detail in Chapter 20, "Security and Encryption."

■ **Disable Agents**—This checkbox, when selected, disables and schedules agents for this database. If you create or enable any default agents in a database, they will not run when this option is turned on. You will learn more about agents in Chapter 15, "Buttons and Agents."

Information Settings

The Information tab displays the following information about the database (see fig. 3.13):

■ The actual size of the database in kilobytes.

■ The number of documents in the database.

■ The date the database was created.

■ The date the database was last modified.

■ The replica ID of the database (this is a very important piece of information that you will learn about in more detail later in this chapter and in Chapter 22, "Notes: Under the Hood").

■ The % used button displays the amount of actual database in a database. In many instances, this will be less than 100 percent, indicating that there is "white space," or free space that is not being utilized in the database. When this number drops below 90 percent, you should compact the database to free-up that white space.

■ The Compact button can free unused white space by compacting the database, thus freeing up valuable disk space.

■ The User Activity button allows you to enable activity tracking, or to view each user's activity in the database if tracking has been enabled.

Fig. 3.13

The Information tab of the Database Properties InfoBox.

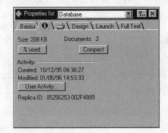

Print Settings

The Print tab allows you to set various options regarding printing documents and views (see fig. 3.14).

Fig. 3.14

The Print tab of the Database Properties InfoBox.

For example, you can insert a header or footer (discussed in more detail later in this chapter), or change the header and footer fonts that are sent to the printer.

Design Settings

The fourth tab, Design, displays information that primarily concerns database designers, such as the Inherit design from templates checkbox and the Database is a template checkbox (see fig. 3.15). These settings are covered in detail in Chapter 9, "Creating New Databases."

> **Caution**
>
> You should not change any of these settings unless you are absolutely certain that you understand what you are doing. These settings can have deleterious effects on other databases!

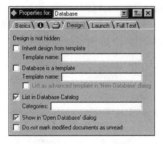

Fig. 3.15

The Design tab of the Database Properties InfoBox.

Launch Settings

The fifth tab, Launch, displays the following checkboxes representing choices that allow you to alter what happens each time a database is opened (see fig. 3.16):

- **On Database Open**—Allows you to choose how the database documents should be initially displayed, and which Navigator to use when the database is opened.

- **Show "About database" document when database is opened for the first time**—Allows you to decide if the About Database document should be displayed upon the first opening of the database.

■ **Show "About database" document if modified**—Allows you to automatically redisplay the modified About Database document when the database is opened only if the About Database document has been modified since the last opening of the database.

Fig. 3.16

The Launch tab of the Database Properties InfoBox.

Full Text (Index) Settings

The Full Text tab provides the following buttons so you can create and modify full text indexes that aid in searching for information contained in the database (see fig. 3.17):

■ **Update Index**—Allows you to create a new full text index, or update an existing index.

■ **Create Index**—Allows you to create a new full text index.

■ **Delete Index**—Deletes a full text index.

■ **Count unindexed documents**—Displays the total number of documents in the database that have not been included in the index. You can use this statistic to determine when you need to update the index.

In addition, this InfoBox displays other pertinent information about how the index was created.

Fig. 3.17

The Full Text tab of the Database Properties InfoBox after creating an index.

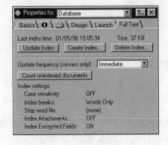

Working with Documents

Now that you know how to access a database, and how its various parts work, you will learn about creating, editing, and saving documents.

To open an existing document, simply select it in a view or folder, and double-click it. If you have Reader access to the database, the document is displayed on your screen in *read mode*, which means that you cannot edit it at this point (see fig. 3.18). An easy way to tell that a document is in read mode is the lack of brackets around any fields.

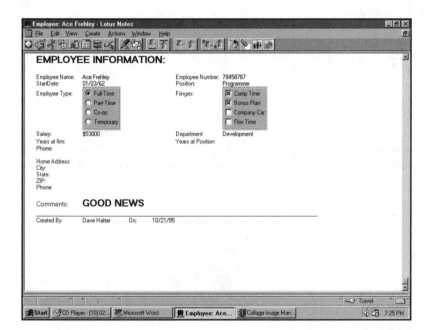

Fig. 3.18

An Employee document for Ace Frehley in read mode.

In read mode, you can see all the data in the document, and can elect to print the document, but you cannot edit it. In order to edit the document, press Ctrl+E. (You can use the Actions Edit Document SmartIcon if you have the appropriate access level.) Once the document is in edit mode (you will be able to see the small, gray brackets around the editable fields), you can change any of the data elements to which you have access (see fig. 3.19).

Fig. 3.19

An Employee document for Ace Frehley in edit mode.

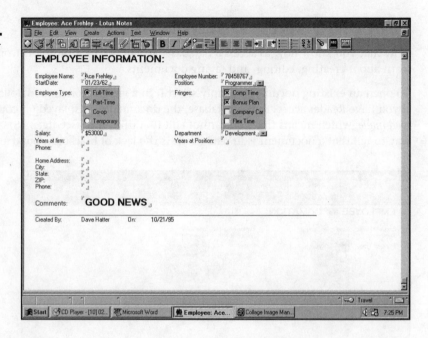

To compose a new document, choose Create, which displays all available forms in the database (see fig. 3.20).

Fig. 3.20

A list of available forms for the Employee database.

As you can see from this figure, there is only one form in the Employee database—Employee. To create a new employee, choose Create, Employee—a new document like the one shown in figure 3.21 is created.

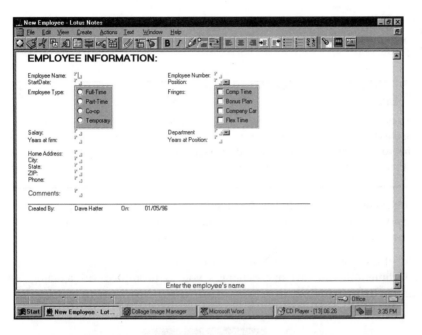

Fig. 3.21

*A new Employee
document.*

Notes Basics

Note

Remember that your ability to read and access documents is controlled by the ACL for each
database. The ACL is set by the database manager.

You can now enter data in the document. Notice that the Created By and On fields
have been set automatically by the system.

Saving and Closing Documents

Now that you know how to compose and edit documents, you need to know how to
save or cancel your changes. When you are finished reading or editing a document,
you can save the document, save and close the document, or just close the document.

To save any Notes document, press Ctrl+S, or use the File Save SmartIcon. This will
not close the document.

To close a Notes document and return to the folder or view, perform any one of the
following actions:

■ Press Esc.
■ Press Ctrl+W.

■ Click the view or folder window's Control-menu box and then choose <u>C</u>lose (the Control-menu box is the small application icon in the upper-left corner of the window).

> **Note**
>
> You will see two Control-menu boxes, one for Notes R4 (in the upper left corner) and one for the view or folder window, just below the program's Control-menu box. Make sure that you click the view or folder's window; because if you inadvertently click the Notes Control-menu box and then click Close, you will exit Notes.

■ Double-right-click anywhere in the document. This is a holdover from Notes 3.x and may not be enabled for your workstation. See Chapter 2, "Customizing Notes," for more information on preferences to learn how to enable this feature.

Performing any of these actions causes Notes to check to see if you have made any changes to a document. If you have made changes, you are prompted with a dialog box like the one in figure 3.22.

Fig. 3.22

The Notes File Save dialog box.

If you want to save your changes, choose <u>Y</u>es. To close the document without saving changes, choose <u>N</u>o. To avoid closing the document (and not saving the document), choose Cancel.

Closing a Database

To close a Notes database, first close any open documents by using one of the methods listed in the last section. Then follow the same steps you would use to close a document.

Copying a Database

The need may arise occasionally to make a copy of a Notes database. For instance, if you wanted to make an archive database that would not replicate with other databases (you will learn about this in Chapter 22, "Notes: Under the Hood"), you would need to make a new copy of the database. To do so, choose <u>F</u>ile, <u>D</u>atabase, <u>N</u>ew Copy or use the File Database New Copy SmartIcon.

Using this command to copy a database is essentially the same as using the operating system to make a copy of the file, except that Notes presents you with some additional choices about database elements that you can copy to the new database. Figure 3.23 displays the dialog box that Notes presents you with after you elect to copy a database.

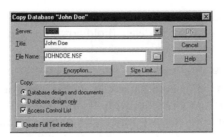

Fig. 3.23

The Copy Database dialog box.

You can choose a different server to receive a copy of the database, give the copy a different title, and indicate a filename for the new copy. In addition, you can elect to copy all the documents and design elements (forms, views, and so on), or only the design elements. You also can choose to copy or not copy the access control list, regardless of the other selections you have made. Finally, you can secure local copies of the database, and specify the maximum size of the database in kilobytes.

Caution

Each database has a *replica ID*, which is a unique identifier that allows it to replicate with other *replica copies* of the same database. When you make a new copy of a database rather than a replica copy, the database gets a different replica ID, which means that the new copy will not replicate with other replica copies. If you want this new copy to replicate with other replicas of the same database, use the File, Replication, New Replica option rather than the New Copy option.

Deleting Database Icons and Databases

There are two ways for you to delete a database from your workpage:

- Delete the database icon from your workpage
- Delete the database permanently from your hard disk or server

Anyone can delete a database icon from their workpage, but only users with Manager access to a database can permanently delete that database. The following sections explain the differences between these two procedures.

Deleting Database Icons from Your Workspace

When you no longer are interested in a particular database, you can delete it from your workspace without deleting the database file from the server or hard drive where it is stored. To do so, follow these steps:

1. Select the workpage on which the database resides, if it is not currently showing.

2. Click the database you want to remove. (Don't double-click, or you'll open the database.)

3. If you want to delete more than one database from the same workpage, Shift + click the other databases you want to delete (hold down the Shift key and then click the other database icons you want to select).

4. Press Del; or choose Edit, Clear; or click the Edit Clear SmartIcon.

5. Notes prompts you with a dialog box that asks if you are sure you want to delete these icons from your workspace (see fig. 3.24). If you are sure, choose Yes to delete the selected icon(s) from your workspace; if you have changed your mind, choose No.

Fig. 3.24

The Remove Database icon dialog box.

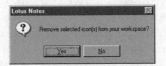

Deleting database icons does *not* actually delete the database file—it only removes the icon from your workpage. Any other users who access the database will still see the database icon on their workpages, and can still access the database. In fact, you can add the same database icon to your workspace again at a later time.

> **Tip**
>
> After you delete database icons from your workpage, there are gaps where the icons used to be. You can fill in the gaps easily by dragging other database icons into these empty positions. Alternatively, you can choose View, Arrange Icons to have Notes rearrange the icons on that workpage so that all gaps are filled in.

Deleting a Database

If you have Manager access through the ACL for a given database, you may permanently delete the database file.

> **Caution**
>
> The following instructions tell you how to permanently delete a database and all its information from the hard disk where the file resides. If you perform this procedure on a database, all data contained in that database will be lost!

To permanently delete a database, perform the following steps:

1. Click the database icon of the database you want to delete—this selects the database.

2. Choose File, Database, Delete. Notes prompts you with a dialog box informing you that you are about to permanently delete the database, and asking if you are sure that's what you want to do (see fig. 3.25).

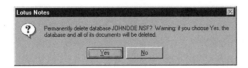

Fig 3.25

*The Delete Database
Warning dialog box.*

3. Choose <u>Y</u>es to permanently delete the database from the server or hard drive, or choose <u>N</u>o to cancel the deletion.

> **Caution**
>
> You have Manager access to all Notes databases that are stored on your workstation. This includes important system databases such as your Mail database, your Notes Log database, and your Private Name & Address Book database. In addition, you have Manager access to your Mail database on the Notes server. You should *not* delete any of these databases without first seeking the advice of your Notes administrator. There is no good reason to remove these icons, as you will find yourself using these databases (particularly your Mail database) very often.

Using the Universal Viewer

Notes 4.0 has a very powerful and useful new feature named the *Universal Viewer* that allows you to easily view the contents of any file attachment, even if you do not have a copy of the application which originally created the file. In fact, you do not even need to know what application created the attachment, because the Universal Viewer is smart enough to determine the file type (in most cases) and display it for you. This can be very handy when you receive file attachments in a format with which you are unfamiliar, when you don't have a licensed copy of the application that created the file, or when you want to quickly view or print the file without launching another application which consumes memory and wastes time.

To invoke the Universal Viewer, double-click any file attachment—this displays the Attachment Properties InfoBox for the attachment (see fig. 3.26).

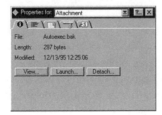

Fig. 3.26

You can choose one of five tabs in the Attachment Properties InfoBox.

Click the View button in the Information tab of the InfoBox to send the Universal Viewer into action. The attachment is displayed for your perusal. While the file is displayed, you can control a variety of display and print settings. To change any of the settings for the file, right-click to get a menu of options (see fig. 3.27).

Fig. 3.27

*You have many options with
the Universal Viewer.*

The Print option displays a Print dialog box. From this dialog box, you can change various print settings and then send the document to the printer. The next menu section lists display options, which vary depending on the file format of the file being viewed. For instance, when a Microsoft Word document is right-clicked, you see options that pertain to the various document display modes in Word. The Options option displays a cascading menu, like the one shown in figure 3.28, that allows you to change many aspects of how the file can be displayed, printed, and copied to the Clipboard.

Fig. 3.28

*The Options menu of the Viewer
pop-up menu.*

If you choose Display, you are presented with the Display Options dialog box, shown in figure 3.29. From there, you can change the default display font, and can decide how, or if, to display files that are unfamiliar to the Universal Viewer. You can choose More to reach additional options, such as how to display database and spreadsheet files.

Fig. 3.29

The Display Options dialog box.

The Print menu option displays the dialog box shown in figure 3.30. This dialog allows you to change a variety of printer output options, such as the printer font, the font used for the document header, whether or not a header prints, the page margins, and a name for the print job.

Fig. 3.30

The Print Options dialog box.

Much like the display options, you can choose More to reach additional options that control how certain types of files will be printed. This causes the More Print Options dialog box to appear (see fig. 3.31). For instance, you can elect to print grid lines and cell headers for spreadsheets, grid lines and field names for databases, and borders for graphics files. In addition, when you print graphics files like bitmaps or drawings, they can be printed in their original size, or can be scaled to fill the entire page.

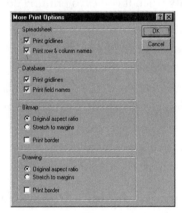

Fig. 3.31

The More Print Options dialog box.

The Clipboard menu displays the Clipboard Option dialog box, which allows you to select a format to place on the Clipboard (see fig. 3.32). As you can see from the figure, there are a variety of format types for the Clipboard. You also can change the Clipboard font. Choosing More displays another dialog box that allows you to change how database and spreadsheet files are copied to the Clipboard.

Fig. 3.32

The Clipboard Options dialog box.

The Universal Viewer is a very powerful utility that can save you time and effort when you need to deal with file attachments.

Printing Documents and Views

Notes has a great degree of flexibility when it comes to printing documents and views. You have several options regarding what should be printed:

- Print a single document
- Print selected documents
- Print the entire view

There are two basic ways to print a single document, each of which is slightly different:

- Printing a selected document from a view or folder
- Printing an open document

Printing a Selected Document from a View or Folder

If you currently are in a view or folder, you can select a document either by clicking it, or by clicking in the view marker column (which puts a check in the view marker column). Then choose File, Print or click the File Print SmartIcon to display the dialog box shown in figure 3.33.

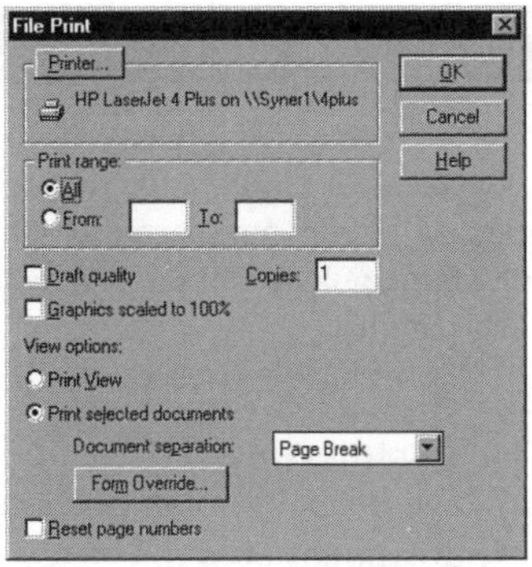

Fig. 3.33

The File Print dialog box as displayed when a single document is chosen in a view.

The File Print dialog box allows you to control many aspects of printing, such as the following:

- Click **Printer** to select a different printer than the one currently selected (this is displayed next to the printer icon) or to change the printer setup for a printer (the next section discusses specifying other printers).

- Choose **Print range** to set a range of pages within the selected document to be printed. This only applies to printing individual documents.

- Select the **Draft quality** checkbox to use lower resolution printing, which speeds the printing process; this might be necessary if the selected printer does not contain much memory.

- Use the **Copies** setting to indicate if you want multiple copies of the document printed.

- Select the **Graphics scaled to 100%** checkbox to print graphics at their original size.

- The most important options presented in this dialog box are in the **View options** section, and are described in the following text.

The selections in the View options section allow you to print only documents that you have selected or print the entire view. Notice that because only a single document was selected in the view, the Print selected documents radio button is selected by default. In addition, you can choose Form Override when printing documents to select a form for printing other than the form that the document was saved with.

Tip

The Form Override feature of Notes can be very useful. For instance, if you use a database where a form is specifically designed to speed data entry, but is not very attractive when printed, then a separate form can be designed for printing. When you decide to print the document, use Form Override to select the form designed for printing, which ensures that the document is printed with the more attractive format.

Document separation allows you to choose from one of three options when printing multiple documents. The first option, Page Break between documents, allows you to eject a page and start printing the next document on a new page. The second option, Extra Line, will not eject a new page; it will literally insert one blank line between each document to help make the printout somewhat easier to read. The final option, No Separation, provides no separation between documents, and the next document in the queue will begin printing on the line immediately following the previous document. When printing only a single document, the Document separation options are not applicable.

Finally, you can select the Reset page numbers checkbox which works in conjunction with the Page Break Document separation option to reset the page number to one for the first page of each document.

Once you have made the proper selections, choose OK to send the document to the printer.

Tip

If you want to see where the pages will break, and words will wrap for a given document before you print, you can open the document and choose View, Show, Page Breaks. A heavy black line is displayed wherever a page break will be inserted.

Printing the Open Document

The second way to print a selected document works for a document currently open in read or edit mode. Choose File, Print, or use the File Print SmartIcon, and you get a slightly altered dialog box that has less choices than the dialog box you would see if you began in a view or folder (see fig. 3.34).

Fig. 3.34

The File Print dialog box for a single document.

The dialog box in figure 3.34 is essentially the same as the one you saw in figure 3.33. Except that, because you are printing a single, open document rather than a view, the following hold true: there are no view options, you cannot select For<u>m</u> Override, and you cannot insert page breaks. Choose <u>O</u>K to send the document to the printer.

Printing Selected Documents

Printing selected documents is very similar to the first option for printing a single document. Open a view or a folder, then select multiple documents by clicking the view marker column next to each document you want to print (a small checkmark in the view marker column indicates that you have selected a document).

Once you have chosen all the documents to print, choose <u>F</u>ile, <u>P</u>rint, or use the File Print SmartIcon. You are presented with the File Print dialog box (refer to fig. 3.33). Your options are the same as when printing a single document, but the View options and Document separation selections take on new importance. Ensure that the Print selected documents radio button is selected, and select Page Break as the document separator. You may also use For<u>m</u> Override to print each selected document with a form other than the form with which it was last saved.

When you have made all your printing choices, choose <u>O</u>K to send the print job to the printer.

Printing a View

There may be times when you are interested in printing the actual view instead of printing documents displayed in the view. Notes makes it quite easy to do this—you simply open the view that you want to print, and then choose <u>F</u>ile, <u>P</u>rint (alternatively you can press Ctrl+P, or use the File Print SmartIcon). You arrive at the familiar File Print dialog box (refer to fig. 3.33). In the View options section, select the Print <u>V</u>iew radio button, which dims the document-specific print settings such as For<u>m</u> Override and Document separation. Set the other print options, such as <u>C</u>opies, to meet your needs, and then choose <u>O</u>K to send the view to the printer.

Printing a List of Documents in a Folder

Printing documents from folders is much like printing documents from views. To print a list of documents from a folder, just select the documents you want to print, and choose <u>F</u>ile, <u>P</u>rint, or click the File Print SmartIcon.

Specifying a Printer

When Windows was installed on your workstation, a default printer driver should have been installed and selected for the printer that you use most frequently. When you print from Notes, the program sends your output to the default printer unless you specify a different printer. Many times it is helpful to have access to a printer other than your default printer—having access to a printer with 8.5"×14" paper is particularly helpful when printing wide views that scroll off the screen—so that you can take advantage of some options that your default printer does not support, such as an envelope feeder. Each time you print something from Notes, you are presented with the dialog box from either figure 3.33 or figure 3.34, depending what type of item you are attempting to print. Each of these dialog boxes displays a Printer button above the currently selected printer (indicated by a printer icon). Click the Printer button, or click the File Print Setup SmartIcon to change printer drivers.

After you click Printer, you are presented with a dialog box that displays all the printer drivers installed on your workstation (see fig. 3.35).

Fig. 3.35

The Print Setup dialog box with installed printers shown.

Click to select a printer driver from the list and then click Setup to display a property sheet for the selected driver. Figure 3.36 displays the dialog box for the HP LaserJet 4/4M driver.

Fig. 3.36

The dialog box for an HP LaserJet 4/4M printer.

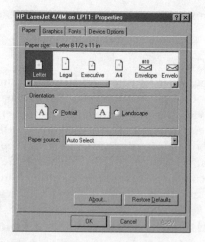

Using Headers and Footers

Another nice feature that Notes provides is the ability to set global *headers* and *footers* for all documents in a database. Headers and footers allow you to further identify documents when printing. A good example of this concept is the headers at the top of the pages of this book. In the header, you see the information such as the title of the book and the page number.

To set a header or footer, choose the Print tab of the Document Properties InfoBox (see fig. 3.37). From this tab, select the Header radio button to create a header, and then enter the text that you want your header to display in the input box below the button. Simply type the text that you want the header to display and then click the green check button to accept the changes, or the red cancel button to reject the changes. Choosing the Footer radio button allows you to enter text to print in the footer, and works exactly the same way as the Header button does.

Click here to
accept the changes ⎤

Click here to
reject the changes ⎦

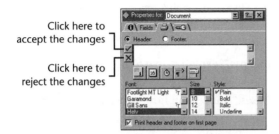

Fig. 3.37

The Print tab of the Document Properties InfoBox.

You can see several icons immediately beneath the text box for the header and footer. These icons make it easy for you to automatically add additional information to the header or footer:

	Inserts a page number, which is displayed in the text box as &P
	Inserts the current date, which is displayed as &D
	Inserts the current time, which is displayed as &T
	Inserts a tab, which is displayed as ¦
	Inserts the code &W, which tells Notes to print the Window title

A header formula, for example, can print the current date and time, insert a tab, print the text `Test Header`, insert another tab, and then print the current page. When printed, the header would look something like the following:

```
10/21/96@10:10PM                Test Header                Page 1
```

From this Properties InfoBox, you can also adjust font settings—such as typeface, size, and style—for the header and/or footer. To change the typeface for the header or footer, simply select a new font from the Font list box. To change the size of the font, select a font size from the Size list box. To change the font style, select the style from the Style list box.

> **Note**
>
> The font settings for the header and footer are mutually exclusive; that is, you can use different font settings for the header and footer.

Notes Basics

From Here...

In this chapter, you learned the basics of using Notes databases: forms, data types, field types, and how to access databases. Now that you know the basics of using databases, Chapter 4, "Getting Started With Electronic Mail," teaches you how to use the NotesMail system. Other chapters you might find useful at this point include the following:

- Chapter 8, "Working with Documents," explains how to use the many advanced features of Notes R4 such as hotspots and doclinks.

- Chapter 9, "Creating New Databases," shows you how to create and distribute new Notes databases.

- Chapter 10, "Designing Forms," explores the creation of Notes applications.

CHAPTER 4

Getting Started with Electronic Mail

Electronic mail (e-mail) is one of the most important and useful tools to come out of the "information era," making it quick and easy to communicate with co-workers, regardless of geographical and time barriers. While Notes provides many valuable services in addition to e-mail, e-mail is probably the single most used service that Notes provides. The Notes e-mail system is a friendly, robust, client/server system modeled after their best-selling, stand-alone e-mail package, cc:Mail. NotesMail makes it very easy to communicate with other Notes users (and with other mail systems, such as Microsoft Mail or Internet mail, if you have the proper hardware and software) and is very flexible; you can not only send messages to other users, you can send file attachments and embed objects such as spreadsheets or graphics in the e-mail. Understanding and using NotesMail is key to maximizing productivity when using Notes.

In this chapter, you learn the basics of sending and receiving mail. Later chapters explain the more advanced mail features and other features of Notes that should help you and your coworkers work together more effectively.

This chapter will help you understand the following:

- Advantages and disadvantages of using e-mail
- How to work with your mailbox
- Workstation-based mail versus server-based mail
- Reading your incoming mail
- Creating and sending mail
- Forwarding, printing, deleting, and archiving messages
- Using the status bar and SmartIcons to handle your mail

Introducing Electronic Mail (E-Mail)

Technological progress has had, and continues to have, a profound effect on the methods people use to communicate. As little as 30 years ago, the U.S. Postal Service was the primary way that people sent messages to one another (paper based mail is sometimes referred to as *snail mail* because it is so much slower than e-mail). But as technology has advanced, new methods such as the fax machine and e-mail have made it easier, faster and, in many instances, less costly to send messages to other people. Since the mid '80s, the popularity of e-mail as a tool to transfer messages has grown exponentially. For proof of this trend, just look at the amount of business cards you now receive that contain the individual's e-mail address.

E-mail has revolutionized internal communications for companies that use it and many companies are now providing e-mail links to their customers and vendors, giving them a significant advantage over competitors who rely on paper based mail. If you ask people who have worked with e-mail for any length of time, most wonder how they ever got by without it, because it makes their jobs easier and more fun. In fact, e-mail is rapidly becoming the preferred method of communication among technologically savvy professionals, and more and more ordinary people are beginning to use e-mail because of the advantages it provides. Before long, e-mail will most likely supplant the postal service for all messages except those that cannot be delivered by e-mail, such as that fruitcake your Aunt Bertha sends you every year for Christmas.

Some of the advantages of e-mail include the following:

- **"Paperless" messaging**—Because e-mail messages are composed and delivered electronically and are generally read and stored electronically, there is little, if any, need to ever print out the message. All e-mail systems provide the option to make a hard copy of the mail message if you desire.

- **Speed**—E-mail messages travel across the wire at the speed of light, which makes for very quick delivery. Most businesses can immediately see a return on investment, because the time it takes for employees to communicate is drastically compressed. This is particularly evident in geographically dispersed companies.

- **Ease of Use**—Most common e-mail systems are very easy to use and work much like a word processor. Once you start the mail software, you can address the mail by pulling up a list of other e-mail users in your network. You then type in your message, add any file attachments you want to send, and send the mail. Some e-mail systems even support spell checking, so you don't have to worry about typographical errors. Since most people would type the letter or memo they want to send, they can save a step by using the e-mail editor to compose the message and send it one step.

- **Message Organization**—Most e-mail systems provide power features that allow you to prioritize, sort, categorize, file, and search for your e-mail, making it much easier to manage your messages than paper mail in traditional folders or filing cabinets. For example, think how handy it would be to search for an important memo from your boss simply by typing in his name rather than digging through all of the papers on your desk looking for the paper version.

■ **Flexibility**—E-mail makes it easy to work with your messages; you can delete mail you're not interested in, forward a message to others, reply to a message, or send the same message to a large number of users just by adding their addresses. With electronic mail, you can do anything you can do with paper mail. Many e-mail systems have other advanced features such as "agents" which allow you to automate mail functions. For instance, you might want a special notification each time you receive mail from your boss.

■ **One stop shopping**—Since you most likely use the computer for other jobs, having the mail available on your computer helps to eliminate redundancy. In addition, since the mail is actually an electronic file, you can export the information into other applications. For example, if I sent you a picture of a new product our company makes, you could include that in a sales brochure that you are producing.

When compared with paper-based mail, e-mail has very few disadvantages. The following examples can be seen as disadvantages:

■ **Expense**—The initial investment in hardware, software, and configuration for an electronic mail system can be quite large. Many of these systems—such as Notes—are expensive in and of themselves; the computers required to use them are expensive and highly skilled people are required to get the system installed and to maintain it. However, most modern offices have computers for their employees, and it is easy to demonstrate the advantages e-mail provides. The system cost is greatly outweighed by the productivity increase it provides.

■ **Facelessness**—Because most e-mail messages are just text, it's hard to convey personal feelings or a sense of warmth. Many would rather receive a handwritten note from a friend than an e-mail, even though they say the same thing. As e-mail packages improve, it's becoming easier to include graphics and sound for that extra touch, but some things still need to be delivered by hand, like a birthday card for your son, or a get well card for a friend.

Now that you have an overview of e-mail, let's examine how NotesMail, the mail system integrated into Notes, works and how it can help you become a more productive Notes user.

Working with the Notes Mailbox

To use NotesMail, you must become familiar with your *mailbox*. Your mailbox is a Notes database (similar to what you read about in Chapter 3, "Using Databases") where all of your mail is stored. Figure 4.1 shows the database icon for a typical NotesMail user.

Notes Basics

> **Note**
>
> Notes provides three core services—Document Databases, Application Development, and Messaging Services. The fact that your mailbox is actually a Notes database points to the tight integration of core services in Notes. Messaging is woven into the database structure so that any database can send and receive e-mail messages.

Fig. 4.1

A NotesMail database icon for John Doe's mailbox.

In most Notes installations, your mailbox is created for you at setup and its icon is placed in a page in your workspace labeled Mail. (This is the normal configuration, but your configuration may be different. If you have trouble finding your mailbox, see your administrator.)

Because your mailbox is really just a Notes database, the procedures and techniques you use to read incoming mail and to create new mail are the same as those you use when working with other Notes databases (see Chapter 3, "Using Databases," for more information). The only thing that makes your mailbox special is that the mailbox user interface closely resembles that of Lotus' cc:Mail product, which facilitates sending, storing, and organizing mail messages to and from other users. As you read this chapter, keep in mind that many of the techniques you have learned for accessing your mailbox and working with documents apply to all Notes databases.

Another important aspect of your mail database (hereafter referred to as *mailbox*) is how you connect to the server to get your mail. If you are primarily a mobile user with no persistent connection to a server, you most likely will be configured for *workstation-based mail*. If you have a persistent connection to the server (usually via a LAN), you most likely will be configured for *server-based mail*. Each of these are covered in more detail in the next section.

Server-Based Mail. If you spend most of your time using Notes connected to a Notes server via a LAN or WAN, you will most likely be set up to use server-based mail. When you are configured for server-based mail, you use your mailbox on the Notes server. Each time you create a new mail document and elect to send it, it is immediately transferred to the Notes server's mailbox (if you also elect to save it, a copy of the document is placed in your mailbox). The Router process on the server then resolves the address of the recipient or recipients and it is routed to its intended recipient. In addition, incoming mail is delivered into your mailbox shortly after it is delivered to your server.

Workstation-Based Mail. If you are primarily a mobile user, or don't have a persistent connection to a Notes server (for instance, you might work in a remote office or at home) and connect to your Notes server occasionally via modem, you most likely are set up for workstation-based mail. When your workstation is configured for workstation-based mail, you work with a *replica copy* of your mailbox and a special Notes database titled Outgoing Mail is created on your workstation; the icon should look like figure 4.2.

Fig. 4.2

The Outgoing Mail database icon for workstation-based mail users.

> **Note**
>
> The Outgoing Mail database (whose actual filename is MAIL.BOX) is created by default the first time you change your location to Travel, Island, or any custom location profile where workstation-based mail is specified. You learn more about location profiles in Chapter 5, "Using the Address Books," and in Chapter 18, "Setting Up To Go Remote."

Unlike server-based mail, when you compose a new mail message and elect to send it, it is not immediately sent to the server's mailbox. Instead, the mail message is temporarily stored in the Outgoing Mail database until your next connection to the server. If you elect to save a copy of the mail, it is stored in your local mailbox, which is a replica copy of your mailbox on the server.

Upon your next connection with the server (if the Transfer Outgoing Mail option is turned on, which it normally is, by default), your outgoing mail is automatically transferred to the server. In addition, if you replicate during this connection, your local mailbox receives all incoming mail from the server. To enable or disable the Send outgoing mail, click the Replicator workspace tab. On the Replicator page, there should be an entry for Send outgoing mail that displays the Outgoing Mail database icon and a small checkbox. If the checkbox has a check in it, the option is enabled and outgoing mail will be sent during each connection. Figure 4.3 shows the Replicator page with the Send outgoing mail option turned on.

Fig. 4.3

The Replicator page shown with Send outgoing mail enabled.

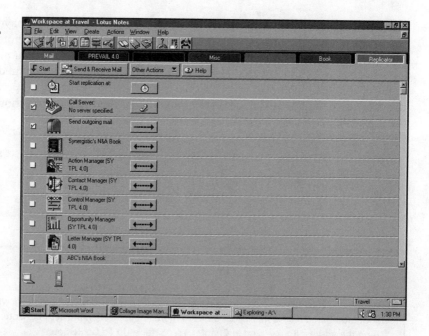

Note

The NotesMail system is extremely flexible and you have a considerable amount of control over it when messages actually get sent. For instance, you can tell Notes to try to make a connection immediately for High Priority mail; you can also tell Notes to make a connection when more than a certain number of mail messages are pending in the Outgoing Mail database.

Tip

If you are using workstation-based mail and your mail is not being delivered, make sure that the Transfer outgoing mail option is enabled during replication.

If you did not have a temporary storage facility for outgoing mail, you would need to make a connection to the server each time you composed a mail message, which would be a major hassle and would severely limit your ability to use Notes on the road. However, much like other remote mail systems such as CompuServe, America Online, and Eudora, Notes provides this temporary storage facility, giving you tremendous freedom in terms of creating and sending mail. You can create a mail message in the plane on your way to a meeting and another while driving down the road to a sales call. When you next connect to the server, the Router transfers the mail messages from your Outgoing Mail database to their intended recipients.

> **Caution**
>
> The Outgoing Mail database is a critical component of the mail system for users who are not persistently connected to a Notes server. Because your mail is stored in this database until your next connection, it is very important that you do not delete this database.

Mailbox Features

Like all Notes databases, to access your mail messages you must first open your mailbox. In most cases, your administrator has put your mailbox icon on your workspace for you; so simply double-click the mailbox icon and the database opens. Remember that if you don't see the database icon you are interested in, check the other pages in your workspace to see if the database you are interested in resides on a different page.

Upon opening your mailbox, you should see something that looks similar to figure 4.4.

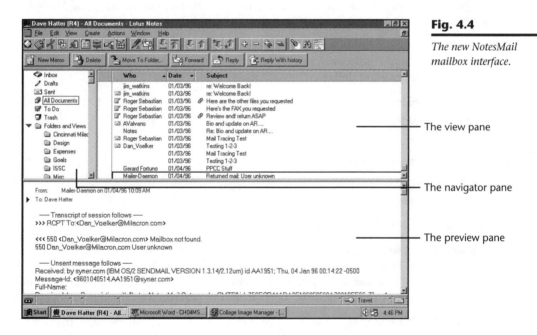

Fig. 4.4

The new NotesMail mailbox interface.

The view pane

The navigator pane

The preview pane

For those who have used NotesMail in the past, you can quickly see from figure 4.4 that the mail interface has changed drastically. As mentioned earlier in this section, Lotus has made the look and feel of the new mail design very similar to that of cc:Mail. If you have used cc:Mail before, you will have a leg up on other users who are converting from Notes 3.x; if you have not used cc:Mail, don't worry, Lotus has made the new mailbox much easier to use.

On the left side of the screen in figure 4.4, you should see the navigator pane, which has been customized for the mail database, but works the same as it does in every database. As you know from Chapter 3, the navigator provides a graphical representation of the elements of a database. Lotus has used this to their advantage in your new mailbox design.

To the right of the navigator is the view pane which is very similar to Notes 3.x views. The various views will be discussed shortly.

One of the most useful new features of Notes R4 is the preview pane. Although you can enable this for any database, it is particularly useful in your mailbox because it allows you to read your mail messages without actually opening the document, which can save you a tremendous amount of time. To enable the preview pane, choose <u>V</u>iew, <u>D</u>ocument Preview.

Remember, the exact display of your mailbox at a given time may depend on any changes that a database designer made to the design of the database and any changes that you might have made, such as resizing the preview pane or disabling the Navigator. Notes R4 offers unprecedented flexibility when working with your mail.

To make the new format of the mailbox as useful and easy as possible, Lotus has designed several default folders and views that you can access by clicking icons from the Navigator. These are as follows:

- Inbox folder
- Drafts folder
- Sent folder
- All Documents view
- To Do view
- Trash folder

The following sections examine each of these new items.

Viewing Inbox Messages. To quickly view all the new mail you have received, click the Inbox icon. Figure 4.5 is an example of the Inbox folder. All incoming mail is stored in the Inbox folder until you move it elsewhere. (See the section, "Moving Your Messages," later in this chapter for details on how to organize your mailbox contents.)

Viewing Draft Messages. To examine your *drafts*, which are mail messages that you have saved but not yet sent, click the Drafts icon. This icon displays a view containing your drafts (see fig. 4.6).

The Inbox icon

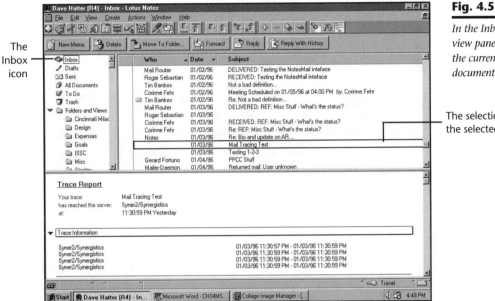

Fig. 4.5

In the Inbox folder, the view pane displays the currently selected document.

The selection bar, indicating the selected document

Notes Basics

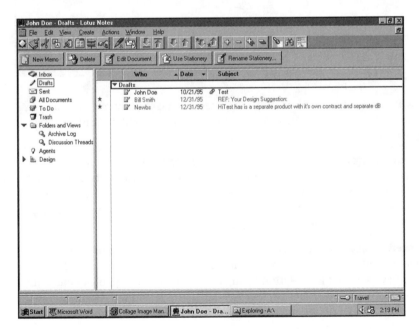

Fig. 4.6

The Drafts view in the new mailbox database.

Once you send a draft, it is automatically moved from the Drafts folder to the Sent folder, unless you specify another folder.

Viewing Sent Messages. To see only the documents that you have actually sent to other users, simply click the Sent icon, which launches the Sent view (see fig. 4.7).

Fig. 4.7

The Sent view in the new mailbox database.

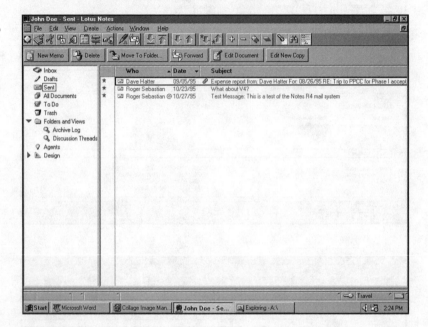

Viewing Task Documents. If you want to only view the tasks you have been assigned, you can click the To Do icon to launch the To Do view which displays tasks sorted and categorized by their status (see fig. 4.8).

Viewing All Documents. If you want to see all of the documents in your mail database regardless of the folder they are in, you can click the All Documents icon, which launches a view that displays all of the documents in the database, irrespective of their status (see fig. 4.9). This view is primarily sorted on the date column. You can, however, click the arrows on the Name and Date columns.

Viewing Deleted Messages (Trash). Documents in the Trash folder have been marked for deletion, but have not yet been deleted. In order to see all of the documents that you have selected for deletion from your mail database, you can click the Trash icon, which displays your Trash folder (see fig. 4.10). If you see documents in the trash folder that you don't want to delete, you can move them to another folder to prevent them from being deleted.

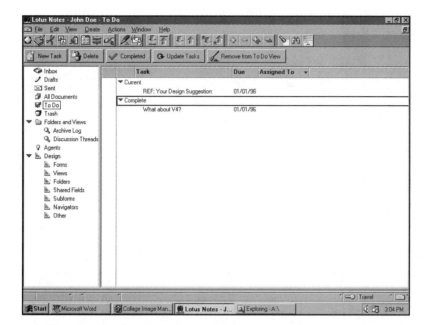

Fig. 4.8

The Tasks view in the new mailbox database.

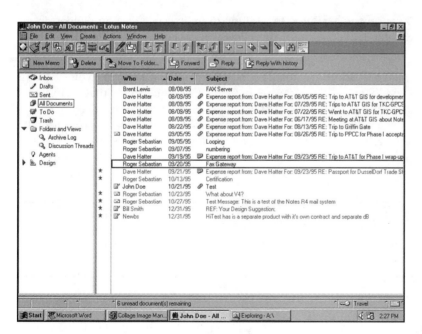

Fig. 4.9

The All Documents view in the new mailbox database.

Fig. 4.10

The Trash (deleted mail) folder in the new mailbox database.

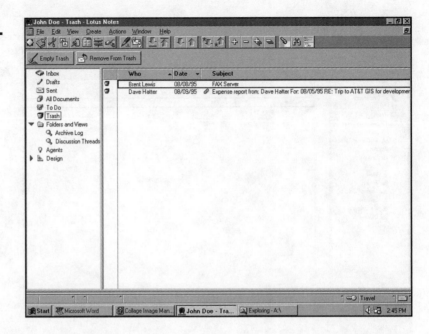

Navigating Through the Mailbox. In addition to the special views and folders in the mailbox, the standard Navigator icons allow you to access other elements of the database.

For instance, the Folder and Views icon can be expanded by clicking it to present a list of other views and folders in the database. In figure 4.11, you can see that there are several other views in your mailbox, each one represented by a yellow magnifying glass. (These views are covered in detail in Chapter 6, "Advanced Mail.") The currently selected view is represented by a blue magnifying glass and its title is displayed in the window title. You can also access these other views by choosing the View menu option and then selecting the specific view you are interested in from the menu.

Note

Although the screenshots used in this book are in black and white, we refer to the colors used in the views so that you can identify them on your screen.

The view pane has been significantly enhanced in Notes R4, but works in a way that is similar to Notes 3.x views (see Chapter 3, "Using Databases," for more information about views and folders). Mail messages in your mailbox are displayed in the view pane. Each of the columns in the view pane represents a field in a mail message, while each row represents an individual mail message. In many of the folders and views in the standard mailbox, the documents displayed are categorized, meaning that documents that have the same category are grouped together and appear under the category in the view pane (refer to fig. 4.9).

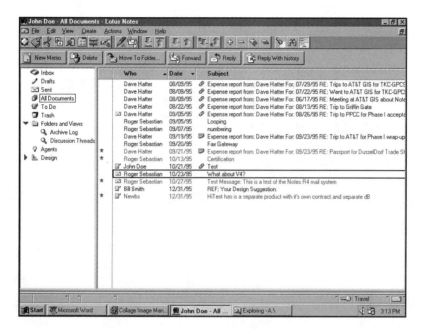

Fig. 4.11

*Other views in the new
mailbox database.*

The following are several columns that display data from each mail message in the
database:

- The leftmost column in the view is a special feature in Notes views and folders.
  It is called the Marker Column and is separated from the other columns in the
  view by a thin vertical gray line that extends throughout the length of the view.
  This column displays a variety of system information. For instance, if you delete
  a mail message, you see a small blue trashcan icon in this column. If you have
  not read a document, a star is displayed in this column—for an example of this,
  look at the message from Brent Lewis, which has a red star in the Marker Column in figure 4.12.

> **Note**
>
> The various icons that are displayed in these views and folders, as well as the colors that
> indicate different parts of the view or folder, are set by the database designer.

- The first column to the right of the Marker Column (which is untitled) begins
  displaying data from the mail messages. In this column, you see the alphabetically sorted name of the person the mail came from. Figure 4.12 shows that in
  some instances, there are several messages from each person, and they are
  grouped under that person's name; this is an example of categorization.

Fig. 4.12

A view showing categorized messages.

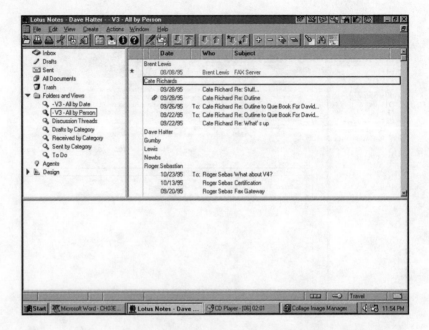

Note

Categories are not documents; they act only as headings so that documents can be logically grouped together. If you click any of the categories in a view, you can expand and collapse the categories. Categorization is a feature that the database designer will build into views and folders. For more information on how categories actually work, see Chapter 3, "Using Databases."

■ The second column (which is also untitled) displays a paper clip icon (which is the default icon for indicating there is an attachment in a document) if there is a file attachment in any of the mail documents.

Note

Lotus Notes allows you to place a copy of a file inside any Rich Text field on any document. Once a file has been attached to a mail message, it can be transferred along with the mail message to all of the intended recipients, who can then detach the file and work with its contents.

■ The third column, titled Date, displays the date of the mail message.
■ The fourth column (also untitled) displays the contents of the To field, which are the mail recipient(s).
■ The fifth and final column displayed in this view is the subject (a brief description of the contents) of the mail message.

Reading Incoming Mail

In order to access the data in a mail message, you must, as a minimum, select the document in a view or folder. Selecting mail messages works just like selecting documents in a regular Notes database. Simply choose the view or folder that is most useful in your search and navigate to the message you want. For instance, if you want to reply to the message your boss sent to you today, the Inbox folder or the All Documents view would probably be the most helpful. Once you have found and selected the message you want (put the selection bar on that document), you are ready to read the mail message.

Alternatively, you can click the All Documents view in the navigator (or choose View, All Documents) and then choose View, Show, Unread Only. Once you have selected a particular document to read, you can enable the preview pane to scan the contents of the document without actually opening the document, or you can double-click the document to open the document in read mode.

Figure 4.13 shows a sample mail message. Notice that the format of the standard Notes mail message, called a *memo*, is somewhat similar to an interoffice memo or standard business letter.

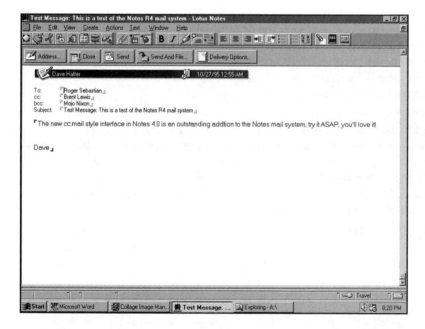

Fig. 4.13

The new Memo form shown in edit mode.

The first four lines (often called the *envelope*) provide the addressing information and provide a snapshot of the contents of the message. The parts of the envelope are as follows:

■ The To field displays the name or names of the primary recipients of the message as well as the time and date (generated by the system) that the mail was sent. If you are reading a message you received, obviously your name appears in this field; if other names also appear in the To field, then those individuals also received the mail.

> **Tip**
>
> When you address a Notes mail message, you can select individual user names, server names, group names (which are lists of users), or database names to send a mail message to. In most instances, you send mail to users or groups. This is covered in more depth in Chapter 5, "Using the Address Books."

■ The cc field displays the name or names of secondary recipients to whom the mail was sent. (cc is an abbreviation for *carbon copy*, a hold-over from the days when carbon paper was used to make copies).

■ The bcc field displays the name or names of other recipients to whom the mail was sent. If you send a mail message with names specified in the bcc field, the recipients named in the To and cc fields will not know that the person or persons specified in bcc also received the mail (*bcc* is an abbreviation for *blind carbon copy*).

■ The From line (the colored bar at the very top of the envelope area) indicates the user name of the sender(s) of the mail message. The name or names in this field are automatically generated by Notes based on the user ID currently in use when a mail message is composed. In addition, the date and time the mail message was sent is displayed in this bar.

■ The Subject line tells you what the mail message is about. When you send a message to another user, it is common courtesy to include a subject so that the user can have an idea of what the message pertains to without opening the message. While you are not required to enter a subject for your mail message, it is recommended that you do so because it makes it easier for the recipients to have some idea of what the message is about and many other mail systems will not accept mail if it contains no subject.

The envelope is followed by the text of the message, commonly referred to as the *body*. The body of a NotesMail message can be virtually any length and can contain embedded objects such as pictures, sound, charts, and so on. It can also contain file attachments. You learn about these other features in Chapter 6, "Advanced Mail."

> **Note**
>
> The body field in a NotesMail message is a special type of field known as a Rich Text field (RTF). You learn more about the powerful features of RTF fields in Chapter 3, "Using Databases," and in Chapter 10, "Designing Forms."

Moving Your Messages. One of the best new features of the new mail interface of NotesMail is the ability to create folders, which allow you to very easily organize your mail based on criteria that you define. For example, you might create a folder named "Accounting" to store all correspondence from the Accounting department. Once you have created a folder, you simply move mail messages into it.

To move a message into or out of a folder, you can click the document you want to move, which should make your mouse pointer display a piece of paper with one edge folded down and a plus (+) symbol above it. You can then drag it to another folder and drop it. You cannot drag a document to a view, only a folder; if you drag it to a view, the mouse pointer changes to the circle and diagonal line (the international symbol for "No") that indicates you cannot perform the requested action. Figure 4.14 shows the first mail message with the subject REF: Your Design Suggestion being moved to the Trash folder. Notice that the mouse pointer has changed from the standard pointer to a document with a plus sign above it.

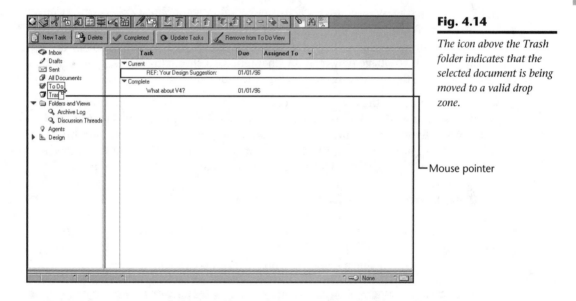

Fig. 4.14

The icon above the Trash folder indicates that the selected document is being moved to a valid drop zone.

—Mouse pointer

Alternatively, you can choose <u>A</u>ctions, <u>M</u>ove to Folder which displays the Move to Folder dialog box (see fig. 4.15).

Fig. 4.15

The Move to Folder dialog box.

You can then select a folder to move the document into, or you can create a new folder.

Mail Notification. Generally speaking, most people want to know if they have new mail as soon as possible. By default, when new mail arrives in your mailbox, Notes plays a short tune to indicate that you have new mail. In addition, if you look at the status bar, there is a small icon in the lower right corner that looks like an envelope. When the envelope is dimmed, you have no new mail; if the envelope turns white, you have new mail in your mailbox.

> **Tip**
>
> If you want to quickly access your new mail, click the envelope icon in the lower right corner of the status bar and choose Scan Unread Mail.

Like most things in Notes, you can control how often Notes checks for mail as well as if Notes should notify you audibly and/or visually when new mail arrives. If you disable the notification features of Notes, you will need to check your mailbox from time to time to see if you have new mail. In Chapter 2, "Customizing Notes," you learn how to edit the default settings for mail notification and scanning.

To take advantage of the notification features, you must leave Notes running constantly on your workstation, even if you are using other applications. You can minimize Notes if you need to run other applications, but ending your Notes session prevents you from getting mail notification. If Notes is minimized and you receive new mail, the Notes icon displays an envelope in addition to its usual graphic.

Understanding the Mailbox Icons

In order to make the new NotesMail interface more intuitive, Lotus has added many new graphics that can be displayed in the mail folders and view so that, at a glance, you can quickly identify certain types of messages and items by seeing a graphic icon. Table 4.1 describes the most common icons you will see in your mailbox.

Table 4.1   Common NotesMail Graphics

Icon	Description	Location
Yellow envelope	Send Mail of Normal or Low importance	View or folder column
Red envelope	Send Mail of High importance	View or folder column
Paper and pencil	Draft (unsent mail message)	View or folder column
Paper clip	Attachment icon	View or folder column
Torn sheet of paper	Truncated document	View or folder column

Icon	Description	Location
Trashcan	Deleted message	View Marker Column
Star	Unread mail	View Marker Column
Checkmark	Selected document	View Marker Column
One piece of paper over another	Stationary	View or Folder Column

Creating Outgoing Mail

The Notes e-mail system is very flexible and supports several different types of mail messages you can send and receive. To send a mail message, choose Create, which displays a menu that lists all of the forms available in your mail database. Figure 4.16 displays the default forms available in the standard mail database.

Fig. 4.16

The Create menu in the mailbox database.

Each of the default forms in the mail database was designed to provide a certain type of functionality. We will now examine the most common and useful forms in detail.

The Memo form is the standard form that you use most of the time when you send mail messages to other users. To create a new memo, choose Create, Memo. A new memo, like that shown in figure 4.17, is displayed on your screen.

At the top of the Memo form, you see the envelope section and you can begin to address the mail. The colored bar at the top replaces the old From and Date fields (in Notes 3.x mail). Notes will compute to display the username of the user ID currently in use at the workstation (this should be your user name if you are sending mail) and the current date and time and place this information into this section. Because I composed the mail, you will see my username and the time and date the message was composed in that section.

Fig. 4.17

A new memo in edit mode.

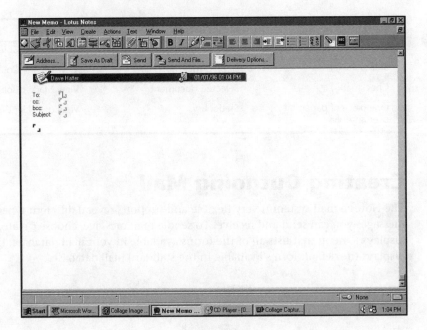

Addressing the Mail

The first editable field, To, is the field you use to list the primary recipient of this message. If you know the exact username of the recipient you can type it in.

> **Note**
>
> Each Notes user must have an account and a Notes ID file that contains that user's Notes username and password (among other information). Notes maintains a directory of each user's username for security purposes and to identify users to the mail system. The Public Name & Address Book serves as the repository for all user information and plays a critical role in the Notes e-mail system. Chapter 4, "Getting Started with Electronic Mail," covers the Public Name & Address Book in detail.

For example, if you want to send a mail to John Doe, you could enter **John Doe** in the To field.

The Memo form has a very handy new feature: you can type the first few characters of a user's name in any of the address fields (To, cc, bcc) and Notes attempts to look up the user's name in the Name & Address Book. If a match is found, Notes completes the name for you; if a match is not found, the status bar displays a message stating that the name was not found in the Name & Address Book.

If you want to send the message to several people, you can enter multiple recipient's names separated by commas. Figure 4.18 displays an example of multiple recipients on a memo.

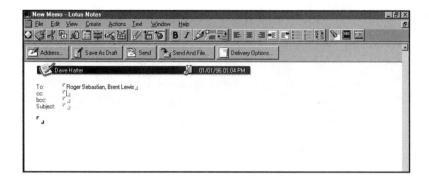

Fig. 4.18

A new memo with several recipients in the To field.

Tip

Alternatively, you can list each name on a new line by pressing Enter after each name but the last. Each time you press Enter, Notes provides additional room for the next name.

Once you have added the names of all of the primary recipients, you can press the Tab key to move to the cc field (or click the cc field). If you want to send a copy of this message to other users, you can enter those names in this field. For example, if you want to send a mail to Roger Sebastian but want Brent Lewis to receive a copy, you would put Roger Sebastian in the To field and Brent Lewis in the cc field (see fig. 4.19).

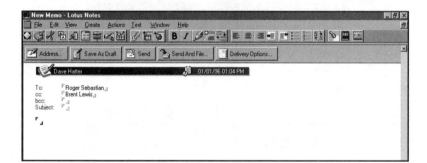

Fig. 4.19

A new memo with both To and cc recipients specified.

Both Roger and Brent will receive the mail, just as if you had included them both in the To field. However, by putting Roger in the To field and Brent in the cc field, you are indicating to Roger that the mail is primarily intended for him, but you also sent the information to Brent. By copying Brent, you let him know what you sent to Roger.

In some instances, you might not want the primary recipient or recipients to know that you have sent a copy of the mail to another party. If this is the case, you can use the bcc field to send copy of the message to other users, but the recipients named in the To and cc fields are not notified that a copy was sent to someone. Figure 4.20

shows a message that is sent to Roger Sebastian, carbon copied to Brent Lewis, and blind carbon copied to John Doe.

Fig. 4.20

A new Memo with To, cc, and bcc recipients specified.

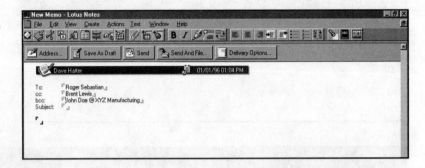

The message sent to Roger Sebastian and the copy sent to Brent Lewis will not display the bcc field showing that John Doe also received a copy; so unless John Doe tells Roger or Brent that he received a copy, they have no way to know that he received a copy.

In addition to the ability to type names directly into the various addressing fields, or using the dynamic lookup capability of the new Memo form, you can press the Address button at the top of the screen to display the Mail Address dialog box, which allows you to choose recipients from the Name & Address Book (see fig. 4.21).

Fig. 4.21

The Mail Address dialog box.

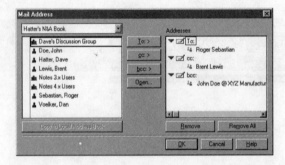

Notes is smart enough to remember the last Name & Address Book you used in the dialog box and chooses it automatically each time you open this dialog box. To Select a different Name & Address Book, click the down arrow to display the list of the Name & Address Books you can see from your workstation. The Name & Address Book drop-down box selects your Personal Name & Address Book by default. The Name & Address Books you are able to access depends on the configuration of your Notes network and the access levels you have been granted by your administrator.

Once you have selected a Name & Address Book, the list box below the Name & Address Book drop-down box displays all of the users and groups in that Name & Address Book.

A *user* is an individual Notes user, while a *group* is just that, a group of Notes users that can be addressed as one entity. Notes resolves the individual address of each person in the group and places each individual name in the field. When using the Mail Address dialog box, users are indicated by a small purple icon that looks like a person, while groups are indicated by a small multi-color icon that looks like a group of people standing together. This is covered in more detail in Chapter 5, "Using the Address Books."

You can use the mouse to scroll through this list to find the user or group you want to send a message to, or you can type the first character of the user or group name you are searching for. Notes will search through the list attempting to find the first entry that begins with the character you entered. For instance, to find Roger Sebastian in the list, you could type **S**. Notes would then move the selection bar to the first item in the list that began with S, in this case Roger Sebastian. This feature is particularly helpful when dealing with a large list of users and groups.

You can also select more than one user or group from the list. This works much like selecting multiple messages from a view or folder, just click in the small empty column (view marker column) next to each name in the list and a small checkmark appears, thus indicating that you have selected that document.

On the right side of this dialog box, you see another list box entitled Addresses. This list box displays small envelope icons representing each of the address fields. If any users or groups have been assigned to a particular field, they are displayed beneath the icon representing that field. For example, in figure 4.21, you can see that Roger Sebastian has been assigned to the To field. Just like a view or folder, these lists can be collapsed or expanded by clicking the twisties in order to save space.

In order to add a user or group to the distribution list, simply select the user or group from the list of Name & Address Book entries and click the button that corresponds to the address field you want to place this username in. For example, to add Mojo Nixon to the To field, you can choose Mojo from the list and press the To button. The Addresses list box immediately reflects the new item. If you decide that you have made an erroneous entry, click the entry you want to remove from the Addresses list and press the Remove button. If you want to delete every entry in the Addresses list, press the Remove All button.

Tip

Many times in large companies there are several users with very similar names. When using the Mail Address dialog box, if you cannot distinguish one user from another, or need more information about a particular user, click the Open button to open the selected person's user document, which should give you all the information you could need about a specific Notes user. This also applies to group documents.

The Copy to Local Address Book button allows you to copy group and user documents from the Public Name & Address Book and add them to your local Name & Address book. This is particularly useful if you are a mobile user, because it allows you to address mail from your Personal Address Book, which eliminates the need for you to know the exact address to type in, or to connect to the server to see the correct address in the Public N & A Book. Just select the entry you want to transfer and press the Copy to Local Address Book button. Once you are finished addressing the mail, to update the mail message with the addresses, click the OK button. To discard your changes, press the Cancel button.

Specifying the Subject

Once you have all of the address information entered, you can tab to the Subject field. This field allows you to enter a brief description of the context of the message and is displayed in the all mail views and folders (see fig. 4.22). Because the subject is the first thing the user will see regarding your message, it should be as explicit and concise as possible. Although you may enter up to 256 characters in the subject, most of the view and folders will not display that many characters for this field and will truncate the text in the display. (Not to worry, your subject will not be affected; this is for display purposes only.)

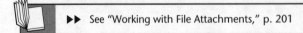

▶▶ See "E-mail Etiquette," p. 155

Fig. 4.22

The new memo form with a completed subject.

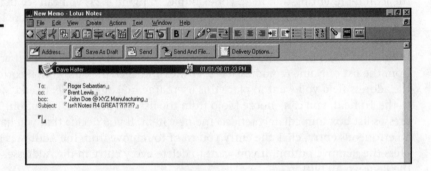

Creating the Body of the Message

Once you have entered the address information and a brief subject, you are ready to enter your actual message, which is known as the body. Although this field appears to be small, you can enter just about as much text as you like. You can also embed objects from other applications, such as a 1-2-3 spreadsheet, or include file attachments. Figure 4.23 shows the completed mail memo ready to send.

▶▶ See "Working with File Attachments," p. 201

Tip

Don't forget to use the integrated spell checker to ensure that you don't have any spelling errors. When you are ready to spell check your message, simply choose Edit, Check Spelling or use the Edit Check Spelling SmartIcon.

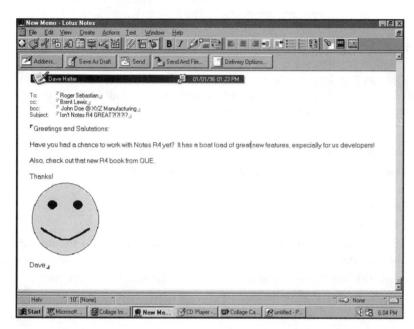

Fig. 4.23

A completed memo ready to be sent.

Mailing Options

If you are familiar with the Notes 3.x mail system, then you know that at the bottom of the old forms there were four fields that allowed you to set certain mailing options. The old fields were the following:

- Delivery Priority
- Receipt Report
- Delivery Report
- Personal Categories

While these fields still exist in many of the new forms, the Memo form has been significantly enhanced and presents these fields in a different way. In addition, they have been given slightly more descriptive names and other mailing options have been rolled into this form. Because of these differences, we will cover each of these options briefly in the following sections, and in more detail in later sections in this chapter.

To examine or change these options, click the Delivery Options button on the Action bar at the top of the form. The Delivery Options button will launch the Delivery Options dialog box (see fig. 4.24).

Fig. 4.24

*The Delivery Options
dialog box.*

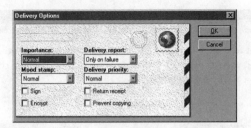

Choosing a Mood. You can use the Mood stamp drop-down list to select a mood for your mail that helps identify to the recipients what tone you want to convey. This is a new field in Notes 4.x. The default mood is Normal, which indicates no tone. You can also select one of any of the following moods which will insert a graphic image between the envelope and the body that represents the tone:

 Confidential tells the recipients that they should not share this information with others.

 Flame indicates that you are angry about something.

 FYI means that this mail message is For Your Information only and no action is necessarily required.

 Personal indicates that the mail is of a personal nature and should not be shared with others.

 Private is similar to confidential; the information contained in the mail is for the distribution list only.

 Thank You immediately let's the recipient(s) know that you are showing your appreciation for something.

 Good Job lets the recipient(s) know that they are being commended for a job well done.

 Joke tells the recipient(s) that the message has a light, jovial tone.

 Question lets the recipient(s) know that the message is a question that they need to answer.

 Reminder indicates to the recipient that they should not forget to do something.

Generating a Delivery Status Report. In most cases, if your mail message cannot be delivered to your intended recipients, the Notes server sends you a message indicating that it had a problem delivering the mail message along with a suggested corrective action to take. If you have sent a message and do not receive a Failure Report message, you can assume that your mail message has been delivered. For very important messages, you may want to have the Notes server send you a Delivery Report to let you know that your mail was delivered successfully.

The Delivery Report drop-down list has four possible settings: Only on failure, Confirm delivery, Trace entire path, and None. The default setting is Only on failure, which only sends a delivery report if a routing error is encountered. You can change the setting by typing the first letter of the setting you want (O, C, T, or N), or by clicking the down arrow and selecting from the list.

If you change the Delivery Report field to Confirm delivery, in addition to sending you notification of the delivery failure, the Notes server notifies you when your mail is delivered. A Delivery Report from the server appears in your mailbox like any other NotesMail message.

Note

A Delivery Report does not indicate that the mail message recipient actually read the message. It only tells you that the mail message was successfully delivered to the recipient's mailbox.

The Trace Entire Path setting will return a confirmation from each hop along the routing path from the sender to the recipient. If you are having trouble sending and receiving mail, this can be a valuable troubleshooting tool because you can see where the mail died on the routing path. If you only communicate with users on the same server, Trace Entire Path probably is not very useful.

If you change the Delivery Report field to None, you do not receive a notification, even if the delivery fails. Though not often used, this setting may be useful if you are sending an unimportant message to many people and don't care if Notes cannot deliver the message to someone. For instance, if you were going to send an FYI type mail to the entire organization, you might use this option.

If you choose Confirm Delivery the Notes server sends you a mail message to indicate that the mail was successfully delivered to the recipient's mailbox. The last option, None, tells the Notes server not to send you a report, even if there is a routing failure.

Setting the Delivery Priority. The Delivery Priority field is similar to the old Delivery Priority field. This drop-down list allows you to choose from the following settings: Low, Normal, and High. Each of these options has an effect on the speed and cost with which the mail is routed by the server. Just as you would expect, High priority mail routes the most quickly, regardless of the cost. Low priority mail routes most slowly and is the most economical. The Normal setting is the default setting and is sufficient for most mail messages. If you only communicate with other Notes users via a LAN connection (persistent connection to the network), this setting has little effect on the speed or cost of routing. If you communicate with other Notes users across leased-line or dial-up connections, this setting becomes more important as it can have a significant effect on the timeliness of delivery and the cost.

For instance, High priority mail is routed immediately, regardless of the routing cost. Low priority mail is only sent between 12:00 a.m. and 6:00 a.m. which is more cost-effective because connect charges are considerably less during the off-peak hours. Normal priority mail is routed according to various settings the Notes administrator sets. If you are cost conscious and the timeliness of the mail is not very important, use the Low setting. Conversely, if the mail is very important and must be delivered as soon as possible, use the High setting.

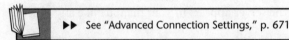 ▶▶ See "Advanced Connection Settings," p. 671

> **Note**
>
> The Notes server software allows the Notes administrator to set up scheduled connections to other Notes servers for routing and replication. As part of this process, the administrator can establish a routing cost that can be used to determine the most economical times and paths for mail routing and database replication.

Requesting a Return Receipt. Return receipt is used to indicate that you want to receive a message from the system when the recipient opens the mail message you have sent. This can be very useful when you need to be sure that a user has received your mail (see fig. 4.25). To enable this feature, simply select the Return receipt checkbox in the Delivery Options dialog box. An *x* should appear indicating that it is enabled. To disable this feature, click the checkbox a second time to remove the *x*.

Fig. 4.25

A return receipt.

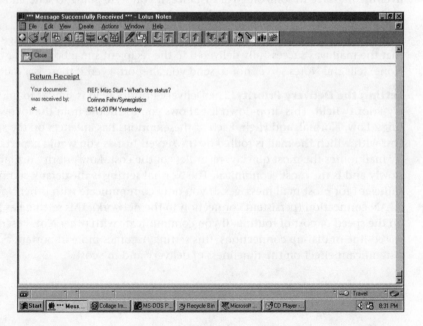

Tip

Many people get irritated when they frequently receive mail that generates a return receipt because it makes them feel pressured to respond to the mail immediately. A return receipt also uses extra system resources because a second mail message must be generated, delivered to you, and stored in your mailbox. While this can be very useful when it's necessary, you should use this feature sparingly.

Encrypting the Message for Security. The Encrypt checkbox allows you to encrypt your mail message with your private key. This provides additional security because even though a user may receive this message, he or she cannot decrypt and read any of the encrypted fields unless he or she possesses a copy of your public key. You learn more about encryption in Chapter 20, "Security And Encryption."

Adding an Electronic Signature. The Sign checkbox allows you to attach an electronic signature to your mail. An electronic signature is derived from your unique key stored in your Notes ID. An electronic signature is virtually impossible to duplicate and guarantees that any mail or document that is signed by your Notes ID actually came from you (or at least your Notes ID). Electronic signatures are discussed in more detail in Chapter 20, "Security And Encryption."

Tip

Electronic signatures and encryption are extremely secure methods for protecting mail messages (or any document for that matter), but are dependent upon the physical security of your Notes ID. Anyone who can access your Notes ID and knows your password can impersonate you! The moral of this story is to keep your ID secure, your password to yourself, and change your password frequently.

Caution

All Notes encryption keys are based on the 64-bit RSA standard which creates almost unbreakable encryption codes and requires a public key and a private key. If you encrypt a mail message or a document and then lose your Notes ID, chances are your information will be irretrievably lost! You should use encryption only when security is paramount.

Disallowing the Reprint of your Mail Messages. Note's new mail interface provides another great new security feature, Prevent copying. You can simply place a check in the Prevent copying checkbox of the Delivery Options dialog box to enable this feature. When you enable Prevent Copying, recipients of the mail message cannot copy the message to the Clipboard, print, or forward the message to other users. This helps to ensure that confidential information can not be leaked to others through the NotesMail system.

Sending Your Message

Once you have selected the settings you want, you are ready to save and/or send your mail message. Press Esc to close the message and display the Close Window dialog box shown in figure 4.26. You can send the message in the following ways:

- The Send and save a copy radio button tells Notes to send the mail and place a copy of the mail message in your mailbox. This is the default option for this dialog box and is recommended for any mail that you might need to refer back to in the future (this is known as CYA—cover your ass).

- The Send only radio button tells Notes to send the message, but does not place a copy of the mail message in your mailbox. If you are sending mail that you don't need to keep, maybe a joke for instance, you can use this option to save space in your mailbox.

- The Save only radio button tells Notes not to send the message, but to save a draft of the mail message in your mailbox. All mail messages that you elect to save without sending will be considered drafts until sent and can be seen in the Drafts view. This can be very handy if you don't have time to finish a mail message and want to come back later and work on it.

- The Discard changes radio button tells Notes to ignore the changes in the mail message. If you are composing a new mail message, this option will cause the new message to be neither sent nor saved; if you are editing a message, all edits will be discarded and the saved mail will remain the same.

Fig. 4.26

The Close Window dialog box for mail messages.

Once you have chosen the option you want, click OK to take the action you have selected. Choose Cancel to ignore the action you have selected and return to the mail message being edited. Pressing Esc while this dialog box is displayed is equivalent to selecting Cancel.

> **Tip**
>
> You can also use the Send or the Send And File buttons on the action bar to send the mail. To send the mail without saving a copy in your mailbox, click the Send button. To save a copy of the mail when it's sent, click the Send And File button.

How Notes Validates Mail Recipients

When you attempt to send the mail, Notes compares each of the recipient's names that you have entered in the various address fields against the user names in your Personal Name & Address Book. If a match is found, then the name is validated and searching stops. If no match is found, the Public Name & Address Book will be searched. If any of the recipient names in your memo doesn't exactly match one of the names in the Name & Address Book, Notes performs what is known as a *soundex search* (a search based on items that sound similar) to present you with a list of users with similar user names.

For example, if you enter the last name Jones, but the actual user name is Will Jones, Notes finds all of the individuals named Jones and displays them in the Ambiguous Name dialog box (see fig. 4.27).

Fig. 4.27

The Ambiguous Names dialog box.

If you see the name of the person you intended, double-click the name, or use the arrow keys to select the name and click OK. Notes inserts the correct user name in place of the invalid user name. If you do not see the correct name in the dialog box, click the Cancel Sending button and use the Address button on the Action bar to pull up a list of valid names.

Tip

Because the Mail Address dialog box pulls its information directly from the Notes Name & Address Books, using it to address your mail messages can save much time and hassle by avoiding invalid user names.

E-Mail Etiquette

Now that you know how to use NotesMail, it's important to know a little about e-mail etiquette so as not to offend your colleagues. The following list presents some tips and conventions you might want to follow when sending e-mail messages:

- Do not type your messages in all UPPERCASE as this is commonly known as shouting and will cause people to get angry with you. Always use proper case unless you want to imply that you are SHOUTING!!

- E-mail is private information, just like the rest of a company's business correspondence, and security is important. You should never send an e-mail message containing company proprietary or confidential information outside the company without prior approval.

- E-mail may seem private, but a business manager may read his/her employee's e-mail with impunity and without informing the employee.

■ E-mail can be edited and forwarded without the originator's knowledge, unless you use the Prevent copying delivery option when you send your mail.

■ Importance and Delivery priority on messages should be set to High only when essential.

■ If you need to provide constructive criticism, or reprimand someone, it is better to do it in person as e-mail may not convey the tone or message you want to get across.

■ People who send frequent or unnecessary messages, or who write dissertations or diatribes, eventually will be ignored, much like the boy who cried "wolf."

■ Subject lines should give the recipient some idea of the content of the message and should be brief.

■ E-mail should be read and edited carefully and then spell checked before sending—typos can make you look foolish, or convey a misleading or incorrect meaning.

■ Too much cute or cryptic use of e-mail shorthand can cause miscommunication. The following list, by no means inclusive, displays many of the common e-mail shorthand and emoticons:

• BTW:	By the way	• GD&R:	Grinning, ducking, and running
• FYI:	For your information	• ;-)	Wink
• LOL:	Laughing out loud	• :-)	Smiling
• ROFL:	Rolling on the floor laughing	• :-(	Frowning
• BRB:	Be right back	• :-D	Big smile
• IMO:	In my opinion	• :-O	Mouth open in amazement
• PMJI:	Pardon me for jumping in	• 8-)	Smile with glasses

Using Other Mail Forms

Your mailbox contains several forms other than the Memo form that are quite useful. After the Memo form, the next two most used forms are probably the Reply form and the Phone Message form. Each of these forms is more like the old style of NotesMail messages, and the differences between the Memo form and these forms is discussed in the next few sections.

Replying to a Message

Many times, you will receive a mail message that needs a reply. You can compose a new memo, but that does not necessarily reference the original mail—and you would have to start from scratch. Notes has a much easier way for you to create a reply.

NotesMail makes it easy for you to reply to a mail message by providing two types of reply forms in your standard mailbox databases, Reply and Reply with History. You can create a reply that references the original mail by choosing Create, Reply, or clicking the Reply button on the Action Bar. This launches a new Reply, and the To and Subject fields are already populated with the correct values. The To field is set to the username of the person who sent you the original mail. The Subject field reflects the subject of the original mail. Enter the text of your reply and send the reply as you would any mail message (see fig. 4.28). Once Notes has sent the reply, it returns you to the original memo.

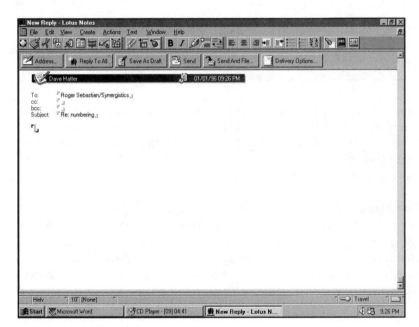

Fig. 4.28

A new reply mail message to a mail message from Roger Sebastian.

The Reply with History is almost exactly like the reply form, except that it copies in the body of the original mail message so that you can reply to specific points raised in the original mail message (see fig. 4.29).

Fig. 4.29

A new reply with history showing the text of the original message from Roger Sebastian.

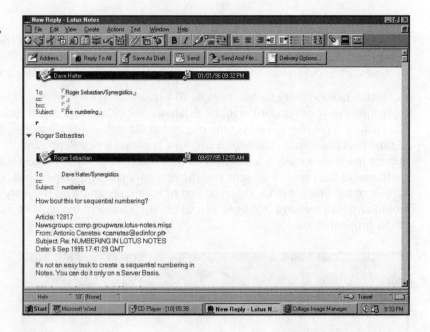

To create a Reply With History message, select the mail message you want to reply to and choose Create, Reply with History, or press the Reply with History button on the Action bar. As in the Reply form, the To and Subject fields will be completed and the body field will contain an exact copy of the original mail message. You can then edit this copy and insert your rebuttals.

Phone Messages

A *phone message* is a mail message with a format similar to that of the standard written phone message. If you take a phone call for someone else, you can use the phone message to let him know he had a phone message via Notes mail, which is not only faster, but sets off the new mail indicators in Notes. To send a phone message, choose Create, Special, Phone Message.

Figure 4.30 shows a sample phone message. Your username appears in the From field, just like a real phone memo pad. The phone message contains additional fields that you can fill in, including Contact and Phone. The message also contains checkboxes for typical comments such as Telephoned and Please Call.

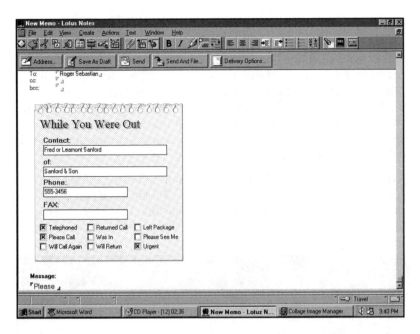

Fig. 4.30

The new Phone Message form in your mailbox.

When you have completed the phone message, send it as you would any other mail message.

Tasks

Those of you who have used Notes 3.x might have used the To Do forms in the old mail database. Notes 4 provides a completely overhauled form named Task that allows you to assign tasks to yourself and others that can be views from the Tasks view. To compose a new Task, choose Create, Task.

The Task field allows you to enter a textual description of the task that needs to be performed. The priority radio buttons can be used to assign a priority to the tasks so that you, or the other assignees, know the importance of the task. None is the default setting for priority. The Start and Due fields allow you to enter dates so that you can track when a task needs to be completed and how many overdue tasks you have. Additionally, you can enter in other comments in the Additional information field. If you want to assign this task to others, you can click the Assign to Others button of the Action bar to display the Assign to and cc fields, which work just like the To and cc fields in the Memo form. Any user or group names entered into these fields will cause all of the named individuals to receive the task via mail.

Bookmarks

Bookmarks are another incredibly useful new feature of the new Mailbox design. An example of a typical use for a bookmark might be if you were browsing a technical support database and found a document that you wanted to share with your team. You could copy the document into a mail message and send it to everyone on the team, but this would be highly redundant as the document already exists in the Technical Support database. You could also send mail that tells the users where to go to find the document, or send them a bookmark, which is a dynamic link to the original document that will take the user there with a single click.

To compose a bookmark, open the document that you want to link to and then, if you are not in your mailbox, choose Create, Mail, Special, Bookmark. If you are in your mailbox, choose Create, Special, Bookmark and a new form that looks like figure 4.31 will be created.

Fig. 4.31

The Bookmark form will link you to another document.

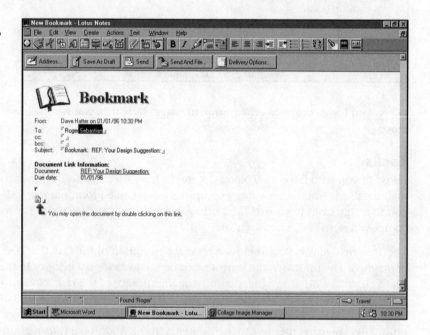

Once you composed the bookmark, you simply put in the address information as you would with another other mail form and send the bookmark. When the recipients receive the bookmark, they can simply follow the instructions beside the red arrow and click the link icon to open the linked document.

Forwarding a Mail Message

Many times you receive a mail message that you want to send to other users who were not included in the original distribution list. To do so, select any mail message and choose Actions, Forward. Notes then presents a new Memo form that looks much like a regular memo, except that the body of the memo contains the entire mail message you were reading (see fig. 4.32). (This is much like the Reply With History option, but does not put the sender's address into the To field, and does not automatically fill in the subject field.) You can address the message using the procedures you learned earlier in this chapter, and you can edit the body of the memo if you need to add to or change the original message, or include additional information with the old message. Send the message as you would any other.

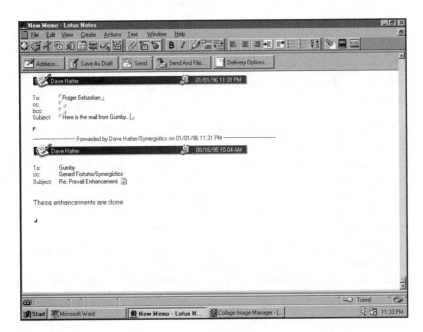

Fig. 4.32

A message forwarded from me to Roger Sebastian.

You can see from the figure that the original mail has been copied into the body of the new mail message, and other text has been added as well. Forwarding mail messages can make it very easy for you to distribute information to other users.

Printing Messages

Even though you work with your mail electronically 99 percent of the time, occasionally you may want to print a copy of a mail message you have sent or received. Printing a mail message is exactly the same as printing any Notes document. The steps that follow serve as a quick reminder on printing documents:

1. Select the message you want to print. (Remember, if you are in a view or a folder, you do not have to open the message to print it.) If you want to print the mail message you are currently reading, proceed to the next step.

2. Choose File, Print, or click the File Print SmartIcon. This causes the File Print dialog box to be displayed. (See Chapter 3, "Using Databases," for more detailed information about this dialog box.)

Notes Basics

3. Select the appropriate settings for this document in the File Print dialog box.

4. Choose <u>O</u>K to print your document.

Closing Messages

When you are finished reading a mail message, you can close the message and return the folder or view you were in by taking any of the following actions:

■ Press Esc.

■ Press Ctrl+F4.

■ Click the view or folder window's Control menu box and then choose <u>C</u>lose (the Control menu box is the small application icon in the upper left corner of the view or folder window).

> **Note**
>
> You will see two Control menu boxes, one for Notes R4 (in the upper left corner) and one for the view or folder window, just below the program's Control menu box. Make sure that you click the view or folder's window. If you inadvertently click the Notes Control menu box, you are prompted to exit Notes. Be sure to click the correct one.

■ Double-click with the right mouse button in the document. This is a hold-over from Notes 3.x and may not be enabled for your workstation. See Chapter 2, "Customizing Notes," for more information on preferences to learn how to enable this feature.

Deleting Messages

As you accumulate mail messages in your mailbox, you will most likely decide that there are a significant amount of messages that you no longer need. Unneeded mail messages clutter your mailbox, making it harder to find the important messages, and occupy precious disk space. (If you keep every mail message you receive, you will begin to consume a large amount of disk space, and your administrator will probably call you to tell you there is some mail you no longer need.)

Consider the following techniques for conserving disk space:

■ After you have read an incoming message, delete it unless it contains information you really need to keep. Similarly, when you send a message to someone else, don't select the <u>S</u>ave checkbox in the Document Save dialog box unless you really need to keep a copy of the mail message in your mailbox.

■ If you frequently need to keep messages for a long time—for example, if you work in a legal department, you might need to keep a message or return receipt message as proof that you responded to a problem—you can print the message and delete the electronic copy. You can also move the message to an archive mailbox, which is discussed in the next section.

■ Regularly scan your mailbox, at most once a month for unneeded messages. Take five minutes to examine your mailbox for messages that you no longer need. When you identify these messages, delete them.

■ Often, you may receive mail messages that have file attachments that you don't really need, but you want to save the mail message. Deleting unneeded attachments can conserve significant space because the attachments are stored within your mailbox as well.

 ▶▶ See "Deleting Attachments," p. 208

Deleting Mail Messages

Because of the way Notes allocates storage space for databases, your mail database can eat up inordinate amounts of disk space if you do not delete mail messages frequently. This is particularly important for remote users, as disk space on most notebooks is usually at a premium. The moral of this story is to delete your unneeded mail frequently; it makes it easier to find mail you need to keep, it saves disk space, and it increases the performance of your mailbox.

As in any Notes database, to delete mail messages, simply open your mailbox and choose the view or folder you find most useful for viewing mail. Then select the message or messages you want to delete and press the Delete key on your keyboard, or click the Edit Clear SmartIcon which marks that message for deletion. Notes does not delete the message immediately; it moves the message into the Trash folder. This is an extremely useful feature, because if you decide that you really don't want to delete any of the marked documents, you can rescue them from the trash.

 ◀◀ See "Emptying Your Mail Trash," p. 68

You also can delete a message while you are reading it by pressing Delete. Notes flags the message (with the trashcan icon in the view marker column) for deletion and immediately takes you to the next message in your mailbox. This procedure works only when you're reading a message, however; the Delete key has a different effect when you are composing a message.

Exiting Your Mailbox

To exit your mailbox, you may use any of the following methods you learned earlier for closing a database:

■ Press Esc.

- Press Ctrl+F4.
- Double-click the control box for your mailbox view.
- Double-click the right mouse button (it doesn't matter what the mouse is pointing at). This method will only work if the right mouse button option is enabled as a user preference on your workstation.

As in any database, if you have flagged messages for deletion, Notes displays a prompt that asks you if you want to permanently delete the flagged documents. If you click Yes, the messages you have flagged are deleted permanently from your mailbox. If you click No, the messages remain in your mailbox and the deletion flag is reset.

Handling Your Mail with the Status Bar and SmartIcons

As you are probably well aware by now, Notes provides many ways to accomplish the same task, particularly in the area of e-mail. One of the most useful features that Notes provides is the envelope in the right corner of the status bar. The Envelope icon on the status bar can make using your mailbox quick and easy.

When the Envelope icon is dimmed, you currently have no new mail. When new mail is transferred to your mailbox, the envelope displays bright white. Clicking this icon displays the menu in figure 4.33.

Fig. 4.33

Mail options are available
from the status bar.

Choose one of the following options from this menu:

- You can select the Create Memo option to open your mailbox and create a new blank mail memo, just as if you had chosen Create, Memo in your mailbox.
- Selecting the second option, Scan Unread Mail, opens your mailbox and opens the first unread mail message in your mailbox. You can then navigate between the unread documents until there are no unread documents left. If no unread mail messages are found, the status bar displays There are no unread documents in your mail file.

> **Note**
>
> When you use this method to read the unread documents, you actually open the documents, which means that Notes no longer considers the mail message unread.

- You can select Receive Mail to initiate a server connection and begin replicating your local mailbox with the server copy of your mailbox. Any new mail that is waiting in your server mailbox is transferred to your local mailbox, but outgoing mail is not sent.

- Selecting Send Outgoing Mail, the fourth option, initiates a server connection and routes pending mail from your workstation to the server's mailbox, but incoming mail is not received.

- The fifth option, Send & Receive Mail, performs the actions of both Receive Mail and Send Outgoing Mail.

- The sixth and final option, Open Mail, opens your mailbox and displays the last view or folder that you used.

In addition to the status bar, when you open you mailbox, Notes provides a context-sensitive set of NotesMail SmartIcons that can make your NotesMail sessions easier and more productive. Table 4.2 contains a listing of each of the default NotesMail SmartIcons and the functionality it provides.

Table 4.2   The Default NotesMail SmartIcons

Icon	Name	Description
	Actions Edit Document	Opens the currently selected document in edit mode.
	Actions Forward	Forwards the currently selected document.
	Navigate Next Main	Goes to the next Main document in the current view or folder.
	Navigate Previous Main	Goes to the previous Main document in the current view or folder.
	Navigate Next	Goes to the next document in the current view or folder.
	Navigate Previous	Goes to the previous document in the current view or folder.
	Navigate Next Unread	Goes to the next unread document in the current view or folder.
	Navigate Previous Unread	Goes to the previous unread document in current view or folder.
	View Expand	Expands the current category.
	View Collapse	Collapses the current category.
	View Expand All	Expands the entire view (All Categories).

(continues)

Notes Basics

Table 4.2 Continued		
Icon	**Name**	**Description**
	View Collapse All	Collapses the entire view (All Categories).
	Edit Find	Launches the Search dialog box.
	View Show/Hide Search Bar	Toggles the full text search bar off and on.
	View Show/Hide Preview Pane	Toggles the document preview pane off and on.

From Here...

In this chapter, you learned how to work with your mailbox—reading, composing, addressing, printing, deleting, and archiving mail. You should now be able to effectively use NotesMail, greatly increasing your ability to communicate with other e-mail users in your company.

For more information on using NotesMail, see the following chapters:

■ In Chapter 5, "Using the Address Books," you learn about the critical role the Name & Address Books plays in all Notes communications.

■ For more information on advanced mailing techniques and securing mail messages, refer to Chapter 6, "Advanced Mail," and Chapter 20, "Security and Encryption."

Using the Address Books

Chapter 2, "Customizing Notes," briefly discussed the Public and Personal Name & Address Book databases and how important they are to Notes operation. In Chapter 3, "Using Databases," you learned how to address mail using the names of users and groups from the Name & Address Book (N & A Book).

In this chapter, you learn about the following:

- Differences between the Personal and Public Name & Address Books
- How these books work together to make your Notes sessions more productive

Understanding the Personal Name & Address Book

Figure 5.1 displays a Public N & A Book icon for ABC Company and a Personal N & A Book icon for Dave Hatter. At first glance, the Personal N & A Book and the Public N & A Book seem very similar in form and function, but they are actually quite different in supporting the enhanced functionality of Notes R4. The Personal N & A Book database is a subset of the Public N & A Book, created on each user's workstation when the Notes client software is installed. It is essentially a directory service that you can use to store information that pertains only to you and your workstation. For instance, if you frequently send mail to a Notes user in another company, but no one else in your organization needs that e-mail address, then store the address in your Personal N & A Book.

The Public Name & Address Book has a much more important role and a larger scope than the Personal N & A Book. In fact, according to the Lotus documentation, the Public N & A Book is the "most important database in a domain." It is shared by all users in a domain and contains the same types of documents as the Personal N & A Book, but it also contains documents that are used by the server for server administration and maintenance.

From an end user perspective, the use of the Personal and Public N & A Books is similar, and many of the forms in each database are identical. Because much of the functionality of the Public N & A Book is administrative in nature, I will discuss the Personal Name & Address Book first.

> **Note**
>
> If you have used previous versions of Notes, you should be familiar with the Public and Personal N & A Book concept. In Notes 3.0, your Personal N & A Book was based on the same database template as the Public N & A Book, which meant that although your Personal N & A Book was not shared with other users, it contained the exact same forms and views as the Public N & A Book. In Notes R4, each of the databases is based on a different template.
>
> The Public N & A Book database is based on the PUBNAMES.NTF template and contains all of the server management forms and views. The Personal N & A Book is based on the PERNAMES.NTF template and contains only forms and views that apply to the workstation. By eliminating forms and views that apply only to the server, the Personal N & A Book is smaller and less confusing.

Figure 5.2 displays the Create menu of a standard Personal N & A Book. As you can see in figure 5.2, the Personal N & A Book contains the following types of documents (described in the subsequent sections):

- Company
- Person
- Group
- Location
- Server Connection

> **Note**
>
> The word *standard* is used to describe the design elements, such as views, folders, and forms, in your N & A Book as they ship from Lotus. What you actually see might vary from the screens displayed in this chapter because each of these forms could be altered by Notes administrators or designers in your organization.

Company Documents

In Notes R4, the Personal N & A Book can serve as a makeshift contact manager. For each company you do business with, you can create a *Company* document (see fig. 5.3).

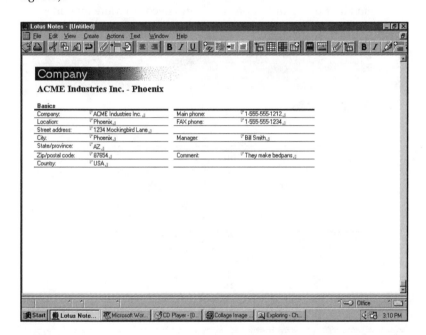

Fig. 5.3

A Company document for ACME Industries.

The usage of this form is very straightforward; you simply fill in information on a company that you want to store in your Personal N & A Book. Company documents are not used by the system; they merely provide a convenient way for you to keep information about companies you commonly deal with in the same place you keep information regarding the specific people you deal with at a given company.

To create a new Company document, choose Create, Company, then enter the information and press Ctrl+S or press Esc. When prompted to save the document, click Yes.

Notes Basics

> **Note**
>
> The line that displays the company name and location immediately beneath the Company graphic on the form will not be displayed until you either save the document, or press the F9 key to refresh the document. Each type of document in the N & A Book has this same functionality.

Person Documents

Person documents are used to identify individual users and to provide Notes with the information it needs to route messages to those users. To make it easy to send mail messages to other Notes users, you can create Person documents in your Personal N & A Book that contain all of the information that Notes needs to route mail messages to them. Figure 5.4 displays a Person document in edit mode.

Fig. 5.4

A Person document for John Doe in edit mode.

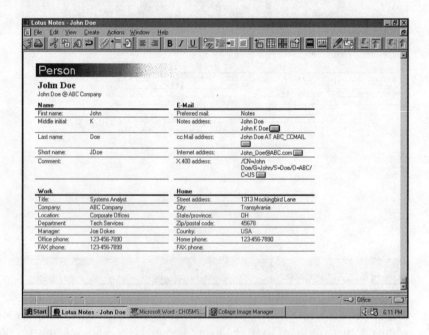

Name and E-Mail Information. The Name and E-Mail sections of the Person document contain important system information used by the Notes server for user authentication and mail routing.

As a minimum, each Person document should have the First name, Last name, Preferred mail, and Notes address fields completed. The First name, Middle initial (which is not required, but should be used because it helps to make a name unique), and Last name fields are the names entered by the administrator when a user is registered. This is the same name stored in the user's ID file.

> **Note**
>
> If the correct password is entered for the user ID in use at the workstation when a user attempts to log in to a Notes server, the server then authenticates the user ID by checking to see if that user exists in its Public N & A Book. If that user exists, it then checks the user's Private Key against the user's Public Key. If it finds a match, the user is authenticated and a communication session with the server is established.

The other fields in these two sections allow you to further describe the user and enter mail addressing information for users who will need to communicate with other mail systems. They are as follows:

■ **The Short name field**—This field can be used to enter a shorter name, such as a nickname, for the user. If a user's name is Jehosephat Van Rumplestiltskin, for example, you might want to give him the short name JVR.

■ **The Comment field**—This field allows you to enter additional information that may be helpful when trying to identify an individual.

■ **The Preferred mail field**—This field is a standard keyword list that displays the Select Keywords dialog box shown in figure 5.5.

Fig. 5.5

The default value for this field is Notes (of course); but if this user employs another mail system, it can be indicated on this list.

■ **The Notes address field**—This is a multi-value text list that allows you to enter several names for identifying a user. (Each one must be unique.) You may enter names directly into this field or press the small gray button next to the field to launch the Notes Mail Address Helper dialog box shown in figure 5.6.

Fig. 5.6

The Notes Mail Address Helper for John Doe.

■ **The Notes Mail Address Helper**—This feature provides some guidance when you enter the names and domain of a user. As you can see in figure 5.6, the names referring to the user are displayed in the User name field, and the user's domain is displayed in the Notes domain field.

> **Note**
>
> Once you have entered the name of the user, you can press the F9 key to refresh the document, and Notes attempts to plug in the e-mail address for you. You will need to check the address to ensure that it is correct.

■ **The cc:Mail field**—This is a multi-value text list that can be used to enter cc:Mail addresses if you need to communicate with someone who uses cc:Mail. Like the Notes Address field, you can press the small gray button to display a dialog box with information on how to enter a valid cc:Mail address (see fig. 5.7).

Fig. 5.7

The Notes cc:Mail Address Helper for John Doe.

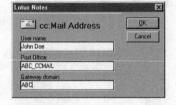

■ **The Internet address field**— This field works exactly like the Notes address and cc:Mail address fields. To communicate with someone across the Internet, enter that user's address in this field. If you are unsure how to enter the address, press the small gray button to display the Internet Address Helper dialog box (see fig. 5.8).

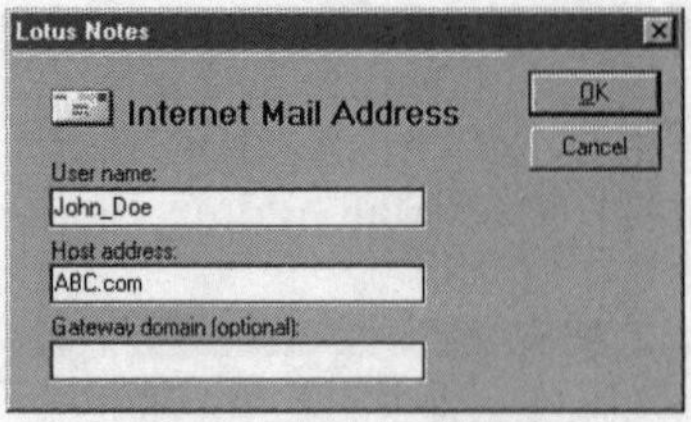

Fig. 5.8

The Notes Internet Address Helper for John Doe.

The last field in the E-Mail section works like the other fields, but is designed to store valid X.400 address for users who use X.400 mail systems. For help entering a valid X.400 address, press the small gray button to display the X.400 Address Helper dialog box (see fig. 5.9). X.400 naming can be quite complicated and confusing. In most cases, you will not be able to use X.400 mail unless you have the recipient's business card with his or her X.400 address on it, or the address has been written out for you.

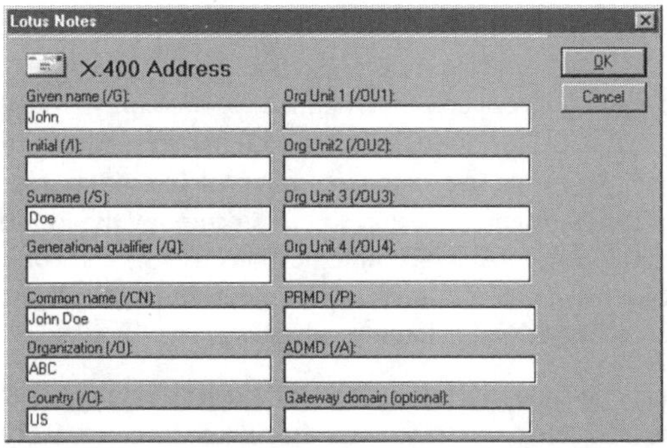

Fig. 5.9

The Notes X.400 Address Helper for John Doe.

The Distinguished Name

Each Notes user has a *distinguished name* that is based on the X.500 naming standard and is broken down into four components: the Common Name (CN), Organizational Unit (OUN, where *N* is the number of the organization unit), Organization (O), and Country (C). The following format is used:

    CN/OU1/OU2/OU3/OU4/O/C

An example of a fully distinguished name is as follows:

    John Doe/R&D/Tech Services/Help Desk/Notes/ABC Company/US

The following list explains each component in the name:

- **Common Name**—Each Notes user must have a Common Name, which can be up to eighty characters long. The common name is derived from the user's first and last names (and middle name if entered), as displayed in the Person document. Examples are John Q. Public or Mojo Nixon. In this example, the common name is John Doe.

- **Organization**—The Organization component of a distinguished user name is typically the name of the company, institution, or organization that is installing Notes. Each Notes user must have an Organization specified as part of their fully distinguished name. Some examples are ABC Company and Mojo Nixon Fan Club. In the John Doe example, ABC Company is the organization component.

- **Organization Unit**—Normally, the Organization Unit is a department or group name that is added to a distinguished user name to make it unique. If two people named Bob Smith worked at ABC Company, for instance, Notes wouldn't know which one you were sending mail to. However, if one worked in the accounting department and the other in the manufacturing department, these department names could be added to their distinguished names as Organizational Units to further qualify each person.

    Although Notes users can have up to four Organization Units in their fully distinguished names, Organizational Units are *not* required. In the John Doe example, *R&D* would be OU1, *Tech Services* would be OU2, *Help Desk* would be OU3 and *Notes* would be OU4.

(continues)

(continued)

■ **Country**—This is a two-letter abbreviation that identifies your country. The country codes are defined by *CCITT*. (CCITT, or The Consultative Committee for International Telegraph and Telephone, is a committee of the International Telecommunications Union, a United Nations treaty organization that studies, recommends, and develops standards for technical and operational telecommunications issues.) This component is optional and is only used when needed to uniquely identify a distinguished name world-wide. In the John Doe example, *US* is the country component.

Whenever you send a Notes mail message to another user, the Mailer module uses the address information that you have entered to look up the distinguished name from the N & A Book. The Router module of the server then uses the distinguished name to route the mail to its recipient. If the recipient is another Notes user, the mail will be delivered based on the mail priority and scheduled connections between servers. If the mail recipient is using another supported mail system such as cc:Mail, Internet, or X.400, you must have a connection to the other system for the mail to be routed. In other words, you must have an Internet mail connection for your Internet mail to be routed to the recipient.

Work and Home Information. The Work and Home sections of the Person document are not used by Notes; therefore, it is not necessary to enter information into these fields. However, this information can be a valuable resource for use within the company because it provides other Notes users within your Domain access to important contact information that can be easily shared and maintained. If this information is known about each user, it is highly recommended that it is entered. For example, if you were trying to solve a critical customer service issue after-hours and needed a team member's home phone number, you could turn to the Public N & A Book to find it very quickly and easily.

Group Documents

Group documents are very useful because they can be used to refer to multiple users, servers, or even other groups, which can save you a significant amount of time when addressing mail messages. For example, you might need to mail the weekly sales numbers to your entire sales team. Rather than enter each of their names into the To field in a mail message (or choose each name from the Address dialog box), just create a group document that references each user, then reference the Group name in the To field of your mail message. Figure 5.10 displays the standard group document in edit mode with the Administration section expanded.

The first section, Basics, contains the fundamental fields needed to define a group—Group Name, Group Type, Description, and Members. The Administration section contains additional information that is useful for identifying who created the group and who maintains the group.

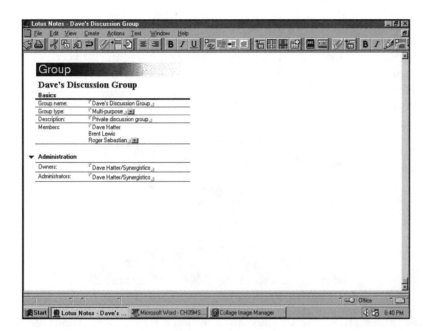

Fig. 5.10

A Group document for Dave's Discussion Group.

Basic Information. You use the Basics fields as follows:

- **The Group name field**—This field is required, as it is the name that Notes will use to find the group. A Group Name might be Widget Sales Team or Accounting. You may enter a maximum of 255 characters in this field. Longer names are recommended because they are more descriptive and generally more unique.

- **The Group type field**—This field is a standard keyword list that allows you to determine how a group list will be used (this field is really geared for use in the Public N & A Book). For instance, you can indicate that the group should only be used for database ACLs, which means when addressing mail, it won't be seen. You can set a group for use in mail addressing only, which means it can't be used in ACLs; or you can use a group to deny access, which means that users in a specific group will be denied access to the server. It can also be a multi-purpose group, meaning that it can be used for any of those functions. This field is not required and in most instances, should be left on the default setting Multi-Purpose.

- **The Description field**—This is an optional text field that you can use to add more detail to a group document. For example, you might want to explain the purpose of a particular group.

■ **The Members field**—This is a multi-value list field that is used to name the members of the group. You can click the down-arrow button beside the field to launch the Names dialog box and add users or other groups to the list very quickly. Figure 5.11 displays the Names dialog box, which works exactly like the dialog box that is launched when you click the Address button in a mail Memo form. Simply choose the users or groups you want, and click OK.

Fig. 5.11

The Names dialog box.

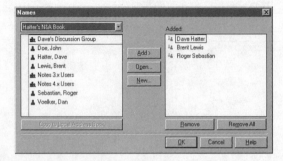

Administrative Information. The Administration section can be expanded and collapsed by clicking the twisty beside the title. Once the section is expanded, the Owners and Administrators fields can be accessed, as follows:

■ The Administrative field can be used to list the user or users who "own" the group. In most cases, this is the person who created the group and it should be left alone.

■ Likewise, the Administrators field can be used to identify the administrator(s) of the group. The group documents found in your Personal N & A Book are identical in function and usage to those found in the Public N & A Book.

Note

Every N & A Book, when it's created, has two groups entered by default. They are the LocalDomainServers and the OtherDomainServers groups. These groups are also entered into every database ACL as Manager when a database is created. If each server in your domain is entered in the LocalDomainServers group, then the servers will be guaranteed access to the database. This ensures that the server can replicate with the local copies of a database.

Location Documents

Location documents are new to Notes R4 and are a very handy way to define location-specific setup information so that you can quickly change your configuration.

For instance, you might have a location document for your office connection via a LAN and a Remote connection via a modem.

When the Notes R4 workstation software is installed on your workstation, four default Location documents will be created in your Personal N & A Book automatically. They are the Office, Travel, Home, and Disconnected documents. If you travel to other sites frequently and need to communicate with Notes from those locations, you can create a Location document for each location.

▶▶ See "Setting Up Locations," p. 658

Figure 5.12 displays a Location document in edit mode. Location documents work hand-in-hand with Server Connection documents. Each Server Connection document contains information needed to connect to a server, such as the server's phone number if a dial-up connection is used. When you attempt to communicate with a Notes server, information from Location documents and Server Connection documents is used to make the connection.

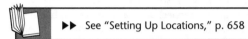

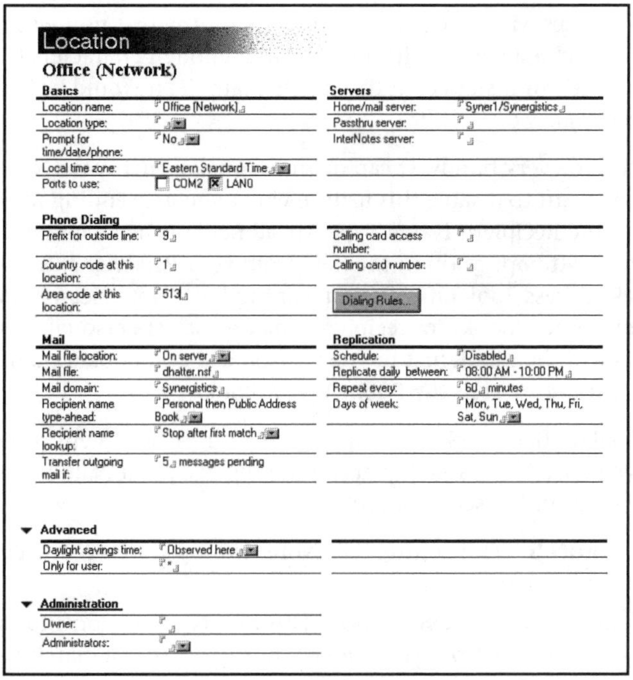

Location

Office (Network)

Basics

Location name:	Office (Network)
Location type:	
Prompt for time/date/phone:	No
Local time zone:	Eastern Standard Time
Ports to use:	☐ COM2 ☒ LAN0

Servers

Home/mail server:	Syner1/Synergistics
Passthru server:	
InterNotes server:	

Phone Dialing

Prefix for outside line:	9
Country code at this location:	1
Area code at this location:	513
Calling card access number:	
Calling card number:	

Dialing Rules...

Mail

Mail file location:	On server
Mail file:	dhatter.nsf
Mail domain:	Synergistics
Recipient name type-ahead:	Personal then Public Address Book
Recipient name lookup:	Stop after first match
Transfer outgoing mail if:	5 messages pending

Replication

Schedule:	Disabled
Replicate daily between:	08:00 AM - 10:00 PM
Repeat every:	60 minutes
Days of week:	Mon, Tue, Wed, Thu, Fri, Sat, Sun

▼ **Advanced**

Daylight savings time:	Observed here
Only for user:	*

▼ **Administration**

Owner:	
Administrators:	

Fig. 5.12

A Location document for your office network.

The Location documents are primarily used when you work remote. See the section "Setting Up Locations" in Chapter 18, "Setting Up To Go Remote," for detailed explanations of the settings in the Location document.

Note

Chapter 18, "Setting Up To Go Remote," assumes that you will be working with a dial-up modem. If you will be connected to the Notes server via a LAN, choose Local Area Network in the Location Type field of the Location document, which will tell Notes to use the LAN card in your workstation when looking for a Notes server.

If you need to have LAN *and* dial-up connections available for a given location, select Both Dial-Up and Local Area Network, which will allow you to access your Notes server either way. The last choice, No Connection, can be used if you will have no connection to a Notes server, but you want to work with local databases on your workstation.

Understanding the Type-Ahead Feature. The Recipient Name Type-Ahead field in the Location document can be used to enable and configure the *type-ahead feature* when addressing mail messages. When type-ahead is enabled, Notes will look into the specified N & A books to find a name based on the characters you have entered in the To, cc, or Bcc field of a message. For example, if you wanted to send a mail message to a user named Mojo Nixon/ABC Company, you could position the cursor in the To field and begin typing the first few characters in the recipient's name. In this example, you could type **Mo** and Notes will search the N & A Book for the first user with a name that begins with the characters *Mo*. It's best to enter enough characters to uniquely identify the name; for instance, in the earlier example, it would be better to enter *Mojo* rather than *Mo*.

Although this feature can be very handy, it can be time-consuming if your N & A Book is very large. If you want to disable this feature when you are sending mail messages, select Disabled in the Recipient Name Type-Ahead field of the Location document. If you only want to attempt to fill in the field from your Personal N & A Book, you can select Personal Address Book Only. If you want to have Notes search both your Personal and Public N & A Books for recipients' names, select Personal then Public Address Book. Notes will then look first in your Personal N & A Book for a match; if one is not found, it will then search the Public N & A Book.

The Recipient Name Lookup field works in conjunction with the Recipient Name Type-Ahead field. If type-ahead is enabled, you can use the Recipient Name Lookup field to determine the scope of the search, as follows:

- **Stop after first match**—This setting tells Notes to stop searching when it finds a match for a user name.

- **Exhaustively check all address books**—This tells Notes to continue searching all N & A Books available from your workstation even after a match has been found. If you have many Notes users in your organization, this option can take some time.

Server Connection Documents

For each server that you communicate with, you must have a Server Connection document. These documents are used to provide specific connection information about each server and, as mentioned earlier, work hand-in-hand with Location documents.

The type of connection that you use to access the server determines the specific information needed in the Connection Type field, as follows:

- If you dial in to the server via modem, select Dial-up Modem.
- If you access the server over a LAN connection, select Local Area Network.
- If you use a Notes passthru server, select the Passthru Server option.
- The Remote LAN Service option should only be used if you will be dialing in to a remote LAN service, such as AT&T Network Notes, to get connected to a server. This is similar to a passthru server.

Dial-Up Modem Connection. A dial-up connection document for the server Saturn is shown in figure 5.13. For details on setting up Server Connection documents for remote access, see the section "Setting Up Connections Records" in Chapter 18, "Setting Up to Go Remote." The other types of connections are described in the following sections.

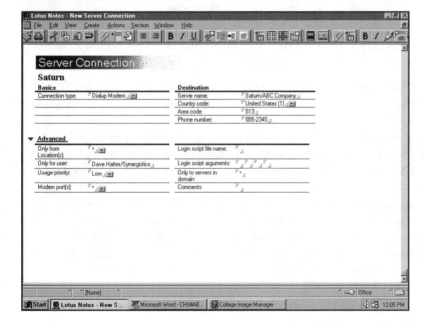

Fig. 5.13

A dial-up server connection document for the server Saturn.

LAN Connection. Figure 5.14 displays a Server Connection document for the server Jupiter. In this example, the connection is via a LAN.

Notes Basics

Fig. 5.14

A LAN Server Connection document for the server Jupiter.

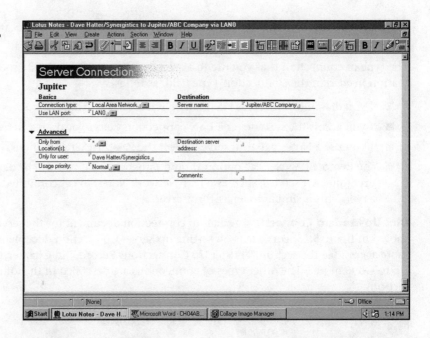

This document has only a few fields that require information (your system administrator will probably do this for you), as follows:

- **The Use LAN port field**—This is a standard multi-value keyword list field that displays the enabled ports on the system. Use this field to indicate which port to use when accessing the specified server.

- **Only for user**—This can be used to limit access to the server through the Server Connection document. To use this field, enter fully qualified user names. This is very beneficial when more than one user is using a particular workstation because this field can limit access to users or groups explicitly stated in the list.

- **The Usage priority field**—This is a standard keyword list field. The Normal and Low choices allow you to select the priority Notes uses when it searches for connection documents. Normal priority documents will be used before Low priority documents. If you generally want to replicate with a specific server, you could set it to Normal priority, and set other servers that you might use in the event the primary server is down as Low priority.

- **The Destination section**—Here you only need to enter the name of the server in the Server Name field.

- **The Destination server address field**

Passthru Server Connection. Figure 5.15 displays a Server Connection document for the Passthru Server Pluto in edit mode. This document is nearly identical to the Local Area Network connection document. The special settings for this type of connection are as follows:

- **The Basic section**—Rather than defining a LAN port, you define the Passthru Server name here.

- **The field Passthru Server Name field**—This is used to define the name of the passthru server that you will connect with.

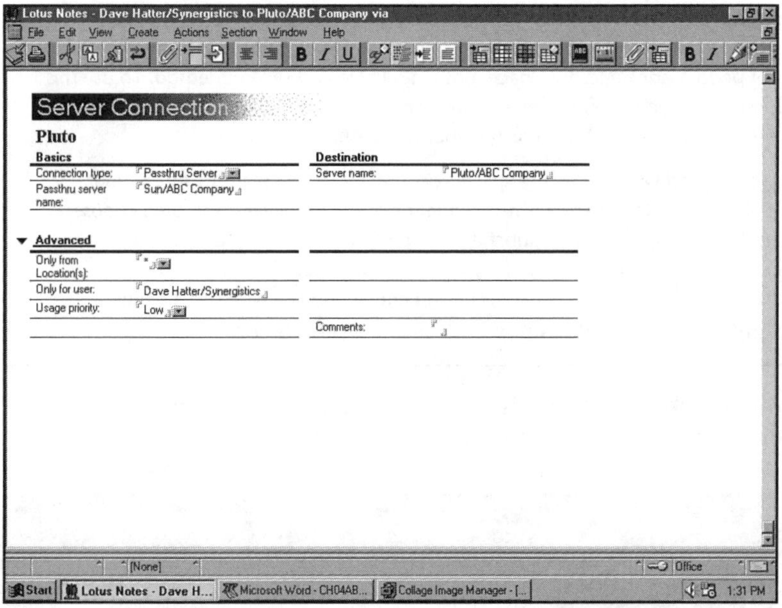

Fig. 5.15

A Passthru Server Connection document for the server Pluto.

Remote LAN Service Connection. Figure 5.16 displays a Server Connection document for the remote LAN service server, ACME_1, in edit mode.

This document is nearly identical to the Local Area Network connection document. The only differences are as follows:

- **The Remote LAN service field**—This is a standard keyword list field that allows you to select the type of remote LAN service you are using. If the service you are using is not displayed in the current list, you may add the name in the New Keywords input box at the bottom of the Keywords dialog box.

- **The Remote connection name field**—This value is used to give the remote connection a name to help identify this connection when displayed in views.

- **The Login name and Password fields**—These are text fields that work hand-in-hand to get you logged in to the remote access server. You should enter your login name and password that you use when accessing the remote access server.

Caution

Unless you secure your Personal N & A Book, someone could access your Remote LAN Service documents and learn your user ID and password for this service. There are two good solutions to protect the confidentiality of your Personal N & A Book.

The first method would be to encrypt the entire database, which would only allow access to someone with your ID and Notes password. This method adds some overhead in terms of performance and disk space, but is a reliable and secure method. To use this method, right-click your Personal N & A Book and choose Database Properties. You can then use the Encryption button to secure your database.

The second method will only secure specific documents. If you want to secure your Remote LAN Service document, right-click that document in a view and then choose Document Properties, which will launch the Properties box. Then click the tab that displays a small key. On this tab you may choose a list of people and groups that can access the document; you can also associate an encryption key with the document, which will protect the contents of your document from prying eyes.

- ■ **The Phone number field**—This is a text field for storing the phone number used to connect to the remote LAN service.

Fig. 5.16

A Remote LAN service connection document for the server ACME_1.

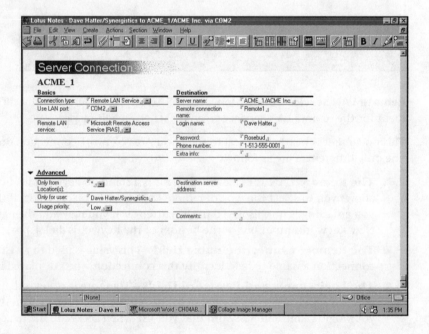

Certificate Documents. Your Personal N & A books will also contain Certificate and Cross-Certificate documents. When you are certified to communicate with a server, you should receive a certificate or cross-certificate document—you must have one to be authenticated by the server.

►► See "Understanding Certificates," p. 725

Creating New Documents

If you need to add users, groups, connections, and so on to your Personal N & A Book, complete the following steps:

1. Select your Personal N & A book.

2. Choose <u>C</u>reate. (An alternative method is to open one of the views that contains the type of documents you want to create and use the Add button on the Action bar to create a new document.

3. Select the type of document you want to create from the following list:

    - <u>C</u>ompany
    - <u>G</u>roup
    - <u>L</u>ocation
    - <u>P</u>erson
    - <u>S</u>erver Connection

4. Fill in the information in the newly created document.

5. Press Ctrl+S, press Esc and choose Yes, or use the File Save SmartIcon to save the document.

Tip

It's easy to add to your Personal N & A Book a user from whom you've received a mail message. Open the mail message and choose <u>A</u>ctions, Add Sender to Address Book. This will automatically create a new Person document in your Personal N & A Book and copy the user's name, mail type, and Notes address into the appropriate fields. You can then add any additional information you have and save the new document. This method is very quick and easy and helps to ensure that the Person document contains valid information.

Understanding the Public Name & Address Book

Although few users utilize the Public Name & Address Book for little more than mail addressing, it is much more than a simple user directory. When the first server in a domain is installed, Notes will automatically create a new Public N & A Book database (the actual filename defaults to NAMES.NSF) from the PUBNAMES.NTF template.

> **Note**
>
> In Lotus Notes, a *domain* is a group of users who share the same Public N & A book. A company that has several locations can have one domain or many domains. The number of domains required is usually determined by security needs and the number of users in each domain. As a domain grows, so does its Public N & A Book, which decreases overall system performance because N & A Book searches take longer and more disk space is consumed. Each user's domain is determined by the server that his or her mailbox resides on.

The Public N & A Book plays dual roles in every Notes installation. First, it provides Directory Services by acting as a central repository for user, server, and group names that can be accessed for communication with others. It also acts as a server management tool for Notes Administrators by providing the Notes server with information on replication schedules, mail routing, automatic tasks, mail-in databases, certificates, and other important system information. Even if you don't use Notes Mail at your company, the Name & Address Book must exist for the Notes server(s) to operate properly.

Because the Public Name & Address Book plays such a crucial role in every Notes installation and can affect every user in a domain, access levels above Reader (which would allow changes to the database) should be limited to a select group of people who are very familiar with its operation. In most cases, you will *not* be allowed to create any type of document in the Public N & A Address Book. If you have an occasion to add a document, say a Person or Group document, to the Public N & A Book, you will probably need to send a request to your Notes Administrator.

In the first half of this chapter, I discussed how the Personal N & A Book contained only a subset of the functionality of the Public N & A Book, and this becomes readily apparent when you examine the Create menu in the Public N & A Book.

As you can see in figure 5.17, many of the forms are the same as in the Personal N & A Book, but there are several additional forms available from the menu. These forms create documents that fall into two basic categories of services that the Public N & A Book provides: Directory Services and Server Management.

Fig. 5.17

The Create menu in the Public Name and Address Book.

Directory Services

Each time you send a mail message or open a database on a Notes server, you will come into contact with the directory services aspects of the N & A Book. Notes keeps track of users and servers in the Public N & A Book. Whenever a mail message is sent, the Notes server will look in the Public N & A book in an attempt to find a document that corresponds to the user, server, or group names listed in the envelope of the mail message. If a match is found, then the message can be routed; if no match is found, then the server cannot route the message.

Likewise, when a user attempts to open a database on a server, the Server examines the database's ACL. (Remember, if you are working with a local database, you have Manager access by default.) If a user is listed in a group in the ACL, the server must find that group in the Public N & A Book to determine if the user is in the group.

In the Public N & A Book, the following three forms fall into the directory services category:

- Person documents
- Server documents
- Group documents

These forms are described in the following sections.

Person Documents. Each Notes user in a domain will be identified by a Person document in the Public N & A Book. A user's Person documents in the Public and Personal N & A Books are identical. The primary difference is that Person documents in the Public N & A Book are shared amongst all users in the domain.

A Person document is automatically created in the Public N & A Book for each user during the new user registration process (which also creates a certified user ID). Certain key fields in the Name and E-Mail sections are populated based on the registration information.

Caution

In most instances, with the exception of your Person document, you will not have sufficient access to the Public N & A Book to make changes to any of the documents it contains. It is critically important that you do not make changes to any documents in the Public N & A Book without first speaking to your Notes administrator, as this can cause a wide variety of serious problems, such as mail not routing. In fact, in almost every instance, you should request that the Notes administrator make any required changes.

Server Documents. Each server in a domain has a Server document in the Public N & A Book (automatically created when a new server is installed).

Basic and Network Configuration Information. Like most forms, the server form is divided into logical sections. The following are the basic fields:

■ **The Server name field**—It contains the name the server was given during the installation process, and is required.

■ **The Server title field**—This is not required, but can be used to help identify a particular server when looking at server views and folders.

■ **The Domain field**—It contains the domain name that was entered for a server during installation, and is required.

> ### Caution
>
> In most cases, unless you are the Notes Administrator for your installation, you will not be able to edit any of the server documents. If, however, you can edit these documents, be especially careful *not* to change the server or domain names unless you are absolutely certain that you know what you are doing. If you inadvertently change either of these fields, you could cause the Notes server to have a variety of problems communicating with other servers and users.

■ **The Administrators field**—This allows you to name users or groups of users who are responsible for the server.

The next section of the server document, called Network Configuration, is a table that defines network information about the server so that users and other servers can communicate with a given server. For example, you can define and enable a port so that it is seen in one Notes Named Network, but not in other Notes Named Networks. For more information on the meaning of each of these settings, see your Lotus Notes R4 documentation.

Restriction Information. The Restrictions section of the document is very important because it enables you to limit users or groups of users to certain tasks, as follows:

■ **The Access server field**—This field allows the administrator to define users or groups who can access the server. If this field is left blank, then any user who has an ID that has been certified by the server in question can access that server. If any names are put in this field, then only those users named can access the server.

■ **The Not access server field**—This field does the exact opposite of the Access Server field. Even if you have an ID that has been certified by the server, you will not be granted access to the server if your name is in this field (or in a group that is in this field).

- **The Create new databases field**—This field can be used to define a list of users who can create databases on a given server. Again, if this field is left blank, any user who can access the server can create new databases. If any names are defined in this field, then only those users can create new databases.

- **The Create replica databases field**—This field works just like the Create New Databases field, except it controls the ability to create replica databases.

> **Note**
>
> In Notes R3, many of the settings that you can now maintain in the Restrictions section of the server document had to be maintained manually in the NOTES.INI file. It is much easier to maintain these settings through the server document.

Contact Information. The Contact section allows you to define the following additional information about a server that helps others determine where a server is and who it belongs to:

- **The Location, Department and Comment fields**—They are not used by Notes and are not required.

- **The Detailed description field**—This can be used to enter as much text as necessary to help identify the purpose and usage of a server. For example, if this server is used only as a replication hub, it might be helpful to note that in this field.

Statistics Reporting. The Statistics Reporting section allows the administrator to establish performance and error reporting for a server, as follows:

- **The Mail-In database address to receive reports field**—This allows the administrator to define a mail-in database that will have the server's reports mailed to it. This is particularly handy in large organizations with multiple servers because these reports can be centralized in a database on one server.

- **The Collection interval field**—This allows the administrator to define how often the server's statistics should be reported. The default collection interval, 60 minutes, should be sufficient in most cases.

Group Documents. Group documents in both the Public and Personal N & A Books are identical and are used in the same way. The primary difference is that Group documents in the Public N & A Book are shared amongst all users in the domain.

The rest of the documents in the Public N & A Book generally fall into the Server Management category.

Server Management Documents

The Public N & A Book contains the documents that are almost exclusively used by Notes Administrators, I will only briefly examine these documents. They are the following:

- **Configuration documents**—These documents are used to control the Notes environment. Examples of Configuration documents are the ACL monitor, Event, Replication Monitor, and Statistics Monitor documents.

- **Certifier and Cross-Certifier documents**—These documents identify each certificate's ancestry. Certifier documents are crucial to the security of a Notes installation.

- **Domain Documents**—These can be created to allow communication and mail routing to other Notes domains or to Foreign domains, such as the Internet. There are two basic types—Foreign Domain documents and Non-Adjacent Domain documents. *Foreign Domain documents* are used to define a Non-Notes domain such as a cc:Mail domain, while *Non-Adjacent Domain documents* are used when you need to communicate with a Notes domain through an intermediary domain. For example, you want to send mail to Ace Frehley in the XZY domain, but you don't have a connection to that domain; however, you do have a connection to the ABC domain which communicates with the XYZ domain. A Non-Adjacent domain document would specify the route to XYZ through ABC.

- **Connection Documents**—These are much like the Connection documents in the Personal N & A Book, except rather than defining user to server connections, they define server to server communication and establish mail-routing and replication schedules.

- **Program Documents**—These can be used to automatically start server tasks, batch programs, or API programs. For example, if you wrote an API program to transfer data from an Access database to a Notes database and wanted it to run each night, you could create a Program document that would run the program at the specified interval.

- **Profile Documents**—These allow the administrator to define a common set of setup elements that can then be applied to multiple users. Profile documents can make adding new users to the system significantly less complicated and time-consuming.

Using Views in the Name & Address Books

Each of the Name & Address Books contains views and folders that can be very useful. Like the documents that each N & A Book contains, many of the views overlap and provide the same functionality, but on a different scale. In this section, I will examine the views that exist in the Personal N & A Book first and then views that only exist in the Public N & A Book. When a view exists in both books, I will point out any differences.

Companies View

The standard Companies view is found only in the Personal N & A Book (see fig. 5.18). This view is very straightforward. The first column, Name, displays the name of each company sorted in ascending order. The second column, Telephone, displays the main phone number for that company.

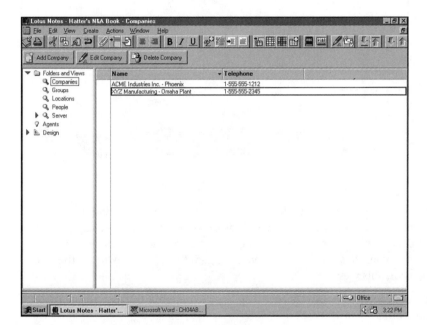

Fig. 5.18

The standard Companies view in the Personal Name & Address Book.

Groups View

The standard Groups view exists in both the Personal and Public N & A Books. The Group column displays the name of each group, sorted in ascending order. The next column, Description, displays the group's description if one was entered.

Locations View

The standard Locations view exists only in the Personal N & A Book. This view displays all of the Location documents that exist in your Personal N & A book, sorted by the first (and only) column, Location, which displays the name of the location (see fig. 5.19).

Fig. 5.19

The standard Locations view in the Personal Name & Address Book.

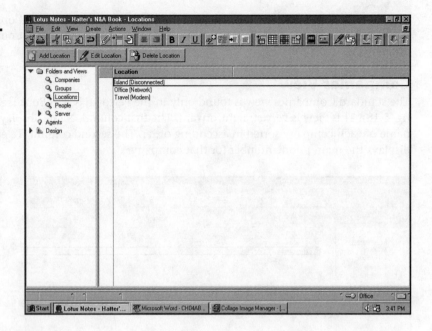

People View

The standard People view is the default view in both the Personal and Public N & A Book. The People view is very useful because it displays every Notes user in the domain if you are looking at your Public N & A Book, or every user you have defined if you are looking at your Personal N & A Book (see fig. 5.20). The following is the information available in this view:

■ The first column in the view, Name, displays the name of the user sorted in ascending order by last name.

■ The next column, Telephone, is a multi-line column. This is another new and very useful feature of Notes R4, which displays the user's office and home phone number if this information has been entered into the document. For example, in figure 5.20, you see that the document for Brent Lewis contains both office and home phone number.

■ The last column in the view, E-Mail address, is pretty much self-explanatory; it displays the user's Notes e-mail address.

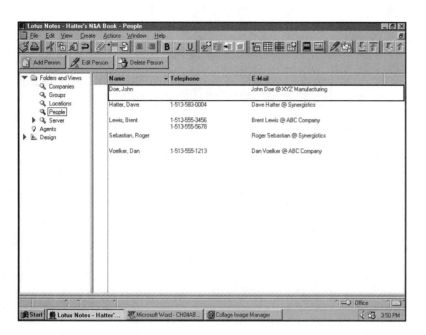

Fig. 5.20

The standard People view.

Notes Basics

Server/Certificates View

The standard Server/Certificates view can be found in both the Personal and Public N & A Books.

Server/Connections View

The standard Server/Connections view in the Personal N & A Book is very similar to the Connections view in the Public N & A Book. A sample of this view is shown in figure 5.21.

This view shows all Server Connection documents in your Personal N & A Book, as follows:

- The first column, Server, displays the name of the server this connection document refers to. It is sorted in ascending order.

- The next column, Port, displays the port that the connection will attempt to use.

- The Via column displays the route the connection will take.

- The final column, Applies to Location(s), displays any location-specific information. An asterisk (*) indicates that this connection document can be used from any location.

Fig. 5.21

The standard Server Connections view.

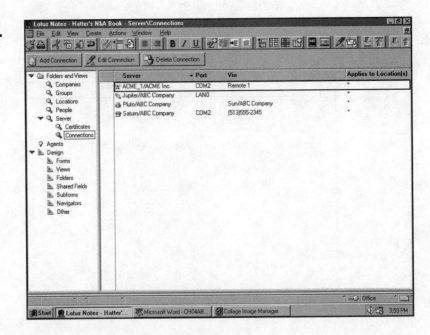

Replicating the Public Name & Address Book

If you are primarily a remote user (that is, you spend most of your time using Notes *not* connected to a LAN), you will probably want to create a replica of the Public N & A book on your workstation so that you can take advantage of the user addresses and groups it contains.

To do so, use the same steps you would use in creating a replica of any database. Select the copy of the Public N & A Book icon on the server, and choose File, Replication, New Replica. The New Replica dialog box is displayed (see fig. 5.22).

Fig. 5.22

The New Replica dialog box.

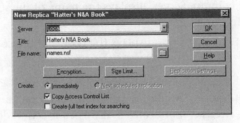

The Server box should be set to Local and the Title box should display the title of your company's Public N & A Book. Enter a new filename for the replica of your Public N & A Book.

> **Caution**
>
> By default, the Public N & A Book on the server has the filename NAMES.NSF. Your Personal N & A Book on your workstation has the same name. If you choose to store a replica of the Public N & A book on your workstation, you must change the default filename given to the replica; otherwise, you will overwrite your Personal N & A Book with your Public N & A Book.
>
> If you forget to change the filename, Notes will warn you that a file with that name already exists and will ask you if you want to overwrite it. Choose No and enter a new filename for the Public N & A Book replica. If no standard exists in your organization for naming local replica copies of the Public N & A Book, you might want to use PUBNAMES.NSF for the actual filename.

You can then use the other settings in the New Replica dialog box to set a size limit for the Public N & A book replica, enter encryption settings, create a full text index, copy the ACL into the replica, and choose when to create the new replica. When you are sure all of the settings are correct, click OK and a new replica stub icon will appear.

Once the replicator has initialized and copied all of the documents into your Public N & A Book replica, you can begin to use the replica as you would the original database on the server.

> **Note**
>
> Remember that you have manager access to all local databases, which means that you will be able to create and modify documents that exist in the replica of the Public N & A Book. However, if the Administrator has done his or her job properly, your changes will be overwritten by the data in the server copy. In short, don't add or change documents in your replica of the Public N & A Book because they will be overwritten. Make them in your Personal N & A Book.

From Here...

In this chapter you learned about the importance of and the differences between the Personal and Public N & A Books and how they are used by Notes. In the next chapter, "Advanced Mail," you will learn how to use the N & A Books to address mail and how to use other advanced features of the Lotus Notes mail system.

For more information on some of the topics discussed in this chapter, refer to the following:

- Chapter 4, "Getting Started with Electronic Mail," teaches you how to work with Lotus NotesMail and the mail forward feature.
- For more information on advanced mailing techniques and securing mail messages, refer to Chapter 6, "Advanced Mail," and Chapter 20, "Security and Encryption."

CHAPTER 6

Advanced Mail

In Chapter 4, "Getting Started with Electronic Mail," you learned the basics of using the Lotus Notes e-mail system. In this chapter, we will examine the advanced features that enable you to use NotesMail with maximum efficiency and effectiveness. The following are some of the specific things you will understand after completing this chapter:

- Organizing your mail
- Working with file attachments
- Using mail-in databases
- Using custom forms
- Sending mail as a fax
- Accessing mail from another workstation
- Sending mail outside your company
- Working with Lotus cc:Mail
- Archiving your mail
- Out of the Office Profile
- Creating letterhead
- Creating stationery
- Mail Tracing

Organizing Your Mail

As you learned in Chapter 2, "Customizing Notes," you can add a certain amount of customization to most views and folders even if you are not a database designer (unless the database designer has specifically disabled some of the features that you can change). However, generally speaking, you have more control over folders than views.

In terms of customizing views, unless you have Designer or higher access to a database, the amount of customization you can lend to a view is somewhat limited compared to a folder. In the standard Notes R4 mailbox, you can make some simple changes to the views that provide greater usability. You can also put your mail into folders that simplify organizing and storing the volume of mail you receive.

> **Caution**
>
> Unlike most databases, you have Manager access (by default) to your mailbox, regardless of whether it resides on the server or is a replica on your workstation. This means that you have the highest level of access to the database and can change the database design. You can even permanently delete the database! In almost every case, the mailbox should provide all of the functionality that you would ever need, and it is highly recommended that you do not attempt to make design changes to the mailbox other than those mentioned in this section. Or, if you feel that changes are required, submit a request to the database design team to make the changes you need.
>
> If you decide to make design changes to the database, you should be very careful because you might make changes that are detrimental to the functionality of your mailbox and that you cannot easily correct. In addition, because your mailbox is based on a template, your changes may be overwritten. You learn more about this issue in Chapter 11, "Designing Views."

Changing the Mail View

In Chapter 4, "Getting Started with Electronic Mail," you learned that when you open your mailbox, Notes displays a list of incoming and outgoing messages in the view or folder that you last used. As with most databases, you can choose any of several different views and folders, each of which presents your mail messages in a different way.

As you know, the View menu lists the available views for your mailbox. Notes provides several standard views, as shown in figure 6.1.

Fig. 6.1

The View menu of the new NotesMail mailbox database.

> **Note**
>
> The word *standard* is used to describe the design elements, such as views and folders, in your mailbox. What you actually see in your mailbox may vary from the screens displayed in this chapter because each of these documents could be altered by Notes administrators or designers in your organization.

The following list describes these standard views:

- **Discussion Threads**—This view displays all messages that are part of the same discussion in a hierarchical manner. Any message that has a reply is displayed with the reply below it, and any replies to a reply are displayed below each reply. This view makes it very easy to keep track of an ongoing e-mail discussion.
- **Archive Log**—This view enables you to see the log documents for each archive session. (This is much like the Notes Log.) You will learn how to archive mail messages later in this chapter in the "Archiving your Mail" section.

Organizing Your Mail into Folders

If you are Notes a 3.x user, then this section will be particularly important to you. In the old version of the mail database, each NotesMail message contained a special field named Personal Categories. This field allowed you to define categories so that you could logically group your mail messages. For instance, if you frequently receive mail from the Finance department, you might have categorized all of the mail from the Finance department as "Finance," while all of the mail from Accounting would be categorized as "Accounting."

You could create as many categories as you needed to help organize your messages into groups and make the views more meaningful and less cluttered.

In the Notes 4 mailbox, each document still contains a Personal Categories field, but it is only there for backward compatibility with older e-mail messages. Lotus has added a more powerful feature to the new mail database: folders. (For a brushup on folders, see Chapter 3, "Using Databases.")

When you are attempting to organize messages, folders can be very useful because you can put messages in a folder that pertain strictly to a specific issue. For instance, you can create a folder called ABC Company and place all mail messages related to ABC Company into this folder. This folder would only contain messages about the ABC Company, so the number of messages it contains would be much smaller than the number of messages that would show up in a categorized view. Searching, manipulation, and viewing are therefore quicker and easier.

Notice that in my mailbox, shown in figure 6.2, I have created several folders, such as the MCS and Synergistics folders, to help organize my mail messages.

Fig. 6.2

User-defined folders in the new mailbox database.

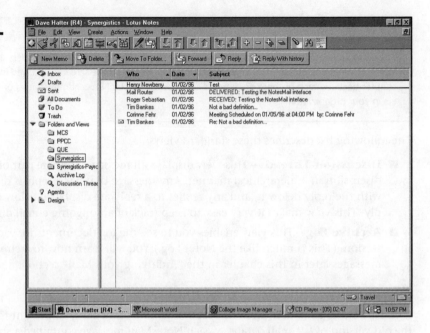

Simply click and drag documents to the folders that you want to store mail messages in. Alternatively, you can use Actions, Move to Folder, or click the Move To Folder button on the Action Bar to display the Move To Folder dialog box (see fig. 6.3).

Fig. 6.3

The Move To Folder dialog box displays a list of folders in my mailbox.

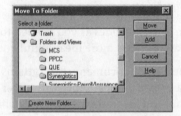

In this dialog box, you can choose a folder from the graphical list displayed in the Select a folder list box. Once you have selected a folder, you can use the Move button to move the document from the folder it's in to the selected folder, or you can choose Add to add a document to the selected folder and leave it in its current folder as well. If you want to create a new folder, simply click the Create New Folder button to launch the Create Folder dialog box, which is covered in the next section.

You can create as many folders as you need in you mailbox to organize your mail messages. In order to create a new folder, choose Create, Folder, and the Create Folder dialog box will be displayed (see fig. 6.4).

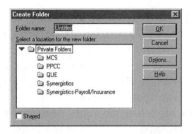

Fig. 6.4

The Create Folder dialog box displays a list of folders in my mailbox.

Notes Basics

The Create Folder dialog box is easy to use. You simply enter a new folder name in the Folder name field and then choose a location for the new folder from the hierarchy of folders shown in the Select a location for the new folder list box (which displays all of the folders and their hierarchy in your mailbox). Simply click the folder where you want the new folder to be placed, and click OK. The new folder will be added to your mailbox, and you can immediately use it.

To begin using your folders, simply select a mail message or messages the same way you would select any documents and then click and drag the messages to the proper folder. It's as simple as that!

Folders are a very powerful and useful new feature of the new NotesMail interface and can make your life easier when working in your mailbox. If you frequently receive mail messages from another department or person, you might want to create a folder to organize those messages. For instance, if you frequently communicate with several departments at the XYZ Company via e-mail, you might create a folder called XYZ for general mail messages from the company and then create several subfolders under XYZ, such as Purchasing, Engineering, Marketing, and Sales, to store mail messages that fall into those areas.

Remember, customize your folders to best meet your needs. You can store a mail message in one or many folders and can move it from one folder to another at any time.

Note

If you are upgrading from Notes 3.x to Notes 4.0, Lotus has included an agent that enables you to convert all of the categories stored in your old mail messages to folders, which can save you a considerable amount of time. (See Chapter 15, "Buttons and Agents," for more information.) To use this agent, open your mailbox and click the Agent icon (the small light bulb) in the Navigator.

Select the Convert Categories to Folders agent and right-click it, which will launch a pop-up menu. Choose Run to start the agent and create new folders for each category. When the agent is finished, Notes will display a brief summary of the actions performed by the agent in the Agent Log dialog box.

Changing the Width of Columns in a View or Folder

In the view pane, the columns in the view are separated by thin gray lines. Most columns in a view are resizable, much like the columns in an Excel or 1-2-3 spreadsheet. When you position your mouse pointer directly over any of the column separator lines, notice that the mouse pointer shape changes to that of a solid black line with an arrow pointing either way. When your mouse pointer changes, you can then "grab" (hold down the right or left mouse button) the column separator and drag it to the size you desire. This can be very handy, as it allows you to dynamically determine how wide a column should be.

> **Note**
>
> The first column in any view or folder is known as the Marker column. It is easily identified by the thin vertical gray line that extends the length of the view and separates it from the other columns. You cannot resize this column. Refer to Chapter 3, "Using Databases," for more information on the special functionality of this column.

Changing the Sort Order

Many of the views in the mailbox, such as the All Documents view, enable you to change the sorted order of certain columns (see fig. 6.5). Any column heading that displays a small arrow pointing up, down, or both indicates that you can click in the column heading to change the sort order.

Fig. 6.5

You can change the sorted order of columns in the All Documents view.

Sorts the column in ascending order

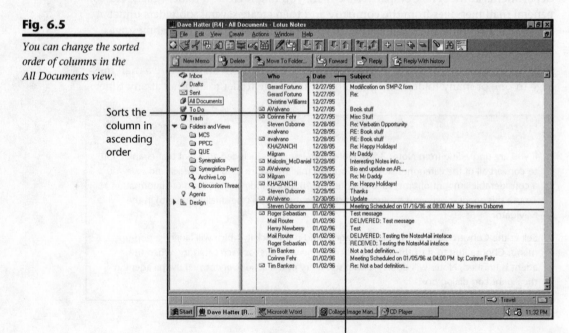

Sorts the column in descending order

In figure 6.5, the Who column displays an arrow pointing up. This means that when you click the Who column header, that particular column is sorted in ascending order. The arrow changes color from black, which indicates that the column is in its default order, to a shade of bright turquoise, indicating that the column is now sorted in ascending order. You can click again to return the column to its default sort order, which is unsorted.

The Date column is already sorted in ascending order (the oldest dates first). The column heading displays the down arrow indicating that you can change the sort order from the default—ascending order—to descending order (most recent dates first). A second click on this column returns the messages to ascending order.

Without getting into the design of a view, those are the only view features that you as an end-user can customize in your mailbox. Folders, on the other hand can not only be customized in the same ways that views can, but can be created from scratch allowing you to build your own folders that can aid in organization of your mail messages.

Working with File Attachments

As a PC user, you most likely need to share files with other users on many occasions and, as you know, this often is much easier said than done. This can be particularly difficult if you work for a geographically dispersed company. Notes, however, makes it very easy to e-mail a file as an *attachment* to your mail message to any other NotesMail user. Perhaps a coworker in Bangladesh needs a copy of the technical documentation you have prepared in Lotus Word Pro, or the plant in Düsseldorf needs your market analysis report created with Lotus 1-2-3.

Before e-mail (and particularly NotesMail), sharing files meant copying the files to a shared disk drive on the LAN or copying them to a floppy disk and using "sneaker net" (you get up and run the disk down to your colleague who needs it) if the recipient was in the office or *snail mail* if he or she was at another location. Notes simplifies tremendously the sharing of files through the capability of attaching a file to an e-mail message. The following sections explain how to work with attachments.

Attaching Files

You can attach a file (or files) to any mail document. The first step is to create a new message. Once the new mail message is on the screen, you work with it just like any other mail message until you are ready to attach the file(s).

You can attach any file, regardless of its format, to a NotesMail message. For instance, if you have an office in Germany, and it needs the latest sales figures, you can attach the 1-2-3 spreadsheet to a mail message and send it to the Germany office. Likewise, you can attach the Access database with the latest inventory data to a colleague in a different office.

To attach one or more files, follow these steps:

1. Place the cursor in the body of the memo, then choose <u>F</u>ile, <u>A</u>ttach or click the File Attach SmartIcon. The Create Attachment(s) dialog box appears (see fig. 6.6).

Fig. 6.6

The Create Attachment(s) dialog box.

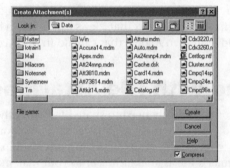

You *must* be in the Body field to attach a file. File attachments can only be attached in Rich Text fields, and Body is the only Rich Text field in the mail message.

◀◀ See "Rich Text Fields," p. 99

2. You can use the File Name drop-down list box to select one or more files to attach to the mail. By default, the Create Attachment(s) dialog box points to the default Notes data directory, in most instances C:\NOTES\DATA. If the files you are interested in are stored in another directory, you can use the Directories list box to choose from the available directories in a particular drive on your workstation. You can use the Drives list box to select from all the valid drives available from your workstation. Use these tools to select the appropriate drive and directory for the file(s) you want to attach.

3. Select all the files you want to attach by clicking the file in the File name drop-down list box (selected files are highlighted with a blue bar). If you want to select more than one file, hold the Ctrl key down as you select files.

4. Choose C<u>r</u>eate. Notes inserts an icon into your document that represents each of the attached files. Notes uses the file extension of each file that you attach to scan the Windows registry in an attempt to identify the source application (the application that created the file) so that an icon representing the application

that created the file can be displayed. For example, if you insert an MS Word document, the MS Word icon is displayed in the mail message to represent the file attachment. If Notes cannot identify the file attachment, an icon that looks like a blank, gray piece of paper with the right edge folded over is inserted. Figure 6.7 shows a sample memo with several file attachments.

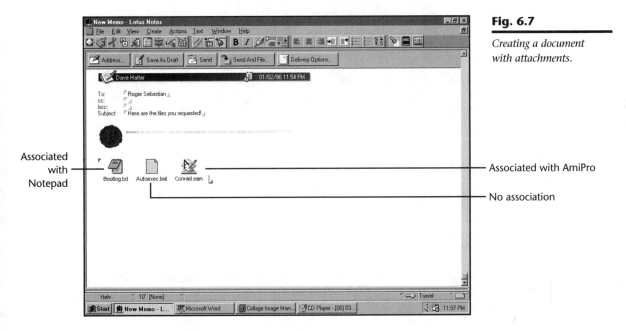

Fig. 6.7

Creating a document with attachments.

Associated with Notepad

Associated with AmiPro

No association

Once you have attached the files, address the mail as you normally would, enter the subject, and add any text to the message body that might help the recipient understand the attachment. After you complete the memo and attach the files, send the message as you would any other.

 ◀◀ See "Sending Your Message," p. 154

A Word about Compression

The Compress checkbox in the Create Attachment(s) dialog box is enabled by default. In most instances, you should leave this option checked so that Notes compresses the file attachment.

During the compression process, Notes searches for repeating patterns within the file. It codes these repeating patterns and strips them out, greatly reducing the size of the file. In many cases, a compressed file attachment is 80 to 90 percent smaller than the original file. Because the files are much smaller, they can be transferred much more quickly than the original file, and consume much less disk space on the server.

(continues)

(continued)

The only disadvantage of compressing attachments is that the attach process takes slightly longer, because Notes must analyze and process each file attachment.

Certain types of files don't contain repeating patterns—for example, any file that has already been compressed by another software package such as PKZIP (the repeating patterns have already been stripped out), or certain graphics files that use a compression scheme by default, such as GIF and JPEG files. Having Notes attempt to compress these files won't cause any damage, but the resultant space savings is negligible and it takes slightly longer.

When the recipient(s) receives the mail message and attempts to extract, launch, or view the attachments, Notes automatically decompresses the file into its original format. The recipient needs to take no special actions.

Detaching Attachments

When you open your mailbox, you should be able to immediately identify mail messages that have attached files because all of the standard views and folders will display a paper clip somewhere in the view pane, as figure 6.8 shows.

Note

The exact position of the paper clip may vary from view to view and folder to folder, but in all of the standard views and folders that ship with Notes 4.0, it is displayed. Be aware that if custom view and folders have been defined for the database, the paper clip icon may not be displayed.

To detach (extract the file from the mail message and store it a file on your disk) one or more of the attached files, follow these steps:

1. Open the mail document that contains attachments. When you open a mail message that contains attachments, you see the corresponding icons in the body.

2. When you select any or all of the attachments, a new menu option, Attachments, appears between the Actions and Window options (see fig. 6.9).

   From this menu, simply choose Detach (actually a bit of a misnomer because it does not detach the attachment from the message, but rather saves the file separately). Notes displays the standard file dialog box asking where you want to copy the file and what the filename should be. The original filename of the attachment is the default value for the new filename; you may, however, give the file a new name. Pick any directory you want, after which Notes detaches the file from the message onto your hard disk.

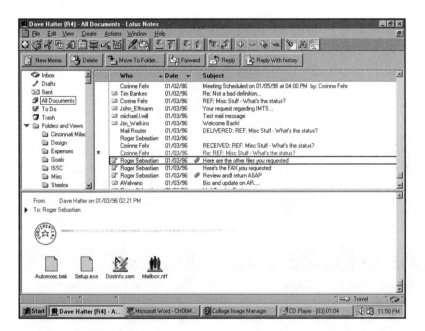

Fig. 6.8

The All Documents view is showing a message that has attachments. Notice the attachments shown in the preview pane.

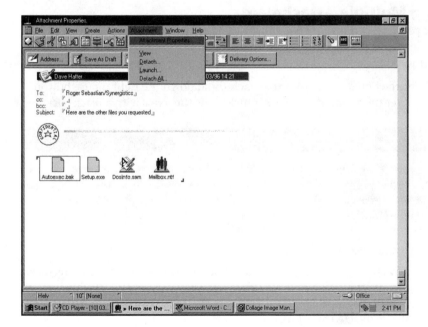

Fig. 6.9

The Attachments menu on the main menu bar.

Alternatively, you can double-click any of the attachments to display the Attachment Properties InfoBox (see fig. 6.10).

Fig. 6.10

The Attachment Properties InfoBox.

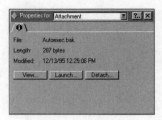

Attached files remain in a mail message even after you detach, launch, or view them (launching and viewing are described shortly). You can extract the attachment as many times as you want. You can detach the files to your hard disk, for example, and then detach them again to a disk (specify A: or B: as the directory). If you forward the message to someone else, the attached files also go with it.

> **Tip**
>
> You can delete attachments from a mail message to save disk space. See the section "Deleting Attachments" later in this chapter for more details.

Detaching Multiple Attachments

Many times, you receive a mail message that has more than one file attached, and it is more convenient to extract several at once. To detach more than one attachment, follow this procedure:

1. Select the attachments you want to detach (hold down the right mouse button and drag over the attachments, which highlights the icons with a black bar).

> **Tip**
>
> Notes doesn't care how much text you select in addition to the attachments, so don't worry about only selecting the attachments. In fact, if you want to detach all attachments in a message, you can select the entire document (and all the attachments in it) by selecting Edit, Select All, which is much faster.

2. Choose Attachments, Detach All Selected.

3. Notes displays the standard file dialog box that enables you to select a directory in which to store the attachments. Choose a directory (all of the attachments will be stored in the directory you select) and select OK, at which point Notes detaches all the selected attachments.

Viewing Attachments

Many times you receive file attachments that you want to examine before you decide to detach them onto your workstation's disk. If you only want to view the contents of an attachment, you can select the attachment and open the Attachment property sheet by double-clicking the icon. You may then click View to open the Universal Viewer and examine the file contents. Alternatively, you can select the attachment to view, and choose Attachments, View.

As discussed in Chapter 3, "Using Databases," the Universal Viewer allows you to examine the most popular file formats, such as Microsoft Word, Microsoft Excel, Microsoft Access, Lotus 1-2-3, Lotus Word Pro, and many others. However, you might receive files that the Universal Viewer cannot understand. For instance, many people use a compression utility such as PKZIP to compress files before they are attached because it provides superior file compression. Because the file is specially encoded, the Universal Viewer is not able to understand the contents of the file and cannot display it correctly.

Launching Attachments

Not only can you extract the files to disk or view and print the contents with the Universal Viewer, you can also launch (start) the application that created the file and begin editing the file immediately.

In order for the Launch function to work correctly, the following two things must be true:

- Unless the attached file is an executable file, such as a Lotus ScreenCam movie, you must have access to the application that created the file attachment, either from the hard disk on your workstation or from a drive on a network server. In other words, you can launch 1-2-3 by double-clicking a file with a WK4 extension only if you have 1-2-3 available on your computer.

- The application that originally created the file must have been successfully installed and configured in the Windows Registry for your system. In the Registry, Windows maintains a database of applications it recognizes and the types of files that are associated with each application. When you choose to launch a file, Windows examines the extension of the attached file and searches the Registry for a match. If a match is found, Windows starts the application and opens the attached file. For example, you receive a mail with the file DOSINFO.SAM (which is an AmiPro 3.1 file) attached. Windows determines from the Registry that files with the extension .SAM are AmiPro files, so it starts AmiPro and the attached file is opened as an AmiPro document.

This method is not foolproof because end users can name a file anything they want, and while a file might look like a 1-2-3 spreadsheet (has the extension WK4), it might actually be an ASCII text file, which means that file will not be launched correctly. If you cannot get a file to launch, consult your operating system manuals and your Notes administrator for more information.

> **Caution**
>
> Some malicious user could send you a virus or other harmful program as a file attachment that infects your computer when launched. (For this to work, the file must be an executable file, not a data file.) If you receive mail that has an executable file from a suspicious source, or you are suspicious of an attached executable file, *do not* launch it! Consult your administrator.

To launch an attachment in its associated program, select the file and open the property sheet by double-clicking the attachment's icon. You can then click the Launch button to open the file with the application that originally created it. When you elect to Launch, Notes starts the application that created the file and opens the file in that application. For example, if the file was created in 1-2-3, Notes starts 1-2-3 and loads the attachment into 1-2-3 for editing. If the file is an executable program, Notes immediately executes the program.

Deleting Attachments

Normally, attached files remain in a message until the message is deleted, which can quickly consume an inordinate amount of disk space. You can, however, decide to keep the mail message but delete the attachments, which saves disk space.

Some reasons for deleting attachments include the following:

- The mail message contains important information, but the file attachments are not needed.
- You elected to detach the files, or launched the files with the host application and elected to save the file to disk. Either of these choices creates a copy of the attached files on disk, meaning you now have duplicate copies of the files on your workstation that quickly consume disk space. By deleting the attachment from the mail, you free up this space.
- Files were erroneously attached to the mail message and you don't actually want to send the files, but you do want to send the mail message. If you delete the message, it deletes the attachments but you must retype the mail message.

To delete an attached file or files, the document must be opened in edit mode. If you are viewing the document in a view or have the document open in read mode, press Ctrl+E to switch to edit mode.

 Once you have the document open in edit mode, select the files you want to delete and press the Delete key or choose Edit, Clear. You could also click the Edit Clear SmartIcon. Notes prompts you with a dialog box indicating that the delete operation cannot be undone. If you are certain that you want to delete the attachment, choose Yes; otherwise, choose No to cancel the delete operation.

Working with Mail-In Databases

Because messaging is at the core of Lotus Notes, mail messages can be sent to any database if it is so enabled. This feature can be especially handy if you need to share information between two databases that do not replicate. For example, you can create a suggestion box-type application where users can mail documents to a database, but they don't need the database available to them. Or if you want to design a workflow application where documents can be routed to individuals who are part of the business process, the Mail-In database capability can be very useful.

A Statistics Collection application is a classic example of Mail-In database usage. For example, you have two Notes servers in your organization, each of which is constantly generating various server statistics. Rather than having to view two different databases on each server to see the statistics, you could create one database on one of the two servers and have the statistics for both servers mailed to this database.

Before a database can receive messages, you or the Notes administrator must create a Mail-In database in the Public Name & Address Book (see fig. 6.11). To do so (remember, you must have Author access or better to create a new document in the Public Name & Address Book), select the Public Name & Address Book and choose Create, Server, Mail-In Database.

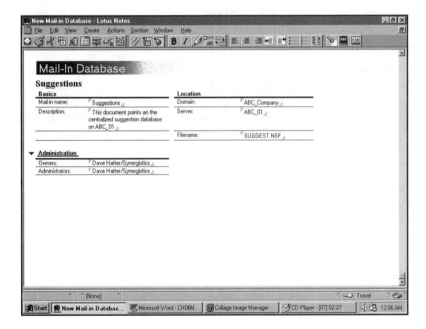

Fig. 6.11

A Mail-In database document for the Statistics Report database.

I

Notes Basics

You must then enter a name for the database (this is the name users enter in the To field of a mail message), the domain of the server where the database is stored, the name of the server where the database is stored, and the filename of the database. Optionally, you may enter a description to help identify the purpose and usage of the database. Be sure to inform users that the new database is available and explain that to send a message to the database, you must use the name defined in the Mail-In Database name field of the Mail-In database document.

Working with Custom Forms in Your Mailbox

Many companies, as they begin to `understand how Notes can increase productivity through workflow automation, expand the default capabilities of the Notes mailbox by adding Custom Forms. Custom Forms usually go hand-in-hand with Mail-In databases. They are Notes forms specifically designed to provide added functionality to your mail system by automating manual processes.

For instance, most companies have a standardized expense report that must be routed to several people for approval before it can be processed for payment. In Notes, a Custom Form modeled from your company's standard paper expense report can be created and added to the mailbox so that the report can be filled out and mailed to the approving authority. If approved, the form is then mailed to the accounting or finance department for payment.

Another example of how Custom Forms can be very useful is in forms routing applications. Take the case where a sales representative in the field needs to request market development funds. The representative fills out a form that is then snail mailed or faxed to his manager, who must approve the funds and pass it off to the VP of Marketing. If the VP of Marketing approves the request, it is then forwarded to accounting so that a check can be cut. This may take several days, or even weeks, and there is a good change the form may get misplaced or overlooked.

In Notes, a Custom Form can be added to the mailbox that allows the sales representative to compose a MDF Request, which is then e-mailed to his or her supervisor. If the form is approved, it is then e-mailed to the VP, and from the VP to accounting. Because the process is automated through NotesMail, the effort required to process the request drops drastically.

To access any Custom Forms that may be in your mailbox, select your mailbox and choose Create, Other. This displays the Other dialog box (see fig. 6.12). You may also choose Create, Mail, Other from the menu if you are not in your mailbox to get the same Other dialog box.

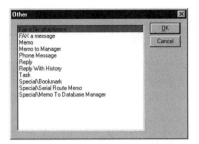

Fig. 6.12

The Other dialog box.

The Other dialog box displays all of the forms available from your mailbox. Simply select the form you want to use from the list and a new form opens. At this point, you work with this form like you would any other mail message.

Although Custom Forms can be designed for any purpose, they are really just special NotesMail messages, which means that in order to be delivered, the messages must be addressed to a Notes user, Mail-In database, or Notes server. In most cases, the database designer who creates the Custom Forms includes a SendTo field as a minimum. He or she may include the cc, bcc, and Subject fields as well, so that when the document is delivered to a mailbox, it is displayed in a manner similar to other mail messages in the folders and views.

In our organization, we have a company-wide, peer-based awards program that allows management and employees to recognize others for doing a good job. In each employee's mailbox is a custom form named Honks. Anyone can recognize a colleague for doing a good job by simply composing and mailing a Honk, which is then sent to every employee in the company as well as to a Honks Mail-In database, so a tally can be kept for each individual. Anyone who accumulates ten Honks receives a cash award. Figure 6.13 displays the Honks form (which is based on Notes R3 design).

The From field on the Honk is automatically calculated based on the user ID of the *Honker* (the person composing the Honk) composing the form. The value in this field is used as the From field for mailing purposes. The Date field is automatically calculated as well and is the Date field of the mail message. The Honk Type radio buttons are used to indicate an individual or group Honk. The Honk Member(s) field is used to store the names of the *Honkees* (the individuals being Honked).

The user presses the gray button to pop up a dialog box listing all of the employees in the company. The Honker then selects the Honkees, which is used as the To field of the mail message. The Honker then enters a Description of the commendable activity. The Honk description is used as the Body of the Mail Message. A formula automatically enters *Honk* for the Subject of the message. When the Honk is saved, it is mailed to all of the Honkees and to the Honk database.

Fig. 6.13

The Honks custom form.

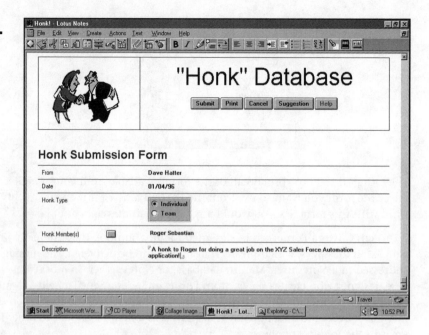

In most organizations, all NotesMail mailboxes are based on a mailbox design template. When a database designer completes the testing of his new custom form, it is placed in the standard mailbox template, which would automatically place the new form in your mailbox on the server. If you use workstation-based mail, the form would be placed in your local mailbox during your next replication.

Sending Faxes with Lotus Notes

The e-mail system in Lotus Notes is very flexible, and through the use of additional software, can be used to send faxes from Notes. If your company purchases the Lotus Fax Server and a machine to run the software on, you can fax any Notes document as well as documents created in other applications, such as Microsoft Word or Lotus 1-2-3. This can be beneficial to your company as it allows multiple users to share the resources of the fax server. You can greatly reduce the need for paper because you can send and receive faxes electronically. In fact, if you couple the fax server with a scanner, you can completely eliminate the need to have a regular fax machine!

Your Notes administrator should be the person who installs this software, because it requires its own machine and significant knowledge of your Notes installation to get it configured and running correctly. Once the Fax gateway is configured and running, you or your administrator will need to install the Lotus Image Viewer software on your local machine. This software installs the printer drivers that allow you to fax documents other than Notes documents and allows you to view incoming faxes.

▶▶ See "The Lotus Fax Server (LFS)," p. 864

▶▶ See "The Lotus Fax Server (LFS)," p. 864

Faxing a Message or File Attachment

After your workstation is configured, when you open your mailbox and choose <u>C</u>reate, you see two new forms in your mailbox—Fax a File Attachment and Fax a Message. When you choose Fax a Message, the old familiar Notes 3.x memo form with two new fields added, Cover page message and Include all names on cover page, is displayed (see fig. 6.14).

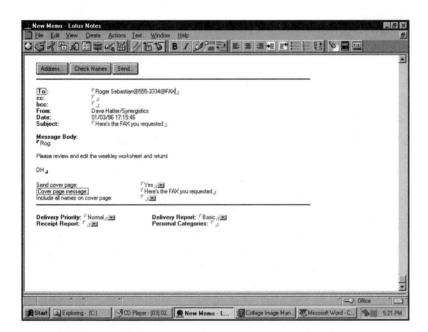

Fig. 6.14

The Fax a Message form for sending faxes through Notes.

Cover page message is a text field that you can use to enter a message that is displayed on the cover page of the fax. Include all names on cover page is a standard keyword field that allows you to display all of the recipients' names on the cover page if there is more than one recipient. If you want all of the fax recipients to be aware of the others who have received this document, choose <u>Y</u>es; otherwise, choose <u>N</u>o.

The Fax a File Attachment form, shown in figure 6.15, is almost identical to the Fax a Message form, except that it has an additional field, Fax File Attachments. Fax File Attachments is a Rich Text field that allows you to attach files, such as Microsoft Word or Lotus Word Pro, that you want to fax. This can be very useful, because you don't have to open the application that created the file and attempt to print the file to the Fax gateway; the Fax gateway attempts to convert the file to graphics and send it as part of the fax.

Fig. 6.15

The Fax a File Attachment form.

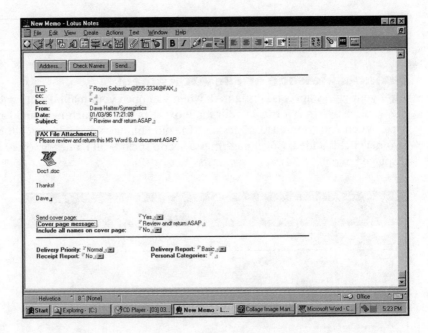

When you elect to Fax a File Attachment, the Lotus Fax software attempts to convert the attached file into graphics that can be sent to the receiving fax machine. Because each file must be converted from its original format, not every type of file can be faxed (most common file types are supported). For instance, a file that was compressed with PKZIP will not fax correctly because the file is in binary format and the fax software cannot convert it. For a complete list of files that can be faxed as attachments, consult the Lotus Fax Server manuals.

In order to tell Notes that this is a fax message and not a regular mail message, you must address it in a slightly different way than you would a regular mail message. If your organization has used the standard settings in the SendTo field, you would enter the address in the following format:

```
User Name@Phone Number@Fax
```

For example:

```
Dave Hatter@1-555-555-1212@FAX
```

The `User Name` portion of the address is used for information only and has no bearing in the delivery of the fax. The `Phone Number` portion of the address is the actual phone number of the recipient's fax machine. The `Fax` portion is the name used to tell Notes that this message should be passed on to the fax gateway for transmission to the recipient's fax machine. The address you enter here is not case-sensitive.

> **Note**
>
> To send the same message to multiple users, simply separate each address with a comma, as you would in a regular e-mail message. The Fax Server software faxes the message to each listed addressee.

Once you have addressed your fax message, send it as you would any e-mail message, and the Fax Server software takes over from there.

Faxing Documents from Other Applications

Another way to take advantage of the Fax Server is to redirect the output of an application, such as Microsoft PowerPoint or Lotus Organizer, to the Fax Server. For instance, you might type up a quick letter with Lotus Ami Pro and fax it to a colleague at another company. Once you have completed the letter, change your printer driver and print your document. Your output is redirected to the Lotus Fax Server, which will launch the Lotus Print-to-Fax dialog box (see fig. 6.16).

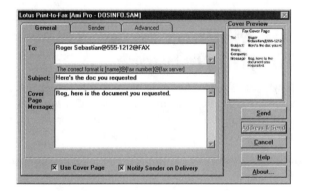

Fig. 6.16

The Lotus Print-to-Fax dialog box for an Ami-Pro document.

As you can see in figure 6.16, the Print-to-Fax dialog box sports a tabbed interface that allows you to set various faxing parameters. In most cases, you will only need to use the settings in the General tab.

The first field, To, works just like a NotesMail message: you simply enter the address of the recipient's fax machine in the standard Notes Fax format. The next field, Subject, is self-explanatory; enter the subject of the fax. The Cover Page Message field allows you to enter text to print on the cover page, just like a regular fax. The Use Cover Page checkbox acts as a toggle: if it's checked, a cover page that looks like the one in the Cover Preview box will be sent with the information you have entered in the aforementioned fields; otherwise, no cover page will be sent. The Notify Sender on Delivery checkbox is similar to a return receipt. When your fax server receives an acknowledgment from the recipient's fax machine, you will get a mail message indicating the fax was delivered.

When you have set the appropriate options, simply click Send, and your fax will be queued at the server until a fax/modem is available to deliver the fax.

Tip

Remember that messaging is one of the core services of Lotus Notes, which means that you can mail any Notes document. This also applies to faxing. For example, you have a lead in your Lead Tracking database who is interested in a service that your friend at another company provides and you want to fax the information to her. To do so, simply open the document that you want to fax and choose Actions, Forward. A new Memo is created and the lead document is copied into the Body field. In the SendTo field, you enter the recipient's name and fax number in the User Name@Phone Number@Fax format mentioned earlier. The router then routes the message to the Fax gateway for faxing.

The Lotus Fax Server, while not cheap, is a powerful and worthy addition to any Notes installation. If your company does not currently have this capability, it is certainly worth investigating.

Accessing Your Mailbox from Another PC on the Network

If you use Notes for any length of time, sooner or later (probably sooner) you will want to use Notes from someone else's PC. For instance, your PC might be down and you need to check your mail to see if you got that big promotion, or you might be in a different location for the day and need to check your mail.

Accessing Notes from another PC within your company is easy, but you must be prepared in advance. The following sections explain what you need to do in order to use Notes from any PC.

Tip

You should take the following actions sometime in the very near future; you just never know when your PC might crash and you won't be able to get your mail or access your databases.

Creating an ID Disk

When Notes was first installed on your computer, a Notes ID file was created for you. This file contains the information Notes needs to allow you access to the Notes server—information such as your user name, password, and other technical information. You can think of your ID file as a key that allows you to unlock the door of the Notes server.

Your ID file, which is normally stored in your Notes data directory (C:\NOTES\DATA\), has the extension ID. Normally, the first part of the actual file name is part of your real name. For instance, John Doe may find a file called JDOE.ID in his Notes directory. If you cannot locate your ID file, choose File, Tools, User ID, which displays the User ID dialog box, similar to the one in figure 6.17.

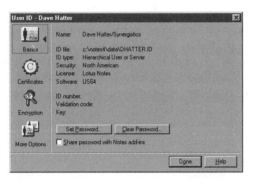

Fig. 6.17

The User ID dialog box for my personal ID file.

As you can see in figure 6.17, the second line, ID file, displays the full path to the file and the actual filename.

Because you must have this file to use Notes, the best plan for using Notes from other PCs is to copy this file to a disk. You can use the same method that you would to copy any file to a disk.

Note

If you don't know how to copy a file to disk, contact your Notes administrator or your Help Desk for support.

After you copy the file to the floppy disk, be sure to put a label on the disk as soon as possible. On the label, identify the disk as your Notes ID, and be sure to write down the filename of the ID file. In addition, write down the name of the mail server on the disk (I explain how to get it shortly). You will use this information to access Notes from the other PC.

Tip

Your Notes ID file is critically important to your success in using Notes. Without an ID file, you are unable to use Notes. If you lose or corrupt your ID file, a new one can be created, but this can cause problems if you have encrypted any documents. So... you should make several backup copies of this file and keep them in a secure location. (Remember, if someone else can get your ID file and knows your password, they can pass themselves off as you!) In addition, you should make backup copies of this file regularly as information stored in the file is subject

(continues)

Notes Basics

(continued)

to change. You can save yourself a lot of pain by making regular backups of this file. Remember, if you change your password in your current ID and then are forced to use a backup copy of your ID file, it may have an old password. The moral of this story is to back up your ID file frequently!

You still need one additional piece of information to be able to access you mailbox from another PC. You must know the name of your mail server (the server where your mailbox database is stored). To get this information, you can find the name of your mail server easily by choosing File, Mobile, Locations. Note the Locations view in your Name & Address Book. Open any of the location documents and you see the Home/Mail Server field in the Servers section in the upper-right corner of the form (see fig. 6.18). As an alternative, click the second box in the status bar (which displays the name of your current location setup) and select Edit Current, which also opens the current location document in your Personal Name & Address Book.

Fig. 6.18

A location document for the Office location.

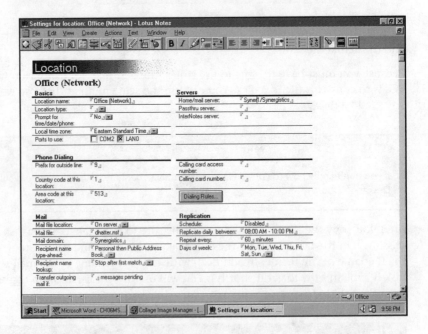

Once you have your ID file on a diskette and know your mail server, you have the ability to use Notes from another PC. To access your mailbox from someone else's PC, you must do the following two things:

- Log into Notes
- Add the icon for your mailbox to the workspace of the workstation you are using

The next two sections cover the steps you need to take to do this.

Note

Because Notes is a truly cross-platform application, you can easily move between workstations that have different operating systems. Notes retains the same general look and feel on all plat-forms. You may, however, have trouble if you try to use a UNIX or Macintosh workstation because those machines may not be able to read a disk that was formatted by DOS, Windows, or OS/2. If you need to use one of these workstations, consult your Notes administrator or Help Desk for advice on creating a Notes ID disk that can be read by these machines.

Logging On to Notes with Your ID Disk

To log on to a Notes server with your ID disk, follow these steps:

1. If Notes is currently running, skip to step 2. If Notes is not currently running on the workstation, start it. You may be immediately asked for a password; if so, choose Cancel and proceed to step 2.

2. Insert your ID disk into the machine.

3. Choose File, Tools, Switch ID.

Notes displays the Choose User ID to Switch To dialog box that shows the filename of the ID file that is currently in use on the workstation (this is ID of the last person to log on to Notes from this workstation) (see fig. 6.19).

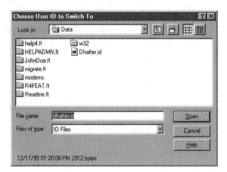

Fig. 6.19

The Choose User ID to Switch To dialog box.

4. Click the down arrow of the Drives box and select the floppy drive that you inserted your disk into.

5. In the File Name list, choose your ID file and then click OK. Alternatively, you can click the File Name box and type the drive letter you put the disk into, fol-lowed by a colon and the name of your ID file (this method is slightly faster if you know the name of your file). For example, if you were switching to John Doe's ID, you would type:

   A:JDOE.ID

6. You are then prompted for your Notes password. Enter your password and click Enter. Notes displays the User ID dialog box that displays certain key information about your Notes user ID, which includes your user name, type of license, and your internal Notes ID number (refer to fig. 6.17).

7. Choose OK.

At this point, you are logged in to Notes, and you can do anything that you can do on your workstation (unless, of course, you have databases on your machine that are not on this machine; you could, however, open them on this workstation). Remember, though, that workspace on this computer has been arranged by the user and that you may not find things arranged the same way you have them arranged on your workstation. For instance, you will not find your mailbox on any of the workpages of this workspace (unless you have added the icon previously). You must add it. The next section explains how to access your mailbox when you are logged on.

> **Tip**
>
> It's generally considered *bad form* to rearrange the workspace on another person's workstation without explicit permission.

Adding Your Mailbox Icon to the Workspace

After you have logged in and are using someone else's workstation, you can access your mailbox, but you must add an icon for the mailbox first. Adding your mailbox is exactly like adding any other database icon.

 ◄◄ See "Accessing a Database," p. 85

To add a mailbox icon to your workspace, follow these steps:

1. Select a workpage on which to add your mailbox. (Courtesy dictates that you should ask the owner of the workspace before you arbitrarily add the icon to any old workpage.)

2. Choose File, Database, Open, or press Ctrl+O.

3. Select the name of the server that houses your mailbox. (You wrote the name of your mail server on the disk label, didn't you? If not, you will need to know the name of your mail server before you continue.)

4. Once you select a server, the Database list displays a list of all of the databases on the specified Notes server. You probably will not see your mailbox in the list; however, if you scroll down through the list of databases, near the end of the list you should see the entry, [MAIL] (the square brackets indicate that this is a directory rather than a database). This is the MAIL subdirectory on the server, which is where mailboxes are stored by default. Select this entry and click Open, or double-click the [MAIL] entry.

> **Tip**
>
> You can type **M** to index down to the first entry that begins with *M*, which is slightly faster than using the scroll bars. This works in all list boxes.

5. The Database list displays all of the mailboxes in the MAIL directory. Each mailbox is identified by the name of the user to whom the mailbox belongs. Scroll through the list of names until you find your own name and then select it. (Remember, you can type the first letter in your name to index to the first mailbox that begins with that letter.) If you want to add the icon and open the database in one fell swoop, click the <u>O</u>pen button, which puts the icon on the current workpage and opens the mailbox. Alternatively, double-click the entry in the Database list. If you only want to add the icon without opening the mailbox, click the <u>A</u>dd button.

You now can access your mailbox from this workstation as from your own workstation. Your mailbox remains available until you or the owner of the workstation removes the icon from the workspace.

If you plan to use this workstation to access your mailbox frequently, you should leave your mailbox icon on the workpage as it saves considerable time. However, if you don't plan to use this machine again, or only infrequently, you should remove the icon from the workspace once you have finished reading your mail. To do so, simply select the icon and press the Delete key.

◄◄ See "Deleting Database Icons from Your Workspace," p. 113

See "Deleting Database Icons from Your Workspace," p. 113

When you open your mailbox on this new workstation, all of your mail messages appear as Unread messages—even if you have read them. This is because the information that tracks which messages have been read is stored on your local workstation. Similarly, if you read messages while using another workstation, Notes displays those messages as unread when you return to your own PC.

Logging Off the Other Workstation

After you finish using another workstation, be sure to clear your user information. If you don't clear your user information, or switch back to the owner's ID, you remain logged in to Notes, as long as that particular session remains active. This means that anyone can access your mailbox and read your mail, or worse, send mail as you. Just imagine, your boss gets a mail from you detailing what a jerk he is… you get the picture, right? In addition, anyone may have access to any of the databases that you have access to.

In order to maintain security (and your job), you should always perform one of the following actions to ensure that you are logged off the system:

- **Exit Notes**—If you did not copy your ID file to the workstation's hard disk, but merely used it from the floppy disk, there is absolutely no way anyone can access your information. If you did copy your ID to the workstation's hard disk, the user must know your password to log in as you (and you'd never tell your password to anyone else, would you?).

- **Press F5**—This key tells Notes to clear all private user information, effectively logging you off the system; anyone then trying to access a mailbox must enter your password.

- **Ask the workstation's owner to log on while you watch**—When the owner of the workstation uses File, Tools, Switch ID to select his ID file and log on to his account, you are automatically logged out.

Logging On After Someone Else Has Used Your Workstation

As soon as someone else logs in at your workstation, your Notes session ends. When you are ready to use Notes again on your workstation, you need to log in to Notes again. The following procedure is almost identical to the one you used to log in on someone else's workstation:

1. If Notes is still running, skip to step 2. If Notes is not running, restart it. If Notes prompts you for the last user's password, select Cancel and proceed to step 2.

2. Choose File, Tools, Switch ID. Notes asks for the location of your ID file. The File name box displays the filename of the ID last used on your machine.

3. Your ID file should be found in the C:\NOTES\DATA directory on your local hard disk. If the path does not currently point to this directory, change the Drive and Directory boxes to point to this directory. The File Name box should display your ID file. (Remember that as a shortcut, if you know the path and name of your ID file, you can type this directly into the File Name box and click the OK button). For example, if your user name is Roger Sebastian, your ID path and filename most likely is C:\NOTES\DATA\RSEBASTI.ID. If you cannot find your ID file, contact your Notes administrator or your Help Desk organization. You cannot reestablish a Notes session without your ID file.

Once you identify your ID file, you are prompted to enter your password. After you have done this successfully, Notes acknowledges that you are logged on, and you can begin to use Notes as usual.

Note

You can also use Notes via a dial-up connection from outside your company. Turn to Chapter 18, "Setting Up To Go Remote," for more information on how to work with Notes remotely.

Sending Mail Outside Your Company

Many companies that use Notes need the ability to send mail to other Notes users outside of their own company, or to users that use other mail systems such as the Internet. As more and more companies discover the benefits of e-mail, the need to link similar and dissimilar mail systems is growing. In fact, this trend is so strong that there is a growing market of add-on products to enable Notes to communicate with other mail systems. Within the next decade, you should be able to communicate with almost anyone via e-mail. The next three sections explain sending NotesMail to other companies that use Notes, sending NotesMail to Internet e-mail users through an SMTP gateway, and a brief overview of the capabilities of sending mail to users of other mail systems such as Microsoft Mail.

Sending NotesMail to Other Notes Users

Providing the ability to exchange NotesMail between companies that use Notes requires coordination and cooperation between the Notes administrators of all the companies who need to communicate, but requires no additional hardware or software.

In order for mail to be exchanged, the following must be in place:

- Each company must have at least one server that is set up to communicate with a server at the other company. Each of these servers must be cross-certified so that they can communicate. Your Notes administrator should perform the cross-certification to enable access for the other server.

- At least one of the servers must call the other servers to establish a connection through which mail messages can be transferred. This dictates a connection document in the Public Name & Address Book for the server that makes the calls.

 ◄◄ See "Server Connection Documents," p. 178

- Scheduled calling times should be configured in the connection documents so that mail is exchanged in a timely, cost-effective manner.

> **Note**
>
> The preceding is only a very brief overview of the actual steps required to make it possible to exchange mail between organizations. If you have the need to exchange mail with another company that uses Notes, see your Notes administrator.

When this setup is in place, sending messages to outside people is only slightly more complex than sending mail to your coworkers. Because users in another company are outside of your domain, they do not appear in your Public Name & Address Book, which means that you must provide more routing information to Notes. When you address a message to someone outside the company, your must include the organization name (which is almost always the company name; your contact at the other company should provide this information for you), preceded by an at sign (@). For example, to send a message to Dan Voelker at ABC Company, you would address the message as follows:

To: Dan Voelker@ABC Company

This notation tells Notes that Dan Voelker is not in your company's Name & Address Book but rather is outside your organization, and this message should be forwarded to the ABC Company server upon the next connection. Once the mail message is delivered to the mailbox on the ABC Company server, it is routed to Dan Voelker by their server.

If you frequently communicate with people in other companies, you can make it much easier on yourself by adding their addresses to your Personal Name & Address Book. To do so, you must add a Person document for each person your want to communicate with, just like you would for people in your own company who are not in your domain. The primary difference for people outside your company is that you must place the person's full mail address in the Forwarding Address field. When Notes sees an address in this field, it knows that the user specified is in another domain or organization and that the mail must be transferred outside the current domain. Figure 6.20 displays a Person document configured to send mail to Dan Voelker at the ABC Company.

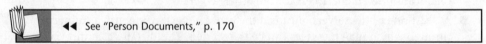

◀◀ See "Person Documents," p. 170

Fig. 6.20

A person document for
`Dan Voelker @`
`ABC_Company.`

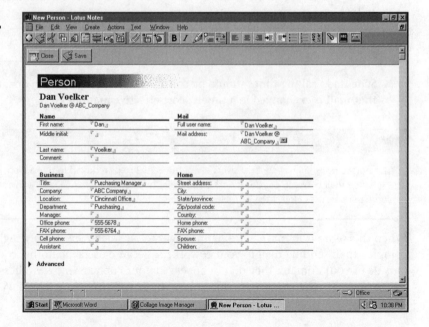

> **Tip**
>
> If you have previously received mail from someone outside your company, you can create a person document for this person by copying the person's address from the mail message. To do so, open the mail message in read mode and select the person's address (in the From field) with the mouse (click in the From field, then hold down the right mouse button and drag the selection bar across the address) and press Ctrl+C to copy the address to the Clipboard. Then create a new Person document in your Personal Name & Address Book. Position the cursor in the Notes Address field and press Ctrl+V to paste the address into this field.

As the popularity of Notes increases, the ability to communicate with other Notes users will become increasingly important. In fact, several third-party service providers such as CompuServe, WorldCom, and AT&T have seen the potential for Notes and have developed large Notes networks that allow you to transfer messages from your company to other Notes users very easily for a small monthly charge. If your company uses Notes, but can't afford the additional support required to enable and maintain external connections, these service provide a very attractive alternative.

Sending Notes Mail Messages to Internet Users

Unless you have been living under a rock for the past five years, you must have at least heard of the Internet and might possibly use it. The Internet is a vast worldwide network of computers that allows millions of people to communicate electronically. Lotus realized the potential of the Internet early on and now provides software that allows Notes users to send and receive Internet mail messages from within Notes.

In order to enable this, the Lotus SMTP (Simple Mail Transport Protocol) gateway must be installed (this is an add-on product, much like the Fax Server software) and your company must have a connection to the Internet. If both of these conditions are met, all you need to send mail to someone over the Internet is an Internet address.

When the Notes administrator installs and configures this software, a special domain is created, much like the Lotus Fax Server software, so that Notes knows that this message is to be forwarded to the Internet. To send a mail message out over the Internet, the SMTP domain should be appended to the user's Internet address.

For example, if you have a friend, Jim Jones, who works at XYZPDQ Manufacturing that has an Internet account, and you want to send a message to him, you create a new mail message and address it as follows:

Jim Jones@XYZPDQ.com@SMTP

When the NotesMail router sees this message, it reads the SMTP portion of the name, knows that the message is intended for the Internet, and transfers it to the SMTP gateway for conversion to the Internet format.

> **Note**
>
> If you frequently communicate with Internet users via NotesMail, you can add these people to your Personal Name & Address Book to make it easier to address mail messages.

Sending Notes Mail Messages to Users of Other E-Mail Systems

Many large companies have a mixture of e-mail systems, such as Microsoft Mail on one LAN and cc:Mail on another. In most cases, this lack of standardization is due to the fact that when LANs and e-mail were first introduced, there was little or no coordination or standardization between departments, which usually meant that each department chose the system it found most suitable.

If your company uses other e-mail systems in addition to NotesMail, additional software products (much like the SMTP gateway or Fax Server software) can be purchased that allow Notes to send and receive messages from most popular mail systems.

Working with the Mail Trace Feature

Mail Tracing is a new Notes 4.0 feature that enables a user to send a mail message that will trace its routing path on the way to its destination. This can be a very useful tool when mail is routing incorrectly because you can tell exactly how far it went before failing. At each *hop* (router) along the path, a verification message is generated, which allows the user or administrator to see the exact route. When the mail reaches its destination, a final verification message is generated. To enable Mail Tracing for a mail message, choose Trace Entire Path for the Delivery Report Delivery option.

The Mail Tools Menu

Lotus Notes 4.0 has a very powerful, flexible e-mail interface that can be highly customized by end users in order to make NotesMail more productive and enjoyable. A good example of this is the folders feature that allows you to define folders to sort and organize your e-mail messages based on your own criteria. This section explores several additional features that enable you to add your own distinctive flair to your mail messages and make your NotesMail sessions easier. Figure 6.21 displays the options available from the Actions, Mail Tools menu. This menu is context-sensitive—it is only available when you are in your NotesMail mailbox.

The rest of this section covers the functionality of the options available in this menu.

Fig. 6.21

The Actions, Mail Tools menu in the NotesMail mailbox.

Archiving Your Mail. Although it is generally a good idea to delete mail messages that are no longer pertinent, the very nature of many jobs requires that you keep some mail messages for long periods of time. For instance, if you work in a purchasing department and conduct electronic commerce with your suppliers via e-mail, you might need to keep copies of these e-mail messages for legal reasons.

If this is the case, you can improve the response time of your mailbox and make it substantially more manageable from an organizational perspective by creating an Archive mailbox and storing old mail messages in it.

> **Note**
>
> Although an Archive Mail database can be very useful when you need to store e-mail messages for long periods of time (but don't want to incur the overhead associated with doing so in your mailbox), you actually consume more disk space because you are storing more mail messages.

If you want to create an Archive mailbox, you first need to decide where it will be stored—on your local machine or on the Notes server.

If you decide to store the Archive mailbox on the Notes server, common courtesy (and the possible wrath of the Notes administrator) dictates that you speak to the Notes administrator of your server before you put the database on the server. In fact, in most Notes installations, only administrators can put new databases on the server, so you may have to consult the Notes administrator for help.

Once you have decided where the Mail Archive database should be stored, it is simple to create the archive. Select your mailbox (if you are not currently using your mailbox) and choose Actions, Mail Tools, Archive Profile. This launches a new Archive Profile form (see fig. 6.22).

Fig. 6.22

An Archive Profile for my local mailbox.

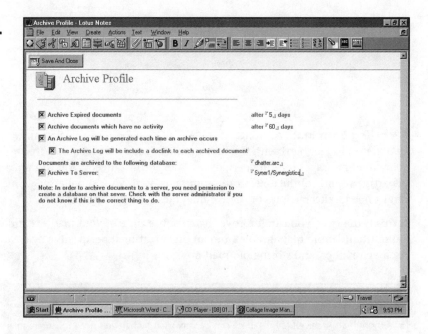

As you can see from figure 6.22, the Archive Profile form is relatively straightforward. The first checkbox, Archive Expired documents, will enabled Archive Expired documents and will display the after ___ days field when checked. You may enter a value for the number of days you want to elapse before expired documents are archived.

> **Note**
>
> Any document can have an expiration date—a date after which the author of the document thinks it will no longer be valuable.

The next checkbox, Archive documents which have no activity, when enabled (checked) will display the after ___ days, which allows you to enter the number of days to wait before an inactive document (a document that has not be edited and saved) is archived.

If you want to generate an archive log, which is a summary of the archive process, you can check An Archive Log will be generated each time an archive occurs to create a log entry that can be viewed in the Archive Log view.

If you enable the archive logging, the next checkbox—The Archive Log will include a doclink to each archived document—will become visible. If you want to be able to open the archive log and quickly jump to any document, enable this feature.

Notes, by default, will fill in the filename of your mailbox database and use the extension ARC. This information is required. You can change the filename if you want, but it is recommended that you go with the default value that Notes plugs in.

The final checkbox, Archive To Server, prompts you for the name of the server on which to create your archive file. You may or may not be able to use this setting, as the form mentions.

Once you have configured your Archive Profile, you are ready to begin archiving your mailbox.

Storing Mail in the Archive. Once the Archive Profile is configured and saved, you can archive mail messages in one of two ways. The first way is through the use of an agent. Lotus provides an archiving agent, Period Archive, that by default will run on a weekly schedule and archive your mail messages based on the criteria you defined in the Archive Profile. (This schedule can be changed; for more information on agents, see Chapter 15, "Buttons and Agents.") To enable the Periodic Archive agent in your mailbox, click the Agents icon in the Navigator, which will display all of the agents in your mailbox (see fig. 6.23).

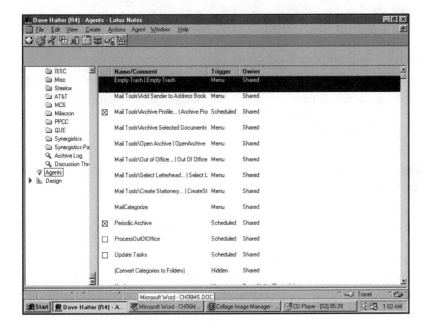

Fig. 6.23

The Agents view.

Notes Basics

On your screen, you can see the Periodic Archive agent with a small empty checkbox to its left. The checkbox is not checked because this agent is not set to run by default. To enable the agent, simply click the checkbox, which will launch the Choose Server To Run On dialog box shown in figure 6.24.

Fig. 6.24

The Choose Server To Run On dialog box.

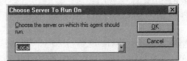

Simply click the drop-down list and choose the server on which this agent should run. If the archive file is stored on your workstation, choose Local; otherwise, choose the name of the server where the archive file is stored. Once you have entered this information, the checkbox will appear checked and periodic archiving will begin.

The second option requires some user interaction. You may, at anytime, select mail messages in your mailbox and choose Actions, Mail Tools, Archive Selected Documents to move the selected documents into the archive file. This can be very useful if you receive a large amount of mail messages and don't want to wait for the agent to run.

> **Note**
>
> Remember that your new Mail Archive database is only a copy of your mailbox—not a replica—which means that the archive only receives new messages when the Periodic Archive agent runs or when you use the Actions, Mail Tools, Archive Selected Documents Menu option.

As you use your Mail Archive database, it most likely will grow very quickly. You should periodically check for mail messages that you no longer need to keep in the archive and can permanently delete.

Using the Archive. Occasionally, you will need to use the mail archive file to refer to old mail or delete messages from it. To use it, open your mailbox and choose Actions, Mail Tools, Open Archive.

Out Of Office Profile. If you have used e-mail before, particularly if you work for a very large organization, then you are probably aware of what happens when you go on vacation or must be out of the office for an extended period: people keep sending you e-mail because they are unaware that you are gone. Upon returning, your mailbox is full and people are angry because you have not responded to their mail messages.

Lotus Notes 4.0 provides a way to solve this problem. If you are going to be out of the office for any extended period of time, you can create an Out Of Office Profile so that users are notified of your absence (see fig. 6.25).

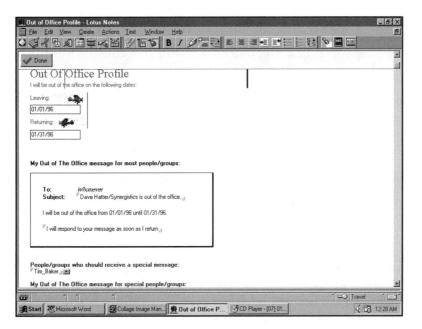

Fig. 6.25

An Out Of Office Profile.

You can enter a Leaving Date and a Returning Date in the Out Of Office Profile. Notes will fill in a default subject and message, which you can edit to say whatever you want. Any mail messages that are sent to you within the time frame defined in this document will cause return mail to be generated to the senders, informing them that you are out for the specified time period as well as any other information you define in the My Out of the Office Message for Most People section. In addition, you can define a special message for certain people in the field People/Groups who should receive a special message, and you can also define a list of people and groups who will receive no message.

Once you have entered the appropriate information, you can click the Done button and you will be asked which server to run this agent on. Be sure to put it in your Home/Mail server. (See the earlier section "Creating an ID Disk," for information on how to determine your Home/Mail server.) Notes will then display the Agent Enabled dialog box (see fig. 6.26).

Fig. 6.26

The Agent Enabled dialog box for Out Of Office Profiles.

This dialog box just tells you that people who send you mail on or between the leaving and returning dates will receive your message. On your returning date, you will receive a "Welcome Back!" message, and the Out Of Office Profile will be disabled.

Creating Letterhead. In Notes 4.0, you can select from several styles of letterhead to display at the top of your mail messages. In the standard mail Memo form, the letterhead is the multicolored bar that displays your username and the time and date the mail was composed. This new capability allows you to display a personal flair on your mail messages. To change your letterhead, open your mailbox and choose Actions, Mail Tools, Select Letterhead, which will display the Select a Letterhead dialog box (see fig. 6.27).

Fig. 6.27

*The Select a Letterhead
dialog box.*

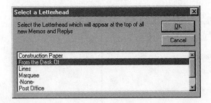

The Select a Letterhead dialog box displays a list of all of the available letterheads in your mailbox. Simply select one of the available letterheads from the list, and this new letterhead will be applied to all of you mail messages. The From the Desk Of letterhead is the default letterhead used in all NotesMail forms.

Creating Stationery. Notes also allows you to create *stationery*, which is a mail message whose format and recipients' list you will use again. This is very useful if you frequently send a mail message to the same people. For instance, if you send a weekly sales report to your sales team, you could create stationery that is well suited for this purpose and defines the recipients list. Use this stationery to send the weekly mail.

To create stationery, open your mailbox and choose Actions, Mail Tools, Create Stationery. This will launch the Create Stationery dialog box (see fig. 6.28).

Fig. 6.28

*The Create Stationary
dialog box.*

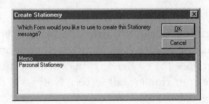

When this dialog box is displayed, a list of the currently defined stationery is shown. Choose one and click OK. The selected stationery will be displayed and can be edited appropriately. When editing is complete, complete the recipient list, add whatever text you need to add to the stationery, and send the message. When the message is sent, you will be asked if you want to save the message as stationery. If you choose Yes, you will then be prompted for a name for the new stationery. Enter a name and click OK. The Save as Stationery dialog box appears (see fig. 6.29).

Fig. 6.29

The Save as Stationery dialog box.

As you can see in figure 6.29, Notes tells you that the new stationery has been saved in the Drafts folder. To compose a new mail message with this stationery, simply open the Drafts view and then open the stationery you want to use.

From Here...

In this chapter, you learned how to perform some of the more advanced functions of the Notes e-mail system: attaching files to mail messages, using different mailbox views, and customizing mail views, folders, and custom mail forms.

Refer to the following chapters in this book for information that you might find useful when using NotesMail:

- Chapter 3, "Using Databases," covers Notes databases in detail. Remember, your NotesMail mailbox is really just a Notes database.

- Chapter 7, "Working with Text," shows you how to make your text aesthetically pleasing.

- Chapter 8, "Working with Documents," shows you many tips and tricks for working with Notes documents. NotesMail messages are really just documents, and any database can send and receive mail—not just your mailbox.

- Chapter 18, "Setting Up To Go Remote," explains such topics as location and connection documents and workstation-based mail in more detail. This will be particularly helpful for mobile users.

CHAPTER 7

Working with Text

In earlier chapters, you learned how to compose simple documents. Although the techniques you learned are adequate for getting information across to your co-workers, you can communicate much more effectively by using the wealth of enhanced features that Notes offers.

In this chapter, you learn how to do the following:

- Add color to your documents
- Use different font styles and sizes
- Cut and paste text
- Use the permanent pen
- Work with styles
- Work with bulleted and numbered lists

These features add emphasis to your writing and facilitate communication as you work with Notes.

Editing Text Fields

If you have used a word processor before—anything from Ami Pro to WordPerfect—you're used to rearranging, highlighting, and manipulating text. Notes includes a sophisticated text processor that provides many of the same features you have come to appreciate in word processors. If you're familiar with Windows-based word processors such as Microsoft Word for Windows, Word Pro, or WordPerfect for Windows, you will find that many of the keystrokes are the same.

Even if you haven't used a word processor before, by now you probably have done some experimenting in Notes and have discovered that you can make some simple corrections by performing the following basic actions:

- Pressing the arrow keys enables you to move up, down, left, and right within your document. The arrow keys also let you move from field to field.

- Pressing the Home key positions the insertion point at the beginning of the line.

- Pressing the End key positions the insertion point at the end of the line.

- Pressing the Page Up and Page Down keys scrolls one screen up or down, respectively.

- Pressing Ctrl+Home positions the insertion point at the beginning of the document; pressing Ctrl+End moves it to the end.

- Pressing Ctrl+left arrow moves the insertion point back a word; pressing Ctrl+right arrow moves it forward a word.

- Pressing the Delete key deletes the character just to the right of the insertion point.

- Pressing the Backspace key deletes the character just to the left of the insertion point.

- You can reposition the insertion point by clicking anywhere within the text.

As you read through this chapter, keep in mind that Notes provides you with a quick mouse trick to bring up a list of some of the most popular formatting selections, as well as the Text Properties InfoBox—which provides you with a wealth of text and paragraph settings to enhance your documents. To use this shortcut, click your right mouse button one time anywhere in the Notes document. Notes displays the context-sensitive menu box shown in figure 7.1.

Fig. 7.1

You can make quick formatting selections by right-clicking your mouse button anywhere in the document.

In the following sections, you learn about more powerful editing commands.

Selecting Text

Some of the most powerful editing and formatting operations involve a two-step process. You first must identify the text that you want to do something to, and then tell Notes what to do with that text. As you read through the next few sections and learn how to perform editing tasks such as copying, changing text styles, and many others, you first must *select* the text as a way of telling Notes that this is the text you want to work with.

Note

If you have not typed text yet, you can set font attributes for the new text first. After setting the font attributes (such as style, size, and color), all of the text you type appears with those attributes until you change them or exit the document.

To select a section of text, place the pointer at the beginning of the text you want to work with, hold down the left mouse button, move the mouse pointer to the end of the text, and release the mouse button. If you prefer to use the keyboard, position the insertion point at the beginning of the text you want to select, hold down the Shift key, and move the insertion point to the end of the text using the directional arrows on your keyboard. By using either method, you can select any amount of text.

After you select the text, it appears in *reverse video*—that is, the text appears as a lighter color with a dark box surrounding it (see fig. 7.2).

Tip

You can select just one word quickly by double-clicking your mouse while the pointer is on the word. This is a great time-saver if you want to check the spelling or change the font attributes of just that one word.

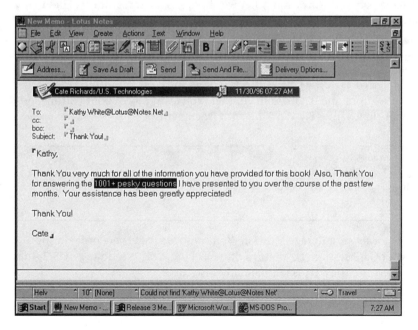

Fig. 7.2

You can select text in documents by clicking and dragging your mouse cursor over it.

After you select the text, you can tell Notes what you want to do to that text.

 One of the simplest and most common operations is deleting the selected text, which you can do by pressing the Delete key. Other ways to delete selected text include selecting Edit, Clear, clicking the Edit Clear SmartIcon, or simply pressing the spacebar.

Another common operation is typing over a selected section of text with new text. After you select the text, start typing new text to replace the old text. The instant you start typing, Notes deletes all the selected text and begins inserting the new text that you type.

Caution

Be careful that you don't accidentally type text while you have text selected. If you type new text while old text is selected, Notes thinks that you want to replace the old text with the new text. Many users have experienced a momentary panic at seeing a large block of selected text disappear because their finger accidentally brushed a letter or a digit. If you make such a mistake, select Edit, Undo Typing before you type anything else, or perform any other function.

Using the Clipboard

The *Clipboard* is a storage area shared among Notes and other Windows, Macintosh, and OS/2 applications. It serves as a temporary holding location for data that you are moving or copying between Notes and other word processors, spreadsheets, and many other programs. You can use the Clipboard to cut text, bitmaps, or other inserted objects (like spreadsheets and other graphic files) from a Notes document—for example, switch to a Windows word processor such as Microsoft Word for Windows or Word Pro—and paste into a Word or Word Pro document. You can also use the Clipboard (also referred to as the *Clipbook* in Windows for Workgroups) to cut and paste a document(s) from one database to another (you learn more about cutting and pasting documents in Chapter 8, "Working with Documents").

Note

You can use the Clipboard to copy data between any applications that are designed to work with the Clipboard.

The Clipboard is a *temporary* storage location. You can store data there only during a single Windows or OS/2 session. If you turn off your PC or exit Windows or OS/2, the Clipboard is cleared and the data is permanently lost.

Caution

Copying something else to the Clipboard will erase whatever you currently have stored there, unless you are appending text to the Clipboard (discussed in a moment). You will lose the old data when you copy new data to the Clipboard.

The following sections explain how to use the Clipboard as a means for copying and moving data with Notes and between Notes and other applications.

While this section discusses the copying, cutting, and pasting of text, these procedures also apply to all objects found in Notes documents. For example, follow these same procedures to copy attachments, graphics, and other objects stored in the database.

Moving Text. As you type your text, you may decide that your thoughts make better sense in a different order, and you may want to move text from one place to another. This process—known as *cutting and pasting*—comes from the days when editors cut snippets of text from a paper document and pasted them elsewhere in the document. As the technique's name implies, cutting and pasting is really a two-step process: you remove the text from its old location (cut it) and insert it into its new location (paste it).

You must be in edit mode to cut and paste data. To enter edit mode, double-click anywhere within a document that is in read mode to open for editing—the field brackets will appear to indicate that you are in edit mode.

To cut and paste text, follow these steps:

1. Select the text you want to move.
2. Press Ctrl+X; choose Edit, Cut; or click the Edit Cut SmartIcon.

   Notes removes the text from your document.
3. Position the insertion point where you want to paste the text.
4. Press Ctrl+V; choose Edit, Paste; or click the Edit Paste SmartIcon. Notes copies whatever text is in the Clipboard into your document wherever the insertion point is.

Copying Text. Copying text is very similar to moving text. As with moving, you want to put the text somewhere else in your current document or another document; but with copying, you also want the text to remain at its current location. You can be in read or edit mode to copy text, but you must be in edit mode to paste it.

Like the procedure to move text, copying text is a two-step process using the Clipboard as an intermediate holding place. Only the second step is different, as you can see in the following steps:

1. Select the text you want to copy.
2. Press Ctrl+C; choose Edit, Copy; or click the Edit Copy SmartIcon.

The text remains where it is, and nothing seems to have happened. Notes, however, has copied the selected text onto the Clipboard.

3. You now can move the insertion point to a new position and paste as described in the preceding set of steps or by using any of the other methods described earlier. Notes copies the text from the Clipboard to the document in the new location.

Tip

If you prefer to use the keyboard whenever possible, you can press Shift+End to highlight all text to the right of the insertion point on a line. However, be careful! If you accidentally press Shift+Insert instead, Notes will copy whatever is on the Clipboard into your document. If this happens, select Edit, Undo Typing immediately to remove the mistake.

Many applications provide cut, copy, and paste operations but use a different set of shortcut keys. Lotus Notes supports two sets of shortcut keys, shown in Table 7.1. If you choose to use the keyboard for editing operations, you can use either set of keys. Keep in mind that the Macintosh uses the Command key—rather than the Ctrl key—when working with the keyboard commands.

Table 7.1 Shortcut Editing Keys

Operation	Standard Keys	Alternative Keys
Cut	Ctrl+X	Shift+Delete
Copy	Ctrl+C	Ctrl+Insert
Paste	Ctrl+V	Shift+Insert
Undo	Ctrl+Z	Alt+Backspace

Copying Multiple Pieces of Data. You may find yourself in a situation where you want to copy several different pieces of text from several different documents and paste them all into a new document. By using the copy-and-paste technique described above, you must copy each piece to the Clipboard and then paste it into the new document before copying the next piece of text. Each new copy operation replaces what is already on the Clipboard.

Notes, however, provides an operation just for this situation:

1. Use the usual key combination—Ctrl+C—to copy the first piece of text to the Clipboard.

2. For a subsequent piece of text, press Ctrl+Shift+Insert. Notes copies the selected text to the Clipboard; but rather than replacing the Clipboard's existing contents, Notes appends the new text so that the Clipboard contains both pieces of text.

You can also hold down the Shift key and choose <u>E</u>dit, <u>C</u>opy or <u>E</u>dit, Cu<u>t</u> for each piece of text you want to add to the Clipboard.

Note

When you copy more than one noncontiguous section to the Clipboard, Notes does not put a space between the last character of the first section copied and the first character of the next, unless you copy a space or blank line at the same time you copy the text. Rather, it simply adds the text at the end of the section you have previously copied.

This may create a messy copy on the Clipboard, in which you will have to spend time "cleaning up" when you paste the information into a new document. If keeping paragraphs, sentences, or words separate is important to you, make sure you highlight the spaces you want copied as well.

By repeating step 2 for additional text, you can accumulate as much text as you need on the Clipboard. Place your cursor in the location in which you want the copied text to appear, and then press Ctrl+V, (or <u>E</u>dit, <u>P</u>aste). Notes pastes the entire contents of the Clipboard into the new location.

More about Moving and Copying Text

After you cut or copy text to the Clipboard, you don't have to paste it into its new location immediately. The text remains on the Clipboard until you cut or copy something else (or until you exit Windows or OS/2). If you need to perform other operations at the location where you cut or copied the text, feel free to as long as you don't cut or copy other text. However, to avoid accidentally losing your data, it is best if you paste the data on the Clipboard into its new location as soon as possible—particularly if you are busy or often distracted and run the risk of forgetting where you left off in your work.

Pasting copies text from the Clipboard into your document, but the text remains on the Clipboard too. If you want to place another copy of the same text elsewhere, you need only to move the insertion point to the new location and paste again. Thus, from a single cut or copy you can perform as many paste operations as you like.

You need not cut (or copy) and paste within the same document. After you cut or copy text to the Clipboard, you can close the current document, open another document, and then paste the text into the second document.

In fact, you need not even paste within the same application or database. You can cut or copy a section of text in Lotus Notes, switch to another application that is designed to use the Clipboard, and then perform a paste into a word processing document or spreadsheet in that application. Similarly, you can perform a cut or copy in other applications, switch to Notes, and perform a paste. This capability to move and copy from one application to another is one of the most important advantages of using applications that support the Clipboard.

Pasting Text into Dialog Boxes. Often, you may want to copy (or cut) and paste information into a field, but the Cut, Copy, and Paste commands are not available to you when you choose Edit. Don't worry, you can use the Ctrl+C to copy (or Ctrl+X to Cut) the information to the Clipboard, and then Ctrl+V to paste the information. This is particularly helpful when you are trying to enter information into a dialog box—where the Edit, Copy and Edit, Paste commands are not available from the menu bar.

For example, you can use this tip when you are trying to fill the contents of a formula box when designing a field in a document. As shown in figure 7.3, the formula in the formula definition box is quite long and would take the designer a good bit of time to write. However, if the designer already has this formula designed elsewhere, she can copy the formula from there and paste it into the field. The designer is now free to customize the formula as needed.

Tip

Often, designers use Notes databases to store copies of formulas—particular complicated ones, in simple text fields. Then, when the formula is needed, the designer simply opens the database document referencing the type of formula needed, copies the formula text, and pastes it into the field formula definition box currently being defined. The designer may need to customize the formula—editing references to other fields, forms, or views, for example—but the formula, with its particular syntax, provides a great template to work from.

Often, this database is stored on a server, and all database designers can contribute and use the formulas. This lets companies maximize the use of database design without having to "reinvent the wheel" every time it is developing a new field.

Fig. 7.3

You can easily paste text into a formula dialog box by copying from one location using Ctrl+C, and then pasting it into the new formula entry field using Ctrl+V.

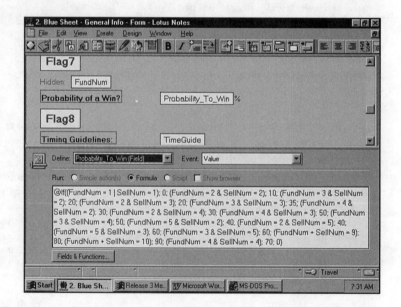

Undoing Changes

Everybody presses the wrong key or chooses the wrong menu option occasionally, and you may wind up cutting when you meant to paste, or deleting when you meant to copy. Fortunately, with Notes all isn't lost.

Whenever you perform an operation that modifies a section of text—such as delete, cut, copy, or paste—Notes offers you a chance to change your mind. You can reverse the effects, or *undo*, the last operation by choosing Edit, Undo; pressing Ctrl+Z; or clicking the Edit Undo SmartIcon.

The exact wording of the first option on the Edit menu varies depending on the last operation you performed. If you last did a cut, the first item on the menu is Undo Cut; if you last did a paste, the command is Undo Paste. If you choose the command, Notes undoes the last operation by restoring the deleted text, removing the pasted text, or reversing whatever action you performed.

Notes also lets you change your mind about Undo—if you undo an operation, like boldfacing text, and you decide you want to perform that function anyway, choose Edit, Redo. The bold text will reappear. Like the Undo menu command, the Redo menu command will change depending on what action you are performing.

Undo is useful only if you realize immediately that you have made a mistake because you can undo only the most recent operation. Suppose that you delete a piece of text and then perform another operation (for example, type another character, or copy another piece of text to the Clipboard). If you realize then that the deletion was a mistake, you're out of luck—it's gone for good.

> **Caution**
>
> The Undo command cannot be used to bring back entire documents that have been deleted from a database.

Understanding Rich Text Fields

The most common type of field you encounter in most Notes documents is a text field. You can enter any kind of text into such a field—words, sentences, names, and so on. In Notes, however, you encounter two types of text fields: *plain text fields* and *rich text fields*.

> **Note**
>
> The body of your Notes e-mail memo is an example of a rich text field, while the Subject field in the memo is a text field.

A rich text field is so called because you can enter text, objects, and formatting information. Associated with any portion of rich text is a particular color, type style, justification, line spacing, and many other characteristics. By changing the characteristics for any portion of rich text, you can tell Notes to display (and print) that portion in any one of various colors, sizes, and type styles. You also can enter tables, graphics, document links, buttons, and other objects.

In the following sections, you learn how to make the most of text attributes. In Chapter 8, you will learn how to insert objects like tables, documents links, and buttons.

> **Note**
>
> Rich text fields are the only fields in which you can change the font attributes, format paragraphs, insert graphics, embedded objects, attachments, tables, document links, pop-up boxes, and other special inserts. They are also the only fields in which you can import data from other applications. If you are trying to use one of these features and the menu command is not available to you, your cursor is not located in a rich text field.
>
> Information entered in rich text fields, however, will not be displayed in views. Text (and other field types) are used when the information needs to be displayed in a view.

Spotting Rich Text Fields

How can you tell whether a field is plain text or rich text? You cannot tell by looking at an empty field, but you can try to use some of the features described in this section. If you try to change the style of the field—by adding color or changing the type style—and Notes will not let you, the field is plain text. Also, with your cursor located in the field, you can look at the Text section of the status bar at the bottom of the Notes window. If the type and size of the font appear, you are in a rich text field; otherwise, you are not.

Finally, you can distinguish between the two types of text fields by placing the insertion point anywhere within the field and pulling down the Text menu. If the insertion point is on a plain text field, most of the menu choices, such as Bold, Italic, and Underline, are grayed out, indicating that they are not available.

Generally, rich text fields are fields in which you may have good reason to use different fonts and type styles, such as the description of a customer problem or notes about a meeting with a client. Other fields that contain simple pieces of data, such as an author's name or the subject of a meeting, are plain text fields.

As you become acquainted with various databases, you may notice that plain text fields tend to contain small amounts of data—name of an addressee, a ZIP code, or a Social Security number, for example—whereas rich text fields tend to include much longer amounts of text, such as a description of a meeting or the body of a memo.

Many documents consist of a few short plain text fields and a single potentially long rich text field. A memo, for example, has several short plain text fields (To:, CC:, BCC:, Subject:) and a single rich text field (the body of the memo), which can contain thousands of lines of text and other objects.

Some database designers will exclude rich text fields from documents to keep users from attaching files in the document. This is the designer's way of trying to minimize database size or maximize the speed in which documents are replicated from one copy of the database to another. If you are using a database in which attaching documents is necessary, then you must contact the database manager to see if the field type can be changed.

Changing the Appearance of Text with the Text Menu

The Notes Text menu provides control over text characteristics, such as text attributes (boldface, italic, underline), fonts, justification, spacing, and others (see fig. 7.4). You can use a single set of procedures to manipulate any of these characteristics. Many of the selections in the Text menu, such as Italic, Bold, and Underline, are quick selections for options that are also available in the Text Properties InfoBox. You will learn about those features when you work through the attribute settings found in the Text Properties InfoBox.

Fig. 7.4

You can change text attributes from the Text menu one at a time, or open the Text Properties InfoBox to change them all at the same time.

You must be in edit mode to type text and change the font attributes. If you do not see open brackets positioned around each field in the document to signify the document is in edit mode, right double-click anywhere in the document. You can use the Actions Edit Document SmartIcon if you have it available in your set of SmartIcons. If you are composing a new document, it is already in edit mode.

Selecting Text To Modify

To control the characteristics of new text that you are about to type, follow these steps:

1. Position the insertion point where you want to type the new text if the insertion point isn't already in the proper location.

2. Choose Text, Text Properties, or press Ctrl+K.

3. Choose the characteristic you want to change (such as Font or Size).

The new text you type at that location will take on the characteristics you selected.

Suppose that you are about to type the phrase **This task is critical to our success**, and you want the word "critical" to appear in bold and in red. Type the first part of the sentence (**This task is**). Next, change the text color to red and then change the style to bold by following these steps:

1. Choose Text, Text Properties (or select the Text Properties SmartIcon).

2. Choose Red in the Text Color drop-down list and choose Bold from the Style list box.

3. Whatever you type now appears in bold red. Type **critical**.

Before you finish the sentence, you need to switch back to plain (non-bold) black, which you can do by following the preceding steps, but choosing Black rather than Red and Normal rather than Bold in step 2. Then finish the sentence by typing **to our success**.

You also can change characteristics for existing text. Suppose that you already have typed the sentence **This task is critical to our success** and then decide that you want "critical" in bold red. Follow these steps:

1. Select the text you want to change—in this example, the word "critical."

2. Choose Text, Text Properties.

3. The Text Properties InfoBox appears. Choose Red and Bold.

The word "critical" changes from black to red. The surrounding text remains normal black. The text you have highlighted remains in reverse video when you select OK to change the font attributes. Simply click the mouse button once anywhere in the document to view your font changes.

Even if you know as you type the sentence that you want the word "critical" in bold red, you may find that typing the complete sentence and then changing the color and style for the word "critical" is easier.

> **Tip**
>
> When you are changing fonts and font sizes, keep in mind that some fonts naturally appear smaller to the reader. For example, Helvetica 10 font is the default and is relatively easy to read on-screen. If you change the font type to Script, and leave the font size 10, you will notice that it is quite difficult to read the text. You will need to increase the font size for the Script font to be readable on-screen.
>
> Also, while Helvetica 10 font is easy to read on-screen, it is often difficult for some to read text with this font size when it is printed. You may want to increase the font size to 12 or greater if you are printing this document or if you are fairly sure the reader will want to print the document.

Working with the Text Properties InfoBox

The first selection from the Text menu, Text Properties, lets you control the appearance of the characters that make up a section of text. The Text Properties InfoBox lets you control the characters' size, color, type style, and other attributes (see fig. 7.5). The Text Properties InfoBox is made up of five tabs. These tabs include the following:

 Font—Controls the font sizes, styles, and colors. The font attributes used by the Permanent Pen are also adjusted through this tab.

 Alignment—Controls how the text in a paragraph aligns in relation to the left margin. The options on this tab also include automatic bulleting and numbering for text and the line spacing for the text in a paragraph.

 Pages/Tabs—Controls the pagination and tab settings for the paragraph. This tab also contains the right margin setting for printing purposes.

 Hide—Controls when Notes displays a paragraph. Notes lets you hide text based on numerous conditions.

 Style—Allows users the ability of defining frequently used paragraph styles. The styles defined through this tab are available for selection in the Style section of the status bar at the bottom of the Notes window.

Each of the settings on these tabs is discussed in detail in the following sections.

> **Note**
>
> If you do not have a mouse and need to select a tab in the Text Properties InfoBox that is not currently displayed, use the right and left arrow keys to cycle through the five tabs until the tab you want to work with is visible. If you press the right or left arrow keys and nothing happens, try pressing the Tab key until you notice a dotted-line box surrounding the current tab's icon. Then press the right or left arrow keys until the tab you want appears.

Fig. 7.5

The font panel of the Text Properties InfoBox is used to change font style, height, color, and other attributes.

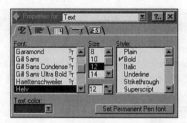

Font Settings. In the Font tab of the Text Properties InfoBox you can select the font type (fig. 7.5 shows Helvetica selected), the size of the font, the color, and the type style.

▶▶ See "Command Reference" p. xxx (App C)

For many common characteristics, Notes provides menu commands and shortcut keys that you can use instead of the Text Properties InfoBox (see Table 7.2). You can access the menu commands using the Text menu. When you choose Text, Notes shows you the shortcut keys opposite their corresponding characteristics. Rather than choose Text, Bold, for example, you can press Ctrl+B and skip the menu altogether (refer to fig. 7.4).

Table 7.2 Text Quick Command Reference

SmartIcon	Command	Shortcut
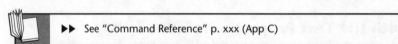	Text, Text Properties	Ctrl+K
N	Text, Normal Text	Ctrl+T
I	Text, Italic	Ctrl+I
B	Text, Bold	Ctrl+B
U	Text, Underline	Ctrl+U
A·A	Text, Enlarge Size	F2
A·A	Text, Reduce Size	Shift+F2
	Text, Indent	F8
	Text, Outdent	Shift+F8

SmartIcon	Command	Shortcut
	Text, Named Styles	F11 (to use Cycle list)
	Text, Permanent Pen	
	Text, Bullets	
	Text, Numbers	
	Text, Color (select color from the list)	
	Text, Align Paragraph, Center	
	Text, Align Paragraph, Full	
	Text, Align Paragraph, Left	
	Text, Align Paragraph, Right	
	Text, Align Paragraph, No Wrap	

You can change the text style to highlight portions of your text in various ways. The style includes characteristics, such as text color and font, and attributes, such as bold-face and italic. Different text styles can add emphasis to important phrases, add interest to your document, and draw your reader's attention to crucial passages.

The following sections show the different text attributes available in the Text Properties InfoBox and some suggested uses.

Change the Fonts. You can choose one of many fonts. Helvetica 10pt is the default font used by Notes (except in Macintosh, in which Geneva is the default font). The following are three examples of typefaces:

Helvetica

Courier

Times Roman

You can also view fonts as Typewriter fonts. The Typewriter fonts option in File, Tools, User Preferences tells Notes to display all information (including database titles, views, and documents) in *monospace fonts*, in which all letters take up the same amount of space. You may find this option useful for checking the width of columns. If a column is wide enough in a monospace font to display the entire contents of the column, it will probably be wide enough when you switch back to a proportional (non-monospace) font. This is a particularly useful feature when you are designing export views.

Notes Basics

Change the Point Size. You can choose from any of the font sizes in the Size list box or type an entry in the box below the list. Clicking the up and down arrows next to the Size text box will cause the text size to increase or decrease one step for each click.

Change the Color. When you click the down arrow next to the Text color selection box, Notes presents a list of 16 colors. Colors are especially helpful in headings and important passages.

Change the Text Style. You can choose from any of the following text styles:

- **Boldface** causes text to stand out from the surrounding text. Typing key points or names in boldface helps your reader spot the topic of a paragraph instantly.

- *Italic* puts extra emphasis on text. Use italic to highlight especially important words or phrases or for foreign phrases.

- <u>Underline</u> also adds emphasis.

- ~~Strikethrough~~ puts a line through the text you have selected. Using strikethrough helps your reader immediately identify areas of the text that you want removed from a document or that you don't agree with.

- ^{Superscript} is used to slightly raise text above the preceding text and make it smaller. This attribute is used in mathematical equations as in 2^2, and with some symbols like copyright or registered trademarks. You can also use it to show degrees.

- $_{Subscript}$ lowers one or more characters below others, as in chemical symbols like H_2O.

You can also enlarge and reduce the size of text one point size at a time through the Text menu commands or by using the following function keys:

- Enlarge Size—Press F2 or choose Text, Enlarge to enlarge text by one point size. Pressing F2 repeatedly makes the text repeatedly larger.

- $_{Reduce\ Size}$—Press Shift+F2 or choose Text, Reduce Size to reduce text by one point size. Pressing Shift+F2 repeatedly makes the text smaller.

You can also change fonts and font sizes quickly by clicking the font name or font size portions of the status bar at the bottom of the Notes window. The font types and sizes available will appear as a pop-up list when you choose the status bar option (see fig. 7.6).

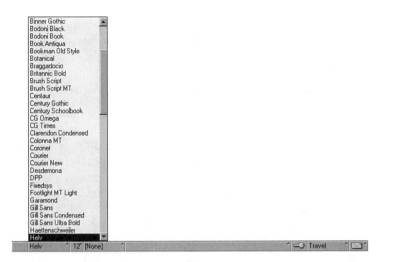

Fig. 7.6

You can quickly change the font and size using the status bar options.

Working with Strikethrough. The Text Properties InfoBox offers a selection called strikethrough, which is very useful, but often overlooked, if you are responsible for editing someone else's documents. For example, if you are reviewing a memo listing the anticipated price on a contract, and you determine that the dollar amount is incorrect, you can simply change it and then save the document. However, this does not leave a "flag" to let the author easily know what has been changed in the document. You can, however, strike through the original figure (and even make the change red), and then enter the new figure to the right of the entry (see fig. 7.7). The author can then review the changes and delete the strikethrough if in agreement.

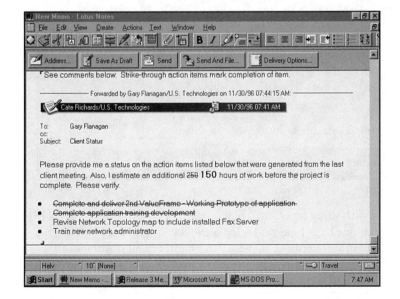

Fig. 7.7

Using the strikethrough command helps you highlight changes you have made to a document.

Another use for the strikethrough feature is in "To-Do" lists in documents. You can use the strikethrough to indicate to others who read the document that an item in the list has been completed, or to indicate edits made to a document (like all of the changes the editors of this book have requested during author review). An example of this application of the strikethrough feature appears in figure 7.7 as well.

Working with Font Attributes. Avoid using characteristics that you cannot print if you are unsure of the audience that is reading the document. You can choose different colors for your text, for example, but most people don't own color printers and thus cannot print in color. Although using color to add pizzazz and emphasis to your document isn't wrong, don't depend solely on the color to convey crucial information. You shouldn't include an instruction that says *All steps in red are mandatory*, for example, because some people may print your document and cannot tell from the printed copy which text was originally red. Similarly, laptop users often have a monochrome display and cannot easily differentiate colors—particularly those colors in the lighter shades. In cases like these, you may want to use font size or bold text to convey your message. These will print, and display on monochrome screens.

Figure 7.8 shows a sample document that uses several different text styles.

Fig. 7.8

You can highlight your text by using different types of styles.

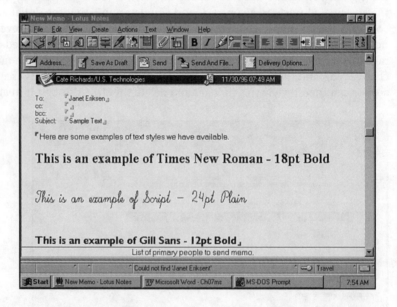

Don't get carried away with using typefaces, color, sizes, and other attention-grabbing characteristics. Bright colors, large type, and attributes such as boldface and italic are meant to emphasize and draw attention. If every paragraph in your document is a different color, size, and style, you may have created a work of abstract art, but you will give your reader a headache trying to find the important parts of the document.

You may find that responding to another user's message by using the Text options is helpful. For example, in figure 7.9, Larry Cook received a memo from Kelly Sloan requesting some information on an upcoming meeting. Larry chose Actions, Forward (or the Forward button in the mail database, as discussed in Chapter 3, "Using Databases") to return the message to Kelly, indicating his responses in bold and red. Kelly then elected to respond further by forwarding the memo back to Larry again, typing her response using a different font attribute. This technique allows individuals to respond to each other's questions while leaving the question in the memo for easy reference. At the end of the "discussion," Larry and Kelly only have to reference the last memo if they want to review all of the material at a later date.

Paragraph Justification Settings. As with any good word processor, you can set margins if you want part or all of your document to have margins different than the one inch default. You can also use tabs to indent text to predefined positions that you select. The following sections explain how to set margins.

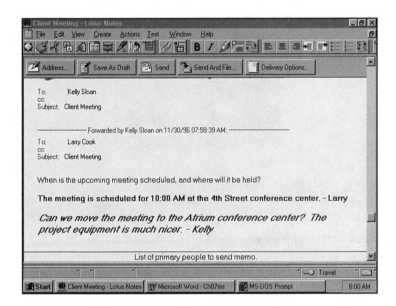

Fig. 7.9

You can use text formatting options to help you communicate with others in a forwarded message.

Although some characteristics, such as type style or size, can apply to any portion of text, other characteristics, such as justification, apply only to whole paragraphs—that is, a section of text that ends with a carriage return. You cannot have part of a paragraph with one kind of justification while another part of the same paragraph has a different type. If you change the justification of *any* portion of a paragraph, the whole paragraph changes.

For these paragraph-only characteristics, Notes provides a shortcut. If you want to adjust a characteristic for a single existing paragraph, you don't have to select the paragraph; just place the insertion point anywhere within that paragraph. Then from the Alignment tab in the Text Properties InfoBox, choose the characteristic you want to adjust. If you want to adjust more than one paragraph, however, you must select the paragraphs as you do any section of text.

To change the attributes for paragraphs, you can open the Text Properties InfoBox by choosing Text, Text Properties, or the menu commands and bullets as described in Table 7.2. To set paragraph alignment, bullet lists, number lists, margin settings, and line spacing, click the Alignment tab (see fig. 7.10). The following selections are available:

- Alignment
- First line
- List
- Left margin
- Spacing

Fig. 7.10

You can change paragraph settings in the Text Properties Alignment InfoBox.

Alignment. Alignment controls how each line of text is aligned along the left and right margins. To set alignment, select the text alignment icon in the InfoBox representing the type of alignment you want to use. The types of alignment are as follows:

- **Left Alignment**—Notes aligns each line of text at the left margin. This style— the same type you see in typewritten text—is especially appropriate for memos. Because the text isn't aligned along the right margin, the right side of the text has a staggered appearance; as a result, this style of alignment sometimes is known as *ragged right*.

- **Center Alignment**—Notes centers text between the left and right margins. You may want to use this kind of alignment for headings.

- **Right Alignment**—Right alignment causes Notes to align each line against the right margin, but not the left, resulting in a ragged left paragraph. This is beneficial if you are trying to align numbers, particularly in column design, but otherwise, this alignment option tends to have little use for the average user.

- **Full Alignment**—Notes aligns each full line of text along the left and right margins. By adding tiny amounts of space almost imperceptibly between words, Notes manages to make each line exactly the same length. For partial lines, such as those at the end of a paragraph, Notes aligns only the left margin.

Newspapers and many books use this type of alignment, which tends to give your document a more professional, pleasing appearance. Many people dislike editing a document with full alignment, however, because Notes' constant changing of the spacing between words during editing distracts them.

■ **None**—Notes displays each paragraph as a single long line. If a paragraph is longer than Notes can display on the screen, you must use the scroll bars or left and right arrow keys to view the rest of the line.

> **Tip**
>
> If you need to edit text that has been fully aligned, you can change the alignment to left align-ment, edit the text, and then change the alignment back to full. This will make it easier for you to edit the paragraph as you won't have to work around Notes' continuous adjustment of the font alignment as you are editing.
>
> You can also set alignment by using the SmartIcons.

First Line Settings (Indent/Outdent). The First Line group of icons tells Notes how to treat the first line of text in a paragraph. You use these settings to indent or outdent the paragraph as the following list describes:

■ **Standard**—Notes does not indent or outdent the paragraph; rather, Notes aligns the first line of text with the rest of the paragraph alignment setting.

■ **Indent**—To indent the first line of the paragraph, select the Indent button and then type in the amount you want to indent the text in the text box that appears to the right. The default setting is .25".

■ **Outdent**—To outdent the first line of the paragraph, click the Outdent button and then type in the amount you want to outdent the text in the text box that appears to the right. The default setting is .25".

You can see an example of these settings in figure 7.11.

Bullets and Numbers. Notes will automatically indent and insert bullets and numbers in documents when you select the Bullets and Numbers buttons in the List section of this tab.

You may also insert bullets and numbers by selecting Text, Bullets and Text, Numbers as needed from the menu command list (see fig. 7.12).

> **Tip**
>
> Select the bullet or number styles prior to typing your text. This will make entering text easier because Notes will automatically add the next bullet, or next consecutive number in the list, while you are typing so that you can keep your thoughts organized as you work.

Fig. 7.11

You can add pizzazz to your documents by indenting or outdenting paragraphs.

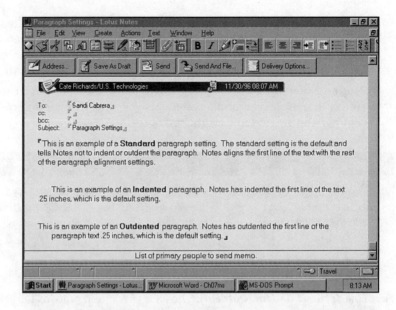

Fig. 7.12

You can add impact (and sometimes fun) in your documents by using the bullet and numbering features.

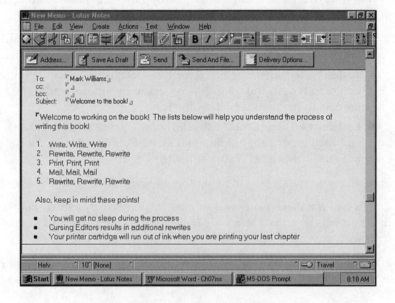

Setting the Left Margin. Enter the left margin setting for the paragraph. You can use whole numbers and decimals to indicate your setting. The standard paragraph left margin setting is 1". The maximum limit for this setting is 22.75"—but you should take care to ensure that the margins are displayed on-screen so that readers of the document are able to see the paragraph.

> **Tip**
>
> You can set margins for a hotspot, button, attachment, or object by highlighting the special item and selecting Edit, Properties. (Notes sets margins for the paragraph that contains the item.) You will learn more about these features in Chapter 8, "Working with Documents."

You can select the Top, Bottom, Left, and Right margin settings for the entire document by choosing File, Page Setup. The Page Setup dialog box appears. Here is where you can alter global document settings. You learn about these settings in Chapter 8, "Working with Documents."

Line Spacing. The spacing options in Notes control the amount of spacing between paragraphs and between the lines of text in a paragraph. The following selections are available:

- **Interline**—How many blank lines Notes inserts between lines within each paragraph.
- **Above**—How many blank lines Notes inserts before each paragraph.
- **Below**—How many blank lines Notes inserts after each paragraph.

When clicking the down arrow next to each of these options, Notes displays a selection list asking for the number of blank lines. Notes uses the same type of notation you may have encountered when adjusting the spacing setting on a typewriter:

- Single (no extra blank space)
- $1\,^1/_2$ (half a line's worth of blank space)
- Double (a full line's worth of blank space)

If you choose Below and then Double, for example, an extra line of blank space follows each paragraph.

> **Caution**
>
> Be mindful that if you select options for both Above and Below for a paragraph, you may be left with up to four lines between paragraphs. If this is not your intention, pick one option or the other.

Pages/Tabs Settings. As you work with Notes, you will have some instances when you want to set the pagination so that Notes inserts a page break where you want it rather than when Notes fills up a page with text. You may also want to adjust tab settings and set the right margin for printing purposes. To perform any of these functions, highlight the paragraph you want to "control" and then open the Text Properties InfoBox. Click the Pages/Tabs tab so that it appears (see fig. 7.13).

Fig. 7.13

The Pages/Tab section of the Text Properties InfoBox lets you specify settings that affect your document when it is printed.

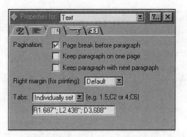

Setting Pagination. The first section on the tab controls pagination. In this section, you can specify the following:

■ **Page Break before Paragraph**—Notes inserts a page break before the selected paragraph. This setting is ideal if you want to insert a page break to ensure that a particular paragraph is printed at the top of the following page. For example, you are writing sections within a proposal document, and you want the heading of each section to begin at the top of a page.

This setting can also be used with your e-mail if you want to print the body of the memo but do not want to include the To, From, Date, and Subject fields. Place your cursor on the first line in the body of the memo, and then select this option. Notes prints the address information on one page, and the remainder of the memo starts at the top of the second page.

■ **Keep Paragraph on One Page**—Notes keeps the lines of text highlighted together when printing. Notes breaks the page either before or after the selected paragraph but not within the text. This is ideal if a user wants to make sure that an entire paragraph prints on the same page to make reading easier.

■ **Keep Paragraph with Next Paragraph**—Notes keeps the selected paragraph on the same page as the following paragraph. Notes breaks the page before the selected paragraph if it does not fit on the same page as the following paragraph. This is ideal for users who are providing an example and want the descriptive paragraph below the example to print on the same page.

Tip

You can also set a page break by pressing Ctrl+L or choosing Create, Page Break. The Ctrl+L option acts as a toggle for setting page breaks; pressing Ctrl+L once will enter a page break, while pressing Ctrl+L again will remove the page break.

A line appears across the page to indicate any page breaks that you specify.

Removing a Page Break. If you decide that you want to remove a page break before a paragraph, place your cursor in the first line of the paragraph immediately following the page break and choose Create, Page Break. Notes will remove the page break. You can also use the Ctrl+L keyboard commands to remove a page break, as mentioned in the previous tip.

Setting the Right Margin for Printing. Use the Right Margin (for Printing) field to specify the right margin. This option applies only to the printed document; the right side of the screen is always the right margin when you display a document, so make sure that you specify this setting based on the paper size. Keep in mind that many printers, (like lasers) will not print any closer than 1/4 of an inch from the edge of the paper—regardless of the margin you specify.

Setting Tabs. You can set tab spacing for your text by using the Page/Tab settings in the Text Properties InfoBox. You can set tab stops for one or more paragraphs by entering specific tab stops in the text entry box provided. Setting tab stops is a two-step process. You must first indicate how you want the tab stops to be set, and then specify the factor Notes will use in setting the tab. Follow these steps to set tabs:

1. Select the down arrow next to the Tabs text box. You have two options to choose from:

- **Individually Set**—This lets you enter the places you want tab stops to occur. You can enter numbers in inches or centimeters (for example, .5" or .5 cm). If you enter more than one tab stop, separate them with semicolons (for example, .5"; 1.35"; 4")

- **Evenly Spaced**—Notes evenly spaces tab stops, based on an interval setting you provide. For example, you can tell Notes to set a tab stop every .45".

There are four types of Tab stops in Notes that can be set by typing their corresponding letter before the tab stop, or by using the mouse to set the tab stop using the ruler (see "Setting Margins and Tabs with the Ruler" later in this chapter for more information on using the mouse.) The following list describes the type of tab stop, its corresponding letter, and the corresponding tab indicator that is displayed in the ruler:

- Right—This is represented by the letter *R* before the Tab stop in the Tabs entry box. Right tabs cause text to be aligned flush right at the tab stop. You often use this setting if you are trying to align currency values.

- Left—This is represented by the letter *L* before the Tab stop in the Tabs entry box. Left tabs cause text to be aligned flush left at the tab stop. You often use this as the standard tab entry.

- Decimal—This is represented by the letter *D* before the Tab stop in the Tabs entry box. Decimal tabs cause text to be aligned according to the decimal point location in the text. This setting is ideal if you are trying to align numbers in a list.

- Center—This is represented by the letter *C* before the Tab stop in the Tabs entry box. Center tabs cause the text to be centered on both sides of the tab stop. This option is ideal if you are trying to display a list of items to a reader.

2. Once you have made your Tabs type selection, specify the interval for the tab settings. If you are individually specifying the tab stops, type in the exact location for each tab, using semicolons to separate multiple entries. If you are telling Notes to evenly space the tab stops, type in the interval space between each tab setting.

> **Note**
>
> You do not have to enter semicolons to separate multiple entries (as illustrated in the following example). If there is a space between the number settings, Notes will insert the semicolon when you save your selections. However, inserting the semicolon helps delineate the individual tab stops when you review your settings—decreasing the chance of you "running" your numbers together and ending up with an incorrect setting.

You have flexibility when setting tab stops. To set tabs at 1.5, 2, and 4 inches, for example, type the following:

1.5 2 4

You don't need to type the quotation mark (or double prime, ") after the number; Notes adds it to all numbers that represent inches.

> **Note**
>
> Notes always displays the current tabs in this box using semicolons, even if you entered the tabs using spaces.

If you prefer to measure a specific tab stop in centimeters, you can type **cm** after a number. For example:

1 2.3 10cm 15cm 6

In this example, Notes will set five tabs. The 1, 2.3, and 6 represent inches, but the 10 and 15 represent centimeters.

If you have chosen Metric measurements as your default measurement (see Chapter 2, "Customizing Notes"), Notes assumes that all measurements you enter are in centimeters unless you enter a double prime (") to indicate that a measurement is in inches. If you have your default set to Metric and set tabs at the following positions:

10 20 6"

Notes sets a tab at 10 and 20 centimeters and at 6 inches.

After you set tabs, you can press Tab to move to the next tab stop in your document. If the insertion point is already past the last tab stop, pressing Tab causes Notes to beep and produces an error message.

Hiding Text. Notes allows you to hide text within a document during particular functions. While this feature is typically used by database designers when designing the forms that will be used, it is discussed briefly here. You will find more information on hiding fields in the database design chapters in Chapter 10, "Designing Forms."

With the Text Properties InfoBox open, click the Hide tab. The Hide tab appears as displayed in figure 7.14.

Fig. 7.14

You can hide text in documents depending on how you are working with the document. You make the hide-when selections in the Hide tab of the Text Properties InfoBox.

Notes provides the following options:

- **Previewed for Reading**—The hidden information isn't visible when users read documents in the preview pane. Users can, however, read the text if they open the document for reading, or have Editor level access and place the document in edit mode from the preview pane—unless additional restrictions are selected as described later.

- **Opened for Reading**—This option hides any text selected when users open a document to read it. Users can, however, read the text if they have editor-level access and place the document in edit mode—unless additional restrictions are selected as described later. This option is ideal in designing documents if the designer wants to provide instructions on completing a field when a user is composing a document but doesn't want the user to be bothered with the instructions when reading the document.

- **Printed**—This tells Notes to print everything but the highlighted text. You can use this option when you want to omit portions of sensitive text when printing a document for someone else to read or otherwise limit the text that prints.

- **Previewed for Editing**—This option lets readers of the document see the text when reading (unless additional restrictions are selected) but not when composing or editing a document when they are viewing the document in the preview pane.

- **Opened for Editing**—This option allows readers of the document to see the text when reading a document (unless additional restrictions are selected) but not when composing or editing a document. This option is usually used by designers who have fields displaying information in a format that is different than when the document is composed. For example, the user selects a keyword series that identifies the product name, price, and catalog number while composing a document, which is easier than having to make three separate selections in three separate fields. The database designer, however, elects to hide that keyword field when someone is reading the document and sets up separate fields to display this information for ease of reading and editing at a later date.

■ **Copied to the Clipboard**—This tells Notes to ignore this text when copying text to and from the Clipboard. It is a handy command when you want to copy all but a part of a document or when the database designer has set security in the fields that should not be overridden if a text is copied to the Clipboard. This setting also affects text when a document is forwarded from a database—the text marked for hiding will not appear in a message forwarded from the database. This setting does not affect entire documents that are copied and pasted at the view level.

■ **Hide Paragraph if Formula Is True**—By entering a qualifying formula in the Formula window, the database designers can set conditions for when the text is hidden. For example, if a designer wants only the author of the document to be able to see the text in the field, then an author formula can be written to provide this criteria for viewing the text. You will learn more about writing formulas in Chapters 13 and 14.

Styles Settings. You can define and save combinations of paragraph and text properties that you use regularly as *named paragraph styles*. This is a handy way of defining particular styles that you use frequently so that you do not have to continuously set the attributes individually through the Text Properties InfoBox. To set up a named paragraph style, follow these steps:

1. Place the document you are working on in edit mode by double-clicking anywhere within the document.

2. Select a paragraph and make all of the attribute settings you want. This is the paragraph style that you will save in the following steps. For example, if you want to create a style to use as a response to other memos in which the text is indented, bold, and red, create these settings for the existing paragraph.

3. Select Text, Text Properties, and then click the Style tab. The Style tab appears (see fig. 7.15).

Fig. 7.15

You can create Styles that can be reused by highlighting a paragraph whose style you want to copy, and then opening the Style tab of the Text Properties InfoBox.

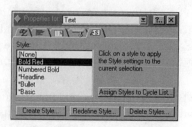

4. Select Create Style. The Create Named Style dialog box appears (see fig. 7.16).

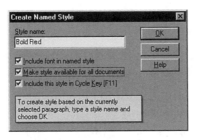

Fig. 7.16

Provide descriptive names in the Create Named Style dialog box to make it easier to remember what the style is used for.

5. Enter a name for the paragraph style in the Style name text box. For example, name the style **Bold Red Response**.

6. Check Include font in named style, which is the default, if you want to include all font settings as well as paragraph settings.

7. Check Make style available for all documents if you want to have this style setting available regardless of the document you are working in. Selecting this option adds the style name to the status bar pop-up selection list at the bottom of the Notes window.

8. Check Include this style in Cycle Key [F11] if you want this style to appear when you cycle through the available styles with the F11 key.

9. Select OK.

Once you have defined the style name, you may highlight a paragraph and select the setting by returning to the Text Properties Style tab or by selecting Text, Named Styles, and then clicking the name of the style you want to apply. If you elected to display the style when pressing F11 to view the cycle key, you will be able to select the style through those options as well. You can also select styles by clicking the Styles option on the status bar to display the list of currently defined styles, as shown in figure 7.17.

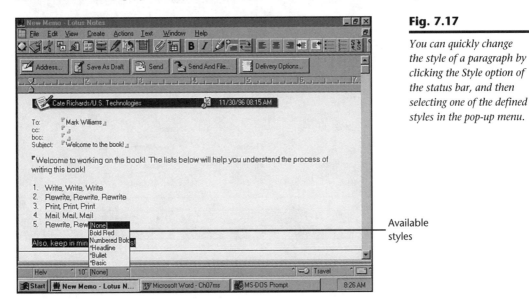

Fig. 7.17

You can quickly change the style of a paragraph by clicking the Style option of the status bar, and then selecting one of the defined styles in the pop-up menu.

Available styles

Notes R4 predefines the following three styles for you that can be selected from the Text, Named Styles menu:

- Headline—This displays the selected text in bold, purple, Helvetica 12pt font.
- Bullet—This displays the selected font in bullet style.
- Basic—This changes the selected font size to Helvetica 10pt, but maintains any other text formatting options previously defined.

You can use the Redefine Style button in the Text Properties InfoBox to redefine a named style based on the current paragraph selection, or you may want to "clean house" periodically and get rid of old styles by pressing the Delete Styles button and then selecting the style to delete.

Setting Margins and Tabs with the Ruler

Notes provides two methods for indicating how you want to set the margins and tabs: you can access the Text Properties InfoBox as discussed earlier in this chapter or use the ruler. Whether you use the ruler method for setting margins and tabs or the Text Properties InfoBox, you may want to have the ruler present to guide you in making your settings.

Displaying the Ruler. When controlling margins and tabs, you may find displaying the Notes ruler helpful. The Notes *ruler* is a bar near the top of the screen marked off in inches like a ruler but with special marks indicating your margins and tab settings (see fig. 7.18). The ruler helps you visualize distances in your document and provides a simple means for setting margins and tabs.

Fig. 7.18

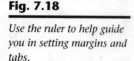

Use the ruler to help guide you in setting margins and tabs.

Ruler ———

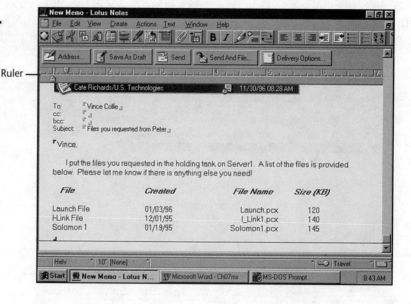

To display the ruler, choose <u>V</u>iew, <u>R</u>uler (or select the View Ruler SmartIcon if it is present in your current SmartIcon group). Along with measuring the document in inches, the ruler shows margins and tabs. Notes displays tabs as arrows pointing up, and the left margin as a pentagon arrow. Choosing <u>V</u>iew, <u>R</u>uler again causes the ruler to disappear.

◄◄ See "Changing the Unit of Measurement" p. xxx (Ch 2)

Note

Table column settings are represented in the ruler by a market that looks like a T. You will learn more about creating tables in Chapter 8, "Working with Documents."

In addition to changing margins, you can use the ruler to set tabs, as explained in the next section.

Setting Margins and Tabs with the Ruler. To change the left margin of the first line using the ruler, click the top pentagon arrow, and drag it to its new location. If you want to adjust the left margin of the paragraph to indicate a setting other than the one set for the first line, click the bottom pentagon arrow, and drag the bottom portion of the arrow to a new location.

By specifying a different left margin for the first line and all other lines, you can create the paragraph styles shown in figure 7.19.

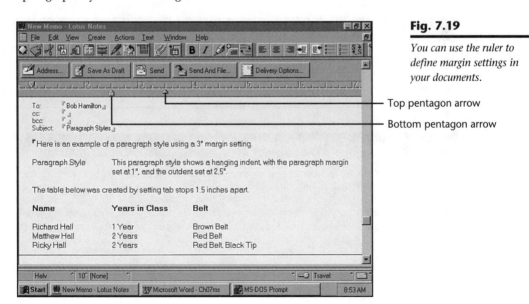

Fig. 7.19

You can use the ruler to define margin settings in your documents.

— Top pentagon arrow

— Bottom pentagon arrow

Notes Basics

You can also set tabs using the ruler. Display the ruler if it isn't showing, and then select the paragraphs you want to change. You can then change the position of a margin by dragging the corresponding triangle to a new position. Recall that the upward pointing triangles are tabs. Figure 7.20 shows all four types of tabs you can define.

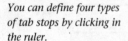

Fig. 7.20

You can define four types of tab stops by clicking in the ruler.

To set a new tab, place the mouse pointer on the ruler at an empty position and click. A tab arrow appears to mark the tab stop. To change the tab setting, click and drag the corresponding tab arrow to a new position and release the mouse button. To clear an existing tab, click the corresponding tab arrow.

As discussed earlier, you can place four types of tabs in your documents. To place these tabs using the ruler, perform one of the following:

- **Left tab**—Left click at the tab location.
- **Right tab**—Right click at the tab location.
- **Center tab**—Shift+right click at the tab location.
- **Decimal tab**—Shift+left click at the tab location.

(Refer to figure 7.20 for examples of each of these tab settings.)

> **Note**
>
> Setting margins and tabs by using the ruler is one of the few Notes operations that require a mouse; there are no corresponding hot keys. If you don't have a mouse, you must choose Text, Properties and use the Pages/Tabs pane of the InfoBox to set margins and tabs.

Setting Margins Fast with the Keyboard

Notes provides several keystrokes for quickly changing margins. After selecting the paragraphs you want to affect, you can do the following:

- Press F7 to indent the first line by a quarter of an inch. By pressing this key several times, you can indent the first line by any multiple of a quarter of an inch. Press Shift+F7 to unindent the first line by a quarter of an inch.

- Press F8 to indent every line by a quarter of an inch. Shift+F8 unindents every line by a quarter of an inch.

You can create a hanging indent (that is, paragraphs in which the first line is further to the left than the other lines) by indenting all lines one or more times by pressing F8 and then unindenting the first line by pressing F7.

Working with the Permanent Pen

The Permanent Pen option lets you use revision marking to quickly add comments that stand out in a document. When you use the Permanent Pen, you don't have to reset the font every time you move somewhere different in the document. For example, if you are answering questions in a document and want to write all of your answers in bold, red font, you can set up your Permanent Pen to use these font attributes. Then you can type text in multiple places in the document without having to redefine the font attributes each time you move to a new location.

Before you use your Permanent Pen, you may want to change the font attributes. To do so, select Text, Properties, and select the font, size, style, and color you want to assign to the Permanent Pen in the Text Properties InfoBox. Once you have made your settings, press the Set Permanent Pen font button to save your selections.

To use the Permanent Pen, use the following steps:

1. Select Text, Permanent Pen.
2. Click once at the beginning of the section you want to add a comment.
3. Type your text. The text you type will be in the style, size, and color you specified for the Permanent Pen.
4. Reposition your cursor in the next position where you want to use the Permanent Pen and type your comments.
5. Continue using the Permanent Pen until you have completed all of your comments.
6. Reselect the Permanent Pen by selecting Text, Permanent Pen to disable this option.

Note

If you want to change the font characteristics for the Permanent Pen, choose Text, Text Properties. In the Text Properties InfoBox, make all of the necessary font, size, style, and color selections you want to use and then select the Set Permanent Pen font button. Notes will redefine the Permanent Pen font characteristics until you repeat this process again.

Using Special Characters

Occasionally, you may have to use special characters that don't appear on your keyboard, such as currency, copyright, and trademark symbols or other special characters. Notes lets you enter hundreds of special characters into a document by pressing special key combinations.

To type a special character, press Alt+F1 followed by the code that represents the special character. Each code, consisting of one or two keys, is selected to remind you of the special character. To type the symbol for the Japanese yen (¥), for example, press Alt+F1, Y, =. Appendix D, "Special Characters," lists more characters available.

Using this feature, you can enter letters that belong to non-English alphabets, enter fractions, international currency designations, and so on.

> **Note**
>
> Not all printers can print all special characters, and Notes may have to drop some special characters when printing documents. In particular, most daisywheel printers are limited in their selection of characters. Keep this limitation in mind when composing documents if you are sharing information with people who use older printers or daisywheel printers.

From Here...

In this chapter, you learned how to create attractive documents by using different colors, text styles, margins, and other text characteristics. In the next chapter, you learn even more Notes features that will add pizzazz and increase functionality when you learn about working with documents.

For more information on some of the topics discussed in this chapter, refer to the following:

■ Chapter 2, "Customizing Notes," shows how to change your ruler's units of measurement.

■ Chapter 4, "Getting Started with Electronic Mail," teaches you how to work with Lotus NotesMail and the mail forward feature.

■ Chapter 10, "Designing Forms," explains how to create hidden fields based on formulas, and further utilizes the text attributes described in this section.

CHAPTER 8

Working with Documents

Lotus Notes 4 has a wide variety of features that help make it a robust environment for communicating with others. These features can be added, or applied, directly to a rich text field within a document that has already been designed. Some of these features, as you will learn in this chapter, can also be built into the design of the database forms. In Chapter 7, "Working with Text," you learned how to use text to enhance your use of Lotus Notes. This chapter covers features that enable you to use the power of Notes to enhance your documents.

In this chapter, you learn how to do the following:

- Use Spell Check
- Search for text and phrases
- Work with unread marks
- Copy and paste documents
- Insert objects, such as links, hotspots, and tables, into your documents
- Insert sections into your documents
- Use folders to organize your documents

Checking Your Spelling

No matter how professional your document appears or how insightful your message, you will not impress readers if misspellings litter your document. And if you are like many who have used word processing software for quite some time, your ability to spell even the simplest words has somehow disappeared! Notes includes a spelling checker that looks for misspelled words and other common mistakes.

> **Tip**
>
> As discussed in "International Settings" in Chapter 2, "Customizing Notes," you can select from one of 28 dictionaries by selecting File, Tools, User Preferences, clicking the International icon, and then selecting the Spelling Dictionary button.
>
> Switching from one dictionary to another is a big plus in organizations that work internationally. A proposal can be written in the U.S., for example, forwarded to the U.K., and spell checked there using the British (ise) dictionary to pick up on differences in spelling between the two countries. (For example, *organization* is spelled *organisation,* with an *s* instead of a *z,* in the U.K.)

To check the spelling of a document, position the insertion point at the top of the document. Then choose Edit, Check Spelling. If Notes finds a misspelled word or detects some other irregularity that it regards as a mistake, it displays the dialog box shown in figure 8.1. In this example, the word *developed* was misspelled.

Fig. 8.1

Use Check Spelling to find misspelled words and other common errors in documents.

> **Tip**
>
> You can check the spelling of just one word or a group of words without having to check the spelling of the entire document. To do so, highlight the word(s) and then select Edit, Check Spelling.

At the bottom of the dialog box you will see the Status field that will tell you the problem Notes finds with each word or phrase it highlights. For example, in figure 8.1, the Status field displays Unknown Word. (That is, the word isn't one that Notes recognizes as correctly spelled.) The offending word is highlighted within your document and displayed in the Replace text box. At this point you must decide what to do among the following options:

- If the word is misspelled, as in the example here, you can fix the word in the Replace box and then choose Replace. Notes replaces the misspelled word in the document with the fixed word. If you misspelled the same word in the same way elsewhere in the document, Notes fixes only the word in one location at a time and will ask you what to do each time it encounters the misspelled word.

- If you agree that the word is misspelled but don't know how to spell it correctly, you can view the guesses that Notes makes. Notes searches its dictionary for words similar to the misspelled word and displays them in the Guess list box. Figure 8.1 shows the guesses Notes produced for *developped*.

Often, the first word in the Guess list box is the correct spelling, and in this example, Notes guessed the correct spelling as *developed*. Select the correctly spelled guess and then choose Replace. Alternatively, you can double-click the correctly spelled word. Notes replaces the misspelled word in the document with the correctly spelled word.

> **Note**
>
> Notes cannot always guess the correct spelling. If too many letters are wrong or if you transpose letters, Notes may not be able to produce with the correct word.

- You may want to prompt Notes to accept an incorrectly spelled word or phrase deliberately. For example, if you intentionally misspell a word or phrase, such as *Ye Ol' Shoppe,* but you want Notes to point out similar misspellings later that may be unintentional, then you can choose Skip to skip just this one incidence of the spelling, or Skip All to always skip this misspelling during this spell checking session.

  This feature is most useful for acronyms and names or technical words that occur several times throughout the document that you know are correct, but you don't want to add to your dictionary.

- If you know the word is spelled correctly and is a word you use often, choose Define. Notes adds the word to your personal dictionary so that Notes will consider the word valid any time you check spelling in the future, whether in this document or another. This feature is most useful for technical terms or proper names that you use often.

- If you want to exit Spell Checking before Notes prompts you that it is completed, select the Done button. Notes will halt the spell checking process at that point and return you to your document.

> **Note**
>
> Words that you define during spell checking sessions are entered into your personal dictionary (USER.DIC). For more information on adding or removing words to or from your personal dictionary, refer to "Changing the User Dictionary" in Chapter 2, "Customizing Notes."

Along with catching misspelled words, Notes watches for other common errors, such as unusual capitalization and repeated words (such as *I saw the the dog*). As with misspelled words, you can tell Notes to ignore the problem, or you can tell Notes how to fix it.

After Notes displays all the questionable words, it displays a final dialog box telling you that spelling is complete. Choose OK to close this dialog box.

> **Caution**
>
> Although the spelling checker is a wonderful aid for producing error-free documents, it cannot replace proofreading. The spelling checker cannot catch grammatical errors or incorrectly used words. Worst of all, it doesn't catch words that you misspell if they happen to be different words that are spelled correctly. For example, if you meant to write *I hear that we have hired ten new people,* but mistakenly omit the *a* in *hear,* Notes will not catch the resulting *her* as a misspelled word. Likewise, if you spelled the word *here,* Notes won't see it as an error, even though it's not the correct usage.

Searching for Text

No good word processor is complete without the capability to locate text wherever it occurs within a document. Notes includes features to enable you to search for text strings and replace one phrase with another. Notes also enables you to search entire databases for text strings, so you can quickly locate documents that relate to the same topic in some manner. Notes contains several ways to search for information in databases. If the database has a full text index, you can do more advanced searches than if the database does not. All Notes databases provide the following capabilities:

- You can search for text in a document that you are reading. If your document is in edit mode, you can also elect to replace the text you find with new text.

- You can search for text in document titles that appear in a particular view. Notes will find and highlight the first document in a view whose title matches your word or phrase.

- You can find all documents that contain a word or phrase anywhere in the document. Using this search method will show the documents in the view, with a checkmark placed next to them. However, the words within the document that match the search criteria will not be highlighted—as they will be if the database is indexed for full text search as described below.

If a database has a full text index, you can enhance the capabilities of your search, as follows:

- You can find all documents that contain a word or phrase anywhere in the document—and have Notes outline the search words with red boxes in the document to highlight them.

- You can use the Search Builder feature to help you quickly create search formulas to find documents.

- You can save search formulas to reuse at a later date.

- You can define your search in the following ways:
  - Make your search case-sensitive
  - Include synonyms of search words
  - Search for words that are located near each other in a document

- Include variations of the same word in your search
- Customize the way your search results are displayed
- Search for documents in multiple databases at the same time

In the following sections, you will learn about all of these features.

Performing General Searches for Text

This section will walk you through searches you can perform whether your database is indexed or not. As you will see, the general search capabilities on any database are pretty powerful!

Searching for Text in a Document You Are Reading. Notes makes it simple to find (and replace if you're in edit mode) a word or phrase in a document. You can search for a word or phrase anywhere within a field by choosing Edit, Find/Replace. Notes displays the Find and Replace dialog box (see fig. 8.2). In the Find and Replace text boxes, enter the word or phrase you want to find.

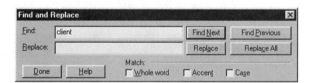

Fig. 8.2

Finding and replacing text is easy when you use the Find and Replace feature in Notes.

Tip

If the phrase you want to find or replace is now on-screen, you can select the phrase so that it appears as the phrase to find when you perform a find or replace operation. Suppose that on-screen you now see a paragraph discussing money market funds and you want to find other places in the document that also discuss them. Select the phrase "money market fund," and when you choose Edit, Find and Replace (or Edit, Find Next), the phrase "money market fund" already appears in the phrase to find.

After you enter the search phrase (if different from the one Notes displays), you can choose any of the following checkbox options in the Match section of the dialog box to change the way Notes performs its search:

- **Whole Word**—Normally Notes looks for the search phrase without regard to word boundaries. If you ask Notes to find *cat,* for example, it stops not only on the word *cat,* but also on *scat* and *catalog* because they both contain the letters *cat.* If you are searching for especially short phrases, however, you can choose Whole Word to tell Notes that you are interested only in the word *cat*, not these three letters within any word.

- **Accent**—Normally when Notes searches text, it ignores diacritical marks for the purposes of finding phrases. If you choose this option, Notes considers diacritical marks when searching for text. Suppose that you are writing a document that includes the name *Björn*. If you want to search for this word and you don't check Accent, Notes finds the word if you enter only *Bjorn*. If you check Accent, however, Notes will find only *Björn* if you enter it with its umlaut. (See "Using Special Characters" in Chapter 7, "Working with Text," for information about entering special characters.)

- **Case**—If you choose this option, Notes looks only for phrases capitalized exactly the way you typed the search phrase. During a search for *cat*, for example, Notes won't stop on *Cat* or *CAT*.

Choose Find Next to begin the search. Notes searches for the phrase from the current insertion point position and repositions the insertion point on the next occurrence of the phrase. If Notes reaches the end of the document without finding the phrase, it displays a dialog box telling you that it cannot find the phrase.

Often, the first occurrence of your phrase that Notes finds isn't the one you want. Choose Edit, Find Next, or press Ctrl+G to repeat the last search. Notes searches for the same phrase, using the same combination of selected options. By pressing Ctrl+G enough times, you can find each occurrence of the phrase throughout the document.

> **Tip**
>
> You also can search for phrases that include tabs and that are separated by a hard right carriage return by typing **\t** and **\n**, respectively. (The \n stands for *new line*.) If you want to find the words *cat* and *mouse* separated by a tab, for example, enter **cat\tmouse** as the search phrase.

Replacing Text. On occasion, you may need to change a phrase that occurs several times throughout a document. For example, a particular function formerly performed by your Denver office may have been transferred to Atlanta, and you need to find all instances of *Denver* within a document and change them to *Atlanta*. You can use the Find feature to find and change each occurrence individually, but Notes provides a related feature, Replace, that makes this kind of wholesale replacement easier.

To perform a replace, you must be in edit mode. Press Ctrl+E to switch to edit mode if you're now in read mode (brackets appear around each field if you are in edit mode). Position the insertion point at the top of your document and choose Edit, Find and Replace. Notes displays the Find and Replace dialog box (see fig. 8.3).

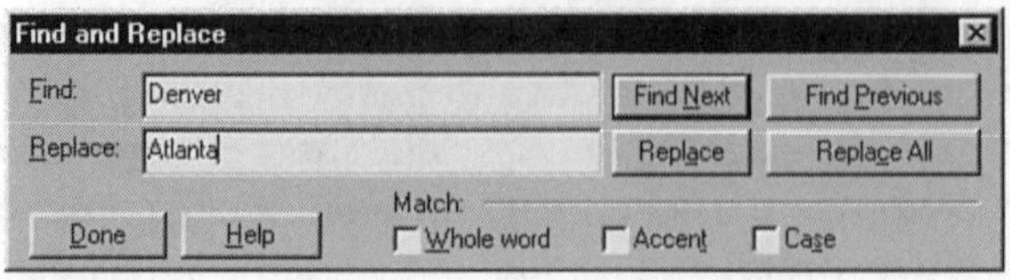

Fig. 8.3

To quickly find and replace text, use the Find and Replace dialog box—but make sure you are in edit mode first.

The Find and Replace dialog box offers exactly the same checkbox options as the Edit Find dialog box, and you use them in the same way. After you enter the phrase to find and the replacement phrase, choose any options that apply and then choose Find Next. Notes locates the first occurrence of the search phrase from the point at which your cursor was located when you began the search, highlights it, and waits for you to choose one of the following buttons:

- If you choose Find Next, Notes leaves the current occurrence of the phrase unchanged and finds the next one.
- If you choose Find Previous, Notes searches for the occurrence directly before the current one (or the cursor location if you are just beginning your search).
- If you choose Replace, Notes replaces the current occurrence with the replacement phrase.
- If you choose Replace All, Notes replaces every occurrence of the search phrase with the replacement phrase.

> **Caution**
>
> Think carefully before using Replace All. If you make a mistake, you cannot undo the operation with the Edit, Undo command. It is much too easy to make incorrect changes to your document that will take you hours to fix. If, for example, a female replaces your male personnel manager, you may want to revise a certain memo by changing *he* to *she*. If you forget to check Whole Word, however, Notes changes *other* to *otsher*, *there* to *tshere*, and similarly messes up all other words that have the letters *he* in them.

- If you choose Done, Notes stops the search, leaving the current occurrence of the search phrase as is.

> **Tip**
>
> Save your document (choose File, Save) before using Replace All. If you make an error in your editing, you can always exit the current document without saving and then reopen the document from its saved version.

Searching for Text in Document Titles. Not only can you search for a phrase within a single document, but Notes also enables you to search in other useful ways when you are looking at a view. You can search for documents within a view to have Notes highlight documents that contain your search word or phrase anywhere within view titles (any of the text showing in the views).

To perform a search within a view, complete the following steps:

1. While in a view, select Edit, Find Next. The Find dialog box appears, as shown in figure 8.4.

Fig. 8.4

To search for a word or phrase within a view, type the text you want to search for in the Find dialog box.

2. In the Find text box, type the text you want to find.

   As an option, you can select Whole word, Accent, and/or Case. (See "Searching for Text in a Document You Are Reading" earlier in this chapter for information on these features.)

3. Select Find Next or Find Previous. If you select Find Next, Notes highlights the first title that contains the text after the location of the cursor. If you click Find Previous, Notes highlights the first title that contains the text before the location of the cursor.

4. Repeat step 3 until you are through with your search for documents.

5. Click Done when you are through with your search.

Full Text Searching in Databases

Notes provides a more powerful search mechanism known as a *full text search*. By using this search feature, you can search for documents that contain several phrases rather than a specific single phrase. Perhaps you want to find documents that discuss stock prices and quarterly earnings, for example. This type of search also enables you to search an entire database or even more than one database at a time—displaying all of the documents that meet your search criteria in a view.

To use a full text search, the database must have been indexed for full text searches. The indexing process creates a special file that enables Notes to determine quickly which words or phrases a document contains. If a database isn't indexed, you can perform only limited searches by choosing Edit, Find, as previously discussed.

Indexing a Database. You can index any databases that you create on your local hard disk. Only someone with Designer access or above, however, can index a database that is shared with other individuals on a server. You can index a database in one of the two following ways:

■ Choose File, Database, Properties to bring up the Properties InfoBox. Select the Full Text tab and then select Create Index to bring up the Full Text Create Index dialog box shown in figure 8.5. This dialog box controls how the database will be indexed.

■ You can also tell Notes you want to index a database by selecting View, Search Bar while in a database that is not indexed already. Notes will open the Search Bar and provide you with a button to Create Index. If you click this button, then figure 8.5 will appear to begin the process.

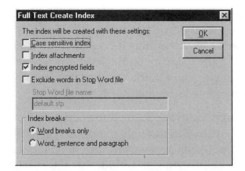

Fig. 8.5

To index a database, open the Full Text Create Index dialog box in the Database Properties Infobox.

> **Note**
>
> As you are the Manager of your E-Mail database located on the server, you can index that database if you want to. However, if your server capacity is low, indexing your mail database may overburden your server as it produces the index and keeps it updated. If your Notes administrator indicates that you should not index your mail database located on the server, then it is usually a sign that the server does not have enough memory or space.
>
> You can, however, create an Archive E-Mail database to cut and paste documents from your active database to the archive one, then index the archive database—typically stored on your hard drive. This is often preferable to Notes users, as there is less need to index the active mail databases where so many changes are taking place every day (requiring continuous updates of your index). Most often, it is older memos that you are trying to search through to find information, and this can be easily done in the archive copy of the E-Mail database.

In the Full Text Create Index dialog box, you should normally accept the default selections, as shown in figure 8.5. These selections provide you with the most compact (small) index possible. The following sections describe the indexing options.

Case Sensitivity. The Case Sensitive Index option enables you to indicate whether you want Notes to distinguish between upper- and lowercase letters. For example, it will treat *cat*, *Cat*, and *CAT* as different entries. If this is unnecessary, which is usually the case, then don't select this option—it can greatly increase the size of the index and may exclude documents that you really wanted to find. Use this option only if case-sensitive searches are required—like if you index a database full of C programming concepts and structures.

Indexing Attachments. The Index Attachments option enables you to indicate whether you want Notes to index any attachments containing text that are inserted in a document. If you select this option, you will be able to search the database for words or phrases stored in Notes documents and any files attached to the documents. For example, if you attached a Word Pro document to a document stored in a database that maintains this selection in its indexing setup, you will be able to search the Notes text and the Word Pro text when you query the database. Choosing this option, however, may significantly increase the length of time it takes to index the database as well as the amount of space the index takes up on the hard drive. Notes is also unable to highlight the words in the search phrase in the attached document. Instead, it highlights the attachment icon in the document.

Indexing Encrypted Fields. If you want to include text in encrypted fields in a full text index, choose Index Encrypted Fields. You can only index encrypted fields if you have the appropriate encryption key, and only people with the encryption key can search the fields. Using this option increases the size of an index by the number of encrypted fields in a database and the amount of text they contain. See Chapter 20, "Security and Encryption," for more information on working with encryption.

Using Stop Word Files. The Exclude Words in Stop Word File option tells Notes not to search for words that are extremely common (*the, and, if, it,* and so forth). These common words are called *stop words*, and are defined in the field located just below this selection. You will probably want to select this option as it reduces the number of documents selected to only those that match the remainder of your search criteria.

However, if your database is local and you find that you need to keep a word in the search, such as *off*, so that a search for articles on Off Broadway, for example, can be successfully run, then you will need to edit the Stop Word file to remove the word *off*. The default Stop Word file name is DEFAULT.STP. It's located in your Notes directory. Although it can be edited using any ASCII text editor, make a copy of the file and then edit the copy. That way, you can revert the original file when needed.

Tip

The line '[0-9]+ in DEFAULT.STP tells Notes not to index numbers. You may want to create a Stop Word file with only this line in it and give it a name that reminds you of its purpose, such as NUMBERS.STP. You can then select this file when users don't need to search for numbers.

You can also create additional Stop Word files and customize them for specific local databases. For example, if you have a local database for computer topics, you can create a Stop Word file for it that includes words, such as *computer, keyboard, mouse,* and so on, that appear so frequently in documents that they're not useful in searches.

If you create an additional Stop Word file, you must do so before you create the index that uses it. Once you create the Stop Word file, you can select it when you create the index. The filename must be eight characters or less and use the extension STP, for example, COMPUTER.STP. The Stop Word file must be located in the program directory—typically in C:\NOTES.

Tip

In large databases, a Stop Word file can reduce the index size by about 20 percent (on average)—according to indexing dynamics. Of course, don't bother searching for "To be or not to be" in a Shakespeare database!

Note

Indexes created with customized Stop Word files do not replicate along with the database—either from server to server or from server to workstation.

Working with Index Breaks. The Index Breaks section has two options: Word breaks only and Word, sentence and paragraph. You will normally use the Word breaks only unless you are trying to perform fancier searches. If you select Word, sentence and paragraph, Notes enables you to perform more complex searches that specify that the search words have to all be in the same sentence or paragraph. This can lengthen the time of your search and also can take up a large amount of space. As most documents you search—particularly in your E-Mail database—are fairly short, selecting Word, sentence and paragraph is not necessary.

Completing the Indexing Process. When you have completed making your selections, Notes tells you that the indexing of the database has been queued if the database is located on the server. If you index a database on your hard drive, you will be informed that Notes is performing a local index. If the database is located on the server, you can continue working in other databases while the database is being indexed, but you won't be able to work in the database the server is indexing until it is finished. You will not get a message that the indexing is completed—you will know it is done when you can open the database. If the database is local, you will not be able to continue working in Notes until the indexing is complete. In local indexing, you will know the indexing is complete when the Indexing Database status box disappears.

When you create a full text index, Notes creates a subdirectory and stores the index files there. Notes names this subdirectory according to the name of the indexed database with the file extension FT. For example, if you index a database named MARKET.NSF, Notes creates the subdirectory MARKET.FT and places it in the same directory as the database—usually the Notes data directory.

Caution

If you are running short on hard disk space, don't index your database. If you begin indexing a database and run out of disk space before the indexing is complete, you will not be able to use the index. You will need to delete the index, clean up space on your hard drive, and then create a new index on the database.

Updating the Index. If you add, delete, or change any documents in a database that has been indexed, the index will no longer accurately reflect the database; new words will have been omitted, and words no longer in any document will continue to remain in the index. This causes your searches to behave in an unexpected manner if you are searching on words that have changed. You will have to periodically update a database index.

If the database is on a server, updating of the index occurs automatically—though you can "force" the replication as well by selecting Update Index from the Full Text tab of the Database Properties InfoBox. You control how often an index update occurs automatically by editing the information in this tab of the Database Properties InfoBox (see fig. 8.6). Open this InfoBox by selecting File, Database, Properties, and then selecting the Full Text tab. Select the arrow next to Update frequency (servers only) selection box, and choose between Immediate (the default), Daily, Scheduled, and Hourly, depending on how often you want the database indexed. Because setting indexing options affects server resources, you should contact your Notes administrator before performing this function.

Fig. 8.6

You update database indexes in the Full Text tab of the Database Properties InfoBox. You also specify the frequency in which a server copy of a database index should be updated from this tab.

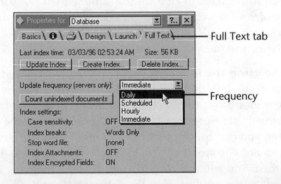

— Full Text tab

— Frequency

If you are working with a database index on your hard drive, you must "force" the indexing by selecting File, Database, Properties, and selecting the Full Text tab. Click the Update Index button. Notes immediately updates the index, presenting you with a status box to show how many documents it is indexing. When the Database Properties InfoBox disappears, you can resume working in Notes with a newly indexed database.

> **Note**
>
> The larger the database and the more complicated the index selections, the larger the file space and memory it will take to maintain it. Make sure that you will really use the indexing feature in a database before you index it.

Indexing in the Background. You can enable background indexing at startup, which creates full text indexes in the background. With this feature set, you can keep working in Notes without having to wait until Notes completes the indexes. To do this follow these steps:

1. Select File, Tools, User Preferences.
2. Select Enable local background indexing and click OK.
3. Click OK when Notes tells you that some preferences will not take effect until you restart Notes.

If background indexing is enabled when you replicate databases, Notes automatically updates each database's full text index and views in the background after replication is completed.

 ▶▶ See "Replicating a Database," p. 681

Deleting an Index. You can delete a full text index if you no longer want a database indexed. You should also delete the index and then re-create it if you are experiencing full text index problems or if you want to change index options. In the latter two cases, create a new index after deleting the original. Do not delete the index from the index subdirectory directly; rather, use the following procedure when you delete an index:

1. Select the database, and then select File, Database, Properties.
2. Select the Full Text tab in the Database Properties InfoBox.
3. Select the Delete Index button. Notes displays the dialog box shown in figure 8.7.
4. Select Yes when prompted to delete the index.

Notes deletes the index for the database, and removes the subdirectory created for this index from your hard drive. If you want to re-index the database after selecting new indexing options or if the index was experiencing problems, follow the procedures to create a full text index described in the earlier section "Indexing a Database."

Fig. 8.7

You can delete database indexes that you no longer use to conserve disk space.

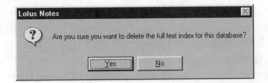

Performing a Full Text Search. If a database has been indexed for full text searches, choosing View, Search Bar causes Notes to display the Search Bar dialog box across the top of the document window, as shown in figure 8.8, which is quite different from the Find dialog box you saw earlier. The Search Bar consists of two areas into which you can enter one or more phrases.

Fig. 8.8

Use the Search Builder to perform queries against indexed databases.

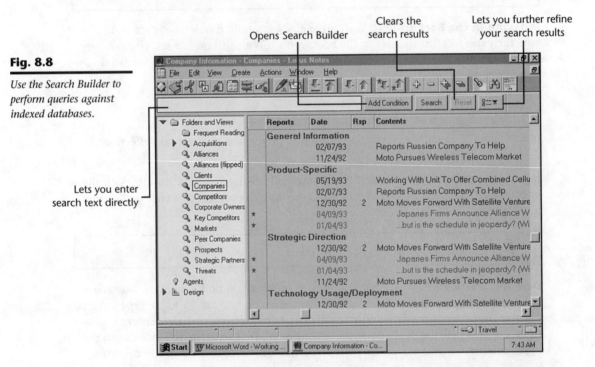

If you are performing a simple search for just a word or phrase, you can type it in the text entry box to the left of the Search Builder, and then click Search. Notes will perform a search on the documents of a database and display the results in the view according to how you elect to see them. You can work with the documents displayed in the view—but if you exit the database, you will clear the results of your search. You can also elect to clear the results of the search by selecting the Reset button in the Search Bar. (You will read more about how Notes displays query results in the next few sections.)

If you want to perform a more detailed query, you can select the Add Condition button to add further detail on the query you want to build in the Search Builder.

When you are finished building a query, you can select Search, and Notes will display the results of your query in the view according to how you elected to see them. This section will walk you through building a query, selecting viewing options, and interpreting your view results.

Tip

You can create complicated, extensive search queries by using any of the search techniques described in the following sections. You can also use a combination of any of these search methods to further refine your search query. For example, you can define a search for a particular author's documents by selecting the By Author search, making your selections, and then selecting OK to save your entry. You can then select another condition and input words or phrases that you want the document to contain to further enhance your query.

Searching for Specified Text. In the previous examples, you learned how to search for a single word or phrase in a database. However, if your database is full text indexed, you can use Search Builder to find documents that contain the words and phrases in a list.

Prior to doing the search, be sure the database is open to the view you want to search, and then perform the following steps:

1. If the Search Bar is not visible, choose View, Search Bar.
2. Click the Add Condition button.
3. In the Condition drop-down list, leave the default value Words and Phrases.
4. Click All to have Notes display only documents that contain all of the words or phrases you enter into the Search Builder. Selecting Any, as described below, will display documents that contain any of the words or phrases you type.
5. Type a word or phrase in as many of the numbered text boxes as you want. Search Builder searches for documents that contain all of these words and phrases (see fig. 8.9).
6. Click OK. Notes displays the query you have built in the text box of the Search Builder. Entries you created in the fields are separated by the word AND to signify that these words and phrases must all be in the document for it to be displayed in the results.
7. Click the Search button in the Search Bar.

Tip

If you need to include more than eight words and phrases in your search, repeat steps 2 through step 6 until all of your criteria have been entered.

For example, figure 8.9 shows a query that has been built to search a products marketing database for all documents that contain the words *telecommunications*, *RBOC*, *wireless*, and the phrase *new legislation*.

Fig. 8.9

Typing words or phrases into each of the entry boxes enables you to narrow your search results by selecting only those documents that meet all of the criteria.

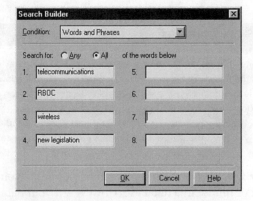

The results from this query would be any documents in the database that contained all of the words and phrases listed above. In this example, only one document, as shown in figure 8.10, contained all of these words and phrases.

Fig. 8.10

The view will display the results of a full text query against a database.

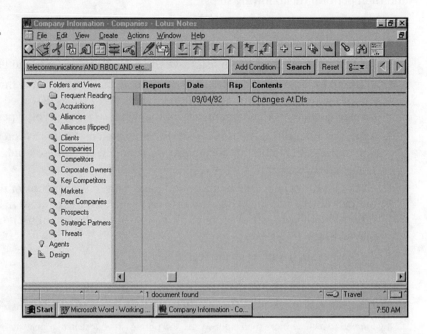

Opening the document displayed in the view will show all of the words and phrases defined in the query highlighted with red boxes, as shown in figure 8.11.

If you want to find documents containing *any* of the words or phrases you have specified, choose *A*ny in step 4. Entries you created in the fields are separated by the word

OR to signify that at least one of these words or phrases will be in the document for it to be displayed in the results.

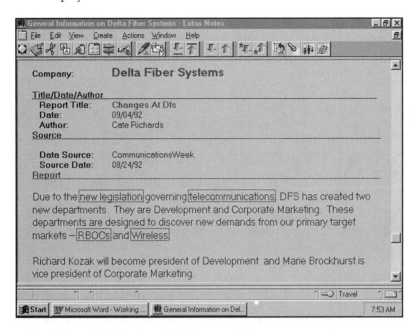

Fig. 8.11

Words and phrases appear with red boxes highlighting them when you open a document displayed after a query when a database is indexed.

Notes will display the results of this query in the view, as shown in figure 8.12. In this example, there are ten documents that meet the criteria defined in the query.

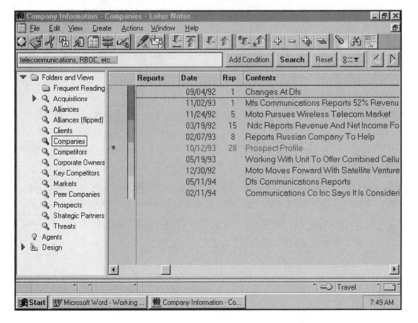

Fig. 8.12

If two or more documents meet the search query, they will be listed in the view according to the criteria you defined.

Notes Basics

Searching Multiple Databases. You can search more than one database at a time, if necessary. To do so, complete the following steps:

1. Select the database icon for each of the databases you want to search (they must all be on the same workpage) by holding down the Shift key and clicking each database icon once.

2. With the Shift key held down, double-click any of the database icons you selected.

3. A view will open in which the titles of the selected databases appear in the Navigator (almost like category titles in a database view), as shown in figure 8.13.

Fig. 8.13

When searching multiple databases for text, the database titles appear in a temporary Navigator when they are selected for query.

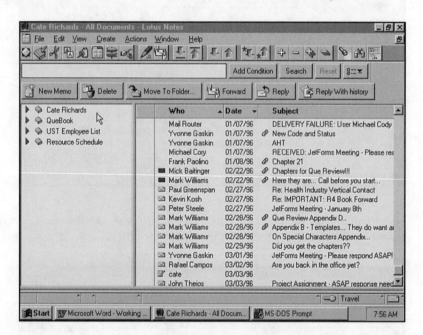

4. Perform a full text search as usual.

5. To see the results of the search in each database, click the small triangle to the left of each database title in the view. That database title will open to display all of the documents found that contain your search criteria. Switch between views and folders as usual in the database to see all documents.

Searching by Author. If your database is indexed, you can define a query to search a database to display all documents composed by a specific author or group of authors.

Prior to doing the search, be sure the database is open to the view you want to search, and then perform the following steps:

1. If the Search Bar is not visible, choose View, Search Bar.

2. Click the Add Condition button. The Search Builder appears (see fig. 8.14).

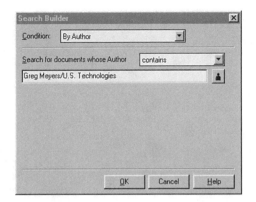

Fig. 8.14

When you query a database for documents By Author, Notes changes the appearance of the dialog box.

I

Notes Basics

3. In the Condition drop-down list, select By Author.

4. In the Search for documents whose Author drop-down list, select contains if you want documents created by the authors you select, or does not contain if you want to exclude documents created by a specific author.

Note

In any query you build, if you elect to exclude an entry based on a selection or term that you enter, Notes will insert the word NOT before the phrase to indicate that Notes should exclude any documents that contain that entry. You can also type this entry directly before any word or phrase to get the same effect. For example, if you want to exclude documents authored by anyone named Larry, enter **NOT Larry** in the search formula by author.

This principal works for all searches you build—not just searches by author.

---

5. Perform one of the following:

- Type the name of an author in the text box. To include more than one name, separate the names with commas.

- Click the Author icon (it appears as an icon of a person) and select the names of the authors you want from the Name & Address Book displayed (see fig. 8.15). If you are working on the network, Notes will display the Public Name & Address Book. If you are working remote (off the network), Notes will display your Private Name & Address Book. If you have more than one Address Book available to you, you can switch between them as usual.

Fig. 8.15

You can select the author(s) you want to search for from your Address Book to make sure you have the correct spelling for your query.

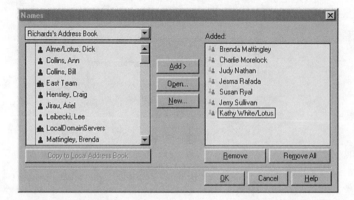

To select a name from the address list, highlight the individual's name (group names have no effect in this search), and then click Add. Notes will add the name you have selected to the list on the right side of the dialog box. Continue to select names until all of the authors you want included in your query are selected.

6. Click OK in the Names dialog box, and then OK again in the Search Builder dialog box.

7. Click the Search button on the Search Bar.

Note

You can search by author in all databases created using Notes Release 4 as long as there is an author field in the design of the database. You may, however, experience difficulty searching databases created in versions earlier than Release 4. You will not be able to search by author in anonymous databases (databases meant to hide the identity of the author of a document).

Searching by Date. If your database is indexed, you can search for documents based on the date they were created or modified. Prior to doing the search, be sure the database is open to the view you want to search and then perform the following steps:

1. If the Search Bar is not visible, choose View, Search Bar.

2. Click the Add Condition button.

3. In the Condition drop-down list, select By Date. Notes will alter the dialog box to appear as shown in figure 8.16.

4. In the Search for documents whose drop-down list, select date created or date modified.

5. In the next drop-down list, select how the date for which you are searching is related to the documents for which you are searching.

6. Type a date in the date text box. If there are two text boxes, type dates in both of them. Make sure you use the format displayed below the list box when typing your dates. The date format is typed according to the format used by your operating system.

7. Click <u>O</u>K. (Repeat steps 2 through 7 if you need to include more dates in your search.)

8. Click the Search button on the Search Bar.

Notes will search the database for all documents that meet your date criteria and display them in the view.

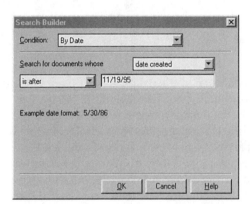

Fig. 8.16

This query searches for documents created after 11/19/95.

Searching by Field Contents. If a database is indexed, you can search for documents that have a specific entry in a particular field. For example, in a Marketing database, you may want to find documents that contain the word *Competitor* in the ClassificationR field.

Prior to doing the search, be sure the database is open to the view you want to search, and then perform the following:

1. If the Search Bar is not visible, choose <u>V</u>iew, Search <u>B</u>ar.

2. Click the Add Condition button.

3. In the <u>C</u>ondition drop-down list, select By Field. Notes displays the dialog box shown in figure 8.17.

4. In the <u>S</u>earch for documents where field drop-down list, select the field you want to include in the search. This drop-down list box contains a list of all of the fields contained in the design of the database.

5. In the last drop-down list, make a relationship choice: either the field contains the entry, or does not contain the entry.

6. In the text box (or text boxes), type the text, dates, or number for which you want to search. For example, type **competitor**.

7. Click <u>O</u>K. (Repeat steps 2 through 7 if you need to include more fields in your search.)

8. Click the Search button on the Search Bar.

Fig. 8.17

This query looks for the word Competitor in the ClassificationR field of the database.

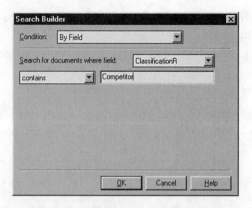

If you are not familiar with the design of the database and do not know the name of the field you want to use in your query, you can review the field design information by highlighting a document in the database view you are searching and selecting Edit, Properties. Notes will display the Document Properties InfoBox for the document. Select the Fields tab. A list of all of the fields will appear in the left list box, as shown in figure 8.18. As you select a field name, Notes displays in the right list box the design and contents of the field for the document you selected. Reviewing this information should assist you in finding the appropriate field to use in this query.

Fig. 8.18

You can view the form's field design in the Fields tab of the Document Properties InfoBox for the document.

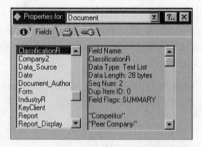

Searching by Criteria in a Form. If your database is indexed, you can search for documents by entering criteria into any database form—as long as the database designer indicated that the form could be displayed in Search Builder.

Prior to doing the search, be sure the database is open to the view you want to search, and then complete the following steps:

1. If the Search Bar is not visible, choose View, Search Bar.

2. Click the Add Condition button.

3. In the Condition drop-down list, select By Form. Notes will display the dialog box shown in figure 8.19.

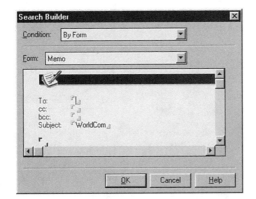

Fig. 8.19

This query checks for the word WorldCom in the Subject field of the memo.

4. In the Forms drop-down list, select the form you want to use in the search. All forms in the database will appear in the drop-down list—unless the database developer designed the forms to not appear. See Chapter 10, "Designing Forms," for more information on form design.

5. In the form you selected, type entries (text, numbers, etc.) in as many fields as you want to include in the search in the fields defined in the database form. What you type in each field is what you search for. You type your entries into the fields that appear in the form—just as if you were typing in a regular Notes document.

6. Click OK.

7. Click the Search button on the Search Bar.

Notes will search for documents that include all of the entries you make.

Searching for Documents Created with a Certain Form. If a database has been indexed, you can use the Search Builder to find documents that were created using a specific form. For example, you can create a query in a Marketing database to show only documents created using the Company form. Typically, you use this type of search when you know that a particular word or phrase appears in many different documents in a database—but you are only interested in information that would be contained in one particular type of form. For example, the word *hotel* may appear many times in a company travel database, but you are interested only in the instances of the word appearing in a Trouble Report form in the database if you are preparing a report on all problems with hotels reported by employees.

Prior to doing the search, be sure the database is open to the view you want to search, and complete the following steps:

1. If the Search Bar is not visible, choose View, Search Bar.

2. Click the Add Condition button.

3. In the Condition drop-down list, select By Form Used. Notes will display the dialog box shown in figure 8.20.

Fig. 8.20

This selection indicates that you want to search in the Company Profile and Activity Report forms.

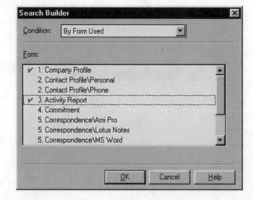

4. In the Forms list box, select one or more forms; a checkmark will appear next to each form selected.

5. Click OK.

6. Click the Search button on the Search Bar.

Refining Your Search Results. Notes provides you many ways to view and alter the results you receive when you run a search query. You can alter the order in which documents are displayed, use synonyms in your search, change the maximum number of entries displayed, and save a search formula. You make these settings through the Options button. When you refine your searches by selecting the Options button on the Search Bar before running the query, the menu in figure 8.21 is displayed.

Fig. 8.21

Selecting the Options button enables you to change the way your results are displayed.

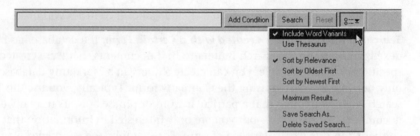

The options available for you to select in this drop-down menu are as follows:

■ **Include Word Variants**—This option tells Notes to include any words in which the base part of the word you are looking for is present. For example, if you enter *training* as the search criteria, documents containing the word *train* would also be selected. If you select *train*, Notes will also display *training*, *trained*, and so on.

■ **Use Thesaurus**—This option enables you to include synonyms of search words in your search. For example, if you search for documents that contain the word *doctor*, Notes also finds documents that contain the word *physician*. This selection will remain active until you reset the Search Builder or exit the database.

■ **Sort by Relevance**—By default, the search results in databases queried with the Full Text Search feature are displayed in the order of significance, which means that the more times the word or phrase is found in a document, the higher up in the list the document will be displayed. You can ascertain the significance of the document in the search by looking to the left of the documents in the view. A vertical bar is displayed to indicate the relevance of each document to the search criteria (see fig. 8.22). The darker the portion of the bar, the more relevant the document.

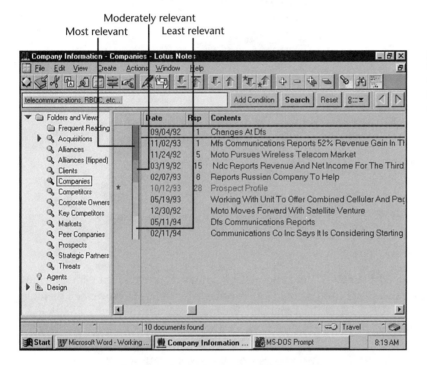

Fig. 8.22

By default, search results are displayed in the view according to relevance.

■ **Sort by Oldest First**—This option displays the documents found in the search according to their compose date, with the oldest documents displayed first. This is an ideal sort order if you are trying to follow a discussion on a topic and want to read the discussion from beginning to end.

■ **Sort by Newest First**—This option displays the documents found in the search according to their compose date, with the newest documents displayed first. This is an ideal sort order if you are looking for the latest information regarding a particular topic. For example, if you are reviewing a database of customer contact reports and want to see what is current for a particular topic.

■ **Maximum Results**—This option enables you to determine the maximum number of documents you will accept in the results of a search. The default setting is 250 documents, which is usually adequate for your needs. If you are only interested in receiving those documents that best suit your query and want to speed up the search process, then reduce this setting.

■ **Save Search As**—This option enables you to save a search formula so that you can use it whenever you use the database in which you created it. If you have Designer or Manager access to the database on a server, you can also make the search formula available to anyone who uses the database by selecting Shared search in the Save Search As dialog box, as shown in figure 8.23. Saved search formulas appear at the bottom of the Options menu in the Search Bar, as shown in figure 8.24.

Fig. 8.23

You can save search formulas in the database in which you used them.

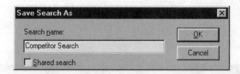

Fig. 8.24

Saved searches are displayed at the bottom of the Options menu in the database in which you saved them.

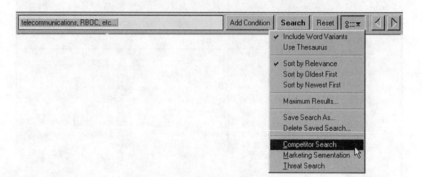

■ **Delete Saved Search**—This option enables you to remove saved search formulas. When you select this option, Notes displays the Delete Saved Search dialog box (see fig. 8.25). Select the saved search name you want to remove and then select Delete.

Fig. 8.25

You should delete old, saved queries that you will no longer use to keep your menu list from becoming cluttered.

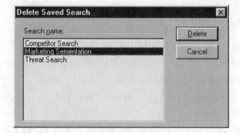

Notes will display a checkmark next to selected items. Once your selections have been made, you can press the Search button on the Search Bar to begin searching the database.

In addition to the methods you have learned in the preceding sections for refining your queries, you can also use the following terms in your query field entries to further enhance your query capabilities.

If you selected Word, sentence and paragraph as Index breaks when you created the full text index, you can use the Proximity operators to increase the relevance ranking of words that are close to each other. The following Proximity operators are available to you:

- **Near**—The closer the words or phrases are to each other, the higher Notes will rank their relevance in the sort view. For example, if you entered **Competitor near Threat** in a query field exactly as shown here, Notes will sort those documents in which these terms are closer to each other at the top of the view.

- **Sentence**—This option works much the same as near, but all of the words or phrases must be in the same sentence. For example, if you entered **Competitor sentence Threat** in a query field exactly as shown here, Notes will sort the documents with both of these terms in the same sentence at the top of the view.

- **Paragraph**—This option works much the same as near, but the words or phrases must all be in the same paragraph. For example, if you entered **Competitor paragraph Threat** in a query field exactly as shown here, Notes will sort the documents with both of these terms in the same paragraph at the top of the view.

You can also use wildcard characters in place of other characters when you search for text, such as the following:

- Use a question mark (?) for a single character. For example, typing **owe?** will return documents containing words such as *owed* and *owes.*

- Use an asterisk (*) for multiple characters. For example, typing **fl*** will return documents containing words like *Florida*, *Floridians*, *flow*, and *flop.*

Wildcard characters work only in text fields; they will not work in fields that contain dates or numbers.

You can also perform a second search on the results of the first search to further refine your query. For example, if your first search against a company information database for company names considered threats to your organization provided so many documents that it was ineffective, you may want to refine the search to include only those companies that are threats and whose product line focuses on the same target market as yours.

You can do this by performing the first query on the database to find those companies that are considered threats, and then with that query's results still displayed, perform another query against documents containing target market names the same as yours. Notes will search only those documents listed in the first query for matches to the second.

Working with Document Read Marks

You have seen that Notes displays a star next to documents that you haven't read. In databases such as your mailbox, these markers can serve as important reminders that you need to read certain documents. Sometimes, however, you may decide that you don't want to read certain documents in a database or in your mailbox at a particular time.

Suppose that your company maintains a database of important scheduled events, which you want to keep abreast of. Someone in your company, however, routinely adds notices about the company softball team, which just doesn't interest you. After a long vacation, you return to your desk and find 14 softball announcements in the database. You really don't want to read them, but they all have the stars next to them, screaming, "Pay attention to me!"

You can use the Unread Marks operation to tell Notes to remove the stars and make the documents appear as though you have read them. To mark documents as read, open the database and choose Edit, Unread Marks. The Unread Marks submenu appears, enabling you to select one of the following four options (see fig. 8.26):

- **Mark Selected Read**—This option marks all selected documents as read.
- **Mark All Read**—This option marks all documents in the database as read.
- **Mark Selected Unread**—This option marks all selected documents as unread.
- **Mark All Unread**—This option marks all documents in the database as unread.

Fig. 8.26

You can mark documents as read to indicate that you have already read them, or as unread to draw your attention to those documents at a later date.

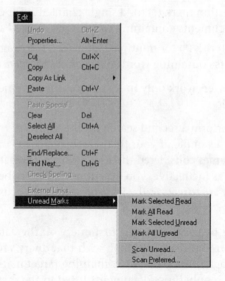

Note that the last two choices enable you to mark read documents as unread; that is, you can read a document and then tell Notes to mark it as though you hadn't read it. At first glance, this capability may seem like a feature in search of a use, but you actually may find it useful, especially if you keep old memos in your mailbox that you think may be important later.

When you open your mailbox, you probably look for the stars that call attention to newly arrived mail. Suppose, however, that you read a message just before quitting time one afternoon and realize that the memo will require significant attention tomorrow. If you close the message, Notes now considers it one of the many previously read messages and removes its attention-grabbing star. However, you can put the star back by marking the document as unread so that it will again attract your notice the next time you read your mail.

 ◀◀ See "Previewing Documents with the Preview Pane," p. 23

Scanning for Unread Documents

Many people work with several different databases and must constantly be on the lookout for new documents showing up in those databases. Suppose that your company has several databases that contain status reports from different departments, and one of your jobs is to monitor those status reports for customer problems. You may find it cumbersome to check each database several times a day to see whether new documents have appeared. Instead, you can use the Scan Unread feature in the Edit, Unread Marks submenu to tell you about new documents.

Scanning Preferred Databases. You can use the Scan Unread feature in several ways, but the most common—and most useful—method involves a two-step process. In the first step, you tell Notes which databases you want to watch for unread documents; these databases are known as your *preferred databases*. Then, at any time, you can ask Notes if there are any unread documents in any of your preferred databases.

To supply Notes with your list of preferred databases, select Edit, Unread Marks, Scan Preferred. The Scan Unread dialog box appears, as shown in figure 8.27. Select Choose Preferred. The Scan Unread Preferred Setup dialog box appears (see fig. 8.28).

Notes lists all the databases on all of your workpages. The workpages themselves are identified with names surrounded by dashes, such as:

    - Misc -

Select the databases that you want scanned for unread documents. You must click on each database title individually. Select OK to save your selections.

Fig. 8.27

You can use the Scan Unread dialog box to begin setting up preferred databases to scan.

Fig. 8.28

You must select each database you want to mark as preferred individually from the list. Workpage names are indicated with a hyphen before and after the name—you cannot select workpage names.

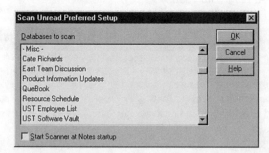

Note

The Scan Unread Preferred Setup dialog box includes a checkbox labeled Start Scanner at Notes startup. If you check this box, Notes will automatically scan your preferred databases for unread documents each time you start Notes.

When you have selected your preferred databases, you can scan them for unread documents by making sure no databases are selected on the workspace (click anywhere in the blank gray portion of the workspace), and choosing Edit, Unread Marks, Scan Preferred. Notes displays the Scan Unread dialog box (refer to fig. 8.27).

The dialog box displays the name of the first of your preferred databases and shows the number of unread documents in the database. You can choose any of the following actions:

- If you choose View First Unread, Notes opens the first document in the first database. You can then read the unread document. Press Tab to move to the next unread document in the database. Press Esc to exit the current document and open the database view.

- If you choose Mark All Read, Notes assumes that you don't want to read the documents and marks them as read from this database only—all other databases you are scanning will not be affected by this selection.

- If you choose Skip This Database, Notes displays the name of the next preferred database and the number of unread documents in that database.

After Notes scans all databases, it loops back to the first and begins scanning again. When you see the same databases appearing again, choose Done to exit scanning.

Scanning a Single Database. To scan a single database for unread documents, high-light the database you want to scan by clicking once on the database icon. Select Edit, Unread Marks, Scan Unread. Notes will open the first unread document in the data-base. Press Tab to open the next unread document. Press Esc to end the scan and exit the document. You will be returned to the database view.

Scanning Multiple Databases. You can select multiple databases and then scan them. To do so, press the Shift key and then select each of the databases you want to scan. Select Edit, Unread Marks, Scan Unread. Notes opens the Scan Unread dialog box. Follow the procedures listed in "Scanning Preferred Databases" in this section to scan the databases you have selected.

Copying and Pasting Documents

Not only can you use the Clipboard to copy pieces of text from one document to another as described in "Copying and Pasting Text" in Chapter 8, "Working with Documents," but you can use almost the exact same technique to move or copy docu-ments from one database to another. Do the following:

1. Open the database in which the documents now exist.

2. Select one or more documents by clicking in the left margin next to each; a checkmark will appear next to selected documents as shown in figure 8.29.

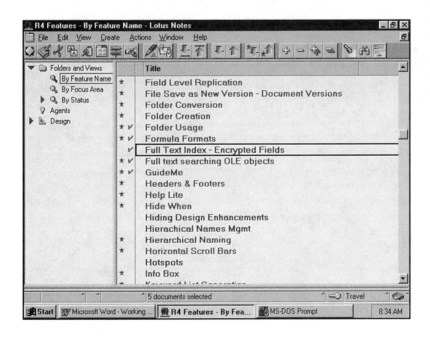

Fig. 8.29

Selecting documents in a view allows you to perform a function—like copying—on all of them at one time.

3. If you want to copy the documents, choose <u>E</u>dit, <u>C</u>opy, or press Ctrl+C, or click the Copy SmartIcon. If you want to move the documents, choose <u>E</u>dit, Cu<u>t</u>, or press Ctrl+X, or click the Cut SmartIcon.

4. Close the current database and open the database in which you want to place the documents.

5. Choose <u>E</u>dit, <u>P</u>aste, or press Ctrl+V, or click the Paste SmartIcon.

Notes inserts the documents into the new database. This procedure works best if both databases contain the form that you used to compose the documents. If, for example, the documents were composed with a form called Client Information and both databases contain that form by that name, Notes can perform the move or copy easily. Otherwise, Notes has to rearrange the fields within the documents to conform to the default form in the receiving database—which may mean you will not see some or all of the text—depending on how successful Notes is at figuring out how to display the information.

> **Caution**
>
> Trying to copy documents into a database that does not contain a copy of the form in which they are created can result in Notes being unable to display any of the information in the form, or displaying the information in a manner than may make it difficult to read. Read Chapter 10, "Designing Forms," for information on working with form design.

> **Applications of Copying and Pasting Documents**
>
> The ability to copy text, fields, or even entire documents is a Notes feature that is often over-looked, but that contains a great deal of power. Some excellent applications of the capability to copy (or cut) documents to the Clipboard are the following:
>
> ■ You can cut documents from your active mail database and store them in an E-Mail Archive database for safekeeping. This enables you to keep your active mail database relatively small, but affords you the capability to keep important documents in case you need to get to them quickly at another time. As mentioned above, make sure that the document's form design is also present in the archive database to ensure that you can read the documents clearly. It is best if your archive mail database is a copy of your active database design. Read Chapter 9, "Creating New Databases," for more information on database design.
>
> ■ You can temporarily protect documents from being lost while you perform other functions in the database. For example, if you are getting ready to run an agent against several documents in a database to replace some text, but you want to make sure the documents are protected against errors—such as being deleted—before you do so, you can copy them to the Clipboard, run your macro, and then verify that your results are as you expected in your original documents.

If something went wrong when you ran the macro, then you can always delete the modified documents and then paste the documents from the Clipboard back into the database so that the information is restored to its original condition before you began the agent.

- Copying and pasting documents within the same database is a time-saver if you want to edit small portions of a document but want to keep the old, unedited document intact, such as a large proposal that someone else in your organization wrote. Copy the document to the Clipboard and then repaste it into the database by selecting Edit, Paste. Open up the copy of the document and edit it. Your document will contain the edits, without disturbing the original document.

Often, depending on the design of the database, your copy of the document will appear slightly indented below the original document as a response document if you highlighted the original document before pasting. (Your database designer may have bypassed your need to do this by selecting one of the following options: New versions become responses, Prior versions become responses, New versions become siblings in the Form Property InfoBox during the creation of the form design. See Chapter 10, "Designing Forms," for more information on the Form Property InfoBox.)

Linking Documents

Often, you will want to guide readers to other areas in which there is related information about the topic they are currently reading about. Perhaps a document that you are composing discusses a topic that also is mentioned in another document.

For example, if you are discussing the health benefits of broccoli, you may want to create a link to another document that contains a recipe for actually making the stuff edible! The link need not even be in the same database as the document you are reading.

You can create links to the following:

- Documents
- Views
- Databases

Links appear as pages of paper with their corners folded down, as shown in figure 8.30. Associated with each link is a location, called the *link point,* within the link document. When the user double-clicks the link, Notes displays the link document showing the section of text containing the link point. When the user closes the link document, Notes returns to the original document that contained the link.

Fig. 8.30

Notes can link a document to other documents, views, or databases.

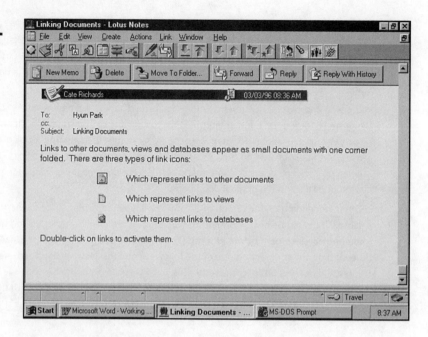

To create a link, complete the following procedure:

1. Start with one of the following:

   • Open the link document (the document you want to link to) and select a link point by clicking the position within that document that you want Notes to display when the doclink is activated. Note that if you open the document in read mode, the insertion point flashes only momentarily on-screen, but Notes still knows where it is.

   • Open the view in which you want to link to (the view does not need to be in the current database). Press F6, and then select the view or folder you want to link to in the navigator pane.

   • Highlight the database you want to link to by clicking its icon once.

2. Choose Edit, Copy as Link.

   Select whether the link you are creating is a Document Link, View Link, or Database Link. Notes puts a link on the Clipboard that corresponds to the link point that you selected. Notes will indicate that the link has been copied to the Clipboard in the Status Bar at the bottom of your Notes window.

3. Open the document in which you want to insert the link. You must open the document in edit mode.

4. Paste the link into any rich text field in the document just as you would a section of text. (Choose Edit, Paste, or press Ctrl+V.)

Caution

The following circumstances may make the links not work for someone trying to use it:

- If the database ID or document ID referenced in the doclink is changed, the link will have to be made again. This often happens if the database is copied to another server (versus having a replica copy made), and then the original database is deleted. It can also happen if the document is cut out of the linked database and stored in another database.

- The user does not have access to the database, server, or directory on the server in which the referenced database is located. The user must have at least Reader access.

- The user does not have form access to read the document referenced in the link. Form access is assigned when the form is created by the database designer—the default is All Users (who have access to the database).

- The user does not have view access necessary to read the view that is linked. The access level for reading a view is created by the database designer—the default is All Users (who have access to the database).

- Remote users will not be able to use the link unless the referenced database is located on their hard drive or they are dialed out to a server hosting a copy of the database.

If you double-click a link and the referenced database is not located on your workspace, Notes will search the servers you have access to and add the database icon to your workspace, opened to the link point.

Because links are simply a set of numbers referencing the database ID and document ID, you can use them in messages to users to have them add a new database to their desktop and open the database to the referenced link point. When you close the database that you have been linked to, you will notice that the database icon has been added to your desktop. The database icon will remain on the workpage until removed by the reader.

This makes an ideal way for database managers to assist users in accessing a new database. There is another way: through the use of buttons that specify exactly which server you should access as well as the name of the database (and possibly the document). You learn more about buttons in Chapter 15, "Buttons and Agents."

Tip

You can use links in the designs of databases to guide users to referenced information automatically. For example, if you have a discussion database, you can create a link in the form design of the response documents to always link back to the parent document should the reader want to review the original topic. You will learn more about designing forms and views in Chapter 10, "Designing Forms," and Chapter 11, "Designing Views."

Adding Hotspots to Your Documents

Hotspots enable you to communicate additional information. Depending on its type, a hotspot may display pop-up text, switch to a linked destination, or perform a Notes action. For example, a pop-up hotspot displays pop-up text, as shown in figure 8.31.

Fig. 8.31

Pop-up hotspots are handy when you want to display information in a document that only some readers will be interested in seeing—like directions to your house.

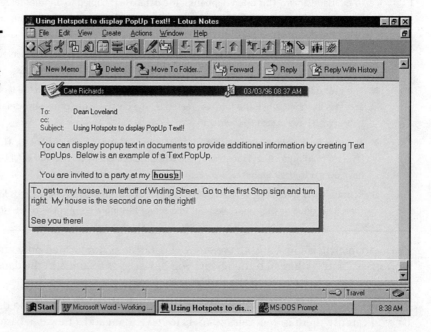

Notes can also use hotspots to link to another document. For example, the document displayed in figure 8.32 shows a document with underlined text. The author of the document created a hotspot for this text so that when users double-click the text, they will open up a related document. You will see many examples of this use of text hotspots in the online Lotus Notes Help database. (The text hotspots appear as underlined green text in the help documents to link you to related information on that help topic.)

Finally, Notes can use hotspots to perform actions. For example, you can define an action to compose a document titled "Registration" whenever someone clicks a hotspot called Register (see fig. 8.33).

> **Note**
>
> Your cursor must be located in a rich text field to create a hotspot, and your document must be in edit mode. You must be in read mode to display or activate a hotspot.

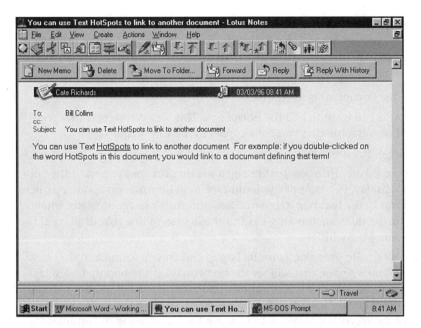

Fig. 8.32

Text hotspots can be used to link readers to a related text.

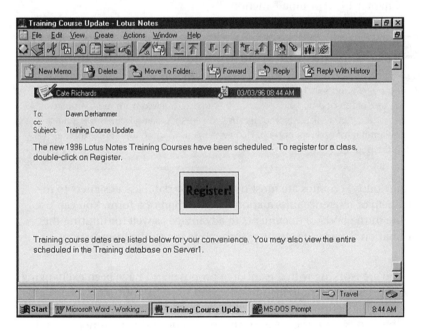

Fig. 8.33

Action hotspots can be used to perform functions—like compose a new form—whenever someone clicks them.

Pop-up Hotspots

If you want text to pop up whenever a user clicks and holds the left mouse button on a particular hotspot, you can define a text pop-up hotspot. Complete the following steps:

1. Make sure the document is in edit mode.

2. Select the area you want to add the hotspot to. This area can be text that you have typed or a graphic that you have copied to the Clipboard.

3. Perform one of the following:

   - Choose Create, Hotspot, Text Popup and enter the text you want the pop-up to display. For example, you can type help information about a particular form in the text box to provide help information—particularly when the instructions are too long to fit in the field help line that displays at the bottom of the window.

   - Choose Create, Hotspot, Formula Popup and enter a formula in the programmer's pane that will set the text you want the pop-up to display. For example, you can set a formula that looks up a list of current products in a product database whenever someone clicks the hotspot. You learn more about writing formulas in Chapter 13, "Working with Formulas," and Chapter 14, "Formula Functions."

Tip

If the text you want to enter has already been typed in another Windows or OS/2 document, you can highlight the text and select Edit, Copy to copy the text to the Clipboard. Then with your cursor in the text of the pop-up field, press Ctrl+V to paste the text from the Clipboard—the Edit, Paste function is not available to you because you are in a dialog box. This is a quick way to put a large amount of text in a pop-up. However, the formatting and font attributes will *not* be present in the pop-up.

As mentioned previously, pop-ups are most often used by database designers to include additional help or reference information in the design of a form. You can use the pop-up feature in the body of documents to advantage as well for limiting the amount of information a reader has to filter through to get to the information needed.

For example, if you are working with a team on a proposal and have been exchanging information about it (close dates, dollar amounts, and so forth), but want to also provide the readers with the definition of some of the terms within the contract, then you can create a pop-up around the terms. If the readers need the definition, then it can be accessed; otherwise, the reader does not need to waste time reading through the definition and can continue on through the rest of the document.

You can also copy information from a previous memo and paste it into a pop-up box when links are not applicable. The reader then has the option of reading prior information, if needed, by clicking the pop-up that you created, or just the current information. To paste text from the Clipboard into a pop-up box, create the pop-up box as usual, and then select Ctrl+V to paste the text from the Clipboard into the dialog box.

Link Hotspots

You can add a hotspot that enables users to switch to another document, view, folder, or database. This is an example of a link hotspot that leads to another document (much as you learned in "Linking Documents" earlier in this chapter). The difference between creating a link and creating a link hotspot is in the appearance of the "trigger" that initiates the link.

In creating links, you paste an object that looks like a document into a document. In creating link hotspots, any area that you highlight will serve as the "trigger" for making the link. For example, you could highlight a graphic of an airplane to have Notes link you to a policy on airline travel in another database.

To create a link hotspot, complete the following steps:

1. Begin by choosing any of these options.
   - In the view pane, click the document you want to link to.
   - In the navigation pane, click the view or folder you want to link to.
   - In the workspace, click the database you want to link to.
   - In a document, click the area of the document you want to link to.
2. Choose Edit, Copy as Link.
3. Open the document you want to add the hotspot to in edit mode.
4. Highlight the area you want to add the hotspot to.
5. Choose Create, Hotspot, Link Hotspot.

Action Hotspots

You can add a hotspot to an area of a document (such as text or a graphic) that enables users to perform a Notes action. For example, you can add a hotspot that creates a document that you can type in and send—like a registration form in a Training database. A good example of action hotspots can be found in many of the new V4 Navigators, in which clicking a graphic opens a view or creates a document for you to enter text.

To create an action hotspot, do the following:

1. Make sure the document is in edit mode.
2. Select the area you want to add the hotspot to by highlighting it. The area can be text or a graphic.
3. Choose Create, Hotspot, Action Hotspot. The programmer pane will appear, as shown in figure 8.34.

Fig. 8.34

To create action hotspots, you will need to work in the programmer pane.

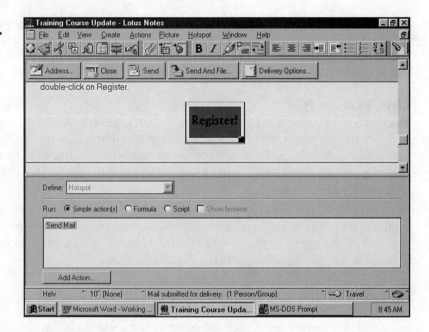

4. In the programmer pane, do one of the following:

   • Specify a preprogrammed action that Notes includes by selecting Simple action(s) and clicking Add Actions. Then select an action, specify any settings Notes needs to perform the action, and click <u>O</u>K.

   • To enter a formula that performs an action, select Formula and enter the formula.

   • To enter a script that performs an action, select Script and enter the script.

> **Note**
>
> You learn about programming simple actions, formulas, and scripts in Part II, "Designing Applications."

5. Click anywhere within the document to close the programmer pane and continue working.

You can remove the green border that surrounds a hotspot by highlighting the hotspot while you are creating it and selecting <u>E</u>dit, <u>P</u>roperties. The Properties InfoBox will appear, as shown in figure 8.35.

Deselect the Show border around hotspot checkbox. You can also hide the hotspot, change fonts, colors, and other text attributes, as well as perform any paragraph formatting options by making the appropriate selections in the hotspot's Properties InfoBox.

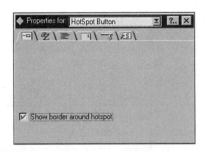

Fig. 8.35

Use the HotSpot Button Properties InfoBox to control how the hotspot is displayed in the document or form.

To use a hotspot, double-click anywhere within the border of the hotspot—with the exception of pop-up hotspots. To use a pop-up hotspot, click anywhere within its borders and hold the left mouse button down. The text will be displayed as long as the mouse button is pressed.

Using Tables in Your Documents

As you use Notes to compose documents, you may find tables handy for representing data. Tables consist of data arranged into rows and columns in any manner you choose. The intersection of each column and row is a *cell*. Most often, lines surround each cell so that the table forms a grid. Like most other advanced formatting features, tables can appear only in rich text fields.

You can include tables in the design of your database forms by following the instructions provided below for creating tables. Rather than entering text into the cells, however, you will define fields instead. An example of a form using a table as part of its design is found in figure 8.36 (in design mode). See Chapter 10, "Designing Forms," for additional information.

In the following sections you learn how to create tables in documents, add data to them, and change their characteristics.

Creating Tables

To create a new table, position the insertion point where you want the table to appear and then choose Create, Table. Notes opens the dialog box shown in figure 8.37.

Enter the number of Rows and Columns you want for this table. Notes immediately creates a table in your document with the numbers of rows and columns you specified. Notes will also add a new menu command to the menu bar at the top of the Notes window: Table. You can use this menu command to control the attributes of the table you are working with.

You can add and delete columns and rows from a table, change the cell widths, change the cell borders, and change other attributes of a table at any time. The following sections provide details.

Fig. 8.36

Tables can be created as part of the form design. Each cell can contain static text—or a separate field design.

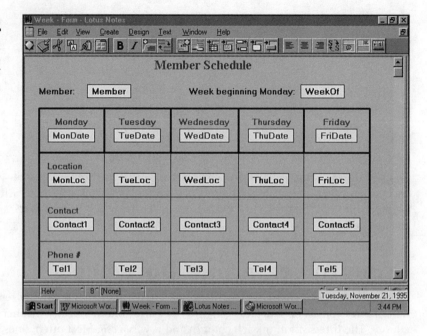

Fig. 8.37

Enter the number of rows and columns for your table.

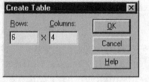

Adding and Deleting Columns

To add a new column to your table, click where you want to add the column. Select Table, Insert Column. Notes adds another column to your table to the left of your cursor location.

If you want to add multiple columns to your table, click where you want to add the columns and select Table, Insert Special. Notes displays the dialog box shown in figure 8.38.

Fig. 8.38

Selecting Table, Insert Special lets you add multiple columns or rows to your table at one time.

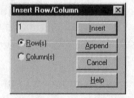

Type the number of columns you want to add in the text box provided, and then select Column(s). Next, select from the following options:

- **Insert**—This inserts the number of columns specified to the left of the current location of the cursor.
- **Append**—This adds the number of columns specified to the far right side of the table.
- **Cancel**—This enables you to exit without adding any columns.
- **Help**—This accesses the online help in Notes.

Notes adds the columns to your table.

You can also delete columns from your table by placing your cursor in the columns you want to remove and selecting Table, Delete Selected Column(s). Notes will prompt you if you want to delete the column. Click Yes. You can delete multiple columns by placing your cursor in the first column in the table you want to delete and then selecting Table, Delete Special. Select Column(s), and specify how many columns you want to remove. When you have made your selections, click Delete. Notes removes the current column and any additional columns to the right of the current one—according to the number of columns you specified.

Adding and Deleting Rows

To add a new row to your table, click where you want to add the row. Select Table, Insert Rows. Notes adds another row above your current cursor location.

If you want to add multiple rows to your table, click where you want to add the rows and select Table, Insert Special. Type the number of rows you want to add in the text box provided, and then select Row(s). Next, choose from the following options:

- **Insert**—This inserts the number of rows specified above the current location of the cursor.
- **Append**—This adds the number of rows specified to the bottom of the table.
- **Cancel**—This enables you to exit without adding any columns.
- **Help**—This accesses the online help in Notes.

Notes adds the rows to your table.

You can delete rows from your table by placing your cursor in the rows you want to remove and selecting Table, Delete Selected Rows(s). Notes will prompt you if you want to delete the row. Click Yes. You can delete multiple rows by placing your cursor in the first row in the table you want to delete and then selecting Table, Delete Special. Choose Rows(s) and specify how many rows you want to remove. When you have made your selections, click Delete. Notes removes the current rows and any additional rows below the current one—according to the number of rows you specified.

Changing Table Attributes

You can change the way your table looks by changing border attributes, column width, space between the columns and rows, and margin settings. To change these attributes, place your cursor in the first column or row you want to modify and select Table, Properties. The Table Properties InfoBox appears with the Cell Borders tab displayed, as shown in figure 8.39.

Fig. 8.39

You can change the borders for your table in the Table Properties InfoBox to add pizzazz to your table and highlight important information.

You can specify single borders, double borders, or no borders for selected cells in a table. To change border settings (the number of lines surrounding your table's cells), complete the following steps:

1. With the Table Properties InfoBox opened to Cell Borders, do one of the following:
   - To set the border on one or more sides, select None, Single, or Double for each side.
   - To set the border on all sides to single, click Set All To Single.
   - To remove the border from all sides, click Set All To None.
2. If necessary, select another cell in the table and repeat step 1 until all of the cell's borders are set as you would like them.
3. Close the dialog box.

Tip

To change borders for the outer sides of the table only, select the entire table by dragging your mouse over it and click Outline in the Table Properties InfoBox. Then select the border styles for each side of the table. This feature makes framing your table with a special border setting easy!

You can also highlight the entire table and remove the border, or select border styles that affect the entire table—including each individual cell's borders.

To make adjustments to the margins, column width, and spacing between rows and columns, select the Layout tab while viewing the Table Properties InfoBox. Notes displays the InfoBox shown in figure 8.40.

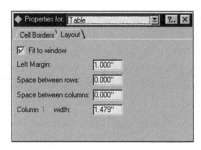

Fig. 8.40

Adjusting margins, spacing, and column width helps add impact to your tables.

The following are the settings you can control:

- **Fit to window**—This setting tells Notes to always adjust the column widths proportionately to fit within the current size window. This enables readers of the table to easily see all columns of the table—regardless of the size of their monitor or window.

> **Note**
>
> Large tables can sometimes be difficult to read if Fit to window is not selected, as the user will have to scroll back and forth in the window to see all of the information.
>
> Also, tables can sometimes be difficult to read on different platforms, screen sizes, and/or resolutions. Keep your user in mind when creating tables in documents.

- **Left Margin**—If you want the table indented, you can enter a larger number than the default (1.25") in this field. Notes will move the left margin of the table accordingly.
- **Space between rows** and **Space between columns**—These options enable you to specify how much blank space Notes displays between the text and the cell's borders. The default is zero.
- **Column width**—This setting enables you to specify the width of each column in inches. You can make the setting for the current column and then click in another column and adjust its column width. Notes records which column you are adjusting next to the Column width text entry box.

When you have made all of your adjustments, close the Table Properties InfoBox to continue working with your table.

> **Note**
>
> Large tables in documents tend to slow down the PC's response time when reading and printing documents. Keep this in mind when deciding to insert a table.

Entering Data in the Table

Suppose that you need to represent revenue figures for each of the past six months in each of your company's four business units. At first, you may think you want a table with four columns and six rows, but an extra row and column would enable you to label each month and business unit. So enter **7** as the number of rows and **5** as the number of columns. When you choose OK, Notes creates the table.

You can enter data in the new table just as you can anywhere in the document. Figure 8.41 shows what the table may look like after data is typed into the cells (but before its characteristics are adjusted to increase its attractiveness). In this example, the data was typed individually into each cell, including the totals. If the table had been part of the design of the form, then a formula can be designed to automatically add the numbers in the Totals row. You read more about creating formulas in Chapter 13, "Working with Formulas."

Fig. 8.41

Tables such as the one shown here communicate information correctly, but are bland, and do not highlight important information.

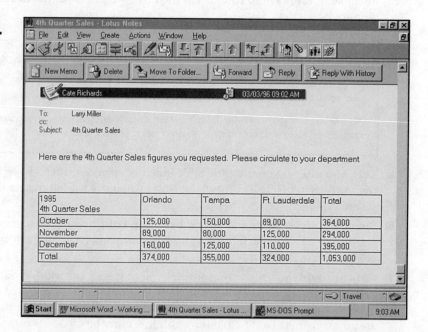

Once you have the design of the table set, you can adjust the borders, cell widths, and other text formatting characteristics to add impact and highlight information that you want to make sure the reader pays attention to. Figure 8.41 displays the same table shown in figure 8.43, but formatted to enhance the presentation of information. As you enter data into a table, keep the following points in mind:

■ You can move around within a table by using the arrow keys just as you can move anywhere within the document. Within a table, however, you also can press Tab to move from one cell to the next and Shift+Tab to move to the preceding cell (that is, the cell to the left or the last cell on the preceding row if you are at the beginning of a row).

- If you enter text that is too wide for the cell, the cell expands into as many lines as necessary to hold the text.

- If you enter a single word that is too long to fit in a cell, Notes expands the height of the cell and splits the word. Notes never increases the width of the cell to accommodate long words. If a word is too long to fit, type a hyphen and then press Enter to divide the word correctly. When you press Enter, Notes adjusts the height of the cell to accommodate the additional line.

Creating a One-Cell Table

You can highlight text in a document to emphasize a point by creating a table that has one cell and one column, as shown in figure 8.42. In this example, the author created a one-cell table with the right and bottom borders defined as double, while the top and left borders were left as single. This provides a shadowing effect that adds some pizzazz to your documents.

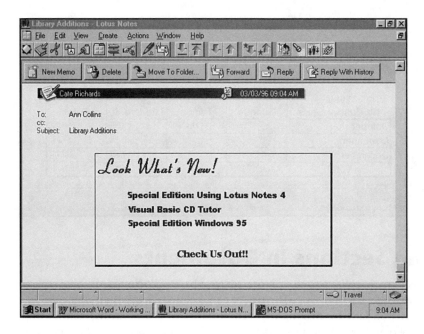

Fig. 8.42

You can use table settings to highlight text in a document.

Once you have created the one-cell table, you can enter text into the box. Notes will not let you put a box around text that has already been typed, so if you want to try this feature with previously entered text, you will need to create the box and then cut and paste the text into it.

Changing Table Text Characteristics

You can change many characteristics of the table text at any time, just as you would any text. You can use the Text menu settings and Text Properties InfoBox to change the color, size, and other font attributes for the text in the table.

Notes Basics

You can also change the justification of an entire column or row: highlight the columns or rows you want to set justification for, and select Text, Align paragraphs. You can specify whether the entire column or row should be Left, Right, Centered, or Full (you can not specify None in tables). In figure 8.43, the columns of numbers have been right-justified so that the numerals line up properly.

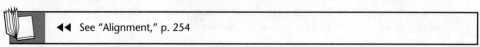

◀◀ See "Alignment," p. 254

Fig. 8.43

You can align text in tables and modify table settings to enhance its readability. This is the same table shown in figure 8.41, but formatted to enhance its presentation.

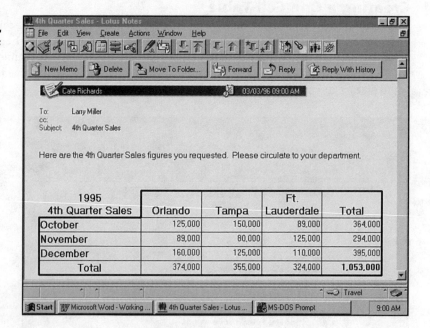

Creating Sections in Documents

You can use sections to collapse one or more paragraphs in a document into a single line—referred to as the Section Title. The reader can see more detail than that displayed on the Section Title by clicking the section indicator (down arrow) next to the Section Title to expand the section to reveal more information. Sections make navigation in large documents easier.

Readers can expand a section when they want to read its contents or ignore the section if it does not apply to them. In the design of forms, database designers can create *hide-when* formulas to provide logic for determining when a particular section can be seen. In this section, you will learn how to create sections in documents. You will learn more about designing forms in Chapter 11, "Designing Views."

> **Note**
>
> You must be in a rich text field to create a collapsed section.

Figure 8.44 illustrates a document about an upcoming meeting, in which sections have been created. One section, "Directions to the office," has been expanded to display further information. You can tell there is a collapsible section by the twistie located to the left of the section title.

Section indicator (twistie)

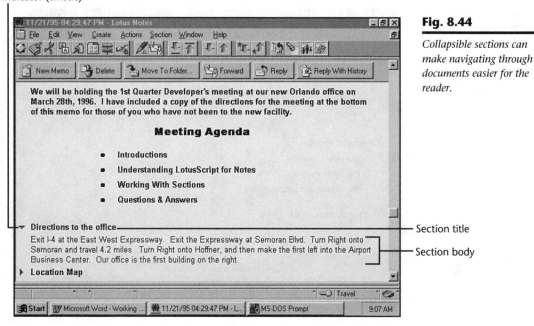

Fig. 8.44

Collapsible sections can make navigating through documents easier for the reader.

Section title

Section body

To create a section, perform the following steps:

1. Highlight the paragraphs you want to collapse into a section.

2. Choose Create, Section. Notes will collapse the section and display the title of the section as the first line of text in the paragraphs that were selected.

If you want to edit the title of a collapsed section after it is created, click anywhere within the collapsed section and select Edit, Properties. Notes displays the Sections Properties InfoBox, as shown in figure 8.45.

You can create nested collapsible sections by highlighting more than one collapsed section and then selecting Create, Sections again. Figure 8.46 displays multiple layers of collapsible sections for an Account Profile document.

Fig. 8.45

Collapsible section titles can be changed in the Sections Properties InfoBox.

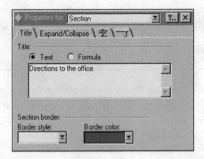

Fig. 8.46

You can create multiple layers of collapsible sections.

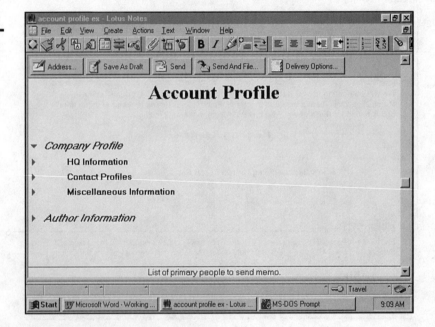

Using Folders To Organize Your Documents

You can use existing folders in a database—or design your own—to organize your documents in a manner that makes sense to you. For example, in your E-Mail database, you may want to create a folder titled Hot Topics to store memos on issues of great importance to you. When you find a document in a view that you want to store in your folder, simply click the document's title and drag it to the folder. When your mouse pointer is located over the appropriate folder (the folder will be highlighted by a box when it is selected), you can release the mouse button. The document will move into the folder. If you click the folder, you will see your document located in it.

Creating Folders

Folders can take on the characteristics of views in that you can copy the column de-sign of the views so that they appear the same in the folder. For example, you can create a folder titled Executive Correspondence and base the folder design on the People view in the database, which sorts documents according to people's names.

To create a new folder, do the following:

1. Select or open the database where you want to create the folder.

2. Choose <u>C</u>reate, <u>F</u>older. The Create Folder dialog box appears (see fig. 8.47).

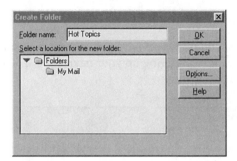

Fig. 8.47

You can enter or edit the name of a folder in the Create Folder dialog box.

3. Enter a name for the folder in the <u>F</u>older name box. The name length should be descriptive and can contain any characters. The name is limited by the number of characters you can type in the <u>F</u>older name box (between 14 and 26 charac-ters—depending on capitalization). If you want to place the folder inside an-other existing folder, click that folder in the <u>S</u>elect a location for the new folder list.

4. Click OK.

Notes creates the folder, and you see it appear in the navigator according to the options you selected.

If you want to select a view on which to base the folder's design, do all of the following:

1. In the Create Folder dialog box, click Op<u>t</u>ions. The Options dialog box appears (see fig. 8.48).

2. Click a view in the <u>I</u>nherit design from list. If you want to change the design of the folder, and want to do so as soon as the folder is created, select the <u>D</u>esign now option. When you click <u>O</u>K to create the folder, Notes will automatically open its programmer pane. You will learn more about designing folders and views in Chapter 12, "Integrating Notes 4.0 with Other Applications."

3. Click <u>O</u>K.

Fig. 8.48

Select the view design that you want the design of your folder to inherit.

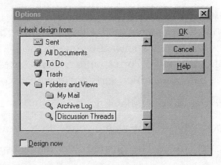

Deleting Folders

Occasionally, you may find that you no longer have a need for a particular folder in your database, and you don't want it cluttering up your navigators. You can easily delete a folder by performing the following:

> **Note**
>
> You must have Designer or Manager level access to delete, rename, or move shared folders (those used by everyone) in a database.

1. Select the folder you want to delete from the navigator pane.

2. Select Actions, Folder Options, Delete Folder.

3. Select Yes when prompted to delete the folder. Notes removes the folder from your navigator.

The documents displayed within the deleted folder, however, have not been deleted. You can switch to any view designed to display the documents to see them.

> **Tip**
>
> You can also delete a folder by highlighting the folder's name in the navigator and pressing F6, and then the Delete key. Select Yes when prompted to delete the folder.

Renaming Folders

There are times when you might want to rename a folder to further define its contents. You can do this by selecting the folder you want to rename, and then selecting Actions, Folder Options Rename. The Rename dialog box appears, as shown in figure 8.49. Type the new folder name in the Name box, and then select OK.

Fig. 8.49

You can also open the Rename dialog box by selecting the folder you want to delete, pressing F6, and selecting Actions, Rename.

Moving Folders

Just as there are times when you might want to rename a folder, there may also be times where you want to move the folder to display within another folder—or to move a folder out of another folder. To move a folder, highlight the folder you want to move and then select Actions, Folder Options, Move. The Move dialog box appears, as shown in figure 8.50. Highlight the location where you want the folder to be relocated, and then select OK. Notes will move the folder to the new location.

Fig. 8.50

You can also open the Move dialog box by highlighting the folder you want to move, pressing F6, and then selecting Actions, Move.

From Here...

In Part I, you learned to work with many of the advanced options available when you are working with documents. You have learned to search text, insert options that enhance your communication, work with tables, create folders, and create sections. You will learn more about many of these features and their use in designing applications in Part II, "Designing Applications."

For more information on the topics discussed in this chapter, refer to the following:

- Chapter 9, "Creating New Databases," teaches you the basics of designing a Lotus Notes database.
- Chapter 11, "Designing Views," teaches you how to design views, and more about creating folders within the design of a database.
- Chapter 13, "Working with Formulas," shows how to create formulas that you can use to customize your hotspots and folders.

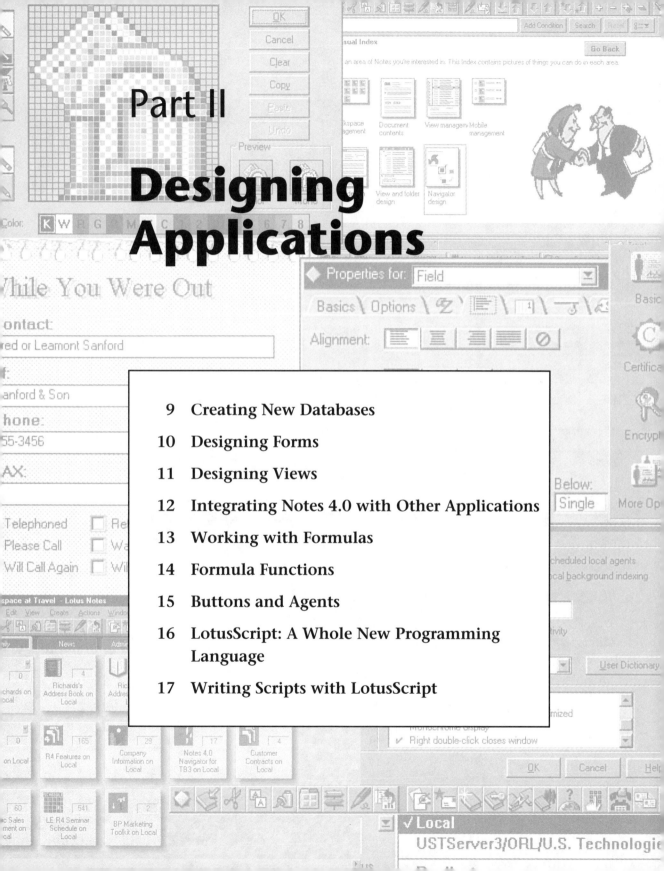

Part II

Designing Applications

CHAPTER 9

Creating New Databases

Throughout this book, you read about the databases that others have created—the Mail database, the Address Book, and others. In this chapter, you learn how to create your own customized databases, which you can use to store and share almost any kind of data you can imagine.

Users of many skill levels can design and build Notes databases. Even beginners with very little computer knowledge and even less Notes experience can learn to build simple-but-useful databases for many purposes, because Notes comes with many helpful templates. Experienced users, especially programmers, find in Notes a wealth of powerful features that enable such users to showcase their programming prowess and generally dazzle others with their database skills. Whatever your skill level, however, building databases in Notes is fun and useful.

Throughout this chapter, you'll learn about the various features for designing and building databases. These features enable you to perform the following actions covered in this chapter:

- Create a database from a template
- Use the design menu/navigator to create and edit forms, views, subforms, navigators, and agents
- Control security to your database
- Create a database icon
- Create Help documents
- Create custom navigators

As you build databases, you might not perform these actions in exactly this order—although creating the database must obviously come first! You might customize an existing form and then customize a view, only then deciding to create a new form. As you read through this chapter, you learn how to perform these steps, which you can perform in the order best suited to your own needs.

> **Note**
>
> Lotus Notes comes in several different flavors designed for varying levels of users. Some Notes clients do not have the capabilities to create and modify Notes databases. If the menu commands described in this chapter aren't available, contact your system administrator and ask how you can upgrade your version of Notes to one with design capabilities.

Using Templates

Notes comes with a collection of templates—ready-made databases—that you can use as a starting point for creating your own databases. A template is a special type of Notes database from which other databases are modeled. You'll use templates to serve as a guideline when you start creating new databases.

The first step in creating a database is deciding which template should serve as the starting point for your new database. In many cases, you might find that one of the supplied templates meets your needs exactly, and you might need to do little more than create the database with that template. If none of the templates matches your needs exactly, a certain template still might contain many of the forms and views you require and therefore can serve as a starting point for creating your new database.

Before you begin to create a new database, think about how you or others are likely to use this database. Are you creating a database to serve as a central storage location for some type of document? Is the database to serve as a discussion group for sharing ideas? Consider the information you want to store in the database and give some thought also to the various ways you want the data displayed and printed.

After you have a clear picture of the purpose of your database, you might be pleasantly surprised to discover that Lotus has anticipated your needs, and that one of the templates is exactly what you need to build your database. In the following sections, you learn how to create a database by using a template. Later in this chapter, you learn how to customize databases to match your precise needs and how to create new databases from scratch.

Reviewing the Notes Templates

Notes comes with more than a dozen templates. A few in particular are extremely useful, and can be used to create your own databases with little or no customization on your part. If you design new databases often, you will find that you keep coming back to these few templates over and over as starting points. Other templates are useful only to system administrators or for use in system databases such as mailboxes. Table 9.1 lists and summarizes several of the Notes templates.

▶▶ See "Database Templates, " p. 949

Table 9.1 Standard Templates Available with Notes	
Template Name	**Description**
Approval Cycle	Used to create sets of databases which will track and follow issues through a cycle of approvals.
Discussion	Enables you to create a Notes discussion database. Discussion databases are informal databases where users can ask questions or post comments that others will find useful. They are a means of sharing and storing knowledge.
Document Library	Used for storing and describing documents. Also allows you to set up document approval cycles. Can be modified for describing a collection of almost anything.
Microsoft Office Library	The same as the Document Library template except you can store copies of documents created with any of the Microsoft Office applications—using OLE2.
Personal Address Book	Used to create multiple Personal Address Books. The template is the same one used for the domain address book.
Personal Journal	Enables you to keep a diary or journal. Allows you to categorize entries into folders.
Room Reservations	Used to manage and track room reservations. It can be easily modified to track reservations for almost anything.

Creating a Database from a Template

Once you decide on a template, follow these steps to create your database:

1. Select the workpage on which you want to create the database.

2. Select File, Database, New; or press Ctrl+N. Notes displays the New Database dialog box shown in figure 9.1.

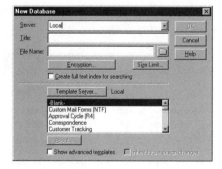

Fig. 9.1

The New Database dialog box.

The top half lets you set the database's location, name, and other options. The bottom half of the dialog box contains a list of available templates.

3. In the Server list, select the server on which you want your database to reside.

> **Note**
>
> When you choose to create a database on Local, you are telling Notes to place the database in your Notes Data directory located on your personal computer.
>
> In addition, sometimes Notes won't permit you to create a database on a specific server. That's because the Notes administrator has control over who is and is not permitted to place databases on a Notes Server. If Notes forbids you from creating a database on a server, contact your system administrator for more information.

4. In the Title box, enter a descriptive title for the database—up to 32 characters long—such as Legal Contract Library or Equipment Requests.

> **Tip**
>
> This title is an easy way to quickly identify this particular Notes database from your workspace, and appears in the title bar at the top of the screen when it is opened. Your database will be much easier for users to find if the title is descriptive and complete.
>
> Notes does not require unique database titles, but you should avoid duplicate titles to reduce confusion among users.

5. In the File Name box, enter the name of the database file. The name should have an NSF extension, such as `CONTRACT.NSF` or `REQUESTS.NSF`. (Notes automatically adds the extension if you leave it out.) Notes does support extended filenames (for Windows 95) and by default, the database filename is the same as the title you just typed in.

6. To encrypt a local database, choose Encryption, select Locally encrypt this database using, then choose an encryption type (see fig. 9.2).

> **Note**
>
> If you encrypt a local database, anyone who uses your computer must enter your password to access the encrypted database. This is especially useful if you have a laptop computer and are worried about someone taking your computer and possibly accessing sensitive information in your notes database.
>
> Desktop security is also useful in an office environment because it helps ensure the confidentiality of the data stored on your personal machine.

▶▶ See "Understanding Database Security," p. 727

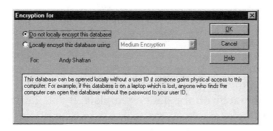

Fig. 9.2

Locally encrypt a database using the Encryption For dialog box.

7. To set a size limit for your database, select Si_z_e Limit. The default size limit of 1 GB is probably enough for most Notes databases, but the limit can be increased to as much as 4 GB.

8. To create a full text index for the database, click _C_reate Full Text Index For Searching.

◀◀ See "Full Text Searching in Databases," p. 276

9. From the template list, select the template you want to use to create your database. When specifying a template, keep the following notes in mind:

- If you select Blank from the template list, Notes creates an empty database with no forms or views. Use this to create a database from scratch.

- The template list contains a list of templates available locally on your computer. To select a template located on a server, select Template Se_r_ver and choose the server on which the template is located. The template list will update to list the templates available on the server you selected.

  Templates may or may not be installed on your personal machine—depending on how the Notes installation was performed. If you don't have templates available on your machine, make sure you look for them on your Template Server.

- If you click Show Advanced Te_m_plates, the template list will include system templates such as the Notes Log and Mail Router Mailbox as well as any other templates marked as advanced templates. In most cases, you will not need to create databases with these templates. If you have upgraded your machine from Notes 3.x to 4.0, other, older templates may also appear in this list. The templates with *[R4]* in their title are specifically geared to take advantage of Notes 4.0 features.

Tip

For more information about a particular Notes template, click the About button from the New Database dialog box.

10. By default, Notes checks the Inherit Future Design Changes check box. Deselect this option if you don't want design changes to be inherited. Keep these issues in mind:

- When this box is checked, the design of your database is automatically synchronized with the design of the template. This is useful if your database will be based exactly on the design template. If you have several databases based on a single template—for example, you have several document library databases—you can change the single underlying template and those changes will propagate out to all databases based on that template. If you are only using the template as a starting point for your database, you should deselect this checkbox.

- If you click Inherit Future Design Changes and later make design changes to your database, you might be surprised to find that your changes were overwritten by the design in the template.

- When a database inherits design changes from a template, it inherits the design from the template on the workstation or server on which the database resides. This means that if you create a database using a template on your workstation and later move the database to a server, you should make sure that the template on the server matches the one on your workstation. Otherwise, the design of your database could be changed without you knowing it—with potentially disastrous results.

11. Click the OK button to create your database. Notes will think for a few moments, create a new file in your Data directory, add a database icon onto your workspace, and open the new database automatically for you.

12. Notes displays an About document, which briefly describes the database. Close the About document by pressing Esc or by double-clicking with the right mouse button anywhere within the document.

After you complete these steps, you see your newly created database—which doesn't contain any documents yet. If the template exactly matched your needs, you are ready to begin entering documents and using your database.

More often than not, however, you must customize the database for it to meet all of your needs. Throughout the rest of this book, you will learn all you need to know to customize your database designs.

Selecting a Location for your Database

As you create a database, you must select a server from the New Database dialog box's Server list and then enter a filename for the database. Together, these two pieces of information determine where the database resides. The location you select for your database will depend on who accesses your database and what directories are on your server.

Note that you should not use network drives to share databases with other people. If multiple people access a database without going through a Notes server, the database could become corrupted.

In the Server list box, you have the following options:

- **Local**—You can select the first entry in the Server list—Local—and the database will be created on your PC's hard drive. Because it's local to your PC, users cannot access the database unless they are using your computer.

- **Server**—You can select a server name from the Server list and the database will be created on the selected Notes server. Since it is on the server, it will be available to everyone on your Notes network—assuming they are given access in the database Access Control List.

Once you have selected a server, enter a filename in the File Name box. You have three options for the filename:

- You can enter a filename such as `PROBLEMS.NSF`. The database will be put into the default data directory for the selected server—for example, if the data directory is `C:\NOTES\DATA`, the full path and filename will be `C:\NOTES\DATA\PROBLEMS.NSF`.

- You can enter a directory and filename such as `DATABASE\PROBLEMS.NSF`. The database will then be put into `C:\NOTES\DATA\DATABASE\PROBLEMS.NSF`, if `C:\NOTES\DATA` is the data directory.

- If you selected Local as your server, you can enter a full path and filename for your database, such as `D:\DATABASE\PROBLEMS.NSF`. This is useful if you want to put your database on another disk drive or a network drive.

Adding and Changing Design Elements in the Database

Now that you have created your database, you are ready to customize its design to fit your needs. You do this by adding, deleting, or changing its design elements. Notes databases have five main design elements that you will use.

- *Forms* define the data that will be entered into a document. They consist of static text, fields, and actions or scripts. The forms are the meat of an application. They are the primary user interface for entering data into your database and contain many of the actions that users invoke while using the application.

- *Views* are a list of documents that includes information about each document. Views are indexes to the information in your databases. A single database usually has many views that list different subsets of documents, different information, or sort the documents in different orders. A well-designed set of views makes information in your databases easy to find and more useful.

■ *Subforms* are reusable groups of fields and other form design elements. They are somewhat of a form within a form. Subforms can include fields, static text, and LotusScript programs. You should use them if you have a part of a form that is common to several forms. By using them, you do not have to add the design elements individually to each form; you can just insert the subform. Also, if you need to make changes to the subform, you can make your change once—in the subform—and it will propagate to all forms using the subforms.

■ *Navigators* are graphical interfaces to your databases. They can contain icons, buttons, bitmaps, hotspots, and static text. Clicking an element on a navigator can execute Simple Actions (such as opening a view or another navigator), @function formulas, or LotusScript programs. Navigators make your applications more intuitive and easier for your users.

■ *Agents* are macros written in either LotusScript or @functions. You can run them at predetermined intervals from a menu selection or event. Agents can be either *private* (created by a user and used only by that user) or *shared* (created by the database designer and used by all users). Some good uses for agents include archiving a set of documents, categorizing documents into folders, or updating groups of documents.

You will access these design elements through the default entry in the navigation pane called Folders—which is created with every Notes database—and the Create menu.

Accessing Existing Elements with the Folders Navigator

The navigation pane, shown in figure 9.3, allows you to access to all existing design elements of your database with just a few clicks. When you are designing a database, the first thing you should do is display the folders navigator (if it is not already shown). If another navigator is currently selected, select View, Show, Folders.

The following headings are under the Design category in the navigation pane:

■ Forms

■ Views

■ Folders

■ Shared Fields

■ Subforms

■ Navigators

■ Other

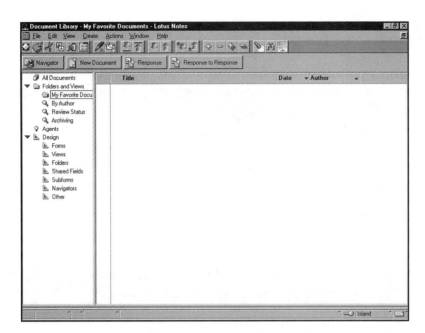

Fig. 9.3

Access existing design elements of a database with the folders in the navigation pane.

Clicking on any of these displays a list of the corresponding existing elements in your database where the current view is normally displayed. For example, selecting Forms lists all of the forms in your database (see fig. 9.4).

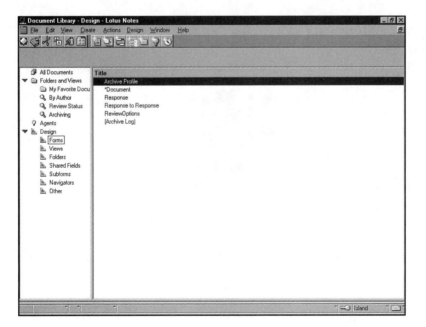

Fig. 9.4

Selecting Forms displays all existing forms.

Designing Applications

II

If you click a form name, you are put into design mode for the selected form (see fig. 9.5). Likewise, if you click views, folders, or any other heading, you will get a list of views, folders, and so on.

Fig. 9.5

The form design screen.

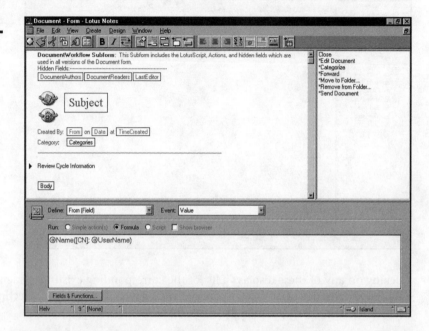

Creating New Elements with the Create Menu

The folders navigator allows you to edit existing elements, but suppose you want to create a new form, view, and so on? You use the Create menu (see fig. 9.6).

Fig. 9.6

*Create new elements using
the Create menu.*

Table 9.2 lists each design element and its corresponding item on the Create menu.

Table 9.2 Creating Elements with the Create Menu	
Element	**Create Menu Selection**
Agent	Create, Agent
Folder	Create, Folder
View	Create, View
Form	Create, Design, Form
Shared Field	Create, Design, Shared Field
Subform	Create, Design, Subform
Navigator	Create, Design, Navigator

You'll learn more about each element listed previously and how to create them in the following sections.

Deleting Design Elements

You can also easily delete design elements from your Notes database. First, choose the type of element you want to remove from the navigation pane on the left hand side of the screen.

For example, you can select Forms to get a list of forms saved within the database. Then choose the actual element (in this case, form) you want to erase from the list on the right by selecting it with your mouse. Next, press the Delete button from your keyboard; choose Edit, Clear from the menu bar; or use the Edit Clear SmartIcon.

Understanding Database Access

Now that you have created a database, you need to decide who should access it. Once you put your database on a server, it is out there for everyone on your Notes network to see. However, you most likely only want certain people to access your database. Even if you want everyone to see the data in your database, you will want to restrict certain functions from users. For example, you probably want only one person—or a group of people—to be able to change the design of your database (chances are, you will be part of the group of people). You will probably want only certain people to edit existing documents, while others will only enter new documents, and still others will only be able to read documents. If you did not restrict these functions to specific people or groups, your data and database design would be in jeopardy since anyone could make changes to your database. This is why controlling access to your database is vitally important.

The key to controlling access is your database's *Access Control List* (*ACL*). Within your ACL, you define what people or groups of people have access to your database and what functions they can perform. Additionally, the ACL defines what servers can access your database and what they can replicate.

> **Note**
>
> By default, the database Access Control List (ACL) affects only databases stored on a server. If the property Enforce Consistent ACL Across Replicas is selected, the ACL is enforced locally. The local enforcement of the ACL is not a security measure—it can be bypassed.
>
> To provide this security, choose File, Database, Access Control from the menu bar. Click the Advanced tab that appears and select the Enforce a consistent Access Control List across all replicas of this database option.

To gain a better understanding of how the Access Control List affects security, we should step back and take a quick look at the entire Notes security framework.

Notes has four layers of security:

- **Server-level security**—Before users can access a database on a server, they must have access to the server. Server access is controlled by the server administrator through the use of certificates attached to users' ID files and server access lists. This is the first and most general layer of security.

- **Database-level security**—Database security for any database on a server is handled by the database Access Control List. The ACL lists users and servers and assigns them rights to the database. Access levels range from Manager—who has total access to the database—to No Access. The database manager creates and controls the ACL. An additional database-level security feature is Local Encryption, which causes local databases to be encrypted, so that only specified users can access them.

- **Document-level security**—Document security consists of the document's Read Access list. The Read Access list is defined by the form's Read Access list, any Reader Names fields in the document, and the Read Access list in the Document Properties dialog box. The Read Access list refines the ACL for that document—meaning that if someone has Reader access or above in the ACL but is not listed in any Read Access list, he or she cannot read the document. If a person is not a reader in the ACL, he or she cannot read the document even if he or she is listed in the document's Read Access list.

- **Field-level security**—Certain fields on a form can be encrypted using encryption keys, so that only users with the correct key can read those fields. The database designer specifies which fields are encryptable, and when a key is associated to the document, all encryptable fields are encrypted with the key.

One good way to think of the various levels of Notes security is as a funnel. At the top level, the administrator controls who has access to a particular server. Then the next level is access to a particular database. Database ACLs can only work within the constraints of what security the administrator has set. All of the security options work like a funnel, where you can control access to a particular level of security only based on what the previous level allows you to.

Within this framework, the ACL is the highest level of security that a database designer can use to control access to a database. Therefore, it is very important that you give serious thought to who will access your database and set up the ACL correctly.

Assigning Access Levels

When planning your Access Control List, you will decide who gets what level of access. There are seven levels you can assign:

- Manager
- Designer
- Editor
- Author
- Reader
- Depositor
- No Access

In the Access Control List, you list users and servers who need access to your database. In the ACL, users and servers are listed together and are given one of the same seven access levels listed above. The access levels have a slightly different, but similar, connotation—depending on if they are given to a person or a server. For a person, the access levels define what actions the user can perform on the database. For servers, access levels define what information the servers can replicate. The access levels for users and servers are outlined in Table 9.3 and Table 9.4.

Table 9.3 Access Levels for People	
Access Level	**Description**
Manager	Users with Manager access can modify the ACL, modify replication settings, set a database for local encryption, and delete the database. A Manager also can perform tasks of lower access levels—Designer, Editor, Author, Depositor, and Reader. Every database should have at least one Manager (usually you have two or more so there is a backup) so that someone is always around to make necessary changes to a database.
Designer	Users with Designer access can change any design elements of a database, modify replication formulas, and index a database for full text searching. Designers also can perform the tasks of lower access levels—Editor, Author, Depositor, and Reader. Normally the person who designed the database has Designer access (at the very least) unless design responsibility was given to another person.

(continues)

Table 9.3   Continued

Access Level	Description
Editor	Users with Editor access can create documents and edit *all* documents in the database. Editors also can perform the tasks of lower access levels. Normally you should limit Editors to those who must edit all documents—too many Editors increases the risk of replication or save conflicts.
Author	Users with Author access can create documents and edit documents they created (if there is an Author Names field in the document with the author's name in it). Authors also can perform the tasks of lower access levels. Author access is the most common level given to users who need to create documents.
Reader	Users with Reader access can read documents in the database. Give Reader access to users who need to read the database but don't need to create new documents or edit existing documents. You want to set the default ACL level for this database to be Reader or better if you are performing an @DbLookup command on the information stored within this database.
Depositor	Users with Depositor access can create new documents but they cannot see any documents in the database. To a Depositor, the database is like a sealed box that they can only put things into but not take anything out.
No Access	Users with No Access cannot compose or read documents. They cannot even open the database or add its icon to their desktop. Often you will set a database's default access to No Access.

Tip

It is useful to create a group in your Public Name & Address Book containing the names of all administrators and provide that group's Manager with access to all databases.

Likewise, you can create a group containing all developers and provide that group's Designer with access to all databases. Using a group, it is easy to control and add people to a database ACL because they are stored in the shared Name & Address Book.

Table 9.4   Access Levels for Servers

Access Level	Description
Manager	A server with Manager access can send ACL changes to replica databases as well as changes allowed by lower access levels. If you want to centrally administer ACL changes from a single server, you should give only that server Manager access to the database and have it replicate with all replica databases.
Designer	A server with Designer access can send changes to design elements and replication formulas to replica databases as well as changes allowed by lower access levels. You can centralize design changes by giving only one server Designer access and having it replicate with all replicas. Keep in mind that if servers do not have at least Designer access to all replicas and the design is changed, it will not be changed in all replicas.

Access Level	Description
Editor	A server with Editor access can send new documents and changes to existing documents to replica databases (deletions will only be sent if the Delete Documents box is checked in the Access Control dialog box).
Author	A server with Author access can send new documents to replica databases. It will send only updates to existing documents if the documents have an Author Names field containing the server name—which is usually not the case. If you want updates to replicate, you should use Editor access.
Reader	A server with Reader access cannot send changes to replica databases. However, it can receive documents from the replica on another server if the other server has at least Author access. For example, if server X has Editor access and server Y has Reader access, new documents and changes on server X will replicate to server Y but no changes on server Y will replicate to server X. Be aware that for a server to receive changes from a replica, the server must have at least Reader access (a server cannot receive changes that it cannot read).
Depositor	A server with Depositor access can send new documents to replica databases. This is an unusual access level to give to servers; if you want to send only new documents, you should give the database Author access.
No Access	A server with No Access cannot send or receive anything from replica databases, regardless of the access level assigned to the other server.

Names, Servers, and Groups in the ACL

Now that we have looked at the access levels you can assign in the Access Control List, we should look at how people and servers are listed in the ACL. Each entry in the ACL is one of the following:

- User Name
- Server Name
- Group Name
- Databases Replica ID

User names in the ACL should be entered exactly as they appear in the user's ID file. If your organization uses hierarchical names, you should enter the fully distinguished hierarchical name—for example, Jane Doe/Marketing/Standard. If the server your database is on and the person you are adding are in the same organization, you can enter just the common name in the ACL, but the fully distinguished name is more secure, since two people cannot have the same fully distinguished name.

◄◄ See "The Distinguished Name," p. 173

Server names are entered in much the same way as user names. You should use the servers fully distinguished name—for example, Server1/Marketing/Standard—but you can use the common name if the servers are in the same organization.

Designing Applications

II

> **Note**
>
> Notes allows you to use the asterisk wildcard (*) to replace any component of a hierarchical name below the organization. Using wildcards, one ACL entry can grant access to everyone within a single organization or organizational unit. For example, the entry */Standard gives access to anyone in the organization Standard (including Bob Smith/Standard or Jane Doe/Marketing/Standard). The entry */Marketing/Standard applies to anyone with an organizational unit Marketing and an organization Marketing (including Jane Doe/Marketing/Standard but no Bob Smith/Standard).

Group names in the ACL can be any group (of people or servers) that is defined in the Public Name & Address Book. Using group names in your ACLs has several advantages over individual names, including the following:

- One group representing many users keeps the number of entries in the ACL low. This makes keeping track of the ACL much easier.

- If a group of people needs its access changed, you only need to change the access for a single group rather than several individual users.

- A single group can be in the ACL in several databases. Simplify administration by centralizing changes within the Public Name & Address Book.

- Using groups, you can list a descriptive name that makes up a set of people, so you don't have to worry about typing in each individual entry, just the group name.

Whenever a background agent acts on a database (either by changing documents or reading documents via an @DbLookup or @DbColumn), the database replica ID should be listed in the ACL with the appropriate access level. The database replica ID is a unique number that Notes assigns to every database created. You can find a database replica ID by clicking on the database and selecting File, Database, Properties.

Standard ACL Entries

There are four standard entries that should be in the ACL for every database: Default, LocalDomainServers, OtherDomainServers, and database creator (the user name of the individual who creates the database). They are created by default in every new database. When you plan the ACL for your database, you should first assign access levels to these four entries. You do not have to include all four of the standard ACL entries, but using them makes your ACLs across databases uniform—making the ACL easier to administer and more secure. The following list describes each entry:

- The *Default* entry defines the access level for anyone who is not listed anywhere else in the ACL. It is recommend that Default be either No Access, Reader, or Author. Your selection depends on the purpose and content of the database. A database with confidential information—such as a human resources database—has a Default of No Access. One with general enterprise-wide information—such as a company policy database—has a Default of Reader. One in which everyone composes documents—such as a discussion database—has a Default of Author.

■ *LocalDomainServers* is a group that is in every domain's Name & Address Book that contains the names of all the servers in your domain. Normally you will give this group Manager access, so that replicas of the database on all servers can replicate the entire database—including changes to the ACL. There are two cases in which you do not give this group Manager access:

  • When you want to control ACL or design changes from a central server. In this case, you will give the group a lower access level (probably Editor) and the central server a Manager access.

  • When you do not want your database replicated to all servers in your domain. In this case, you will give the group No Access.

■ *OtherDomainServers* is also a group in every domain's Name & Address Book. It contains the names of servers in other domains within your organization with which you regularly replicate. This group typically has Designer access if the database is replicated to other domains (to keep the designs in sync among replicas). If the database is not replicated to other domains, the group has No Access.

■ The *database creator* is put in the ACL with Manager access. You do not have to keep this person in the ACL, but Notes does require that at least one person is given Manager access to the database. If there isn't a Manager, it's possible that everyone could be locked out of a database with nobody able to add people to the ACL.

Caution

Notes will allow you to give the Default group any access level—all the way up to Manager. But you should never set it higher than Author for a database in production; this poses a serious security threat. Even Author access should be used sparingly. In fact, many organizations impose a standard that Default is given only Reader or No Access.

If you need to give a large group a high access level, you are better off leaving Default no higher than Reader; create a group in the Public Name & Address Book that you can grant a higher access level.

Note

If you replicate with servers in other domains outside your organization, those servers are usually listed in the *ExternalServers* group in the Name & Address Book. OtherDomainServers only refers to servers in other domains within your organization.

Beyond these standard entries in the ACL, you will add additional entries for users, servers, and groups of users or servers. These additional entries will affect the bulk of the database users.

Creating the ACL

In the previous sections, you learned about the access levels and entries that make up the Access Control List. Now it is time to put that knowledge to work and actually create an ACL.

The first step you take in creating the ACL is to plan who needs access to your database. As part of this process, you collect all the names of your users and organize them into any necessary groups. If you use any groups, now is the time to either create the groups yourself or ask the administrator to create them for you.

The groups you create should have a descriptive name. You can describe either the tasks of the group (for example, PO Approvers) or the members of the group (for example, Account Managers). A descriptive name tells you who belongs in a certain group when ACL changes are made (possibly months or years down the road).

If you have an administrator create the groups for you, make sure he or she includes you as a group owner. As an owner, you can add or remove people from the groups you use. Therefore, if an administrator is not available, you can make access changes immediately.

Table 9.5 lists a sample ACL. It contains the standard server groups (LocalDomainServers and OtherDomainServers), two individual names, two groups of users, one name using wildcards, and the Default entry.

Table 9.5   Sample ACL Entries

Entry	Access Level
LocalDomainServers	Manager
OtherDomainServers	No Access
Jane Doe/Marketing/Standard	Manager
Bob Smith/Marketing/Standard	Manager
Document Editors	Editor
Account Managers	Author
*/Marketing/Standard	Reader
Default	No Access

Once you have defined who need access to the database, you are ready to create the ACL. You create the ACL using the Access Control List dialog box. To display the dialog box, follow these steps:

1. Click the database icon for which you want to set up an ACL and select File, Database, Access Control. Or right-click on the database and select Access Control (see fig. 9.7).

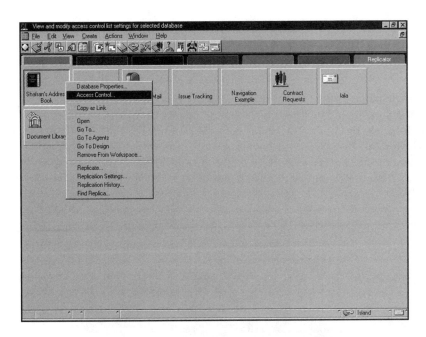

Fig. 9.7

Right-click on a database to view its pull-down menu.

2. Notes prompts you for your password—if you have not already entered it—and then displays the Access Control List dialog box (see fig. 9.8).

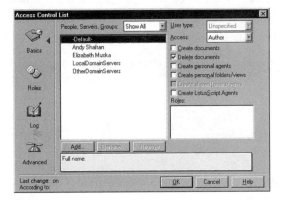

Fig. 9.8

The Access Control List dialog box.

People, Servers, <u>G</u>roups lists all the entries in the ACL. You can add, delete, or update entries in the list. Use the following procedure to add names to the list:

1. Click the A<u>d</u>d button (located below the list of people, servers, and groups). Notes displays the Add User dialog box (see fig. 9.9).

Fig. 9.9

Enter names into the Add User dialog box.

2. Enter a single name in the Person, server, or group box. Or click the Person button in the Names dialog box, which is used for looking up names in a Name & Address Book (see fig. 9.10). This dialog box is very similar to the one you use to address NotesMail. You can select names from the list on the left and click Add to add them to the list on the right. In addition, you can also select groups of individuals from the Name & Address Book.

Fig. 9.10

Add names from an Address Book in the Names dialog box.

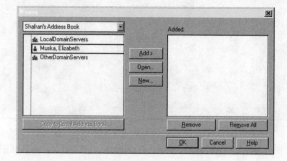

3. When you have added all of the names, click OK. The names will now show up in the People, Servers, Groups list.

To rename an item in the list, followthese steps:

1. Select the name you want to rename and click Rename. The Rename User dialog box appears (see fig. 9.11).

Fig. 9.11

The Rename User dialog box.

2. From this point on, the procedure is the same as for adding new names (except that the name you enter will replace the one you selected). Notes tries to reconcile a name in the ACL with one in your Name & Address Book and looks for spelling and phonetic matches.

To delete a name from the list, select the name you want to delete and click Remove.

Once you have entered the correct names, you can assign access levels to those names using the following procedure:

1. Select a name from the list of People, Servers, Groups listbox.

2. If you want, select a user type from the Üser type pull-down list (see fig. 9.12).

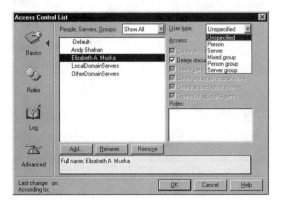

Fig. 9.12

Selecting a user type.

3. Select the appropriate access level from the Access pull-down list (see fig. 9.13).

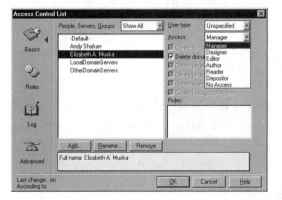

Fig. 9.13

Selecting an access level.

4. Below the Access list are six checkboxes that you should check to further refine a user's actions. The actions available for selection depend on the access level you assigned the user. For example, the Create Documents box is unavailable for a user with Reader access because a reader, by definition, cannot create documents. Any unavailable items are grayed out.

5. Finally, you can select any roles assigned to this user—if any are defined—in the Roles list box.

You can also set other ACL-related options by clicking the icons on the left side of the Access Control List dialog box. Figure 9.14 shows the advanced options you can set.

II

Designing Applications

Fig. 9.14

Setting other ACL related options.

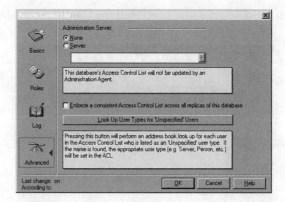

With these advanced options, you can control whether this database's ACL can be updated by an agent automatically, and enforce the ACL for databases on local workstations:

- **Basics**—This option is used to set up names and access levels.
- **Roles**—This option allows you set up roles for the database. Roles let you define more specific security entries for a database. For example, if your default access was Depositor, you could create a role which allowed certain users to author a particular document instead of giving them blanket Author access to the whole database.
- **Log**—This option displays a history of changes to the ACL.
- **Advanced**—This option allows you to select advanced options, such as Enforce a consistent Access Control List across all replicas of this database.

Customizing Database Icons

An *icon* (a tiny picture that Notes displays on your workpage to help you spot the database at a glance) is associated with each database. Most database templates have a default icon associated with them that the Lotus designers considered appropriate for that type of database. Sometimes the icons are clever, sometimes they are not. Figure 9.15 shows the icon that Notes assigns to a database created from the Document Library template as described earlier in this chapter.

Fig. 9.15

The Document Library icon.

You should create at least a simple icon for every database to help users distinguish databases on the desktop.

Having common icons for similar databases can cue the user to the type or purpose of the database.

Using the Icon Editor

You can modify the icon as you want or even create new icons. To edit or create a new icon for your database, double-click it from your Notes workspace. Once opened, click Design in the navigation pane on the left hand side of the screen and then select Other. Notes displays several unique aspects of the database you can change in the view pane on the right hand side of the screen. Double-clicking Icon opens up the Design Icon dialog box, the built-in icon editor (see fig. 9.16).

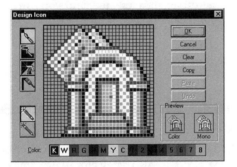

Fig. 9.16

The Design Icon dialog box.

If you want to showcase your originality and creativity, you can change the current icon by choosing a Color from the colored squares at the bottom of the dialog box and clicking points in the large icon image. You can experiment with the various tools on the left side of the Design Icon dialog box; the tools enable you to fill large areas of the icon with certain colors and perform other special editing.

You can draw an entirely new icon by first clicking the Clear button, which erases the current icon and gives you a clean drawing area. When you are finished making changes, click the OK button to save your changes.

Copying and Pasting Icons from Another Source

Even if you aren't artistic, you still can add more interesting icons to your databases. If you know of another database that has an interesting icon, for example, you can "borrow" that icon for your database. To copy another database's icon, follow these steps:

1. Open the database that has the icon you want to use.

2. Click Other under Design on the folders navigator and select Icon. The Design Icon dialog box appears.

3. Click the Copy button. Notes copies the icon to your computer's Clipboard.

4. Click Cancel to close the dialog box (which ensures that you haven't made any changes to this icon) and then press Esc to close the database.

5. Open the database for which you want to use the icon.

6. Again, click Other under Design on the folders navigator and select Icon to access the Design Icon dialog box.

7. Click the Paste button. The icon you copied from the other database appears in the icon editor area of the dialog box.

8. Click OK to close the dialog box. Your new icon is in place.

You can use icons from other sources also. If you have access to Windows and OS/2 icons and can copy them to the Clipboard, you can paste them into the icon editor of the Design Icon dialog box. You might also have access to an icon library database that contains all kinds of icons that others have created, and you can use them for your databases.

Remember that when an icon is changed for a database on a server, people won't see the new icon until the next time they access that database on their PC.

Creating Standard Help Documents

Every database has two standard help documents—an About document and a Using document. These standard help documents will help your users by telling them the purpose of your database and how to use it. Also, they eliminate some of the questions asked of you. You should therefore take some care in creating these documents before deploying your database.

The user can access these documents from the Help menu. If, for example, the user is reading the Company Procedures database, the Help menu will show two items— About Company Procedures and Using Company Procedures.

Creating an About Document

A database's *About document* tells people about the database—what kind of information the database contains, who should use the database, and how to get the most benefit from that particular database. If you create a database for your private use, you probably will not create an About document. However, if your database will be used by others who might not be familiar with it, an About document can provide those other users with vital information about the database.

The About Document can also display default information, your company logo, or perform automated events when a database is opened—propagating information to all database users in a simple way.

To create or modify an About document, open the database. Click Design in the navigation pane, and then select Other. Now select the About Database Document from the view pane on the right hand side of the screen.

Notes displays the current About document (or a blank screen if no About document exists) and enters an edit mode very similar to the one used to edit forms (see fig. 9.17). You can type new text, delete existing text, or perform almost any editing function on your About document.

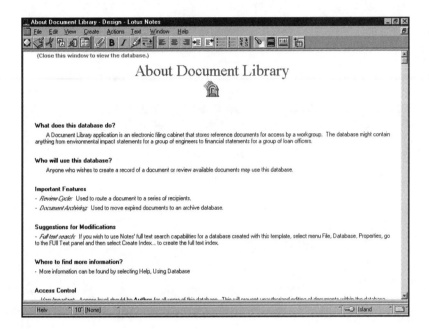

Fig. 9.17

Sample About document for the Company Procedures database.

After you complete your About document, close the window. When Notes asks if you want to save your changes, select Yes.

> **Tip**
>
> You should list any important database contacts (such as the database owner or manager) in the About document. That way, the users will know who to contact if they have any problems.

Creating a Using Document

A *Using document* is very similar to an About document except it describes how to use the database. It usually describes the forms and views in the database and how they function.

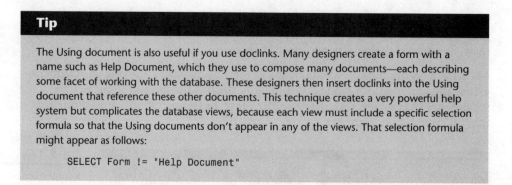

> **Tip**
>
> The Using document is also useful if you use doclinks. Many designers create a form with a name such as Help Document, which they use to compose many documents—each describing some facet of working with the database. These designers then insert doclinks into the Using document that reference these other documents. This technique creates a very powerful help system but complicates the database views, because each view must include a specific selection formula so that the Using documents don't appear in any of the views. That selection formula might appear as follows:
>
> ```
> SELECT Form != "Help Document"
> ```

Figure 9.18 shows how a portion of the database Using document might appear.

Fig. 9.18

Sample Using document.

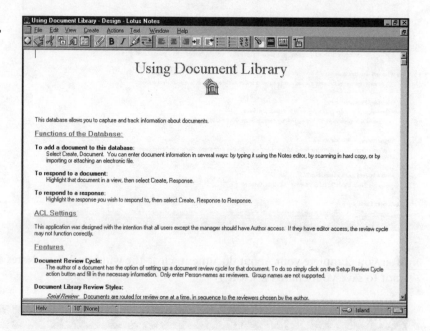

Creating Graphical Navigators

Once you have created forms and views for your database, you will want to build a user interface that helps users maneuver around it. *Graphical navigators* are that interface. Navigators provide a graphical way for users to do such things as switch views, open documents, file documents into folders, and just about any other action you can program in Notes.

Navigators are made up of objects (text, pictures, or shapes) that cause actions to occur when they are clicked. One common use for navigators is a graphical table of contents. The Notes Help Database uses this style of navigator (see fig. 9.19).

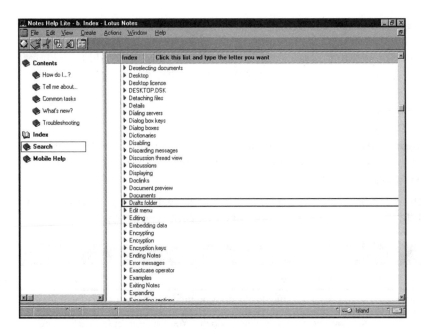

Fig. 9.19

A table of contents navigator from the Notes Help Database.

You have already worked with at least one navigator, the default navigator. Each database automatically has a navigator which splits up your screen into two different panes which allows easier access to your Notes information.

Even though the navigator provides a good interface to a database, you undoubtedly are going to want to create your own specialized navigators.

Working with Navigator Objects

Navigators are a collection of navigator objects which are graphical shapes and images that can have actions assigned to them. To work with these objects, choose Create, Design, Navigator from the Notes menu or use the Create Navigator SmartIcon. All of these objects can be added to a Navigator by using the Create menu.

There are six types of navigator objects:

- **Graphic Backgrounds**—A graphic background is a bitmap that is pasted into the navigator. Each navigator has only one background, and you cannot attach actions to it. In fact, a graphic background is the only element that cannot perform an action. You can think of a graphics background as wallpaper behind the information that appears on the screen.

- **Graphic Buttons**—Graphic buttons are small images that can be pasted into a navigator. They can appear like icons on-screen and perform specific actions when clicked upon.

- **Graphical Shapes**—Similar to buttons, graphical shapes can be rectangles, polygons, polylines, or ellipses. They are drawn using Notes drawing tools and can be any shape you choose. Like graphic buttons, you can assign Notes tasks to be performed when they are clicked upon.

II

Designing Applications

- **Hotspots**—Hotspots are extremely similar to graphical shapes except they're displayed on-screen in a more discreet manner. For example, a hotspot might be a green pop-up box that appears around text. When clicked on, additional information might appear. They are transparent so that they don't take up a lot of room on-screen.

- **Textboxes**—Textboxes are simply blocks of text that can be placed on the navigator which also can have an action associated with it.

- **Command Buttons**—Command buttons are normal buttons with a text captions on their face. Command buttons are useful for initiating any actions that don't have graphical depictions.

Navigator objects can be created or drawn within the navigator design space using the Create menu. Table 9.6 shows the procedure to create each type of object.

Table 9.6   Creating Navigator Objects

Object	Procedure
Graphic Background	Create a picture in any drawing program, copy the picture to the Clipboard, and select Create, Graphic Background. The graphic will be pasted into the navigator. You can also set the background color of the Navigator by editing its properties (choose Design, Navigator Properties).
Graphic Button	Create a picture in any drawing program, copy the picture to the Clipboard, and select Create, Graphic Button.
Graphical Shapes	From the Create menu, select the type of shape you want to draw. Then use the mouse to draw the shape.
Hotspots	Select Create, then either Hotspot Rectangle or Hotspot Polygon. After drawing the hotspot, double-click it to display its Properties InfoBox. Select the HiLite tab. In this box, you can specify if the hotspot should highlight when touched or clicked.
Textbox	Select Create, Text and draw a box using the mouse. After you draw the box, the Text Box Properties InfoBox opens. Enter the text you want to display in the Caption box and close the Properties InfoBox.
Command Button	Select Create, Button and draw the button with the mouse. The Button Properties InfoBox will appear. Enter the text for the face of the button in the Caption box and close the Properties InfoBox.

Working with Navigator Actions

Up to this point, we have referred to objects having actions associated with them. But what can these actions do? An action can be one of three types:

- A simple action
- A formula
- A script

You define actions in the bottom portion of the navigator design screen (see fig. 9.20).

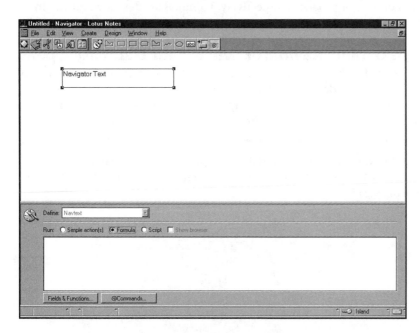

Fig. 9.20

The navigator design screen.

To define an action for an object, you should first click the object. This activates the bottom portion of the design screen. Then click the radio button corresponding to the type of action you will define—either Simple action(s), Formula, or Script.

If you select Simple action(s), you must select an action from the Action pull-down list. Table 9.7 describes the type of simple actions you can select.

Table 9.7   Types of Simple Actions

Simple Action	Description
Open another Navigator	This Action causes the current navigator to close and another to open in its place. When you select this option, another list box opens from which you select the navigator to which you want to switch.
Open a View	This Action switches the user to the specified view. When you select it, another list box opens from which you select the view to which you want to switch.
Alias a Folder	This Action causes any documents dragged from the view pane onto the object to be placed in a specified folder (like your mail database). When you select this, a list box opens from which you select the folder you want to alias.
Open a Link	This Action opens a specified document. Before selecting this option, go to a document and select Edit, Copy as Link. The object will link to the specified document.

If you select either a Formula or Script, a box opens where you can write any @function formula or LotusScript program, respectively. Formulas are described further in Chapter 14, "Formula Functions," and LotusScript is discussed in Chapters 16 and 17.

Displaying a Default Navigator When Your Database Opens

Once you have created several navigators, you might want to select one navigator and have it open every time the database opens. Setting a default navigator in this way ensures that the same screen will always display on startup. By creating a default navigator, you can link to different views, documents, and other navigators, creating a graphical user interface to your Notes database.

To select a default navigator, open the Database Properties InfoBox (from the workspace, right-click the database icon and select Database Properties) and select the Launch tab (see fig. 9.21).

Fig. 9.21

Select a default navigator in the Database Properties InfoBox Launch tab.

There are two options you can select in the On Database Open pull-down list regarding navigators:

- **Open Designated Navigator**—This option opens the designated navigator within the normal three-paned window (the navigator is on the left, the view is on the right, and the preview is on the bottom).

- **Open Designated Navigator In Its Own Window**—This option displays only the navigator when the database is opened; the three-paned window won't appear until the navigator is closed.

Tip

Opening a navigator in its own window is a convenient way to display a welcome screen each time the database is opened.

From Here...

Now that you know how to create a Notes database, the next several chapters further explore creating forms and views. That is followed by chapters that cover writing formulas and LotusScript programs. For more information on the topics discussed in this chapter, refer to the following:

- Chapter 10, "Designing Forms," describes how to create and design custom forms for your database.

- Chapter 11, "Designing Views," shows how to create views to display the documents created from your forms.

- Chapter 16 "LotusScript: A Whole New Programming Language," teaches the basics of the powerful LotusScript programming language, which can be used to manipulate objects and links.

II

Designing Applications

CHAPTER 10

Designing Forms

Now that you've learned how to create a new database, you're ready to create a form. Forms contain the fields you'll use in your application. Lotus Notes uses forms for data entry, displaying data, and controlling the field structure in documents. When users open documents, they see the data "through" the form. A database may have a variety of forms used for displaying different data, or even for displaying the same data in different formats.

The form can contain fields, static text, tables, graphics, buttons, popups, and other objects such as subscriptions or OLE links. When you design a form, you place the objects (like those listed above) where you want them displayed; you can also select formats to control how the data appears on the screen.

In this chapter, you learn how to do the following:

- Define your database structure through Create Design Form
- Create forms by defining static text and form attributes
- Create fields to be utilized on the form
- Designate the data and field types for the fields
- Use field formulas to manipulate data
- Format the fields to display on the form

What's Contained in a Form?

A *form* contains multiple components that define the structure of your database. These components could be fields, static text, graphics, buttons, popups, layout regions, tables, and objects (OLE, Subscriptions, FX fields) that link Notes to other products and a variety of other components.

Following is a list of the most widely used components for designing forms:

- **Fields**—You can place fields anywhere you want on a form. A field can be unique to that form, shared among forms within a database, or based upon a design template and used in multiple databases. Fields are the basis for how data is stored and displayed from within Notes. Besides storing data you can use fields to calculate data and even add LotusScript programs that run when users move to or from certain fields. Text attributes (such as bold type or color) applied to fields are reflected in the way data is displayed in the finished document. Fields can also be Notes/FX fields that exchange information with other products.

- **Text**—You can place static (unchanging) text anywhere on a form, and you can apply any text attributes to it—color, size, different typefaces, and so on. You generally want to label fields with text that helps users understand the purpose of each field.

- **Graphics**—You can place a decorative graphic anywhere on a form and it will appear on every document created with the form. For example, if you are designing a form for correspondence, you can place your company logo at the top of the form to create a letterhead.

- **Actions and hotspots**—Form actions and hotspots allow users to click them to accomplish simple tasks that mimic the Notes menus or complex tasks that are defined by formulas or a LotusScript program. Form actions can be displayed on the action bar and the Actions menu. Hotspots are placed directly on the form. Hotspots, in the form of pop-up text, actions, links, and formulas, are a useful way to automate static text and decorative graphics.

- **Tables**—Tables are useful for summarizing information or lining up fields in rows and columns. A table placed on a form appears in every document created with the form. You can disable the cell borders (lines that surround each table cell) if you want to create an "invisible" table.

- **OLE objects**—A form that has an Object Linking and Embedding (OLE) object enables you to use a Notes document to view and update data created in another product. For example, an Employee Information form can include an OLE object that links to a Word Pro file where the employee annual performance reviews are stored.

See Chapter 12 "Integrating Notes 4.0 with Other Applications," for details on using OLE with Notes.

New Design Logistics in Notes R4

If you have previously developed in Notes 3.x or earlier, you will notice a profound change in the appearance of Notes R4, especially when first developing a database. Don't worry, Lotus has actually made your life easier. Though the menu and options have changed for accessing and designing a form, the basic principles of database design have not. As a developer, you still need to define your form types, fields, field types, static text, objects, and the formulas within the fields.

Designing forms in Notes R4 is now easier, more accessible, and more visually appealing. If you are designing or modifying forms, always verify that the Design options are displayed by selecting <u>V</u>iew, <u>S</u>how, <u>D</u>esign. Figure 10.1 shows a sample database in design mode, which was created using the sample discussion (`DISCUSS4.NTF`).

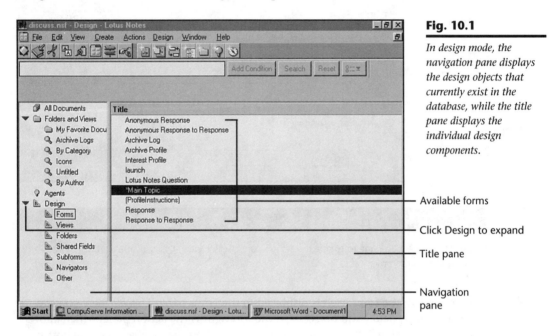

Fig. 10.1

In design mode, the navigation pane displays the design objects that currently exist in the database, while the title pane displays the individual design components.

Notice that in the navigation pane you see the various components of the database, such as the folders and views, agents, and design. Click Design to expand the design components. This displays the views, forms, folders, shared fields, subforms, navigators, and other components that exist in the database.

When you double-click Forms in the navigation pane, the title pane on the right displays all of the forms that exist in the database. You can now double-click one of these forms to go into edit mode. Figure 10.2 displays the Response form in edit mode. (Page down in the form pane to skip over the hidden fields.) Once in form design mode you can show up to three different window panes.

Fig. 10.2

While editing a form, you can easily maneuver between panes to design the form and its attributes.

Form pane —

Action pane —

Programmer pane —

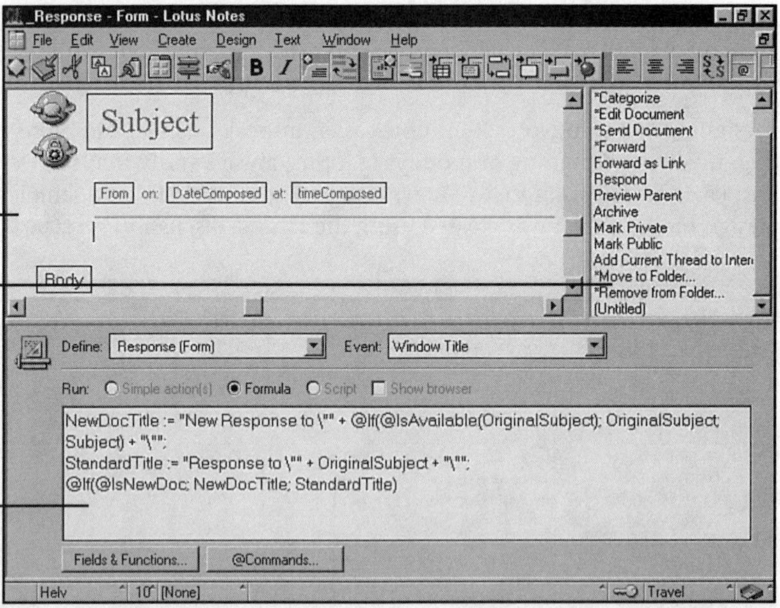

Tip

Select <u>V</u>iew, <u>A</u>ction pane to toggle the Action pane. Select <u>V</u>iew, <u>D</u>esign Pane to toggle the design or programmer pane.

On the top left, the form itself is displayed in the Form pane. This is where you can enter static text, fields, and objects. On the top-right is the action pane, which allows you to define various actions that can be performed on the database. On the bottom center is the design pane, which allows you to define the formulas, scripts, and actions for the form and the fields on the form and their corresponding formulas.

Now that you are aware of the new features and logistics that are encountered when designing a form, we can begin creating a form. The next few sections detail how to define a form and its attributes.

Understanding Form Hierarchy and Types

Before jumping in and selecting <u>C</u>reate, <u>D</u>esign, <u>F</u>orm to create a new form, you need to understand the structure or hierarchy of a Notes database. Each form created for any application has a form type associated with it. The following three types of forms can exist in a Notes database and they follow a hierarchical order:

- Document
- Response-to-document
- Response-to-response

Document is the default form type and the highest-ranking form in the form hierarchy. If you create only one form in the database, it should be of document type.

Response-to-document and *Response-to-response* type forms are used to create responses to documents and other responses. It is important to remember that the relationship between the document and the response is created by highlighting the appropriate document before composing the response. Also, when building views, Notes distinguishes between these three types of documents by indentations and column formulas to enable Notes to thread discussions correctly. Figure 10.3 shows an example of response documents in a hierarchical view.

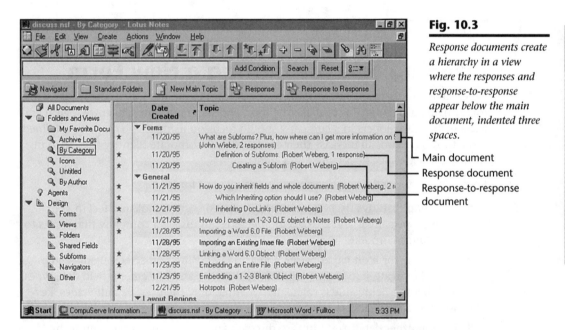

Fig. 10.3

Response documents create a hierarchy in a view where the responses and response-to-response appear below the main document, indented three spaces.

Main document
Response document
Response-to-response document

II

Designing Applications

Note

Response-to-response type forms provide the user with more flexibility when composing documents because they can be associated with either a document or any response-type document.

Table 10.1 summarizes the three different form types.

Table 10.1 The Three Form Types	
Form Type	**Description**
Document	Used to create any main document. Independent of all other documents.
Response-to-document	Used to create responses associated to a main document. Dependent upon the main document. In a view that uses a response hierarchy, a response document appears underneath the main document that is highlighted when the user chooses Compose, and is indented three spaces under a main document. You can display 32 levels of responses.
Response-to-response	Used to respond to either a main document or another response document. Indented under another response document. Multiple levels are allowed.

Planning and Formatting a New Form

When laying out a form, you should always attempt to act the way a user would when inputting data. Your goal is to make the form appealing and the data entry logical and free-flowing. Developers in a company should focus on using their company's defined formatting standards to increase their organization's corporate identity (e.g., logo in the left corner, a specific font size and color).

Keep in mind the following tips when designing your forms:

- You should always try to keep a standard or consistent look and feel in your forms, especially if you are developing applications for a company that wants to maintain a corporate image.

- Sketch the form on paper before you actually create it on-screen. Your sketch should indicate static text, graphics, field names and placement, field data types, whether the field value is calculated or entered by the user, default values, keyword lists, graphics, and help text.

- Look at other databases' forms to discover and learn new form design techniques. Open them up and learn. If appropriate, copy and paste desired parts of other forms.

- You should consider how your forms will appear when used in various screen size resolutions and attempt to use light-colored backgrounds for easy viewing.

- Utilize tab settings for consistent alignment and do not use too many fields as users become frustrated when forced to enter large amounts of data entry.

Creating a New Form

When first designing a new form, you can define the fields, graphics, text, margins, and tabs because Notes does not create any predefined structure on the form. To create a form, you need to perform the following steps:

1. Select the database you want to add the form to.

2. Choose <u>C</u>reate, <u>D</u>esign, <u>F</u>orm to create a blank, untitled form as displayed in figure 10.4 (or you can choose the Create Form SmartIcon).

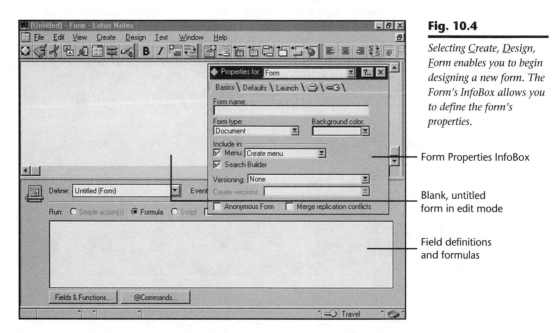

Fig. 10.4

Selecting <u>C</u>reate, <u>D</u>esign, <u>F</u>orm enables you to begin designing a new form. The Form's InfoBox allows you to define the form's properties.

Form Properties InfoBox

Blank, untitled form in edit mode

Field definitions and formulas

II

Designing Applications

3. To define the form properties for a form, you need to select <u>D</u>esign, Form <u>P</u>roperties to display the Form Properties InfoBox. Notice in the Properties For list box that Form is automatically selected. The Form Properties InfoBox enables you to modify the settings for your form, such as its name, what to do when the document is opened or closed, and other default options.

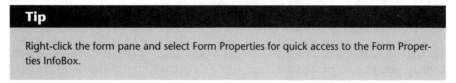

Tip

Right-click the form pane and select Form Properties for quick access to the Form Properties InfoBox.

4. Lay out the form by placing fields, text, graphics, and other objects on the form as needed.

5. Save the form by choosing File, Save (Ctrl+S). If you have not named the form in the Form Properties InfoBox, you will be prompted to name the form before saving. The form name is significant because Notes can reference it from within field formulas, form formulas, selection formulas, and view column formulas.

Adding Static Text to a Form

All forms need *field labels*. Field labels are static text that describe the field. You can add static text to a form in design mode the same way you type characters into any Notes document: type directly on the form exactly where you want the text to appear. Figure 10.5 shows a form in design mode with static text.

Fig. 10.5

Static text identifies and labels your fields.

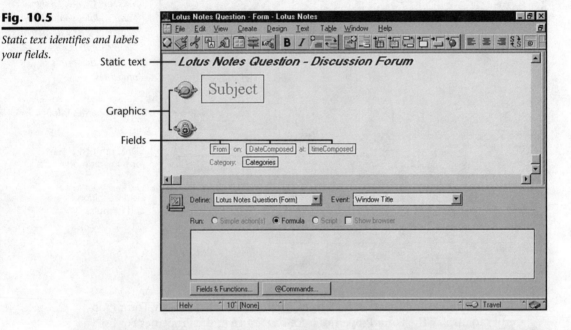

The Tip

Information entered into a field is usually variable. For example, a customer name field would be variable while a social security number field would be constant. Thus, position fields on the form to accommodate the longest piece of data that might be contained there.

The default font and color for static text on new forms is Helvetica 10-point in black. Usually, you should create static text with a different color or size, or utilize boldface, to set it off from the field contents.

Choose Text, Text Properties; press Ctrl+K; press the Text Properties SmartIcon; or right-click and select Text Properties to change the size, color, and other attributes of static text. The following table shows some of the most common text attributes and the different methods you can use to apply them.

◀◀ See "Changing the Appearance of Text with the Text Menu" p. 245

SmartIcon	Command	Keyboard	Description
B	Text, Bold	Ctrl+B	Boldfaces selected text or turns on boldfacing
U	Text, Underline	Ctrl+U	Underlines selected text or turns on underlining
I	Text, Italic	Ctrl+I	Italicizes selected text or turns on italics
A·A	Text, Enlarge Size	F2	Enlarges selected text one point size
A·A	Text, Reduce Size	Shift+F2	Reduces selected text one point size

II

Designing Applications

> **Tip**
>
> Add tabs by using the ruler to align fields. To toggle the ruler display, choose View, Show Ruler or press the View Ruler SmartIcon. To set margins and tabs using the ruler, you must use a mouse.

◀◀ See "Setting Tabs," p. 259

Copying a Form from Another Database

Occasionally, you may want to copy a form from one database and use it in another, possibly modifying it to meet the new application's needs. This procedure can save you a lot of development time, especially if you begin using consistent formatting standards in your databases.

▶▶ See "Database Templates," p. 949

To copy and paste a form, complete the following steps:

1. Select the database containing the source form.
2. Verify that you are in design mode (View, Show, Design).

3. In the navigation pane, click Design to expand the design components.

4. Click Forms to display the available forms in the database in the Title pane.

5. Select the form you want to copy from the Forms list.

> **Tip**
>
> You can select a range of forms by clicking and holding down the Shift key or the Ctrl key to select individual forms.

6. Select Edit, Copy or click the Edit Copy SmartIcon.

7. Switch to the database where you want to paste the form and click Design in the navigation pane and then click Forms to display the list of forms.

8. Select Edit, Paste or click the Edit Paste SmartIcon. The new form's name will appear in the Forms list.

> **Caution**
>
> If you are copying and pasting a form from the same database, the form is pasted into the list of forms but is renamed by appending the form with "Copy of."

▶▶ See "Naming a Form," p. 367

Form Properties

Adding static text is just the initial step in creating a form. You also need to define the form's overall attributes, such as its name, the type, read access, compose access, whether to hide the form, whether to make it the default form in the database; and then you will be ready to add the fields. Form attributes are defined in the Form Properties InfoBox, which is accessed by selecting Design, Form Properties (see fig. 10.6). The following sections describe how to use the settings on the various tabs in the InfoBox.

> **Note**
>
> You must be designing or editing a form to select Form Properties.

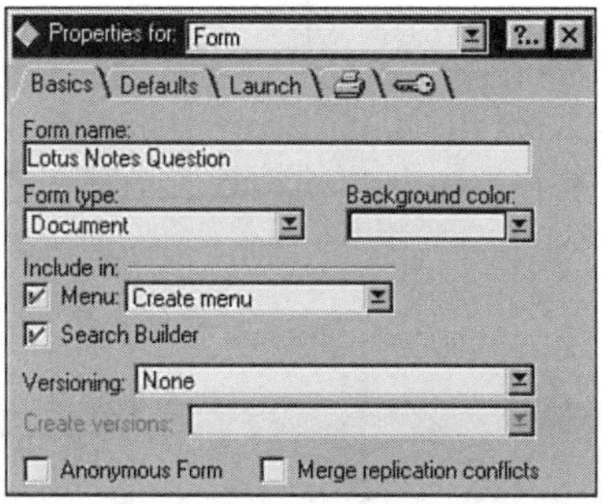

Fig. 10.6

The Form Properties InfoBox enables you to define the properties of a form. Each tabbed section enables you to define different attributes.

Basic Settings

The Basics tab in the Form Properties InfoBox for a form is the default tab, which you will always encounter first. In this section, you can name the form, select the form's hierarchy in the database structure, and decide whether to include it in the Create menu.

The following sections explain in more detail the available options that can be utilized to define a form's properties or attributes in the Basics tab.

Naming a Form. In the Form name box, enter a name for this form. The name can be any combination of characters, including spaces, and it is case-sensitive. A name can have as many characters as you want, but only the first 32 will appear on menus and characters in dialog boxes.

Keep the following items in mind when naming a form:

- **Use descriptive names**—The form names appear on the Create menu. Essentially, the form name is the Create command to create a specific document, so its name should indicate its purpose. For example, if it's a response form, try to use the word "Response" in its name. I like to precede form names by "frm" (though not necessary) to clearly identify the form name, which is especially useful if the form name is used in formulas. For example, frmResponse, frmMainDocument, frmLoan, etc.

- **Use accelerator keys**—The first unique letter in the form name is used as the form's accelerator; the accelerator is underlined in the Create menu. To force Notes to use a different letter as the accelerator, insert an underscore (_) before that letter. For example, to force the letter "A" to be the accelerator key for a form named Loan Analysis, enter the name as **Loan _Analysis**. Even though you can designate the same letter multiple times as an accelerator key, it is good practice to use a different letter for each form that will appear under the Create menu.

■ **Use cascading form names**—Enter the top-level form name, followed by a backslash (\) and the additional form name. For example, entering **Loan Analysis\Initial Review** causes the name Loan _Analysis to appear on the Compose menu and the Initial Review form to cascade from it as shown in figure 10.7. Notes allows one level of cascades.

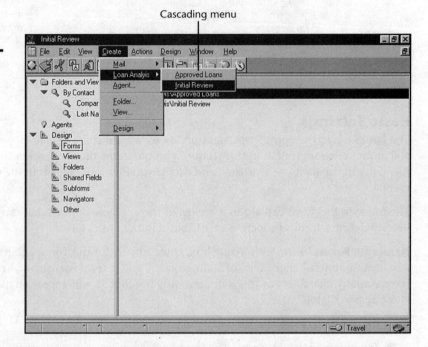

Cascading menu

Fig. 10.7

Cascading form names are useful for organizing your forms under the Create menu.

■ **Use synonyms**—Synonyms enable you to change the form's name on the Create menu without tracking down and rewriting formulas that reference the original form name, which is a great time saver. For example, if you changed the Loan Analysis\Initial Review form to Loan Analysis\Initial Loan Review, you would attain errors in various formulas that reference that form.

To use synonyms, enter the form name, followed by a vertical bar (|) and the synonym's name. The synonym is only used internally in the Form field; the first name in the Name box is the name that appears on the Create menu. If you're using both a cascade and a synonym, put the cascade name before the synonym.

Specifying the Form Type. As mentioned before, three types of forms are in a Notes database: Documents, Responses-to-documents, and Responses-to-responses. In the Form type drop-down list box, you can select the desired form type (see fig. 10.8). The default form listed is Document.

Fig. 10.8

Select the desired form type in the Form type drop-down list box. To fully understand the hierarchy of forms, see the earlier section "Understanding Form Hierarchy and Types."

Including the Form in the Create Menu. Select the Include in Menu option if you want to display the form in the Create menu. If you deselect this option, the form is effectively hidden from the database's users. For example, your Notes mail database has several hidden forms that are used only for displaying information. Developers use this feature to prevent users from composing a certain form, but to enable them to use the form for reading documents.

Tip

If you want a limited number of users to use the form, keep it in the Create menu, but then create an access list for the form.

Caution

Deselecting Include in Menu does not guarantee that the form is truly hidden. This is because users could use it in form formulas (to select which form will be used in a particular view) and print it by choosing File, Print, Form Override. To permanently hide a form, you can place parentheses around the form's name in the Form Name box (*form name*). Using parentheses not only hides the form on all menus, but prevents users from using Form Override to print the document. The form, however, can still appear in form formulas. Developers like to use this technique to hide an old form that they want to store for future use or backup.

You could select the Include in Menu option and then choose the Create–Other dialog box option in the displayed list box. This removes the form from the Create menu and moves the form to the Other menu dialog box, which is accessed from the Create menu (see fig. 10.9). This is useful if you don't expect a form to be used frequently, but want to shorten the list of forms shown in the Create menu.

Fig. 10.9

The Other dialog box is accessed by selecting Create, Other.

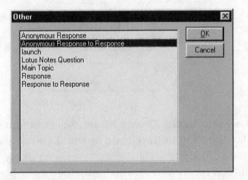

Including the Form in the Search Builder. If a database manager has created a full text index for a database, the Include in Search Builder option enables you to use the form in a Search Builder for full text search. In a full text search, users can select a form to use in a search and enter search criteria in the fields on the form (see fig. 10.10). This option even enables users to search for text in attachments and embedded objects.

 ◀◀ See "Performing a Full Text Search," p. 282

Tip

If the form is used to display documents, it generally should be made available for queries so that users can attempt a full text search using a familiar layout versus having to enter more complex query commands when a form is not made available.

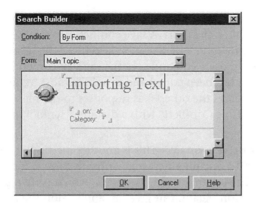

Fig. 10.10

The Search Builder enables you to select the condition By Form and then the desired form to be used in conducting a query.

Tracking the Version. Normally, every time you save an updated document, it re-places the original document, which is lost forever. With the versioning option, you can allow this to happen or force a saved update to become a new response document. Figure 10.11 displays the available options that would enable you to begin version tracking, meaning that when a user creates a response to the current document, the new document can become either.

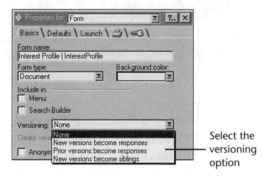

Select the versioning option

Fig. 10.11

Versioning enables you to incorporate whether documents become responses or siblings upon being updated. This is a great way to track who and how often documents are being used.

The following options are available for incorporating versioning into your database:

■ **None**—This is the default option that designates no versioning to occur.

■ **New versions become responses**—This enables you to incorporate document version control in your application. If a document created with this form is modified, the original remains intact and all updated copies are stored as re-sponses to that original, providing a history of changes. This method of version control is immune to replication and save conflicts. For example, if users on different servers modify and save the same main document, their versions are treated and displayed as two separate response documents when the databases replicate.

II

Designing Applications

A replication conflict occurs when two or more users edit the same document in different replicas between replications. A save conflict occurs when two or more users edit the same document in a database on a server at the same time. At the next replication, after two users edit and save the same document, Notes designates the document that has been edited and saved the most frequently the main document and displays the other(s) as responses to the main document labeled "[Replication or Save Conflict]" with a diamond symbol in the left margin.

■ **Prior versions become responses**—This is another method of version control, except in this case if a document created with this form is modified, the updated copy replaces the original main document, which is then stored as a response to the new version. Again, this gives an application the ability to maintain a history of changes.

■ **New versions become siblings**—In this situation, the original document is listed first, and all successive versions or siblings follow as additional main documents. You should choose this option if you want to leave the original document as a main document without introducing the risk of replication or save conflicts, which can occur if the database resides on multiple servers.

> **Tip**
>
> Distinguish sibling and response documents from their main parent documents by adding labels such as "New Version:" or "Revised:" to the column formula that is displayed in a view column.

◄◄ See " Understanding Form Hierarchy and Types," p. 360

Selecting a Background Color. The Background Color option enables you to select the form's background color. Notes R4 offers a larger variety of colors than previous versions of Notes. Keep in mind that monitor resolution and size affect color, and that background color affects the visibility of text. Select light colors such as white, light blue, and yellow for easier viewing.

> **Note**
>
> Be especially careful when choosing form colors if you have mobile users who still use laptops with mononchrome screens.

Troubleshooting

I have attempted to order these three non-alphabetically but have been unsuccessful. How can this be done? The three forms are currently named Weekly Timesheet, 401K Enrollment, and Expense Reimbursement.

The trick is to rename the forms by preceeding the existing form names with a number. For example, rename each form listed above to the following: "1. Weekly Timesheet," "2. 401K Enrollment," and "3. Expense Reimbursement." Then they are listed in numerical order in the Create menu.

After creating a new form I noticed that it is not appearing in the Create Menu. Why?

Make sure that you did not deselect the option Include in Menu in the Form Properties InfoBox. Also, verify that you did not use parentheses around the form name. For example, naming the form "(Expense Reimbursement)" would not display the form in the Create menu.

Default Settings

In the Defaults tab of the Form Properties InfoBox, you can select options that enable you to define a form for specific actions. Some of these options are familiar to Notes 3.x developers, such as designating default forms, storing the form in the document, and automatically refreshing fields; but developers will be excited about several new options, such as automatically enabling a document in edit mode and inheriting the whole document into one rich text field. Figure 10.12 displays the Defaults tab options for the Form Properties InfoBox.

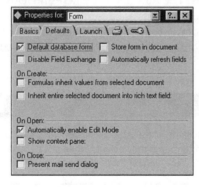

Fig. 10.12

The Defaults tab in the Form Properties InfoBox enables you to specify the default characteristics for how your form acts.

The following sections describe the options that are available in the Defaults tab.

Specifying the Form as the Default Form. Selecting the Default database form option makes the current form the default form for the database. A database must have exactly one default form. Figure 10.13 displays the list of available forms in the database with the default form designated by an asterisk.

Fig. 10.13

The default form in the current database is always indicated by an asterisk (*) in the Title pane.

Asterisk——

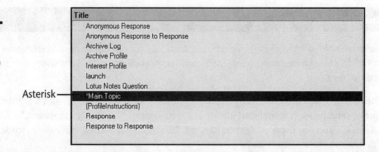

Title
Anonymous Response
Anonymous Response to Response
Archive Log
Archive Profile
Interest Profile
launch
Lotus Notes Question
*Main Topic
(ProfileInstructions)
Response
Response to Response

Caution

When you designate a form as the default form, another form in the database that might already have that designation loses default form status. The new default form setting takes precedence.

Using a default form ensures that if a form is renamed without a synonym or is deleted from the database, users can still view documents created with the obsolete form by displaying them with the default form. For example, if you created a document with a form six months ago and then that form name was changed or deleted, Notes would need to use the current default form to display the document because no form exists with the original name. Unfortunately, this default form may not display the desired information that is contained in the document because each form has its own set of fields and static text. Therefore, you may want to re-create a form to display the appropriate data.

Automatically Refreshing Fields. The Automatically Refresh Fields option recalculates all of the form's computed fields (fields are described later in this chapter) every time the user moves the mouse pointer to the next field during data entry. This allows you to update calculated fields for users automatically as they move through the document during data entry.

Caution

If the form contains many computed fields, constant recalculation will slow data entry and irritate the user. Therefore, use this option sparingly or only when it is necessary to see the result of a calculation when proceeding to the next field.

Tip

The user can always update the fields manually by pressing F9.

Storing Forms in Documents. Normally, only the data in the fields of a document are stored within a database. The Store Form in Document option, when selected, automatically stores the form with the document allowing you to retain the layout of that form with that document. This is a relatively significant setting, because documents that are created with this setting are not updated when the form is changed, they are like that forever.

You should use this option when you want documents to display correctly even in databases where the form has not been defined, or where the form has been renamed or even deleted. Also, if the document is copied to a database that doesn't contain this form, the data still displays correctly. If you don't use this option, the document is displayed using the new database's default form.

Caution

Use this option sparingly, as it requires a lot of overhead in disk space and memory to store the form in each document. If you expect the documents to be used in other databases, store a copy of the form itself in those databases.

Enabling Field Exchange. With the Enable Field Exchange option, you can enable field exchange to occur between a Notes document and an object from another application that supports Notes/FX technology. Notes/FX uses OLE technology to enable Notes and any OLE server application to share data fields. The contents of fields in an OLE server application file can automatically appear in a corresponding field in a Notes document, and vice versa. Furthermore, depending on the type of field, the contents of the field can be updated from either direction.

Inheriting Default Field Values. In the On Create section of the Defaults tab, select the Formulas Inherit values from selected document option if you want documents created with this form to inherit or copy values from the highlighted document when the user chooses the form from the Create menu. In this scenario, the highlighted document becomes the parent document of the new child document. An example of inheriting field values would be if the field CustomerName contained "ABC Company, Inc."—this same value appears in the response document's CustomerName field upon creation.

This option is very useful in discussion databases where you utilize the three different types of forms (Document, Response-to-document, and Response-to-response) and want to have similar information filter down to the child documents. For example, you may want to copy relevant information (such as the subject) from a main discussion document to a Response document in the discussion database. The Discussion template (`DISCUSS4.NTF`) has two forms—Response and Response-to-response—that utilize this option, and is an excellent starting point in learning this Notes development technique.

From a developer's standpoint, inheriting fields from parent documents is useful for making a Notes database more closely associated to "relational" database rather than the general "flat-file" Notes database. This technique helps significantly when designing views because associated main documents, responses, and responses-to-responses have data that is the same in all three because of the designated inheritance feature. In a sense, the parent and child documents are joined by this inherited field.

Turning a Response Document into Rich Text. A new feature in Notes R4 for developers is the Inherit entire selected document into rich text field option. If selected, you can choose how you want the response document to appear: as a link, collapsible rich text, or rich text. For instance, a new response document can automatically inherit the contents of its main document. Just make sure that you have created a rich text field to store the inherited document. After selecting Inherit entire selected document into rich text field, you can select the rich text field you created. Then select one of the following full document display options:

- **Collapsed rich text**—This option displays the parent document as a collapsed section and gives users the opportunity to review the parent document, but it doesn't clutter the form.
- **Rich text**—Rich text inherits the fully expanded contents of the parent document.
- **Link**—This creates a doclink to the original parent document.

Figure 10.14 displays an example of a document if Link was selected as the inherit option.

Automatically Opening a Document in Edit Mode. Your users will appreciate this new feature in Notes R4. If the Automatically enable Edit Mode option is selected, an accessed document is placed in edit mode. Earlier versions of Notes opened the document only in read mode upon double-clicking

You can also govern how a document appears when it is open by selecting the Show Context pane option and its associated appearance option—either Doclink or Parent. For example, figure 10.15 displays how the context pane for a Contact Profile response document appears when opened if the Parent option is selected for the Show Context pane option.

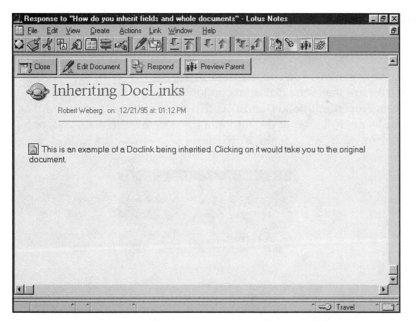

Fig. 10.14

Doclinks allow users to quickly navigate between documents in databases. The Link option allows developers to automate the creation of doclinks.

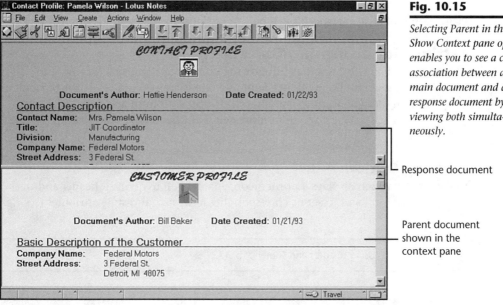

Fig. 10.15

Selecting Parent in the Show Context pane option enables you to see a clear association between a main document and a response document by viewing both simultaneously.

Response document

Parent document shown in the context pane

Mailing Documents When Saving. Did you know that any document can be mailed to a fellow user by choosing Forward from the Mail menu? Occasionally, in applications that require work-flow procedures, you may want to automate this procedure.

To facilitate document mailing, you could include a Text field called SendTo on the form. Then if the Present mail send dialog box option is selected in the On Close section of the Form Properties InfoBox, and a SendTo field exists on the form with an individual's name, Notes will prompt the author of the document to mail, save, or discard the document, as shown in figure 10.16.

Fig. 10.16

The Close Window dialog box appears automatically when saving a document if a SendTo field exists on the form. The document will be sent to the name that has been entered in the SendTo field by the developer.

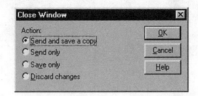

This is a great feature if you want to mail-enable forms in your databases and is especially useful for creating work-flow type applications, such as sending approvals.

Settings for Launching Objects

The Launch tab in the Properties InfoBox for a form initially displays only Auto Launch drop-down list box with a default to None. Here you can select the object type or application that you want to launch from within your form and any associated actions. These actions are covered in more detail in Chapter 12, "Integrating Notes 4.0 with Other Applications."

Printing Options

The Print tab, which displays a printer icon, enables you to define a header and/or footer in your form and to set its corresponding font, size, and style attributes (see fig. 10.17).

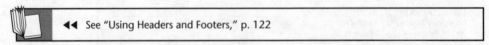

◀◀ See "Using Headers and Footers," p. 122

Tip

To specify a multi-line header or footer, press Enter at the end of each line of the header or footer.

Fig. 10.17

It is easy and flexible to set the Header and Footer options for your form when printing. Unfortunately, these options are not WYSIWYG and you are forced to printout the header and footer to see how they print.

Security Settings

At times, you will want to restrict who can create or read specific documents. The Security tab, which displays a key icon in the Form Properties InfoBox, enables you to establish whether a user can read or create a certain document with this form (see fig. 10.18). The following sections describe these options.

Fig. 10.18

The Security tab in the Form Properties InfoBox enables you to define who can and cannot see specific documents using this particular form.

Restricting Read Access. By default, anyone with at least Reader access to the database can read all documents. You can define a read access list that restricts the form so that documents created with the form are available only to a limited list of people. Then every document created with the form receives this list.

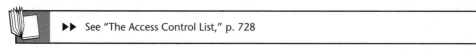

▶▶ See "The Access Control List," p. 728

Follow these steps to define the list of users allowed to read documents composed with this form:

   1. Deselect All readers and above in the Default read access for documents created with this form section.

   2. Select each user, group, server, or access role you want to include.

II

Designing Applications

> **Note**
>
> The database ACL and any access roles should already be defined by the manager using File Database Access Control.

3. If a person does not exist in the ACL, you can click the Person icon to select a name from a Public or Private Address Book.

   Repeat steps 2 and 3 for each name that you want added to the list. To remove a name, click the name again to remove the checkmark.

4. Save the form.

> **Note**
>
> The read access list defines the ACL, but it cannot override the ACL. If a user does not already have Reader access to the database, he or she will not be able to read the documents created with this form, even if you list them in the read access list.

Create Access. You can restrict the form to a limited list of people when creating. The create access list is designed just like the read access list. By default, anyone with at least author access to the database can create documents with any of the database's forms. To define the subset of users who will be needing a specific form, perform the following steps:

1. Deselect All authors and above in the Who can create documents with this form section.

2. Select each user, group, server, or access role you want to include.

3. If a person does not exist in the ACL, you can click the Person icon to select a name from a Public or Private Address Book.

   Repeat steps 2 and 3 for each name that you want added to the list. To remove a name, click the name again to remove the checkmark.

4. Save the form.

Other Methods of Securing Forms. The Security tab in the Form Properties InfoBox also enables you to select the following options:

- **Disable printing/forwarding/copying to Clipboard**—This option prevents users from printing, forwarding, or copying restricted information. This feature really helps to prevent accidental or intentional distribution of confidential information. This does not prevent a user from using a screen capture program, however.

- **Default encryption keys**—This option enables you to select and associate any defined encryption keys for the form. To use this feature, you must define one or more fields on the form as encryptable. Every document created with the form will automatically have its encryptable fields encrypted, using the keys you specify here (be sure to distribute the keys to people who will be using the form).

 ▶▶ See "Understanding Encryption Keys," p. 732

Adding Fields to a Form

Once you've defined a form, you can add fields to it. Fields are the means by which you enter data into Notes and display the data stored in Notes. A form can only accept and display data for which there are fields; for example, if you want users to enter their employee ID numbers on the form, you must add the EmployeeID field to the form layout.

You create a field by giving it a name and selecting some attributes for it, such as the data type, field type, and format. Notes then places the field on your form.

The following sections explore the various types of fields you can use in your forms.

Single-Use and Shared Fields

Notes supports two types of fields: single-use and shared.

A *single-use field* is a normal field. You define it, select attributes for it such as its data type, and then place it on a form. If you want to use it again in a different form, define a new field using the same name and attributes, but the new field has no relation to the original. Single-use fields are stored within the form itself and are available only on that level.

Shared fields are separate entities stored within the actual database structure and can be accessed by any fields. Its definition is stored in the Insert Shared Field dialog box; which lets you reuse the existing field definition instead of creating a new one. Shared fields enable you to reuse a field in any number of forms within a particular database. Every time you update one instance of the shared field, all other instances are automatically updated too because they use the same field definition. For example, if you make a shared field a text field instead of a number field, all instances of that shared field are updated automatically to reflect your changes.

Shared fields are useful when you want to use the same field in multiple forms, or even in multiple databases, and want to make sure that the exact same definition is used everywhere. For example, your database might use the InterestRate field in three different forms. To make sure that all the forms use the same field definition, you define a single shared field called InterestRate, and then "use" it in each form.

To create a new field, follow these steps:

II

Designing Applications

1. Place your mouse pointer on the form where you want the field to appear.

2. Select Create, Field, or press the Create Field SmartIcon to insert a single-use field. Notes inserts a new field called Untitled on your form and displays the Field Properties InfoBox (see fig. 10.19). You can now rename the field and change other properties of the field.

Fig. 10.19

Inserting a new field onto a form. A single-use field is identified by its light rectangle outline.

Inserting a single-use field—

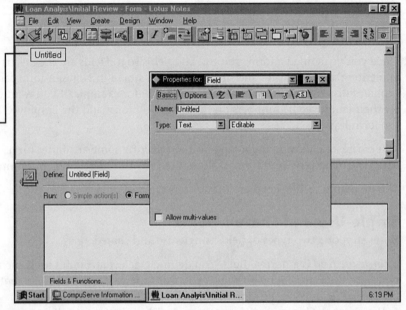

3. Select Create, Insert Shared field or press the Create Insert Shared Field SmartIcon to display the Insert Shared Field dialog box as shown in figure 10.20. Select the shared field and then click OK to insert the field onto the form (see fig. 10.21).

   If you have not defined a shared field, this dialog box will be blank. To define a shared field, you must return to the navigation pane, select Create, Design, Shared Field, and then name and define the shared field. Once saved, this newly named shared field will appear in the Insert Shared Field dialog box for reuse.

Tip

You can copy and paste fields between forms by using the Clipboard. However, shared fields will revert to single-use fields when copied and pasted because its definition is not stored with the field.

If you define a shared field and then place it in a form that has the Store Form in Documents option selected, that instance of the field is automatically converted to a single-use field whenever a document is created and saved using that form. This ensures that if the document is mailed or pasted into another database, the field will be accessible even if the new database doesn't contain a copy of the shared field's definition.

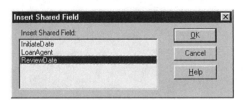

Fig. 10.20

Inserting a shared field called ReviewDate onto a form.

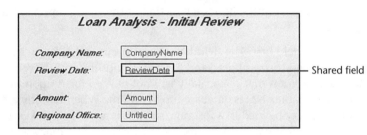

Fig. 10.21

The shared fields are designated by a heavy bold rectangle.

— Shared field

If you delete a shared field from a form, the data entered through that field cannot be displayed. There is no message, and the data itself cannot be altered, but it can still be displayed by adding the field to another form. The contents of the field are still considered part of the document, but because there is no field to display them in, they are displayed on the form itself as text—you cannot edit or delete this text.

Note

You could use another form or create a new field to write a formula to see the contents of that deleted shared field.

Defining Fields

Once you've chosen whether the field on the form is single-use or shared, you must define the field's characteristics—its data type, field type, format, paragraph attributes, etc. This is accomplished in the Field Properties InfoBox.

Tip

Double-click an existing field, select Design, Field Properties, or press the spacebar while a field is selected to display its Field Properties dialog box.

Basic Settings. Use the Basics tab section to name the field, select the data type, and then select the field type. Figure 10.22 displays the Basics tab of a Field Properties InfoBox.

II

Designing Applications

Fig. 10.22

The Properties InfoBox for a field enables you to define the attributes for the fields in your form.

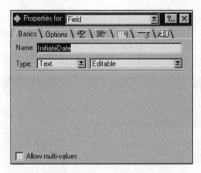

The following options appear in the Basics tab section of the Field Properties InfoBox when defining a field:

- **Name**—Name the field first. The field name must begin with a letter, but it can include numbers and the symbols _ and $. Fields beginning with $ are internal type fields used by Notes that you usually will not have to focus upon unless you begin more complex Notes database programming. When naming a field, remember that it may be used in a formula, so you should try to pick a short name that's easy to remember. There are about a dozen field names, such as Categories, SendTo, and Sign, that hold a special meaning in Notes. Fields that have these reserved field names behave in a predefined way. The name may contain up to 32 bytes (if you're using multibyte characters, 32 bytes is different from 32 characters).

- **Type**—Notes supports nine data types for fields. Select a data type to indicate how this data will be stored and used. These data types are discussed later in the next section.

- **Allow multi-values**—If multiple values will be accepted in a field, select the Allow multi-values checkbox. This is generally used with a standard Keywords field. Multi-value fields are useful if you have a field that can contain more than one value. For example, a Region keyword field could contain Southeast, Southwest and Northwest. Keyword fields are fields defined to contain a list of predefined selections that you can choose from.

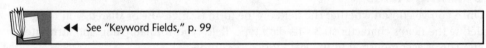

◄◄ See "Keyword Fields," p. 99

Choosing Options. In the Options tab, you can define help descriptions, address security issues, and define multiple-value separators (see fig. 10.23). The following list details those options:

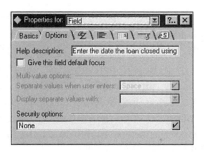

Fig. 10.23

The Options tab section in the Field Properties InfoBox is where you supply help instructions and apply multi-value features.

- **Help Description**—If provided, the optional Help description appears as a one-line prompt at the bottom of the form window when the mouse pointer is placed in that field. For example, "Enter the date the loan closed" is a poor example of field help description because it fails to inform the user how to enter the date. A better example would be "Enter the date the loan closed using the format MM\DD\YY."

> **Tip**
>
> Try to make the Help Description useful and indicate the field's general purpose. Use a popup on the form if you cannot fit all the information into this Help. To toggle Display field help, select View, Show, Field Help

- **Give this field default focus**—This is a great feature new to Notes developers. It enables you to automatically move the mouse pointer to a particular field location. If not selected, the cursor moves to the first editable field on the form.
- **Multi-value options**—This section enables you to handle multi-values in a field. You need to define either Separate values when user enters or Display separate value with and then the corresponding separator value (Space, Comma, Semicolon, New Line, or Blank Line).

The Separate values when a user enters an option allows you to give users choices for entering text. If the field is editable, it's best to allow several kinds of separators so users can separate entries as they want, and Notes can still identify the following individual entries:

    Europe; Asia, North America.

If you allow only one separator, such as a comma, users must use that separator to prevent Notes from reading multiple entries as a single entry.

The Display separate value with option allows you to define how the multi-value entries appear. To align and separate multiple values on the form, use the ruler (Ctrl+R) to create a hanging indent where the field begins. Select New Line for both the input and display separator.

■ **Security Options**—Here you can select Sign if mailed or saved in section, Enable encryption for this field, and Must have at least Editor access to use to enable security features for particular situations.

Select Sign if mailed or saved in section to determine if mailed documents are signed or encrypted automatically during mailing. These override the users' settings in the Document Save dialog box. Select the Enable encryption for this field option to activate the encryption of a field when it is saved. Select the Must have at least Editor access to use allows you to define if a user with at least Editor access can modify the field.

Setting the Font. The Font tab displays an icon with the letters *a* and *Z* in custom fonts (see fig. 10.24). The options on this tab enable you to easily set or modify the field's font, size, style, and text color. You can also set the permanent pen font for adding comments to a document in a different font.

◄◄ See "Working with the Permanent Pen," p. 267
◄◄ See "Font Settings," p. 248

Fig. 10.24

The Font tab section in the Field Properties InfoBox.

Alignment Settings. The Alignment tab section permits you to define how a field appears. Figure 10.25 displays the available alignment options on the Alignment tab (the tab sports an icon with left-aligned rows of text). You can specify the field's alignment, where the first line begins, whether the field is displayed within a list using bullets or numbers (a new feature that I really like), where the left margin begins, and the desired spacing of lines.

> **Note**
>
> Make sure these alignment settings work in tight conjunction with your static text fonts and alignment settings.

◄◄ See "Alignment," p. 254

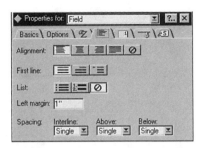

Fig. 10.25

The Alignment tab section in the Field Properties InfoBox.

Pagination Settings. In this section, you can specify how a form is paginated. A form could have a Page break before a paragraph, Keep paragraph on one page, or Keep paragraph with next paragraph. The Page break before a paragraph option allows you to keep all the lines in one paragraph on the same page. The Keep paragraph on one page and the Keep paragraph with next paragraph options allows you to keep consecutive paragraphs on the same page.

You can also specify the right margin when printing and the spacing of tabs. Figure 10.26 details the available pagination options (the Pagination tab icon looks like a page with the number 1 displayed).

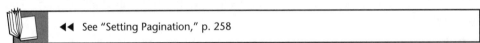

◀◀ See "Setting Pagination," p. 258

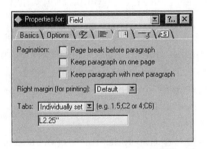

Fig. 10.26

The pagination tab has features that are very useful when printing documents.

Options for Hiding Fields. The options on the Hide tab (it displays a window shade icon—see fig. 10.27) are used a lot by Notes developers to hide data when users are either reading or editing a form. Occasionally, you may want to use fields on a form for such purposes as easing the use of entering data (checkboxes for a keyword list), performing calculations, or tracking modification dates. However, the users could typically care less about seeing these fields once calculated or entered. You can hide such fields in the form layout.

II

Designing Applications

Fig. 10.27

You can hide lines of your form depending on whether a user is reading, editing, previewing, or printing a form.

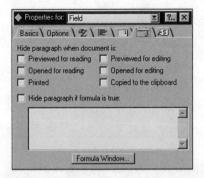

> **Caution**
>
> Hiding fields is more useful as a formatting option than as a security measure. Hidden data (such as Salary) could always be seen by a user who selects File, Document and then the Fields tab in the Document Properties InfoBox when a document is selected. If you want to ensure that data is hidden from users, you should encrypt those fields.

The following options for hiding fields are available in the Hide tab of a Field Properties InfoBox:

- **Previewed for reading**—This option hides the text or field when the document is being read in a preview pane. It can still be seen when being read or edited.

- **Opened for reading**—This hides the text or field when the document is being read. Whenever you hide information in read mode, it is automatically hidden during printing, too.

- **Printed**—This hides the text or field when the document is printed. The data is not hidden when the document is being read unless you also select Opened for reading.

- **Previewed for editing**—This option hides the text or field when the document is being edited in a preview pane.

- **Opened for editing**—Hides the text or field when the document is being edited.

- **Copied to the clipboard**—Hides the text or field when the document is copied, so that the hidden information is not copied to the Clipboard.

- **Hide paragraph if formula is true**—You must provide the formula. For example, this formula would hide the paragraph that contains the Categories field if it contained the keyword "General":

```
@If(Categories = "General";1;0).
```

Note

If you select Opened for reading, Notes automatically selects Previewed for reading and Printed. If you select Opened for editing, Notes automatically selects Previewed for editing.

To hide a field or paragraph using any of these options listed, perform the following steps:

1. Select the paragraph(s) or field(s) you want to hide. You can only hide entire lines or paragraphs (delimited by a hard return).

2. Select the Hide tab and in the Hide paragraph when document is section, you can select any of the options detailed previously.

Tip

Some developers like to place all of their hidden fields that are only to be displayed when edited at the very bottom of the form with a "Hidden Fields" label. This makes the hidden fields easy to locate if the form has to be modified.

Caution

Notes calculates fields from top to bottom, left to right in a document. Thus, beware of placing all of your hidden fields at the bottom if it is required to complete a calculation in another field above it, because the hidden field must be encountered before the field that uses its data.

Saving Paragraph Properties as Styles. You can use the Style tab to save combinations of paragraph properties that you use regularly (such as alignment, indentation, and margins) as a named paragraph style. These named styles can then be used to quickly format existing paragraphs.

For example, suppose that you often write financial reports in italic text with a 2.25" left margin. You could save the italic and left margin paragraph properties as a named style called Reports. Then when you write financial reports, you could format them with Reports without having to specify the italic and left margin properties individually each time. You could select Reports from the Text, Named Styles menu, or you could assign Reports to the cycle key F11, which lets you cycle through each of the named styles you've created and assigned to the key.

To create a named style, perform the following steps:

1. Create and customize a paragraph to your liking. With the paragraph selected choose Text, Text Properties to display the Text Properties InfoBox.

II

Designing Applications

2. Select the Style tab and choose Create Style to display the Create Named Style dialog box.

3. Enter a name for the paragraph style as shown in figure 10.28.

Fig. 10.28

Creating a named paragraph style is a great time-saving tool for quickly formatting lines in a form.

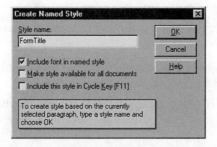

4. (Optional) Deselect Include font in named style if you don't want to save the selected paragraph's font in the named style.

5. (Optional) Select Make style available for all documents to make the style available when you format paragraphs in other documents in the database.

6. (Optional) Select Include this style in Cycle Key [F11] to make the style available when you press F11 to cycle through named styles.

7. Click OK to save your style.

After you create named styles, you can format paragraphs with those styles. To format a paragraph with a named style follow these steps:

1. Make sure the document is in edit mode.

2. Select the paragraph(s).

3. Perform one of the following:

    • Choose Text Named Styles and select a style from the menu Notes displays.

    • Click the Named Styles indicator on the status bar and select a style from the list Notes displays.

4. Press F11 or click the Text Style Cycle Key SmartIcon to cycle through the named styles when you format paragraphs.

Understanding the Data Types

Nine data types are available when creating a field. The data type definition enables you to define what type of data can be entered into the field. In most cases, you will be dealing with Text fields that can accept alpha-numeric data such as phone numbers or regional offices names. However, you will encounter situations in which your form will require use of the other data types, such as Time, Number, Rich Text, Reader, Author, and Keyword type fields.

It's easy to select and format these field types. However, once you begin developing more complex formulas that manipulate the entered data, you will want to know how each data type is stored. The following sections explain in further detail each of the available data types.

▶▶ See "Formula Functions," p. 533
▶▶ See "Working with Formulas," p. 495

Text. Text consists of letters, punctuation, spaces, and numbers that are not used mathematically. Company names, addresses, and phone numbers with hyphens are all good examples of the Text data type. Individual text within a Text data type field cannot be styled by the user (bold, color, and so on); it can only be plain. However, the developer of the form can globally change the format for all of the data contained in the field.

Note

To allow a user to change individual pieces of text in a field, you should use rich text as the data type. Here a user can designate bold, underline, and color for various text, lines, and paragraphs.

Caution

Carefully consider the need to use Rich Text fields versus Text fields which are easier to manipulate in formulas. Rich text fields cannot be evaluated for content. For example, if the field BodyText is a rich text field, you cannot display its contents or convert it to plain text by specifying @Text(BodyText). However, you can access the attributes of the field. The following formula tests for the availability of a rich text field:

```
@Prompt([OK]; "Is BodyText Available"; @If(@IsAvailable(BodyText);
"Yes"; "No"))
```

Time. The Time data type is comprised of both the time and the date, it is made up of letters, numbers, and punctuation. You must use the Time data type if you want Notes to recognize a value as a time-date value, otherwise it is treated as text.

The following are examples of valid Notes time formats. When the Time data type is selected, the Field Properties InfoBox changes to display the available time and date options (see fig. 10.29).

Fig. 10.29

Notes can format time data in several different time, date, and overall time formats. It's as simple as selecting the displayed option.

Dates can range from 1/1/1000 through 12/31/9999, while times can range from 00:00:00 through 23:59:59 in the 24-hour format and from 12:00:00 A.M. through 11:59:59 P.M. in the 12-hour format.

> **Note**
>
> You can use formulas to convert text fields to date fields or vice versa. For example, @TextToTime("07/31/64") converts the text string "07/31/64" to the date 07/31/64. On the other hand, @Text(@Today) converts the value of today's date to text.

See Chapter 13, "Working with Formulas," for details on writing formulas to convert data types.

Numbers. The Number data type is used to represent all numbers that need to be displayed or calculated mathematically. It can include any of the ten numerals (0 to 9), the minus and plus signs (– and +), the decimal point (.), scientific notation (E), and the constant (e).

When the data type Number is selected, the Field Properties InfoBox displays the available number options as shown in figure 10.30.

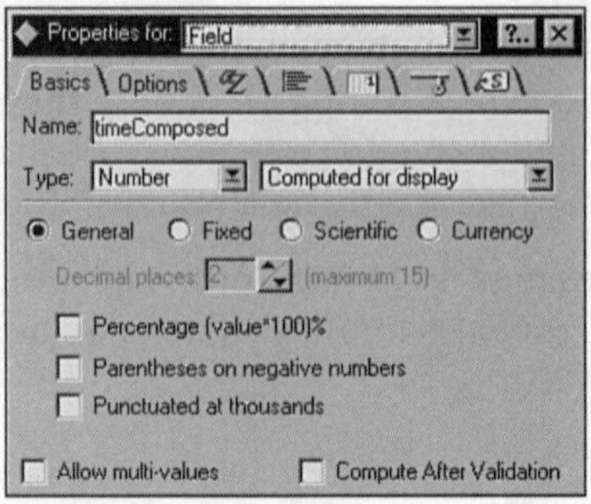

Fig. 10.30

The number section on the Basics tab enables you to define the format for your number field, which is how it will be displayed in Notes.

The available Number formats are as follows:

- **General**—Displays numbers as they are entered, with zeroes being suppressed.
- **Fixed**—Displays numbers with a fixed number of decimal places as specified in the Decimal Places list box.
- **Scientific**—Displays numbers using exponential notation.
- **Currency**—Displays values with a currency symbol and two digits after the decimal point.

You can also choose whether to display percentages, parentheses, and punctuation at thousands. Table 10.2 Summarizes the available number formats.

Table 10.2 Number Formats	
Format	**Examples**
Integers	123, –123
Decimal fractions	1.23, 0.12, –.123
Scientific notation	1.23E4, 1.23E-4, –1.23E4
Currency	$1.23, ($1.23)

Keywords. Keywords are a list of predefined values for a field that a user can select from. For example, you may want the user to select from a list of keywords for a field named BranchOffice. Notes stores keywords as text, but the keywords do not have to be made up of text characters. Using keywords lends consistency to the values that appear in the database documents, because each user has the same set of values to choose from when entering information into a keyword field.

To create a Keyword list, follow these steps:

1. After creating the field, select Keywords as the data type in the Type list box.

2. In the Choices list box, select one of the following:

- **Enter Choices (one per line)**—This is the most widely used option when building keyword lists.
- **Use Formula for choices**—Developers like to use this technique to query other databases (mainly Notes) and bring in a view column of key words. This can be accomplished using @Dblookup or @Dbcolumn.

 ◀◀ See "Working with Formulas," p. 495

- **Use Address dialog for choices**—This enables you to use the Address book as the keyword list which is convenient to use if building a keyword list of names contained in your Address book.

- **Use Access Control List for choices**—This enables you to pull in the predefined Access Control List for the current database to build the keyword list. This is a handy new feature that Notes developers will appreciate because now you can build more flexible security features into a database like possibly allowing users to choose who can access a document that they create.

- **Use View dialog for choices**

3. Select whether the field is to be editable or computed. Most keywords are generally editable because you want the user to choose the desired keyword versus having a field calculate and automatically choose the keyword based upon some previously entered data.

4. In the keyword text section, enter each keyword followed by a hard return. Figure 10.31 displays a "one per line" keyword list using Illinois, Iowa, and Minnesota. You can sort the lists after entering by clicking the Sort button.

Fig. 10.31

Creating a simple keyword field will enable the user to select from predefined lists of data when entering data.

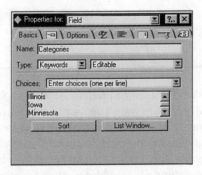

5. Select Allow values not in list if you want users to be able to enter additional keywords to your list. You can also select Allow multi-values to enable a user to select multiple entries from the keyword list.

Tip

Select Allow multi-values when you want to associate a document to multiple keywords. This is very useful when building views that require a document to be shown in multiple categories.

Caution

Any keywords entered by users will be accepted in the field, but will not be added to the list permanently. The newly added keyword will appear in the keyword list only for that document.

To determine how you want the keyword list to be displayed, select the Display tab (second tab) in the field's Properties InfoBox to select an interface style for displaying the keywords (see fig. 10.32). You can choose from three methods for displaying the list of keywords to users, plus designate the frame type and number of columns:

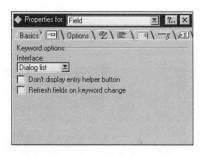

Fig. 10.32

Selecting the interface style for your keyword list enables you to creatively display your available options when a user inputs the data.

- **Dialog list**—Presents a standard field interface. Users can press the spacebar to cycle through the list, type the first letter of the appropriate item to display it, or press Enter to display the keyword dialog box listing all the items. This interface gives you the option of allowing users to enter items not included on the list (select Allow values not in this list); however, the additional items are not added to the list for future use.

- **Checkboxes**—Presents a vertical list of checkboxes, each representing one list item as shown in figure 10.33. Users can select more than one of the available keywords.

Fig. 10.33

Keywords can be formatted with checkboxes using a 3D frame with one column. Checkboxes enable users to select multiple keywords.

- **Radio buttons**—Presents a vertical list of radio buttons, each representing one list item. Users can select only one item. Figure 10.34 displays how radio button keywords will appear.

Select Don't Display entry help button if you do not want to display the entry help button (see fig. 10.35). This is only available for dialog box list keywords. I like to keep this button to help the user easily identify keyword lists when inputting data and it allows them to enter the data with only the mouse instead of hitting a key in the field.

II

Designing Applications

Fig. 10.34

Keywords can be formatted with radio buttons using a 3D frame with two columns. Radio buttons enable users to select only one keyword.

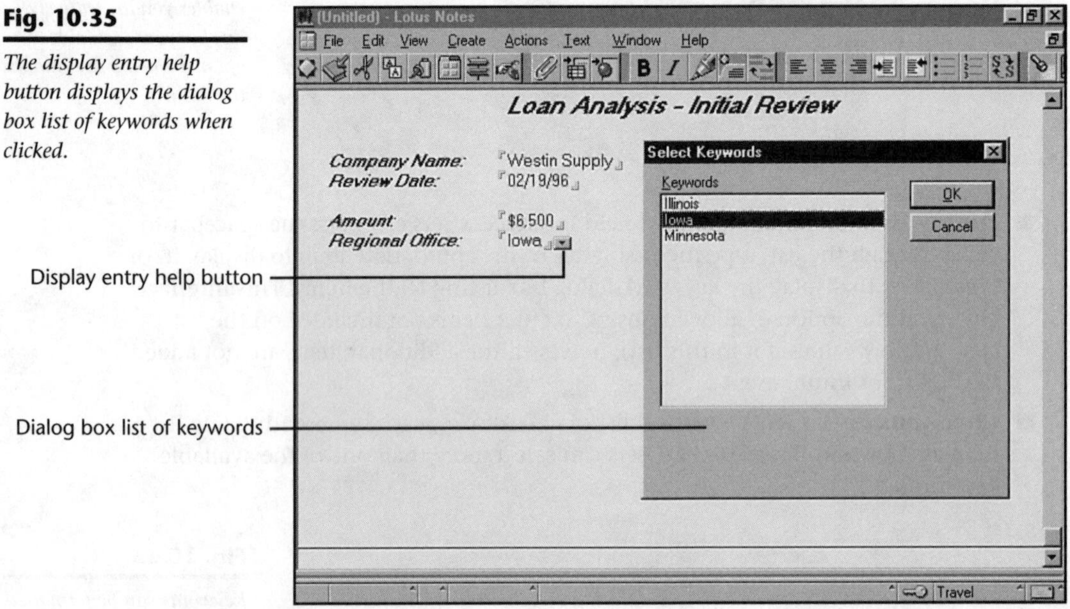

Fig. 10.35

The display entry help button displays the dialog box list of keywords when clicked.

Display entry help button ———

Dialog box list of keywords ———

You can also select Refresh fields on Keyword Change to automatically change other fields within the document that may be using that keyword selection in a formula. This is important if other fields are based upon the current keyword selection, because you want them to be updated to display the correct information.

 After you finish setting up the keyword field, apply any formatting options desired, close the Field Properties InfoBox, and save the form (or press Ctrl+S or the File Save SmartIcon).

Note

Always test out your keyword list by selecting the saved form from the Create menu, and verify its interface style and the list of options.

Tip

Select <u>D</u>esign, <u>T</u>est Form to quickly test changes in your form.

You can also create synonyms for your keywords, so that if the keyword itself changes, any formula referencing the synonym still works. Keyword synonyms are designated by using | followed by the synonym. The following shows a keywords list for a Type of Loan field with synonyms:

- ▪ Commercial ¦ C
- ▪ Private ¦ P
- ▪ Real Estate ¦ R

The leftmost name is displayed within the document, while both the name and the synonym (the rightmost name after |) are stored internally. If you categorize a view based on a keywords field, the keyword synonyms will be used as the category names. The important point to remember is that synonyms allow you to use a shorter name.

Rich Text. Rich text information may contain text, tables, embedded objects, or graphics. The text in a rich text field can be individually styled (bold, color, and so on) with the Text Font command. Text fields cannot be individually styled and all of its contents are the same font and size.

Rich text fields are more versatile than Text fields, but they have two limitations: they cannot be combined with other data types in an @function, and they cannot be displayed in a view.

Authors. Authors is a data type that contains a text list of user names (group names and access roles may also be used) that indicates who can edit a given document (see fig. 10.36). Authors fields are an interesting and integral part of security in Notes applications and documents because they provide another level of security beyond the ACL.

Authors fields are also useful for any application that requires restricted access to particular documents or for workflow applications that pass documents from person to person, where each is responsible for updating a specific set of information.

▶▶   See "Security," p. 806

If a form contains an Authors field, only those users listed in that field when the document is saved can edit it. The Authors field cannot override the access control list, it can only refine it. This means that users who have been assigned Reader access or No Access to a database can never edit a document, even though you have listed them in the document's Author Names field.

Fig. 10.36

An Authors field enables you to indicate who can edit a given document.

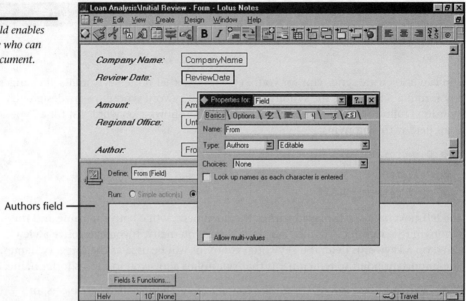

Authors field ————

In most situations, you will want the user who originally composed a document to be able to edit the document later. To enable this, include at least one field that is an Authors data type. This field should be a Computed when composed field that has @UserName as the default field formula.

A document can contain multiple Authors fields; this is useful when you want to display the name of the document's original author in one field, and then designate Editor access to additional users with another field. Any user listed in any of a document's Authors fields can edit the document.

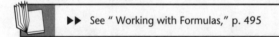 ▶▶ See "Working with Formulas," p. 495

Caution

If the Authors field on a document is blank, it acts as if the field is not there. The original author, unless he/she has Editor access or above in the ACL, will not be able to edit the document. This occurs quite often if you do not include @UserName in the formula of a Computed when composed field or if you allow the field to be editable and the user accidentally removes their name as the author.

Tip

Click and hold the Authors field in the read or edit mode to display the contents of the $UpdatedBy field.

Note

If a user says he or she cannot edit his own documents, verify that an Authors field exists and that it contains the user's name.

You can generate the list of choices in the Authors field by choosing one of the following options in the Choices list box on the Basics tab:

- **None**—In this situation, you must rely on a formula or on the authors to create the list of names.
- **Use Address dialog for choices**—This option displays the Names dialog box so users can select names from a Personal or Public Address Book. Select Look up names as each character is entered to help users fill in a name quickly. Notes looks up a match for the character in the open Address Book.
- **Use access control list for choices**—This option brings up a list of people, servers, groups, and roles in the access control list, which is a smaller subset than the Address book.
- **Use View dialog for choices**—This option brings up a dialog box containing entries from a column in a Notes database view. Select the database to look up, select a view, and select a column number. This is similar to using @DbColumn formula to bring in a list of users.

Note

You must select Allow multi-values for an Authors field to store a text list with multiple names. Concatenate the names in the formula with colons.

Readers. Similar to the Authors data type is Readers, which contains a text list of user names (group names and access roles may also be used) that determines who can read documents.

If provided, users can control read access to a particular document. If the document also contains a read access list, the two lists are combined. If a Readers field does not exist, the ACL defines who can read the documents. Users not included in a Readers field (regardless of ACL rights) cannot see the document in any view and therefore cannot read the document. This includes Managers and Servers; if Servers are not included, the document will not replicate the database on other servers.

II

Designing Applications

A Readers field has available the same choices to generate a list of readers as an Authors field. See the previous section, "Authors" for an explanation of these choices.

> **Note**
>
> Readers is similar to Authors, except that it limits read access to a document instead of granting edit access. It is important to remember that Readers and Authors fields can further restrict, but cannot extend a user's capabilities.

Names. Names provides a means of displaying distinguished names in various formats. Distinguished names are always stored internally in their canonicalized format, listing all components of the name along with their labels. The Names field displays only the Common Name component of a distinguished name (that is, the person's first name and last name).

 ◄◄ See "The Distinguished Name," p. 173

A Names field converts hierarchical names to a cleaner, abbreviated form, like the following, for example:

    Steve Stiles/Supervisor/US

instead of the following:

    Steve Stiles=CN/Supervisor+O/US=C

Use this type of field when you want to show user names as they appear on Notes IDs.

Use the Names field to display a list of user names or server names where an Author Names or Reader Names field is inappropriate because you are not trying to assign any type of read or write rights, like when using a SendTo field in a workflow application

Field Types

The field type determines whether the data is user-entered or calculated. Not all field types are available for all data types, so be sure your selection makes sense. The four field types are: Editable, Computed, Computed for display, and Computed when composed.

All three of the Computed field types are non-editable, meaning the developer supplies the data or value automatically via a formula—the user cannot modify it. The purpose of Computed fields is to automatically generate data, such as time and author names, and then protect that information from being updated by the user.

Editable

Editable fields are probably the most commonly used fields because you usually want the user to enter some data. Plus, they can be used with all data types. After the user enters data, it is stored with the document. You can optionally define a default value formula that forces an initial value to appear when the user composes the document, or utilize an input translation formula or an input validation formula, or even begin utilizing the LotusScript programming language to create an event.

Computed

Computed fields are automatically calculated upon composing and can be used with any data type except rich text. Computed fields only allow one formula. This formula is entered in the programmer pane by selecting the event Value. As a developer, you supply the value by either a constant or a formula that calculates the value.

Computed fields are used so that the user cannot modify them. It is important to remember that this value is recalculated every time the document is edited and saved. A perfect example of the use of Computed fields is to capture the name of the document's Author in an Authors field and the date it was created in a date field (see fig. 10.37).

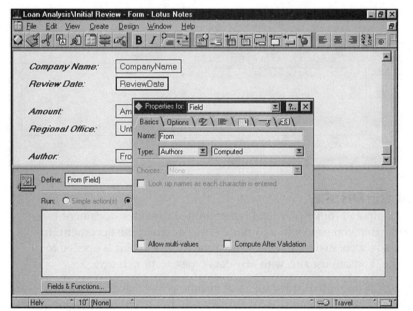

Fig. 10.37

The formula for this simple Computed field will capture the author's name.

  ▶▶   See "Working with Formulas," p. 495

Computed When Composed

This field is very similar to a computed field, except that the value is calculated when the document is originally composed and is never recalculated again, even though the document may be modified. The value is then stored with the document and can be used with any data type except rich text. Fields that inherit information from another document are often Computed when composed fields, as shown in figure 10.38. See the earlier section in this chapter, "Understanding Form Hierarchy and Types," detailing response documents. These values are not permanently locked because these and other fields can still be changed through other field formulas or agents that are contained in the document.

Fig. 10.38

This field in a Response document would inherit the Subject field from its parent document. The field name OriginalSubject dictates that the form will inherit the Subject data in the parent document.

Formula

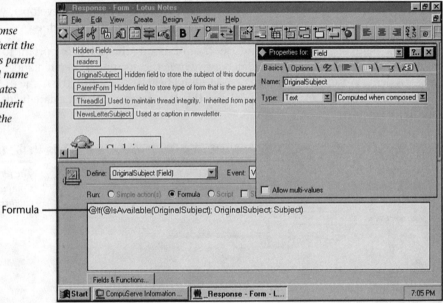

Computed for Display

The value of a Computed for Display field is determined when the document is retrieved. The value that you supply in a formula is not stored in the document. Instead, the value is recalculated for display every time the document is opened for reading or editing. You can use this with any data type except rich text.

A good example of its use is to display the current time or the date the document was created. Developers also use Computed for Display field to present information previously entered by users in an Editable in a different format.

> **Caution**
>
> You cannot display the contents of a computed-for-display field in a view because it is not a value stored in the document. This could be a problem if you need to display a value shown in computed-for-display field in a view or perform some other calculation based upon that value. Also, do not use a lot of these fields on a form because they can slow down the performance of a form.

> **Note**
>
> For computed or computed-when-displayed fields you can delay computing until after input validation formulas have been run by selecting Compute after validation. Input validation formulas are used to verify that the information entered in a field meets specific criteria or to verify that a required field has been filled in. This can help you speed up data entry.

Editable Field Formulas

Every field type accepts at least one formula, as described below. Editable fields can accept up to three formulas for the field while Computed (non-editable) can contain one formula. The three field formulas for editable fields are Default Value Formula, Input Translation Formula, and Input Validation Formula.

The formulas are optional, meaning you do not have to supply a formula for any of the three, but if you want to manipulate or automate data entry you will have to provide formulas. For example, after the user enters his data, you could convert the entry to uppercase letters and then validate the entry to make sure it meets certain requirements.

Formulas are written in the programmer pane, which is located at the bottom of the screen when editing a form. This is displayed by selecting View, Design Pane. You can easily switch between the various fields by selecting the desired field in the Define list box to display the field's corresponding events (like Default, Input Translation, and Input Validation formulas) in the Event list box.

When building formulas, you can also easily click the Fields & Functions button in the programmer pane to display a list of available Fields and Notes programming functions.

Default Value Formula

Default Value Formulas provide an initial value for the field, which the user can either accept or edit. Providing a default value ensures that the field gets filled in, and often removes the need for users to enter data such as their names or the date.

II

Designing Applications

You can supply a constant such as "U.S.A." for a text field or 0.05 for a number field, or a formula that resolves to an appropriate value, such as Subtotal * 1.05. To construct the default formula, just write the expression; no assignment statement is needed (see fig. 10.39). However, if the Subtotal field used in the formula Subtotal * 1.05 is blank, an error will occur.

Fig. 10.39

Supply the constant "IL" for the text field CompanyState.

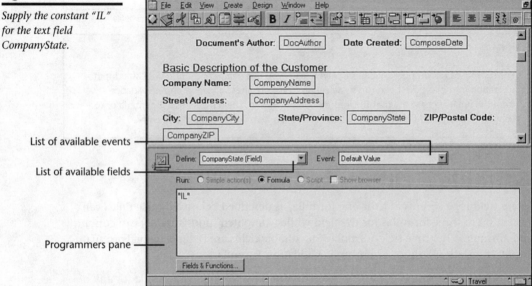

List of available events ———

List of available fields ———

Programmers pane ———

Note

The default field value is calculated only once when the document is first created and never changes after the document is saved.

Tip

If you want a text string in the formula entered as text (literally), you must enclose it in quotation marks (""). For number fields you need to enter the number, for example, 100 enters the number 100. You may want to have the default formula use another field and its value, for example, entering Price in the formula enters the value of the field named Price. Field names don't need quotation marks.

Input Translation Formula

An input translation formula converts information entered by the user to adjust the field value or make the field conform to a format. Developers generally use them to convert text to proper case or capitalization, or to trim out blank spaces. It is important to remember that this formula executes when the document containing the field is saved and it must evaluate to a value suitable for storage in the current field.

When constructing the formula, be sure to reference the field name. For example, an input translation formula for the State field might convert its text to proper case (see fig. 10.40), and for the phone field, remove any spaces.

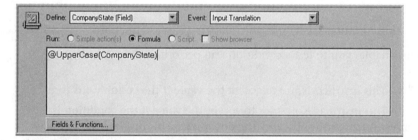

Fig. 10.40

@UpperCase(Company State) *in the Input Translation Formula converts the CompanyState field to uppercase.*

Input Validation Formula

The Input Validation Formula compares the data entered by the user with criteria specified by you in the formula. If the data satisfies the criteria, it is accepted; otherwise a message is displayed. For example, an input validation formula for the CompanyName field might ensure that a value exists, as shown in figure 10.41. The important point to remember is that this formula executes *after* the input translation formula.

Tip

Be careful not to use a lot of validation formulas on one form, because the messages tend to annoy users when entering data.

Fig. 10.41

The formula in this example verifies that a CompanyName exists; if it doesn't, a message is displayed.

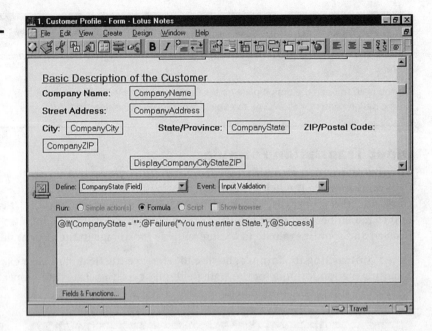

An input validation formula usually uses the following three @functions:

- **@If**—This enables you to test a condition and perform actions based on the result.

- **@Success**—This instructs Notes to accept the value if the condition is true.

- **@Failure**—This instructs Notes not to accept the value if the condition is false and to prevent the user from saving the document. This displays the message that you supply as an argument in this @function. Be sure to display a message that clearly indicates what is wrong and how the user can correct it.

> **Tip**
>
> If a field is required, you should indicate this in the field's Help description.

Layout Regions

Notes R4 has added a great new design feature called layout regions, which enables you to more easily design visually enticing forms. In earlier versions of Notes, forms designers had to insert fields, objects, tables, etc., in one region—the form itself. With layout regions in Notes R4 you can now have regions within the form, allowing for more graphical features. The Personal Journal template (JOURNAL4.NTF) has an excellent example of a layout region in the Docinfo form. Figure 10.42 displays the Docinfo form being used in the database, while figure 10.43 displays the layout region for that form in design mode.

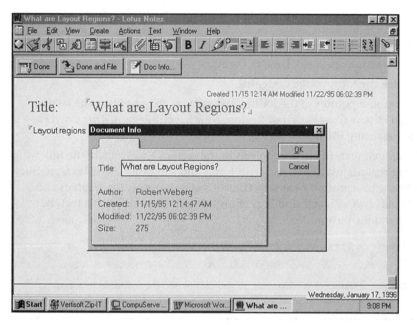

Fig. 10.42

Clicking the DocInfo button on the Journal Entry form opens the DocInfo form. Notice the folder graphic, static text, and fields. These have been placed in a layout region.

Static text   Layout region   Fields

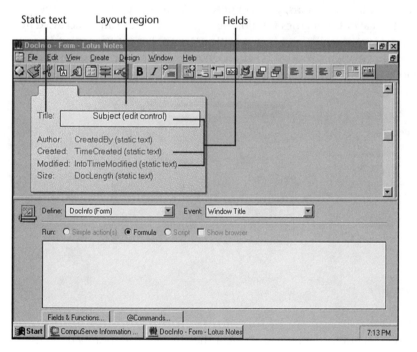

Fig. 10.43

Editing the DocInfo forms reveals how the layout region has been constructed with a graphic, static text, and the fields.

Follow these steps to create a layout region:

1. Select the database and choose <u>V</u>iew, <u>D</u>esign.

2. In the navigation pane, click <u>D</u>esign, <u>F</u>orms.

3. Double-click the form you're designing.

4. Move the mouse pointer to the location where you want to place the layout region and choose <u>C</u>reate, <u>L</u>ayout Region, <u>N</u>ew Layout Region. This inserts a frame representing the layout region.

5. Add the desired text, fields, and objects in the region. You can add the following to a layout region, just as you can with forms and subforms: static text, graphics (either in the background or as selectable objects), hotspots for graphics and text, all fields (with greater numbers of display options) except rich text, buttons, and graphic buttons.

> **Note**
>
> Layout regions cannot contain rich text, so you cannot add the following to a layout region: links, tables, objects, attachments, pop-ups, sections, and rich text fields.

When creating layout regions, you will need to define the properties for the region in the Layout Properties InfoBox (see fig. 10.44). This can be accessed by selecting the layout region and then selecting <u>D</u>esign, <u>L</u>ayout Properties. Here you can define margins, widths, 3D effects, borders, snapping to grid, and hiding options.

Fig. 10.44

The Layout Properties Infobox allows you to choose various options for your layout region.

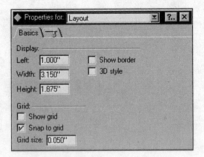

6. Save the form.

Subforms

A subform is an excellent form-building shortcut that enables you to store often-used fields and other form elements together. In an earlier version of Notes, you needed to add fields individually; now you can place subforms that consist of group fields on the form. Subforms are very similar to shared fields because they allow you to use fields in multiple forms within the database, except subforms are like groups of fields.

The Microsoft Document Library (DOCLIBM4.NTF) provides an excellent example of using a subform numerous times in the many forms contained in the database. Figure 10.45 displays the subform Document Workflow and its elements. Figure 10.46 shows this subform inserted in another form within that same database. This development technique will save you a lot of time.

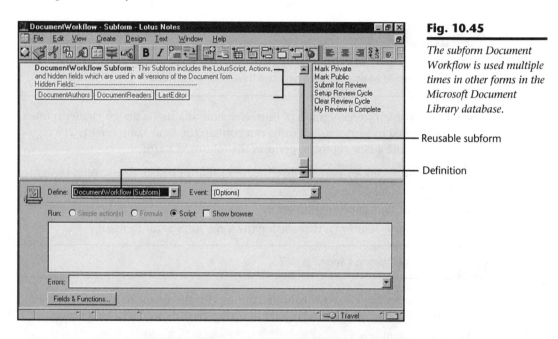

Fig. 10.45

The subform Document Workflow is used multiple times in other forms in the Microsoft Document Library database.

Reusable subform

Definition

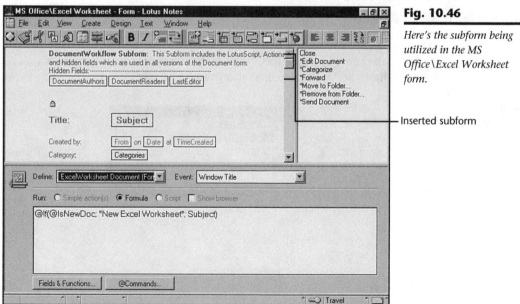

Fig. 10.46

Here's the subform being utilized in the MS Office\Excel Worksheet form.

Inserted subform

> **Note**
>
> Previously created subforms can be edited by clicking on them directly in a form or by selecting Design Subforms in the navigation pane.

> **Caution**
>
> You cannot add other fields to the form that have the same name as those on the subform because this would be an attempt to have two fields with the same name on one form.

The subform (which stores a group of form elements as a single design element) must have been created in advance. Subforms can contain the same components as a regular form. To create a new subform, perform the following steps:

1. Select the database that will have the new subform and choose Create, Design, Subform.

2. Choose Design, Subform Properties.

3. Give the new subform a name using the same rules as for forms.

 ◀◀ See "Naming a Form," p. 367

4. In the Basics tab, choose the desired options for the subform: Include in Insert Subform dialog, Include in New Form dialog, or Hide Subform for R3 users.

5. Save the Subform.

To insert a previously created subform, perform the following steps:

1. Open the desired form in edit mode and place the insertion point where you want to paste the subform and choose Create, Insert Subform. The Insert Subform dialog box is displayed, as shown in figure 10.47.

Fig. 10.47

The Insert Subform dialog box enables you to place previously created subforms into your forms. Think of subforms as libraries of grouped fields that can be reused.

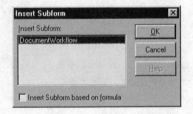

2. Select the subform you want to use and click OK to insert the subform into your form.

3. Save the form.

> **Note**
>
> Just as a form formula attached to a view changes how a whole document is displayed, a subform formula can be attached to a form to change how a portion of the document is displayed under different circumstances.

 ▶▶ See "Working with Formulas," p. 495

Tables

Tables are useful for summarizing information or lining up fields in rows and columns. A table placed on a form appears in every document created with the form. You can use tables to organize information or line up fields in rows and columns. Tables within forms can contain text, buttons, objects, or graphics. You can even omit the cell borders if you want to create an "invisible" table.

To create a table on a form, perform the following steps:

1. In the selected form, move the mouse pointer to the location where you want to place the table.

2. Choose Create, Table.

3. Specify the starting number of rows and columns for the table and click OK. Figure 10.48 displays a 3-row, 2-column table.

Use the Table Properties InfoBox to change border styles and spacing for the highlighted area or even highlight the table or individual rows or columns and choose Text, Text Properties to change the style of text or to hide text for the highlighted area.

 ◀◀ See "Using Tables in Your Documents," p. 309

4. Click the form; then save it.

Fig. 10.48

Tables in forms are great for organizing and aligning fields. Use the Table menu or the Table Properties InfoBox to modify your tables.

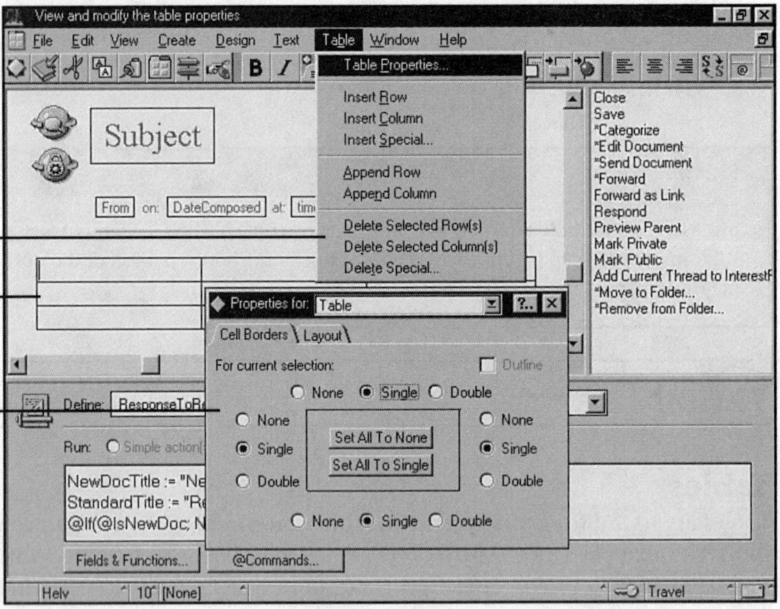

Table menu

Inserted table

Table Properties InfoBox

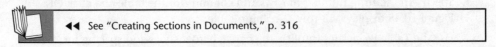

Sections

Sections are useful for organizing documents that contain a lot of information. You can use sections to collapse one or more paragraphs in a document into a single line or to limit access to specific areas of a form. Sections make navigation in large documents easier. Readers can expand a section when they want to read its contents. Developers like to group related information in a large document into different sections.

◀◀ See "Creating Sections in Documents," p. 316

To create a collapsible or controlled access section, perform the following steps:

1. Open the desired form in edit mode.
2. Select and highlight the paragraph(s) you want to collapse into a section.
3. Select Create, Section, Standard or Create, Section, Controlled Access.

Tip

Notes uses the first paragraph as the section title by default. To change a section's title, you must use the Section Properties InfoBox.

Hotspots

Hotspots are very useful for displaying pop-up text, using buttons to utilize a formula, switching to linked destinations, or activating a Notes action.

◀◀ See "Adding Hotspots to Your Documents," p. 304

You can add a hotspot to an area of a document (such as text or a graphic). To create a hotspot, perform the following steps:

1. Open the desired form in edit mode.
2. Select the area you want to add the hotspot to.
3. Choose Create, Hotspot. You can now select either of the following:

   - **Link Hotspot**—This enables you to link to a specific document (such as a Help document designed for your database). You must first use Edit, Copy as Link a portion of text on a target document prior to selecting this hotspot option.

   - **Button**—Use this option to create a button and corresponding formula to perform some type of task.

   - **Text Popup**—This enables you to enter the text you want the popup to display.

   - **Formula Popup**—This enables you to enter a formula in the programmer's pane that will set the text you want the popup to display.

   - **Action Hotspot**—Use this option to create an action hotspot that performs a specific action defined in the database.

Figure 10.49 displays the available hotspots.

Designing Applications

II

Fig. 10.49

Hotspots are useful for displaying help information, switching to linked destinations, and performing Notes actions.

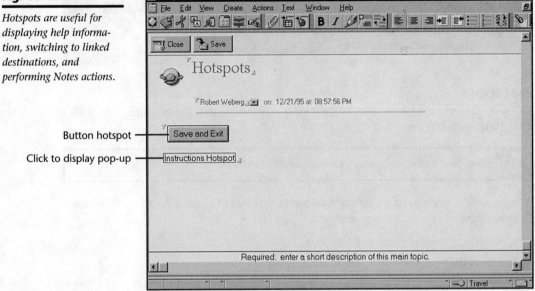

Button hotspot —

Click to display pop-up —

From Here...

This chapter taught you how to begin creating forms. Forms are the building blocks and the basic structure of your database, because it is the forms that contain the general layout, the field names, the field data types and formats, and any formulas that the field needs to calculate information. To learn more about how Notes uses the forms that you create, read the following chapters:

- Chapter 8, "Working with Documents," covers how to edit existing documents that could contain objects.

- Chapter 11, "Designing Views," shows how to create views to display the documents that store your objects.

- Chapter 16, "LotusScript: A Whole New Programming Language," teaches the basics of the powerful LotusScript programming language, which can be used to manipulate objects and links on your forms.

Designing Views

The secret to developing and building views in Notes is knowing the database's structure and having a vivid understanding of what you want to accomplish with the view. You need to understand what fields, data types, and forms exist in your database. Once you know that information, creating views is very easy.

In a Notes database, a view lists documents and provides a means of accessing them. Views are essentially tables of contents listing the documents in a Notes database. Unlike most printed books, a database can have many tables of contents, each of which selects, sorts, or groups the documents in the database in a specialized way.

Every database must have at least one view; most have multiple views. A view may display all of the documents in the database or show only a subset of existing documents. Often, you may want to view the same information in different ways. For example, you may want to see the information in a Contact or Address database organized and listed by Last Name, by State, by the date they were created, by who created them, just to name a few of the possibilities.

Notes enables you to create multiple views for each database. You can design views that display only those documents that you want to see, and sort the documents in a way that makes it easy to interpret the information.

In this chapter, you learn how to perform the following tasks in designing a view:

- Creating the view
- Assigning the view attributes
- Creating and formatting the view columns
- Using the selection formula to select documents to include in the view
- Using form formulas to select the form with which to display documents in the view
- Defining the view's sort order with categorization and sorts

The Logistics of Views

As mentioned above, views are lists of documents in a Notes database. Depending on how they're designed, views can select, sort, or categorize documents in a variety of ways. Views can also show many types of information about the documents listed in them, such as author's name or date of creation. It is important to remember that views may show all documents in a database or only a selection of documents. You can split a view into three panes: the navigation pane, the view pane, and the preview pane.

Tip

Select <u>V</u>iew, Document <u>P</u>review to toggle the preview pane.

Note

If the database's design allows for it, you can resize columns by dragging, or change the sorting in a column by clicking its title.

The views are created by the designer of a database. Users can customize panes and columns to some extent, but they can't affect a view's design. Each view consists of one or more columns, each of which displays a field or the results of a formula. I like to think of views as a form of a report with each column in the report displaying the field information for the individual documents (rows).

Each line (row) in a view usually represents a single document (Notes R4 allows for multiple rows for a single document or word wrapping). Columns represent one type of information (field) available in the document. The developer writes a selection formula for each view, which picks which documents will be displayed in that view. The formula can select all the documents in the database, or select only those that meet certain criteria.

As a user, you can perform several tasks in a view. You can open a document, navigate between documents, find unread documents, forward documents (mail) to other Notes users, select documents to act upon (print, export, refresh fields, and so on), delete documents, copy documents, and refresh the view.

Views can either be shared or private. Shared views are available to all database users, unless restricted by a read access list assigned to the view. Private views can be seen only by the person who creates it. Private views are useful when a user wants to see the documents organized in a particular way. I like to think of private views as predetermined ad hoc queries created by the user. However, a user's private view can display only those documents to which the user already has access; encrypted data will not be displayed.

Planning a View

Before creating a view in Notes, you should sketch the idea on paper. Your sketch should include the following information and should answer questions that may arise when creating views:

- Identify and state the purpose of each view. If the database is made up of main and response documents, its a good idea to have at least one view of the database that shows each main document associated with its response documents. It's also a good idea to have a flat, nonhierarchical view that sorts documents by date.

- Which subset of documents will be displayed? Do you want to see all of the documents or just a subset?

- Decide how to sort documents in the view. To reduce the number of views, use columns that users can sort themselves.

- Try to visualize the columns of information (fields). Do you want to include all of the fields in columns or just some specific fields?

- Will unread markers be displayed? Do you want unread documents to appear in a different color and/or be marked with a star?

- Will the column display the field data or be manipulated in a column formula? Sometimes developers combine two fields, such as City and State, into one column using a column formula like `City + ", " + State`.

- Should Responses be indented beneath the parent document to display the hierarchy relationship? Indenting enables you to organize your related parent/child documents for easier viewing.

- Do you want to include any view statistics? For example, you may want to indicate whether a contact entry has had five call reports (responses).

- Do you want to categorize any columns? Categorization enables you to sort and organize your data to locate data.

- Decide if access to read the documents in each view is restricted. For tighter security, you can add access lists to forms rather than views.

- Decide if any shared or private-on-first-use folders are needed.

- Identify any hidden columns that are needed for special sorting or for other applications' lookups.

- Decide on the view style, such as colors for view elements, and the view background and the number of lines per row.

- Decide on column colors, type styles, and widths (either resizable or set).

Creating Views

After designing and planning the view, you can create a view in Notes by performing the following steps:

1. Select <u>C</u>reate, <u>V</u>iew or press the Create View SmartIcon to display the Create View dialog box, as displayed in figure 11.1. The <u>S</u>elect a location of the new view list box defaults to creating a Private view.

Fig. 11.1

The Create View dialog box enables you to name and select the type of view that you want.

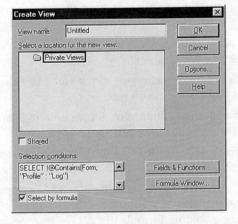

2. In the <u>V</u>iew name box enter a name for the view. This can be left as Untitled and changed from within the View Properites Info box.

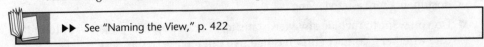

▶▶ See "Naming the View," p. 422

3. Click S<u>h</u>ared if you want to create a Shared view. This can be further defined by selecting <u>P</u>ersonal on first use. Notice that the <u>S</u>elect a location for the new view list box changes to display the current view folders (see fig. 11.2).

Fig. 11.2

Notice how the Create View dialog box changes to reflect a Shared view.

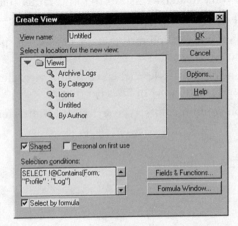

> **Note**
>
> A Personal on first use View combines the attributes of the shared and private views. It is created as a shared view, but after it is used by an individual user for the first time, it becomes a private view. Developers use this option when they want to create specialized private views for each userbut they don't want to have each users name on the View menu.

4. Click OK to create and save the view. The newly created view appears in the design pane when Design Views is selected in the navigation pane (see fig. 11.3).

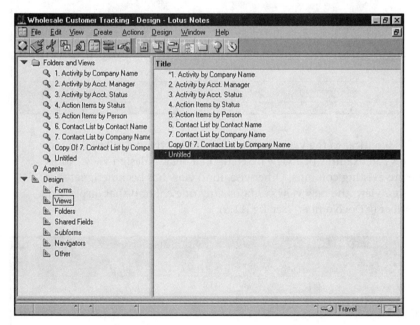

Fig. 11.3

The view Untitled appears in the design pane after being created and saved. If you named the view, its name would appear.

Double-click the new view to open the view in edit mode, as shown in figure 11.4.

Fig. 11.4

The newly created untitled view is opened in edit mode. Here is where you begin defining the structure of the view.

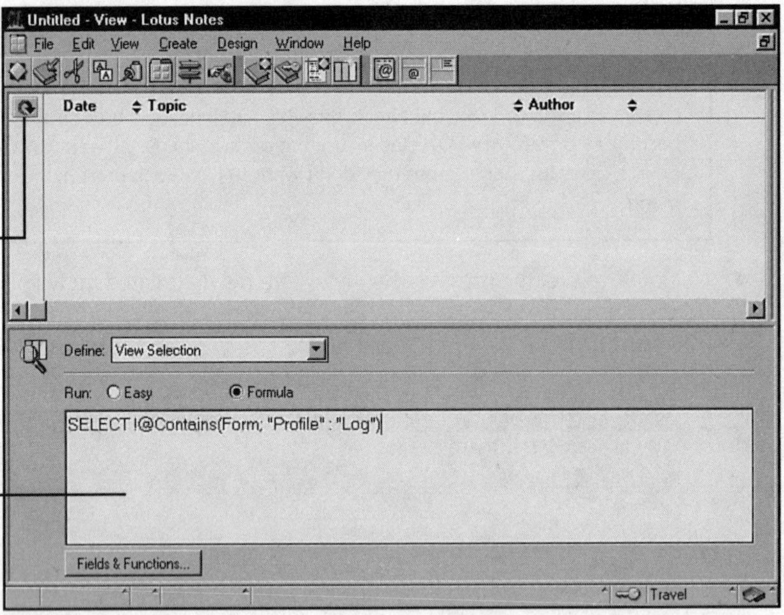

Refresh button

Formula box

The new view is identical to the view that is designated as the default design view. Figure 11.5 shows an example of a view based upon a default design view. Notice that there are pre-existing columns. Otherwise, if no view has been designated as the default design view, the new view contains only one column that displays the document number (@DocNumber) (see fig. 11.5).

Fig. 11.5

This is an untitled view opened in edit mode that has not been based upon a default design view. Notice that the new view contains only one column to display the document number.

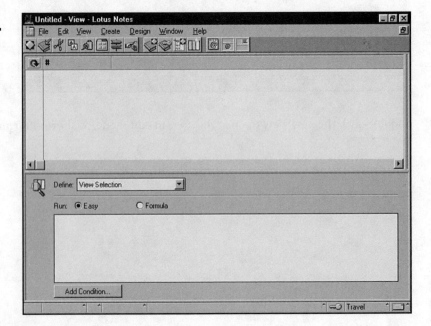

At this point you can now modify the view by adding and modifying columns and their corresponding attributes.

Copying a View

Occasionally, you may want to copy a view from one database and use it in another, possibly modifying it to meet the new application's needs.

 ▶▶ See "Database Templates," p. 949

To copy and paste a view, perform the following steps:

1. Select the database containing the source view.
2. In the navigation pane, select Design Views to display the available list of views in the Title pane.
3. Select the view you want to copy from the Views list.

> ### Tip
> You can select more than one view using Ctrl+Shift.

4. Select Edit, Copy or press the Edit Copy SmartIcon.
5. Switch to the database where you want to paste the form.
6. Select Edit, Paste and the new view's name will appear in the views list.

> ### Caution
> If you are copying and pasting a view from the same database, the form is pasted into the list of forms but is renamed by appending the view with "Copy of." This can be renamed using the View Properties InfoBox.

 ▶▶ See "Naming the View," p. 422

Defining View Attributes

Before you begin laying out columns in the view, you will need to define some basic attributes, such as the view's name, styles, and default options, in the view's Properties InfoBox.

To open this InfoBox, perform the following steps:

1. Open the desired view in edit mode.
2. Select Design, View Properties or right-click and choose View Properties.

The Basics tab in the View Properties InfoBox, as shown in figure 11.6., essentially enables you to supply a name, alias, and comment for the view.

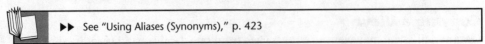

▶▶ See "Using Aliases (Synonyms)," p. 423

Fig. 11.6

The Basics tab in a view's Properties InfoBox is used to define the Name, Alias, and any Comments for a view.

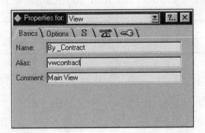

Naming the View. The name you type in the Name text box can be any combination of characters including spaces, and it is case-sensitive. A name can have as many characters as you want, but only the first 32 will appear on menus and in dialog boxes. View names appear on the View menu; thus, when you name a view you are naming a command. The name should be logical and indicate the criteria or sort order (e.g., View By Contact). The following sections describe in more detail the specifics of naming a view.

Specifying Accelerator Keys. When naming a view, you should also use accelerator keys. The first unique letter in the form name is used as the view's accelerator. To force Notes to use a different letter as the accelerator, insert an underscore before the desired letter. For example, in By _Contact, the underscore forces the letter *C* to be used as the accelerator.

Ordering View Names. Consider how the views are ordered on the View menu. The View menu automatically sorts names in alphabetical order. If you want more highly used views to appear first, you can use numbers as the first character. For example:

```
1. By Contact
1. By Lender
3. By Date
```

Tip

View names with numbers provides easy accelerators for users, because the numbers are unique and become the accelerator keys.

Grouping Views with Cascading Menus. You can use cascading views to group a series of views in a cascading submenu under a single name. This shows the user that the views are related and can save space on the menu. You define a cascading view by entering the top-level view name, followed by a backslash (\) and the additional view name. Notes allows one level of cascade. For example, these two view names would appear under <u>V</u>iew, By Contact:

```
By Contact \ Last Name
By Contact \ Company Name
```

When the user chooses <u>V</u>iew and highlights 1. By Contact, a cascading menu appears, as displayed in figure 11.7.

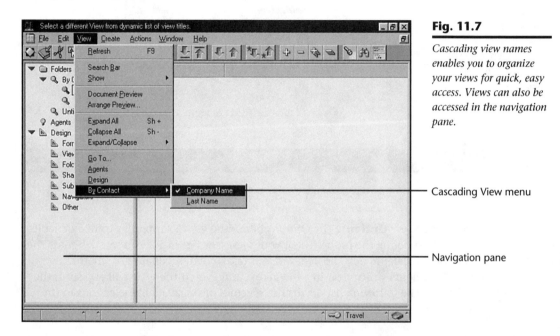

II

Designing Applications

Fig. 11.7

Cascading view names enables you to organize your views for quick, easy access. Views can also be accessed in the navigation pane.

Cascading View menu

Navigation pane

Hiding a View. Occasionally, you may want to "hide" a view from the database's users by not displaying it on the <u>V</u>iew menu. Developers like to hide views for keyword lookups or to save views for future use. To hide a view, enclose the view name in parentheses. For example:

```
(1. By Contact \ Last Name)
```

Caution

Hidden views usually exist for use with formulas or LotusScript and Agents. Hiding a view is not a security measure. Users can still make a private view and see its data if they have Reader access to the database.

Using Aliases (Synonyms). *Aliases* (also called *synonyms*) in views work exactly like using synonyms in forms. Aliases enable you to change the view's name on the <u>V</u>iew menu without tracking down and rewriting formulas that reference the original name. If you didn't use aliases, these formulas and even doclinks from other databases would generate errors. Figure 11.8 displays an example of naming a view with an alias.

> **Caution**
>
> If you want to rename a view, be sure to keep the original name as a synonym so any doclinks pointing to that view can still be opened.

Fig. 11.8

You should use logical names for your views, plus utilize aliases to prevent any future programming agony.

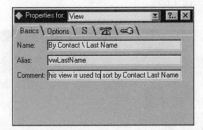

> **Tip**
>
> I like to precede my alias names with vw, thus indicating that it is a view alias name.

Setting the View Options. The Options tab in the view's Properties InfoBox enables you to further define the properties of your view (see fig. 11.9). You can designate the view to be the default view, how view opens (expanded or collapsed), whether response documents will appear in a hierarchy, and even if the view will appear in the View menu. The following list details the specifics of the available selections in the Options tab:

Fig. 11.9

The Options tab displays various default options for your view.

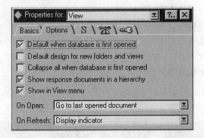

■ **Default when database is first opened**—This designates the view as the default view, and when the database is first added and opened by a user this view will appear. Only one default view is allowed per database. The default view is marked with a star in the list of views in the Title pane.

> **Note**
>
> Selecting this option in one view automatically deselects this option for another view, because there can be only one default view.

- **Default design for new folders and views**—This enables the developer to use the view as the default view when designing other views in the database. If selected and creating new views, the new view will initially be identical to this view.

- **Show response documents in a hierarchy**—You can indent response documents and response-to-response documents under their parent documents. This option enables you to indent response documents an additional three spaces under main documents. A response hierarchy is useful when readers want to see the progression of a discussion or want to see related topics grouped together. Discussion databases often use this format in a main view. Figure 11.10 shows a view where the option Show response documents in a hierarchy has been selected.

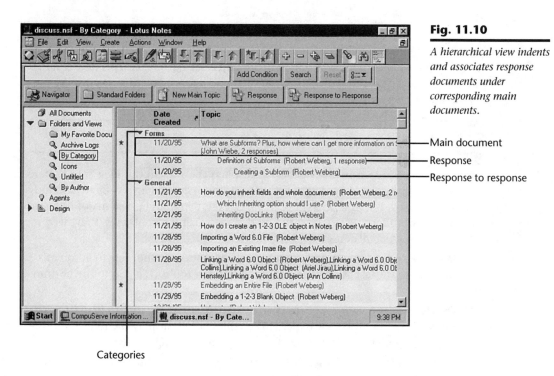

Fig. 11.10

A hierarchical view indents and associates response documents under corresponding main documents.

A flat, nonhierarchical view doesn't distinguish between main and response documents. This is useful when the listing isn't focused on topics, such as in a By Author view or where there are no response documents, as shown in figure 11.11.

Fig. 11.11

A nonhierarchical view does not indent response level documents under their corresponding main parent documents. This view is categorized by Author Name and sorted by ascending Date.

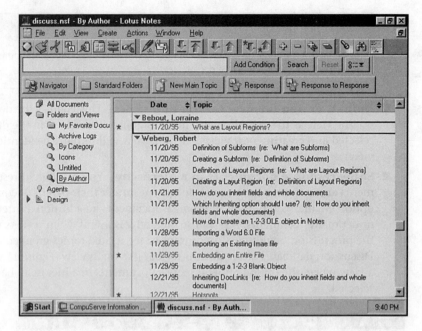

To indent response-to-response documents, create a column immediately to the left of the column that contains your main documents (see fig. 11.12). This new column will need to have Show Response Only selected and a formula written to display the response documents.

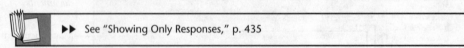

▶▶ See "Showing Only Responses," p. 435

- **Show in View menu**—This option displays the view in the View menu. Deselecting this is sort of synonymous with adding ( ) around a view name and hiding the view. But in this case the name does not contain ( ). The major difference is that when formulas refer to the hidden view using parentheses, they need to include the parentheses.

- **On Open**—Here you can instruct Notes when opening the view to automatically Go to the last opened document, Go to the top row, or Go to the bottom row.

- **On Refresh**—A view that's ready to be refreshed has the refresh icon in the top-left corner of the view pane. This enables you to display the refresh indicator button when a refresh is needed for the view (see fig. 11.13).

- **Collapse all when database is first opened**—This initializes the view to collapse the existing categories when the view is opened.

Responses only column   Main document column

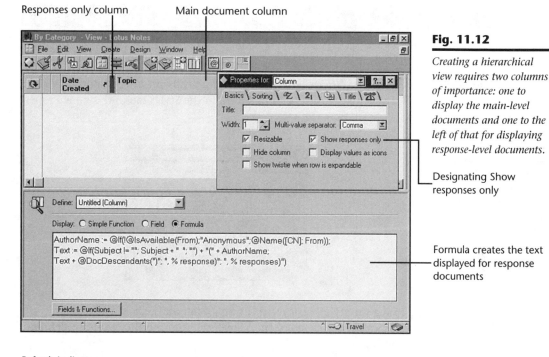

Fig. 11.12

Creating a hierarchical view requires two columns of importance: one to display the main-level documents and one to the left of that for displaying response-level documents.

Designating Show responses only

Formula creates the text displayed for response documents

Refresh indicator

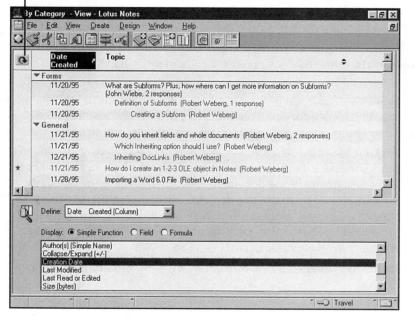

Fig. 11.13

The refresh indicator is displayed when the view needs to be refreshed to display any new documents that have been created.

II

Designing Applications

> ### Tip
>
> I like to use this option to allow users to easily locate categorized documents in a view.

Setting the Style for the View. Notes R4 has dramatically improved upon how a view can appear. These new features can be found in the Styles tab of the View Properties InfoBox, as shown in figure 11.14.

Fig. 11.14

The Styles tab enables you to set properties, such as color, and whether to use multiple rows for headings and rows. Some are new features to Notes R4.

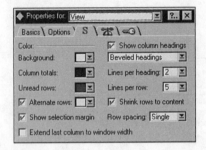

Developers can find a variety of options in the Styles tab that enable them to affect how a view appears. In the Styles tab of the View Properties InfoBox, you can define the color of the following:

- **Background**—Generally, a light-colored background is easier to view data. White is the default.

- **Unread Rows**—This indicates by its color whether a document in a view has been read. Black is the default.

- **Column Totals**—This enables you to have column totals stand out from the other data. Grey is the default.

- **Alternate Rows**—This is a new feature that enables developers to interchange row colors and highlights for easier reading. For example, one row might be highlighted in yellow, the next row white, the next yellow, and so on.

- **Show Selection Margin**—The *selection margin* is used for selecting documents. If you need a clean space that shows only documents without other identifier information, you can remove the document selection margin at the left. Only in rare development situations would you deselect this option to prevent the users from marking or selecting documents to copy or refresh. Readers can still select documents by holding Shift as they click document names, but they won't be able to see which documents are selected.

- **Show Column Headings**—If deselected, the view's column headings will be hidden.

- **Beveled or Simple Headings**—In the Show Column Headings list box, you can indicate how you want the column headings to appear. The Beveled option is the default option that bevels the appearance of view columns. The simple headings option displays the view columns with out column separators using black text on white background (see fig. 11.15).

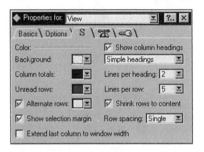

Fig. 11.15

A view using the Simple headings option to display the column headings.

■ **Lines per heading**—You can now select the number of rows (1-5) the column heading can have. This is a great feature for using long column heading names, as shown in figure 11.16.

Two-line heading

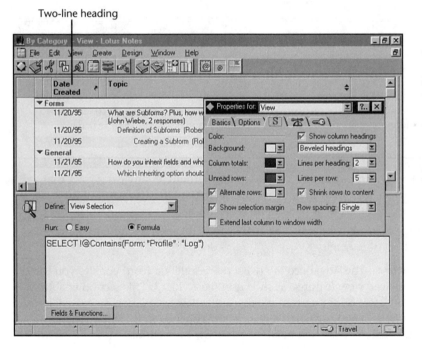

Fig. 11.16

You can increase the size of your column headings; this example uses two lines. You can even hide the selection margin on the far left. This improves how views can be viewed and printed.

■ **Lines per row**—Another new feature is the ability to have multiple rows in the view. This gives you the opportunity to utilize word wrapping and improve the reporting capabilities of Notes (see fig. 11.17).

II

Designing Applications

Fig. 11.17

The ability to designate multiple rows for each row in the view enables you to utilize word wrapping.

Word wrapping the column text

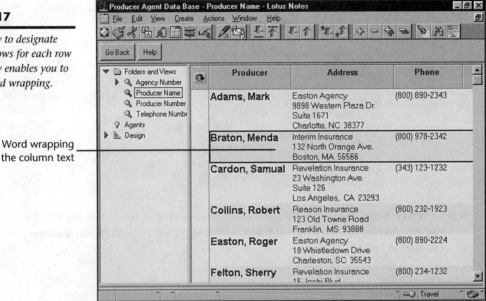

> **Note**
>
> Since rich text fields cannot appear in a view and they normally contain long strings of text that you would want to word wrap, you may want to convert the rich text field to a text field prior to attempting to utilize the word wrapping feature for a field in view column.

■ **Shrink rows to content**—This essentially eliminates any extra rows that are not used by a document if you have indicated the Lines per row option to be more than one, thus saving view and reporting space.

■ **Spacing**—Spacing, which is the vertical space between documents, can be specified as either single, $1\,^1/_4$, $1\,^1/_2$, $1\,^3/_4$, or double.

Advanced Features. The Advanced tab (with the beanie hat icon) enables you to select more advanced view features, as shown in figure 11.18. This section enables you to specify when Notes should refresh or discard the view index, how to display unread marks, and which forms to use when a document is opened in this view. The attributes you can designate are described in the following sections.

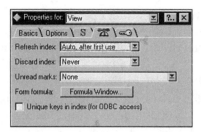

Fig. 11.18

The Advanced tab enables you to establish when to refresh or discard the view index, plus designate a Form formula.

Refreshing the View. In the Refresh Index list box you can select Auto, after first use; Automatic; Manual; and Auto, at most every. A view index (unrelated to a full text search index) is an internal filing system that lets Notes create the most current list for a view. When documents change, the view index must be refreshed to display the changes. To improve performance time, you can change how frequently the view index is refreshed by selecting one of the following options:

- **Auto, after first use**—The default option, this updates the view every time the view is opened after the first time by adding changes incrementally to the view index. Users never need to be concerned about whether the view displays the latest changes, but it takes a little longer for a view to display the first time the view is opened.

- **Automatic**— This option keeps the view updated whether or not users ever open the database, by adding changes incrementally to the view index. Users never need to be concerned about whether a view displays the latest changes, and views open more quickly.

- **Manual**—This option relies on the user to refresh the view. This option is useful with large databases, if it isn't critical for the view to be kept up–to–date, because it enables large databases to open faster. If users want to look for a new document, they can refresh the view by clicking on the refresh indicator.

- **Auto, at most every**—This option enables you to specify how frequently the view index should be updated. This is also a good compromise between Automatic and Manual Indexing for large databases that change fairly often. The view's index is updated automatically only at the specified interval. If a user opens a database in which changes have been made since the last indexing, a yellow question mark appears at the top left of the view to indicate that changes have been made that are not visible in the view. Users have the option of manually refreshing the view to see the updates.

Discarding the Index. Change Discard index from Never to one of the other choices to save disk space, if slower view displays are acceptable. If the view index is deleted, users have to wait for the view index to be recreated. You have the following options:

II

Designing Applications

- **Never**—This option preserves the view index permanently; updates are added to the existing index. The view index never has to be recreated, but this option takes up more disk space than the other options. Use this for views that users frequently need, so they don't have to wait for a new view index to be created when they open the database. For large databases, this can take several minutes.

- **After each use**—This option deletes the view index as soon as the database is closed. This option saves the most disk space, but the index must be rebuilt the next time the view is opened. Select this option when the view is used infrequently, but on a predictable basis; for example, only on Friday afternoons when an agent is run.

- **If inactive for n days**—This option deletes a view index only if the view hasn't been used in the specified number of days. If the view is deleted, the view index is rebuilt the next time the database is opened. (This option doesn't affect local databases.) Select this option when a database is used infrequently on an unpredictable basis as a compromise between the Never and After each use options.

Displaying Marks for Unread Documents. In the Unread Marks list box, the Standard (compute in hierarchy) option displays asterisks for unread main documents and response documents, and for any collapsed categories containing unread main or response documents. Because this choice displays unread marks for every level, it displays the view the slowest, but gives the readers the most information about documents they need to read. You also have the following choices:

- **Unread documents only**—This option displays asterisks only for unread main documents. Unread marks do not appear next to response documents or collapsed categories. This choice displays the view faster than the Standard display and is a good compromise between showing unread marks at every level and not showing them at all.

- **None**—This option does not display unread marks; it displays the view fastest, but doesn't help users see which documents they haven't read. Use this only if users don't need to see asterisks next to new or modified documents they haven't read. Users can still navigate to the next unread document by using SmartIcons.

Security Options. You can select the Security tab (with the key icon) to define a limited list of users who can access this view. Figure 11.19 shows the Security options for a view. The default option is All readers and above, which utilizes what has been defined in the ACL for the current database.

To refine this list further, follow these steps:

1. Deselect All readers and above.

2. Click the Person icon to select a name or group from a Personal or Public Address Book.

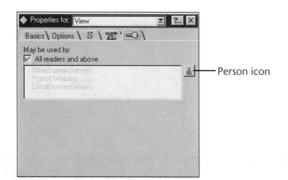

Fig. 11.19

The Security tab enables you to decide who (users and groups) can access the view. The initial list shown resides in the ACL; however, you can refine the list using the Address Book.

 ◄◄ See "Restricting Read Access," p. 379

Creating Columns in a View

To fully create a view, you need to create columns. A column displays the contents of a field or the result of a formula (which may involve one or more fields). A new view always includes a column labeled # (using the formula @DocNumber to number the documents in the display) or columns that were included in the default design view.

Keep the following tips in mind when creating columns:

- Delete any columns that you do not want to use by selecting them and hitting the Del key or by choosing Edit, Cut if you want reuse and paste the column in another location.
- You can add as many columns as you desire.
- It is advisable to fit the columns on the screen so the user is not forced to horizontally scroll the display to see them.
- Always try to place the most useful columns toward the left edge of the screen.

To create a column, perform the following steps:

1. Click where you want the column to appear.

2. Choose Create, Insert, New, Column to insert a column to the left of the currently highlighted column. If you want to add another column to the right of the last column in the view, choose Create, Append New Column instead.

3. Double-click the new column header to display the column's Properties InfoBox, as shown in figure 11.20.

Fig. 11.20

The column's Properties InfoBox enables you to establish how the column will appear.

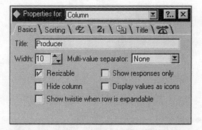

> **Tip**
>
> Right-click the column header and select Column Properties to display the Properties InfoBox.

> **Caution**
>
> If you are editing a view that contains documents and you change the view by adding a column or modifying an existing column, you should click the Refresh indicator button to update the view.

Basic Settings

In the Basics tab of the column's Properties InfoBox you can enter the name of the column, set the width of the column, decide whether to hide the column, and several other options. Figure 11.20 in the preceding section displayed the Basics options that are available for a column. The following sections describe these options.

Adding a Column Title. In the Title box, enter a title to be displayed at the top of the column. Using a title is optional. If the title is longer than the defined column width, it will be truncated to fit the width (unless you have designated multiple rows for the column header). See "Setting the Style for the View" earlier in this chapter for more information about the Lines per Heading option.

> **Note**
>
> Columns that are only one or two characters wide rarely call for titles. Generally, these type of columns are categorized and the categories themselves are self-evident for naming purposes.

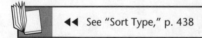

◀◀ See "Sort Type," p. 438

Determining the Column Width. Enter the desired width of the column, in characters, in the Width box. Notes assigns a default width of ten characters to new columns, but you can make a column as narrow or as wide as you want. Depending on the font name and size, a variable amount of characters will fit in the length, not just ten characters.

Tip

Drag the column header lines with the mouse to size the column.

Choosing a Separator for Multiple Values. If the column shows several values (usually generated by a multi-value field), you can specify how you want to separate the values with the Multi-value separator field. If None is selected the multiple value field is displayed as a single text string.

◀◀ See "Keyword Fields," p. 99

◀◀ See "Basics Settings," p. 367

Controlling Column Resizing. Select the Resizable option if the users have the capability of adjusting the column header themselves as they're using the database. The width reverts to the design setting when the database is closed.

Hiding Columns. The Hide column option is useful for columns that do not display information needed by users, but which are needed by the view's design, such as a column used only for sorting purposes. Figure 11.21 shows an example of a hidden sort column using the ResolutionStatus field. Notice that the column formula assigns a numerical value to the Resolution Status entry allowing the view to be sorted by the numbers in that column.

Note

Hidden columns are not hidden when designing a view in design mode. They are only hidden when viewed in the view pane.

Showing Only Responses. Select the Show responses only option to display the column only if the document is a response or a response-to-response document. All response documents are displayed under their corresponding main documents; each level of response is indented an additional three spaces. This option is widely used in discussion databases or databases where you will want to show the parent (main document) to child (response) relationship. See "Setting the View Options" earlier in this chapter for more information on the Show response documents in a hierarchy option.

Fig. 11.21

A hidden sort column is used to force a sort on pre-existing fields.

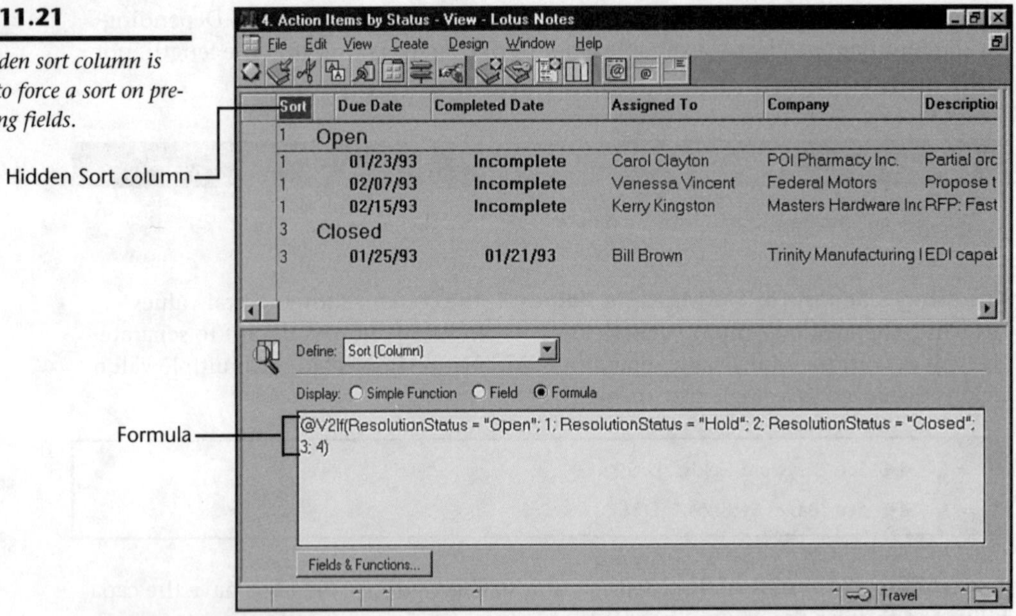

Hidden Sort column —

Formula —

Troubleshooting

Why do you place a Show response only column to the left of columns that display only main document information?

When I first began designing views in Notes, I thought that this was one of the most difficult concepts to comprehend and I was always asking the same question. Notes allows only for information to be displayed within the limitations of a column's width normally. But when Show Responses Only is selected, that restriction is bypassed.

To see the difference, use Ctrl+X to cut the column containing the Show responses only and refresh the view. Notice how the view changes. Paste (Ctrl+V) the column back into the view.

Displaying Values as Icons. Select the Display values as icons option to display one of over 300 predefined icons in the column to graphically represent special values, such as attachments. Write a formula for the column; the result of the formula determines which icon is displayed. The following formula determines whether a document has an attachment and, if so, displays the attachment icon (number 5):

```
@If(@Attachments;5;0)
```

Use 0 as the false case when you want to leave the column blank. The formula above returns 0 when the document has no attachments, so nothing is displayed. Figure 11.22 displays a view using this formula.

Indicating Expandable Rows. The Show twistie when row is expandable option displays a green triangle, which users can click to see categorized documents within a collapsed view or folder (see fig. 11.23).

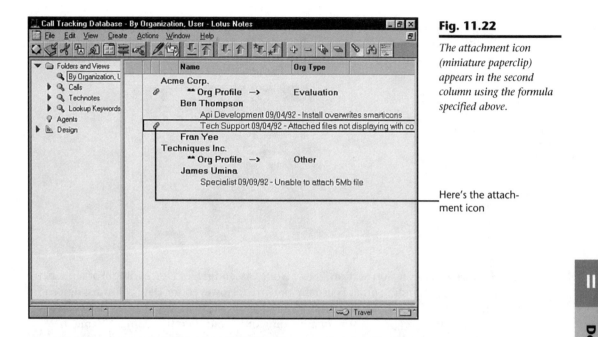

Fig. 11.22

The attachment icon (miniature paperclip) appears in the second column using the formula specified above.

Here's the attachment icon

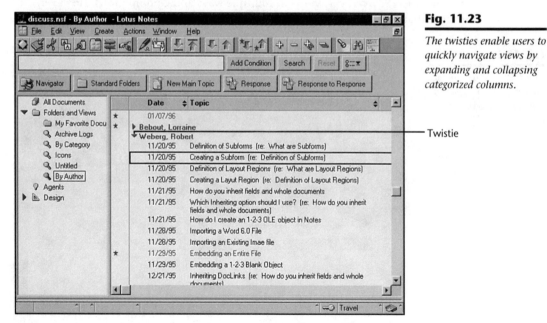

Fig. 11.23

The twisties enable users to quickly navigate views by expanding and collapsing categorized columns.

Twistie

Sorting Options

Sorting and categorizing is the fun and exciting part of building views. It enables you to be creative in how you will display your documents to users. You should always sort the view on at least one column; otherwise, documents and responses appear in the order they were composed.

The Sorting tab in the column's Properties InfoBox, displayed in figure 11.24, enables you to define how the column will be sorted and categorized. The options available are described in the following sections.

Fig. 11.24

The Sorting tab allows you to specify the sorting and categorization attributes for your view.

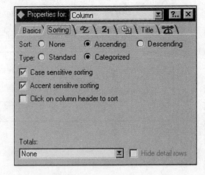

Sort Order. In the Sort section, select None, Ascending, or Descending. For alphabetical listings, ascending order is usually preferred. However, for Date columns, descending is preferred to display the most recent documents first. Figure 11.25 shows a view that sorts the Company Name in ascending order and then the Contact Name in ascending order. You can sort views in multiple ways and combinations. However, remember that columns are sorted from left to right.

Fig. 11.25

This view is sorted first by the company and then the contact. Notice there is no categorization of columns.

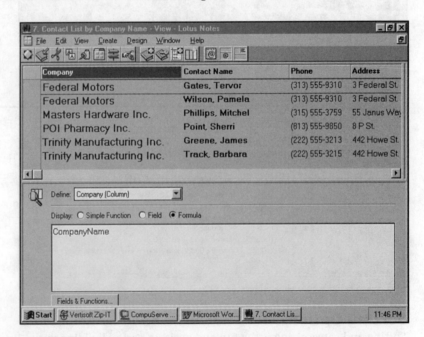

Sort Type. In the Type section, choose Standard or Categorized. Standard is the default option, but you should select Categorized if the view will contain categories. Figure 11.26 contains a view with categories.

> **Note**
>
> If sorting a view by chronological order, you must design a column and sort using a formula with @Created. The formula function @Created returns the date the document was created. Using this time value you can sort the column in ascending or descending order.

 ▶▶ See "Formula Functions," p. 533

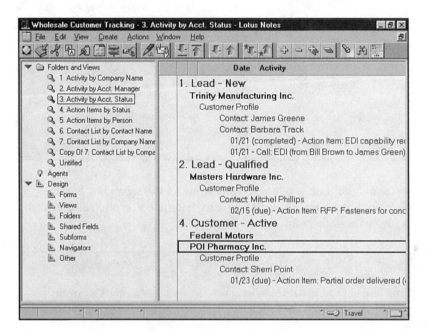

Fig. 11.26

This view has been sorted by the status field and then subcategorized by the Company Name. Each category enables users to drill down on information.

Designing Applications

Sorting on Demand. You can designate one or more columns in a view as sortable on demand. Users click these special columns and choose a sorting method to see the documents in the order they choose.

To establish this feature select the Click on Column Header To Sort option. You can choose between Ascending, Descending, Both, or Change to view. The Change to view option lets you select a view that Notes will switch to when the user clicks the column. In the column header, the Ascending option is represented by an upward pointing arrow, the Descending option displays a downward pointing arrow, the Both option displays both arrows, while the Change to view option displays a curved arrow. Figure 11.27 shows a column heading with the Click on Column Header to Sort option selected using Change to view. Notice the curved arrow indicates that it switches to another view if selected.

Fig. 11.27

Users click these special columns and choose a sorting method to see the documents in the order they choose. You can designate one or more columns in a view as sortable on demand.

Sortable on demand column

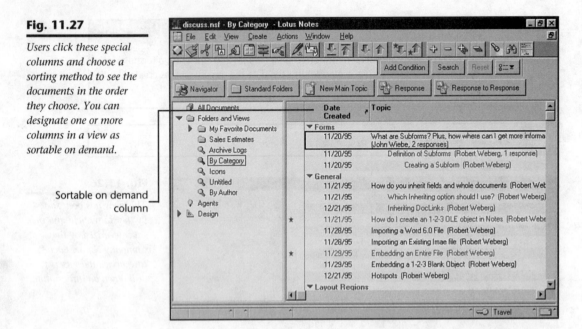

If Ascending, Descending or Both is selected, you can select the Secondary Sort Column to display option to list boxes that allow you to designate a second column and it's sort order to automatically sort upon.

Note

Use the column heading title text to warn users what will happen if they use the Change to view option. For example, you might title the column "Click here to switch to the By Author view." Plus, the view they switch to should probably have this same option specified to return to the original view to prevent the user from getting lost.

Case-Sensitive and Accent-Sensitive Sorting. Deselect the Case-Sensitive Sorting option if you do not want the sort to be case-sensitive.

Deselect Accent-sensitive sorting if you do not want the sorting for this column to be accent-sensitive.

Displaying Totals. The Totals option enables you to specify how you want totals to appear. The options are None, Total, Average per document, Average per sub-category, Percentage of parent category, and Percentage of entire view. You can click Hide details to hide the details row for the rows but show the totals for the categories.

Defining the Style for the Column

The Styles tab (its icon shows *a* and *Z*) in the Column Properties InfoBox enables you to define the style attributes for the selected column. Figure 11.28 displays the Styles tab options available in the column's Properties InfoBox. Here you can define the following attributes to improve the appearance of your view:

- Font
- Size
- Style (Select any predefined styles)

 ◀◀ See "Saving Paragraph Properties as Styles," p. 389

- Text Color
- Justification (Align the data in your column to be Left, Right, or Center)

Fig. 11.28

The options in the Styles tab are very logical. You can select font, size, color, etc., to make your view stand out when viewing and printing.

Tip

Select Left when working with text and time-date values, Right when displaying numbers (especially numbers with decimal places), and Center when working with small values that you want to stand out (like Yes and No).

One new feature developers will appreciate is that style changes are automatically reflected in the view. This saves an immense amount of time, since you don't have to close a dialog box to preview any changes. Also, you can click Apply to All to apply any changes made to all of the existing columns in the view, so you don't have to individually change each column.

Displaying Numbers

The Numbers tab in the column's Properties InfoBox (its icon is a large 2 and a small 1—see fig. 11.29) enables you to define how columns with numbers will appear. You can choose between the following four number formats:

- **General**—This option displays numbers as they are entered. Zeroes to the right of the decimal point are suppressed; for example, 8.00 displays as 8.
- **Fixed**—This option displays numbers with a fixed number of decimal places; for example, 8 displays as 8.00. You can select the desired number of places from the Decimal Places list.

- **Scientific**—This option displays numbers using exponential notation; for example, 80,000 displays as 8.00E+04. You can select the desired number of decimal places from the Decimal Places list.

- **Currency**—This option displays values with a currency symbol and two digits after the decimal point; for example, $8.00.

Fig. 11.29

The Numbers tab enables you to define the numbering format for the column.

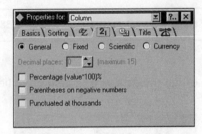

After choosing the numbering format, you can also set the following options:

- **Percentage (value * 100)%**—This displays values as percentages; for example, displays .80 as 80%.

- **Parentheses on negative numbers**—This displays negative numbers enclosed in parentheses; for example, (8) instead of –8.

- **Punctuated at thousands**—This displays large numbers with the thousands separator; for example, 8,000.

Time and Date Settings

The Time and Date tab in the column's Properties InfoBox (displaying a clock and calendar icon—see fig. 11.30) enables you to define the following time and date attributes:

- **Show**—You have four choices for controlling combinations of time and date: Date and time, Date only, Time only, and Today and Time. If you select the last choice, values indicating the current date will display Today instead of the date. Values indicating the previous day will display Yesterday instead of the date. All other values will display the date.

- **Date format**—You can select MM/DD, MM/YY, and MM/DD/YY.

- **Time format**—You can select HH:MM or HH:MM:SS to display the time using a 12-hour or 24-hour clock format.

- **Time zone**—You can select Adjust time to local zone, Always show time zone, or Show only if zone not local. Adjust all times to local zone displays the time relative to the time zone of the reader. For example, a document created at 3:00p.m. in New York that is read by a user in Los Angeles adjusts to Pacific Standard Time; the creation time is displayed as 12:00p.m.

The Always show time zone displays the time zone where the document was created. With this option, the creator's time zone is always shown. The Show only if zone not local option displays the time zone where the document was created only when the document is read by someone in a different time zone.

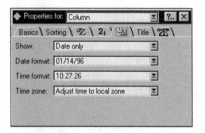

Fig. 11.30

Here you can select the date, time, and time zone formatting attributes.

Changing the Style of the Column Title

This is one of the most desired design features that developers have been wanting incorporated into views. Previously, column headings were not editable. Now, using the Title tab in the column's Properties InfoBox, you can modify how the column headings appear.

The available options are identical to the styles tab, except that any changes made are reflected in the column title. You can also use multiple rows in the header by switching to the view's Properties and selecting the Style tab. See "Setting the Style for the View" earlier in this chapter for more information on the Lines per heading option.

Defining Column Formulas

Column formulas specifies what information should be displayed in this column of the view. Usually, the formula is a field name if you want to display the data for a particular field. However, developers do require more complex formulas than just the field name.

To start writing a column formula, open the desired view in edit mode. Display the programmer pane if necessary.

Then select the column heading you want to write the formulas for. You can also click the Define list box in the programmer pane to select the desired column. Figure 11.31 displays the first column in the selected view and its corresponding formula.

Entering the formula into the Formula box is easy. You must select one of these Display options to enter your formula—Simple function, Field, or Formula (these options are described in the following sections).

Note

A column formula must evaluate to a text string.

Fig. 11.31

This column formula specifies the column contents to be CompanyName.

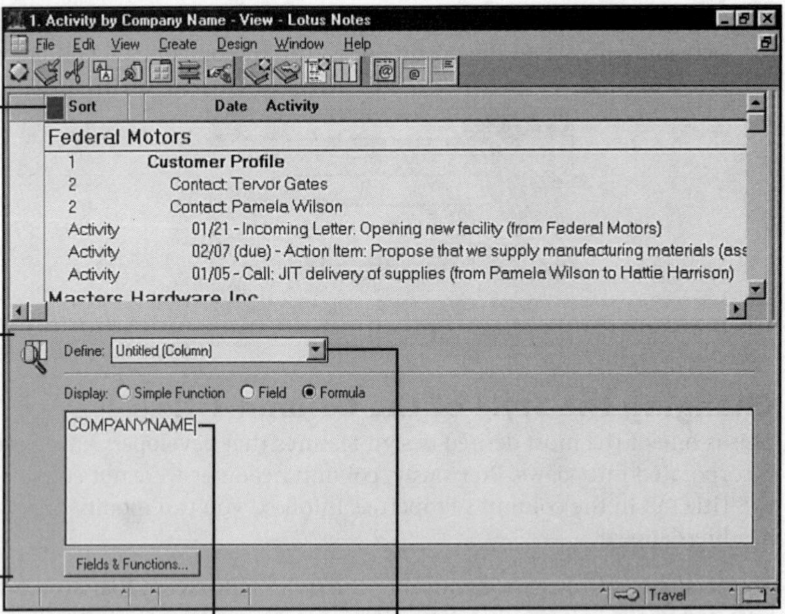

Column selected —

Programmer pane —

Formula   Define list box

Simple Functions

Selecting the Simple Function option displays a list of multiple, simple, often-used functions that save you time in writing formulas from scratch. These functions let the columns you're designing display information about authors, attachments and documents, time and date, responses, the view, or folder. Figure 11.32 displays a column using the simple function Creation Date. This quick shortcut is identical to selecting Formula as the display option and writing the formula @Created in the formula window.

Following is the list of available simple functions:

- **Attachment Lengths**—Uses @AttachmentLengths to return the size(s) of the document's attachment(s). The data type is a number list.

- **Attachment Names**—Uses @AttachmentNames to return the file names of the document's attachments. The data type is a text list.

- **Attachments**—Uses @Attachments to return the number of files attached to the document. The data type returned is a number.

- **Author(s) (Distinguished Name)**—Uses @Author to return the names of the document's author(s) in fully distinguished format, as in Amanda Lauster/Marketing/IBM.

- **Author(s) (Simple Name)**—Uses @Name([CN];AUTHOR) to return the author's name without its fully distinguished format, as in Michael Solger.

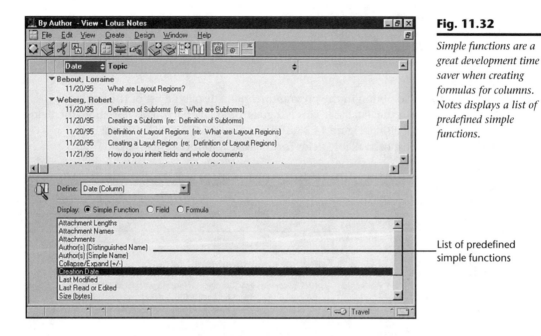

Fig. 11.32

Simple functions are a great development time saver when creating formulas for columns. Notes displays a list of predefined simple functions.

List of predefined simple functions

- **Collapse/Expand (+/-)**—Uses @IsExpandable to return a plus symbol (+) if the view entry has descendants that are not visible because the main document or category is collapsed or a minus symbol (-) if there are no subordinate documents, or if subordinate documents are currently visible.

- **Creation Date**—Uses @Created to display the time and date a document was created. The data type is a time-date.

- **Last Modified**—Uses @Modified to determine when a document was last saved. The data type is a time-date.

- **Last Read or Edited**—Uses @Accessed to determine the last time and date a document was read or edited. The data type is a time-date.

- **Size (bytes)**—Uses @DocLength to return the size of the active document in bytes. The data type returned is a number.

- **# in View (e.g., 2.1.2)**—Uses @DocNumber to display a number for each document indicating its order in the view. Responses are numbered in outline style under Main documents; for example, the first response to the first main document would be 1.1.

- **# of Responses (1 Level)**—Uses @DocChildren to return the number of direct descendant (response) documents for a document or next-level subcategories for a category. The data type returned is Special text.

- **# of Responses (All Levels)**— Uses @DocDescendants to return the total number of descendant (response and response-to-response) documents for a document or subcategories for a category.

II

Designing Applications

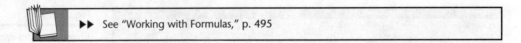

▶▶ See "Working with Formulas," p. 495

Fields

Selecting the Field option in the programmer pane displays a list of the fields currently available in the database. This is a great time saver if you do not know the fields or their correct spelling. Figure 11.33 displays the COMPANYNAME field being selected from the list of available fields for the first column of this view.

Fig. 11.33

You can choose from the list of available fields. This quick shortcut is the same as selecting Formula as the display and typing the field name.

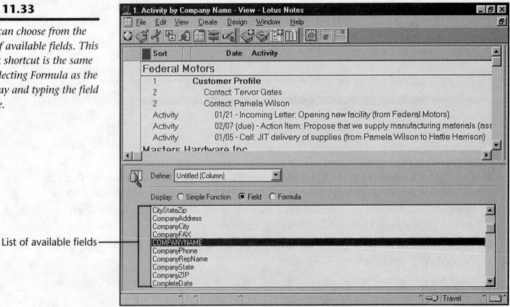

List of available fields ⎯

Formulas

Choosing the Formula option is the traditional Notes 3.x way to enter a column formula. You will encounter situations where the Simple Function and Field display are not enough to perform detailed column formulas, as shown in figure 11.34.

 Once in the formula window, you can enter the formula. You can even click the Fields & Functions button to display a list of available fields and functions that can be pasted into the formula.

The following formula specifies the column contents as the Subject field followed by a blank (or nothing, if the Subject field is empty), followed by the From field in parentheses. By default (the first line), the From field contains the name of the author of the document:

```
DEFAULT From := @Author;
@If(Subject != ""; Subject + " "; "") + "(" + From " ")"
```

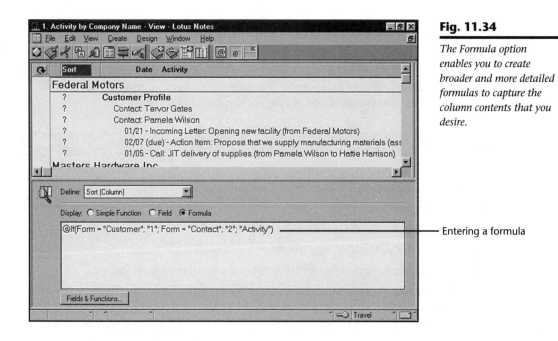

Fig. 11.34

The Formula option enables you to create broader and more detailed formulas to capture the column contents that you desire.

The following formula specifies the column contents as the number 1 for fields with a Status "Closed" and 2 for all other Status designations. This type of formula is useful to force sorting in a hidden column:

```
@If(Status = "Closed"; 1; 2)
```

The following formula reformats the contents of From to put the last name first followed by a comma, a space, and the first name. (i.e., Solger, Michael):

```
@If(@Contains(From; " "); @Right(From; " ") + ", " + @Left(From; " ");
From)
```

The following formula is useful for a categorizing column that displays each month as a category name. Dates need to be converted to a text value to be displayed in a view:

```
m :=@Text(@Month(Date));
@If(m = 1; "January"; m = 2; "February"; m = 3; "March";m = 4; "April";m =
5; "May"; m = 6; "June";m = 7; "July";m = 8; "August";m = 9; "September"; m
= 10; "October"; m = 11; "November"; m = 12; "December"; "")
```

To show people's names and phone numbers together in one column, create a column that is sorted in ascending order. The following formula separates the two field values with a blank space:

```
Name + " " + Phone
```

The following example joins the fields City, State, and Zip into one column.

```
City + ", " + State + " " + Zip;
```

Defining Selection Formulas

Usually, in each database you design a main view that displays all of the documents. However, it is often useful to have one or more selective views that only include those documents that are relevant to a particular topic or meet certain criteria. The view's selection formula selects which documents are displayed in a view.

Note

Every view has a selection formula. If you do not define one, Notes defaults the formula to SELECT @All, which selects every document in the database.

To create a selection formula, perform the following steps:

1. Open the desired view in edit mode.

2. In the programmer pane select View Selection from the Define list box.

3. Write the selection formula in the formula box and refresh the view to see if your formula evaluates correctly. Figure 11.35 shows a sample selection formula that selects only those documents where the field ContactName equals Tervor Gates.

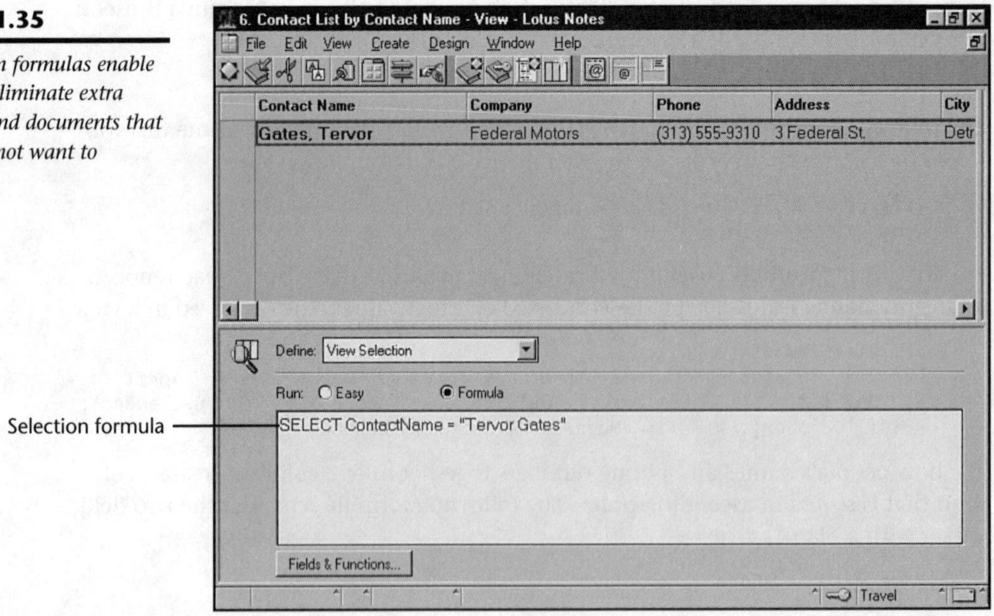

Fig. 11.35

Selection formulas enable you to eliminate extra forms and documents that you do not want to display.

Selection formula

Using Form Formulas

What would you do if you wanted to have users compose a document using one form, but then have them view the data entered in an entirely different form? Well, you could use Form Formulas.

The form formula decides which of a database's forms is used for composing and displaying documents, depending on the conditions. This enables you to display the same information in different ways, order fields differently, or omit some fields in the alternate form. For example, the Address Label view of a Contact Information database could use the form formula frmAddressLabel to display documents using the Address Label form. The frmAddressLabel form could be a shortened version of the Contact Information form that only includes the Name and various Address fields.

The form formula is optional. If you do not create one, Notes will either display the documents in the view using the default form designated in the database (Design, Form Properties), the form used if the Store form in document option was selected when the document was created, or the form with which the document was created.

◀◀ See "Specifying the Form as the Default Form," p. 373

◀◀ See "Storing Forms in Documents," p. 375

Note

If a document is created with a form that has the option Store form in Document selected, the form formula is ignored and the document is displayed using the stored form. Storing the form in documents allows documents to display correctly even in databases where the form has not been defined, or where the form has been renamed or deleted.

To create a form formula, perform the following steps:

1. Open the desired form in edit mode and select Design, View properties to display the view's Properties InfoBox.

2. Click the Advanced tab.

3. Click Formula Window, which displays the Design Form Formula dialog box (see fig. 11.36).

4. Write the form formula and then click OK. A form formula must evaluate to the name of a form.

II

Designing Applications

Fig. 11.36

This formula creates new documents using the Open New Discussion form and accesses existing documents using the Main Topic form.

Troubleshooting

Why do I get an error in my keyword field called Loan Type that my Loan Type Lookup view does not exist? I am using an @DbColumn formula to build the keyword list.

Make sure that you have not renamed the view. For instance, you may have hidden the view by placing parentheses () around the name, or you may have modified the name. You should use an alias name and then refer to that alias in your @DBColumn formula. This prevents future errors if the view names change.

After creating a Form Formula for my view that uses the New Loan form if a new document is being composed and then uses the New Loan for Viewing if it's being loaded, why doesn't the New Loan for Viewing form get used when opening a previously created document?

Make sure that the New Loan form does not have the option Store form in Document selected. If it does, you need to remove this option. Any new documents created will display the viewing form; however, existing documents will still not be displayed. Either re-create these documents to remove the stored form, or run a macro on them that refreshes the fields and their contents.

Using Folders

Folders are very similar to views. In fact, you design a folder nearly the same way you design any Notes view. Why create folders? Designing a folder is useful when none of the existing views of a database shows information the way you want to see it. Folders let you store and manage related documents without putting them into a category, which would require a categories or keyword field in the form used to create the documents. In fact, you can easily add and remove documents from folders by dragging selected documents. Figure 11.37 displays the Discussion template database with the folder "My Favorite Documents," which displays documents that have been selected and moved into this folder.

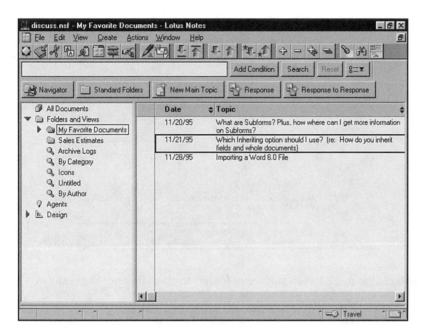

Fig. 11.37

Folders allow you to organize selected documents. This is especially useful if an existing view does not display the desired information.

When you create a folder, its design is automatically based on the design of the default view of the current database. You can choose to base the folder's design on a different existing view, or to design the folder from scratch. After you create a folder, it appears in the navigation pane until you delete the folder.

Designing Folders

You can keep a folder private, or share it with other users of a database. No one else can read or delete your private folders. To create private folders in a database, you must have at least Reader access to the database. To create shared folders in a database, you must have at least Designer access.

▶▶ See "Understanding Database Security," p. 727

When you create a private folder, Notes stores it in one of two places:

■ If the manager of the database has allowed it, your folder is stored in the database, letting you use the folder at different workstations.

   To see whether a database allows storage of folders, select the database, choose File, Database, Access Control, and see whether Create personal folders/views is turned on (see fig. 11.38).

Fig. 11.38

The Access Control List dialog box allows you to see whether you can create personal folders/views.

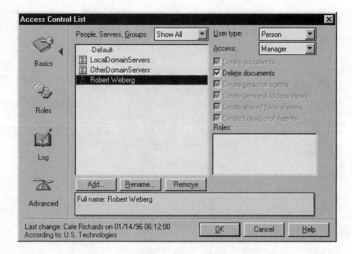

- If the manager has not allowed storage of folders in the database, Notes stores your folder in your desktop file (DESKTOP.DSK).

Creating a Shared Folder. If you can't find a folder that is similar to the one you need, create a new folder. Its initial design is copied from the default design, or from the default view if you haven't set a default design. Follow these steps:

1. Select or open the database where you want to create the folder and choose Create, Folder. The Create Folder dialog box appears.

2. Enter a name for the folder in the Folder name box.

3. Select Shared. See Chapter 9, "Creating New Databases," to learn more about creating private folders.

4. Click Folders to store this folder at the top folder level, or click the name of another folder to place this new folder inside another existing folder.

5. Select Personal on first use if this is a private folder that you're distributing to multiple users.

6. (Optional) To select a view to base the folder's Inherit design on, select Options. This will allow you to choose the desired folder or view.

7. Click OK to create the folder.

If a view or folder already exists in the database that is similar to the one you need, you may be able to use it with only minor modifications. To copy a folder, perform the following steps:

1. In the selected database, choose View, Design.

2. In the navigation pane, click Design, Folders.

3. Click the folder you want to copy and choose Edit, Copy (or press Ctrl+C).

4. Choose Edit, Paste or Ctrl+V. This will automatically create a copy of that folder starting with the name "Copy of." If no existing view or folder suits your

purpose, create a new one. Its initial design is based on the default design you've set for new views and folders, or on the default view if you haven't set a default design. You could also copy a folder from another database.

Folder Properties. After creating the folder, you may want to further define its properties. Using the Properties InfoBox, you will be able to define basic properties like the folder name and alias, and the more advanced properties like its style and security levels. To do so, perform the following steps:

1. In the selected database, choose <u>V</u>iew, <u>D</u>esign.

2. In the navigation pane, click Design, Folders and then double-click the desired folder. This opens the folder in design mode.

3. Click the right mouse button and choose Folder Properties or select <u>D</u>esign, Folder <u>P</u>roperties. This will display the Folder Properties InfoBox (see fig. 11.39).

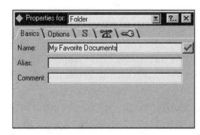

Fig. 11.39

The Folder Properties InfoBox allows you to select and define the attributes for your folder.

II

Designing Applications

While designing a folder, you can also create more advanced options using actions and navigators that will enable the user to automate moving documents between folders. Folder actions allow users to perform specific tasks on documents without having to open them, while navigators enable the user to easily switch and move between folders.

Renaming and Deleting Folders. You can rename or delete any private folder, and any public folder to which you have Designer or Manager access. To rename a folder, follow these steps:

1. In the navigation pane, select the desired folder.

2. Choose <u>A</u>ctions, <u>F</u>older Options, <u>R</u>ename to display the Rename dialog box.

3. In the Name box, enter a name of up to 60 characters.

4. Click OK.

To delete a folder, perform the following:

1. In the selected database, choose <u>V</u>iew, <u>D</u>esign.

2. In the navigation pane, click <u>D</u>esign, <u>F</u>olders.

3. Highlight the folder you want to remove.

4. Choose <u>E</u>dit, <u>C</u>lear, or hit the Delete key.

5. Click Yes to confirm the deletion.

Moving Folders. You can move the folders under Folders and Views in the navigation pane into other unrelated folders but not into its parent folder, any of its children, or itself. To do so, perform the following steps:

1. Display the navigation pane.

2. If Folders and Views is collapsed (its triangle is pointing to the right), click the triangle.

3. Drag the folder you want to move into the folder you want to move it to.

4. Using the menu, select the folder you want to move.

5. Select Actions, Folder Options, Move.

6. In the Choose a folder list, click the folder into which you want to move the selected folder.

7. Click OK to move the folder.

From Here...

Views are lists of documents in a Notes database. This chapter discussed how to create views that can be used to select, sort, or categorize documents in different ways to make documents easier to locate. After a view has been designed, your users could open documents, copy and paste documents, delete documents, print documents or the view, forward selected documents to other Notes users, refresh the view to see new documents, and even search for documents containing specific text. To learn more about using the views that you create, review the following chapters:

■ Chapter 8, "Working with Documents," covers how to edit existing documents that could contain objects.

■ Chapter 10, "Designing Forms," describes how to create and design forms in Notes R4.

■ Chapter 13, "Working with Formulas," covers how to write formulas using the available @functions and @commands in Notes.

■ Chapter 16, "LotusScript: A Whole New Programming Language," teaches the basics of the powerful LotusScript programming language that can be used to manipulate objects and links.

CHAPTER 12

Integrating Notes 4.0 with Other Applications

Notes allows workgroup members to attain great productivity by using discussion databases, exchanging information via electronic mail, and managing a variety of documents. But workgroup members can also use Notes to share documents and data created in other applications, and use those documents to collaborate on ideas, issue reports, track clients, monitor projects, and customize workgroup processes.

I like to think of Notes as a network enabler. It enables you to integrate data from other programs by importing, exporting, linking, and embedding the information. Once you have integrated your data with Notes, you can utilize the power of Notes—and its great security and replication features—to manage your documents. This is more powerful, secure, and manageable than saving files to a shared group network drive.

This sharing concept is enhanced by a technology called *Notes/FX* (Application Field Exchange) to share information between Notes document fields and OLE embedded applications. Notes/FX and OLE allow you to create stunning work-together applications.

This chapter explores the following topics:

- Importing and exporting data
- Linking data files to Notes documents
- Embedding OLE 2.0 objects in rich text fields
- Creating useful integrated applications with Notes/FX

Importing and Exporting Data with Other Applications

Lotus Notes provides several ways to import information from other programs into Notes documents or views. Conversely, Notes data can be exported to other software programs and file formats.

In Notes, the File, Import command and File, Export command enable you to transfer information through a variety of standard file formats. Whether you want to exchange data with a Windows, OS/2, or DOS application, or with your company's mainframe, you'll discover an easy way to do it.

Transferring data to and from Notes is performed from a view or from within a specific document. Views are used to exchange tabular information between the Notes database and another application. Documents are used when you only want to transfer data from a specific document. In most cases, you probably will import or export large numbers of records, and therefore will need to work from a view.

To import or export tabular data from the view level, switch to the desired view, select File, Import or File Export, choose the desired file format, and then name or select the file to be imported or exported. Notes supports the following file formats when exporting or importing tabular data at the view level:

- Lotus 1-2-3 worksheet (WKS, WK1, WRK, WR1, WK3, and WK4 extensions)
- Structured text
- Tabular text
- Lotus Agenda (STF extension)

When exporting or importing rich text data at the document level, Notes supports the following file formats:

- Lotus Ami Pro (1.x or later)
- ANSI metafile
- ASCII
- Binary with text
- BMP image
- DisplayWrite DCA
- GIF image
- Interleaf ASCII
- JPEG image
- Lotus 1-2-3 worksheet
- LotusPic
- Manuscript 2.0/2.1
- MultiMate 3.3, 3.6. 3.7
- Microsoft Excel 2.1, 3.0, 4.0, 5.0
- Microsoft Word for Windows 1.x, 2.0, 6.0
- Microsoft Word RTF
- PCX image
- TIFF image 5.0

- WordPerfect 4.1, 4.2, 5.0, 5.1, 6.0/6.1 (4.1 or later)
- WordStar 3.3/3.31, 3.45, 5.0/5.5

Importing a File into a Document

You can easily convert data from another application so that a Notes document can use the data. To import a file from another document, perform the following steps:

1. Open the document in edit mode, then click where you want the imported data to appear.

2. Choose File, Import, or click the File Import SmartIcon to display the Import dialog box (see fig. 12.1).

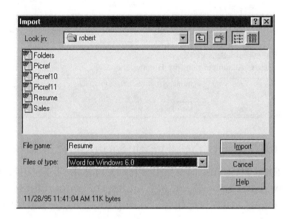

II

Designing Applications

Fig. 12.1

The Import dialog box allows you to specify the file to import into your Notes document. This example is importing the file RESUME.DOC, *which was created in Word for Windows 6.0.*

3. In the List Files of Type list box, select a file type. Locate the desired file using the Drives and Directories list boxes, and then select the file; alternatively, just enter the path and filename in the File Name box.

4. Click Import to import the file. Figure 12.2 displays a file imported into a Rich Text field.

Importing Pictures

You can use the Clipboard to copy pictures into a document. You can also import picture files into a document using File, Import.

To copy a picture or graphic object into a document, perform the following steps:

1. Copy the picture in the source application (choose Edit, Copy or Ctrl+C).

2. Switch to Notes and open in edit mode the document you want to add the picture to (press Ctrl+E or choose File, Open).

3. Click where you want to place the picture.

Fig. 12.2

The file is imported into the Notes document. You may need to adjust margins and tab settings to align some portions of your imported file.

Imported résumé —

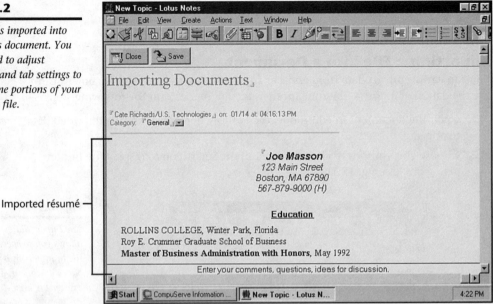

4. Choose Edit, Paste, Ctrl+P, or click the Edit Paste SmartIcon.

You can import Lotus PIC files (PIC), ANSI metafiles (CGM, GMF), JPEG files (JPG), and TIFF 5.0 files (TIF), as well as BMP, GIF, and PCX files. It is important to note that pictures can only be imported in a rich text field. To import a picture file into a document, perform the following steps:

1. Open the Notes document in edit mode (press Ctrl+E or choose File, Open).

2. Click where you want to place the picture.

3. Choose File, Import, or click the File Import SmartIcon to display the Import dialog box (see fig. 12.3).

Fig. 12.3

The Import dialog box is used here to import a BMP image file. You can select from a variety of image file types when importing into a Notes document.

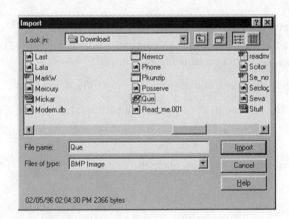

4. Specify the file type and name of the picture file, then click <u>Im</u>port. The image is inserted into Notes (see fig. 12.4).

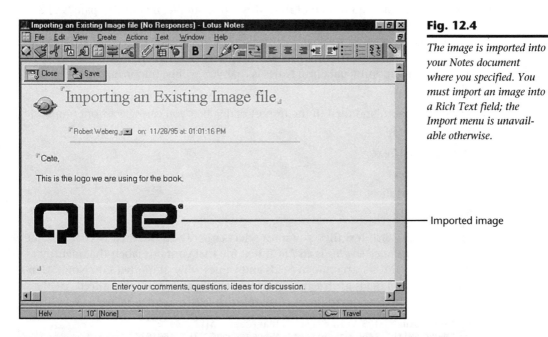

Fig. 12.4

The image is imported into your Notes document where you specified. You must import an image into a Rich Text field; the Import menu is unavailable otherwise.

Imported image

Tip

If the file type for your image file is not displayed, open the image in its source application, and use a copy/paste procedure to copy the image into Notes.

Troubleshooting

The pictures that I import come in very large. How can I change their appearance in Notes?

Once a picture file has been imported into Notes, you can easily adjust or resize the graphic. To do so, click the picture once and then drag the box in the picture's lower right corner in the desired direction to resize. Notes treats the picture as one unit, so you must resize the entire picture. To help you gauge the picture's dimensions, Notes displays the picture's current width and height as a percentage of its original width and height above the status bar.

After resizing a picture, I discovered the original dimensions of the imported picture was more appropriate. How do I return a picture to its original size?

Open the document containing the picture in edit mode and click the picture. Next, choose Picture, Picture Properties to display the Properties InfoBox. Click the Basics tab and then click the Reset width and height to 100% button.

Importing Structured Text Files

Importing data from ASCII files is relatively painless, and with a little preparation and setup, Notes can offer quite a bit of flexibility. For example, if your company's MIS reporting department provides your group with customer mailing lists in ASCII file format (generally mainframe downloads are in ASCII or tabular-text format), you can set up Notes to make importing the data a simple matter. The important step to re-member when importing data into Notes is that you will be importing from the view level.

Choose File Import, and then in the Import dialog box you can select from four basic types of data files:

- Structured Text
- Tabular Text
- 1-2-3 Worksheet
- Agenda STF

If working with ASCII text files, you must select either the Structured Text or Tabular Text type. A *structured text file* is an ASCII text file that contains labels that identify each field. It retains its structure in fields and values when imported into Notes. Generally, records and fields in structured text files are separated by a form-feed ASCII character or delimiter. The following example displays a comma-delimited text file:

```
"Joe Lotus","123 Main Street","Bartlett","IL","60103"
"Mary Smith","456 Oak Street","Streamwood","IL","60107"
```

When you import a structured text file into a view, the field names in the text file must correspond to the field names in the Notes document. To do this, you create a form that contains the names of the fields you're importing. Figure 12.5 shows an example structured text file that imports data into a contact list database.

To import structured text files into Notes, follow these steps:

1. Choose File, Import, or click the File Import SmartIcon. The Import dialog box appears (see fig. 12.6).

2. In the List Files of Type list box, select Structured Text as the file type. Then select the path and name of the structured text file.

3. Choose Import. Notes displays the Structured Text Import dialog box (see fig. 12.7).

Field names   Data

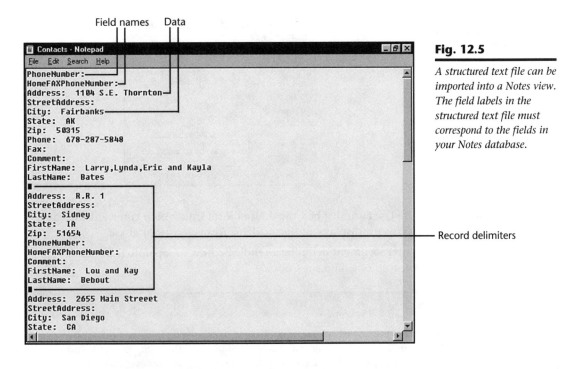

Fig. 12.5

A structured text file can be imported into a Notes view. The field labels in the structured text file must correspond to the fields in your Notes database.

Record delimiters

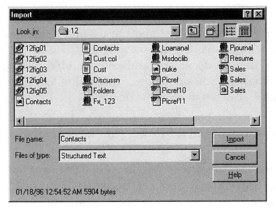

Fig. 12.6

This example displays the structured text file, CONTACTS.TXT, being imported.

II

Designing Applications

Fig. 12.7

Specify how to import the CONTACTS.TXT *file into your Notes database.*

4. Select in the Use Form list box the desired form into which you want the data imported. This list displays all the available forms in the database.

5. Select an interdocument delimiter to indicate how to separate the records—either Form-feed or Character-Code.

> **Note**
>
> The order of the labeled fields does not have to match the order of the fields in your Notes form. Each record could have fields of various sizes. However, you must separate records with a specific delimiter, such as ASCII Code 12 (the form-feed character).

6. Leave Main Document(s) selected in the Import As list unless you are creating Response documents. For example, if you have a Notes database that has contact information contained in main documents and call report information contained in response documents, you would select this option to import call report data into a corresponding call report response document.

7. Leave Justify selected in the For body text list to wrap text to fit the Notes window, or you can choose to maintain the existing line breaks in the source file by adding a return character at the end of each line of text.

8. If you want the imported documents to contain every field of the form you selected, select Calculate fields on form during document import. This will create any of the fields that exist on the form, even if you are not importing them.

9. Click OK. Notes imports the data into the fields in your Notes database using the selected form (see fig. 12.8).

   You can now utilize existing views or design new views to display the imported data in any desired way. For example, you could design a view that sorted the contact information alphabetically that included contact name and address information. This view could then be exported to an external application for printing mailing labels.

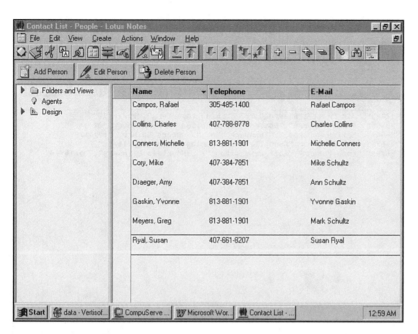

Fig. 12.8

The records are imported into the view using the selected form. Opening the individual documents would reveal that the data was imported into the appropriate fields.

◄◄ See "Designing Views," p. 415

◄◄ See "Adding Fields to a Form," p. 381

Importing Tabular-Text Files

Reports from mainframes or client-server databases are downloaded in the format of tabular-text files. *Tabular-text files* contain data in distinct rows and columns, because records and fields are separated with equal amounts of tabs, spaces, or other delimiters. If you have a Notes database with a view that exactly matches the contents of the tabular view, in terms of both field names and widths, you might be able to import it directly into the view with little trouble. However, the tabular-text file doesn't always provide data for all the target fields, and also might not properly identify to Notes the contents of each field. Situations like this arise if you are attempting to import a file that has not been parsed. A nonparsed file is an ASCII file in which delimiters or tabs have not been defined.

Thus, if you are frequently importing one type of file into a view or if the ASCII file and Notes view have a different format, create a *column format descriptor file (COL file)* to parse the ASCII file so its individual components correspond to columns in the Notes view or document fields. A COL file is used by Notes to specify and map how a comma-delimited or tabular-text file is imported into a Notes database.

Suppose that you have a listing of customer information from your company's customer contact system. This file is to be downloaded in comma-delimited format (see

Designing Applications

fig. 12.9). Each field in a comma-delimited file is surrounded by quotes, then each field is separated by a comma. Each record must contain the same number of fields or items.

Fig. 12.9

The comma-delimited file CUST.TXT *shows records as rows; the field data is separated by commas.*

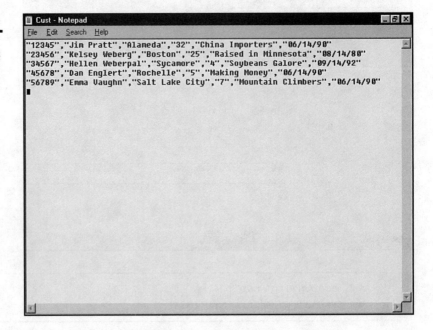

```
Cust - Notepad                                                          _ 8 X
File  Edit  Search  Help
"12345","Jim Pratt","Alameda","32","China Importers","06/14/90"
"23456","Kelsey Weberg","Boston","25","Raised in Minnesota","08/14/88"
"34567","Hellen Weberpal","Sycamore","4","Soybeans Galore","09/14/92"
"45678","Dan Englert","Rochelle","5","Making Money","06/14/90"
"56789","Emma Vaughn","Salt Lake City","7","Mountain Climbers","06/14/90"
```

Next, suppose that you want to import this file into a Notes database you have de-signed. The Customer form you are importing into the database should contain the fields listed in the CUST.COL file shown in figure 12.10. You can create a COL file with any ASCII text editor and give it the extension COL. The target form can contain more fields than the tabular-text or comma-delimited file, and the fields can be in a different order.

After creating the COL file, switch to Notes and the desired database that will receive the imported data. Then perform the following steps:

1. Choose File, Import or click the File Import SmartIcon to display the Import dialog box.

2. Select in the List files of Type list box, and then select the text file that will be imported in the File Name list box, using the Drives and Directories list boxes if necessary.

3. Click Import to display the Tabular Text Import dialog box (see fig. 12.11).

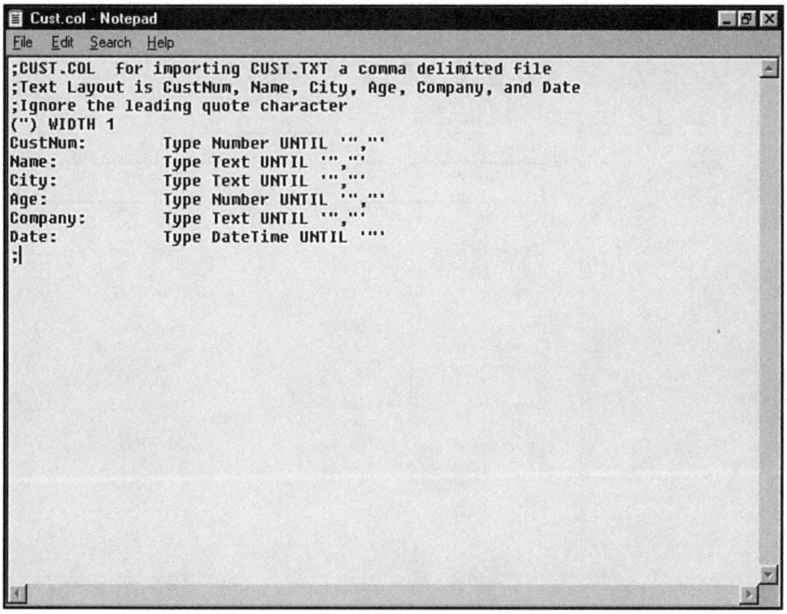

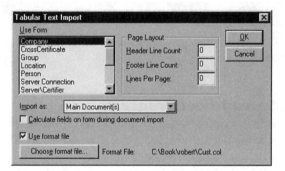

Fig. 12.10

The CUST.COL *file tells Notes how to interpret and import the contents of the comma-delimited text file shown in figure 12.9 into documents, using a specified form in the database.*

Fig. 12.11

The Tabular Text Import dialog box allows you to choose various options needed to import the comma-delimited file.

4. Select the desired form in the Use Form list box.

5. Select Use format file, then click Choose format file to display the Choose an Import Format File dialog box. This allows you to select the COL file that you created.

6. Click OK to import the data based upon the COL file.

Figure 12.12 displays the sample CUST.TXT file that was imported into a Notes database.

Designing Applications

II

Fig. 12.12

The CUST.TXT *file has been imported into the database. You should create views that logically display your imported data so you can verify that the data was imported correctly.*

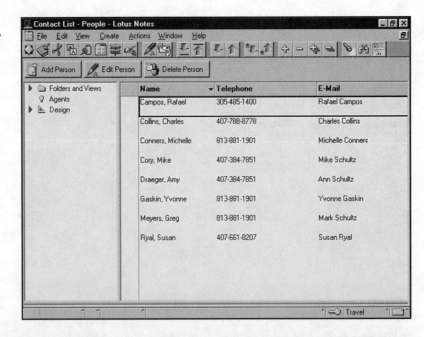

Tip

To quickly see if the data was imported in the correct fields, open a document or choose File, Document Properties, and the Fields tab.

Using Notes with Spreadsheet Programs

Occasionally, you might need to extract Notes data into a format that enables you to perform what-if analysis or to build graphs for financial analysis. To meet that need, you can export the Notes data to a spreadsheet program. Since Notes can export and import data to and from Lotus 1-2-3 worksheet file format, any program that can read or write a WK* file can effectively share data with Notes.

Note

In order to export Notes data into Microsoft Excel for Windows, you must export the view data into Lotus 1-2-3 format, and then use 1-2-3 to save the data as an Excel spreadsheet.

Exporting Notes Data to a 1-2-3 Worksheet. To export data from Notes to a 1-2-3 worksheet file, you must first start from a view, because you can't export to a worksheet file from within an open document. When you export a view to a worksheet, each document becomes a worksheet row and each field becomes a worksheet column, with field contents becoming cell contents. The view does not need to display all the fields available in the Notes database, but it must contain all the fields you want to export.

◄◄ See "Creating Views," p. 418

►► See "Working with Formulas," p. 495

Suppose that you want to export the sales information from the view shown in figure 12.13.

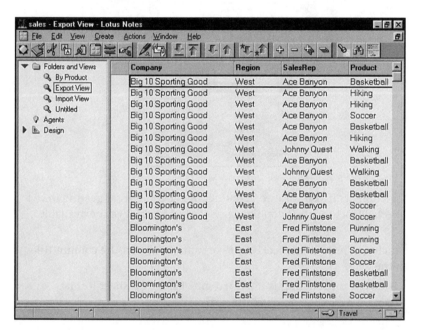

Fig. 12.13

This database contains sales information. A view named Export View has been created to prepare Notes data for export—you can export any view that exists in the database.

With the desired view selected, perform the following steps:

1. Choose File, Export or click the File Export SmartIcon to open the Export dialog box (see fig. 12.14).

2. Enter a filename in the File Name box. Then choose Lotus 1-2-3 Worksheet in the Save File as Type list box.

3. Specify the Drives and Directories where you want to save the file, then click the Export button. The 1-2-3 Worksheet Export dialog box appears (see fig. 12.15).

Fig. 12.14

The Export dialog box allows you to enter a filename and extension for the export file, choose the appropriate file type, and specify the drive and directory where you want to save the file.

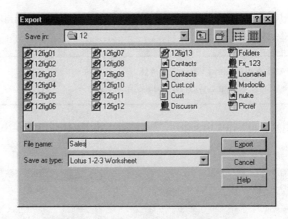

Fig. 12.15

The 1-2-3 Worksheet Export dialog box allows you to specify how you want to export the data.

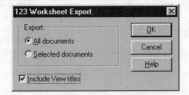

4. Select <u>A</u>ll Documents if you want to export all the documents appearing in the view, or <u>S</u>elected Documents if you have preselected a subset of the available documents.

5. Select the <u>I</u>nclude View Titles checkbox if you want to export the column titles along with the data.

6. Click <u>O</u>K. The view information is imported into 1-2-3 worksheet format.

If you open the exported file in 1-2-3, you see something like figure 12.16.

Caution

When you export a view to a new spreadsheet file, Notes exports the file as plain worksheet data without any formatting or styles, regardless of the file extension you specify. When you open the exported file in 1-2-3, you may receive the message `File or extension converted`, indicating that the worksheet has been converted to the appropriate format for the 1-2-3 version that you're using. Also, you may need to reformat data like time values into the desired format. Reformatting will be necessary when working with other programs, such as Excel, Word, and Quattro Pro.

Importing Spreadsheet Data. Importing data into Notes from a spreadsheet file requires more preparation than exporting from Notes requires, because when importing you should assign a range name to the data range in the file that you want to import, and you might need to build a view to receive the spreadsheet data. When you import a spreadsheet into a view, each spreadsheet row becomes an individual document, and each spreadsheet column becomes a field, with the cell contents becoming field contents. You must create both a form and a view before you import a spreadsheet file into a view.

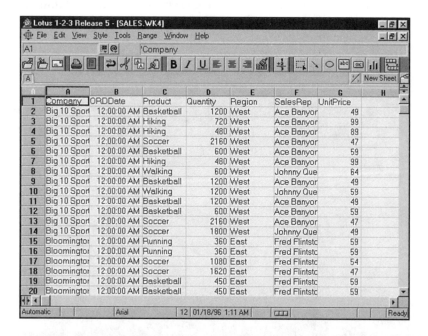

Fig. 12.16

The exported data from the Notes view is now displayed in 1-2-3. The fields in the original view have become columns, and every document has become a row.

Caution

Notes imports only the first sheet in a multiple-sheet worksheet/workbook/notebook, or a specified range in the first sheet.

Tip

Don't include any column headings in this range name; if you do, Notes imports the column headings as a document.

To understand how to import a spreadsheet, let's import the data SALES.WK4 we just exported (refer to fig. 12.16). This worksheet data will be imported into a view designed to receive the worksheet data. Follow these steps:

Tip

Before importing large amounts of data, always import small test files. Before importing an entire spreadsheet, for example, you might want to import a named range of several rows and columns.

1. Create and save the view that will import the spreadsheet data. Figure 12.17 displays a view that has columns ordered and fields designated to accept the data. The columns in the receiving view should not be categorized and must exactly match the columns in the worksheet. For example, if the first column in the worksheet's range contains a name, you should set the first column of the view to contain those names.

Fig. 12.17

The Import View view has been designed to receive the worksheet data. Notice that the columns in the view are ordered exactly as the worksheet is ordered.

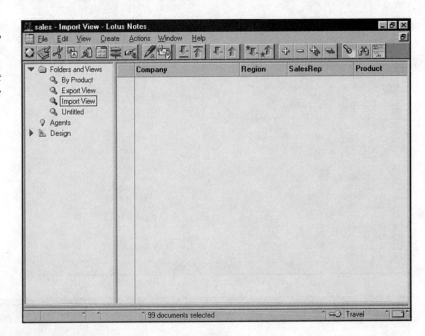

◄◄ See "Creating Views," p. 418
◄◄ See "Sorting Options," p. 437

2. Switch to the view into which you'll be importing the data. Choose File, Import to display the Import dialog box (see fig. 12.18).

3. Specify 1-2-3 Worksheet in the List Files of Type list box.

4. Select the file in the File Name box using the Drives and Directories list boxes if necessary.

5. Click Import to open the Worksheet Import Settings dialog box (see fig. 12.19).

6. In the Use Form list, choose the form that will receive the data. This form should be the one that contains the fields that exactly match the data you are importing.

◄◄ See "Creating a New Form," p. 363

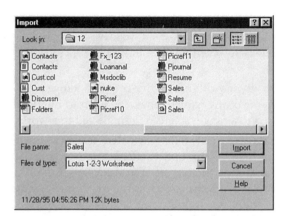

Fig. 12.18

The Import dialog box is similar to the Export dialog box. Use it to select the file type and filename to import.

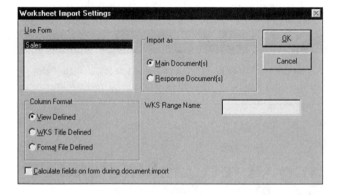

Fig. 12.19

In the Worksheet Import Settings dialog box, choose the appropriate Notes form and other options to use for importing the data.

Designing Applications

7. Next, select the desired column format. This example uses <u>V</u>iew Defined because you're mapping the columns in the spreadsheet to the Notes view. The following list describes when to use the different column format options:

- **<u>V</u>iew Defined**—Select this option if the format of the worksheet columns exactly matches the format of the columns in the view. The columns in the view must contain the field name; otherwise the data will appear in the view after the import, but will not be contained in the corresponding field.

- **<u>WKS</u> Title Defined**—Select this option if the cell contents in the first row of the worksheet file are to become column headers in the database. These cell contents must be labels or text. Field names will be created from the column titles and can be used in the database forms.

- **Forma<u>t</u> File Defined**—Select this option (the most reliable import method) if you have created a separate column format descriptor file (COL file).

8. In the Import As section, select the desired option. Generally, you want to import each worksheet row as a main document, so leave the Main Document(s) option selected. If needed, however, you can import the spreadsheet data into Response Document(s).

9. If you're importing the whole worksheet, leave the WKS Range Name box blank. Otherwise, enter the name of the named range you want to import. A named range is a name assigned to a range of cells or a single cell in a worksheet.

10. If you are importing data that needs to be calculated, select Calculate Fields on Form during Document Import. This option enables Notes to calculate any computed fields on the form during the import procedure. For example, if you have a computed field called "Region" that contains the following formula:

```
@If(State = "IL";"Midwest";State = "CA";"West";State =
"OH";"Mideast"; State = "NY";"East";"")
```

this would calculate the Region field based upon this formula.

> **Caution**
>
> Notes imports information more quickly when you do not select Calculate Fields on Form because it is not required to calculate each field on the form when importing.

11. Choose OK or press Enter to import the data into the Notes database.

Understanding Object Linking and Embedding (OLE)

Notes enables you to copy and paste data from other Windows applications. You can paste text into any standard editable field. Pasting text is a great time saver, but with today's Object Linking and Embedding (OLE—pronounced *oh-lay*) technology, you can do so much more—like pasting and embedding rich text, pictures, and bitmap objects—to make your Notes documents more robust. You could embed objects, such as a 1-2-3 worksheet, a Word 6.0 document, a Word Pro document, or a Freelance presentation.

OLE 2.0, which is supported by Notes R4, is the second generation of OLE. OLE facilitates integrating and linking data between different Windows applications. OLE information can generally be linked, embedded, or both.

To use OLE 2.0, customers must have two OLE 2.0 compliant applications: a server and a client. The server application contains the source data, while the client application is the recipient of the source data. For example, if you embed a 1-2-3 worksheet object into a Notes database, 1-2-3 is considered the server application and Notes the client application. *Linking* an OLE object means getting a copy of the object or data from the server, placing it in the client, and maintaining a link to the server application so that the client is kept up-to-date.

> **Note**
>
> OLE linking is similar to Dynamic Date Exchange (DDE) linking in that the link is dynamic because the data updates when the original file changes. Unlike DDE, however, users can double-click an OLE link and load the server application to modify or update information. With a DDE link you would need to first load the source application and locate and open the file to modify the data. Check your source application to determine if it is DDE or OLE 2.0 capable.

Embedding an object means placing the entire object into the client application. Unlike linking, the connection is not dynamic. There is no continuing link to the server application. As a result, if a user changes data in the server application, it will not change in the client application; an embedded object immediately becomes a physical, static part of the client application.

Linking an Object

A *linked object* is a pointer to data in another file. If you make any changes to the original source file, those changes are automatically reflected in the Notes document containing the linked object because of the link that was created. To link a file created with another application to a Notes document, perform the following steps:

1. Select the desired data in the file and copy it to the Clipboard using Edit, Copy (or Ctrl+C).

> **Caution**
>
> If the application is a DDE server but not an OLE server, make sure that you keep the server application and linked file open when updating a link between the DDE server and the Notes document containing the linked object.

2. Switch to Notes and open in edit mode the document to which you want to add the linked object (press Ctrl+E to place the document in edit mode).

3. Position the cursor where you want the object to appear.

4. Choose Edit, Paste Special or click the Edit Paste Special SmartIcon to display the Paste Special dialog box (see fig. 12.20).

5. Select Paste link to source to create a linked object. You could select the Paste option to paste the object without any linking features (see fig. 12.21).

6. In the As box, select a display format for the object. The options available in the As box will change depending on the type of source data.

7. If available and desired, select Display As Icon to display an icon instead of the linked data. To display a different icon, click Change Icon and choose a different one. You may want to choose this option if you do not want to display all that's copied or don't want the object to take up a lot of space in your Notes document.

8. Click OK.

II

Designing Applications

Fig. 12.20

The Paste Special dialog box allows you to link an object in a Notes document to the object's source file.

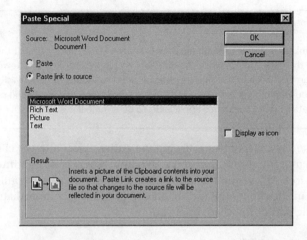

Fig. 12.21

The linked Word 6.0 object (in this case, a table) is inserted into the Notes document.

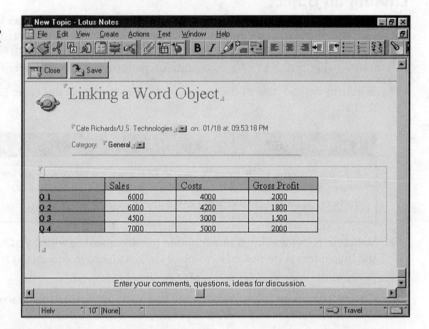

This inserts a picture of your Clipboard contents into your document. Paste link to source creates a link to the source file so that any changes to the source file will be reflected in your Notes document. If any changes are made to the source file, Notes prompts you to update the linked object when you open the document (see fig. 12.22).

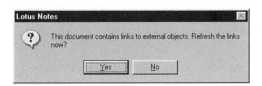

Fig. 12.22

Notes detects if the object is linked, and prompts you to update the object in the Notes document if desired.

You can update linked objects automatically upon activation or update them manually. To change a linked object's update type, perform the following:

1. With the document in edit mode, click the object.

2. Select Edit, External Links to display the External Links dialog box. This lists the links that are currently available in your document and allows you to edit the link, update the link, open the source, or break the link.

3. Select Automatically to update the object each time you activate it or Manual to update the object as needed.

4. Click OK to save your changes.

> **Tip**
>
> It's useful to manually update objects that take a lot of time to update, such as large bitmaps, by pressing F9 each time they are edited.

> **Tip**
>
> To display or edit an object's data when the object is displayed as an icon, double-click the icon.

When you link a file to a Notes document, keep the following in mind:

- You must be in a Rich Text field to add an object.

- The source file must be saved. Without a filename, Notes does not know what file to link to.

- If the server application is an OLE server, Notes creates an OLE object. If the server application is a DDE server but not an OLE server, Notes creates a DDE object. When you create or activate a DDE object in Notes, you must have both the server application and Notes open.

- Notes lets you display objects in four display formats (rich text, bitmap, picture, and text) as well as a format corresponding to the server application (for example, Word Pro document). However, the server application determines which display formats are available. If you select a display format the server application does not provide, Notes displays the object in picture format instead.

- Notes displays an icon instead of linked data if you select bitmap format, picture format, or the Display As Icon option, or if the data in the original file uses multiple display formats.

- If you select the Display As Icon option, Notes displays the server application's icon by default. To display a different icon, click the Change Icon button, which appears when you select Display As Icon. This displays the Change Icon dialog box, which enables you to choose between the current and various default icons available for that application, or even choose a different file to select another icon.

Embedding Part or All of a File

Recall that an embedded object is basically a copy of data from another file. Changes made to the original source file are not reflected in the Notes document.

To embed a portion of a file, perform the following steps:

1. In the source application, select the data you want to embed; then copy it to the Clipboard by choosing Edit, Copy (or pressing Ctrl+C).

2. Switch to Notes and open in edit mode the document to which you want to add the embedded object (do so by choosing File, Open or pressing Ctrl+E).

3. Position the cursor where you want the object to appear.

4. Choose Edit, Paste Special or click the Edit Paste Special SmartIcon to display the Paste Special dialog box (refer to fig. 12.20).

5. Select Paste.

6. In the As box, select how you want the pasted data to appear.

7. If available and desired, select Display As Icon to have Notes display an icon instead of the embedded data.

◄◄ See "Linking an Object," p. 473

8. Click OK.

This inserts an embedded picture of your Clipboard contents into your document. It looks the same as a linked object, but it acts differently in that any changes you make to the source file will not be reflected in your Notes document. In fact, double-clicking the object activates a new file based upon the original object that can be modified and saved back to Notes. Embedding files is ideal for document versioning applications.

◄◄ See "Tracking the Version," p. 371

When you embed an object in a Notes document, keep the following in mind:

- You must be in a Rich Text field to add an object.

- If you select the Display As Icon option, Notes displays the server application's icon by default. If Display As Icon is selected, you can click Change Icon to choose a different icon to be displayed.

- If Notes cannot determine the format of the data in the original file, it will display the server application's icon instead of the data.

- If you embed a blank object using a server application that can also serve as a client application, then you can embed other objects into the object you're creating. For example, you could embed a Word 6.0 document into a Notes document and then within that same Word 6.0 document you could embed an Excel 5.0 object. This allows you to build compound documents using different source applications.

To embed an entire file in a document, perform the following steps:

1. In Notes, open in edit mode the document to which you want to add the embedded object (press Ctrl+E).

2. Click to position the cursor where you want the object to appear.

3. Choose Create, Object, or click the Create Object SmartIcon to display the Create Object dialog box (see fig. 12.23).

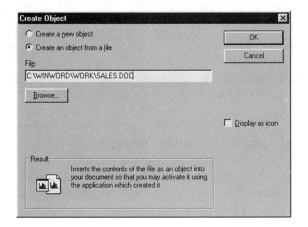

Fig. 12.23

The Create Object dialog box enables you to select the object type and file to insert.

4. Select Create a new object to display the available options. Notes displays the object types that have been registered to your operating system.

5. Optionally, select Create an object from a file and then in the File box, enter the path and filename; alternatively, you can click the Browse button and select the desired file.

6. If desired, select <u>D</u>isplay As Icon to have Notes display an icon instead of the embedded data.

7. Click OK to insert the object file, as displayed in figure 12.24. Double-click the embedded file to activate it for editing; if the application which created the embedded file is not currently running, Notes starts the application.

Fig. 12.24

This is the SALES.DOC *file inserted as an object in a Notes document.*

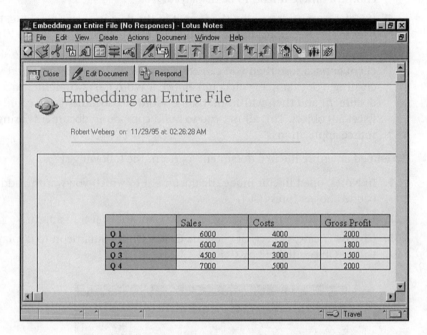

This is a new and separate object that is not related or linked to the existing object. Any changes or updates made in the original file will not be incorporated into this object.

Embedding a Blank Object in a Document

You can embed a blank object in a Notes document. Embedding blank objects is useful when you want to insert a new object not based on any pre-existing data. Also, if you embed a blank object using a server application that can also serve as a client application, then you can embed other objects into the object you're creating.

> **Note**
>
> Notes will display only the object types that have been installed on your system. For instance, Lotus Approach would not be shown as an object type option if it was not installed or registered. Check your WIN.INI and REG.DAT files for more details.

When you add a blank object, Notes opens a blank work file in the application you select, so you can enter data. After selecting File, Save within the server or source application, the data and embedded object will be saved in Notes. Follow these steps:

1. In Notes, open in edit mode the document to which you want to add the embedded object (press Ctrl+E).

2. Click to position the cursor where you want the object to appear.

3. Choose Create, Object, or click the Create Object SmartIcon to display the Create Object dialog box.

4. Select Create a new object to display its available options (see fig. 12.25).

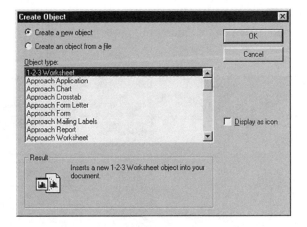

Fig. 12.25

Here you can select a 1-2-3 worksheet object to insert into the current document. This activates 1-2-3 for Windows, allowing you to enter desired data and then update and save the object in Notes.

5. In the Object type list box, select the desired object type.

6. Select an object type that corresponds to the application you want to use (for example, Freelance Presentation or 1-2-3 Worksheet).

7. If desired, select Display As Icon to have Notes display an icon instead of the embedded data.

8. Click OK to insert the selected object into your Notes document.

9. You now can create new data in the blank work file.

   After working with the file and if the embedded object is OLE 2.0-compliant, you can click anywhere on the Notes document to save the object data and return to Notes. You can easily double-click the object to activate the object to edit and modify.

Using the OLE Launch Features in a Form

You can design document management databases that automatically open blank embedded objects when you create a new document. This type of Notes database is more ideal for organizing and managing databases than using a network drive because users

II

Designing Applications

may not have access to your network drive or may not know the correct path where the files are located. Using Notes, any user with the appropriate access (designated in the Access Control List) can locate documents using the views in the database. The Microsoft Library template (MSOFT4.NTF) is an example that utilizes this workflow.

To create a form that automatically launches another application, perform the following steps:

1. In the database where you want this to happen, create a new form or edit an existing one. Add fields to store the desired information (for example, AuthorName, Category, Title, DateCreated, and Body).

2. Choose Design, Form Properties to display the form's Properties InfoBox, or click the Design Form Properties SmartIcon.

3. Click the Launch tab to designate the launching properties for this form (see fig. 12.26).

Fig. 12.26

MS Office/Excel Worksheet form in the DISCUSS4.NTF template database provides an excellent example of using the Launch options. When a new form is created, OLE is launched; after completion of the Excel object, the object is saved in the Body field.

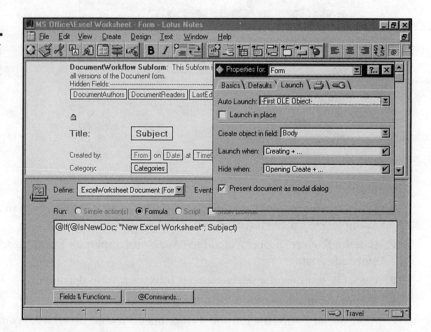

4. In the Auto Launch list box, Notes will display the available applications installed on your PC that your operating system recognizes. You can select the application that you want to automatically launch. Also, Notes will display the following three options if an object or attachment already exists on your form:

- **First Attachment**—This will automatically launch the first file attachment contained in the form.

- **First Document Link**—This will automatically launch the first linked document contained in the form.

- **First OLE Object**—This will automatically launch the first OLE object contained in the form. Selecting this option will display more options to further define how this object will launch.

5. You can select from the following options if you previously selected First OLE Object in the Auto Launch list box:

◄◄ See "Settings for Launching Objects," p. 378

- **Launch in place**—This launches the object in place, which enables the user to edit the object directly within Notes. This is called in-place editing because the menu in Notes changes to adapt to the corresponding application versus having to launch the embedded object's application and then having Notes switch to that application.

- **Advanced Options**—This displays additional options such as hiding and creating when selected.

- **Create object in field**—This enables you to select either None or First Rich Text Field. If another rich text field is available in the form, you could select it here. This will save the object in the indicated field.

- **Launch when**—This instructs Notes when to launch the indicated object. You can have the object activated when Creating, Editing, or Reading. The option Creating launches the embedded object when the document is created. The option Editing launches the object when the user edits a document that was created with this form. The option Reading launches the object when the user opens a document created with this form and uses it in read mode.

- **Hide when**—This instructs Notes when to hide the object. You can hide the object upon Opening Create, Opening Edit, Opening Read, Closing Create, Closing Edit, and Closing Read. Some of these options will be grayed out depending on the option selected in Launch when. You can design a form that hides the Notes document during any of these activities, and you can select more than one available option.

  Opening Create hides the Notes document when users create the document; Opening Edit hides the document when users edit a document; Opening Read hides a document when users read a document; Closing Create hides a document when a user closes a document after creating it; Closing Edit hides a document after a user closes a document after editing it; and Closing Read hides a document after a user closes a document after reading it.

- **Present document as modal dialog**—This option displays a dialog box with the form upon returning from the object; otherwise, the form is presented in a full pane. Figure 12.29 displays an example of this option. The user can also select actions not shown in the modal dialog box by clicking the Action button.

II

Designing Applications

6. Save the form.

Depending upon what options you selected, you can now create a new form by selecting it from the Create menu. Figure 12.27 displays a Microsoft Word document object that is automatically launched when a user selects the form from the Create menu. The user can enter data into the document, and then save the data and switch back to Notes.

Fig. 12.27

This figure displays the automatic launching of a Word 6.0 object. The user enters data, and then returns to Notes.

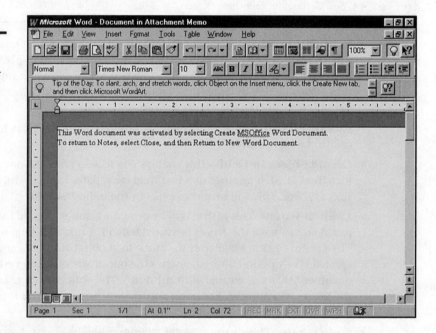

In this example, the Document Info dialog box appears when the user returns to Notes, prompting the user for the document's title and category (see fig. 12.28). Once it is saved, the document appears in the database's views, as shown in figure 12.29.

Fig. 12.28

The Present document as modal dialog option was selected in this example, so the user is prompted to enter a title and category.

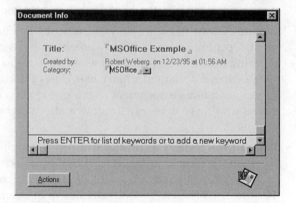

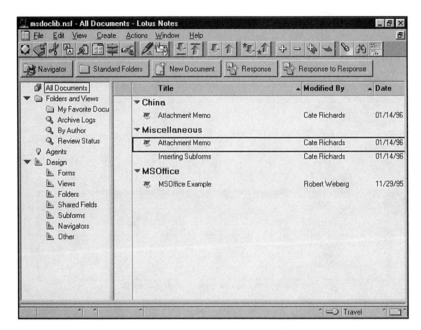

Fig. 12.29

The Notes document containing the embedded Word document is now displayed in the database. In this example, opening the document automatically launches the stored Word document.

New Features of OLE 2.0 Available in Notes R4

OLE 2.0 offers several enhancements to OLE 1.0, and provides for more versatility in Notes R4. For example, if a customer double-clicks an object that was created by an OLE 1.0-compliant application, but that object is contained within an OLE 2.0-compliant application that supports in-place editing, a new editing window is activated in the OLE 1.0 style.

Note

OLE 2.0 is backward-compatible with OLE 1.0, which means that programs written to the OLE 1.0 specification can interact with OLE 2.0-compliant applications (and operating systems) as if both used OLE 1.0.

The following list describes some new features of OLE 2.0 that are available in Notes R4:

■ **In-place activation**—This allows users to directly activate objects within documents without switching to a different window. The menus, toolbars, palettes, and other controls necessary to interact with the object temporarily replace the existing menus and controls of the active window.

For example, double-clicking the Word 6.0 object displayed in figure 12.30 shows an in-place activation window within Notes R4.

II

Designing Applications

Fig. 12.30

This example displays an object being edited using the OLE 2.0 in-place activation feature.

Menu changes to Word 6.0

Object being edited within Notes

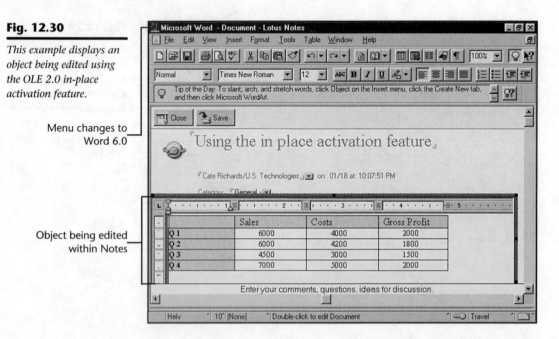

- **Nested object support**—This allows users to directly manipulate objects nested within other objects, and to establish links to nested objects. Essentially, this means you can have embedded objects within other embedded objects.

- **Drag-and-drop**—This enables users to drag objects from one application window to another, or to drop objects within other objects.

  For example, an illustration can be dragged from a Word 6.0 application window and dropped into a Notes document (see fig. 12.31).

- **Storage-independent links**—This allows links between embedded objects that are not stored as files on disk but within Notes documents. In other words, embedded objects within the same or different documents can update one another's data, whether or not the embedded objects are recognized by the file system.

- **Adaptable links**—This enables links between objects to be maintained in certain move or copy operations. Meaning that if you move a linked object to a new file path, the link will be maintained and recognized in its new location.

- **Programmability**—This enables the creation of command sets that operate both within and across applications. For example, a user could use LotusScript to invoke a command from Notes R4 that sorts a range of cells in a spreadsheet created by Excel.

- **Logical object pagination**—This allows objects to overlap page boundaries and break at logical points.

- **Version management**—This allows objects to contain information about the application that created them, including what version of the application was used. This feature gives programmers the ability to handle objects created by different versions of the same application.

- **Object conversion**—This allows an object type to be converted so that different applications can be used with the same object. For example, an object created with one brand of spreadsheet can be converted so that it is interpretable for editing by a different spreadsheet application.

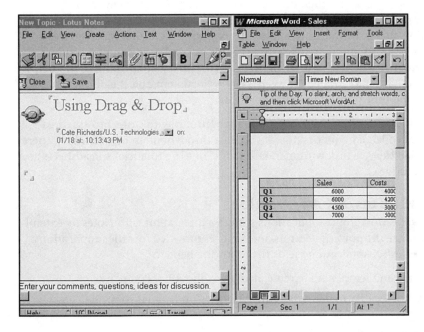

Fig. 12.31

You can drag and drop a Word 6.0 object into a Notes document, which will then be embedded.

The following sections describe in more detail some of the new OLE 2.0 features in Notes R4 that enable you to create remarkable compound documents using the power of Notes/FX.

Using Application Field Exchange

The latest releases of most productivity applications—1-2-3, AmiPro, Word Pro, Freelance, Word for Windows, PowerPoint, Excel, and so on—support a powerful feature of application integration called *Notes Field Exchange* (*Notes/FX*).

Notes/FX uses OLE technology to enable Notes and any OLE server application to share data fields, or to swap information. The contents of fields in an OLE server application file can automatically appear in a corresponding field in a Notes document, and vice versa. Furthermore, depending on the type of field, the contents of the field can be updated from either application.

> **Note**
>
> Lotus SmartSuite products use Notes/FX 1.1, the latest version, which includes enhancements to the handling of OLE objects; however, Microsoft Office products still utilize Notes/FX 1.0, an older version.

This Notes-driven technology greatly extends the application potential of Notes. For example, you can use 1-2-3 to create sophisticated worksheets or use Word Pro to create robust documents, and then users can save, categorize, and view these worksheets or documents in a Notes database. By working within Notes, you leverage the information stored in Notes and exploit the workgroup collaboration services of Notes. Why is Notes/FX more useful than just using object linking and embedding documents? Notes/FX expands the capabilities of OLE by enabling you to build fields of information that can be shared between a Notes document and the object. These fields can then be shown easily in either application.

From the desktop perspective, you now have a powerful way to store, browse, organize, share, and collaborate on desktop documents throughout an organization. There will be no more "Here's a disk with marketing files" or "The financial spreadsheets are somewhere on drive G."

Benefits of Notes/FX Applications

Notes/FX provides workgroup applications seamless integration with Notes by extending Notes to utilize the powerful editors and features provided by other applications. Designing a Notes/FX application yields the following benefits:

- Documents and templates are replicated throughout the company.
- You can use security and access control features from Notes to regulate data access.
- You can use version control to implement and maintain documents.
- Approval management can be automated.
- You can build groupware applications quickly using existing desktop applications, thereby facilitating rapid application development.
- Desktop documents can be categorized and sorted.
- Search and retrieval occurs quickly.

You can build a variety of business applications using Notes/FX. Table 12.1 lists a few potential business applications that could be used in developing a Notes/FX application.

Table 12.1 Business Applications of Notes/FX	
Application	**Examples**
Managing workflow	Travel planning, expense authorization, customer support, call tracking
Collaboration and review	Budget planning, sales projections, contract management, document versioning
Sharing documents	Presentation libraries, form letters, marketing materials, corporate policies

How Does Notes/FX Exchange Data?

Notes/FX utilizes OLE embedded objects to exchange information with fields in a Notes form. For example, if you embed a 1-2-3 worksheet document in a Notes database using OLE, then 1-2-3 makes data in cells and ranges available to Notes, along with some document information. Notes can use these fields in views or calculations, and can return new values to the 1-2-3 worksheet.

Note

For Notes/FX to exchange data with an OLE-enabled server application, the field names in the embedded file (server) must correspond exactly to the field names in the Notes form being used.

Note

For more information about fields in any other application that exchanges data with Notes, see the Help documentation for that application.

Caution

Make sure that SHARE.EXE (the DOS Share program) has been loaded in your Windows session; otherwise, Notes/FX will not work. You might need to add the following line to your AUTOEXEC.BAT file:

```
C:\DOS\SHARE
```

II

Designing Applications

Using Application Field Exchange

There are three major steps involved in setting up a Notes/FX application:

1. Create the application document that will be used with Notes, then copy a portion or all of the document to the Clipboard using Edit, Copy.

2. Embed the application in a Notes document or form. By embedding the object, you are initializing a live OLE link that enables the field exchange.

3. Define the user-defined fields that will be used to exchange information (as described by your application's Help instructions).

The following example creates a Notes/FX application using 1-2-3 and Notes that tracks expense reports. The expense reports are created in a 1-2-3 worksheet, then stored in Notes for easy document management and categorization.

All that's required is for you to identify and match Notes field names with 1-2-3 range names or cell addresses. To exchange data between 1-2-3 and Notes, a 1-2-3 worksheet object needs to be embedded in a Notes form. In the worksheet object, you need to create a two-column table of data you want to exchange.

Preparing the Notes Form. The Notes form needs to be designed to store the fields that will exchange data with the object (in this case, a 1-2-3 worksheet), and to store the 1-2-3 worksheet object itself. To create such a form, do the following steps:

1. In Notes, select or create a new database. Choose Create, Design, Forms or edit an existing form if desired.

◀◀ See "Creating a New Form," p. 363

2. Create and name fields to contain text and numbers from the 1-2-3 worksheet object (see fig. 12.32). Use descriptions and instructions to inform database designers how the form is designed to work.

3. Choose Design, Form Properties to display the form's Properties InfoBox; then click the Launch tab to reach the options shown in figure 12.33.

4. Select First OLE Object in the Auto Launch list box. This indicates that you want Notes to launch the first OLE object encountered on the form. (You embed this object in the next section.)

5. Save the Notes form.

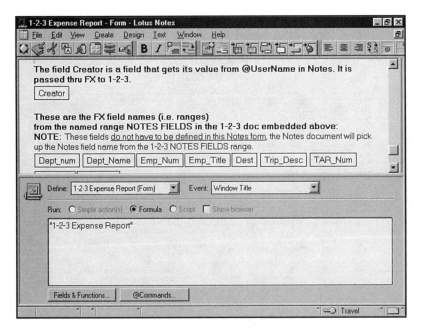

Fig. 12.32

The design of this Notes form will contain the necessary fields to exchange data with the object.

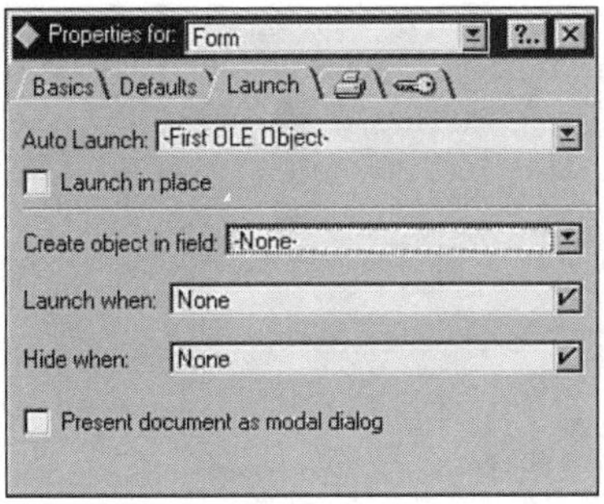

Fig. 12.33

The form's Properties InfoBox enables you to select the available Auto Launch options.

Designing Applications

Preparing the Embedded Object. To create a Notes/FX application using 1-2-3 and Notes, perform the following steps:

1. Open the desired 1-2-3 worksheet or create a new file. Figure 12.34 displays the 1-2-3 worksheet object that will be embedded into a Notes form.

2. Create the fields to exchange data with Notes. This is a two-column table in the worksheet (see fig. 12.35). The first two columns are essential for Notes/FX to work. The first column lists the field names in the Notes form that will receive and send 1-2-3 data. The second column defines the range names of the corresponding information in the 1-2-3 worksheet. This range of field names is then named with the range name, Notes Fields, which enables FX to find and exchange the field information.

Fig. 12.34

This is the 1-2-3 expense worksheet that will be used in the Notes/FX application.

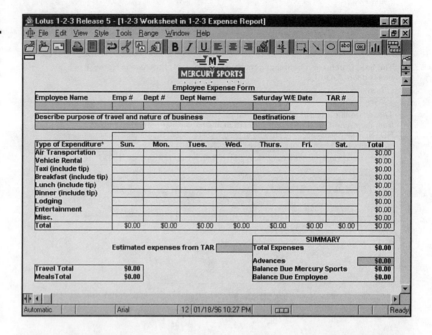

Fig. 12.35

The range Notes Fields is required for Notes to exchange data with a 1-2-3 object.

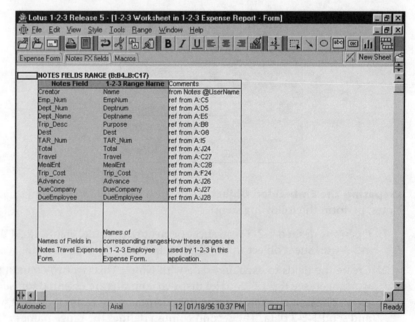

> **Note**
>
> The headings in the first row are not part of the Notes Fields range—these are for reference only. They are not necessary for Notes/FX to occur, and should not be included in the Notes Fields range.

> **Tip**
>
> Use Range, Name, Add in 1-2-3 Release 5 to name the two-column table Notes Fields.

3. Arrange and position your worksheet area. Highlight a portion or all of the document and then choose Edit, Copy to copy the part of the worksheet that you want to display in the Notes form (see fig. 12.36). The selected range does not have to display the information that you want to exchange, but it is easier to recognize in Notes if the copied range is displayed.

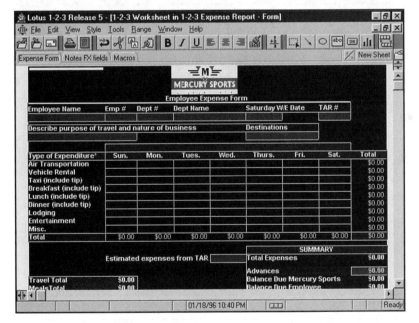

Fig. 12.36

Copy a range of data to display in Notes.

4. Switch to your Notes form, then click to position the cursor where you want the object to appear.

5. Choose Edit, Paste Special to display the Paste Special dialog box.

6. Select Paste and then 1-2-3 Worksheet in the As list box to embed the 1-2-3 worksheet object in the form.

7. Save the Notes form.

Using the Notes/FX Application. You now can begin using your Notes/FX application designed above. To create a new Notes document using the embedded 1-2-3 worksheet object, perform the following steps:

1. Choose Create and then select the name of the form that you just created. If you selected First OLE Object in the Properties InfoBox, Notes creates a new 1-2-3 worksheet document based on the embedded object.

2. Edit the data in the 1-2-3 expense worksheet.

3. Choose File, Update to update the worksheet object.

4. Choose File, Exit & Return to have Notes close 1-2-3 and return to Notes; or choose File, Close to close the worksheet object without exiting 1-2-3. The fields in the Notes document that match the 1-2-3 data are updated.

5. Your new document appears in the view, including the new data entered in the 1-2-3 expense report template (see fig. 12.37).

Fig. 12.37

The 1-2-3 expense report templates are saved in Notes. You now can utilize the power of Notes to sort, categorize, and total the existing documents.

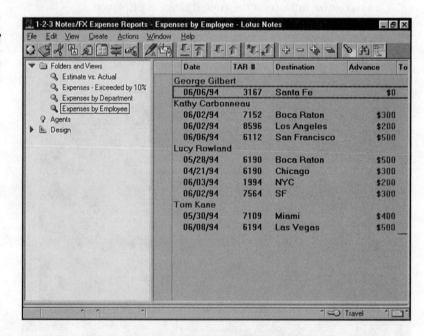

Note

You can update the existing templates by opening the document that launches the 1-2-3 object. In 1-2-3, make any necessary changes, then update the document and return to Notes. The fields you modified in 1-2-3 are reflected thereafter in Notes.

From Here...

This chapter discussed how to begin integrating Notes R4 with other applications. You can easily export and import data to and from external data sources and applications; you also can utilize OLE 2.0 to increase the functionality of your Notes documents. Notes/FX allows you to interchange data between Notes and other applications. To learn more about building Notes applications and working with Notes documents that can contain OLE objects, turn to the following chapters:

- Chapter 8, "Working with Documents," covers how to edit existing documents that can contain objects.

- Chapter 10, "Designing Forms," describes how to create and design forms in Notes R4.

- Chapter 11, "Designing Views," shows how to create views to display the documents that store your objects.

- Chapter 16, " LotusScript: A Whole New Programming Language," teaches the basics of the powerful LotusScript programming language, which can be used to manipulate objects and links.

II

Designing Applications

CHAPTER 13

Working with Formulas

Lotus Notes has three different ways to program custom features for a Notes database. You can use simple actions, formulas, or LotusScript. Simple actions are just that; you can select from a small range of actions. Formulas allow you to do everything that simple actions do and more. You can define variables, perform loops, and use if-then-else logic. LotusScript goes one step beyond formulas—you can create procedures and functions.

This chapter discusses the following:

- The concept of formulas and how they are evaluated
- How constants, operators, remarks, and functions are used in formulas and what each is
- Where formulas can be used and some examples

What Is a Formula?

Simply put, a *formula* is an expression that Notes evaluates to find a value. This value is then used in whatever context is appropriate at the time of evaluation. A lot of formulas are simply evaluated and have no side effects. For example, the following is a simple formula:

```
100 + 100
```

It adds 100 to 100 which, of course, equals 200.

However, some of them do have side-effects. For example, a formula might use the @Prompt function which will cause a message box to appear:

```
@Prompt([Ok];"Reminder";"Don't forget to run backup tonight.")
```

When this formula is evaluated, the result is a dialog box that displays the message Don't forget to run backup tonight.

 ▶▶ See " Understanding Function Basics," p. 533

Taking the side effects even further, formulas can also be a sequence of expressions which comes close to being a program—in essence, all side effect and little evaluation. If fact, some people would argue that they are little programs in their own right.

So, writing a formula is a type of programming. Through formulas, you instruct Notes to accomplish some task. If happen to be a programmer, you will find similarities between formulas and programming languages with which you are familiar. In fact, you might be more comfortable using LotusScript. If you're not a programmer, don't panic; you don't need a computer science degree to use formulas.

▶▶ See "What Is LotusScript?," p. 589

As mentioned in the introduction of this chapter, you can create variables and use control logic in formulas. Most of the complicated tasks that formulas do require use @functions. These functions like @Today, @If, or @SetField are discussed in Chapter 14, "Formula Functions." This chapter, while using @functions in examples, is more concerned with the basics.

Notes formulas perform calculations according to strict instructions you provide. In almost any situation where Notes needs to use or display a value, you can provide a formula that tells Notes what steps to take to calculate the value. They also let you express relationships between fields, cause Notes to choose between courses of action based on the values of fields, calculate values, and perform other complex actions.

One of the most common uses for formulas—and probably the easiest to understand—is using formulas in the columns of a view. Each column is usually set to a field name, and therefore, the value of that field is displayed. Simply by specifying the field name you have created an extremely small formula. A more complicated formula might be computing a totalCost column by multiplying a numberOfItems field by a costPerItem field. Figure 13.1 shows the totalCost column in a view.

> **Tip**
>
> By taking advantage of Notes' built-in formatting, you can make columns more readable with very little work. The columns are right-aligned and two of the columns display dollar signs to indicate that they represent currency information. The total price column is also sorted in descending order so that the largest cost is shown first.

When editing a column formula in Notes, you can see the whole view in the top section of the Notes window. This makes checking your formulas very easy.

▶▶ See "Creating Columns in a View," p. 433

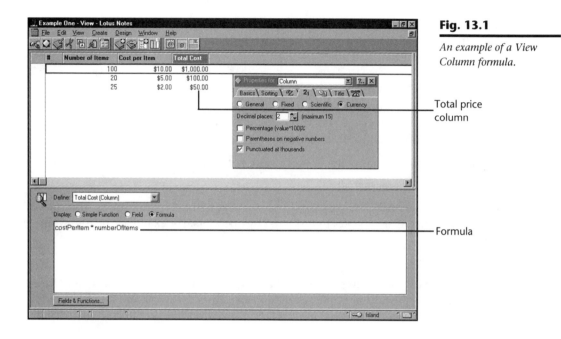

Fig. 13.1

An example of a View Column formula.

Total price column

Formula

II

Designing Applications

The following are some other situations where formulas can be useful:

■ When you define a view, you can define a formula that selects which documents Notes displays in the view.

■ When you design a view, you create columns where Notes displays information about each document. When you create a column or edit the definition of an existing column, Notes enables you to enter a formula that tells how to compute the value you want to display.

■ When you define a form, you can define a formula that specifies the title bar text that Notes displays when someone reads or composes a document. For example, the title bar text of the dialog box in figure 13.1 is Example One - View.

■ When you design a form, you create fields in which to store information. For each field, you can use a formula to define the default value for the field in the Default Value Formula box.

■ For each field, you can provide an input translation formula that tells Notes to perform some type of automatic conversion each time the user enters a value into the field. For example, you could write a formula to change all the characters in a field to uppercase—"Peter and Richard" could be changed to "PETER AND RICHARD."

■ For each field, you can provide an input validation formula that enables Notes to determine whether data entered by the user is acceptable. If you expect the user to enter a number representing a month, for example, an input validation formula enables Notes to verify that the user entered a number between 1 and 12.

This short list does not describe all of the ways that you can use formulas in Notes. Later in this chapter, the section "Where Are Formulas Used?" details every formula type in Notes and gives examples of each.

Evaluating Formulas

When you use a formula in a view, the value Notes displays isn't stored in the document or database. Notes calculates the value of the formula each time it is displayed, using other information in the document.

The most basic formula is a simple expression. For example, the following formula:

```
"This is an expression"
```

consists of a single *string constant* (an unvarying text item). Expressions can also consist of a field name or variables interspersed by operators. For example, the following formula:

```
storeCost * 1.2
```

shows how to calculate a 20 percent markup on the original price of some item. The *operator*, in this case *, or multiplication, serves to connect the variable and a numeric constant. Operators are discussed in the "Using Operators" section later in this chapter.

Notes formulas can also consist of multiple expressions. When this happens, the last expression evaluated becomes the value of the entire formula. This is where some programming comes into play because variables are usually involved. For example, a two step process might be involved in determining some total cost column:

```
customerCost := customerPrice * 1.2;
taxToAdd := customerCost * .06;
customerCost + taxToAdd
```

The first line uses customerCost as a temporary variable to simplify the calculation. It also helps to isolate the different parts of a formula. If the customerCost expression needs to change in the future, only one line needs to be changed. Temporary variables only last as long as the formula does. When the formula is finished, the temporary variables vanish.

Notice that the := sign is used to assign a value to a temporary variable. It is also important to note that a semicolon ends each line. The semicolon tells Notes that the expression is complete and that it should be evaluated before continuing.

The last line is used to give a value to the entire formula. Whatever it evaluates to is what Notes will display in the column.

Every formula must evaluate to some value; and every value must be one of the following four data types:

- **Numeric values**—These are numbers and include fields that you define as numbers. The example of `storeCost * 1.2` used above would evaluate to a number.

- **Time/Date values**—These values represent a time or date and include fields that you define as time or date. Formulas that evaluate to Time/Date values are useful in column formulas. For example, you can use the `@Adjust` function to calculate when an invoice should be paid. The `@Adjust` function can add 14 days to the invoice date to arrive at the due date.

- **Truth values**—These values don't correspond to fields you define in a document. They always represent the answer to a question that can be expressed as "true" or "false." For example, when database replication is controlled by a formula, it must evaluate to true for those documents which get replicated and false for those documents that are left behind.

- **Text values**—These values include most other types of fields, including those you defined as text, rich text, or keyword. Because Notes is document oriented you will probably find yourself using text values quite often. For example, you might want to change a person's name to all uppercase characters to make searching easier. You could use the `@Uppercase` function to do this.

- **List values**—These values contain more than one element. The elements can be either number, text, or Time/Date value. However, usually each list only contains one type. For example, a list of cities or a list of birthdates. Notes provides special functions that let you perform different types of list processing.

As you write formulas, you will discover that some calculations make sense only when you apply them to certain types of data. To multiply two fields together, for example, both fields must be numeric—multiplying an interest rate by a principal amount makes sense, but multiplying a name by an address doesn't. Similarly, asking Notes what day of the week the number 437 falls on doesn't make sense; such a question is meaningful only when you apply it to a date. Essentially, all of the items in a single expression must have the same data type.

▶▶ See "Converting Data Types," p. 542

Now, let's discuss constants and how they can be used in formulas.

Using Constants

Constants enable you to specify values that never change. For example, a formula that computes average monthly sales may sum the sales of each month and divide by 12 (the number of months in a year). Because the number of months in a year won't change, a constant can be used.

In the next few sections, you will read about number, text, date, and list constants.

Designing Applications

II

Number Constants. Perhaps the most familiar constants are numeric. If you see the number 3.1415, you might recognize it as pi—one of the most famous numeric constants. When constants are used in formulas, nothing special is done, you just type in the number—for example, 36.23 or 4. Notes also recognizes a style of writing numeric constants called *scientific notation*; see the sidebar "Understanding Scientific Notation" for more information.

One of the simplest formulas is one that simply consists of a constant. For example, the default value of a state tax field might be 0.06, which represents six percent. As you design the field, you might create a default value formula of:

```
0.06
```

From then on, Notes will set that field to 0.06 each time a new document is composed. The user can change it as needed.

Text Constants. You can also specify constant text. This is done by surrounding a group of characters with quotation marks (" "). Suppose that you are defining a `city` field in a form, and you expect that in *most* cases the user wants to enter **Orlando**. Specify the default value for the field as the following:

```
"Orlando"
```

The quotation marks are crucial to a proper text constant; without the marks, Orlando looks like a field name. If you omit the quotes, Notes thinks that you want to initialize the `city` field with the value in the `Orlando` field, and you will get an error if your document doesn't have an `Orlando` field.

> **Tip**
>
> If you are having trouble with a formula, check to make sure that the quotes are correct. You might be referencing a field name when you meant to use a text constant.

Time/Date Constants. The Time/Date constant is probably the least used. It is specified by enclosing a time or date in brackets ([ ]). Times can include AM or PM, and can include a time zone. For example, suppose you have a database in which you track company meetings. Most meetings begin at 8:30 AM, so you might initialize the field that contains the meeting start time with the following time constant:

```
[8:30 AM EDT]
```

You can write dates as numbers, separated by slashes or dashes, depending on whether your computer is running Windows or OS/2. If you're using Windows, use slashes for dates:

```
[11/9/96]
```

If you're using OS/2, use dashes:

```
[11-9-96]
```

Tip

When using Date/Time constants in formulas, you need to be aware of where the formula is being evaluated—the server or the workstation. Use the Date/Time format (slashes or dashes) associated with the operating system of the machine that evaluates the formula.

List Constants. Lists constants are the most powerful and complicated type of constant. A list constant consists of one or more elements of the same data type. If the list constant has more than one elements, the elements are separated by a *list concatenation operator* (:). For example, the following is a list containing the names of four cities:

```
"Boston" : "New York City" : "Orlando" : "Flanders"
```

Notice that each element is a text constant. You could also use number or date constants to form a list. For example, the following might be a list of quarterly billing dates:

```
[03/15/96] : [06/15/96] : [08/15/96] : [12/15/96]
```

To summarize, you write text constants surrounded by quotes, date and time constants surrounded by brackets, and number constants surrounded by nothing; and list constants are combinations of other constants connected by the list concatenation operator.

Understanding Scientific Notation

To express very large and very small numbers, Notes supports *scientific notation*, which most often is used by scientists and engineers. A number expressed in scientific notation consists of a number (technically called the *mantissa*), the letter E, and one or two digits called the *exponent*, representing a power of 10:

```
1.73E14
```

You can read this number as "1.73 times 10 to the 14th power," which in turn is 173,000,000,000,000. (In general, don't type commas in numbers; Notes will not recognize them.)

You can also use negative exponents to represent numbers that are smaller than 1. For example, the following:

```
1.73E-4
```

is equal to 0.0173.

People who must deal with very large or very small numbers appreciate this notation because you can tell at a glance how large the number is. Unless you are involved in some type of scientific endeavor, you're not likely to run into this notation.

II

Designing Applications

Performing Calculations

Most formulas perform simple calculations—adding, subtracting, multiplying, and dividing numbers to compute values. The following sections explain how to use operators.

Using Operators. Notes provides symbols, called *operators*, that represent actions that Notes can perform on data. Four of the most common operators, shown in Table 13.1, represent the basic arithmetic operations.

Table 13.1   The Four Most Common Arithmetic Operators

Operator	Description
+	Addition
–	Subtraction
×	Multiplication
/	Division

Notice the symbols for multiplication (×) and division (/). You must use these symbols for these operations. You cannot, for example, use x for multiplication as you would if you were writing a formula on paper.

Suppose that your database contains documents which contain information about a sale your company made last month. In each document is a field called customerPrice. Normally, this field is displayed without a shipping charge. However, in one view's column, you need to display the price including a $6.00 shipping charge.

When you define the Total Price column, you can enter:

```
customerPrice + 6
```

as the default value formula. Yes, this default value formula is a bit overworked as an example...but you will use it a lot in real life also.

The first operand of the expression, customerPrice, represents the value of the customerPrice field in a document. The 6 is a numeric constant. The plus sign (+) tells Notes to add two values together—the value in the Price field and the number 6—for each document and display the resulting value in the column.

You also can perform calculations that involve several fields. Suppose you have the fields shown in the following table.

Field	Description
productCost	The amount you paid for the product
laborCost	Your cost for getting the product set up and ready for delivery
customerPrice	The price the customer paid for the item

In one column of the view, you might want to display the profit for each sale. When you define the column, however, you cannot enter a simple field name as the formula, because no field in the documents contains the profit on the sale. Instead, you can enter a formula that calculates the amount of the profit by subtracting the cost of the product and the labor from the price, as follows:

```
customerPrice - productCost - laborCost
```

As Notes reads this formula from left to right, it takes the value of `customerPrice`, subtracts `productCost`, and then subtracts `laborCost`. The result of this expression is the value Notes displays in the profit column, using the appropriate values for each document.

> ### Tip
>
> Remember that a formula is *not* an equation. Notice that there is no equal sign in the formulas.

To take this example one step further, perhaps you want to display the preferred customer's price, which reflects a discount off the customer price. The discount percentage isn't contained in any of the fields in the document, but is always 85 percent of the regular customer price. So the formula for the `discountPrice` column would be as follows:

```
customerPrice * 0.85
```

Notes evaluates this formula and then displays the resulting value in the column.

Suppose you had a `Discount Price` column that also showed a `Profit After Discount` column. This column uses the following formula:

```
(customerPrice * .85) - productCost - laborCost
```

Notice that the discount price formula is simply embedded into the profit formula by enclosing it in parentheses. More information about how to use parentheses and what they mean can be found in the next section.

Operator Precedence. As Notes computes the value of a formula, it usually reads the formula from left to right. For example, if you write the following:

```
fudgeFactor + increaseAmt - decreaseAmt + otherAmt
```

Notes takes the value of the `fudgeFactor` field, adds the value of the `increaseAmt` field, subtracts the value of the `decreaseAmt` field, and adds the value of the `otherAmt` field.

The *operator precedence*, or the order in which the operators are evaluated, is the same for addition and subtraction.

If a formula uses addition or subtraction mixed with multiplication or division, however, Notes does the multiplication and division first. This means that multiplication and division have a *higher* precedence than addition or subtraction.

II

Designing Applications

Let's look at the evaluation order more closely. Suppose that a document contains information about an employee's pay, and one of the formulas looks like this:

```
empBonus + hoursWorked * hourlyRate
```

If you read this formula strictly left to right, you may think that Notes adds empBonus and hoursWorked, and then multiplies the result by hourlyRate. But Notes does the multiplication first, computing the value of hoursWorked times hourlyRate, and then adding the result to empBonus.

Thus, the *order of operations* is multiplication first and then addition. This order of operations can be seen in Table 13.2. You can see that multiplication has a precedence level of 3 and addition has a precedence level of 4. A precedence level of 1 is considered the highest. Therefore, the multiplication operation is performed first.

Table 13.2   Notes Operators and their Precedence Levels

Operator	Operation	Precedence
:=	Assignment	N/A
:	List concatenation	1
+, –	Positive, Negative	2
*	Multiplication	3
**	Permuted multiplication	
/	Division	
*/	Permuted division	
+	Addition, Concatenation	4
*+	Permuted addition	
–	Subtraction	
*–	Permuted subtraction	
=	Equal	5
*=	Permuted equal	
<>	Not equal	
!=	Not equal	
=!	Not equal	
><	Not equal	
*<>	Permuted not equal	
<	Less than	
*<	Permuted less than	
>	Greater than	
>*	Permuted greater than	

Operator	Operation	Precedence
<=	Less than or equal	
*<=	Permuted less than or equal	
>=	Greater than or equal	
*>=	Permuted greater than or equal	
!	Logical NOT	6
&	Logical AND	
|	Logical OR	

▶▶ For more information about the conditional operators (those operators with a precedence level of 5), see the section "The @If Function," p. 535

▶▶ For more information about the logical NOT, AND, and OR operators, see the section "Logical Operators," p. 538

The assignment operator does not have a precedence level because it is only used in assignment statements. The permuted operators are used for list operations. Both of these topics will be covered in a moment.

The Assignment Operator. It is sometimes convenient to break a formula into smaller parts. This is usually done to make the formula more understandable and easier to document.

The assignment operator is used to assign parts of a formula to a variable. For example:

```
empWage := hoursWorked * hourlyRate;
empWage + empBonus
```

This two-statement formula shows the assignment operator being used to calculate an employee's wage. Compare this example to the following:

```
(hoursWorked * hourlyRate) + empBonus
```

Using the variable empWage makes the formula easier to understand because it reduces the complexity of the formula's statements.

The next section shows you how to use parentheses to explicitly change the order of operations. They are also useful as an aid to documentation to show future users of your formulas that you intended the formula to be evaluated in a certain way.

Using Parentheses to Prioritize Operations. Usually, Notes performs arithmetic left to right, except when the order of operations dictates otherwise. However, you can force Notes to perform specific operations first by surrounding portions of a formula with parentheses. In essence, the parentheses are telling Notes that the operators inside have a higher priority and need to be evaluated first.

II

Designing Applications

Suppose that you want to display a discount price in a column, and you compute the discount price by adding the item cost and the item profit and multiplying by 90 percent. You might try to create a formula like the following:

```
itemCost + itemProfit * .9
```

If you have an `itemCost` of $10 and an `itemProfit` of $2, then this formula would be $10 + $2 × .9 or $8.20.

However, this is not correct. Notes performs multiplication first, therefore it multiplies `itemProfit` by .9, and then adds the `itemCost`. To get the results you want, you need to explicitly tell Notes what to evaluate first, like this:

```
(itemCost + itemProfit) * .9
```

When the same values as before (an `itemCost` of $10 and an `itemProfit` of $2) are used this version of the formula becomes ($10 + $2) × .9 or $7.20.

Surrounding the addition portion of the formula with parentheses forces Notes to add first, and then multiply.

You can also nest parentheses if needed. Here is a contrived example simply to show you the technique. If you consistently get a two percent reduction in the `itemCost` because you pay your bills in cash, you might represent the fact in the formula as follows:

```
((itemCost * .98) + itemProfit) * .9
```

In this formula, the `itemCost` is multiplied by .98 to reflect the two percent reduction for cash payment. This is enclosed in parentheses so that it will be the first operation performed. Then Notes will add the result to `itemProfit` and multiply that result by .9.

Using the previous values (an `itemCost` of $10 and an `itemProfit` of $2) the formula becomes (($10 × .98) + $2) × .9 or $7.02.

Concatenating Text

Concatenate means to connect end to end, an operation you often want to perform on text. When the plus sign (+) appears between two text values, it tells Notes to concatenate two pieces of text. By using plus signs interspersed between text or fields, you can concatenate as many pieces of text information as you need.

Suppose that a form contains two fields that contain a person's first name and last name, respectively. And in a view, you want to display the last name, a comma, and the first name. You can use the following formula to define the column:

```
lastName + ", " + firstName
```

This formula evaluates to a single text value that contains the last name, followed by a comma and a space, and then the first name.

> **Note**
>
> Remember that using quotes in a formula causes Notes to use the text inside the quotes exactly as is. In the case of `lastName`, however, you don't actually want it to use the word "lastName" in constructing the person's full name; instead you want it to access the value of the `lastName` field and use the field value. If you used quotes, it would print the literal word `lastName`.

Reusing Operators (or Overloading)

Notes uses the plus sign (+) to represent two different operations—addition and concatenation. Computer scientists like to call the dual use of a symbol *operator overloading*. This is done a lot in the C++ language.

When you enter a plus sign between two numbers, Notes adds them; when you write a plus sign between two text values, Notes concatenates them. The data types determine the operation.

This dual meaning for the plus sign is similar to the English language. A single group of letters, for example, can have more than one pronunciation and more than one meaning. Consider the dual meaning of *lead* in the sentence, "You can *lead* a horse to water by chasing him with a *lead* pipe." You learn to look at the other words to distinguish between the various meanings of *lead*; Notes looks at the types of values on either side of the plus sign to determine whether it represents addition or concatenation.

List Operations

Earlier in the chapter, you saw that list constants looked like the following:

```
"Boston" : "New York City" : "Orlando" : "Flanders"
```

Each city is an item in this four-element list. In Notes, the colon (:) acts as a list concatenator in the same fashion that the plus sign (+) acts as a text concatenator.

You can use the assignment operator to store this list into a variable:

```
destinationCities := "Boston" : "New York City" : "Orlando" : "Flanders"
```

Now the variable `destinationCities` has a list with four elements. If you needed to expand this list, you could do the following:

```
expandedList := destinationCities : "Roseland"
```

The `expandedList` variable holds a five-element list. This formula shows that the list concatenation operator works on list variables as well as list constants.

This section will look at the different operations that you can perform on lists. List operations fall into the following types:

II

Designing Applications

■ **Pair-Wise**—These operators act on two lists in parallel fashion. The first element in list A pairs with the first element in list B. If one list is shorter, the last element in the shorter list is repeated for each remaining element in the longer list.

■ **Permuted**—These operators act on two lists by pairing each element in list A with every element in list B. Thus, every possible combination of values (all permutations) is used.

Of the four basic arithmetic operators, only the addition operator will be discussed since the addition, subtraction, multiplication, and division operators all work on lists in a similiar fashion.

List Addition. The addition operator works differently depending on whether the lists being added are numeric or text. The numeric lists act as you probably would expect them to. The following formula:

```
listOne := 5 : 10;
listTwo := 1 : 2;
listOne + listTwo
```

will result in a list consisting of the following:

```
6 : 12
```

which is 5 + 1 and 10 × 2.

If one of the lists is longer than the other, the last element of the shorter list is repeated as many times as needed to make up the difference. For example, the following:

```
listOne := 5 : 10 : 20 : 30;
listTwo := 1 : 2;
listOne + listTwo
```

will result in a list consisting of the following:

```
6 : 12 : 22 : 32
```

which is 5 + 1, 10 + 2, 20 + 2, 30 + 2. Notice that the 2 in the listTwo variable is repeated twice.

Text lists, when added, result in the concatenation of an element in list A to an element in list B. For example, the following:

```
listOne := "A" : "B";
listTwo := "1" : "2";
listOne + listTwo
```

will result in a list consisting of the following:

```
A1 : B2
```

which is "A" + "1" and "B" + "2"

Again, if one of the lists is longer than the other, the last element of the shorter list is repeated as many times as needed to make up the difference.

Permuted List Addition. Let's use the previous examples to show permuted addition. The following example:

```
listOne := 5 : 10;
listTwo := 1 : 2;
listOne *+ listTwo
```

will result in a list consisting of the following:

```
6 : 7 : 11 : 12
```

which is 5 + 1, 5 + 2, 10 + 1, and 10 + 2. All possible combinations of values are used.

Lists with mismatched lengths do not need any special consideration when doing permuted operations. For example, the following:

```
listOne := 5 : 10 : 20 : 30;
listTwo := 1 : 2;
listOne *+ listTwo
```

will result in a list consisting of the following:

```
5 : 6 : 11 : 12 : 21 : 22 : 31 : 32
```

which is 5 + 1, 5 + 2, 10 + 1, 10 + 2, 20 + 1, 20 + 2, 30 + 1, and 30 + 2. Again, all possible combinations of values are used.

Permuted text list addition worked exactly as you might expect. For example, the following:

```
listOne := "A" : "B";
listTwo := "1" : "2";
listOne *+ listTwo
```

will result in a list consisting of the following:

```
A1 : A2 : B1 : B2
```

which is "A" + "1", "A" + "2", "B" + "1", and "B" + "2"

Note

The elements from the first list control the ordering of the resulting list. The first element of the first list is matched against the first element of the second list, and then the second element of the second list, and so on.

This may be important if you need to know the order of the list. I don't know of any situation where this is critical but you never know when a fact like this might save you a couple of hours of frustration looking for a bug in your formula.

II

Designing Applications

Formula Keywords

You have read about the basics so far; let's look at some more complicated things. There are several things that make formulas into little programs—the temporary variables and the multiple expressions might be the most important.

However, Notes also has keywords that can be used in formulas. These statements are more executed than evaluated, and so might also fuel the "formulas are small programs" argument. No values are associated with keywords, just actions.

There are five keywords that are used with formulas:

- DEFAULT
- ENVIRONMENT
- FIELD
- REM
- SELECT

The next five sections discuss each of them.

The *DEFAULT* Keyword. This keyword lets you assign a default value to a field. It will also let you create a temporary field (which lasts while the formula is being evaluated) with a default value. And, since you can use the statement more than once in the same formula, you can have dynamic defaults.

The syntax of the DEFAULT keyword is as follows:

```
DEFAULT variableName := value ;
```

The Notes online help has a great example of how this statement might be used. You can use the following column formula:

```
@If(@IsAvailable(keyThought); keyThought; topic);
```

to display the topic field if the keyThought field is not available.

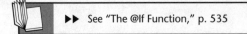 ▶▶ See "The @If Function," p. 535

You can perform this same task by using the DEFAULT statement:

```
DEFAULT keyThought := topic
keyThought
```

You might consider the second method easier to understand and less error-prone. It says if the keyThought field does not exist, temporarily create it, using the topic field as the default value. If the field also exists and has a value, the DEFAULT keyword is ignored.

The *ENVIRONMENT* Keyword. This keyword is used to create and/or set environment variables in the NOTES.INI file under the Windows, OS/2, and UNIX operating systems and the Notes Preferences file under the Macintosh operating system. This means that each machine (and probably each user) can have different values for the same environment variable.

The syntax of the ENVIRONMENT keyword is as follows:

```
ENVIRONMENT variable := textValue ;
```

Notice that environment variables must be text values. If you need to use numbers with environment variables, check out the @Text and @TextToNumber functions in Chapter 14, "Formula Functions." They can be used to convert between text and number data types.

> **Note**
>
> The @Environment function can retrieve the value of an environment variable. It can also be used, along with the @SetEnvironment function, to set the value. Both of these functions are discussed in Chapter 14, "Formula Functions."

Environment variables are frequently used to create sequential numbers for Notes applications. The idea is that the first time you access the variable, it does not exist. So you create it with a value of 1. The next time you need a sequential number, read the value, increment it, set the environment with the new value, and use the new value in your document as needed.

Environment variables are also used to personalize databases since each user can have a different value. For example, if your company uses regional sales offices, the address of the local sales office can be stored in an environment variable and used in default value formula in fields. For example:

```
@Environment("salesOfficeAddress")
```

You also need to be aware of where the formula is being evaluated. Some formulas are evaluated at the server and the NOTES.INI or Notes Preferences file will be different than the one on the client workstation.

The Notes online help topic "Examples: @Environment, @SetEnvironment, and ENVIRONMENT" does a good job of explaining the details and intricacies of this keyword.

The *FIELD* Keyword. The FIELD keyword is used to assign a value to a field. It is also used to tell Notes which fields will be assigned values later in the formula. Before using the @SetField function, you need to use the FIELD keyword to tell Notes about the field before you try to set its value.

The syntax of the FIELD keyword is as follows:

```
FIELD fieldName := value ;
```

II

Designing Applications

> **Caution**
>
> If `fieldName` does not already exist in the document, it will be created. Make sure that you want a permanent field and not a temporary field when using the `FIELD` keyword. Also, when you use `FIELD` intending to create a new field, make sure that you are not overwriting an existing field by accident.

When using the `FIELD` keyword to tell Notes that you might set its value later, you can use this form of statement:

```
FIELD myField := myField;
```

This formula sets `myField` to the value stored in `myField`. In other words, the value does not change. You can blank out a field by using the following:

```
FIELD myField := "";
```

If you are not certain that the value of the field will be changing in your formula, set the field equal to itself. Only set the field equal to blank text if you intend to never use its value again.

The `FIELD` statement can also be used to delete fields by combining it with the `@DeleteField` function:

```
FIELD myField := @DeleteField;
```

This keyword does not work in column, selection, hide-when, window title, or form formulas.

The *REM* Keyword. *Remarks*, also known as *comments*, are notes that you make, as part of your formula, to explain to yourself or others how your formula works. Lotus Notes completely ignores remarks but keeps them as part of your formula so that you can see them when you examine your formula.

If you become very proficient with formulas, some day you may work on a very complex formula for hours before getting it to work just right. If you—or worse, someone else—needs to make a change six months later, the nuances of the formula may have been forgotten. Perhaps you had the foresight to jot down a few notes about what your formula does in some internal documentation. But, of course, those are gone also. Adding comments to your formulas will avoid this problem.

The syntax of the REM keyword is as follows:

```
REM " [remark text] ";
```

For example:

```
REM "This formula selects only dogs without rabies vaccine";
REM "Written 08-12-96 by Waswaldo, Head Programmer";
```

Good programmers know that no matter how fresh your thoughts are in your mind today, six months from now they may be stale. You may not have the slightest idea why you wrote a formula the way you did.

In complicated formulas, you can use remark statements to separate different sections of the formula. For example:

```
REM "----------";
REM "Setup the first list";
REM "----------";
listOne := 5 : 10;
REM "                    ";
REM "********************";
REM "Setup second list   ";
REM "********************";
listTwo := 1 : 2;
REM "                    ";
REM "----------";
REM "Add the two lists.  ";
REM "----------";
listOne + listTwo
```

Of course, you use any character to create the line; some people use underscores, some use asterisks. It all depends on what you find readable. Both dashes and asterisks are used in the previous example. You should be consistent and always use the same character.

The *SELECT* Keyword. The SELECT keyword is used to target specific documents. When used, only those documents that match its criterion will be seen by the formula. The SELECT keyword is used before the expression that changes the documents.

The SELECT keyword defines criteria for the selection of documents in an agent that runs a formula, in a view, or during replication. You use a SELECT statement *before* an expression to define the set of documents that you want to change, see in a view, or replicate.

The syntax of the SELECT keyword is as follows:

```
SELECT expression ;
```

You can use the formula:

```
SELECT @All;
```

to have your formula see all of the documents in the database. Or you can have a complex expression, as in the following:

```
SELECT Form = "myForm";
```

This SELECT statement ensures that only documents created using the form named myForm will be seen be the formula.

> **Note**
>
> The Form field is a field that Notes automatically adds to each document. Its value is the name of the form used to create the document.

Designing Applications

This keyword does not work in column, hide-when, section editor, window title, hotspot, field, form, or form action formulas.

Where Are Formulas Used?

One of the things that makes Notes so powerful and flexible is that there are so many different ways to customize your databases using formulas. Notes has almost 30 different types of formulas that can be used.

This section describes each formula type. This brief description lets you know the context in which this type of formula is found. For example, Column formulas can only be found in the View design mode.

You also see an example of each formula type. This small example gives you an idea of how each formula type can be used and what data type the formula needs to return. Some formula types, like a Replication formula, must only return a `true` or `false` value. SmartIcon, Agent, Action, Button, and Hotspot formulas do not require any return value. Instead, they are designed to *do* something.

The description also points out any @functions that are designed to work well with that particular formula type. For example, the `@All` function can only be used in Replication, Agent, and View selection formulas.

Another important consideration is where the formula will be evaluated. If the formula is evaluated on the server, you will not be able to access information stored in INI files as environment variables at the client.

Formulas can be generally assigned to categories such as workspace formulas, form formulas, and so forth. However, some formulas fit in multiple places. We'll look at these first.

Action Buttons

Action buttons enable a user to perform tasks with the click of a mouse. Each action button is associated with either a view or a form and is displayed in the area just below the SmartIcons palette. This action bar area is nonscrollable so users can look at long documents and still be able to access an action button. Figure 13.2 shows you what action buttons look like. You can see that the three buttons are: Categorize, New Clean Sheet, and Move to Folder.

There are six predefined actions to which you can attach buttons:

- Categorize
- Edit Document
- Send Document
- Forward
- Move to Folder
- Remove from Folder

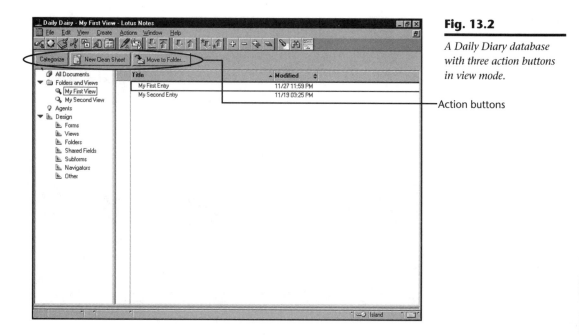

Fig. 13.2

*A Daily Diary database
with three action buttons
in view mode.*

Action buttons

Each of these actions are atomic. You can't add anything to them and you can't change them. If the action does not do what you want, you can't use them and you will need to define your own custom action instead.

The next section on action button formulas shows you how to create custom actions.

Action Button Formulas. In addition to the six predefined actions, you can create your own custom actions. The Personal Journal template that comes with Notes shows a good use of action button formulas.

Figure 13.2 showed three action buttons from the default view of the Daily Diary template. Now let's take a look at one of the definitions. In the navigator pane, select Design, Views and then double-click ($All). This puts you into design mode. Now choose View, Action Pane and then double-click the New Journal Entry action in the action pane that appears. This screen should look similar to figure 13.3.

This is a really busy figure. At the top left, the columns for the view are displayed. The top right holds the action pane. The bottom half holds the programmer pane with the action button formula. And lastly, the InfoBox at the bottom right is where you can decide the various options that affect the action buttons. You'll notice that the Include action in button bar option has been checked.

The New Journal Entry action, the selected one in the action pane, has the following formula:

```
@Command([Compose];"JournalEntry")
```

Fig. 13.3

The ($All) view in design mode with the action and programmer panes and the InfoBox displayed.

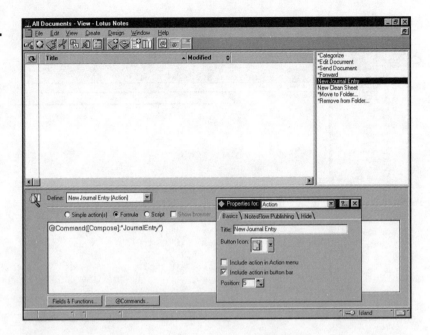

When the action button is pushed, Notes evaluates the formula which results in the creation of a new JournalEntry form. The @Command function is used to invoke a menu option from inside a formula.

You can also create action buttons—and their formulas—that are associated with a given form. When a given form is displayed, only the action buttons that are a part of that form are displayed.

Form action formulas are a good place to automate some tasks for the user, or to control field values. A simplistic example of this might be to use a form action formula to control a status field. For example, consider the following lines of code:

```
FIELD docStatus := docStatus;
question := "Has account been verified?"
response := @Prompt([YESNO]; "Caution"; question);
fld := "docStatus";
@if(response; @SetField(fld ; "OK"); @SetField(fld; "unknown"));
```

This formula asks the user if an account has been verified. If it has, the status field is changed to OK. When controlling field content like this, you might want to change the field type to computed.

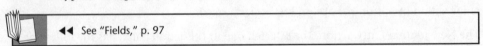

◄◄ See "Fields," p. 97

Notice that the FIELD statement is needed in this formula. Before passing a document field to the @SetField function, you need to declare it with the FIELD statement. You could assign any value you'd like to the field in the FIELD statement. In this example, we leave the value unchanged.

The @Command, @PickList, @PostedCommand, @Prompt, and @SetField functions and the FIELD statement are designed to work well in action button formulas.

The @IsDocBeingEdited, @IsDocBeingLoaded, @IsDocBeingMailed, @IsDocBeingRecalculated, and @IsDocBeingSaved functions can't be used in an action button formula.

Hide Action Button Formulas. The hide action button formulas are used to control when actions are shown to the user, either in the Action menu or the Action bar. When the Hide Action formula evaluates to true, the actions will be displayed.

This ability might come in handy if your weekend staff has a different set of tasks to perform than your weekday staff. The following formula:

```
day := @Weekday(@Now);
@If(day = 1 ¦ day = 7; 0; 1)
```

displays a given action only on Sunday (day equals 1) and Saturday (day equals 7).

Figure 13.4 shows the Hide tab of the Action Properties InfoBox for the action. When the formula shown in the InfoBox is true, the action will be hidden if the checkbox is checked.

Fig. 13.4

An InfoBox showing a Hide When formula.

You can display the Action Properties InfoBox by double-clicking the action in the action pane or selecting the Design, View Properties menu option.

Each view or form action button also has an associated hide action button formula that you can set.

Hotspots

A hotspot is a highlighted object that does some task when clicked. A hotspot can display text in a pop-up window, execute a hypertext link, or perform an action. Hotspot formulas can be added to words in rich text fields, rectangles and polygons in Navigators, and buttons in layout regions.

The next section discusses how hotspots can perform actions and display pop-up windows.

Hotspot Formulas. Hotspot formulas are evaluated when the hotspot is clicked. The formula must evaluate to some text suitable for displaying in a pop-up window.

You might want to use a hotspot to let your user get some commentary or you might link the hotspot to a field on the document. Figure 13.5 shows a trivial example of a hotspot formula.

Fig. 13.5

A hotspot formula.

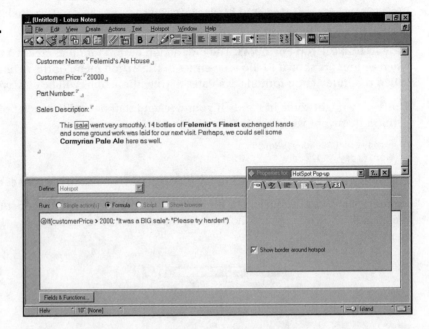

If the customer price is above $2,000, then the text It was a BIG sale is displayed when the reader clicks the hotspot text; otherwise, the text Please try harder is displayed.

You can also use a hotspot formula to display a dialog box to request additional details. For example, your main form might be an inventory control form. If you need to display additional information about a supplier or detailed information about stock on hand in a particular warehouse, you can use a layout region and a dialog box to display the additional information. More information can be found in the topic "Showing users a dialog box instead of a document" in the HELP4.NSF database that comes with Notes.

You can create hotspot formulas for rectangles and polygons in Navigators. Their use in a Navigator is unrestricted. Whatever you can dream up, you can do. For example, you might create a Navigator to act as a graphic-based menu. In this case, each menu item might have a hotspot rectangle formula to execute whatever menu option is selected.

Hotspot formulas also come in handy when editing a document. You can create a hotspot formula simply by selecting words in a rich text field and then choosing Create, Hotspot, Formula Popup. The most common formula to add is probably a text constant that could act as commentary to the normal text. For example, the following formula:

```
"World Wide Web"
```

could be linked to the abbreviation "WWW." Later, readers of the document could click the hotspot to see an expansion of the abbreviation.

If the hotspot is already defined, the programmer pane is reached through the Hotspot, Edit Hotspot menu option.

The @Command, @DbColumn, @DbLookup, @DialogBox, @Platform, @Prompt, @Return, and @SetField functions are designed to work well in hotspot formulas. The SELECT statement can't be used in hotspot formulas.

Buttons

A *button* is a clickable object that you can add to a form. A Notes user can also add buttons inside a rich text field. When the button is clicked, Notes executes the actions, formula, or script associated with it. You look at button formulas in the next section.

Button Formulas. A good use of a button might be to automate switching to another form. For example, the following formula:

```
@Command([ViewSwitchForm]; "Medical Info")
```

could be used to look at the medical information form. This technique is useful when the main document is long or complicated. The second form would simply focus on one part of the information.

This might be a good time to pause a moment and reflect that this new version of Notes lets you perform a task many different ways. This example could also be used in an action button formula or as an agent. You could also create the medical information as a subform. There is no one right way to program in Notes. It all depends on the style that you are comfortable using.

The @DbColumn, @DbLookup, @IsDocBeingMailed, @IsDocBeingRecalculated, @IsDocBeingSaved, @IsNewDoc, @MailSend, @Platform, @Prompt, @Return, and @SetField functions and FIELD statements are designed to work well in button formulas.

If you want to use the @Command function in a button formula, you must make sure that the formula switches to the right context. For example, view-level menu options won't work unless Notes is in view mode.

Workspace Formulas

Formulas that act at the workspace level are global to all databases. They can perform any menu command and manipulate databases.

SmartIcons. A *SmartIcon* is a customizable button that performs actions. It acts just like the buttons on toolbars that you see in many Windows applications. Each SmartIcon has a formula associated with it. There are over 100 predefined SmartIcons, with formulas that map to one of the menu commands. Many people find that click-ing a SmartIcon is faster than selecting menu options and easier than recalling key-board shortcuts.

You can create you own SmartIcon by choosing File, Tools, SmartIcons and clicking the Edit Icon button. Then select one of the customizable icons from the list, enter a description, click Formula, and enter a formula.

SmartIcons come in sets. Among others, there is a set for editing a document and a set for designing a form. When you create a SmartIcon, you need to assign it to an exist-ing or new set.

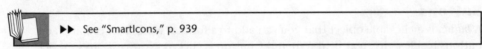

▶▶ See "SmartIcons," p. 939

Figure 13.6 shows the SmartIcons dialog box, the Edit SmartIcons dialog box, and the SmartIcons Formula dialog box. The formula shown will open the Names database and display the people view.

Fig. 13.6

A SmartIcon formula to display a database view.

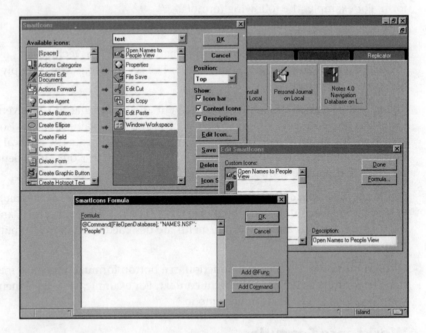

The @Command, @DbColumn, @DbLookup, @IsNewDoc, @MailSend, @Platform, @Prompt, @Return, @SetField, and @ViewTitle functions are designed to work well in SmartIcons formulas.

Database Formulas

There are two types of formulas that act at the database level. One type, the Replica-tion formula, controls replication. The other type, an *agent*, replaces the macros used in R3 of Notes.

Replication Formulas. A replication formula controls which documents will be replicated. It is applied to each document in the database. The formula is evaluated wherever the database is located, usually at the server.

You might use a replication formula to replicate all client documents that came from IBM or Compaq, as in the following:

```
SELECT Form="Client" & (Source="IBM" ¦ Source="Compaq")
```

If the formula evaluates to true, then the document is replicated.

By using @IsResponseDoc in a replication formula, you cause all response documents in a database to replicate, not just those that meet the selection criteria. To avoid this, use @AllChildren or @AllDescendants instead.

The @All, @AllChildren, and @AllDescendants functions and the SELECT keyword are designed to work well in a replication formula. In fact, all replication formulas must end with a SELECT statement.

The @DbLookup, @Environment, @Now, and @UserName functions can't be used in a replication formula.

Agent Formulas. An *agent* is a procedure that can be made of simple actions, a formula, or a script. You can have the agent triggered manually, from another agent, when new mail arrives, when documents are created or changed, when documents are pasted, or on a preset schedule.

Formula-based agents can be run on all documents in a database, all new or modified documents since the last run, all unread documents, all documents in a view, all selected documents, or the current document. In addition, you can use a SELECT statement to determine which documents will be looked at. The formula is applied to each document, one at a time.

The agent is run at the client if the agent is triggered manually, when documents are created or changed, and when documents are pasted. The agent is run at the server when the trigger is new mail or a preset schedule.

You might use an agent to set the status of a field. For example, let's say that your organization needs to highlight valued customers for a beginning-of-the-month sales promotion. You could create an agent triggered monthly that looks at new or changed documents since the last run, and the formula might look like the following:

```
SELECT monthlySales > 200000;
FIELD promoStatus := "Valued";
```

This formula sets the promoStatus field to Valued for any customer with monthly sales over $200,000.

The @All, @Command, @DbColumn, @DbLookup, @DeleteDocument, @DeleteField, @DocMark, @MailSend, @Platform, @Prompt, @Return, @SetField, @Unavailable, and @ViewTitle functions and the SELECT keyword are designed to work well in agent formulas.

II

Designing Applications

View Formulas

Formulas that operate at the view level are used to control what information is seen in each view column, which documents are seen, and which forms are used to display information.

Column Formulas. A column formula controls what information is shown in a view column and must evaluate to a value that can be converted into text. It is evaluated either at the client or the server, depending on the database's location.

The column formula may be the most-used type of formula because views are built from columns. And views are the way that information is communicated most frequently in Notes.

 ▶▶ See "Creating Columns in a View," p. 433

Columns are very versatile in Notes. Here is a simple column formula that will let you know whether a document was created on a weekend or a weekday:

```
day := @Weekday(@Created);
@If (day = 1 ¦ day = 7; "WeekEnd"; "WeekDay")
```

The @Created function has a value that represents the time/date when the document was created.

The @Weekday function looks at a time/date value and indicates which day of the week the time/date value falls on. A value of 1 represents Sunday, 2 represents Monday, and so on. This value is then assigned to the day variable.

The second line, with the @If function, looks at the value of the day variable and decides between two text constants, WeekEnd or WeekDay. If the day variable is equal to Sunday (1) or Saturday (7), then the value of WeekEnd is selected; otherwise the value of WeekDay is used.

The @DocChildren, @DocDescendants, @DocLevel, @DocNumber, @DocParentNumber, @DocSiblings, @IsCategory, @IsExpandable, and @Platform functions are designed to work well in column formulas. In fact, the @IsCategory and @IsExpandable functions can only be used in column formulas.

The @Command, @DeleteDocument, @DeleteField, @DialogBox, @Do, @DoesDbExist, @GetDocField, @IsAgentEnabled, @IsDocBeingEdited, @IsDocBeingLoaded, @IsDocBeingMailed, @IsDocBeingRecalculated, @IsDocBeingSaved, @MailDbName, @MailSend, @NewLine, @PickList, @PostedCommand, @Prompt, @SetDocField, @SetField, @Unavailable, @UserPrivileges, @UserRoles, @Version, @ViewTitle, and @WhatIsUserAccess functions and the FIELD statement can't be used in a column formula. In addition, none of the DDE functions can be used.

The @IsNewDoc function always has a value of `false` or `0` in a column formula.

Form Formulas. A form formula controls which form is used to display the document information and must evaluate to the name of an existing form. The formula is evaluated on the client. A form that is stored in the document will take precedence over the form formula.

Tip

You can store the form used to create each document inside the document. This, of course, will probably eat up a lot of disk space. But, if you avoid changing the form after creating a document, this might be a good option.

This feature is turned on by selecting Design, Form Properties while editing a form, and then selecting the Defaults tab in the InfoBox window. Check the Store form in document checkbox.

One of the most common uses for a form formula is to display a different form when an existing document is viewed versus when a document is being created. The following formula:

```
@If(@IsNewDoc; "New Inventory Item"; "Inventory Item")
```

displays the form called New Inventory Item when new documents are created. Later, when the document is seen again, the Inventory Item form is used. This is useful when a lot of information is needed to add an item to inventory (like supplier information, discounts, costs) and everyday users do not need those details.

A form formula might also come in handy if you want to run some functions (perhaps to display some message) when a new document is composed, but not for existing documents. You can do this with the following formula:

```
msg := "Check all information before saving.";
@If (@IsNewDoc; @Prompt([OK];"Warning"; msg); "");
Form
```

Figure 13.7 shows the Design Form Formula dialog box with the preceding formula entered. You can use the Zoom In button to display a larger dialog box to make editing easier. In addition, you can use the Add @Func and Add Field buttons to select from lists of functions and fields.

Notice that the last line of the formula simply says Form. As mentioned previously in the chapter, the Form variable is automatically valued by Notes to the form name used to create a document. The Form variable is set before the form formula is evaluated. Therefore, you can use it here to indicate that Notes should use whatever the default form name is.

II

Designing Applications

Fig. 13.7

A form formula that displays a warning messages when composing new documents.

The @Environment and @IsDocBeingLoaded functions are designed to work well in form formulas.

The @Command, @IsDocBeingEdited, @IsDocBeingMailed, @IsDocBeingRecalculated, @IsDocBeingSaved, @Modified, @NewLine, @Now, @PickList, @PostedCommand, @SetField, and @Unavailable functions and the FIELD statement can't be used in form formulas.

Selection Formulas. A selection formula controls which documents appear in a view. The formula should begin with the keyword SELECT and be followed by a condition expression. The condition expression must evaluate to either true or false and is applied to each document in the database. Any document where the expression evaluates to true is included in the view. Selection formulas are evaluated at the database's location, either at the client or at the server.

You might use a selection formula that lists all customers with a negative account balance. For example, consider the following statement:

```
SELECT accountBalance < 0
```

If you have a database that includes several different forms, you might decide to show only a single form in a view. For example, in a database of veterinarian patients you can select only cats—composed with the Feline Profile form—with this formula:

```
SELECT Form = "Feline Profile"
```

> **Tip**
>
> The special field, Form, is a part of every document and contains the name of the form used to compose that particular document.

If you don't specify a selection formula, Notes will use a default formula of:

```
SELECT @All
```

Form Formulas

Formulas that work at the form level have an effect when a form is being viewed. They help you to control actions, buttons, events, hotspots, paragraphs, subforms, and titles.

Event Formulas. Event formulas are evaluated whenever a specific event happens. There are seven different events for which you can create formulas: Queryopen, Postopen, Postrecalc, Querysave, Querymodechange, Postmodechange, and Queryclose. Table 13.3 lists these events and tells you when they will be run.

Table 13.3 When Are the Event Formulas Run?	
Event	**Formula Is Run...**
Postmodechange	...after changing into or out of edit mode
Postopen	...after a document is displayed
Postrecalc	...after a document has been refreshed
Queryclose	...just before a document is closed
Queryopen	...just before a document is displayed
Querymodechange	...just before changing into or out of edit mode
Querysave	...just before a document is saved

Most of the time, you want to use an Event formula to do validation of field values or to display information automatically. For example, the Postmodechange Event formula can be used to reset some field information when going into edit mode. You do this with the following formula:

```
FIELD custDiscount := "unknown";
select @all
```

This formula automatically changes the customer discount to unknown when the form is in edit mode. You may want to do this so that no discount is given accidentally when a document is changed. A Queryclose Event formula may check the discount against other field values to make sure that it is being updated correctly.

Hide Paragraph Formulas. The Hide Paragraph formula can be used to hide individual paragraphs depending on a given set of conditions. For example, you could hide paragraphs depending on which state is being viewed. This can be very useful for an employee handbook where the rules in California are different from those in New York. One source document could serve both states. Paragraphs that are unique to New York might have the following Hide Paragraph formula:

```
@Environment("State") != "New York"
```

and paragraphs that are unique to California would use:

```
@Environment("State") != "California"
```

These formulas assume that some setup procedure created the State value in the NOTES.INI file. Notice that these formulas use the not equals operator (!=) so that the unique paragraphs are hidden if not displayed in that state.

You can also make paragraph visibility depend on a value in fields on the same document. For example, if someone over 65 is filling in a form, additional medical information may be needed. One possible hidden paragraph formula might be:

```
applicantAge <= 65
```

Again, the condition might be the opposite of what you expect to see. Remember that the formula evaluates to true if the paragraph is hidden. In this case, if the applicant is 65 or under, the paragraphs will not be seen.

Tip

Users can also hide paragraphs inside of Rich Text fields, if needed.

Insert Subform Formulas. Subforms are a good way to group a bunch of related fields together so that multiple forms can access them. This helps to keep form designs consistent. At times, you might want to dynamically determine which subform(s) to use with a given form. This is when the Insert Subform formula comes in handy.

An Insert Subform formula lets you dynamically determine the name of a subform to display in your form. It must evaluate to the name of an existing subform or a runtime error will result. This formula is run on the client.

Continuing with the inventory control system for your examples, you can use subforms to display different information depending on the inventory type. Your formula may look like:

```
@If(invType = "Medical"; "Medical Detail"; "Standard Detail")
```

Insert Subform formulas are only evaluated when the document is opened. If the basis for the condition (such as the inventory type) changes, you must close and reopen the document to reevaluate the Insert Subform formula.

Section Access Formulas. Sections let you group portions of a document together. When a section is collapsed, only a title shows. When expanded, the section contents are readable. Sections are a good way to organize information because you can group related information into one section.

In addition to a standard section, you can create an access-controlled section to limit who can edit the information in the section. This type of section uses a Section Access formula to control access.

> **Note**
>
> The Session Access formula specifies who can *edit* the section, not who can read it. In addition, the formula will not override the access control list of the database.

Section Access formulas must evaluate to a name or list of names. This formula will run on the client.

You can simply specify names explicitly in the formula, like this:

```
"Jane Doe" : "John Doe"
```

which restricts edit access to just those two users. Or you might want to use a view and the @DbColumn, like this:

```
@DbColumn(""; ""; "(View of Section Readers)"; 1)
```

which looks at the list of names in the first column of the View of Section Readers view in the current database.

The @Command, @IsDocBeingLoaded, @Modified, @PostedCommand, and @ViewTitle functions and the SELECT statement can't be used in Section Access formulas.

Section Title Formulas. A Section Title formula is used to determine what is displayed as the section title. The formula must either be a single field or evaluate to a text or numeric value.

If you use sections to collapse a series of fields, perhaps the education information in a personnel form, you could use a Section Title formula to display some key information in the title. For example, examine this formula:

```
"Education: (" + yrGraduated + ") " + @Left(collegeName; 25)
```

This formula might display Education: (1964) Rutgers University when evaluated. Pulling out the most important information in this way can make your forms easier to understand and appear less cluttered.

> **Tip**
>
> Users can also create sections inside of rich text fields and create their own section title formulas, if needed.

Window Title Formulas. Window Title formulas determine the text that is displayed as the title for each document that is viewed. The formula is evaluated on the client.

You might use a Window Title formula to display one title for new documents and another for existing documents. For example, if your database describes an animal

II

Designing Applications

patient at a veterinarian's clinic, you may want to use the title *New Patient* when the document is first composed, and then use a title with the pet's and owner's names when read later. The following formula accomplishes this task:

```
@If (@IsNewDoc; "New Patient"; patientName + " (" + ownerName + ")")
```

You can also make very complicated window title formulas. The next example will display `New Patient` for new documents, `patient (Owner)` for existing documents, and `patient (Unknown Owner)` for existing documents whose owner is unknown. It's a contrived example but the technique is useful nonetheless:

```
isFldThere = @IsAvailable(ownerName) & ownerName != ""
ifFldYes = patientName + " (" + ownerName + ")"
ifFldNo = patientName + " (Unknown Owner)"
@If(@IsNewDoc; "New Patient"; @If(isFldThere; ifSFldYes; ifFldNo))
```

The key element in this example is the first line:

```
isFldThere = @IsAvailable(ownerName) & ownerName != ""
```

which sets the variable `isFldThere` to `true` or `false`. The last line actually determines which text is displayed in the title.

Like Section Title formulas, the Window Title formula must either be a single field (except for rich text fields) or evaluate to a text or numeric value.

Field Formulas

Field level formulas are used to control what happens when buttons are clicked; they also determine default values, check for valid input and, in general, deal with things that happen when users are actively entering information into a document.

Default Value Formulas. Default value formulas enable you to specify the value that appears automatically in a field when a user composes a document.

A good example of a default value is a field that represents the current user's name. You could create a field called `lastEditor` with a default value formula of:

```
@UserName
```

The `@UserName` function equates to the name of the user reading or editing the document. Each time the document is edited, Notes inserts the user's name. If you want the keep the name of the original created, make the field computed-when-composed.

Another example a default value that is often used is a field that holds the current date. This is done by using the following function:

```
@Today
```

The `@Today` function returns the current date. When used in field level formulas, it is evaluated at the client.

Input Translation Formulas. Input translation formulas let you tell Notes to perform some type of automatic conversion on the information in a field. Notes executes the formula when the document is saved.

For example, you might want to make sure that all supervisors' names start with a capital letter and that the rest of the letters are lowercase. Notes has a function called @ProperCase that does this for you. Using it in an input translation formula would look like the following:

```
@ProperCase(supervisor)
```

When a user enters a value into this field in lowercase letters, @ProperCase provides the correct capitalization as the document is saved. For example, if the user enters the text "felemid mcfal," the above formula would convert it to "Felemid Mcfal."

Input Validation Formulas. Input validation formulas enable you to explain to Notes how to determine whether or not data entered by the user is valid. These formulas differ from other kinds of formulas because they answer only a yes or no question: Is the data valid?

Almost all input validation formulas contain an @If function that determines whether the field contains valid data. Two special functions, used exclusively in conjunction with input validation formulas, tell Notes whether the data is valid: @Success means the value in the field is acceptable; @Failure means that the value isn't acceptable.

Suppose that you have a field called partNumber, which should contain the number of a part for a product that your company produces. Part numbers always are supposed to be six characters long. You can use the @Length function to determine the length of the field, so the entire validation formula for the field may look like the following:

```
failMsg = "Part number must be 6 characters in length";
@If (@Length (partNumber) = 6; @Success; @Failure (failMsg))
```

The @If function determines whether the length of the partNumber field is six characters; if so, it signals to Notes (through the @Success function) that the data is valid. Otherwise, it uses the @Failure function to signal that the data is invalid. @Failure requires you to provide a description of the problem, which Notes displays as an error message (see fig. 13.8). Further, Notes doesn't let the user save the document until he or she fixes the problem (in this example, the user needs to make the part number six characters long).

You may have an opportunity to use the more complex form of the @If statement, because the data may not be acceptable for several reasons. Suppose that the part number must be six characters, *and* the first character must not be an X. This formula checks for both conditions and displays an appropriate message in either case, as you see from the following:

Designing Applications

```
msgNotSix := "Part number must be 6 characters in length";
msgX := "Part number must not begin with an X";
@If (@Length(PartNumber) != 6;
    @Failure(msgNotSix);
    Begins(PartNumber; "X"); @Failure(msgTwo); @Success)
```

Fig. 13.8

This is a sample error message produced through a validation formula.

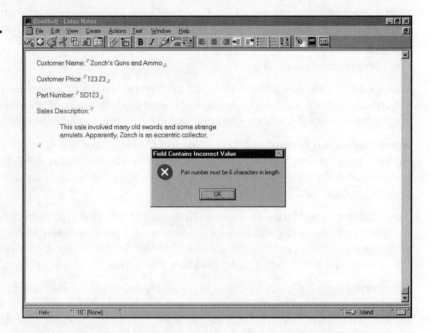

This formula tells Notes that if the length of the partNumber field isn't 6, the data is unacceptable; if the part number begins with an X, the data is unacceptable; otherwise, the data is acceptable. With this format, you can validate up to 99 separate conditions and print an appropriate error message for each possible problem.

The "Examples: @Environment, @SetEnvironment, and ENVIRONMENT" and the "Examples: @SetDocField" topics in the Notes online help system have more good examples of input validation formulas.

Computed Field Formulas. Document fields can be editable, computed, computed for display, and computed when composed. All of the computed field types need to have a formula associated with them. When evaluated, the result data type must agree with the data type of the field. A text value needs a formula that evaluates to the text string. A date field needs a formula that evaluates to a date.

For example, you might want a computed numeric field that calculates the sum of other document numeric fields. You could do this with the following formula:

```
monRevenue + tueRevenue + wedRevenue + thuRevenue + friRevenue
```

Unlike spreadsheets, there is no function to sum a series of numeric fields. You simply list each numeric field and add them together.

Keyword Field Formulas. Keyword fields are used to display a list from which a user can select the information that will be used in a field. The list can be explicitly created by the form designer or a formula can be used that will evaluate to a list.

One of the most common @functions used in keyword field formulas is @DbColumn, which is used to get a list of keywords from a column in a view. For example, to get a list of all dog breeds in your database you might use this formula:

```
@DbColumn(""; ""; "List of Dog Breeds"; 1)
```

Figure 13.9 shows this formula in use in an InfoBox that is reached by choosing Design, Field Properties when a field is selected.

Fig. 13.9

The Field Properties InfoBox shows the keyword value formula and its options.

If you check the Allow values not in list checkbox in the Field Properties InfoBox, then the user can add information to the list as needed. Otherwise, you'll need to create another way to update the view to add selections.

Tip

These dynamic lookups are very powerful and make creating lookup tables very easy to do. At least they'll be easy once you get the hang of it. However, dynamic lookups are *slow*. Don't use too many of them or your users will complain about poor response time.

Figure 13.10 shows the result of using this formula. Notice that to the right of the Dog Breed input field, there is a little down arrow button (immediately above the mouse pointer). When you click it, the Select Keywords dialog box is displayed.

From the Select Keywords dialog box, the user can select from the list or type a new one in the box at the bottom of the dialog box.

II

Designing Applications

Fig. 13.10

An example of a keyword field formula.

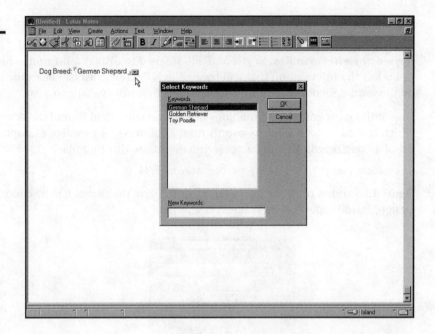

From Here...

In this chapter, you learned about formulas. You saw that a formula can be a numeric or string constant, a field name, or an expression. Formulas can have variables and keywords and consist of multiple lines.

At great deal of discussion was spent on where formulas can be used and examples of how to use them. This chapter, of course, just skims the surface of what you can do with formulas. When used creatively, there seems to be few limits.

To continue your exploration of formulas and Notes programmability, consider the following:

- Chapter 10, "Designing Forms," and Chapter 11, "Designing Views," refresh the basics if some of the examples were confusing.

- Chapter 14, "Formula Functions," discusses all of the @functions that you can use in formulas.

- Chapter 17, "Writing Scripts with LotusScript," talks about the next level of Notes programming.

- The Notes online help has good examples of each type of formula and keyword. Take advantage of the full text search capability to look for specific information that you need.

Formula Functions

Although you can do a lot with the constants, operators, and keywords discussed in Chapter 13, "Working with Formulas," the real power of formulas is in Notes' collection of functions. A *function* is a Notes operation that processes data and provides a value that you use in some way. Notes has numerous functions that can process data in many different ways, as you will learn in this chapter.

This chapter contains the following:

- A description of functions and how they are used
- A description of the @If function and how it is used to make choices inside formulas
- A listing of Notes @functions in alphabetic order
- Some function listings broken up into categories
- A listing of every @command keyword in alphabetic order

The two alphabetic listings are not meant to be comprehensive descriptions of the @functions and @command available in Notes. They are intended to be used as a reference.

Quite frequently, programmers find it useful to be able to browse the function reference without being tied to a computer. This chapter will give you that chance. You can look through the lists and get a feel for the vast amount of control that the @functions and @commands give to you.

Understanding Function Basics

At first glance, functions appear to be similar to fields in some ways. Like fields, functions have names, and when you use the name of the function in a formula, Notes finds a value for the function to use in evaluating the formula. However, a field represents data in a document, and a function represents an action that you are requesting Notes to perform.

In other words, when you ask Notes to find the value of a field, it will go look for that value in the database. When you ask Notes to find the value of a function, it will need to perform some task associated with that function. The @Today function requests Notes to find the current date. In order to determine the current date, Notes does not need to reference the database.

> ### Tip
>
> Function names are easy to distinguish from field names because all function names begin with an *at sign* (@), as in @Success or @Year.

Let's look at another example. Suppose that you defined a column with the formula

```
effectiveDate
```

which consists of a single field name. For each document, Notes fetches and displays the value of the effectiveDate field.

Compare that with the formula

```
@Created
```

which consists of a single function name. You can tell that @Created is a function because its name starts with @. @Created causes Notes to find the date that the document was created. So if you use this function in a column formula, Notes displays the date that each document was created. If you use this function in a default value formula, the creation date becomes the value of the field.

Function Arguments

Most functions require you to specify information with which they can work to produce a result. For example, if you want a function to determine what day of the week a certain date falls on, you must tell Notes exactly which date you are interested in.

The @Weekday function calculates the day of the week on which a date occurred; in order for this function to do its work, you must give it a date. Pieces of information that are required by functions are called *arguments*. Some functions, such as @Created, don't require any arguments, but most functions require a specific number and types of arguments, which you must provide in parentheses after the name of the function. In the case of @Weekday, you need to provide a single date argument. Consider the following formula, which might appear in the definition for a column:

```
@Weekday(effectiveDate)
```

The data in parentheses—the value of the effectiveDate field—is the data that @Weekday uses. @Weekday, in return, provides a number from 1 through 7, indicating a day of the week (Sunday through Saturday, respectively).

If a function requires more than one argument, you must list all the arguments inside the parentheses, separated by semicolons. Suppose that your documents contain a homePhone field, which you use to store home phone numbers with area codes. Suppose next that you want a column to display just the area code for each person. The @Left function enables you to extract characters from the left end of a text field. You must provide @Left with a text field and the number of characters you want. To display the leftmost three characters, for instance, enter the following:

```
@Left(HomePhone; 3)
```

Nesting Functions

You can use the result provided by one function as the data for another function to process, a technique called *nesting*. You have already seen that @Created gives you the date that a document was created, and @Weekday takes a date and tells you on what day of the week that date occurred. Thus, to display a number that represents the day of the week on which the document was created, you can write the following:

```
@Weekday(@Created)
```

Notes starts inside the parentheses and works its way out. @Created tells Notes to compute the date that the document was created; then @Weekday uses that date to compute the day of the week on which the creation occurred.

The *@If* Function

One of the most widely used functions is @If, which enables you to write a formula that chooses between several possible values based on the outcome of a question.

In its simplest form, the @If function returns one of two values. You supply a *condition expression*, a *true expression*, and a *false expression*. The first step that Notes takes is to evaluate the condition expression—it must evaluate to true or false. Next, one of the two other expressions is evaluated and its value becomes the return value of the @If function. If the condition evaluates to true, then the truth expression is evaluated. If the condition evaluates to false, then the false expression is evaluated.

For example, suppose that each document in a customer database contains a field named creditRating, which contains an A or B value. The A customers have credit limits of $10,000; the B customers have $3,000 limits. The following formula defines a column that displays the customer's credit rating:

```
@If(CreditRating = "A"; 10000; 3000)
```

Notice the three required parts:

- The first part is a condition that can be true or false. In this case, the condition asks whether the creditRating field is equal to A.

- The second part is the expression used if the condition is true; in this case, the value is 10000.

- The third part is the expression used if the condition is false; in this case, the value is 3000.

In effect, this function says if the value of the creditRating field is A, display the value 10000; otherwise, display 3000.

Now, suppose that each document in a database describes one of your customers, and has a field named areaCode which contains a customer's area code. Your courier considers every destination with a area code that starts with 328 to be local; all other destinations are long-distance calls, and thus are more expensive. In a column, you want to display either *Local* or *Long Distance*. Consider this function:

```
@If(@Left(areaCode; 3) = "328"; "Local"; "Long Distance")
```

This example is much trickier than the preceding example. The condition asks whether the first three digits of the area code are 328. If so, Notes displays Local; otherwise, it displays Long Distance.

The text constants in this example could be replaced with any Notes expression. This means that you could use field names, operators, and @functions to accomplish different tasks. For example:

```
localCost := .10
longCost := .30
@If(@Left(areaCode; 3) = "328";
    callTime * localCost;
    callTime * longCost)
```

In this example, the text constants have been replaced with expressions that represent the total cost of the phone call to the customer. If the phone call is local, then the first expression is evaluated. If the phone call is long distance, then the second expression is evaluated.

The Conditional Operators

Notes provides operators that you can use in the @If condition expression for comparing values. These are summarized in Table 14.1.

Table 14.1   The Conditional Operators

Operator	Description
=	is equal to
!=	is not equal to
=!	is not equal to (same as !=)
<>	is not equal to (same as !=)
><	is not equal to (same as !=)
<	is less than
<=	is less than or equal to
>	is greater than
>=	is greater than or equal to

You can also use predicate functions and logical operators in conditional expressions. See the "Predicate Functions" and "Logical Operators" sections that follow for more information.

For example, you can use the following formula in a column formula to alert you to customers who have spent too much:

```
@If (currentBalance > creditLimit; "Over Limit"; "")
```

This formula decides which of two values to display in the column. The formula asks whether the value of the currentBalance field is greater than the value of the creditLimit field; if so, Notes displays the value Over Limit; otherwise, Notes displays nothing, specified as two adjacent quotes with nothing in-between.

> **Note**
>
> The true expression and false expression can include any functions or combination of functions that you need. You are not limited to using constants as we have done in most of these examples.

The @If function has a related format that enables you to select from any number of values. In this format, the @If function includes any number of pairs of conditions and values. Notes begins checking conditions. As soon as Notes finds a condition that is true, the @If function selects the value that follows that condition.

Suppose that your company manufactures cameras. Throughout the course of its existence, the company has manufactured cameras with three different kinds of focusing mechanisms. All the cameras made before March 1981 were manual focus. After that date, manual cameras were discontinued, and all your factories produced cameras with fixed focus, except the Cleveland factory, which produced auto-focus cameras.

If each document in the database describes a camera and includes fields for the date and place of manufacture, you can define a column formula that displays the type of focus mechanism the camera uses:

```
@If (mfgDate < [3/1/91]; "Manual"; mfgSite != "Cleveland"; "Fixed"; "Auto")
```

This formula gives Notes the following orders: If the manufacture date is before 3/1/91, display Manual; otherwise, check the manufacture site—if it's not Cleveland, display Fixed; otherwise, display Auto.

Predicate Functions

Many Notes functions don't manipulate data, but instead examine data, testing for the existence of some condition. These functions—called *predicate functions*—are meant to be used with the @If function so that you can take some action if a specific condition exists.

For example, suppose that you want to change the title of a document to read:

```
Customer Complaint Meeting (James Owens)
```

when a user reads or edits a document. The first part of the title will be pulled from the document's `subject` field, and the name in parentheses will be the document author's name.

When a user first creates a document, however, the document doesn't have a subject, so a better title might include the words *New Document* with the author's name, as follows:

```
New Document (James Owens)
```

You can use the predicate function `@IsNewDoc` to distinguish between an existing document and one that is in the process of being created. By using the `@IsNewDoc` function as the condition of an `@If` function, you can construct one Notes formula to display either of the needed titles. The window title formula might look like this:

```
@If (@IsNewDoc; "New Document"; Subject) + " (" + @Author + ")"
```

This formula tells Notes to determine whether this document is new, and to display the phrase `New Document` if it's new, or the value of the `Subject` field if it isn't new. Onto that value, Notes should concatenate an opening parenthesis, the author's name, and a closing parenthesis. The resulting text becomes the title of the document window.

Logical Operators

In some situations, you may need to test for combinations of conditions. You can test for these combinations by combining individual conditions with one of two special operators.

The *And operator* (&) enables you to determine whether all of two or more conditions are true. For example, let's say that you want to determine which magazine subscribers are eligible for renewal so that you remember to contact them. One way to do this is to create a column formula that displays "Renewal" if their subscription expires this month and they have a good credit rating. The column formula might look like this:

```
@If (@Month(@Today) = renewalMonth & creditRating = "Good";
    "Renew";
    "")
```

This `@If` function has two conditions separated by the And operator. When evaluated, Notes selects one of two values to display: `Renew` or `""` (nothing). The `@Today` function returns today's date; the `@Month` function determines what month that date occurs in. Notes determines whether that month is equal to the value in the `renewalMonth` field. It also checks whether the `creditRating` field contains the value `Good`. For Notes to display `Renew`, both conditions must evaluate to true; otherwise, Notes displays nothing.

The *Or operator* (|) enables you to determine whether any of two or more conditions are true. Suppose that your rental car fleet database contains documents describing vehicles in your corporate fleet, and you want to display an asterisk (*) in a column if the vehicle is due for maintenance. Vehicles are scheduled for maintenance every 3,000 miles or if the driver complained of a problem during his last run. The column formula might look like this:

```
@If (currentMiles > lastServiceMiles + 3000 | complaint = "Y";
    "*";
     "")
```

This @If function selects between displaying an asterisk or displaying nothing. If the value in currentMiles is greater than lastServiceMiles plus 3000, or if the complaint field is equal to Y, Notes uses the asterisk—only one of the conditions has to be true.

The *Not operator* (!) changes true values to false and false values to true. Continuing with the rental car fleet example, let's say that you have a very rich peculiar customer who insists that her rented car be red in February and December and blue in all other months. The following formula will evaluate to either Blue or Red:

```
@If (customerName = "Morganna" &
    !(rentalMonth = "February" | rentalMonth = "December");
        "Blue" :
        "Red")
```

When trying to understand a complex statement like this, always start with the innermost parentheses. In this case, it means looking at the part about the rental months:

```
(rentalMonth = "February" | rentalMonth = "December")
```

This formula clause or fragment will evaluate to true if the rental month is either February or December. However, the original formula has a NOT (!) operator directly in front of this clause:

```
!(rentalMonth = "February" | rentalMonth = "December")
```

This reverses the value of the clause so that it will be true only if the rental month is *not* February or December.

Now, you can look at the next larger clause which checks the customer name. If the customer name is Morganna and it's not February or December, then the whole formula will evaluate to Blue—otherwise it will evaluate to Red.

Conditional expressions can get pretty complicated. But if you start in the middle and work your way outward, they can be understood one bit at a time.

Function Reference by Category

Notes includes more than a hundred functions. To help you organize them, this section groups the functions into different types. For example, some functions deal with text manipulation and others are mathematical.

Designing Applications

In order to save space, only the function names are listed here. The syntax and a brief description of each function is listed in the "Alphabetical Function Reference" section later in this chapter.

The User Environment

The *user environment* is the client computer unless the formula is being evaluated in the following situations: replication formula, agent whose trigger is If New Mail Has Arrived or On Schedule, selection formula, or column formula.

The following functions are useful when dealing with the user environment:

@MailDbName	@Name	@OptimizeMailAddress
@Password	@UserName	@UserRoles
@Version		

Defining Columns

Because column formulas and views can make up a large part of a Notes application, there are quite a few functions that are useful in defining columns:

@Begins	@Category	@DbCommand
@DbLookup	@DocChildren	@DocDescendants
@DocLength	@DocLevel	@DocNumber
@DocParentNumber	@DocSiblings	@DocumentUniqueID
@Elements	@Ends	@If
@InheritedDocumentUniqueID	@IsAvailable	@IsCategory
@IsExpandable	@IsNotMember	@Keyword
@Length	@Matches	@New
@NoteID	@Subset	@Unique
@UserRoles	@WhatIsUserAccess	@Word

Manipulating Dates and Times

Notes has several functions that let you manipulate date and time values. Functions such as @Month and @Day enable you to determine the parts of a date or time. @Adjust enables you to compute a time or date in the future or past—for example, you can compute the date 30 days from today. Most useful of all is @Today, which gives you today's date. This function is especially helpful as the default value formula of a date field, because it enables you to specify the current date as the initial value for a field when the user creates a document.

The following functions also are useful in dealing with dates and times:

@Accessed	@Adjust	@Created
@Date	@Day	@Hour
@Minute	@Modified	@Month
@Now	@Second	@Text
@Time	@Today	@Weekday
@Year	@Yesterday	@Zone

Working with the Selected Document

When writing formulas that act on the selected document the following functions are useful:

@All	@AllChildren	@AllDescendants
@AttachmentNames	@AttachmentLengths	@Author
@Attachments	@DeleteDocument	@DeleteField
@DocLength	@DocMark	@DocumentUniqueID
@InheritedDocumentUniqueID	@IsAvailable	@IsDocBeingEdited
@IsDocBeingLoaded	@IsDocBeingMailed	@IsDocBeingRecalculated
@IsDocBeingSaved	@IsNewDoc	@IsResponseDoc
@IsUnavailable	@MailSend	@NoteID
@Response	@SetField	@Unavailable

The DEFAULT, FIELD, and SELECT statements also are important when working with a selected document.

Manipulating Lists

The following functions are useful when dealing with lists:

@Elements	@Explode	@Implode
@IsMember	@IsNotMember	@Keywords
@Member	@Replace	@Subset
@Unique		

II

Designing Applications

Manipulating Numbers

Manipulating numbers is done by mathematical functions. For example, the @Max function returns the largest number from a list of parameters that you pass it.

Here is a list of the functions that are useful in dealing with numbers:

@Abs	@ACos	@Asin
@ATan	@ATan2	@Cos
@Exp	@Integer	@Log
@Ln	@Min	@Modulo
@Max	@Pi	@Power
@Random	@Round	@Sign
@Sin	@Sqrt	@Sum
@Tan	@Text	

Manipulating Text

Text functions enable you to manipulate text in various ways, and to convert data from text to another type, or vice versa. Earlier in this chapter, you learned about the @Left function, which enables you to extract the beginning portion of a text value. Other text functions enable you to check for the length of a field, manipulate text in various ways, and extract any portion of the field.

Suppose that a document requires the user to enter a part number in a field named partNumber. Letters in this field always are supposed to be in uppercase, but you want the user to be able to enter them in uppercase or lowercase. You can specify the following input translation formula:

```
@UpperCase (partNumber)
```

The following functions allow various types of text manipulation:

@Begins	@Contains	@Date
@Ends	@Explode	@Implode
@Left	@LeftBack	@LowerCase
@Middle	@MiddleBack	@ProperCase
@Replace	@Right	@RightBack
@Trim	@UpperCase	

Converting Data Types

When working with different data types, you frequently need to convert from one data type to another. For example, let's say that you have a time/date field that holds the order date of an invoice. And you would like to create a window title formula that shows the customer name and the year of the invoice. The window title, when finished, should look like this:

```
John Doe - 1996
```

Here is the formula that will accomplish this:

```
@ProperCase(customerName) + " - " + @Text(@Year(orderDate))
```

You've seen the `@ProperCase` function before—it makes sure that each word is capitalized. Let's concentrate on the right side of the formula. The `@Year` function looks at the `orderDate` field and extracts the year as a number date type. In order to concatenate it to the `customerName` field and the text constant, the year needs to be changed into a text data type. The `@Text` function does this for you.

> **Note**
>
> In order to create or edit a window title formula, you must first edit the associated form. Then in the programmer pane, select the form name in the Define drop-down list and the window title in the Event drop-down list.

The following functions allow various types of data type manipulation:

@Implode	@Explode	@Text
@TextToNumber	@TextToTime	@Time

Alphabetical Function Reference

Some functions presented in this chapter operate with features not discussed in this book. They are listed here, however, so that you will have a complete reference available as you learn about features beyond this book.

In addition, while the function parameters are shown, they are not explained. They are here simply to serve as a memory jogger. After you use a particular function a few times, the parameters should become self-explanatory.

The Notes online help for functions can be reached by choosing Help, Help Topics and then selecting Search in the Navigator pane.

> **Note**
>
> If you have not used the online help, the database might not be indexed for full text searching yet. You can index it by choosing File, Database, Properties, clicking on the Full Text tab, and then clicking Create Index.

At the search view, click the Display search bar action bar if the search bar is not displayed. Type the name of the function that you need help with, and press Enter. Notes displays a list of topics that mention the function.

II

Designing Applications

Function	Description
@Abs(*anyNumber*)	This function returns the absolute value of a number.
@Abstract([commands] ; size ; beginText ; "bodyFields ")	This function abbreviates the contents of one or more fields, controlled by 19 different commands. You could elect to abbreviate common words or remove vowels. This function only works with single-byte character sets.
@Accessed	This function returns the time and date when the document was last accessed, either for reading or editing. @Accessed is good in workflow databases to see how long it's been since someone did something with a document.
@Acos(*cosine*)	This function returns the arc (inverse) cosine.
@Adjust(*dateToAdjust* ; *year* ; *month* ; *day* ; *hour* ; *minute* ; *second*)	Adjusts the dateToAdjust parameter by the amounts in the year, month, day, hour, minute, and second parameters. The adjustment can be forward or backward in time. Use 0 for those parameters that you do not need.
@All	This function returns the value true. It is designed to be used with the SELECT statement.
@AllChildren	This function is designed to be used with the SELECT statement. For example, SELECT custName = "General Motors" | @AllChildren will select the set of documents with General Motors as the customer, and all immediate response documents.
@AllDescendents	This function is similar to the @AllChildren function except that response-to-response documents will also be selected.
@Ascii(*string* ; [AllInRange])	This function converts a string from LMBCS (Lotus Multi-Byte Character Set) to ASCII. The [AllInRange] option forces the return of a null string if the characters in the string parameter are not in the 32–127 ASCII range.
@Asin(*sine*)	This function calculates the arc (inverse) sine.
@Atan(*tangent*)	This function calculates the arc (inverse) tangent.
@Atan2(*x* ; *y*)	This function calculates the arc tangent using the tangent y/x of an angle.
@AttachmentLengths	This function returns the approximate length(s) of the document's attachment(s) as either a number or a number list.
@AttachmentNames	This function returns the filename(s) of the document's attachments as either a string or a string list.
@Attachments	This function returns the number of files attached to a document. You can use the column formula @If(@Attachments;5;0) to display a paper clip icon if you also check off the Display values as icons box in the Column Definition dialog box.
@Author	This function returns a text list containing the name(s) of the author(s) of the current document.
@Begins(string ; substring)	This function finds out whether a specified string is contained at the very beginning of another specified string, then returns a value of true if it's contained and false if it isn't. This function is case-sensitive.

Function	Description
@Certificate([*Variable*], Certificate)	This function pulls information from the encoded Certificate field in the Name & Address Book.
@Char(*codePageNumber*)	This function converts an IBM Code Page 850 code number (any number between 0 and 255) into a corresponding display character.
@Command([*command*] ; *parameters*)	This function executes a Notes command. It will not work in column, selection, hide-when, section editor, window title, field, or form formulas, or in agents that run on a server.
@Contains(*string* ; *substring*)	This function finds out whether *substring* is contained anywhere within *string*. It returns a value of true if it is contained and false if it is not present. *Substring* can be a text list, in which case, all elements of the list are tested to see if they are contained anywhere within *string*.
@Cos(*angle*)	This function calculates the cosine of an angle.
@Created	This function returns the time and date a document was created.
@Date([*time-date*])	This function accepts the individual components of dates and times, and converts them into the Notes time-date data type.
@Day(*timeDateValue*)	This function extracts the date from the *timeDateValue* parameter. For example, @Day("[09-20-96]") would evaluate to 20.
@DbColumn(ODBC : NoCache ; *data_source* ; *user_ID1* : *user _ ID2* ;"*password1*" : "*password2*" ; table ; column : null_handling ; Distinct : sort)	This function looks up and returns an entire column of values from a view or folder in either the active database or another Notes database.
@DbCommand(ODBC : NoCache ; *data_source* ; user_ID1 : user_ID2 ; "password1" : "password2" ; *command_string* : null_handling)	This function uses information from the ODNC.INI file to activate an ODBC driver and pass the *command_string* to the *data_source* database. It returns the data sent back from the database.
@DbExists(*server* : *file*)	This function checks to see if a given database file exists on a server. *Server* is the name of the server where the database should reside. Use an empty string ("") when checking for a local database. *File* is the path and filename of the database file.
@DbLookup(ODBC : NoCache ; *data_source* ; *user_ID1* : *user_ID2* ; "*password1*" : "*password2*" ; *table* ; *column* : *null_handling* ; *key_column* ; *key* ; Distinct : *sort*)	This function retrieves information from a Notes database or uses information from the ODBC.INI file to activate an ODBC driver and retrieve information based on the *table* and *column* parameters.
@DbManager	This function returns a list of the users, groups, and servers who have Manager access for the specified database. In a window title formula, only the first item in the list is returned.

II

Designing Applications

(continues)

(continued)

Function	Description
@DbName	This function returns a text list with two elements: the name of the current Notes server and the path and filename of the database. If the database is local the server name will be the null string ("").
@DbTitle	This function returns the title of the current database.
@DDEExecute(*conversationID* ; *command*)	This function, which is only available in Windows and OS/2, passes *command* to the DDE application specified by *conversationID*.
@DDEInitiate(*application* ; *topic*)	This function, which is only available in Windows and OS/2, starts a DDE conversion.
@DDEPoke(*conversationID* ; *location* ; *data*)	This function, which is only available in Windows and OS/2, places data into *location* inside the DDE application specified by *conversationID*.
@DDETerminate (*conversationID*)	This function, which is only available in Windows and OS/2, ends a conversion with a DDE application.
@DeleteDocument	This function, typically used in agents, deletes the current document.
@DeleteField	This function, typically used in agents, deletes the selected field. For example, FIELD oldField:=@DeleteField.
@DialogBox(*form* ; [AutoHorzFit] : [AutoVertFit])	This function displays a form inside a dialog box. The users then interact with the new form. When done, they return to the original form and continue working with it. This function does not work in column or selection formulas, or in agents that run on a server (mail and scheduled agents).
@Do(*expressions*)	This function evaluates expressions left to right. The last expression evaluated becomes the return value of the @Do expression. This function does not work in column or selection formulas. It typically is used to execute or evaluate multiple expressions from within another function, such as the @If function.
@DocChildren(*zero-string* ; *one-string* ;*defaultString*)	This function returns a string that represents the number of direct descendant entries of the current document or category in a view. Response-to-response documents are not counted. This function works only in column and window title formulas.
@DocDescendants(zero-string ; one-string ;defaultString)	This function returns a string representing the total number of descendant entries of the current document or category in a view. This function works only in column and window title formulas.
@DocFields	This function returns a list of all fields in the current document.
@DocLength	This function returns the approximate size of a document in bytes.
@DocLevel	This function returns the level of the document or category number. This function works only in column and window title formulas.

Function	Description
@DocMark([NoUpdate])	When used in an agent formula, this function indicates if changes made to a document should be saved. Using the [Update] parameter tells Notes that changes should be saved. The [NoUpdate] parameter tells Notes not to save the changes.
@DocNumber("")	This function returns the entry number of a view entry, and only works only in column and window title formulas. For example, 1.4 indicates that the document is the fourth entry under the first entry.
@DocParentNumber("")	This function returns the entry number of the parent document. The parent document can be another document or a category (in a categorized view). This function works only in column and window title formulas.
@DocSiblings	This function returns the number of entries at the level of the current entry (either a document or a category). The number returned includes the document itself. For example, if the current document has an @DocNumber of 3.3, and 3.1, 3.2, and 3.4 also exist, then there are four document siblings, and 4 is returned.
@DocumentUniqueID	This function returns a 32-character string that uniquely identifies the document. If two documents have the same ID, they are replicas of one another.
@Domain	This function returns the current Notes domain of the user.
@DoesDbExit()	While Test Build 3 does have documentation for this function, Notes will not recognize its use. Please use the @DbExists function instead.
@Elements(list)	The function returns the number of text, number, or time-date values in a list.
@Ends(string ; substring)	This function finds out whether *substring* is contained at the very end of *string*; the function returns true if it is at the end, and false if it is not at the end.
@Environment (variable ; value)	This function sets or returns an environment variable stored in the NOTES.INI file. The variable parameter can be a string or a string list. The @SetEnvironment function and ENVIRONMENT keyword perform the same tasks as @Environment.
@Error	This function lets you establish an error condition (@ERROR) within an expression; this is ideal for identifying a data-entry error in a field. You must use the @IsError function to test for the @ERROR condition.
@Exp(power)	This function raises e (roughly 2.718282) to power. This operation is useful in scientific calculations. The *power* argument is limited to 14 decimal places.
@Explode(string ; separator ; includeEmpties)	This function returns a list composed of the elements of *string*. The *string* parameter is broken into elements based on spaces between words or the *separator* parameter. @Explode is the opposite of the @Implode function.

II

Designing Applications

(continues)

(continued)

Function	Description
@Failure(string)	This function, mainly used in input validation formulas, displays *string* as an error message. It is used to check for valid data, and to make a field entry required.
@False	This function returns the number 0. It is equivalent to the @No function.
@GetDocField(documentUNID ; fieldName)	This function returns the value of *fieldName* in the document specified by *documentUNID*. Frequently, the special variable $Ref is used as the *documentUNID* parameter to refer to the parent of the current document.
@Hour(timeDateValue)	This function returns the hour, extracted from the *timeDateValue* parameter.
@If(condition1 ; action1 ; condition2 ; action2 ; ... ; condition99 ; action99 ; else_action)	This function evaluates the condition expressions; if one evaluates to true, the action immediately after that condition is performed, and the @If statement ends. Otherwise, the else action is performed.
@Implode(textlistValue ; separator)	This function returns a string consisting of the concatenation of all members of the *textlistValue* list. It is the opposite of the @Explode function.
@InheritedDocumentUniqueID	This function returns the parent's unique ID.
@Integer(numberValue)	This function truncates numbers (to get the integer value) by dropping any decimal places. The *numberValue* parameter can be either a number or a number list, and will return either a number or a number list.
@IsAgentEnabled(agent)	This function returns true if the scheduled *agent* is enabled. This function does not work in column or selection formulas.
@IsAvailable(fieldName)	This function checks documents and returns true if *fieldName* exists, false if it does not exist.
@IsCategory(trueString ; falseString)	This function returns *trueString* if any item in the current row of the view is defined as a category; otherwise, *falseString* is returned. This function is intended for use only in column formulas.
@IsDocBeingEdited	This function returns true if the current document is being edited, false if not. This function does not work in column, selection, agent, form, or view action formulas.
@IsDocBeingLoaded	This function returns true if the current document is being loaded into memory for display, false if not. This function does not work in SmartIcon, button, selection, column, agent, section editor, hotspot, form action, or view action formulas.
@IsDocBeingMailed	This function returns true if the document is being mailed, false if not. This function does not work in column, selection, agent, window title, form, or view action formulas. It is useful when tracking the number of times a document has been mailed or forwarded.

Function	Description
@IsDocBeingRecalculated	This function returns true if the current document is being recalculated, false if not. It does not work in column, selection, agent, window title, form, or view action formulas.
@IsDocBeingSaved	This function returns true if the current document is being saved, false if not. It does not work in column, selection, agent, window title, form, or view action formulas.
@IsError(*value*)	This function returns true if *value* is an @Error value, false if not. For example, the formula @IsError(1/0) returns true because you cannot divide by zero.
@IsExpandable(*trueString* ; *falseString*)	This function returns trueString (or + if no parameters are specified) if the row in a view can be expanded. This function only works in column formulas.
@IsMember(*textListValue1* ; *textListValue2*)	This function returns true if the first parameter is contained in the second parameter. This function is case-sensitive. When processing lists, *textListValue1* must be a subset of *textListValue2* in order for true to be returned.
@IsNewDoc	This function returns true if a document has not yet been saved to disk, false if it has.
@IsNotMember(*textListValue1* ; *textListValue2*)	This function is the opposite of the @IsMember function.
@IsNumber(*value*)	This function returns true if *value* is a number or number list, false if not.
@IsResponseDoc	This function returns true if the current document is a response document, false if not. New documents have no type, so false is returned for them.
@IsText(*value*)	This function returns true if *value* is a string or string list, false if not.
@IsTime(*value*)	This function returns true if *value* is a time-date or time-date list, false if not.
@IsUnavailable(*fieldName*)	This function returns true if *fieldName* exists in the current document, false if it does not exist.
@Keywords(*textList1* ; *textList2* ; *separator*)	This function returns the intersection of two lists. Any items in *textList2* that are also in *textList1* are returned. This function is case-sensitive.
@Left(*stringToSearch* ; *subString*)	This function returns either the first *numberOfChars* characters of *stringToSearch* or all the characters in *stringToSearch* that are to the left of *subString*. For example, @Left("53: Testing"; 2) returns 53, and @Left("53: Testing"; ":") returns 53. Even though the arguments are different, the result is the same.
@LeftBack(*stringToSearch* ; *startString*)	This function starts at the end of a string and either chops off *numToSkip* characters from the tail of *stringToSearch* or searches *stringToSearch* for *startString* backward from the tail. If startString is found, everything to its left is returned.

II

Designing Applications

(continues)

(continued)

Function	Description
@Length(*stringlist*)	This function returns the length of *string*, or a number list containing the lengths of each member of *stringlist*.
@Like(*string* ; *pattern* ; *escape*)	This function returns true if *string* matches *pattern*, false if not. It conforms to the ANSI SQL standard. The *escape* parameter can be used to mark wild-card characters in pattern so that Notes will ignore them (this is called *escaping* the characters). For example, @Like("_TEST_"; "/%/_"; "/") uses the / character to escape the underscore wild-card character.
@Ln(*number*)	This function returns the natural logarithm of *number*. The *number* parameter must be greater than zero. @Ln is the inverse of @Exp.
@Log(*number*)	This function returns the common logarithm of *number*. The *number* parameter must be greater than zero. @Log is the reciprocal of scientific notation.
@LowerCase(*string*)	This function converts the uppercase letters in *string* to lowercase letters.
@MailDbName	This function returns the name of the Notes server and Mail database of the current user. It does not work in column formulas. The returned value is formatted as a two–item text list specifying the Server;Directory\Database.NSF. For example, NOTESMAIL;LEGAL\DLEE.NSF.
@MailSend(*sendTo* ; *copyTo* ; *blindCopyTo* ; *subject* ; *remark* ; "*bodyFields*" ; [*flags*])	This function mails the current document or composes a new memo to be mailed using the parameters that you supply. It does not work in column, selection, hide-when, or window title formulas.
@Matches(*string* ; *pattern*)	This function returns true if *string* and *pattern* match, false if not. The *pattern* parameter can contain wild-card characters. The ? wild-card character can match any single character in *string*. The * wild-card character can match any sequence of characters in *string*. You can use the \ character to escape the wild-card characters, which means that Notes will view them as normal characters instead of wild-cards.
@Max(*number1* ; *number2*)	This function returns the larger of *number1* and *number2*. The parameters can be numbers or number lists. For example, @Max(10; 15) returns 15, and @Max(32:12:67; 5:100:45) returns 32;100;67. If the list lengths are mismatched, the last element of the shortest list will be repeated for each element of the longer list.
@Member(*value* ; *stringlist*)	This function returns the position of *value* in *stringlist*. If *value* is not contained in *stringlist*, 0 is returned.
@Middle(*string* ; *startString* ; *numberchars*)	This function returns a substring of *string*. The starting point is either *offset* or one position after the end of *startString*. The ending point is either *numberchars* after the beginning or wherever *stopString* is found.
@MiddleBack(*string* ; *startString* ; *numberchars*)	This function returns a substring of *string*. Unlike @Middle, it starts searching and counting from the tail of *string*.

Function	Description
@Min(*number1* ; *number2*)	This function returns the smaller of *number1* and *number2*. The parameters can be numbers or number lists. For example, @Min(10; 15) returns 10, and @Min(32:12:67; 5:100:45) returns 5;12;45.
@Minute(*timeDateValue*)	This function returns the minute, extracted from the *timeDateValue* parameter.
@Modified	This functions returns the time-date when the document was last modified and saved. This function does not work in mail agent, paste agent, hide-when, section editor, or form formulas.
@Modulo(*number1* ; *number2*)	This function returns the remainder of *number1* divided by *number2*. The parameters can be numbers or number lists.
@Month(*timeDateValue*)	This function returns the month, extracted from the *timeDateValue* parameter.
@Name([*action*] ; *name*)	This function lets you manipulate hierarchical names.
@NewLine	This function inserts a carriage return into a text string. This function does not work in column, selection, hide-when, window title, form, or @prompt formulas.
@No	This function returns the number 0. It is equivalent to the @False function.
@NoteID	This function returns the ID number of the current document.
@Now	This function returns the current time-date. It does not work in form formulas.
@OptimizeMailAddress (*address*)	This function returns *address* with all unneeded domains removed.
@Password(*string*)	This function returns an encrypted version of *string*. It is often used in input translation formulas.
@Pi	This function returns pi, or 3.14159265358979, accurate to 15 decimal places.
@PickList([Name])	This function displays a dialog box with a view, or with all available Name & Address books. When a view is displayed, the function returns a column value. When the Name & Address books are displayed, the function returns the names that are selected. This function does not work in column, selection, mail agent, scheduled agent, hide-when, window title, or form formulas.
@Platform	This function returns the name of the currently running platform version of Notes.
@PostedCommand([*command*] ; *parameters*)	This function executes a Notes command after the rest of the formula has been evaluated. It emulates the way that Notes R3 evaluated Notes commands. All the standard menu commands can be used, and several specialized commands are available. See the "@PostedCommand Commands" section later in this chapter. This function does not work in column, selection, hide-when, section editor, window title, field, or form formulas, or in agents that run on a server.

(continues)

II

Designing Applications

(continued)

Function	Description
@Power(*base* ; *exponent*)	This function returns base raised to the power indicated by exponent.
@Prompt([*style*] : [No Sort] ; *title* ; *prompt* ; *defaultChoice* ; *choiceList*)	This function displays a dialog box, and returns the user's response. This function does not work in column, selection, mail agent, or scheduled agent formulas.
@ProperCase(*string*)	This function converts the words in *string* to proper-name capitalization: the first letter of each word is uppercase, all other letters are lowercase.
@Random	This function returns a random number between 0 and 1, inclusive. You can use (y - x)*@Random + x to generate a random number between any two numbers x and y.
@Repeat(*string* ; *number* ; *numberchars*)	This function returns a string that contains *string* repeated *number* times. If the *numberchars* parameter is present, the resulting string is truncated to *numberchars* length (if needed). In any case, the resulting string can't be longer than 1,024 characters.
@Replace(*sourcelist* ; *fromlist* ; *tolist*)	This function performs find-and-replace operations on a string list. The *sourcelist* is scanned for items in *fromlist*; if they're found, they are replaced by items in *tolist*.
@ReplaceSubstring (*sourceList* ; *fromList* ; *toList*)	This function replaces specific words or phrases in a string with new words or phrases that you specify. This function is case-sensitive.
@Responses	This function returns the number of responses for a document. Only responses in the current view are counted. @Responses works only in window title formulas.
@Return(*value*)	This function immediately stops the evaluation of a formula, and returns *value*.
@Right(*stringToSearch* ; *subString*)	This function returns either the rightmost *numberOfChars* characters of *stringToSearch*, or all characters in *stringToSearch* to the right of *subString*.
@RightBack(*stringToSearch* ; *subString*)	This function works exactly like @Right except that it starts counting or searching from the tail of *stringToSearch*.
@Round(*number* ; *factor*)	This function rounds *number* to the nearest whole integer. The *number* parameter can be a number or a number list. The *factor* parameter, if present, acts as a rounding factor.
@Second(*timeDateValue*)	This function returns a number of seconds, extracted from the *timeDateValue* parameter.
@Select(*number* ; *values*)	This function returns the value in the *number* position of the *values* parameter. The *values* parameter can be any number of values separated by semi-colons—including numbers, strings, time/dates, or lists. For example, @select(3; "One"; 2; 3 : 3; "[04-04-96]") would evaluate to the list 3 : 3.

Function	Description
@Set(*variableName* ; *value*)	This function assigns value to a temporary variable, *variableName*. It is intended for use within another function, such as @If or @Do. Before you use a variable, it must have been declared in the formula. You can do this by assigning it a null value in the beginning of the formula, like this: TemporaryVariable:=.
@SetDocField(*documentUNID* ; *fieldName* ; *newValue*)	This function sets the value of *fieldName* in the document specified by *documentUNID*. Frequently, the special variable $Ref is used as the *documentUNID* parameter to refer to the parent of the current document. This function does not work in column or selection formulas.
@SetEnvironment (*variableName* ; *value*)	This function sets or returns an environment variable stored in the NOTES.INI file. The *variable* parameter can be a string or a string list. The @Environment function and ENVIRONMENT keyword perform the same tasks as @SetEnvironment.
@SetField("*fieldName*" ; *value*)	This function sets *fieldName*, which is stored in a document, to *value*. It is intended for use inside other functions. This function does not work in column, selection, hide-when, window title, or form formulas. Before you use a variable, it must have been declared in the formula. You can do this with: FIELD Fieldname:=Fieldname.
@Sign(*signedNumber*)	This function returns –1 if *signedNumber* is negative, 0 if *signedNumber* is zero, and 1 if *signedNumber* is positive.
@Sin(*angle*)	This function returns the sine of *angle* accurate to 15 decimal places. The *angle* parameter is expressed in radians.
@Soundex(*string*)	This function returns the Soundex code for a specified string. It is useful when searching for information that sounds like *string*.
@Sqrt(*number*)	This function returns the square root of *number*. The *number* parameter must be positive.
@Subset(*list* ; *number*)	This function returns *number* items from *list*. If *number* is negative, Notes starts counting from the end of *list*. For example, @Subset("A":"B":"C":"D":"E"; 2) returns "A";"B", and @Subset("A":"B":"C":"D":"E"; –2) returns "D";"E". The @Implode function can be used to convert the resulting list into a string suitable for displaying.
@Success	This function always returns true. You can use @Success with the @If function in input validation formulas to indicate success.
@Sum(*numbers*)	This function returns the summation of the *numbers* parameter, which can be a number or a number list. For example, @Sum(5 : 5; 10 : 10) sums the two lists and returns 30, while @Sum(annualResults) sums the contents of the annualResults field. The "Examples: @Sum" topic in the Notes help database shows how to sum a column.

(continues)

II

Designing Applications

(continued)

Function	Description
@Tan(*angle*)	This function returns the tangent of *angle*. The *angle* parameter is expressed in radians.
@Text(*value* ; "*format-string*")	This function returns a string that consists of *value* converted into a text string using *format-string* as a guide.
@TextToNumber(*string*)	This function returns a number by converting *string* into a number, where possible. It is useful for converting a text field into a number that can be used in a calculation. For example, @TextToNumber("10") would evaluate to a value of 10. However, @TextToNumber("TEN") would evaluate to a value of @Error.
@TextToTime(*string*)	This function returns a time-date by converting *string* into a time-date value, where possible. It is useful for converting a text field into a time-date that can be used in a calculation. Like the @TextToNumber function, the @Error value is returned when the string can't be converted.
@Time(*year* ; *month* ; *day* ; *hour* ; *minute* ; *second*)	This function returns a time created by converting the individual parameter components into a time-date value. The *year*, *month*, and *day* parameters are ignored if present.
@Today	This function returns the current date as a time-date value.
@Tomorrow	This function returns tomorrow's date as a time-date value.
@Trim(*string*)	This function returns a string created by removing all leading, trailing, and redundant spaces from *string*. If *string* is a list, then any blank elements are removed before *string* is returned.
@True	This function returns 1. It is equivalent to the @Yes function.
@Unavailable	This function has no return value. It is used to make a field unavailable for use, in this way: FIELD fieldName = @Unavailable Use the @IsUnavailable function to check availability status. Be careful when using this function because if you mistype the field name you might cause unpredictable results in your databases.
@Unique(*textlist*)	This function returns a random, unique text value, or else removes duplicate values from *textlist*. This function is case-sensitive.
@UpperCase(*string*)	This function converts all lowercase letters in *string* to uppercase letters.

Function	Description
@UserName	This function returns the current user or server name.
@UserPrivileges	This function returns a text list of the current user's privileges. It returns only the position of each privilege in the privilege list, not the name of the privilege. This function does not work in column, selection, mail agent, or scheduled agent formulas.
@UserRoles	This function returns a list of roles for the current user. It only works on databases residing on a server—local databases return a null list. This function does not work in column, selection, mail agent, or scheduled agent formulas.
@V2If(*condition1* ; *action1* ; *condition2* ; *action2* ; *condition99* ; *action99* ; *else_action*)	This function performs the same actions as the @If function. The @V2If function is needed if some of your users use Notes R2 or you have old databases that were never updated.
@Version	This function returns the build number of Notes. For example, it returns 114 under Notes R3, and 116 under Notes v3.0c. This function does not work in column, selection, mail agent, or scheduled agent formulas.
@ViewTitle	This function returns the name of the current view. Aliases and synonyms are returned in a list. This function does not work in column, selection, mail agent, paste agent, scheduled agent, section editor, window title, or field formulas.
@Weekday(*timeDateValue*)	This function returns a number from 1 (Sunday) through 7 (Saturday) that indicates the correct weekday for timeDateValue.
@WhatIsUserAccess (*server* : *file*)	This function returns the current user's level of access to the database. This function does not work in column or selection formulas, or in agents that run on a server (mail and scheduled agents).
@Word(*string* ; *separator* ; *number*)	This function returns a specified word from a text string. The word is defined as a part of a string that is separated from other parts of the string by a defined separator.
@Year(*timeDateValue*)	This function returns the year, extracted from the *timeDateValue* parameter.
@Yes	This function always returns 1. It is equivalent to the @True function.
@Yesterday	This function returns yesterday's date as a time-date value.
@Zone(*timeDateValue*)	This function returns the time zone settings of the current computer if no parameter is specified. If a parameter is specified than the time zone of *timeDateValue* will be returned.

II

Designing Applications

@Command and *@PostedCommand* Action List

In addition to the functions already discussed, you have a couple of other functions at your disposal. You can access any of Notes' menu options through the @Command and @PostedCommand functions.

Both @Command and @PostedCommand can handle the same actions—the key difference is when the actions are performed. @Command performs an immediate action in the Notes environment, while @PostedCommand defers actions until the end of the formula.

From Here...

This chapter discussed function basics, including how functions operate, how to call functions, and what arguments to pass to specific functions. The chapter also suggested broad categories of functions so that you could begin to make sense of the large numbers of functions available in Notes.

Much of the chapter was devoted to an alphabetical function reference. This section should serve you well in the future when you know that a function exists but have forgotten what it is called or what its arguments are.

Any true Lotus Notes guru spends much time learning formulas and functions. The wealth of functions and @command actions that Notes provides can keep you busy learning them for months. Don't try to memorize the list, though—you'll find that learning as the need arises allows you to view Notes as a less intimidating environment.

When you are ready to tackle some more challenging stuff, take a look at the following:

- Chapter 16, "LotusScript: A Whole New Programming Language," gives you more information about programming.
- Chapter 22, "Notes: Under the Hood," provides an understanding of what happens internally when you run Notes.

CHAPTER 15

Buttons and Agents

The world is filled with buttons these days! They've changed our lives. My stereo, TV, VCR, and tape deck all have them. Four remotes controlling one component each. Each one with a dozen buttons creating clutter on my table. Then one day, I saw it at the electronics store...the smart remote! Yes, it too had buttons but I could program these to do the things I wanted. Salvation!

The idea of these user programmable buttons has spread to computer programs. While buttons aren't new to Notes, the way they're programmed and the things you can do with them have been enhanced with a new interface and LotusScript functionality.

In Notes Release 4, there's more flexibility than ever before in defining tasks or executing script programs. Behind a button may be some quite complex code, yet the user is presented with a simple, non-intimidating interface. But programmability can have a downside, which we'll discuss in the chapter.

Agents allow you to automate daily tasks or to build powerful tools that you may use to execute complex programs. Users of previous versions of Notes will recognize the similarity of the Agent Builder window with that of the Macro Design window from Notes 3.x. Basically, agents are macros, but more powerful and updated to include the new LotusScript capabilities.

> **Tip**
>
> If you've recently migrated to Release 4 of Notes, you may want some assistance in converting your knowledge of Release 3.x menus to the current version. Choosing Help, Release 3 Menu Finder will activate a stay-on-top window showing the conversions in a display window as you click the familiar Release 3 menu interface.

Don't be intimidated by the idea of automating your database applications. After working with buttons and agents for awhile on local databases, you'll be ready to begin adding them to some production databases. In this chapter, you'll learn basic concepts and some advanced tips that you can begin using today. This chapter covers the following:

- Types of agents
- Creating and naming agents
- Programming agents
- Selecting documents
- Running agents
- Building search queries
- Buttons and hotspots
- Testing your creations

Understanding Agents

Thirty years ago the media was full of predictions about the future. We were supposed to be flying around with jetpacks while machines took care of those pesky manual tasks like cooking dinner and cleaning the house. Computers were going to make work easy and paperless, remember? I don't have a jetpack yet and still cook and clean for myself. Although my computer *is* helping me do more work, I'm still buried in paper.

Perhaps programmable agents are the beginning of that future. Agents can automate daily tasks, help you organize yourself and keep you better informed. Agents carry out your instructions, pull information from other sources, and file it away until you need it. You can use them to answer mail and let others know you're flying off on your jetpack for a few days of rest and relaxation.

Agents can be run manually from the Notes menu, can be scheduled to execute on their own, can run in response to a database event (such as new mail being received), or can run at the touch of a button.

The type of agent that a user creates depends upon their access level (determined by the database's ACL) and their intended audience.

Public Agents

Public, or *shared*, *agents* are meant to be run by other users and are typically created by administrators and application designers. An example might be an agent that automatically searches a sales contract database, sending a reminder to the appropriate salesperson of clients with an approaching contract renewal date.

To create a public agent, you must have at least Designer access to the database. In order to run an agent, you must have at least Reader access. Agents are sensitive to the access level of the user and do not allow them to perform tasks they wouldn't be able to do manually.

Agents are stored within the database in which they are created. In order for Notes to activate an agent, the database must be stored in the Notes data directory (usually C:\NOTES\DATA) or one of its subdirectories on the computer where the database is kept. Directory links, which are text files pointing to data storage locations other than the Notes data directory, can be utilized; however, that link file must be stored in the Notes data directory.

> **Note**
>
> Once an agent is designated as public or private, that designation cannot be changed. If you create a private agent and want to make it public (or shared) later, you'll need to create a new agent and designate it as shared. A public agent is designated by selecting the Shared Agent checkbox in the Agent Builder window.

Private Agents

Users, with ACL access below Designer, can create agents for their own use. These private agents are stored in the database, and may act on their own computer or on public databases.

You might want to create a private agent, for example, to organize your mail database or copy documents from a public database to a newsletter database.

A user must have at least Reader access to a database to run an agent. Private agents can't carry out a task that the user wouldn't be able to do manually in a given database. For example, an agent cannot update a document if the user doesn't have, at least, Editor access to the database.

Creating Agents

With Designer or better access to a database, you can create both public and private agents. If you have Editor, Author, or Reader access, you are limited to creating private agents. Agents can be created in one of three ways:

- You can copy an agent that performs a function similar to the one you require from the same database you're designing.

- You can copy an agent from another database.

- You can create an agent from scratch using the Agent Builder window reached through the Create, Agent menu choices. Again, you need Designer or better access to create public (or shared) agents and at least Reader access to create agents for your own use.

The following sections cover each method.

Copying an Agent in the Current Database

To copy an agent from the current database, follow these steps:

1. Choose View, Agents and highlight the agent you want to copy.

II

Designing Applications

2. Choose Edit, Copy; press Ctrl+C, or use the Edit Copy SmartIcon.

3. Choose Edit, Paste; press Ctrl+V; or use the Edit Paste SmartIcon. Notice that the copied agent will have the name "Copy Of *agentname*."

4. Double-click the newly pasted agent to open the Agent Builder window. Edit the agent to fit your needs. If you have Designer level access and want to create a shared agent, select the Shared Agent checkbox in the Agent Builder window.

5. Press Escape and choose Yes to save your changes.

Copying an Agent from Another Database

To copy an agent from another database, follow these steps:

1. Highlight the icon of the database containing the agent you want to copy and choose View, Agents.

2. Highlight the agent you want to copy and choose Edit, Copy; press Ctrl+C; or use the Edit Copy SmartIcon.

3. Press Esc to close the database.

4. Open the database you want to paste the agent into.

5. Choose View, Agents.

6. Choose Edit, Paste; press Ctrl+V; or use the Edit Paste SmartIcon.

7. Double-click the newly pasted agent to open the Agent Builder window. Edit the agent to fit your needs. If you have Designer level access and want to create a shared agent, select the Shared Agent checkbox in the Agent Builder window.

8. Press Esc to close the database and choose Yes to save it.

If you copy an agent from a database that is a design template, you'll be asked if you want to accept future design updates (see fig. 15.1). Choose Yes if you want to receive design updates from the original template. Choose No if you want to update it yourself. See Chapter 9, "Creating New Databases," for more information on working with database template files.

Fig. 15.1

Agents copied from databases designated as a template can be updated automatically when those in the template are changed or updated.

It is possible to change this option later. To accept or deny changes to an agent after it has been created, follow these steps:

1. Click the agent name.

2. Choose Agent, Agent Properties; or right-click the agent name and choose Agent Properties. The Agent Properties InfoBox appears.

3. Click the Design tab in the InfoBox (see fig. 15.2).

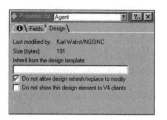

Fig. 15.2

Choose the Design tab in the Agent Properties InfoBox to change template update choices.

4. Choose the Do not allow design refresh/replace to modify option.

> **Note**
>
> You may also want to erase the template name from the Inherit from the design template field to ensure the reference is gone. However, this will also prevent you from changing your mind again in the future.

5. Close the Agent Properties InfoBox.

In Chapter 9, you learned that Notes ships with example databases that can be used as templates for new databases. These databases are also an excellent place to find agents that you can use in other databases you create.

To access the template databases that are available to you, choose File, Database, New from the menu or press Ctrl+N. Notes will display the New Database dialog box which allows you to choose the destination of the new database as well as designate a Title and File Name (see fig. 15.3). You can also choose templates from another server if there isn't one available locally that appears useful. Enable the Show advanced templates checkbox in the New Database dialog box to see additional template files.

Fig. 15.3

Choose the destination of the new database in the New Database dialog box.

You may want to make a separate Workspace Page, by choosing Create, Workspace Page from the menu, and place icons for template databases there. This way you'll have a ready reference library to explore for ideas.

II

Designing Applications

For example, an employee responsible for collecting articles for a monthly newsletter might want to advise people sending items to be included in the next newsletter that they will be on vacation for two weeks. This user can do one of the following:

- Add the Mail(R4) database template to their workspace.
- Copy the Out Of Office form as well as the Mail Tools\Out of Office and ProcessOutOfOffice agents to the newsletter database.

This will create a Mail Tools menu choice under the Actions menu. By choosing Mail Tools, the employee can complete an Out Of Office form. The way the form is completed determines the message that someone submitting a newsletter item receives as a reply.

The employee can choose to send a general message, a special message to certain users, or no message at all in response to a submission.

The ProcessOutOfOffice agent will send the appropriate responses once each day. The employee can schedule this agent to run weekly, or even hourly, if desired.

Creating an Agent from Scratch

You can build an agent from scratch if you cannot find one suitable to copy and edit. Keep these tips in mind when building agents from scratch:

- Write down the steps you'd follow if you were going to proceed manually. This will help you get the basic steps in the right order. Next, consider making a flowchart of the agent. This can help you to identify any holes or gaps in the process.
- Consider creating a "library" database to store copies of agents that you find useful. Agents can be copied here for later reference by you or other developers. This can be a big time-saver, especially when using complex formulas and LotusScript programs!

Before building an agent, consider the following:

- What do I want the agent to do? The things that agents can do have greatly increased with this version of Notes. Simple Actions allow users to create agents even without knowledge of Lotus' @functions. The addition of LotusScript lets you answer this question in ways users of previous versions only dreamed about. Have a clear idea of the tasks the agent should accomplish and how to have Notes do it.
- What should I name the agent? What you name a Notes agent matters. If you're creating public agents for others to use, you'll want to think about using descriptive names. Your users will thank you and you'll spend less time answering questions about why you named an agent X when it obviously should be called Y!

    Users who create private agents have only themselves to consider here. The workday can be frustrating enough without adding complications yourself. Do yourself a favor and use descriptive names so you don't have to remember exactly what "Delete" is going to do when you run it.

■ When do I want the agent to run? For planning purposes, consider the time(s) that your agent will run. Are there periods during the day that you use your computer more than others? Are there times when the server you're using is busier than others, or perhaps unavailable? Consider scheduling agents that are resource-intensive (those requiring more time or processing power to complete) at times when resources are least strained.

The details of scheduling your agent will be covered in the "Choosing When To Run the Agent" section later in the chapter. Right now, be aware that agents can be scheduled to run manually, in response to a database event (such as received mail), at a particular time, or repeatedly. For example, agents that archive public databases should be run when those databases aren't in use. Mail agents should run at least daily. You may want some agents only to be run manually.

■ Which database elements should it act on? The scope of the actions for your agent should be considered. Agents can be run against an entire database, a particular folder, selected documents, or a single document. It is important to understand and plan your agent so that it affects only those database elements you desire. Otherwise, you could lose important information, or negatively affect other people's jobs or your own!

By thinking about these questions before you begin, you'll find that you have the necessary elements in your grasp to easily create a useful agent.

Using the Agent Builder Window

To build an agent, follow these steps:

1. Highlight the icon of the database you want to design the agent in.

2. Choose Create, Agents. The Agent Builder window opens (see fig. 15.4).

3. Choose the desired options in the Agent Builder window. If you have Designer level access and want to create a shared agent, select the Shared Agent checkbox in the Agent Builder window.

4. Specify the action, formula, or script for the agent. Check the format of your formulas by clicking the green checkmark to the left of the programmer pane. If there is an error in the format, a pop-up window will appear with text summarizing the problem. Make the necessary changes to the formula and click the checkmark again to verify that at least the formula is valid.

5. Press Esc.

6. Make sure you test the formula before allowing it to be used on live data. Use the simulated run option to verify that the agent will select the intended documents and act the way it's intended. You may place important data at risk, otherwise. Refer to the section "Testing Your Creations" later in this chapter for more details on testing agents.

Fig. 15.4

Open the Agent Builder by choosing Create, Agent from the menu or double-clicking the name of an existing agent to edit choices for that agent.

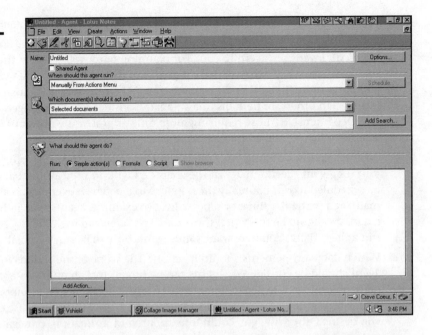

Some options in the Agent Builder window are not available for all agents. Agents that are run manually from the Actions menu present the greatest number of options to the creator. Agents that run in response to defined actions like new mail or pasted documents are more limited since they only run on the documents that have changed.

As you may suspect, there are four elements required of an agent:

- Name
- Schedule
- Document selection
- Actions

The following sections describe the options for these required elements.

Simple Actions and @function formulas can be combined using the @function Simple Action. @Function formulas cannot be combined with LotusScript programs. However, you can create agents that trigger other agents, so it is possible to link components to accomplish a task.

Note

A comprehensive explanation of @functions and LotusScript are outside the scope of this chapter. See Chapters 13 and 14 for more information on @functions, and Chapters 16 and 17 for information on LotusScript programming.

Choosing a Name

First give your agent a name so users can refer to it. Naming it first lets you refer to the agent by name as you work. If you save an agent without a name, it will appear as Untitled in the menu. Naming conventions aren't as innocuous as you might suspect.

Using Descriptive Names. An agent's name should be descriptive of its actions—for example, "Save to Newsletter folder."

A descriptive name will help users decide which agent to run from the Actions menu. Since your agent names can contain up to 32 alphanumeric characters (including spaces and punctuation), you should be able to create names that describe the function of an agent. This can reduce mistakes and user anxiety. The function of an agent named Send article to Sales team is easy to understand.

Descriptive names reduce the work of users building their own agents. They'll have an easier time determining that an agent performs a task similar to the one they need, enabling them to copy that agent into another database and edit it for their purposes.

Naming Conventions. Standardized naming conventions help users to work efficiently since agents with similar functions will have similar names in all of the databases they use. It also provides a more cohesive look and feel to your company's Notes environment. This is especially important if you're considering publishing databases on the Internet.

Specifying Name Order. Notes will sort agent names, on the Actions menu, in alphabetical order (see fig. 15.5). If you want your agents to appear in a particular order on the menu, you'll have to name them appropriately. For example, if tasks are carried out in a particular order, you'll want to set the order of agent names accordingly.

Fig. 15.5

Agents names sorted alphabetically.

You can use numbers to name your agents. However, Notes will sort the numbers as text so 10 will be listed before 1, not after 9 as you might expect (see fig. 15.6). Circumvent this problem by using 01, 02, 03, and so on when naming instead of 1, 2, 3. Notes will then list the agents in "numeric" order (see fig. 15.7).

Fig. 15.6

Agent names numbered conventionally.

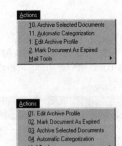

Fig. 15.7

Agent names numbered with preceding 0.

Specifying Accelerator Keys. Windows, OS/2, and UNIX users can select an agent by typing the first letter of its name or the underlined letter in the agent's name. These are referred to as *accelerator keys* and can be programmed by the agent's creator. To do so, place an underline character (_) in front of the letter you want to use as the accelerator key when naming the agent.

If you do not specify one, Notes will create a default accelerator key for you. Since the first unique letter in the agent's name will be used, the program's choice may not be intuitive to the user. For example, if you have two agents whose names begin with *Copy*, the first will use *C* as its accelerator key and the second will use *O*.

Naming agents alphabetically will allow users to select an agent by simply typing that letter. If two agent names begin with the same letter, the default accelerator key will be the first unique letter in the name of the second agent (see fig. 15.8).

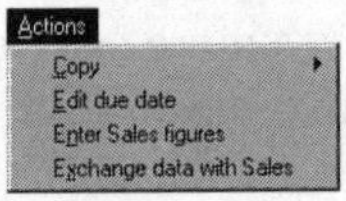

Fig. 15.8

Note that the accelerator key for the first agent is E, followed by N for the second and X for the third.

Consider renaming agents alphabetically so that the first letter in each name is unique. If this isn't possible, force Notes to use a more intuitive choice by using an accelerator key.

Grouping Agents with Cascading Menus. If a database contains several agents that perform similar functions, consider creating a cascading menu. This presents a more cohesive and efficient menu to the user by grouping agents together by function. When you click the first level, a submenu appears with additional choices. This option is helpful in reducing clutter on the Action menu.

To set up a cascading menu, first decide on a descriptive name for the top level menu the user will see. For example, if there are several agents that copy selected documents to different folders, place them under one menu item with a name such as Copy To Folder.

When naming the agent, begin with the name from the preceding step followed by a backslash (\). Next, type the agent name the user will see in the submenu. For example, to create the menu shown in figure 15.9, name the agents as follows:

```
Copy \ Documents to Finance folder

Copy \ Documents to Marketing folder

Copy \ Documents to Sales folder
```

Fig. 15.9

Agents grouped by function.

Notes will support one level of cascaded names. These appear on a submenu. Each agent name cannot contain more than 64 bytes. Multi-byte characters (such as the \ character in the cascading name) will limit the number of characters, as opposed to bytes, the name may contain. The name of the top menu can be up to 32 bytes in length and the cascaded names can be up to 30 bytes.

Choosing When To Run the Agent

Some agents require user intervention to run. These manual agents are useful for tasks that are run at the user's discretion. Agents can also be set to run on a schedule or in response to certain database events. Let's look at how to create these agents and consider some examples of situations where they might be useful in your day to day work. The following choices are available in the field When Should This Agent Run?:

- Manually From Actions Menu
- Manually From Agent List
- If New Mail Has Arrived
- If Documents Have Been Created or Modified
- If Documents Have Been Pasted
- On Schedule Hourly
- On Schedule Daily
- On Schedule Weekly
- On Schedule Monthly
- On Schedule Never

> **Tip**
>
> If you're a laptop user and choose to receive truncated documents during replication (see the Receive summary and 40 KB of rich text only option under replication), agents will not run against these documents.

(continues)

II

Designing Applications

> (continued)
>
> You may also choose not to receive agents when replicating a database. If you don't want agents to replicate to a local copy of a database, follow these steps:
>
> **1.** Click the icon of the replica database.
>
> **2.** Choose File, Replication, Settings, Advanced.
>
> **3.** Under the Replicate incoming field, clear the checkmark from the Agents option.

Running Manually from the Actions Menu. Database designers who create public agents for use by others will find the Manually From Menu option the most useful. This allows users to run an agent by highlighting a database icon, clicking the Actions menu, and choosing an agent by name (see fig. 15.10).

Fig. 15.10

Choosing Actions in the menu displays a list of available agents.

This option can be useful when testing the component pieces of a complex agent before changing its run option to Manually From Agent List. Checking the function of component agents can save you from repairing the damage caused by unexpected results.

Hiding Agents/Running Agents from Other Agents. You may choose to hide an agent so that it doesn't show up in the Actions menu. Hidden agents can be run from another agent or by highlighting it in the Agents view and selecting Actions, Run. To hide an agent, choose Manually From Agent List in the When Should This Agent Run? field in the Agent Builder window. Keep the following in mind:

■ Use the Actions, Run option to test hidden component agents when creating large or complex agents. The Agent Log will appear after the hidden agent runs using the Actions, Run menu options while in the Agents view.

■ Use the Run Agent action in the programmer pane to combine existing agents. (If you want to run an agent from another database, you'll have to copy it into your database.) Use this technique to combine component agents using Simple Actions, @function formulas, or LotusScript into a single agent.

■ Actions will be carried out sequentially, in the order in which they occur in the agents. Document selection is performed by the primary agent. The main agent (perhaps one chosen from the Actions, Run menu) runs and passes the resulting information to a secondary agent for its processing. For example, the first component agent searches for all documents within a folder for a particular author name and marks them unread. The next component agent performs the programmed action on all of the documents selected by the first agent.

Scheduling Agents. Scheduled agents require no user intervention to run. They do exactly what their name implies. This also makes them one of the most useful tools in the never ending battle to stay informed in a constantly changing market.

In the When Should This Agent Run? section of the Agent Builder window, choose the desired schedule:

- On Schedule Hourly
- On Schedule Daily
- On Schedule Weekly
- On Schedule Monthly
- On Schedule Never

A Daily agent can be used, for example, to run periodic checks of published databases that you subscribe to. This might be useful if you need to keep informed of your competitor's movement within a given market. Several companies now publish news and information databases for users of Notes. AT&T's Network Notes service allows companies to publish databases for use by subscribers to the service. Lotus' Newsstand also provides another source of published databases.

Perhaps you are responsible for the department newsletter or a weekly meeting. You might use a weekly agent to remind others to submit an article or complete an action item (or just to show up for a meeting).

> **Tip**
>
> If you are responsible for the company newsletter and you're one of the millions of people surfing the Web nowadays, check out Lotus' Newsstand. There's a neat list of published databases you can subscribe to providing industry and special interest information. For an up-to-date list, point your Web browser at **http://www.lotus.com/nwsstnd/**.

An agent that runs monthly might be useful for copying documents more than six months old to an archive database for storage and reference. This could also serve to keep the size of a production database smaller, thus reducing the need for disk space on remote servers in branch offices.

The On Schedule Never option is reserved for background macros from Notes 3.x that were scheduled to run Never. If you want one of these to run, change the schedule to one of the Release 4 options.

Keep in mind that an agent runs on the computer where the database is stored. If you're running an agent from a database on your local machine, you can do more since you have Manager access, unless Local Security is enabled. Running an agent from the server requires you to pay closer attention to the user's Access Control rights.

To run scheduled agents when you start Notes, follow these steps:

1. Choose File, Tools, User Preferences.

2. Select Enable scheduled local agents.

3. Click OK when you get the message that some changes won't take place until Notes is restarted.

4. Click OK.

Using the Schedule button on the Agent Builder window, you can do the following (see fig. 15.11):

■ Decide which server or workstation an agent runs on.

■ Set the starting and ending dates.

■ Set the frequency and starting and end times of hourly agents.

■ Set the start time for a daily agent.

■ Set the day of the week and time of day a weekly agent runs.

■ Set the day of the month and starting time of monthly agents.

Fig. 15.11

Click the Schedule button in the Agent Builder window to choose the times this agent will run. Note that the agent in the example can be found in the Room Reservation template file.

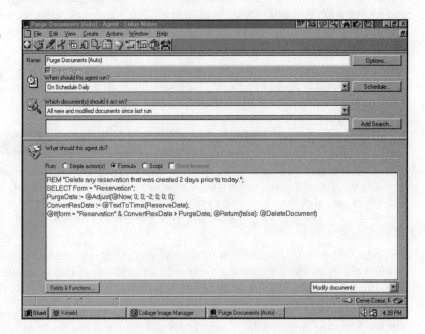

These options will be handy for agents that run time- or system resource-intensive tasks, such as archiving large databases or compiling a report. You can choose when you can afford to dedicate those resources. Some tasks lend themselves to being run during off hours.

A salesperson who's on the road visiting a customer may want his computer to dial into his home server at night, while the phone rates are less expensive, and pull all the orders he wrote for a client between the 1st and 20th of the month from the company's Projected Sales database, for example. Perhaps, he also wants those orders that mention a certain part or product. Agents can also be set to query other databases for documents by certain authors, dates, even those including or excluding certain keywords. Look at the "Building Search Queries" section later in this chapter.

Triggering Agents with Events. An agent that is set to activate whenever new mail arrives in the database might, for example, check the user name and Delivery Priority fields and forward any High Priority item from the District Vice President to your assistant for action while you're on vacation. To activate the agent with e-mail, choose If New Mail Has Arrived in the When Should This Agent Run? section of the Agent Builder window.

Agents may also be set to activate when a document is modified or if a document has been pasted into a database. Any important document from an employee work schedule to a customer contract might need to be sent to a Person or Group defined in the Name and Address Book if it were modified. To choose one of these options, select If Document Has Been Modified or If New Documents Have Been Pasted in the When Should This Agent Run? section of the Agent Builder window.

Specifying Documents Affected by the Agent

Deciding which documents within a database an agent will act upon is required for the successful creation and execution of any agent:

- Manual agents present the greatest number of selection options. They will allow the agent to select a single document, folder, view, or the entire database.

- Scheduled agents can be run against all documents in the database or on documents that were added or modified since the agent last ran.

- Change-activated agents present the user with the fewest selection options because they will run only against those documents specified by the type of change that occurred—for example, new mail items, pasted documents, or documents modified since the agent was last run.

To specify what documents will be affected by the agent, select one of the following options in the Which Document(s) Should It Act On? section of the Agent Builder window:

- **All documents in the database**—The agent will attempt to modify all of the documents within the database.

- **New and Modified documents**—Only documents which have been created or modified since the agent last ran will be processed.

- **All unread documents**—The agent will run against documents marked as unread. You may use another agent to select documents by author, for example, and mark those unread before triggering a secondary agent.

- **Selected documents in the open view**—This option may be most useful to process documents selected by another agent or you may select documents manually and then run the agent from the Actions menu.

- **All documents in the open view**—This choice instructs the agent to run against all documents within the view that is currently open.

- **Current document**—The agent will make changes only to the document currently open.

- **Pasted documents**—Documents that are pasted into the database will be acted upon when the agent runs.

Building Search Queries. The use of search queries allows you to fine-tune document selection by agents. This section will introduce you to the options available using search queries.

The Add Search button in the Agent Builder window allows you to define search parameters for an agent (refer to fig. 15.11). This feature allows you to, more specifically, define criteria to select which documents should or shouldn't be acted upon by your agent.

Clicking the Add Search button displays the Search Builder dialog box, in which you can choose search options for documents including author names, dates, field values, or forms used (see fig. 15.12). You can build compound searches by adding parameters to more than one of the option fields in the Search Builder window.

Fig. 15.12

Use this dialog box to target all documents, for example, by a given user or all but those authored by the specified user.

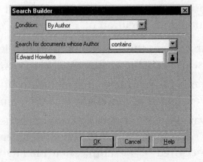

For example, you may want to search a folder for documents by a particular author, created in a given date range. To do this, just complete the necessary fields in the By Author, By Date, and In Folder options in the Condition field. The resulting query will be shown in the field to the left of the Add Search button in the Agent Builder window.

Notes allows searches of encrypted fields and file attachments as long as the database is full-text indexed and the index was created to include these items. If it does not, contact the Manager of the database and ask for a new index to be created that includes attachments and encrypted fields.

> **Note**
>
> If the database is full-text indexed, make sure that it is current—otherwise your results might not be accurate. Databases that are full-text indexed will produce better results than those that aren't.

To check the criteria used for the database's full-text index, follow these steps:

1. Highlight the database icon on the workspace.
2. Right-click your mouse on the icon.
3. Choose Database Properties.
4. Select the Full Text tab.

Databases that are stored on a server can use scheduled updates of full-text indexes. Contact your Notes Administrator for assistance in setting up a schedule that meets your needs. Remember that full-text indexes require both disk space and processor resources. The administrator can help balance the need for indexing with the resources available on the server.

The following sections describe each type of search.

Searching by Author. Any document that contains an Author Names field can be searched. You may specify documents that were either created by or not created by a specific author. You may also access either a Public or Private Name & Address Book to search for the author's name to ensure accuracy. In the example shown in figure 15.12, the agent will search for documents authored by Edward Howlette. This type of search is very useful if you remember who authored a document.

Searching by Date. You can search for any documents that were (or were not) either created or modified on or within a certain date range. The example shown in figure 15.13 will search for any documents created on March 15th of 1996. Using this parameter, you can narrow your search to a specific timeframe. Used in conjunction with other search parameters, this is useful in large databases.

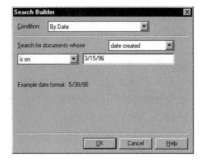

Fig. 15.13

Use the By Date parameter to target all documents by the date(s) they were created or modified.

Searching for a Field Value. You can search any field within the given form, via a pull-down menu, for the presence or the absence of a certain value. The example shown in figure 15.14 will search documents with the AvailableResources field for the occurrence of the term *Conference Room*.

Fig. 15.14

Use the By Field parameter to target terms either contained or not in a specific field on a database form.

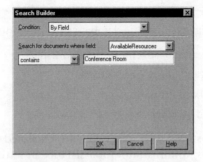

Searching Multiple Fields on a Form. You cansearch multiple fields on a particular form with the By Form option (see fig. 15.15). The forms available in the database are selectable from a pull-down menu. A representation of the form you choose will appear in the bottom portion of the Search Builder dialog box. Type the values you want to search for in the fields on the form.

Fig. 15.15

Use the By Form parameter to search for specific values in single or multiple fields on a selected database form.

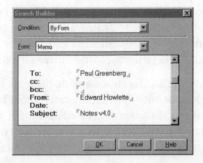

> **Note**
>
> Problems with the By Form type of search include misspellings and values in fields Computed for Display, since the values are not stored within the form but computed when the document is opened.

Searching by Form Used. You can search by the form used in a database. Multiple forms can be selected. Clicking the name in the list of database forms creates a checkmark next to the form name. Notes will search the selected forms for documents meeting your selection criteria. This is a useful search parameter to isolate forms with similar fields and data. The example in figure 15.16 will search any document created using the Action Form, Memo, and Phone Message forms.

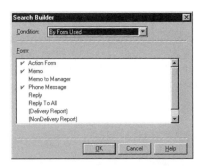

Fig. 15.16

Use the By Form Used parameter to target specific forms within the database.

Searching by Folder. You can search documents in a particular database folder or view. A menu tree appears in the bottom of the Search Builder window enabling you to scroll through the database and select the folder or view to search (see fig. 15.17). Unlike the search by Form Used, you can only select one folder or view at a time.

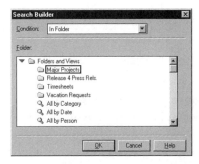

Fig. 15.17

Use the In Folder parameter to specify which folder the agent should search.

Searching for Words and Phrases. You can search for documents that contain either any or all of the words entered in the fields in the lower part of the Search Builder window. Up to eight words and/or phrases may be entered.

The example shown in figure 15.18 will search for documents containing any of the words shown. This parameter is useful for selecting documents to be acted upon by a second agent.

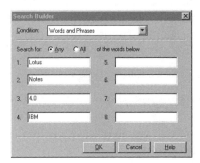

Fig. 15.18

Use the Words and Phrases parameter to search for documents containing either any or all of the listed terms.

Programming the Agent's Function

Up to this point, you've learned the details to consider when naming an agent. You've considered, in general terms, when it should run and on which elements of the database it should act. Now you'll look at the *how* part of agents. Using the programmer pane, you'll define the specific functions that an agent actually carries out (see fig. 15.19).

Fig. 15.19

The programmer pane is the portion of the screen that asks the question: What should this agent do?

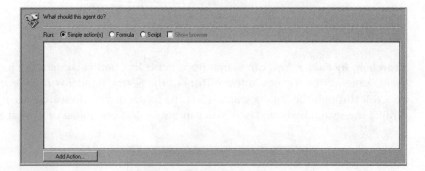

An agent doesn't have to be complex to be useful. There are three ways to program an agent's function:

- Using Simple Actions (predefined Notes functions), a user can create an agent with no programming experience. Simple Actions are discussed in the following section.

- Using @function formulas, which enable you to select and process documents. Agents that use @function formulas require an understanding of the @function commands but allow more flexibility than Simple Actions.

- Using LotusScript, Lotus' BASIC-compatible scripting language, you can interact with other scripting languages, such as Visual Basic.

Agents using LotusScript are the most complex of the three methods. LotusScript allows creation of powerful programs that can manipulate databases in ways not possible with Simple Actions or @functions.

Using Simple Actions. Simple Actions are predefined Notes functions that can be strung together to carry out a desired task. These allow manipulation of documents, fields, mail, and folders. You can use Simple Actions to trigger other agents allowing you to combine component parts into a larger, complex agent.

To program the agent with Simple Actions, follow these steps:

1. With the Agent Builder window open, click Simple action(s) in the programmer pane.

2. Click the Add Action button on the bottom of the programmer pane. The Add Action dialog box appears on-screen (see fig. 15.20).

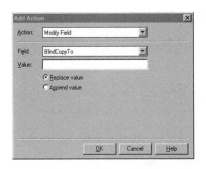

Fig. 15.20

Clicking the Add Action button in the programmer pane allows you to program one of Notes' predefined functions.

3. Click the arrow on the right side of the <u>A</u>ction field to see a drop-down list of the actions available. You can choose from these 15 Simple Actions available in Notes 4:

- Copy to Database
- Remove from Folder
- Reply to Sender
- Run Agent
- Send Document
- Send Mail Message
- Send Newsletter Summary
- @Function Formula

- Move to Folder
- Copy to Folder
- Delete from Database
- Mark Document Read
- Mark Document Unread
- Modify Field
- Modify Fields by Form

> **Note**
>
> You can combine Simple Actions and @functions by choosing the @Function Formula action and writing a @function formula.

4. Note that the fields in the lower part of the Add Action dialog box change, depending upon the <u>A</u>ction that you choose. Complete the fields in the lower part of the dialog box.

5. Press <u>O</u>K to save or Cancel to close the box without saving your choices. The resulting command will be shown in the programmer pane.

Notes will carry out multiple Simple Actions in the order listed in the programmer pane. To program an agent to carry out multiple Simple Actions, repeat steps 2 through 5. Each command you add will be shown in the programmer pane next to the preceding command (see fig. 15.21).

Designing Applications

II

Fig. 15.21

Programmer pane shows the multiple Simple Actions selected.

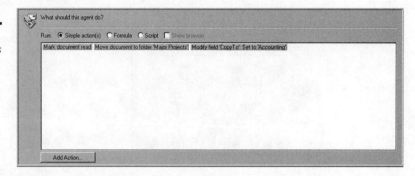

Using @Function Formulas. Using @functions, you can do the following:

- Modify and save existing documents.
- Create new documents by making a copy of an existing document and modifying the copy, preserving the original.
- Select documents in a view but not process them. Use this option to test your selection formula before actually processing documents.

> **Note**
>
> Use of the @command functions are limited within agents. @Command and @PostedCommand can only be used with agents that act upon the currently selected document. Scheduled agents cannot use @DbColumn or @DbLookup to access information in databases on another server. They may, however, be used to access other databases on the same computer that the agent resides on.

Agents defined as formulas in the Run field on the programmer pane cannot be combined with Simple Actions or LotusScript programs in a single agent. Refer to Chapters 13 and 14 for detailed information on working with @functions.

Use @function formulas to select and process documents within a database. To program an agent using @functions, follow these steps:

1. Choose Formula in the Run field on the programmer pane.
2. Click the Field & Functions button. The Fields and Functions dialog box appears on-screen (see fig. 15.22).

Fig. 15.22

Select the Fields & Functions button to display a list of @functions and field names to add to your formula.

3. Choose either the Eunctions or Fields button:

- Selecting Eunctions will show a list of @function commands that can be pasted into the programmer pane. The keywords ENVIRONMENT, FIELD, REM, and SELECT are also available. These must be the first word used in a formula statement. Highlight the desired selection and click Paste to add it to your formula.

- Selecting Fields will show a list of the fields defined in the database. Highlight the desired selection and click Paste to add it to your formula.

4. Write an @function formula in the programmer pane. As you enter parameters in the programmer pane, you'll note the appearance of a green checkmark and a red X to the left. Clicking the green checkmark allows you to check the format of the @function formula you've written. If the formula's format is incorrect, clicking the checkmark will produce a dialog box with a summary of the problem. Clicking the red X will clear the programmer pane.

5. On the bottom right side of the programmer pane is a pull-down menu; open the menu and select one of the following options:

- Modify Documents will modify the original and save the new document.

- Create New Documents will make a copy of an existing document and modify the copy, preserving the original.

- Select Documents In View will mark documents with a checkmark but not process them. Use this option to select documents to be processed by an agent or to test your selection formula before actually processing documents.

Using LotusScript Programs. Agents defined as Script in the Run field on the programmer pane cannot be combined with Simple Actions or formulas in a single agent. Refer to Chapters 16 and 17 for detailed information on working with LotusScript.

Use LotusScript to create sophisticated programs that can process database documents, act on the database ACL, or interact with other programming languages.

To program an agent using LotusScript, follow these steps:

1. Choose Script in the Run field on the programmer pane.

2. Write or copy-and-paste a LotusScript program that selects the documents you want to process and performs the actions you desire. You can check the Show browser checkbox to show a list of LotusScript commands that can be pasted into the programmer pane (see fig. 15.23).

Fig. 15.23

Enable Show Browser to display a list of LotusScript programming parameters.

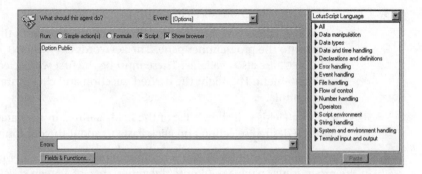

Completing the Agent

After you finish specifying what you want the agent to do, save the agent. Then test it to be sure it works as expected. Begin writing agents in local database copies so you won't corrupt important data. Begin testing your agent with the Simulated Run option which identifies the changes that would occur if you actually ran the agent.

> **Tip**
>
> Refer to the "Testing Your Creations" section of this chapter for information on how to test your agent before running it on live data. The more complex an agent is, the more places things can go wrong. Consider creating several subagents that may be tested individually, and linked together after the bugs are ironed out. This can make troubleshooting any problems easier.

Using Buttons and Hotspots

A button is a graphical representation of a push-button that you can place in a Rich Text field to carry out Notes commands or run a script (see fig. 15.24). Buttons allow users to run agents, formulas, or scripts from the form or document level by double-clicking. Again, users may complete only actions allowed by their access level defined in the ACL.

Fig. 15.24

This button will open the Year-end Report document database.

The button interface has been updated in Notes R4. You have more options than with previous versions in creating and displaying the button itself, as well as in programming the underlying code. From the Button Properties InfoBox, you can determine if a button appears on a form and format the text, alignment, and style.

Notes 4 adds a new design element called a *hotspot*. While a button is an independent graphic, a hotspot usually appears as text or a graphic, with a green border around it.

Like a button, users can click a hotspot to perform Notes actions or run scripts. You can use hotspots, like hypertext, to link documents together. For example, if a memo mentions a corporate policy, consider using a link hotspot to allow the user to read the policy document for clarification (see fig. 15.25). Hotspots can be used to annotate phrases and graphics, test formulas, or carry out a script.

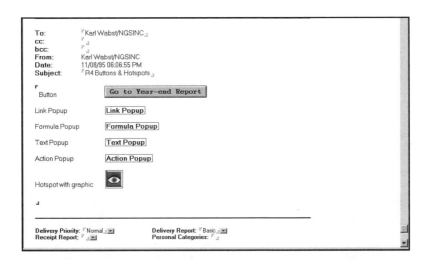

Fig. 15.25

Hotspots can be linked to text or graphics. They carry out Notes' commands and actions much like buttons. Although they usually appear as a green border around text or a graphic, their power depends on the underlying code.

Designing Applications

Creating and Removing Hotspots

Hotspots can execute Simple Actions, @functions, and LotusScript just like buttons. The presentation is the major difference between a hotspot and a button. While a button appears as a graphical object, a hotspot can appear as a bordered area of text— and even the border can be removed! In essence, a hotspot can do what a button can without taking up additional space in the document.

To add a hotspot, follow these steps:

1. Open the document or form you want to add the hotspot to.

2. When adding a hotspot to an existing document, choose Actions, Edit Document. While in edit mode, select the area in the Rich Text field where you want the hotspot. When creating a hotspot in a new form, highlight the Rich Text field where you want the hotspot to appear.

3. Choose Create, Hotspot.

4. Choose the type of hotspot to be created:

   - Link Hotspot
   - Text Popup
   - Button
   - Formula Popup
   - Action Hotspot

5. If you choose a Formula Popup or Action Hotspot, you need to write a formula in the programmer pane which appears on-screen. Format the hotspot as desired, and close the Properties InfoBox for the hotspot. Test your formulas to ensure the actions taken are what you want, before using them on live data.

6. Save the form.

To remove a hotspot, right-click the hotspot while in edit mode and choose Remove Hotspot from the menu.

Link Hotspots. *Link hotspots* can be used to create a link to another document or database—these are similar to doclinks. To create the link, follow these steps:

1. Go to the document or graphic object you want to link to this hotspot.

2. Choose Edit, Copy As Link.

3. Close the object.

4. Open the document or form you want the hotspot in.

5. Highlight the area of the Rich Text field you want to link. This can be text or even a graphic.

6. Choose Create, Hotspot, Link Hotspot.

> **Note**
>
> When you create a link hotspot, Notes doesn't copy the object into the field but uses a pointer to the destination. If the object you link to is not reachable due to ACL levels or if the server the object resides on is unavailable, Notes will present a menu asking where it should search for the object. For this link to function properly, ensure that the object will be available to the intended user.

You can find the object linked to a hotspot by double-clicking the hotspot. Clicking once and holding the left mouse button down will show the destination of the linked object.

Text Pop-up Hotspots. *Text pop-ups* display text when the left mouse button is clicked once and held down while on the hotspot. This can be used to provide commentary or explanation for the text. To create a text pop-up hotspot, follow these steps:

1. Highlight the area of the Rich Text field you want the text to appear by when the hotspot is activated.

2. Choose Create, Hotspot, Text Pop-up. The HotSpot Pop-up Properties InfoBox appears (see fig. 15.26)

3. In the Properties InfoBox, enter the text you want to appear when the hotspot is activated.

4. Click the green checkbox in the left border to accept the text as entered. Click the red X in the left border to clear the text box.

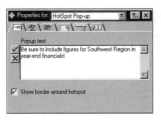

Fig. 15.26

The text entered into the HotSpot Pop-up Properties InfoBox appears when the hotspot is activated.

Formula Pop-up Hotspots. *Formula pop-up hotspots* will allow programming of an @function formula in the programmer pane. A user will see the result of this formula by clicking and holding the left mouse button down on the hotspot. The result of the hotspot formula must be a text string, such as True or False.

To create a formula pop-up hotspot, follow these steps:

1. Highlight the area of the Rich Text field you want the result of the @function formula to appear by when the hotspot is activated.

2. Choose Create, Hotspot, Formula Hotspot. The HotSpot Pop-up Properties InfoBox appears along with the programmer pane.

3. Enter an @function formula in the programmer pane.

Figure 15.27 shows a formula hotspot in progress, while figure 15.28 shows the result of the formula when the hotspot is activated.

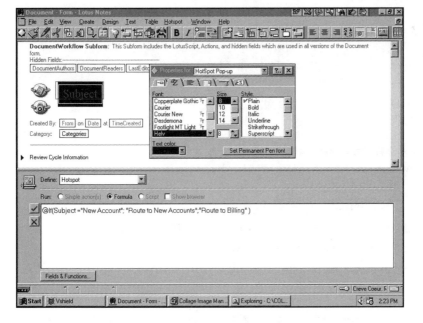

Fig. 15.27

Formula hotspot in progress.

Designing Applications

II

Fig. 15.28

The result of the formula is displayed when a formula hotspot is activated.

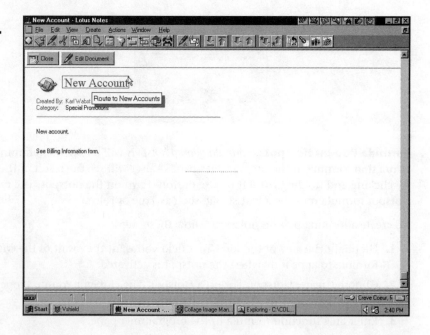

Action Pop-up Hotspots. *Action pop-up hotspots* allow a user to execute an @function or @command when the hotspot is double-clicked, provided he or she has adequate ACL access to the necessary functions.

The following steps show how you create them:

1. Highlight the area of the Rich Text field you want the hotspot to appear.

2. Choose Create, Hotspot, Action Hotspot. The HotSpot Properties InfoBox appears on-screen along with a programmer pane.

3. In the programmer pane, enter Simple Actions, an @function formula, or a LotusScript program to control the hotspot.

Making a Hotspot Invisible

You can remove the green border from around the hotspot, making it "invisible" to the user. To do so, follow these steps:

1. Click the inside of the hotspot.

2. Choose Hotspot, Hotspot Properties. The HotSpot Properties InfoBox appears.

3. Deselect Show Border around Hotspot. You'll see that the border disappears.

4. Close the HotSpot Properties InfoBox and save the form or document.

Editing a Hotspot's Function

You can edit the function of a formula or action hotspot, replacing or editing the underlying actions or formula. Button formulas are edited in a similar fashion:

1. Open the document or form in edit mode.

2. Click the hotspot (or button).

3. Choose Hotspot, Edit Hotspot from the main menu. (If editing a button, use the Button, Edit Button menu choice.) The HotSpot Properties InfoBox appears along with the programmer pane.

4. Make your changes to the code.

5. Save the changes and close the document.

Creating Buttons

Buttons manually execute Simple Actions, @functions, or LotusScript programs with the double-click of a mouse. They add automation to the database. Users don't have to use the menus to choose commands or the name of the agent necessary to carry out the actions programmed into a button.

To create a button, follow these steps:

1. Open the document or form you want to add the button to.

2. While in edit mode, place the cursor in the Rich Text field where you want the button to appear.

3. Choose Create, Hotspot, Button. A small button will appear on the form at the point you selected with your cursor. The Button Properties InfoBox and programmer pane will appear on the screen (see fig. 15.29).

Fig. 15.29

The Button Properties InfoBox.

4. Click the first tab of the Button Properties InfoBox (it looks like a button on a document).

5. In the Button label text box, type the label you want the user to see on the button.

6. The formatting options for buttons are the same as those for normal text. (These were discussed in greater detail in Chapter 7, "Working With Text.") With the formatting options in the Button Properties InfoBox, format the button as desired:

   • Click the Fonts tab to format the attributes of the font used for the button's label.

   • Click the Alignment tab to format the alignment and spacing used for the text in the button's label.

- Click the Pagination tab to format pagination, printing margins, and tab spacing for the text in the button's label.

- Click the Style tab to choose or manage the style of the button's text.

7. When you have finished selecting options for the button, close the Button Properties InfoBox.

8. In the programmer pane, program the actions the button will carry out. As with agents, program the buttons using Simple Actions, @function formulas, or LotusScript. Again, the code doesn't need to be complex in order to be useful. Buttons that transport users to a related document or add a database icon are relatively easy to create, and save time over completing the same action manually.

The default button settings create a functional button. To edit the properties of an existing button, follow these steps:

1. Open the document in edit mode by pressing Ctrl+E or selecting Actions, Edit Document from the menu.

2. Right-click the button and select the Button Properties option to bring up the Button Properties InfoBox. (Alternatively, you can choose Button, Edit Button from the menu.)

3. Select the tab of the property you want to edit (button title, text, etc.).

4. Make the desired changes. As you make changes, they are reflected in the button on-screen. If you edit the button label, a green checkmark appears next to the Button Label field. Click the checkmark for the changes to the label to take effect.

5. Close the InfoBox.

Hiding Buttons and Hotspots

The Properties window has an additional choice that allows control over the display of a paragraph, including buttons, hotspots, sections, or attachments.

You might want to hide a paragraph due to either formatting or security concerns. For example, when a form is printed, buttons and other graphic objects may detract from its ascetic appeal. Humans are visual creatures. The way a form looks often affects whether or not it even gets read! You may also want to hide sections with confidential or non-essential information. Refer to Chapter 13, "Working With Formulas," and Chapter 14, "Formula Functions," for more ideas on using this option.

You may choose to hide a paragraph under conditions defined here. The options in the Button Properties InfoBox are relatively self-explanatory. You can hide a paragraph while the form is being read, printed, edited, or copied.

In the InfoBox, you'll notice the option to Hide paragraph if formula is true. Below this is a formula window that allows you to enter an @function formula. By clicking the Formula Window button at the bottom of the InfoBox, a larger window is displayed.

The Field and Functions button on the bottom allows selection of @functions and field names. You might want to utilize this ability, for example, to hide the button/ hotspot from certain users or groups.

Testing Your Creations

In this chapter, we've learned that agents, buttons, and hotspots can automate Notes databases. What you may have realized by now is that, improperly programmed, they could potentially cause a good deal of grief as well!

Think about what would happen if you created an agent on a Sales Commission Reports database that erased documents or worse, deleted the file. How many other files or records can you think of that would have disastrous results if they were to be lost or altered erroneously?

To save yourself and others a lot of grief, think about ways to test your agents, buttons, and hotspots before they're used on live data. Following are some ways to accomplish safe testing without pain.

Use Local Databases

When you're starting out with a new development project, consider using copies of the database(s) you're developing agents for on a local workstation instead of a server. This will limit your exposure if an error should occur. This is especially true with vital databases such as the server's Name & Address Book.

Considering the functionality of LotusScript or the inexperience of a new developer, it's a good safeguard.

Protect Server Data

If your agents are acting upon mailed documents, the test database needs to be on a server. Anytime you test on a server, take precautions to protect your investment. The first precaution should be involving your Notes administrator. He or she can advise you on server resources, data availability, index issues, and the best time to conduct testing.

Using these steps on your workstation or server will protect your data:

- Perform a clean backup of the server prior to testing agents that will interact with the Public Name & Address Book or other databases that are likely to be open when the server is running.

- Create a non-replica copy of the database you're affecting and rename it. Have the agent interact with the renamed database instead of that containing your live data.

- If possible, choose an execution time that will affect the fewest users if the unthinkable happens.

> **Tip**
>
> You can turn off all scheduled mail or change activated agents within a database by following these steps:
>
> **1.** Choose File, Database, Properties.
>
> **2.** Select the Disable agents for this database option.
>
> This may prove to be useful while troubleshooting problems with agents on workstations or servers.

Simulation—Test Option

Notes provides a feature that will let you simulate the execution of an agent. To simulate an agent, follow these steps:

1. Highlight the database to be tested.

2. Highlight the agent to be tested.

3. Choose Actions, Test.

4. Look at the Test Report, which shows the number of documents that would be processed and describes the actions that would be taken if the agent was actually run.

5. Fix any problems encountered in the agent's code and test again.

6. Repeat until everything checks out. Close and save the agent.

Testing Complex Agents

When testing complex agents or scripts, break them apart into component parts and execute each in the order they will execute when run as a single agent or action. You can use the simulated run option to test individual components. Check the test log to identify problems with each component. This will allow you to easily and quickly isolate the problems that occur.

From Here...

This chapter has shown you how to create your own agents, buttons, and hotspots. Automating databases with these techniques can either save users time or cripple their ability to perform their jobs. Making life easier is the whole idea of database automation! Keep it simple and protect your company's investment in its people and data.

Other chapters you should read to enhance your ability to create effective automation include the following:

- Chapter 14, "Formula Functions," discusses all of the @functions that you can use in formulas.

- Chapter 16, " LotusScript: A Whole New Programming Language," teaches the basics of the powerful LotusScript programming language, which can be used to manipulate objects and links.

- Chapter 17, "Writing Scripts with LotusScript," talks about the next level of Notes programming.

LotusScript: A Whole New Programming Language

In previous chapters, you learned how to use the Notes @functions and @commands. In this chapter, you learn about a new feature of Notes called LotusScript. LotusScript lets you stretch the capabilities of Notes in ways previously impossible. It also simplifies many programming tasks from previous versions of Notes, where complicated combinations of @functions and @commands were often the only way to get things done.

This chapter helps you with the following:

- Using and understanding LotusScript
- Creating LotusScript scripts

Note

LotusScript is a programming language resembling Visual Basic. Teaching you to program using LotusScript is beyond the scope of this book. In this chapter and Chapter 17, however, you learn to apply LotusScript to Notes. If you need to learn how to program using a scripting language, contact Lotus Education for information on LotusScript courses, or look into taking a course on Visual Basic (or other scripting languages) to learn the fundamentals required to use LotusScript. These chapters assume that you understand programming in scripting languages.

What Is LotusScript?

LotusScript is a programming language that is used by numerous Lotus products, including Word Pro, 1-2-3, and Notes R4. LotusScript lets you automate your work in Lotus products, and is an offshoot of Microsoft's Visual Basic, with very few commands that are different. If you are a competent VB programmer, then learning and using LotusScript is quite easy.

You can use LotusScript rather than Notes formulas to do a wide variety of tasks, from creating agents to writing complex Notes scripts.

LotusScript and formulas provide an integral programming interface to Notes. You use LotusScript to write scripts to perform various functions and tasks in Notes—just as you use Notes formulas. You attach scripts and formulas to various objects in Notes, depending what you need to accomplish. For example, you might use a Notes formula to compute a field, and you might use LotusScript to create an agent to run against documents at a scheduled time.

LotusScript versus Formulas

LotusScript is a structured, object oriented programming environment—with classes, methods, and properties—very similar to Visual Basic. LotusScript's interface to Notes is through predefined object classes. LotusScript is based on ODBC, and provides read and write access to back-end databases for data update and synchronization. Notes oversees the compilation (interpreting of the visual text script you have entered as a series of instructions your computer can read), and loading of user scripts—automatically including the Notes class definitions.

Notes formulas are expressions that have program-like attributes. For example, you can assign values to variables, and use a limited control logic. The formula language interface to Notes is through calls to @functions. If you have ever created macros in Lotus 1-2-3 or Microsoft Excel, then you probably are familiar with many of the @functions you can use in Notes.

You can attach LotusScript and Notes formulas to the following various objects in a Notes database:

- Fields
- Views
- Agents
- Buttons
- Actions
- Hotspots

The particular object determines which of the two programming options you should use—you can't use both at the same time. For some objects, either LotusScript or Notes formulas can be used. For other objects, only one or the other should be used. Discussions later in this section indicate specifically when you should use which.

In general, Notes formulas are best used for working with the object that the user is currently processing. For example, to return a default value to a field, or to determine selection criteria for a view, you do best with a Notes formula. LotusScript is better used for accessing existing objects—for example, to change a value in one document based on values in other documents, or to print the access control list (ACL) of a database. LotusScript provides some capabilities that Notes formulas do not, such as the ability to manipulate a Notes database's ACL, and the ability to print a list of all databases that reside on a server or local hard disk. Notes formulas provide better performance than LotusScript and might be more convenient. The use of LotusScript versus Notes formulas is ultimately determined by the experience of the Notes application developer and the application requirements of your Notes databases.

LotusScript and Formulas for Agents. An *agent* is a user procedure that you can trigger in a number of ways, including a menu command, a preset schedule, the arrival of mail, and the pasting of documents. You can write LotusScript scripts and @formulas to create agents, and you also can use Notes-supplied agents. Before writing your own agent, see if a Notes-supplied agent will do the job.

@Formula-based agents run in iterations on the documents in the database. You can apply search criteria to specify which documents in the database are to be processed— a SELECT statement in the formula limits the search to particular documents. If you do not include a SELECT statement, all documents in the database are processed by the agent.

LotusScript-based agents, in contrast, run once and have no associated search criteria. You supply the search criteria and process flow when you construct the LotusScript instructions.

An agent runs at either of the following locations:

- The user's workstation, if the agent's trigger has been set to either Manually, Document Has Been Modified, or Document Have Been Pasted
- The server or workstation containing the agent, if the agent's trigger has been set to either If New Mail Has Arrived or Is On Schedule

Scripts and Formulas for Actions. An *action* is a custom procedure that you can associate with a view or form. When you open the view, or open a document based on the form, the associated action becomes available as a command on the Actions menu, or as a button on the action bar.

You can conditionally suppress availability of an action on the menu or action bar with a Show action formula. Availability is suppressed if the formula evaluates to false.

Actions are run on the user's workstation by clicking the action button on the Action line or by selecting Actions from the tool bar and clicking an action listed.

Writing a Button Script or Formula. A *button* executes a LotusScript script or formula when you click it. An example of a LotusScript script button is a button that modifies the ACL of a database. A button to print a document would be an example of a formula button.

Writing a Hotspot LotusScript or Formula. A *hotspot* is a highlighted object in a document or form design that performs an action when you click it. The available actions are pop-up text, pop-up text from a formula, go to a link, run a formula, and run a script.

Writing Event Scripts. An *event script* is a custom procedure that runs when an event associated with a form or field occurs. The form events are: Opening, Closing, Initialize, and Terminate. The field events are: Entering, Exiting, Recalc, Initialize, and Terminate. Form and field objects are available through the Object menu in the LotusScript user interface. The events are available through the Item menu in the LotusScript user interface.Event scripts run on the user's workstation.

When To Use LotusScript versus Formulas

Table 16.1 outlines the programmable objects in Notes. The third column specifies whether LotusScript (Script) or Notes formulas (Formula) should or can be used.

Table 16.1   Notes Script and Formula Examples

Scope	Notes Object	Type	How To Design and Activate
Workspace	SmartIcons	Formula	To design, choose File, Tools, SmartIcons. Click the icon, choose Edit Icon, and then choose Formula. Activated when the user clicks the icon.
Database	Replication formula	Formula	To design, choose File, Database, Properties. Choose Basics, Replication Settings, and then Advanced. Click Replicate a subset of documents and choose Select by formula. Activated when replication occurs.
	Agent	Script Formula	To design, choose View, Agents. Select the agent and choose Actions, Edit, or choose Create, Agent. Click Simple Action, Script, or Formula for Run option. Activated according to a schedule, manually from Actions Menu, manually from Agent list, when mail arrives, when a document is modified or created, when a document is pasted, Schedule Hourly, or when the user chooses Actions, the name of the agent, or (while in View, Agents) Actions, Run.
View design	Form formula	Formula	To design, choose View, Design and click Views in the design pane. Double-click the view, or choose Create, View and name the view in the Create View properties box. Choose Design, View Properties, click the propeller head, and then click Formula Window. Activated when a document is opened from the view.
	Selection formula	Formula	To design, choose View, Design and click Views in the design pane. Double-click the view, or choose

Scope	Notes Object	Type	How To Design and Activate
			Create, View and name the view in the Create View properties box. Select View Selection for Define and click Formula for Run, enter the formula. Activated when the view is opened.
	Column formula	Formula	To design, choose View, Design and click Views in the design pane. Double-click the view, or choose Create, View and name the view in the Create View properties box. Select the column for Define and click Formula for Run, enter the formula. Activated when the view is opened.
	Action	Script Formula	To design, choose View, Design and click Views in the design pane. Double-click the view, or choose Create, View and name the view in the Create View properties box. Choose View, Action Pane and double-click the action in the action pane, or choose Create, Action, name the action, and click the X. Click Simple action, Formula, or Script for Run. Activated when the user chooses Actions, the name of the action, or clicks the action button.
	Show action formula	Formula	To design, choose View, Design and click Views in the design pane. Double-click the view, or choose Create, View and double-click the new view. Choose View, Action Pane and double-click the action, or choose Create, Action. Click Hide and Hide action if formula is true. Activated when the view is opened.
Form design	Window title formula	Formula	To design, choose View, Design and click Forms in the design pane. Double-click the form, or choose Create, Design, Form. Select the name of the form in the Define box. Select Window Title in the Event box. Activated when a document based on the form is opened.
	Section title formula	Formula	To design, choose View, Design and click Form (or Subforms) in the design pane. Double-click the form (or subform) or choose Create, Design, Form (or Subform). Select a standard section, or choose Create, Section, Standard and select the new standard section. Choose Section, Section Properties and click Formula;

(continues)

II

Designing Applications

Table 16.1	Continued		
Scope	**Notes Object**	**Type**	**How To Design and Activate**
			enter the formula. Activated when a document based on the form is opened.
	Section access formula	Formula	To design, choose View, Design and click Form (or Subforms) in the design pane. Double-click the form (or subform), or choose Create, Design, Form (or Subform). Select a controlled access section, or choose Create, Section, Controlled Access. Click the Formula tab; enter the formula. Activated when the section is accessed.
	Insert subform formula	Formula	To design, choose View, Design and click Forms in the design pane. Double-click the form, or choose Create, Design, Form. Choose Create, Insert Subform. Click Insert subform based on formula. Activated when a document based on the form is opened.
	Hide paragraph formula	Formula	To design, choose View, Design and click Forms (or Subforms) in the design pane. Double-click the form (or subform), or choose Create, Design, Form (or Subform). Choose Text, Text Properties, click the window blind icon, and select Hide Paragraph if formula is true. Activated when the text is accessed.
	Action	Script Formula	To design, choose View, Design and click Forms (or Subforms) in the design pane. Double-click the form (or subform), or choose Create, Design, Form (or Subform). Choose View, Action Pane and select the action, or choose Create, Action, enter the action name, and click the X. Click Simple action, Formula, or Script. Activated when the user chooses Actions, choose the name of the action, or clicks the action button.
	Hide action formula	Formula	To design, choose View, Design and click Forms (or Subforms) in the design pane. Double-click the form (or subform), or choose Create, Design, Form (or Subform). Choose View, Action Pane and select the action, or choose Create, Action. Click the Hide tab. Select Hide action if formula is true. Activated when a document based on the form is opened.

Scope	Notes Object	Type	How To Design and Activate
	Event Formula	Script	To design, choose View, Design and click Forms (or Subforms; but only the events for the first subform in a form will work) in the design pane. Double-click the form (or subform), or choose Create, Design, Form (or Subform). Select the form in the Define box. Select Queryopen, Postopen, Postrecalc, Querysave, Querymodechange, Postmodechange, Queryclose, Initialize, or Terminate in the Event box. Activated when the event occurs.
	Button	Script Formula	To design, choose View, Design and click Forms (or Subforms) in the design pane. Double-click the form (or subform), or choose Create, Design, Form (or Subform). Select a button or choose Create, Hotspot, Button. Click Simple action, Script, or Formula for Run. Activated when the user opens a document based on the form and clicks the button.
	Hotspot	Script Formula	To design, choose View, Design and click Forms (or Subforms) in the design pane. Double-click the form (or subform), or choose Create, Design, Form (or Subform). Select a hotspot, or select some text and choose Create, Hotspot, Formula Popup or Action Hotspot. Click Script (Action Hotspot only) or Formula for Run. Activated when the user clicks the hotspot text.
Navigator design	Hotspot	Script Formula	To design, choose View, Design and click Navigators in the design pane. Double-click the navigator, or choose Create, Design, Navigator. Select an element or choose Create, Graphic Button, Hotspot Rectangle, Hotspot Polygon, Graphic Button, or Button. Click Simple action, Script, or Formula for Run. Activated when the user clicks the hotspot.
Layout region design	Hotspot	Script Formula	To design, go into form or subform design. Select a layout region or choose Create, Layout Region, New Layout Region. Select a hotspot or choose Create, Hotspot, Button. Activated when the user clicks the hotspot.

(continues)

II

Designing Applications

Table 16.1 Continued			
Scope	**Notes Object**	**Type**	**How To Design and Activate**
Field design	Default value formula for editable field	Formula	To design, go into form, subform, or shared field design. In form design, select the field or choose Create, Field. Select Default Value in the Event box. Activated when the document is created.
	Input translation formula for editable field	Formula	To design, go into form, subform, or shared field design. In form design, select the field or choose Create, Field. Select Input Translation in the Event box. Activated when the document is saved or recalculated.
	Input validation formula for editable field	Formula	To design, go into form, subform, or shared field design. In form design, select the field or choose Create, Field. Select Input Validation in the Event box. Activated after input translation.
	Value formula for computed field	Formula	To design, go into form, subform, or shared field design. In form design, select the field or choose Create, Field. Select Value in the Event box. Activated when the document is saved or recalculated.
	Keyword field formula	Formula	To design, go into form, subform, or shared field design. In form design, select the field or choose Create, Field. In the properties box, select Use formula for choices in the Choices box. Activated when the field is edited.
	Event	Script	To design, go into form, subform, or shared field design. In form design, select the field or choose Create, Field. Select Entering, Exiting, Initialize, or Terminate in the Event box. Activated when the event occurs.
Rich text field	Button	Script Formula	To design, go into form or subform. Select the button and choose Button, Edit Button, or choose Create, Hotspot, Button. Click Simple action, Formula, or Script for Run. If you click Script, select Click, Initialize, or Terminate in the Event box. Activated when the user clicks the button.

Scope	Notes Object	Type	How To Design and Activate
	Hotspot	Script	To design, go into form or subform. Select the hotspot and choose Hotspot, Edit Hotspot or choose Create, Hotspot, Formula Popup or Action Hotspot. Click Formula or Script (Action Hotspot only) for Run. If you click Script, select Click, Initialize, or Terminate in the Event box. Activated when the user clicks the hotspot text.
	Section title formula	Formula	To design, go into form or subform. Select a standard section, or choose Create, Section and select the new standard section. Choose Section, Section Properties and click Formula. Activated when a document based on the form is opened.
	Hide paragraph	Formula	To design, go into form or subform. Choose Text, Text Properties, click the window blind icon, and select Hide Paragraph if formula is true. Activated when text is accessed.

Script and Statement Construction Rules

A *script* is composed of statements in the LotusScript language. Each *statement* consists of the following, written according to the syntax rules for the particular kind of statement:

- Keyword
- Operators
- Literals
- Names
- Punctuation

LotusScript includes dozens of statements, and recognizes five kinds of language elements in the statements in a script. Every statement is a sequence of these elements, and different syntax rules can apply to each kind of statement. Table 16.2 shows the kinds of language elements available within LotusScript.

Table 16.2 Language Elements	
Language Element	**Description**
Literal	Either a numeric literal, such as 777 or 77.7 or 7.77E+02, or a string literal, such as "777 Sixth Avenue".

(continues)

Table 16.2 Continued	
Language Element	**Description**
Identifier	A name you give to a variable, a subprogram, or other user-defined element in a script, such as a label or a user-specified type. Examples of identifiers are Seven, six_up, Seven77, Hyperlist, RevByYear, rollup, and PATHOCASE. In the LotusScript documentation, identifiers are referred to as *names*.
Operator	One or more characters, or a word, representing a built-in LotusScript operation. Operations are performed on one of these types of values: literals, values that are represented by names, or values that are represented by expressions. For example, an asterisk (*) operator represents multiplication of two numeric values, and the <= operator represents a less-than-or-equal-to comparison of two numeric values or string values. Some operators are also keywords; for example, the keyword Not is the operator for logical negation of a value.
Keyword	A word with a fixed spelling and a particular meaning in the LotusScript language. A keyword is distinguished from a name by the fact that you do not get to choose a keyword's spelling and meaning, as you do with a name. Some keywords (such as Print) represent actions; others (such as Dir and Sin) represent built-in functions; others (such as Not) represent operators; others (such as Double) represent data types; and so on.
Special character	As their name implies, special characters are characters with miscellaneous but particular uses. For example, some special characters punctuate statements and lines in the script; some designate a particular data type when attached to a name. Some special characters are used in more than one way.

Within a statement, one element is sometimes separated from the next by white space (a space or a tab). Where white space is legal, a single space usually separates two elements. Extra white space can be used to make a statement more readable, but has no effect on the script being processed.

White space is needed primarily to separate names and keywords, or to make the use of a special character unambiguous. It is not needed with most non-alphanumeric operators, and is often illegal around a special character, such as a data type suffix character appended to a name.

Literals

There are two kinds of *literals*—numeric and string:

- A *numeric literal* represents a number. Numeric literals are also called *literal numbers*, or just *numbers*.

- A *string literal* represents text. String literals are also called *literal strings*, or just *strings*.

Numbers. A numeric literal represents numbers expressed in one of the following forms: decimal (1.11), scientific notation (1.11E+02), decimal integer (111), binary, octal, or hexadecimal.

Strings. A literal string in LotusScript is a string of characters enclosed in either double quotations (") or vertical bars (|). A literal string can include any character. Its maximum length is 32K. The *empty string* (*null*) has no characters at all and is represented by "".

To include a quotation mark in a string enclosed in quotation marks, use two quotation marks (""). For example,

```
PRINT "This is a quotation mark "" within a string."
```

prints the following line:

```
This is a quotation mark " within a string.
```

Likewise, to include a vertical bar in a string enclosed in vertical bars, use two vertical bars. A string enclosed in quotation marks differs in only one way from a string enclosed in vertical bars—a vertical bar string can include newline characters, while a quotation mark string cannot.

You can concatenate two strings together using the plus sign (+) or ampersand (&). For example,

```
PRINT "This is" + "more text."
```

prints the following:

```
This is more text.
```

Identifiers

You can and should give identifiers and labels meaningful and descriptive names. As you are designing and coding your LotusScript scripts, think about each identifier or variable, determine what it is to be used for, and choose a name that is informative.

An *identifier* is the name you give to a variable, constant, type, class, function, sub, or property.

The following rules govern the construction of identifiers in LotusScript:

- The first character in an identifier must be an uppercase or lowercase letter.
- The remaining characters must be letters, digits, or underscore (_).
- A data type suffix character (%, &, !, #, @, or $) can be appended to an identifier. It is not part of the identifier.
- The maximum length of an identifier is 40 characters, not including the optional suffix character.

Labels

A *label* gives a name to a statement and is built the same way as an identifier. It is followed by a colon (:). It cannot be suffixed with a data type suffix character. This section provides the guidelines for you to understand and work with identifiers and labels.

The rules that govern the use of labels in LotusScript are the following:

- A label can only appear at the beginning of a line.
- A label can appear on a line by itself.
- A given statement can have more than one label preceding it, but the label must appear on different lines.
- A given label cannot be used to label more than one statement in the same procedure.

The following statements transfer control to labels from some area within the LotusScript script:

- `GoSub`
- `GoTo`
- `If...GoTo`
- `On Error`
- `On...GoSub`
- `On...GoTo`
- `Resume`

Operators and Expressions

An *expression* consists of operands combined with operators.

- An *operand* is a language element that represents a value. Operands include constants, literals, variables, functions, and properties.
- An *operator* determines how the value of the expression is computed using the operands.

Keywords

Recall that a keyword is a word with a reserved meaning in the LotusScript language. The keywords name LotusScript statements, built-in functions, built-in constants, and data types. Four keywords are used to name subs that you can define in s script (`Initialize`, `Terminate`, `New`, and `Delete`). Other keywords are not names, but appear in statements, for example, `NoCase` or `Binary`. Some of the LotusScript operators, such as `Eqv` and `Imp`, are keywords.

You cannot redefine keywords to mean something else in a script, with one exception: keywords can name variables within a type, and variables and procedures within a class.

The following list shows all the LotusScript keywords:

Abs	Date	FreeFile	Lib	Random
Access	Date$	From	Like	Randomize
ACos	DateNumber	Function	Line	Read
ActivateApp	DateValue	Get	List	ReDim
Alias	Day	GetFileAttr	ListTag	Rem
And	Declare	GoSub	LMBCS	Remove
Any	DefCur	GoTo	Loc	Reset
Append	DefDbl	Hex	Lock	Resume
As	DefInt	Hex$	LOF	Return
Asc	DefLng	Hour	Log	Right
ASin	DefSng	If	Long	Right$
Atn	DefStr	IMEStatus	Loop	RightB
Atn2	DefVar	Imp	LSet	RightB$
Base	Delete	In	LTrim	RmDir
Beep	Dim	Input	LTrim$	Rnd
Bin	Dir	Input$	Me	Round
Bin$	Dir$	InputB	MessageBox	RSet
Binary	Do	InputB$	Mid	RTrim
Bind	Double	InputBox	Mid$	RTrim$
ByVal	Else	InputBox$	MidB	Second
Call	ElseIf	InStr	MidB$	Seek
Case	End	InStrB	Minute	Select
CCur	Environ	Int	MkDir	SendKeys
CDat	Environ$	Integer	Mod	Set
CDbl	EOF	Is	Month	SetFileAttr
ChDir	Eqv	IsArray	Name	Sgn
ChDrive	Erase	IsDate	New	Shared
Chr	Erl	IsElement	Next	Shell
Chr$	Err	IsEmpty	NoCase	Sin
CInt	Error	IsList	Not	Single
Class	Error$	IsNull	NOTHING	Space
CLng	Evaluate	IsNumeric	Now	Space$
Close	Event	IsObject	NULL	Spc
Command	Execute	IsScalar	Oct	Sqr
Command$	Exit	IsUnknown	Oct$	Static
Compare	Exp	Kill	On	Step
Const	FALSE	LBound	Open	Stop
Cos	FileAttr	LCase	Option	Str
CSng	FileCopy	LCase$	Or	Str$
CStr	FileDateTime	Left	Output	StrCompare
CurDir	FileLen	Left$	PI	String
CurDir$	Fix	LeftB	Preserve	String$
CurDrive	For	LeftB$	Print	Sub
CurDrive$	ForAll	Len	Private	Tab
Currency	Format	LenB	Property	Tan
CVar	Format$	LenBP	Public	Then
DataType	Fraction	Let	Put	Time

Time$	Trim$	UChr	UseLSX	While
TimeNumber	TRUE	UChr$	UString	Width
Timer	Type	Uni	UString$	With
TimeValue	TypeName	Unicode	Val	Write
To	UBound	Unlock	Variant	Xor
Today	UCase	Until	Weekday	Year
Trim	UCase$	Use	Wend	Yield

Special Characters

LotusScript uses special characters, including punctuation characters and others, for several purposes. Special characters are used to do the following:

- Delimit literal strings
- Designate variables as having particular data types
- Punctuate lists, such as argument lists and subscript lists
- Punctuate statements
- Punctuate lines in a script

Table 16.3 lists the special characters used in LotusScript.

Table 16.3   LotusScript Special Characters

Character	Usage
" (quotation mark)	Opening and closing delimiter for a literal string on a single line.
| (vertical bar)	Opening and closing delimiter for a multi-line literal string. To include a vertical bar in the string, use double bars (||).
{ } (braces)	Delimits a multi-line literal string. To include an open brace in the string, use a single open brace ({). To include a close brace in the string, use double close braces (}}).
: (colon)	Separates multiple statements on a line. When following an identifier at the beginning of a line, designates the identifier as a label.
$ (dollar sign)	When suffixed to the identifier in a variable declaration or an implicit variable declaration, declares the data type of the variable as String. When prefixed to an identifier, designates the identifier as a product constant.
% (percent sign)	When suffixed to the identifier in a variable declaration or an implicit variable declaration, declares the data type of the variable as Integer. When suffixed to either the identifier or the value being assigned in a constant declaration, declares the constant's data type as Integer. Designates a compiler directive, such as %Rem or %If.
& (ampersand)	When suffixed to the identifier in a variable declaration or an implicit variable declaration, declares the data type of the variable as Long. When suffixed to either the identifier or the value being assigned in a constant declaration, declares the constant's data type as Long. Prefixes a binary (&B), octal (&O), or hexadecimal (&H) number. Designates the string concatenation operator in an expression.

Character	Usage
! (exclamation point)	When suffixed to the identifier in a variable declaration or an implicit variable declaration, declares the data type of the variable as `Single`. When suffixed to either the identifier or the value being assigned in a constant declaration, declares the constant's data type as `Single`.
# (pound sign)	When suffixed to the identifier in a variable declaration or an implicit variable declaration, declares the data type of the variable as `Double`. When suffixed to either the identifier or the value being assigned in a constant declaration, declares the constant's data type as `Double`. When prefixed to a literal number or a variable identifier, specifies a file number in certain file I/O statements and functions.
@ (at sign)	When suffixed to the identifier in a variable declaration or an implicit variable declaration, declares the data type of the variable as `Currency`. When suffixed to either the identifier or the value being assigned in a constant declaration, declares the constant's data type as `Currency`.
* (asterisk)	Specifies the string length in a fixed-length string declaration. Designates the multiplication operator in an expression.
( ) (parentheses)	Groups an expression, controlling the order of evaluation of items in the expression. Encloses an argument in a sub or function call that should be passed by value. Encloses the argument list in function and sub definitions, and in calls to functions and subs. Encloses the array bounds in array declarations, and the subscripts in references to array elements. Encloses the list tag in a reference to a list element.
. (period)	When suffixed to a type variable or an object reference variable, references members of the type or object. As a prefix in a product object reference, designates the selected product object. As a prefix in an object reference within a `With` statement, designates the object referred to by the statement. Designates the decimal point in a floating-point literal value.
.. (two periods)	Within a reference to a procedure in a derived class that overrides a procedure of the same name in a base class, specifies the overridden procedure.
[ ] (brackets)	Delimits names used by certain Lotus products to identify product objects.
, (comma)	Separates arguments in calls to functions and subs, and in function and sub definitions. Separates bounds in array declarations, and subscripts in references to array elements. Separates expressions in `Print` and `Print #` statements. Separates elements in many other statements.
; (semicolon)	Separates expressions in `Print` and `Print #` statements.
' (quote)	Designates the beginning of a comment. The comment continues to the end of the current line.
_ (underscore)	When preceded by at least one space or tab, continues the current line to the next line.

II

Designing Applications

The statements in a script are written as lines of text. These lines are processed one after another by the LotusScript compiler to produce a module that LotusScript can run.

Directive Statements

A special kind of statement, called a *directive*, is treated specially by the compiler. There are two types of directives:

- %REM...%ENDREM—The keywords %REM and %ENDREM indicate the beginning and end of a comment of any length. The compiler ignores all lines that appear between these keywords.

- %INCLUDE filename in quotes —When the compiler encounters %INCLUDE in a script, it inserts the contents of another designated file of ASCII text in the script at that point, and then continues compiling line by line, beginning with the first line of the included file.

A script also can include one-line comments that the compiler ignores. These can be the contents of a REM (remark) statement, or anything following an apostrophe (') on any line.

Understanding Statements and Lines

The statements of a script are written as lines of text. The text on a line can begin at the left margin, or it can be indented on the line without affecting the meaning. The script can include blank lines without the meaning of the script being altered.

Statements are commonly written one to a line, as in the following example:

```
DIM A AS STRING
A = "This is a test line"
PRINT A
```

Except as described below, LotusScript regards a new line as marking the end of a statement. The next line starts a new statement.

To write a statement on two or more lines, use an underscore (_) as a *line continuation character* at the end of each line that needs to be continued. The following example is the same script as above, but with a line-continuation character included at the end of the first line:

```
DIM A _
AS STRING
A = "This is a test line"
PRINT A
```

Although it certainly was unnecessary for this short DIM statement, you will find this technique important in many situations. It enables you to break a long statement to make it more readable, or so that it is displayed conveniently on several lines. An underscore used to continue a line must be preceded by at least one space.

Including Comments in a Script

An apostrophe (') designates the rest of the current line as a comment. When LotusScript processes the statements in a script, all comments are ignored. The following script has exactly the same results as the preceding example:

```
DIM A _ 'Declare A to accept a constant
AS STRING
A = "This is a test line"
PRINT A
```

Multiple Statements on a Line

Any number of statements can appear on the same line; that is, as many as will fit. A colon (:) separates one statement from the next statement on the same line. The line

```
DIM A AS STRING : DIM B AS VARIANT
```

is equivalent to the following two lines:

```
DIM A AS STRING
DIM B AS VARIANT
```

With a few exceptions, any statement can start in the middle of a line, after another statement and a colon. The exceptions are:

- %INCLUDE directives—This must be first and only LotusScript item on a line.

- %REM...%ENDREM directives—%REM and %ENDREM each must be first on a line.

- Any labeled statement—The statement must be first on a line.

Block Statements

Some statements, called *block statements*, appear on multiple lines and are delimited by two or more keywords; these often contain other statements.

For example, the FOR...NEXT statement is a block statement. It begins with FOR and ends with NEXT, and includes one or more statements that are executed a specified number of times. Its syntax is as follows:

```
FOR count = first TO last [STEP first]
    statements to be executed
NEXT [count]
```

The following list describes all the block statements in LotusScript. For detailed examples of these block statements, refer to the online Help included with Lotus Notes Release 4.

- Declarations for subprograms:

    FUNCTION...END FUNCTION

    SUB...END SUB

    PROPERTY GET/SET...END PROPERTY

■ Declarations for classes and types:

```
CLASS...END CLASS
TYPE...END TYPE
```

■ Control statements in which other statements are executed

```
DO...LOOP
FOR...NEXT
FORALL...END FORALL
IF...THEN...ELSE...END IF
SELECT CASE...END SELECT
WHILE...WEND
```

The Notes Programming Environment

The programming environment has three main components—the programmer pane, the script debugger window, and the utilities pane.

The programmer pane becomes available at the bottom of any window in which you can use LotusScript (see fig. 16.1). It lets you write LotusScript code, and then check the code's syntax.

Fig. 16.1

Here is an example of LotusScript in the programmer pane.

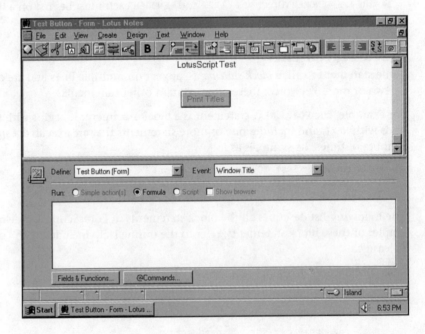

The script debugger window becomes available when a LotusScript script is executed in Lotus Notes and you have requested it by choosing File, Tools, Debug LotusScript (see fig. 16.2). It executes LotusScript one line at a time, or lets you set a breakpoint so that the script stops executing at a predetermined location.

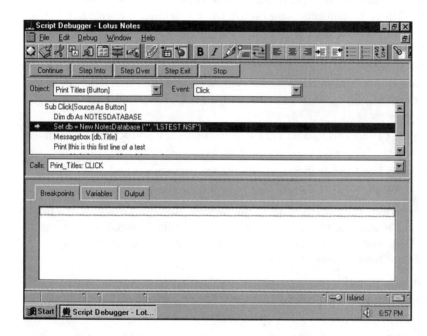

Fig. 16.2

You can debug LotusScript using the script debugger window.

The utilities pane becomes available at the bottom of the script debugger window, and lets you do the following:

- View a list of all the breakpoints set for LotusScript script in the current document
- View variables and edit their values
- Enter and execute lines of script as a means of testing them

These three main components are discussed further in the following sections.

Using the Programmer Pane

The programmer pane is displayed at the bottom of any Notes window that allows LotusScript script. You can also use the programmer pane to write @formulas. For LotusScript, you can use the programmer pane to do the following:

- Drag the horizontal bar separating the programmer pane from the rest of the window up or down to size the pane to your preference. This step can be performed at any time while the programmer pane is visible.
- Create or select the field or button for which you want to write a script, or use the Define box to attach the script to a Notes object such as a field, button, or action.

- Select Script for the Run option.

- If necessary, use the Event box to select an event to trigger execution of the script.

- Use the script editor to write, edit, and view a script, and to check the syntax of the script. The script editor becomes active when you enter the large box in the programmer pane. The top of the pane is where Notes fields and buttons are present.

- Select the Show browser option to view the browser, which appears as an additional pane to the right of the programmer pane. Drag the vertical bar separating the two panes if you want to adjust their sizes. Deselect Show browser to hide the browser.

- Click Fields & Functions to obtain a list of the fields and @functions you can use in your script.

- Use the Errors box to view messages describing syntax errors and other errors that occur during script entry and compilation.

The Define box reflects the current focus in the window above; for example, if a field named FirstName is selected, then FirstName is selected in the Define box. In some windows, the Define box is not present—for example, when you create an agent—because you do not have to select an object.

The Define box also includes (Global), which gives you access to a script where you can define subprograms and declare variables that are available to all objects in the current document.

Depending which Notes object (field or button) you're working with, the following events can be selected:

- (Declarations) applies to all scriptable objects.

   This provides an area where you view and declare variables and types that are available to all events in the object. Use the (Declarations) event for the (Global) object to view and declare variables and types for all events, for all objects in the document.

- Click applies to actions, buttons, and hotspots in the document. Selecting the Click action activates the LotusScript script that is associated with action.

- Entering and Exiting apply to editable fields on a Notes form. Tabbing or positioning the cursor into (for Entering) or out of (for Exiting) a field activates the associated script.

- Recalc applies to all field objects, not button objects. Choosing View, Refresh fields activates the associated script for all fields in the current document.

- Opening and Closing apply to documents only. Opening a document activates the Opening script; closing a document activates the Closing script.

■ `Initialize` and `Terminate` apply to all scriptable objects. Opening or closing an object, respectively, activates the associated initialize or terminate script. When a document is opened, events occur as follows: initialize document, initialize fields, open document. When a document is closed, events occur as follows: close document, terminate document, terminate fields.

The browser provides syntactical entries for the following categories of components:

■ Notes classes

■ Notes constants

■ Notes subroutines and functions

■ Notes variables

■ LotusScript script language elements

Select the component from the box, and open the component categories by clicking the arrows.

To put an entry into the script area, select the entry in the browser, then click Paste. If no errors exist, the message box is empty. If errors exist, they appear in the message box in the order in which they occurred. Messages have the following format:

```
Object: event: line#. errormessage
```

When you select an error from the message box, the corresponding line in the script is highlighted.

Using the Script Editor

The *script editor*, the large box in the programmer pane, lets you do the following:

■ Move the insertion point (mouse pointer) while you edit a script

■ Select text

■ Cut, copy, and paste text

■ Format a script automatically

■ Create an additional script

■ Complete a block statement

■ Complete a directive automatically

■ Delete a script

■ Rename an object or subprogram

■ Save a script

Moving the Insertion Point While Editing a Script. Table 16.4 lists keys and key combinations that move the insertion point.

Table 16.4 Moving the Insertion Point

Key Combination	Effect
Right arrow	Moves the insertion point one character to the right
Left arrow	Moves the insertion point one character to the left
Up arrow	Moves the insertion point up one line
Down arrow	Moves the insertion point down one line
Home	Moves the insertion point to the beginning of the current line
End	Moves the insertion point to the end of the current line
PgUp	Scrolls up, one screen retaining one line from the previous screen
PgDn	Scrolls down, one screen retaining one line from the previous screen
Ctrl+Right arrow	Moves the insertion point to the first character in the next word
Ctrl+Left arrow	Moves the insertion point to the first character in the previous word

Ways to Select Text. There are two ways to select text when editing a LotusScript script:

- Selecting text with key combinations (see Table 16.5)
- Selecting text with the mouse (see Table 16.6)

Table 16.5 Selecting Text with Key Combinations

Key Combination	Effect
Shift+Left arrow	Selects the character to the left of the insertion point
Shift+Right arrow	Selects the character to the right of the insertion point
Shift+Up arrow	Selects the text starting one character to the left of the insertion point and ending at the character on the line above and one character to the right of the insertion point
Shift+Down arrow	Selects the text starting one character to the right of the insertion point and ending at the character one line below and one character to the left of the insertion point
Shift+Home	Selects the text starting with the character to left of the insertion point and ending with the first character on the line
Shift+End	Selects the text starting with the character to the right of the insertion point and ending with the last character on the line
Ctrl+Shift+Left arrow	Selects the previous word, or selects the first part of the word if the insertion point is in the word
Ctrl+Shift+Right arrow	Selects the next word, or selects the remainder of the word if the insertion point is in the word

Key Combination	Effect
Ctrl+Shift+Up arrow	Selects the text starting to the left of the insertion point and ending at the character one line above and one character to the right of the insertion point
Ctrl+Shift+Down	Selects the text starting one character to the right of the insertion point and ending at the character one line below and one character to the left of the insertion point

Table 16.6   Selecting Text with the Mouse

Key Combination	Effect
Shift+click	Selects the text from the insertion point to the position of the mouse
Click and drag	Selects the text from the position of the click to the final position of the mouse
Double-click	Selects the entire word and any following blank space

Cutting, Copying, and Pasting Text. Text must be selected by one of the above methods before it can be cut, copied, or pasted. After selecting the desired text, do one of the following actions:

■ Choose Edit, Cut to cut selected text to the Clipboard.

■ Choose Edit, Copy to copy selected text to the Clipboard.

■ Choose Edit, Paste to insert a copy of the current contents of the Clipboard at the location of the insertion point.

Formatting a Script Automatically. The script editor automatically enforces the following capitalization and coding conventions for LotusScript:

■ LotusScript keywords appear with the initial letter capitalized.

■ Lines within a block statement (for example, a FOR...NEXT statement) are indented one tab.

Creating an Additional Script. A number of LotusScript scripts—such as Initialize, Terminate, Click, Entering, and Exiting—are automatically defined as events for the current Notes object. You select them from the Event box after you have selected the Notes object (field or button). You can create additional scripts and other block structures as shown in Table 16.7. After a new script is created, you can access it from the Event box also.

Table 16.7 Creating Additional Scripts	
What You Type	**What LotusScript Does**
Sub *name*	Creates an empty SUB...END SUB block called *name* for the current object, and adds it to the Event box. Positions the insertion point in the subroutine.
Function *name*	Creates an empty FUNCTION...END FUNCTION block called *name* for the current object, and adds it to the Event box. Positions the insertion point in the function.
Property Get *name*	Creates an empty PROPERTY GET...END PROPERTY GET block called *name* for the current object, and adds an item called *name* Get to the Event box. Positions the insertion point in the subprogram.
Property Set *name*	Creates an empty PROPERTY SET...END PROPERTY SET block called *name* for the current object, and adds an item called *name* Set to the Event box. Positions the insertion point in the subprogram.
Type *name*	Creates an empty TYPE...END TYPE block called *name* for the current object, and adds it to the end of the (Declarations) script for the object. Positions the insertion point at the beginning of the TYPE...END TYPE block.
Dim *name*	If the Dim statement is typed outside of a subprogram, adds a Dim statement for *name* to the end of the (Declarations) script for the current object. Positions the insertion point at the Dim statement.
Option *string*	Adds an Option statement to the beginning of the (Declarations) script for the current object. Positions the insertion point at the Option statement.
Deftype *letter_range*	Adds a Deftype statement to the beginning of the (Declarations) script for the current object. Positions the insertion point in the (Declarations) script at the Deftype statement.
Class *name*	Adds a Class statement to the beginning of the (Declarations) script for the current object. Positions the insertion point in the (Declarations) script at the Class statement.

Completing a Block Statement Automatically. The following block structures are automatically terminated, and the insertion point is placed in a new indented line within the block structure:

- A FOR statement is automatically terminated by a NEXT statement.
- A DO WHILE or DO UNTIL statement is automatically terminated by a LOOP statement.
- A FORALL statement is automatically terminated by an END FORALL statement.
- An IF...THEN statement is automatically terminated by an END IF statement.

- A SELECT CASE statement is automatically terminated by an END SELECT statement.

- A WHILE statement is automatically terminated by a WEND statement.

Completing a Directive Automatically. LotusScript completes some LotusScript directives automatically, as follows:

- If a script contains an %IF directive without a matching %ENDIF directive, LotusScript inserts a new line containing %ENDIF immediately below the %IF directive when the script editor is closed or loses focus, or when a different object or script is selected.

- If a script contains a %REM directive without a matching %END REM directive, LotusScript inserts a new line containing %END REM immediately below the %REM directive when the script editor is closed or loses focus, or when a different object or script is selected.

Deleting a Script. Deleting a script is accomplished when you are in the programmer pane. You delete a script with the following steps:

1. Select the object (button, filed, action) containing the script.
2. Select the script from the Event box (Entering, Exiting, Initialize, Terminate, Click).
3. Highlight the LotusScript script.
4. Delete the complete text of the script by pressing the Delete key, spacebar, or Backspace key.

> **Tip**
>
> When deleting a LotusScript script, make certain that all script lines are deleted, including the Sub and End statements. If Sub or End is present, the script will give you an error at runtime, though not during compilation.

Saving a Script. After you have made all the changes or enhancements to a LotusScript script, you need to save it, using one of the following methods:

- Choose File, Save to save the document along with all its associated scripts, formulas, and forms.

- Exit the Notes form on which you are working, and choose Yes to save changes.

- Choose Design, Test Form and then choose Yes to save changes.

Compiling Scripts. Compilation of LotusScript scripts occurs automatically in the following ways:

- A partial compilation occurs as you enter the script. Syntax errors and other per-line errors are reported at this time.

- A complete compilation occurs when you save the script. All remaining compile errors are reported at this time.

- A complete compilation occurs when you click the insertion point outside of the script entry portion of the programmer pane. All remaining compile errors are reported at this time.

You should correct all compile errors before you save a script and exit the Notes form or agent. LotusScript script errors are reported again when a document using the script is opened. The document might or might not open, depending on the severity of the errors and where they are in the document.

Using the Debugger

The script debugger allows you to step through a script one line at a time, or to stop script execution at preset breakpoints. By doing this, you can see how the script is executing, and what values are being assigned to particular variables; this might help you to determine where a faulty script is aborting. Each line of the script is displayed in the top half of the screen, and as lines are executed the arrow moves from line to line, always positioned on the line that is to be executed next.

The debugger provides the following capabilities:

- Runs in debug mode
- Selects a subprogram
- Provides ways to step through a LotusScript script
- Stops LotusScript script execution
- Provides ways to use the LotusScript script utilities

Running in Debug Mode. The script debugger does not run automatically. The only way to use the debugger is to start it before you execute or open the Notes document that contains the script to be debugged. To run the debugger, do one of the following:

- Choose File, Tools, Debug LotusScript to enable the debugger.
- Perform the action that starts the script: opening a document, clicking a button in a document, or choosing an action.
- Click and drag the horizontal bar separating the two window panes if you want to adjust the relative sizes of the two panes.
- Choose File, Tools, Script Debugger to stop the debug mode process.

Looking at the debugger in action should help you understand the following discussions on using the debugger (see fig. 16.3).

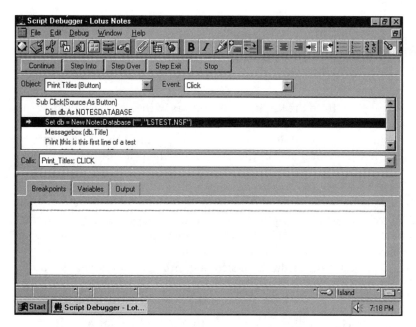

Fig. 16.3

Use the debugger to find errors in your script.

When you are in debug mode and a script executes, execution pauses at the first line of the script. The debugger opens with the following components:

- A Debug menu on the menu bar
- Debug action icons below the menu bar
- A Debug pane at the top of the window that appears
- A window to let you watch the script being debugged
- A Define box for the object containing the script
- An Event box for the event containing the script
- A Calls box for a list of subprograms currently on the execution stack
- A utilities pane at the bottom of the window with tabs for breakpoints, variables, and outputs

When you run a LotusScript script in debug mode, the script is in one of three states:

- When a script is interrupted at a breakpoint, the debugger has control.
- When a script is being stepped through, control passes to the script, but is returned to the debugger after a single statement in the script is executed.
- When a script is continuing, it runs uninterrupted until a breakpoint is reached. If you do not set any breakpoints in a script, it runs as if the debugger were not present.

Selecting a Subprogram. As you execute the script, the current subprogram appears in the debugger window.

The Calls box contains a list of the subprograms currently being executed—in order of execution—with the currently executing subprogram at the top of the list. Subprograms are listed as objects and events. For example, if the list contains Print Document: Click, then Print Document is a button on the Notes form, and Click is the event that will occur when the button is pressed.

If you select a subprogram from the list, its script appears in the debugger window. If you select the subprogram that is currently executing, the current pointer points to the statement about to be executed. If you select another subprogram, the current pointer points to the statement that calls the next subprogram.

If the source or a subprogram is not available (as with an external script file), the name is dimmed.

Stepping through a Script. The script debugger has three ways to step through the script—Step Into, Step Over, and Step Exit. Each of these steps tell the script debugger to start and stop execution of LotusScript script statements in different ways. The debugger provides the following facilities for stepping through a LotusScript script:

■ **Step Into**—Click the Step Into action button, choose Debug, Step Into, or press F8 to execute the next statement in the script. If the current statement calls a subprogram, the debugger displays the script for the subprogram, and sets the current line to the first executable statement in the subprogram script. If no source script is available for the subprogram (because it is an external file), Step Into behaves the same as Step Over.

■ **Step Over**—Click the Step Over action button, choose Debug, Step Over, or press Shift+F8 to execute the next statement in the current program unit. If the statement calls a subprogram script, the debugger executes the entire subprogram as if it were a single statement, and sets the current line to the next statement in the calling program script.

■ **Step Exit**—Click the Step Exit action button, choose Debug, Step Exit, or press Ctrl+F8 to continue executing the current subprogram script, and stop in the subprogram that called it at the line following the call. If the subprogram was not called by another, execution continues to the next breakpoint or to completion.

Continuing Execution of the Script without Stopping. To execute the remaining script statements without stopping for any subprograms or other script statements, click the Continue action button; alternatively, choose Debug, Continue (or press F5).

Debugging with Breakpoints

As discussed earlier in the chapter, you can set breakpoints to interrupt the execution of a script. The debugger halts execution just before any statement at which a breakpoint is set. While script execution is interrupted, you can examine and modify the values of variables, or use other debugger features.

After you set a breakpoint, you can permanently clear it, temporarily disable it, or enable it again. Breakpoints are displayed as red stop signs when enabled; yellow slashes are added when they are disabled.

You can set a breakpoint at any executable statement. If the statement has multiple lines, you can set a breakpoint only on the first line of the statement. If you edit a line of script that has a breakpoint set, the breakpoint remains there unless the line no longer meets the rules just described.

Setting and Clearing Breakpoints. To set a breakpoint, you must be in the LotusScript script statement portion of the script debugger. Perform the following steps to set a breakpoint:

1. Click to select a statement at which no breakpoint is currently set—one that has no red stop sign beside it.
2. Double-click the statement, choose Debug, Set/Clear Breakpoint, or press F8.

A red stop sign is displayed beside the statement, and execution of the script will stop whenever it reaches the statement.

To clear a breakpoint that has been set, perform the following steps:

1. Click to select the statement at which the breakpoint is set.
2. Double-click once if the stop sign has a yellow slash, or twice if the stop sign is solid red. Choose Debug, Set/Clear Breakpoint, or press F9.

To clear all breakpoints from all scripts in the active document, choose Debug, Clear All Breakpoints.

Enabling and Disabling Breakpoints. An enabled breakpoint appears with a red stop sign beside the script statement. A disabled breakpoint appears as a red stop sign with a yellow slash through it. To disable a breakpoint, perform the following steps:

1. Click to select the statement at which the enabled breakpoint is set.
2. Double-click the statement, or choose Debug, Disable Breakpoint (or press Shift+F9).

To disable all breakpoints for all scripts in the active document, choose Debug, Disable All Breakpoints.

To enable a previously disabled breakpoint within a script, perform the following steps:

1. Click to select the statement at which the disabled breakpoint is set.
2. Double-click the statement twice, or choose Debug, Enable Breakpoint.

To enable all breakpoints for all scripts in the active document, choose Debug, Enable All Breakpoints.

Continuing Script Execution after a Breakpoint. To start executing the current script, or to resume execution after the script is interrupted at a breakpoint, click the Continue action button, or choose Debug, Continue. This starts the script running to its completion without stopping unless an invalid script statement is encountered.

Stopping Script Execution. To stop script execution while the debugger is open, choose Debug, Stop. Any script that is at a breakpoint is stopped as if the end of the script has been reached. No further LotusScript script statements will be executed until the LotusScript script is started again.

Using the Breakpoint Panel. Click the Breakpoints tab to access the breakpoints panel; alternatively, you can choose Debug, Breakpoints to reach this panel. The panel displays the current breakpoints in the following formats:

```
Object. event: line
```

If the breakpoint is disabled, (Disabled) is appended.

Using the Variables Panel. Click the Variables tab to access the variables panel; alternatively, you can choose Debug, Variables to reach this panel.

In the variables panel, the variables defined for the current procedure appear in a columnar display, showing the name of each variable, its data type, and its value. To view array or type members, click the arrow to the left of the variable name.

To change the value of a variable, do the following:

1. Select the variable by clicking the variable to be changed.
2. Type the value in the New Value box, and press Enter.

Using the Output Panel. Click the Output tab to access the output panel; alternatively, you can choose Debug, Output to reach this panel.

Script output—for example, the output from a Print statement—goes to the output panel. You can do the following in this panel:

- View the output.
- Clear the contents of the panel by clicking Clear All.
- Copy selected output by choosing Edit, Copy. (Choose Edit, Select all to select the entire contents of the panel.)

From Here...

Now that you have learned about LotusScript syntax, script structure, the programmer pane, and the debugger pane, you are ready to move on to actually write and execute LotusScript programs. You might want to turn to the following chapters:

- Chapter 14, "Formula Functions," discusses all of the @functions that you can use in formulas.
- Chapter 17, "Writing Scripts with LotusScript," looks at writing LotusScript scripts to perform simple Notes functions.
- Chapter 22, "Notes: Under the Hood," provides an understanding of what happens internally when you run Notes.

Writing Scripts with LotusScript

Chapter 16, "LotusScript: A Whole New Programming Language," introduced you to LotusScript, and reviewed the language's syntax and parts, including the programmer pane and script debugger window. With this background, you can build a sample Lotus Notes database that uses some of the LotusScript techniques you learned in Chapter 16.

In this chapter, you will do the following:

- Build a database
- Write a script to print the name of the database
- Review some LotusScript code
- Write a script to retrieve a Notes document field variable
- Write a script to change a Notes document field variable
- Discuss the LotusScript keywords specific to Notes

Creating a Form and Button

The first thing you need to do is to build a Notes database. You have read in previous chapters how to do this, and the following steps should refresh your memory:

1. Choose File, Database, New. The New Database dialog box opens (see fig. 17.1).
2. For Server, use Local.
3. Enter the title of the database to be built; for this example, type **LotusScript Test**.
4. By default, the filename is determined based on the first eight characters of the title; change it to **LSTEST.NSF**.
5. Click OK.

Fig. 17.1

Create a new database by completing the entries in the New Database dialog box.

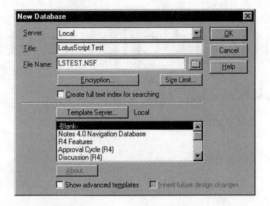

Your example database has now been built, and you are ready to start building a document form. After that, you can write and test your first script.

To create a new form, choose Create, Design, Form. The programmer pane displayed in figure 17.2 appears. This is where you will be entering the design of the Notes form and the LotusScript script that will be executed.

Fig. 17.2

This is the programmer pane.

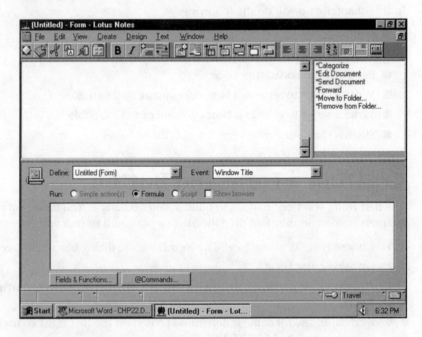

The LotusScript script that you will be coding during this example will run each time the user clicks a button on the Notes document form. But before you can run any LotusScript script, you must first create the Notes form using the following steps:

1. Type **LotusScript Test** on the first line to serve as the form's title.

2. Select the text you just typed, then choose Text, Align Paragraph, Center to center the text on the line.

3. Place the insertion point at the end of the heading line, then press Enter twice to create two blank lines.

4. Choose Create, Hotspot, Button to create a button on the form. The Button Properties InfoBox appears (see fig. 17.3).

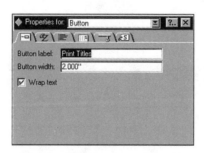

Fig. 17.3

Choose the button label and width in the Button Properties InfoBox.

5. In the Button label text box, type **Print Titles**.

6. Close the Button Properties InfoBox. Your Notes form now should resemble figure 17.4.

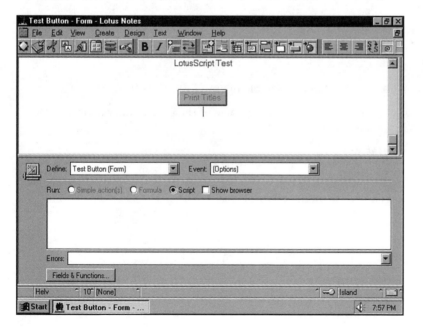

Fig. 17.4

This is the programmer pane with the Notes form built.

II

Designing Applications

7. In the programmer pane, click the Define drop-down list box and select Print Titles (Button). Your form should now look like figure 17.5.

Fig. 17.5

This programmer pane shows Print Titles selected in the Define drop-down list box.

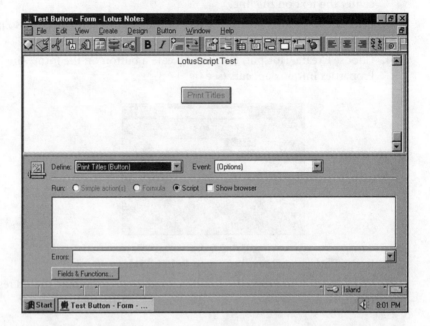

8. Select the Script radio button.

9. Make sure that Click is displayed in the Event drop-down list box. If it isn't, select it.

The programmer pane now should resemble figure 17.6.

Enter the following lines into the LotusScript area of the programmer pane, between the Sub and End Sub statements.

```
Dim db as NotesDatabase
Set db = New NotesDatabase ("", "LSTEST.NSF")
Messagebox (db.Title)
```

Your programmer pane now should resemble figure 17.7.

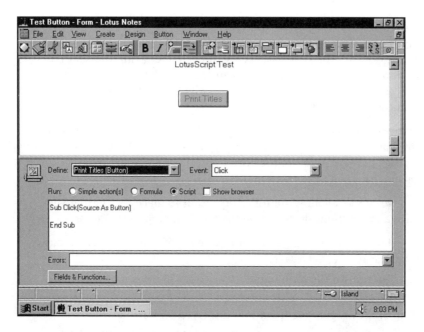

Fig. 17.6

Here you see the programmer pane after selecting Print Titles for Define and selecting Script for Run.

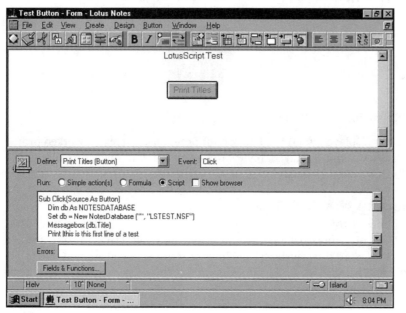

Fig. 17.7

This programmer pane shows LotusScript entered for the Print Titles button.

Compiling and Testing the Script

The LotusScript is now ready to be compiled and tested. *Compiling* is the process by which LotusScript validates the syntax of each script statement, and translates the LotusScript statements into a form that Notes can execute. Notes compiles the button script when you close and save the document, click the top portion of the programmer pane, or choose Design, Test Form.

For now, click the top half of the programmer pane. This will perform validation of the LotusScript that was entered previously. When the script has been checked for any errors and no errors have been found, the bottom of the programmer pane becomes blank, and you are ready to test the button.

Now that you have checked your script for errors, test it to make certain that what you entered runs and functions properly. Do the following to test the script:

1. Choose Design, Test Form. The Save Form As dialog box is displayed because your design has not yet been saved.

2. Type **Test Button** for the form name.

3. Click OK. The form is saved, with the message Compiling Script displayed on the bottom of the programmer pane and displayed on-screen.

4. Click the Print Titles button; a message should be displayed (see fig. 17.8).

Fig. 17.8

The message box that results from pressing the Print Titles button.

5. Click OK to return to the form.

If the message was displayed, then the LotusScript program you created worked properly. If the message was not displayed, review the form design to make sure that you typed the script statements correctly.

Understanding the Script

To understand how LotusScript works, you need to review the script line by line. The lines of script that you wrote used a Lotus Notes keyword (NotesDatabase) and a standard LotusScript keyword (Messagebox). The lines of script that you entered told Notes to do the following:

1. Access the LSTEST.NSF Lotus Notes database on the local hard drive.

2. Retrieve the name of the database.

3. Display the name of the database.

Now you can review line by line the LotusScript script that has been entered and executed.

Begin a Subroutine. `Sub Click(Source As Button)` defines the beginning of a *subroutine*, or *sub*. This line was created for you by Lotus Notes when you selected `Script` as the Run option. Every subroutine in LotusScript begins with a `Sub` statement and ends with an `End Sub` statement. These two lines tell LotusScript the beginning and end of a sub program.

Declare an Object Variable. `Dim db As NotesDatabase` declares a variable named `db`, which is an instance of the `NotesDatabase` class. Whenever a variable is declared as an instance of a class, the variable is called an *object*.

`Dim` tells LotusScript that you are declaring an object variable. You use `Dim` along with `As` any time you declare a variable. For example, the following are valid declarations:

```
Dim x As Integer
Dim name As String
Dim view As NotesView
```

`db` is the name of the object; `NotesDatabase` is the name of the class.

Set the Value of the Object. `Set db = New NotesDatabase("","LSTEST.NSF")` sets the value of the object `db` to refer to the `LSTEST.NSF` database file on the local hard drive. Prior to LotusScript executing the following statement, `db` has a value of nothing, since nothing has been set or assigned to this object. Let's examine the various parts of the statement:

- `Set db =`—Tells LotusScript that you want to set `db` equal to the value retained by `New`.
- `New`—Tells LotusScript that you want to construct a new object.
- `NotesDatabase`—Tells LotusScript that the new object should be an instance of the `NotesDatabase` class.
- `""` and `"LSTEST.NSF"`—Tell LotusScript how to create the new object you want. The first parameter is the name of the server; here it's an empty string (`""`) because the database is on your local hard drive. Had the database been located on a Notes file server called NotesServer1, the first parameter would have been NotesServer1. The second parameter (`"LSTEST.NSF"`) is a string containing the filename of the database. This is the same format that is used in the `@DbLookup` Notes formula.

Print a Property of the Object in a Dialog Box. `Messagebox(db.Title)` gets the title of the database that `db` represents, and prints it in a dialog box on the screen:

- Messagebox—This is a LotusScript keyword that takes a string and prints that string in a dialog box. Messagebox is part of the LotusScript language.

- db.Title—This statement returns a string containing the title of the database. Title is a property defined in the NotesDatabase class. To access or modify a property within a script, you need the following three things:

  - The name of the object—in this case, it's db
  - A period (.)
  - The name of the property—in this case, it's Title

A property is only useful if you know which object it pertains to—that's why you need to use it in conjunction with an object name. The Title property, for example, is only useful if you know which database it pertains to, so you used the db object to access it. If you had a different NotesDatabase object, you could use the Title property the same way, but would get different results:

```
Dim anotherdb As NotesDatabase
Set anotherdb = New NotesDatabase ("","TestName.NSF")
MessageBox (db.Title)
```

This script would print the title of the database TestName.NSF. (To find out what other database properties could be displayed, refer to Table 17.2 later in this chapter.)

End Sub. End Sub defines the end of a subprogram or script—it tells Notes that the script has finished. Notes automatically creates this line for you.

A Script that Prints a List of Databases

The following LotusScript runs from a button in a Lotus Notes database. This script performs the following actions:

1. Opens an output print file named DBNAMES.PRT in the root directory of drive C.
2. Retrieves the current date.
3. Prints two lines of printer header information, and then one blank line.
4. Gets the first database on the local hard drive.
5. Loops through, printing the title and filename of each Notes database on your hard drive, until there are no more database entries.
6. Closes the print file to save it.

The script only works with a user's local Notes databases. It does not reference the Notes server database. You could modify the LotusScript script to do this, by changing line 3 to contain the name of the Lotus Notes server for which you wanted the databases reported.

To use this script, you have to create a Lotus Notes database or use an existing one. Then create a button, and write the following LotusScript script for the Click event of the button:

```
Sub Click(Source As Button)
    Open "c:\dbnames.prt" For Output As #1
    Dim Server As New notesdbdirectory ("")
    Dim DataBase As notesdatabase
    PrintDate = Date()
    Print #1, "DataBases on System"
    Print #1, "Printed on "; PrintDate
    Print #1, ""
    Set DataBase = Server.getfirstdatabase(DATABASE)
    While Not (DataBase Is Nothing)
        PrintTitle = DataBase.title
        dbname = DataBase.filename
        Print #1, PrintTitle; Tab(45); dbname
        Set DataBase = Server.getnextdatabase()
    Wend
    Close #1
    Print "Script processing completed"
End Sub
```

Understanding the Script

This section describes how each LotusScript statement or group of LotusScript statements are processed to produce the final output result.

Begin a Sub. `Sub Click(Source As Button)` defines the beginning of the subroutine.
This line was created for you by Lotus Notes when you selected `Script` as the Run
option in the programmer pane.

Open the Printer Output File. `Open "c:\dbnames.prt" For Output As #1` tells
LotusScript to open an output file named DBNAMES.PRT in the root directory of drive C,
and to refer to it as #1 throughout the rest of this script. Caution should be taken
with an open statement like this one, because whatever filename is specified will be
overwritten. This means that if this file existed before the Open statement is executed,
the original file will be lost. For example, if you specified `"C:\NOTES\NOTES.EXE"`, you
would delete and overwrite the NOTES.EXE file.

Set the Value of the *NotesDBDirectory* Object. `Dim Server As New notesdbdirectory`
`("")` sets the value of the object `Server` that refers to the Notes database directory on
the local hard drive.

Declare an Object Variable. `Dim DataBase As notesdatabase` declares a LotusScript
object named `DataBase` that will be used to refer to the Notes databases on the local
hard drive.

Get Current Date and Print Headers. `PrintDate = Date()` gets the current system
date for printing as part of the header.

The `Print` statements print the three lines of printer header information on the
printed output report:

■ `Print #1, "DataBases on System"` tells LotusScript to print the literal string
`"databases on System"` to output file #1.

- Print #1, "Printed on "; PrintDate tells LotusScript to print the value of the current date (PrintDate) to output file #1.
- Print #1, "" tells LotusScript to print a blank line to output file #1.

Get First Database. Set DataBase = Server.getfirstdatabase(DATABASE) instructs LotusScript to get the first database name from the local hard drive, and store that value in the variable db. Since the value of srv is blank, the GetFirstDatabase LotusScript command looks only on the user's local Notes location to find Notes databases. If you wanted LotusScript to look on a Notes file server, then the variable srv would have to be set to your server name; for example, Set Server = "Test Notes Server".

Loop To Read the Lotus Notes Databases. Line 10, While Not (DataBase Is Nothing), and line 15, Wend, instruct LotusScript to perform a loop—and continue to perform that loop—until the variable DataBase has no value associated with it.

Retrieve the Database Name and Title. PrintTitle = DataBase.title retrieves the title of the database currently contained in DataBase.

dbname = DataBase.filename retrieves the filename of the database currently contained in DataBase.

Print Title and Filename. Print #1, PrintTitle; Tab(45); dbname prints the title of the database, tabs 45 characters to the right, and prints the name of the database. Tab(45) was an arbitrary number of spaces to insert before printing the name of the database.

Get Next Database. Set DataBase = Server.getnextdatabase() instructs LotusScript to retrieve the next Notes database, and place its values into the variable DataBase.

Wend. Wend instructs LotusScript to loop back to the While statement to repeat the process, as long as there is a value in the variable db. If no value is present in db, then the looping stops and processing proceeds to line 16.

Close the Output. Close #1 closes the file #1. Recall that #1 is the output print file to which all the information processed by LotusScript so far has been printed. It is a file named DBNAMES.PRT located on drive C.

Indicate That Processing Has Ended. Print "Script processing completed" prints a statement in the status bar on the Notes workspace to indicate that the processing of this LotusScript is completed.

End Sub. End Sub defines the end of the LotusScript. Lotus Notes creates this line for you.

Sample of LotusScript Output.
```
DataBases on System
Printed on 1/9/96
```

```
Notes Help                        HELP4.NSF
Notes Administration Help         HELPADMN.NSF
Install Guide for Workstations    WRKINST.NSF
Migration Guide                   MIGRATE.NSF
Web Navigator Admin Guide         WEBADMIN.NSF
Web Navigator User's Guide        WEBUSER.NSF
Install Guide for Servers         SRVINST.NSF
Test Build Release Notes          README.NSF
```

A Script that Prints Database Built-In Properties

The following LotusScript script only works with a local Notes database—it does not reference a Notes server. This script asks for a Notes database filename, then prints various built-in database properties.

To use this LotusScript script, you have to create a Lotus Notes database or use an existing one. Then create a button, and write the following script for the Click event of the button:

```
Sub Click(Source As Button)
    Dim db As New NotesDatabase("", Inputbox$("Filename"))
    Print "Title              " db.Title
    Print "File name          " db.FileName
    Print "Path name          " db.FilePath
    Print "Replica ID         " db.ReplicaID
    Print "Size               " db.Size
    Print "Created            " db.Created
    Print "Last Modified      " db.LastModified
    Managers = db.Managers
    Forall Manager In Managers
        Print "Manager          " manager
    End Forall
End Sub
```

The values that are printed as a result of the Print statements are displayed on-screen in the status bar at the bottom of the Notes workspace. Since no Open, Print #, or Close # statements are in the script, the output of this script will not be printed to a file. If the output is to be printed to a file, then add the Open, Print #, and Close # statements to this script. Refer to the prior LotusScript script to see how these statements were used.

Using LotusScript in Lotus Notes

Now that you have written and tested some LotusScript examples, the remainder of this chapter covers the script classes that Lotus Notes defines for LotusScript; these classes allow you to access Notes structures at two levels:

- The *database (back-end) classes* let you access named databases, views, documents, and other Notes objects. You can access back-end objects from any LotusScript program.

■ The *user interface (UI) classes* let you access current objects that the user is working on. You can access UI objects from any LotusScript program except an agent.

Table 17.1 outlines the LotusScript classes defined by Lotus Notes.

Note
Accessing a back-end object through a UI object is possible but not supported.

Table 17.1 LotusScript Classes for Lotus Notes

Level	Class	Description
Back-end	NotesACL	Represents a collection of all the access control entries for a database.
	NotesACLEntry	Represents a single entry in an access control list.
	NotesAgent	Represents an agent.
	NotesDatabase	Represents a Notes database.
	NotesDateTime	Provides a means to translate between LotusScript and Lotus Notes date/time formatting.
	NotesDbDirectory	Represents the database files on a server or the local machine.
	NotesDocument	Represents a document in a database.
	NotesDocumentCollection	Represents a collection of documents.
	NotesEmbeddedObject	Represents embedded objects, links, and file attachments.
	NotesItem	Represents a piece of data on a document.
	NotesNewLetter	Is a summary document that contains information from, or links to, several other documents.
	NotesRichTextItem	Represents items that can contain rich text.
	NotesSession	Represents Notes environment information, providing access to environment variables, Address Books, information about the current user, and information about the current Notes platform and release number.
	NotesView	Represents a named view of a database.
UI	NotesUIWorkspace	Provides access to the current workspace (document).
	NotesUIDocument	Models the behavior of a Notes document window.

All LotusScript features work in Notes exactly as specified in generic LotusScript (the basic LotusScript language) with a few exceptions and clarifications, which are explained in the following sections.

Using the *%Include* Directive

%Include directives must be placed in the (Declarations) event for an object. Do not place %Include directives in the event containing the execution script.

Closing a File

You must explicitly close all files that you open. Otherwise, the files will remain open and lock out other attempts to open them until the user exits Notes. This applies to files opened and closed with the Open and Close script statements, not to Notes databases accessed through Notes objects.

In the section "A Script that Prints a List of Databases," had the Close #1 statement not been in the LotusScript script, the file would have remained open until you exited from Notes. This would have meant that the contents of the output file could not be viewed or printed to a printer. In attempting to print or view the file, the error Sharing violation would be displayed.

Using the Evaluate Statement

The evaluate statement in Lotus Notes has the following syntax:

```
returnValue = Evaluate(NotesFormula [,NotesObject])
```

NotesFormula must be a string. *NotesObject* is optional and provides context where needed for the formula; for example, if the formula accesses a field, *NotesObject* must be the NotesDocument object that contains the field. The return value is an array whose type and number of elements reflect the formula result: a single data element value is retrained to the first element (element 0) of the array.

You must use the Set statement to assign an object reference to a variable. For example, you might use the following:

```
Set db = srv.GetNextDatabase()
```

You must not, however, use the Set statement for any other type of assignment, including the assignment of an array of object references to a variable. For example, you cannot enter the following:

```
Views = db.Views
```

But you can enter this:

```
set View = db.Views(0)
```

Calling a Function or Subroutine

Use the Call keyword to call a function where no return value is wanted, or to call a subroutine. Enclose the argument list in parentheses. For example, you might use the following:

```
Call db.Open("",Inputbox$("File Name?"))
```

The parentheses can be omitted if the function or subroutine takes no arguments, as in the following example:

```
Call db.Close
```

You can omit the Call keyword, but if you do omit it, then do not enclose the argument list in parentheses. The result is something like the following:

```
db.Open "", Inputbox$("File Name?")
```

Using Parentheses To Pass by Value

You can pass an argument by value by enclosing it in parentheses, as in the following example:

```
Call subabc((11),(22))
```

This syntax can be confusing, especially if it appears in a subroutine call that does not use the Call statement. For example, this statement passes one argument by reference:

```
subabc 11
```

This statement passes one argument by value:

```
subabc (11)
```

Accessing Notes Databases

The NotesDatabase and NotesDbDirectory classes provide means for locating and opening Notes databases. A NotesDatabase object provides access to NotesView, DocumentCollection, and NotesDocument objects. NotesDocument objects can be accessed directly through a NotesDatabase object, or by first obtaining a NotesDocumentCollection or NotesView object.

Table 17.2 lists the NotesDatabase built-in data type properties. You can directly manipulate the properties that are of built-in data type. The rest of the properties are the Notes objects; for these you must use the associated properties and methods.

Table 17.2 NotesDatabase Properties

Property	Data Type	Description
Agents	NotesAgent Array	Agents in the database
Categories	String array	Categories in the database
Created	Date/Time	Date and time the database was created
DesignTemplateName	String	Database's design template, if any
FileName	String	Database filename

Property	Data Type	Description
FilePath	String	Database path
IsFTIndexed	Boolean	True if the database is full-text indexed
IsOpen	Boolean	True if the database is open
IsPrivateAddressBook	Boolean	True if database is Private Name & Address Book
IsPublicAddressBook	Boolean	True if database is Public Name & Address Book
LastFTIndexed	Date/Time	Date and time a full-text index was last updated
LastModified	Date/Time	Date and time the database was last modified
Managers	String array	Users who have Manager access to the database
Parent	NotesSession	Current Notes session
ReplicaID	Sting	Database replica ID in hexadecimal
Size	Integer	Database size in bytes
TemplateName	String	Database template name, if applicable
Title	String	Database title
Views	NotesView array	Named views in the database

Accessing Notes Views

The NotesView class lets you locate documents within views, and perform operations on views. The NotesView class does not have a New method. You access views through the GetView method and the Views property of the NotesDatabase.

Table 17.3 lists the view properties. You can directly manipulate the properties that are of built-in data type. The Parent property is a NotesDatabase object; you must use the associated properties and methods.

Table 17.3   NotesViews Table

Property	Data Type	Description
Created	Date/Time	Creation time and date
Columns	NotesViewColumn array	Columns that are in the view
IsDefaultView	Boolean	True if this is the default view
IsFolder	Boolean	True if this is a folder
LastModified	Date/Time	Date and time the view was last modified
Name	String	Name of the view, including cascades
Parent	NotesDatabase	Database containing this view
UniversalID	String	Universal ID of the view

Designing Applications

Accessing Notes Information

The NotesDocument class lets you examine and manipulate document properties and contents. You gain access to a NotesDocument object through methods in the NotesDatabase, NotesView, and NotesDocumentCollection classes.

Table 17.4 lists the document properties. You can directly manipulate the properties that are of built-in data type. For a property that is an object, you must associate properties and methods.

Table 17.4	NotesDocument Table	
Property	**Data Type**	**Description**
Authors	String array	Names of users who have saved the document
Created	Date/Time	Date and time the document was created
EmbeddedObjects	EmbeddedObject array	All objects embedded in the document
EncryptionKeys	String array	Keys used to encrypt the document
EncryptOnSend	Boolean	True if the document is encrypted when mailed
FTSearchScore	Integer	Relevance value (number of occurrences of the criteria) if the comment was retrieved from a full text search
HasEmbedded	Boolean	True if the document has embedded objects
HasItem	Boolean	True if the document has a specified item
IsNewNote	Boolean	True if the document is created but does not yet exist on disk
IsResponse	Boolean	True if the document is a response document
IsSigned	Boolean	True if the document is signed
Items	NotesItem array	All the items in the document
LastAccessed	Date/Time	Date and time the document was last accessed
LastModified	Date/Time	Date and time the document was last modified
NoteID	String	Note ID of the document
ParentDatabase	NotesDatabase	Database that contains the object
ParentDocumentUNID	String	Universal ID of the parent if the document is a response
ParentView	NotesView	View from which the document was retrieved

Property	Data Type	Description
SaveMessageOnSend	Boolean	True if a message is saved when mailed
SentByAgent	Boolean	True if the document was mailed by an agent using the Send or SendTo method
Signer	String	Name of signer if the document is signed
SignOnSend	Boolean	True if the document is signed when mailed
UniversalID	String	Universal ID of the document
Verifier	String	Name of user verifying the signature if the document is signed

Accessing Notes Items (Fields)

The NotesItem and NotesRichTextItem classes let you examine and manipulate document properties and contents. You gain access to a NotesItem or NotesRichTextItem object through various methods in the NotesDocument class. The NotesRichTextItem class inherits from NotesItem. With these classes you can do the following:

- Access item properties
- Get an item and its value
- Create an item and assign values
- Copy an item
- Remove an item
- Work with a rich text item
- Work with an embedded object

Table 17.5 lists the item properties. You can directly manipulate the properties that are of built-in data type. The Date, Parent, and EmbeddedObjects properties are NotesDatabase objects; you must use the associated properties and methods to access them.

The Values property is an array except for rich text items. For a single value, access element 0. If the item contains multiple values, access each array element—for example, in a Forall loop. Access a rich text item as a simple value, not an array.

The Text property of NotesItem displays the complete Values array with the display separator, typically the semicolon (;), between elements.

Table 17.5 NotesItem Table		
Property	**Data Type**	**Description**
DateTimeValue	NotesDateTime	Date/time value of an item of type
EmbeddedObjects	NotesEmbeddedObject	Embedded objects in the item
IsAuthors	Boolean	True if the item is of type authors
IsEncrypted	Boolean	True if the item is encrypted
IsNames	Boolean	True if the item is of type names
IsProtected	Boolean	True if Editor access is required to modify
IsReaders	Boolean	True if the item is of type reader names
IsSigned	Boolean	True if the item is signed
IsSummary	Boolean	True if the item can appear in a view
Name	String	Name of the item
Parent	NotesDocument	The document that contains the item
Text	String	Plain text representation of the item's value
Type	Integer constant	ATTACHMENT, EMBEDDEDOBJECT, ERRORITEM, NOTELINKS, NOTEFERS, NUMBERS, RICHTEXT, SIGNATURE, TEXT, DATETIMES, UNAVAILABLE, UNKNOWN, USERDATA, and USERID
ValueLength	Integer	Size in bytes of an item's value
Values	Variant array	Values that an item holds

Accessing Notes Sessions

The NotesSession class provides a means for accessing attributes of the user environment, and persistent information about agents. It also provides methods for accessing environment variables.

The *user environment* is the server or workstation containing the formula's database in the following cases: replication formula, agent whose trigger is If New Mail Has Arrived or On Schedule, selection formula, or column formula. Otherwise, the user environment is the Notes workstation.

A script has only one Notes session, so successive calls to the New method return the same session handle. You do not need the session handle to access a database or perform other operations in Notes, but you do need it to access the session properties and methods.

You can close a session at any time with the Close method. The Close method is implicit upon program termination.

Table 17.6 lists the session properties. You can directly manipulate the properties that are of built-in data type. Some of the properties are other Notes objects; for these, you must use the associated properties and methods. For example, the CurrentDatabase property must be set to a NotesDatabase object, where the NotesDatabase properties and methods are used to access it.

Table 17.6 NotesSession Table

Property	Data Type	Description
AddressBooks	NotesDatabase	Accessible Public and Private Name & Address Books
CurrentAgent	NotesAgent	Agent in which the program is running
CurrentDatabase	NotesDatabase	Database in which the program is running
EffectiveUserName	String	Person who created the current program
IsOnServer	Boolean	True if the program is running on a server
LastExitStatus	Integer	Status the last time the program ran
LastRun	Date/Time	Date and time the program last ran
NotesVersion	String	Version of Notes being used
Platform	String	Operating system platform
SavedData	NotesDocument	Document that stores data between program invocations
UserName	String	User name from the Notes ID

Accessing the Notes User Interface

You can access the document that is currently open through the NotesUIWorkspace and NotesUIDocument classes. The NotesUIWorkspace class has one property, CurrentDocument, which is a reference to the current document. The NotesUIDocument class has numerous properties and methods for examining and manipulating the current document.

These classes are used to retrieve document information to be used to set and get information from a field in a Notes document.

The NotesUIDocument class has the following read-only properties:

■ Document is a reference to the NotesDocument object associated with this document window, giving you access to the back-end properties and methods. If you modify and save an item using the NotesDocument object, the item is automatically updated in the workspace.

■ IsNewDoc is true if the document is not yet saved.

- `CurrentField` is the name of the current field if the document is in edit mode.
- `WindowTitle` is the name of the window title.

Table 17.7 shows the read-write properties for the `NotesUIDocument` class. Reading the property gets its status; writing the property sets its status.

Table 17.7 NotesUIDocument Properties		
Property	**Data Type**	**Description**
EditMode	Integer	True for edit mode
PreviewParentDoc	Integer	True if the lower pane containing the parent document is displayed
PreviewDocLink	Integer	True if the lower pane containing the preview document is displayed
Ruler	Integer	True if the ruler is visible
HorzScrollBar	Integer	True if the horizontal scroll bar is visible
HiddenChars	Integer	True to display hidden characters
FieldHelp	Integer	True to display field help

From Here...

This chapter has shown you how LotusScript can be constructed and used in Notes; this wraps up the part of the book that covers designing applications. You now are ready to learn how to set up and work remote. In particular, you might want to look at the following chapters:

- Chapter 14, "Formula Functions," discusses all of the @functions that you can use in formulas.
- Chapter 16, "LotusScript: A Whole New Programming Language," offers more information on LotusScript and how to use it within Notes.
- Chapter 22, "Notes: Under the Hood," provides an understanding of what happens internally when you run Notes.

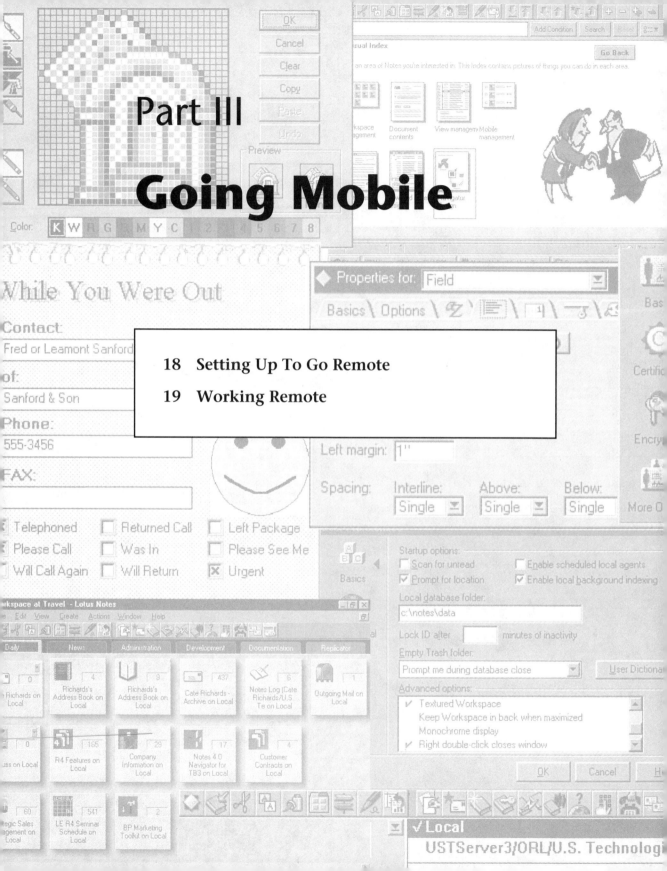

Part III

Going Mobile

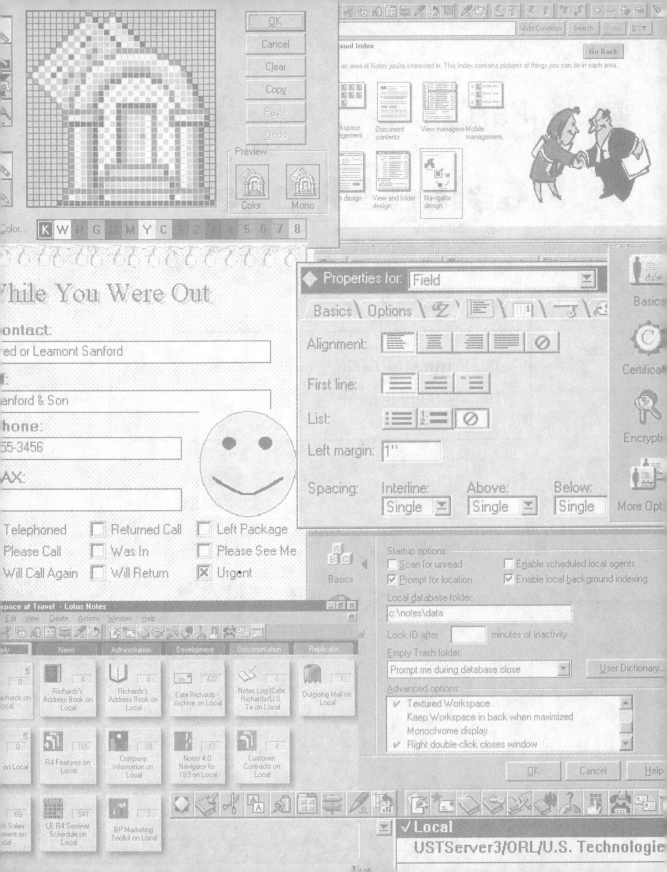

CHAPTER 18

Setting Up To Go Remote

This chapter is for Notes users who need to set up their PCs to work on Notes away from the office—that is, users who aren't connected to a Notes server through a local area network. You can work remote all the time (referred to as *remote only*) or part of the time (referred to as *network/remote*). With Lotus Notes' remote capability, you can easily send and receive mail, use public databases, and participate in Notes discussions as though you are working on-site.

In this chapter, you learn the following:

- What Notes needs to work when you are not connected directly to a server
- How to set up your network ports for remote usage
- How to set up your modem to work remote
- How to set up your location and server connections so that you can make contact with your Notes server(s)

This chapter will take you further into the world of working remote by walking you through setting up your Notes Mail to work off (and on) the network, connecting to a server via telephone lines, creating replica copies of your databases, exchanging information remotely, and tips on working smart while away from the office.

What Does It Mean To Work Remote?

When you connect to a Notes server through a local area network, your PC, whether it is a desktop or a laptop, is connected by cables directly through a LAN to one or more servers. You have direct access to databases on the servers in your network. Usually, you also have access to printing resources and other *file servers* (servers used to store files and applications for you). This access often enables you to work with a large amount of information without having to have a large hard disk to store it all. You also can work with the current database information and send and receive e-mail instantly.

Notes works quite differently, however, when you work remote. When you set up Notes on your remote PC, you must use a modem to connect to a Notes server through a telephone line connection. You create copies of all the databases you want to use and store them on your PC's hard disk (unless you are working strictly through Interactive Connection, which Chapter 19 discusses). If you are using a printer, then you typically have the printer cables attached directly to your PC. In other words, you have to be in physical possession of just about everything you need to work with when you are off the network; and you control the times when information is passed between you and others on the network because you must initiate the call to the server to begin the communication process.

Most often a remote PC is a laptop that you use when you travel. You also can work remote with Notes on a desktop PC at home or in another office. Regardless of the type of equipment you use, keep in mind that you will require more disk space when working remote because you will have to store replica copies of databases on your hard drive. You will learn more about replica copies as you read through the rest of this chapter, and Chapter 19, "Working Remote." The size of these copies depends on the amount of information the databases store and how much of the information you elect to carry with you remotely. In Release 4, the maximum size a database can grow to is four gigabytes. Although most databases will not grow to their maximum allowable size, they can be quite large and can require a significant amount of space. The minimum recommended amount of free hard disk space for running Notes, and working with the databases you need on your remote PC, is 100 MB—and that may be cutting things close if you are accessing multiple databases! You will find tips on minimizing your hard disk space usage in Chapter 19, which explains how to make and use databases while working remote.

Considering Disk Space When Going Remote

If you are getting ready to work remote, but have not yet purchased the PC that you will use, talk with your Notes administrator to find out how much disk space you will need to successfully work remote and access all of the applications you will require within your company. If you install the full version of Notes on your PC (all of the operating files, Help files, documentation files, sample databases, and so on), you are looking at using at least 55 MB of disk space before you make the first copy of a database you will use from the server! Keep in mind that most operating systems do not perform efficiently if you don't allow for at least 5 MB of free disk space to be used as swap file space while you are working.

You can elect to install Notes without all of the documentation and sample databases to minimize the disk space used. This type of installation is recommended if you are working only part of the time away from the office and you have access to these files when you are on the network if you need them. Typically, individuals who are planning to design (or customize) new databases and want to have an example of a database to use for ideas or as a template use the sample databases stored in a subdirectory titled EXAMPLES. If you're not planning to design databases, you can safely elect not to install these databases on your hard drive. Documentation databases, which are stored in a directory titled DOC, are online copies of Notes documentation. You may want to install the documentation databases, and then delete the databases you don't find useful for your needs.

The Notes Help database (HELP4.NSF) is very large, but it provides online help for most Notes questions. When you were installing Notes 4, you or your Notes administrator also installed a database titled Notes Help Lite, unless you deselected this option during the installation. The filename for Notes Help Lite is HELPLITE.NSF, and it is stored in your C:\NOTES\DATA subdirectory (unless you specified a different data directory during setup). Help Lite contains a subset of the Notes Help documents. It provides help while you travel, but it uses less disk space than the full Help database. Help Lite contains information you are more likely to need when you use Notes away from the office, such as information on working remote. It does not contain a lot of information on non-remote topics, such as database design.

If you work remote all of the time, you may want to delete the Help Lite database (by highlighting its icon and selecting File, Database, Delete, Yes) and keep the full Notes Help database, because you will most likely need to access help information on topics not covered in Help Lite. You can conserve some disk space by not carrying two copies of the same information on your hard drive.

However, if you typically work remote only a part of the time, you may want to delete the full Notes Help database from the hard drive of your PC and carry only the Help Lite database on your hard drive to conserve disk space. You can always access the full version of the Notes Help database from the network when you are working in the office.

Your Notes administrator can help you decide which of these databases you need while working remote. It is always recommended that you consult with your Notes administrator to ensure that you are working within the standards set for your company.

What You Need To Work Remote

To work remote, you need the following:

- A PC with Notes 4 installed
- A modem connected to your PC with an asynchronous (serial) port enabled and a modem (MDM) file that's compatible with your modem
- The exact name of the Notes server(s) you will access
- The phone number(s) for the modem connection to the Notes server(s)
- The Notes server(s) names
- A direct-dial, analog phone line
- A certified Notes User ID

Your Notes administrator also must do the following:

- Grant you appropriate access to the Notes server(s)
- Set up the Notes server(s) to receive incoming calls through a modem
- Enable network ports on the Notes server

III

Going Mobile

In the following sections, you learn about modems and phone lines. The remainder of this chapter walks you through configuring your PC to work remote.

Using Modems

Modems, which are the most common type of communications processor, convert the digital signals from your computer at one end of a communications link into analog frequencies, which can travel over ordinary telephone lines. At the other end of the communications line, a modem converts the transmitted data back into digital form that the receiving computer can process.

You can buy several types and speeds of modems today. An *internal modem* (located inside your PC) is certainly more convenient when you travel with a laptop, but it is not always the recommended type of modem for your needs and is not supported in some older laptops. An *external modem* connects through a port outside your PC. External modems are now available in desktop models (meant for stationary use) and pocket models, known for their compact, lightweight, portable features.

> **Note**
>
> Most new laptops support PCMCIA cards—often referred to as PC cards—which are about the size of a credit card, and fit into small slots on the side of your laptop. One of the most popular PCMCIA cards is the modem card. These small, credit card-size modems are very popular due to their high-speed data transmission capabilities—typically 14,400 baud to 28,800 baud—and their lightweight, compact features (which helps keep the laptop weight down when you are lugging around a PC all day!). They are also popular because they are easy to take in and out of a laptop.

When you choose a modem, one of the most important factors is the modem's speed, which is measured in bits per second, also known as the *baud rate*. A higher baud rate means your PC and the server can exchange information more quickly, which results in a shorter (and cheaper) phone call. In business settings today, most users use 9600 to 14,400 baud modems. The least expensive modems in wide use today are 2400-baud modems, which have longer exchange times and higher phone costs. Several popular modem models on the market today offer speeds from 2400 baud to 14,400 baud. Recent modems have speed capabilities even greater than 14,400 baud.

Paying attention to what type of baud rate the modem speed is manufactured for is also important. *Fax modem speed* refers only to the speed that a fax can be transmitted through the modem; *data modem speed* refers to how fast data can be transmitted through the modem. A 9600/2400 fax data modem, for example, enables you to transmit faxes at 9600 baud and data at 2400 baud. Lotus Notes transfers data (the information you are exchanging when you work in databases). Therefore, you must pay attention to the data baud rate that your modem supports. You should try to get a modem that supports at least 14,400 baud to help keep your phone calling costs down, as well as to keep the server from being tied up for lengthy periods of time. Table 18.1 illustrates just three average times for data transmission based on the baud rate of the modem you and the server are using.

| Table 18.1   Comparison Transmission Times for Three Baud Rates ||
Time	Baud Rate
25 minutes	9600
15 minutes	14,400
7 minutes	28,800

> **Note**
>
> When working with Lotus Notes remotely, you will be prompted when you have connected with the remote server and be told at which speed you have connected. The prompt information tells you the port connection speed, which is the speed at which your port is transmitting data to the port on the server. However, in many cases, this speed is not the actual speed at which data is being transmitted. The speed in which the carrier can successfully transmit data is also a factor. For the purposes of using Notes remote, think of a *carrier* as everything in between your modem and the server's modem, including the phone lines, hotel switchboards, and so on. When connecting internationally, through old phone systems, or even through hotel switchboards, the carrier speed may be greatly reduced. You may receive a prompt that you have connected to the server at a port rate of 9600 baud, for example, but everything will seem to be happening in slow motion. This problem is most likely due to the slow carrier speed for the transmission.

Notes can work with all the many different makes and models of modems that you can find, as long as you can locate or create a modem command file for your modem (see the following paragraph). Many manufacturers sell modems that are known as *Hayes compatible*, indicating that software can control them using commands that were standardized by a company called Hayes. Notes works well with these types of modems.

Notes comes with files called *modem command files*, which have MDM file extensions. These files provide the commands PCs need to use your modem. If you use a non-Hayes compatible modem, you need to search for a modem command file configured for your modem or spend time editing a modem command file to meet your needs. Editing a modem command file can be a considerable chore, and it's best done by an expert or at least, with assistance from one.

III

Going Mobile

Caution

Before you buy a modem, check with your Notes administrator to make sure that your modem is compatible with the server's modem. Otherwise, you may experience problems with your modem connections, have to connect only at very low speeds, or sacrifice some of the special functionality of your modem in order to talk with the Notes server. Typically, Hayes-compatible modems are your best bet because Notes runs very well with them.

Note

If you purchase a new modem, and find that your particular modem's file is not currently available in Notes, you can check with your modem's manufacturer to see if they have an updated file, or check the Internet services (like CompuServe), which often have modem files stored in libraries by their manufactures. You can also check out the Modem Survival Kit which houses many of the latest modem files available. You can find this database in CompuServe by typing GO LOTUSC and checking out the Library in this forum, or accessing the database from Lotus' Web page or in the Lotus Notes Knowledge Base. You learn more about accessing Lotus through their Web site, and about the Knowledge Base in the "Lotus Notes Support" section of Chapter 24, "Inside Lotus Development Corporation."

Getting Help with Your Modem Setup. If you have trouble with your modem, you have resources to turn to for additional help. Your Notes administrator is the first resource available to you for assistance with modem installation and troubleshooting.

The modem's manufacturer and the documentation that accompanied your modem may also provide the key to getting your modem set up properly. Look for a section in your modem documentation that indicates the appropriate modem files that may be compatible with your modem, as well as any special settings that may be required.

Also available from Lotus is the Modem Survival Kit database, which provides debugging information for problems with modems, as well as additional modem files that may work better with your particular modem. This database, if it's available to your company, will most likely be installed on a Notes server(s) on your network. Check your network's Database Catalog to see whether this database is available to you. If you do not see it listed, ask your Notes administrator if this database was acquired for use by your company through partnership agreements.

Finally, several other outside resources, bulletin boards, and help services may be available to you if you have substantial trouble with your modem. Chapter 24, "Inside Lotus Development Corporation," discusses these services in more detail.

Phone Line Requirements

When you communicate with a server remotely, the modem you are using converts the data signals sent from your PC into analog signals that can be sent over a telephone line. The modem on the server then converts the analog signals back into digital form that your PC can understand. Having the proper type of phone line to transmit the signals being sent from your modem is therefore important.

To work with a modem, you need a direct-dial analog phone line, also referred to as a *voice line*. Most residential locations have an analog line into the house. *Digital lines* transmit digital signals that your modem cannot interpret—you typically find digital lines in office buildings.

You also must make sure that special telephone services such as call waiting and call park (similar to putting a call on hold), which may interrupt communications on your line, are discontinued or disabled when you work with your modem. Even a split-second interruption in the phone signal can cause your modem connection to be terminated. Contact your local phone company for details on the specific services they offer that may interfere with your modem.

Tip

If you can temporarily disable a special telephone service by pressing a particular number/character sequence (*70 on a touchtone phone or 1170 on a rotary phone in most North American areas), you may also be able to disable this service through Notes each time you dial the server. Enter the number sequence as part of the prefix number when you call a server. You may need to experiment or contact your phone company for additional information. More information on how to enter phone numbers is provided in the section titled "Setting Up Connections Records" later in this chapter.

Ideally, you would have a dedicated phone line to use if you are planning to work a great deal with Notes from your home. If you want to install a phone line, specify to the phone company that you want a POTS (plain old telephone service) line. This request ensures that you receive the type of line you need to work remote. You may also consider getting Integrated Services Digital Network (ISDN) service—particularly if you are planning to communicate a lot of data back and forth with a server(s). ISDN sends digital signals, which are more compatible with computer systems than analog systems, and the speed in which the data is transmitted is much greater. However, this type of service is more expensive, and you will need to get a special modem to use it.

Getting Started

Although Lotus Notes provides you with all the software capability you need to work remote, you first need to set up your system before you can work away from the network. Each step is discussed in detail later, but the following list gives you an overview of the steps you must perform on your PC:

1. Enable a port.
2. Enable your modem.

III

Going Mobile

3. Create a location(s).

4. Create a server connection(s).

The remainder of this chapter discusses these steps in more detail. An additional step, setting up Notes for remote mail, is covered in Chapter 19 because the settings you make will depend on how you elect to work with the Notes server.

Enabling a Port

Before you can work with Notes remote, you must make sure that the proper communications ports are set up correctly on your system. Communications ports serve as a gateway through which your PC can "talk" with other hardware through special connections. To use Notes on a network, you enable a LAN port, which is denoted by the letters *LAN* and a number (such as *LAN0*). When you are working remote, you use a communications port, which is denoted by the letters *COM* and the number of the port (such as *COM1*). Notes makes setting up the type of communications ports you need to work with easy.

> **Tip**
>
> If you use your computer to work on a LAN at one site and to work remote at another, you can enable the LAN port and the COM port at the same time. Notes switches to the appropriate port as necessary based on the location you select for your working session. You will learn more about setting up locations shortly.

Follow these steps to verify, change, or set up your network port(s):

1. Choose File, Tools, User Preferences to open the User Preferences dialog box.

2. Select the Ports icon to display the Ports Setup panel, as shown in figure 18.1.

> **Note**
>
> You may not see as many ports listed in your Ports Setup pane as shown in figure 18.1. The number of ports displayed is dependant on the setup of your computer.

3. In the Communication Ports scroll box, select the COM port attached to your modem. (COM2 often is used with modems for portable PCs, particularly internal modems. COM1 is often used for external modems. Check your PC's user manual to determine which COM port you need to choose.)

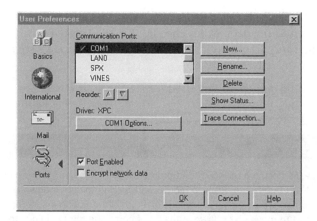

Fig. 18.1

*To set up your communica-
tion ports, you use the
Ports Setup panel of the
User Preferences dialog
box.*

4. To see the status of the COM port you have selected, select the COM port in
Communication Ports scroll box, and then select Show Status (see fig. 18.2). If
you see any message indicating that the COM port is performing a function,
select another COM port for your modem. The Port Status dialog box in figure
18.2 indicates that no activity is taking place. Select Cancel to close this dialog
box and return to the Ports Setup panel.

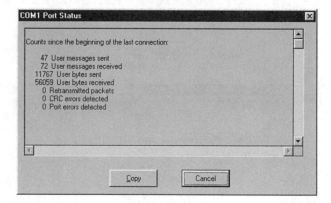

Fig. 18.2

*Opening the Port Status
dialog box is a fast way of
determining whether
another device is utilizing
the port you have selected.*

III

Going Mobile

5. Select Port Enabled so that a checkmark appears in the checkbox and next to the
selected COM port in the Communication Ports scroll box.

6. If you need to encrypt the data as it's sent over the modem, choose Encrypt
Network Data. (This selection slows down the transmission of data by turning
off the ability to use data compression. It is really not recommended unless you
are transmitting highly sensitive data or suspect that someone is tapping into
your transmissions.)

Encryption causes Notes to encode data in such a way that anyone wiretapping a phone line cannot read the data. Notes encodes the data before transmitting it over the phone line and decodes it at the other end. Eavesdroppers see meaningless data if they try to analyze the line.

Leave the Ports Setup dialog box open. You need it to set up your modem in the next section.

Tip

You can reorder the way the ports are sorted in the Communication Ports scroll list by highlighting the COM or LAN port name you want to reorder and clicking the up or down arrow next to the Reorder option below the Communication Ports scroll list. Clicking a Reorder arrow causes the highlighted port to move up or down in the list of ports. Use this technique to move the port names you work with frequently to the top of the list for easier reference.

Defining a New COM Port

If you do not see any COM ports listed in the Port List scroll box, you must define one before you can move forward. This procedure is very simple. When you add a port, you are telling Notes what communications port on your PC to use and specifying what driver and buffer size to use. With the Port Setup dialog box open, follow these instructions to define a port:

1. Select <u>N</u>ew to display the dialog box shown in the following figure.

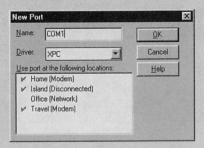

2. Enter the following information in the appropriate text fields:

- <u>N</u>ame—Enter the COM port that you want to set up. For example, enter **COM1**. If you are unsure of which port you need to activate, consult your PC and modem documentation.

- <u>D</u>river—Select XPC to specify the driver for dialup use.

- Select which location(s) will use this port name in the <u>U</u>se Port at the following locations list box. (You learn more about locations later in this chapter.)

Your new port setup should look similar to the example in the preceding figure if you are setting up a COM1 port.

3. Select OK to return to the Port Setup panel.

Setting Up Your Modem

Before you can use your modem, you need to specify the particular modem command file to work with your modem, the modem speed (baud rate) for your modem, and whether your dial setup is pulse or tone. You also may want to customize some additional settings. To set up your modem, follow these steps:

1. If you are not already in the Port Setup panel of the User Preferences dialog box, select File, Tools, User Preferences, and then select the Ports icon; otherwise, skip to step 2.

2. Choose the port's Option button. You will find this button located below the Driver information label in the center of the dialog box. The title of this button changes, along with the defined driver based on the port you have highlighted in the Communication Ports list box. The Additional Setup dialog box appears (see fig. 18.3).

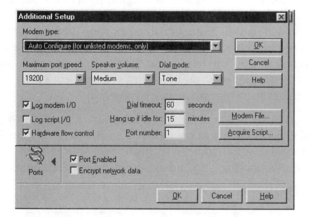

Fig. 18.3

You can adjust modem settings in the Additional Setup dialog box.

3. From the Modem type list box, choose the type of modem you are using.

If your exact modem type isn't available, choose the closest compatible type. Refer to your modem's user's guide to determine modem compatibility. If your modem type is not listed, see the next section, "What To Do If Your Modem Is Not Listed."

4. Adjust the remaining modem settings, if necessary. (The settings are described in later sections.)

III

Going Mobile

> **Note**
>
> Ignore the buttons labeled Acquire Script and the Log script I/O checkbox. Script files are written and managed by Notes administrators on the Notes servers and are not covered in this book. Script files are similar to modem command files in that you use both to set up communications equipment to work in your environment. For example, if you try to connect to CompuServe's Lotus Notes server to send e-mail out to non-Notes users, you will need a script file provided by CompuServe to log on and navigate you through its complex services to reach the Lotus Notes servers. Your Notes administrator will contact you if you need to make adjustments to these features.

5. Choose OK, and then choose OK again to save your modem and network ports selections.

What To Do If Your Modem Is Not Listed

If your modem type is not listed in the Additional Setup dialog box, choose Auto Configure (for unlisted modems only). Notes will usually be able to adapt to the modem connected to your PC. If you later change your modem type, Notes automatically tries to adapt to the new modem if this file is selected.

If your modem type isn't listed, and the Auto Configure (for unlisted modems) MDM file does not allow your modem to connect with the server, try selecting modem files that may be similar to your modem. If you still cannot get your modem to work with an existing MDM file, you will need to create or edit an existing modem command file. You can do so by choosing one of the generic or null modem files to use as a template, and then selecting the Modem File button. Editing or creating a modem command file is not an easy task for most users; consult your modem's user guide or your Notes administrator for the technical assistance you need.

Choose a modem file specifically designed for your modem when possible. Often, when you use a modem file that is close to the type you need, but is not quite like it, you experience some problems, or lose some of the features of your modem. Refer to Appendix F, "Remote Troubleshooting," if you have problems making connections with your modem.

> **Note**
>
> If you cannot see any modem files listed when you open the Additional Setup dialog box, you may have a line missing from your NOTES.INI file. Exit to your command prompt and edit the NOTES.INI file to include the following line:
>
> ```
> ModemFileDirectory=C:\Notes\Data\Modems
> ```

> If you specified a different data directory when you installed Notes, you will need to modify the entry above to show the path to your MODEMS subdirectory. Save your new NOTES.INI file and exit. You must restart Windows and Notes before the edits will take effect. For more information on editing your NOTES.INI file, read Chapter 2, "Customizing Notes."

Port Speed

In the Additional Setup dialog box, the Maximum Port Speed option specifies the fastest speed at which transmission can take place, depending on the type of modem you use. If you chose Auto Configure as the modem type, choose 19200; Notes automatically adjusts to the appropriate speed during each session for your particular modem.

Lotus Notes uses data compression when passing information across the phone lines, unless the data you are sending is encrypted. Data compression, for the most part, effectively doubles the speed at which the data is passed across the connection. For example, a modem with a maximum baud rate of 9600 can transfer data at the relative speed of 19,200 baud with data compression because twice the amount of data is being passed within the same amount of time.

The speed actually used will be the lesser of the maximum speed you select in this setting and the maximum speed specified in the MDM file you have selected. For example, if you selected 19,200 bps in the Maximum Port Speed option, and the MDM file limits your modem to 9600 bps as the maximum, you will see a warning like the one shown in figure 18.4.

Fig. 18.4

This sample error message signals an incompatible modem speed.

If you dial from a hotel or on noisy phone lines, you may need to choose a slower speed than the maximum allowed by your modem to improve your connection. The large amount of electronic noise being processed by your modem at the same time as it is trying to process the data can cause connection problems, and the hotel's PBX switch may not be able to handle high-speed transmissions. Lowering the baud rate helps your modem to distinguish between what is data and what is noise.

Speaker Volume

The Speaker Volume option in the Additional Setup dialog box determines what you can hear when you dial the server. To hear the modem as it dials, choose any option except Off. If you listen to the modem, you can determine whether your modem is

III

Going Mobile

dialing, whether the carrier connection is established, and whether the server's modem and your modem are "shaking hands" (sort of a "Darth Vader with a cold" sound). Hearing the modem is also useful if you manually dial into the server. Choose to hear the modem tones unless you are scheduling your PC to call the server during times where you need quiet, like during the night in your hotel room!

Dial Mode

Use the Dial Mode option in the Additional Setup dialog box to specify what mode of dialing you should use: Tone (as used in a touchtone phone) or Pulse (as used in a rotary phone). The mode of dialing refers to how you dial to make a phone connection, not how the data is transferred (see the earlier discussion on analog signals). If you use a rotary phone, or have a modem style that does not support touchtone dialing, select Pulse under Dial Mode. Tone is the most common selection in most North American countries. You may need to experiment if you are working internationally or on old phone systems. To verify a tone line, lift the receiver of the telephone connected to the analog phone line and enter a phone number. If the tones on the line vary depending on the numbers you have pressed, you are working in tone mode. If the tones for all of the numbers sound the same, you are working in pulse mode.

> **Note**
>
> Keep in mind that if you travel, you may need to make changes to the dial mode based on where you are trying to dial from. If you try to dial a server, and you receive an error message indicating that a dial tone cannot be found or another strange error message, try changing the dial mode. Typically, locations with relatively modern phone systems support a tone mode for dialing.

Dial Timeout

The Dial Timeout option in the Additional Setup dialog box sets the number of seconds to wait for a connection to a server before canceling the call. The default setting is 60 seconds. If you have problems connecting to a busy server, are dialing overseas, include a calling card number in your dialing, or find that your modem is particularly slow, increase the Dial Timeout setting. You can also increase the Dial Timeout setting for a particular session in the Call Server dialog box. You will learn more about this setting in the next chapter.

Notes uses this setting to determine how much time it will spend trying to successfully dial and connect (log on) to the server. Don't increase this setting to too high of a number, or you will find yourself waiting for long periods of time if there is an error in trying to dial a server. Also, don't set it too short, or you will rarely connect to the server in the time allotted! You may need to adjust this setting a few times if you experience problems connecting with the server within the default 60 seconds. Typically a setting of 60 will work, and a maximum setting of 90 seconds is usually the upper limit you will need.

Hang Up/Idle Time Setting

Use the Hang Up If Idle For option in the Additional Setup dialog box to set the number of minutes your system stays connected to the server without any activity taking place against the server. The default time is 15 minutes. Increase the setting if you need more time. Decrease the amount of time if you don't need a long waiting period. You save in telephone costs and tie up the server for less time if you keep this setting low.

The Hang Up If Idle For setting is based on activity with the server, not activity being performed solely on your hard drive. For example, if you are reading a document in a server copy of a database while connected from a remote location, Notes does not count the time spent reading the document as performing a function against the server because the document is local to your workstation once you open it. Notes begins the idle countdown from the time you open the document until you perform another activity that accesses the server, such as indexing the database, opening another document, saving the document, and so on. You will know the server is being accessed when you see a small lightning bolt appear in the lower left corner of the Notes window.

> **Caution**
>
> If you set up your PC to perform any selection that "talks" to the server while you are connected at least once during the time that is specified in the Hangup If Idle For section, you will not be disconnected after the Hangup If Idle time is met, even if you leave the room or otherwise stop working on the server. Three direct examples come to mind: if you have set up your Mail Preferences to check for mail in the File, Tools, User Preferences, Mail panel more often than the time set in the Hang Up If Idle for setting; if you have set up a macro that accesses a server database to perform its task while you are working on the server as well; and, if you set up your locations to replicate with the server more often than the time set in the Hang Up If Idle For setting.

The server also has a Hangup If Idle setting, and the shorter of the two times is used. If increasing the Hangup If Idle time on your system doesn't keep you from disconnecting from the server before your work is finished, contact your Notes administrator.

Logging Modem Input/Output

The Log Modem I/O setting in the Additional Setup dialog box enters modem responses in your system's log entries. Under normal circumstances, you don't need this option, but it can help if you need to troubleshoot modem problems.

If you select Log Modem I/O, each time you try to make a call (or perform just about any function in which your modem is involved) a document will be written in your Notes Log database, which is stored on your hard drive. After a while, this database becomes quite large, depending on how often you call your server. Refer to the section "Working Smart Remote" in Chapter 19 for tips on keeping your hard drive clean.

III

Going Mobile

Using Log Entries

Notes provides a special template that creates a Notes log on your PC that records all modem activity if you choose Log Modem I/O. (Your server also has a Log database that logs all of the activity—calls, replications, database access, and so on.) When Notes logs a modem activity, it creates a document that lists the details about the call. The log reports successes and failures in dialing remotely and provides you with a record of what occurred during communication with the server. To view this information, add the Notes log from your C:\NOTES\DATA directory to your desktop (the log filename is always LOG.NSF), and then open the modem log as you would any other database. The Notes log is very beneficial in helping you troubleshoot problems while working remote.

Hardware Flow Control

The Hardware Flow Control option in the Additional Setup dialog box specifies what Notes should do if more data exists than can fit in your system buffer when receiving and transmitting. (In Notes 3.0, this option was called RTS/CTS Flow Control.) Choose this option unless your modem or serial card cannot support flow control. (Consult your modem/serial card documentation.) Activating this setting is especially recommended for transmission speeds of 9600 baud or greater in order to protect against impaired performance.

Editing the Modem File

You can edit your modem command file, if necessary. For example, if you are receiving a large number of errors indicating that the modem cannot detect a dial tone (perhaps Notes does not recognize an international dial tone, or you are trying to dial through or out of a PBX system, which can be found in many offices and hotels), and Notes does not recognize its dial tone, you may want to edit the modem command file you are using.

To edit your modem file, highlight it in the Additional Setup dialog box, and select the Modem File button to open the Edit Modem Command File dialog box displayed in figure 18.5. Scroll through the settings you want to change and edit them as you would any other text in Notes.

For this example, you would scroll down to the section headed [commands] and look for a line that starts with SETUP and contains the string of characters X4. You may need to look closely because this string is often hidden in a cluster of command strings. In figure 18.5, the I-beam pointer is next to the appropriate character string for this modem file.

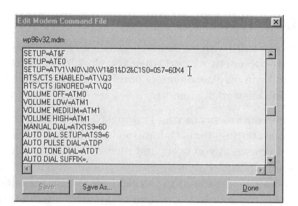

Fig. 18.5

Use this dialog box to change your modem file to deal with special circumstances.

Change the X4 command to X1. This command tells Notes to ignore listening for dial tones, ringing, and so forth, and continue to try to make connection with the server. You will not need to change the command file back to its original state once you can make connections successfully. Notes will continue to function well with the change in any situation.

A great application for this edit is when an individual is overseas and wants to use the company's 1-800 phone number or other corporate phone access to connect to a Notes server through its internal phone mail system (provided that the company's PBX system will allow this situation to happen). This individual can then take advantage of cheaper rates and possibly have a direct connection to the server. Keep in mind that in some countries, like Mexico, special arrangements may need to be made with the local phone company to set up connections to 1-800 phone numbers.

Select Save to save the new settings, Save As to save the new settings under a different name that you specify, or Done to exit the dialog box. If you try to exit the dialog box and have not already saved any changes you have made, Notes prompts you to do so. Select No if you do not want to save your settings, Yes to save your changes, or Cancel to return to the dialog box.

Caution

If you are editing a command file, make a backup copy of the file, or save the edited file under a different name. This copy will allow you to easily return to the original modem command file if you have made errors in the edited one or switch to a new modem that requires the original configuration. If you have never edited a modem command file, you may want to get assistance from someone experienced in doing so before attempting it yourself.

III

Going Mobile

Setting Up Locations

A *location* is a place where you work with Notes using specified communication settings. For example, you may use a network port when you work in the office and are connected to a network, and you may use a remote port (COM) when you are disconnected from the network and are working remote.

Notes lets you create location documents in your Personal Name & Address book to store specific communications settings for each location in which you work. You can create as many location documents as you want, and then switch to those locations when you want. The location document tells Notes how you are working in Lotus Notes (remote or network-based), how to call the server, how to treat mail during your work session, and many other communication details as discussed later in this chapter. The location document you select when you begin your work session also defines the databases you elect to replicate. You will learn more about replicating databases in Chapter 19, "Working Remote." In the location document, you specify the following items:

- The port (network or remote)
- Mail delivery type (server-based or workstation-based)
- Phone information (such as dialing prefixes)
- Replication information

When you first installed Notes, you automatically created the following four location documents in your local Name & Address book:

- Island (Disconnected)
- Office (Network)
- Travel (Modem)
- Home (Modem)

You can edit these documents and customize them, or create your own. You can then choose between the different locations you have defined to tell Notes how it will work with the server and mail the work session.

With locations, a remote user can easily define multiple types of location connections to use while working away from the network, and then quickly switch back to the network when in the office by selecting a network-defined location. Some suggested tips for location settings include the following:

- If your home and office are typically in different area codes, create a location called Home, and specify a 1 and your office's area code as a dialing prefix. When you use the Home location to call a server, Notes automatically dials 1 and the area code before it dials the server's phone number.

- If you work in an office that is disconnected from a network and is located in a different area code, create a location called My Office, and specify a 1 and your office's area code as a dialing prefix. When you use the My Office location to call a server, Notes automatically dials 1 and the area code before it dials the server's phone number.

- If you are working from a hotel room, and typically use a calling card when you make long-distance calls from hotel rooms, create a location called Hotel and specify your calling card number. Then when you use the Hotel location to call a server, Notes automatically uses your calling card number. You may also want to specify a prefix for gaining an outside line when calling from a hotel room.

Entering a New Location

Location documents are stored in your Personal Name & Address book, which is usually defined as your last name followed by the words *address book*. You can view your current location documents by opening your personal address book and selecting the Locations view from the navigator as shown in figure 18.6 or by selecting the File Mobile Edit Locations SmartIcon.

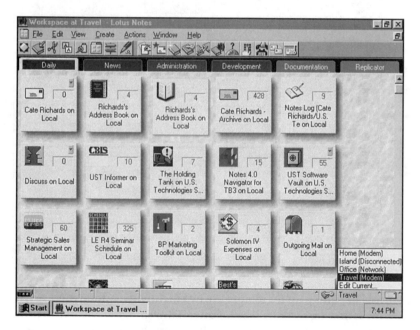

Fig. 18.6

Check out your defined location documents in your Personal Name & Address book.

Figure 18.6 shows the three default locations created when you first install Notes 4. You can customize these locations, or create new ones. To create a new location, follow these steps:

1. While viewing the Locations view, select Create, Location. The New Location document will appear as shown in figure 18.7.

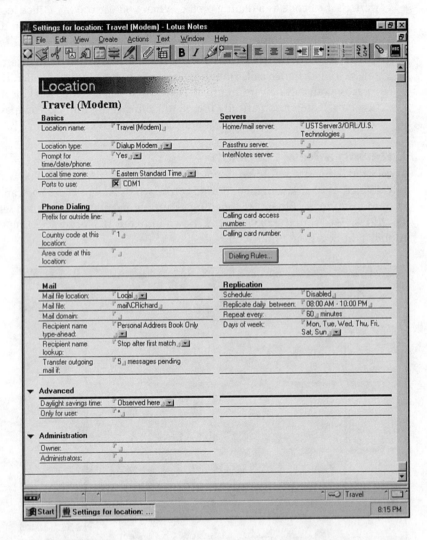

2. Specify that you are setting up for remote use by entering the information as described in the following sections. The Location form shows six sections for this type of setup—Basics, Phone Dialing, Mail, Servers, Replication, Advanced, and Administration. Make the appropriate entries. (Entries for each section are discussed later in this chapter.)

3. When you have completed your entries, press Esc to exit the document, and then Yes to save it. You will see your new location document appear in the view.

To edit an existing location document, open the location document you want to edit, and then double-click anywhere within the body of the document. Notes will place the location document in edit mode for you to make the necessary changes. Exit and save the document as described in the preceding step 3.

> **Note**
>
> The New Location document uses a new Notes 4 technique called Hide-When. The sections and field entries for this form change as you enter information into the preceding fields. This section discusses those options available to you when you select that you are working as a Dialup Modem location. For additional information on the personal address book, read Chapter 5, "Using the Address Books."

Basic Location Settings. The first section of the location document, Basics, controls the basic information Notes uses to determine how you are working. The following are your options:

- **Location Name**—Type in the name of the location. This name can be anything you want to use that is descriptive of the location in which you would want to use this profile. For example, you could type `Hotel (Calling Card)` to define a location document that you plan to use when staying at hotels where you want to have the call billed to your calling card. You could enter another location document called Hotel (Direct Dial) to use when you stay at hotels that do not accept calling cards for dialing long distance.

- **Location Type**—Select Dialup Modem to tell Notes that this location is used when you are disconnected from the network.

- **Prompt for time/date/phone**—Select Yes if you want Notes to prompt you for these settings each time you start up Notes. If you select Yes, the dialog box shown in figure 18.8 appears whenever you switch to this location or start Notes with this location defined. This option is recommended if you frequently work from different locations, particularly if you frequently work on and off the network, or if you frequently cross time zones.

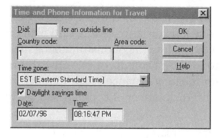

Fig. 18.8

The Location Setup dialog box appears if you tell Notes to prompt for time, date, and phone in the New Location document.

- **Local time zone**—Select the time zone that is typically used for this location. For example, if you typically use this location profile when you are working in Georgia, you would select Eastern Standard Time. This selection changes the time/date information that Lotus Notes uses during the work session to meet that of the local time zone.

- **Ports to use**—Select the ports to use for this location. The available selections are determined by the ports you defined when you set up your modem. To select a port, click in the box located to the left of the port's name. For example, figure 18.7 indicates that the port COM 1 will be used to connect to the server from this location.

Phone Dialing Information. The Phone Dialing section of the location is used to enter the phone dialing information you will use in conjunction with the phone number defined in the connections record. (You will learn about the connections record in the next section.) Notes adds the information you specify to a server's phone number as a prefix (outside line prefix, country code, area code, and calling card access number) or as a suffix (calling card number). In the Phone Dialing section, you set up the dialing instructions to connect with the server, as well as modify any server numbers that you may call when working from this particular location:

- **Prefix for outside line**—Enter any dialing prefix you must use to get an outside line when dialing the server from this location. For example, if you are in a hotel and must dial a 9 to get an outside line before you can call the server, enter **9** in this field. (See the sidebar "Entering Prefixes and Suffixes" for more details.)

- **Country code at this location**—Enter a country name if you always call the same country from this location, or the actual country code if the country is not defined. Notes automatically converts the country name into the correct dialing code for the country.

- **Area code at this location**—Enter the area code for this location if you did not enter this information directly with the phone number in the connections record. Typically, if you define a connections record for access to a server that is always outside your area code, you will enter 1-*area code* and the remainder of the number in the connections document.

- **Calling card access number**—If you plan to use a calling card when using this location, and your phone long distance calling card plan requires you to enter an access number before dialing the phone number, enter that number in this field. You may want to include a comma or two after this number to have Notes pause to give time for the long distance access number to register. You may need to experiment with the number of commas you use to reach your long distance service.

- **Calling card number**—If you plan to use a calling card when using this location, enter the calling card number you would normally dial after you have dialed the phone number. You may want to add a comma or two before this entry to have Notes pause between dialing the server number and entering your calling card number. You may need to experiment with the number of commas you use to successfully enter your calling card number.

■ **Dialing Rules**—Select the Dialing Rules button to open the Dialing Rules dialog box, as shown in figure 18.9. This dialog box displays the list of all of your connections records and the phone numbers defined for each of those records. Select the server names to view the phone numbers that will be dialed when working from this location. You may want to edit these phone numbers for dialing from this location only to meet your needs. You will learn more about defining server phone numbers in a following section, "Setting Up Connections Records." Select <u>O</u>K to save your changes and return to your locations document.

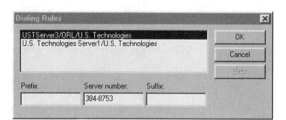

Fig. 18.9

Check out your connections records in the Dialing Rules dialog box.

Entering Prefixes and Suffixes

When you are entering dialing instructions, keep in mind that the phone number can include any numbers that you normally dial before or after a phone number, including calling card numbers. Insert commas after the prefix and before calling card numbers for each two seconds you normally would pause between dialing the phone number and entering your card number:

```
,,calling card number
```

Two commas are usually adequate before the calling card number, but you may need to experiment. It is best that you be able to hear your modem dialing when trying to work with calling card numbers to help you determine whether the entry is correct.

If you dial out of a hotel, and an operator comes on the line to ask for the calling card number you are dialing, you most likely need to increase or decrease the number of commas between the server phone number and the credit card number. If the pause between these numbers is too long, an operator will come on to ask you what number you want to dial before Notes dials the credit card number. You will need to hang up, remove a comma, and try again. If the pause is too short, your modem will try to enter the card number before the phone system is ready for it, and then an operator will come on the line to try to assist you. You will need to hang up, add a comma or two, and then try again.

If your modem is an older model, check the modem's documentation to determine the maximum number of digits it can dial. To fit as many numbers as possible into the sequence, don't

(continues)

III

Going Mobile

(continued)

use any hyphens in the phone number defined in the connections document or prefix and suffix entries in this document, and use as few commas as possible.

Some hotel phone systems may not enable you to use your calling card number for remote dialing. If not, you may need to dial directly and charge the call to your hotel room bill. Also, pay attention to the calling information in your hotel. Some hotels are set up to have you enter a 9 when making some outside calls and an 8 when making others. If you are unsure of which prefix to use, contact your hotel operator.

Finally, some hotels are using an older PBX system that will not allow you to use your modem, or let you use your modem only at very slow speeds. Though this situation is rare in North America, it can be quite common elsewhere. Refer to Appendix F, "Remote Troubleshooting," for additional help before you give up completely!

Mail Settings. The Mail section of the location document identifies how Notes treats your mail when you are working remote. Make the following entries when setting up your locations records:

■ **Mail file location**—Select Local if you want Notes to use the copy of your mail file stored on your hard drive; choose On Server if you plan to work interactively with your Mail database file that is located directly on the server.

> **Note**
>
> When you select Local, Notes stores all of the mail you send in your Outgoing Mail database, which acts as a holding tank for your outgoing mail until you call the server and replicate your mail to pass it on to the recipients. When you select On Server, Notes immediately transfers the mail to the recipients when you send it, so you must be directly connected to the server to use this selection. It is recommended that you select Local for this option when working remote. You will read more about how mail is used when working remote in Chapter 19.

■ **Mail file**—Specify the exact path and filename of your mail file. If you selected Local for your mail file location, you need to specify the path and filename of the mail file on your hard drive. Typically, your mail file is located in the mail subdirectory of your data directory and is titled with the first initial of your first name, followed by the first seven letters of your last name. For example, the mail filename for Robert Richards would typically appear as follows:

```
mail\Rrichard.NSF
```

If you selected On Server for your mail file location, you need to specify the path and filename of your mail file on your mail server. Typically, this mail file is also located in the mail subdirectory on your server and appears similar to the preceding example.

> ### Tip
>
> When possible, it is best to always name and store your mail file on your hard drive exactly as it is stored on your mail server. This setup makes it easy to change the mail file location without having to edit the mail filename.

- **Mail domain**—Enter the mail domain to be used for this location. This entry is not required. If you are unsure of your mail domain, contact your Notes administrator.

- **Recipient name type-ahead**—Select where you want Notes to look for address names when using the type-ahead feature of Notes R4 (see Chapter 5, "Using the Address Books"). You can specify one of the following:

  - Selecting the Personal Address Book Only option means that Notes looks only in your Personal Address Book for entries. If a match is not in the Personal Address Book, Notes quits trying to use the type-ahead feature and accepts whatever you type in the recipient fields of a memo.

  - Selecting the Personal then Public Address Book option means that Notes looks first in your Personal Address Book for entries, and if a match is not found there, Notes searches the Public Address Book. To use this entry, you must be connected to the server when addressing a memo.

  - In the Recipient name lookup field, select Stop after first match to have Notes find only the first name that matches the recipient name when you send mail from the location. Select Exhaustively check all address books to have Notes find all of the names that match the recipient name when you send mail.

  - Selecting the Disabled option causes Notes to disable the type-ahead feature completely. If you don't have any names listed in your Personal Name & Address book, and do not have a copy of the Public Name & Address book stored on your hard drive, you may want to select this option so that Notes does not bother to look for the spelling when you mail a document.

- **Transfer outgoing mail if**—Enter the number of outgoing mail messages you want to automatically initiate a call to the server. For this feature to work, your modem must be connected to a phone line, and you must have background replication running for this location. (You will learn more about setting up background replication later in this chapter.)

Server Settings. The Servers section of the location document specifies your Home/mail server, as well as Passthru and InterNotes servers, if applicable. Make the following entries in the Servers section:

- **Home/mail server**—Specify the exact name of your Mail server (often referred to as your Home server). This is the server in which your mail file is located. If you are unsure of your Mail server name, highlight the network copy of your

III

Going Mobile

Mail database and select <u>V</u>iew, Show <u>S</u>erver Names (a checkmark appears when this option is highlighted). The server name displayed in the icon of your network mail icon is the entry you must make in this field.

- **Passthru server**—A Passthru server configuration enables you to dial into one server location and access any other servers defined in the network through that dialup connection. If your company uses this configuration, enter the server's name exactly as it is defined by the Notes administrator in the Public Name & Address book. If you do not know your Passthru server name, contact your Notes administrator for assistance before you make an entry in this field.

- **InterNotes server**—If your company uses the Lotus InterNotes product, you can define the InterNotes server in this field. Contact your Notes administrator for particulars about this entry.

Replication. You can create entries that tell Notes how often you want to replicate with your server(s) when you are set up for a particular location. *Replication* is the process of calling the server and exchanging information. You learn more about replication in Chapter 19.

To use these settings, you must be set up for background replication. You will learn how to set up for background replication later in this chapter. To set up a replication schedule, make your entries in the following fields:

- **Schedule**—Select Enabled if you want Notes to perform background replications with the server at set times during the day. Select Disabled if you want to prompt Notes each time you want to perform a replication with a server.

- **Replicate daily between**—Specify the time frame in which you want Notes to try to call the server. Notes will try to dial the server during this time frame, based on the settings you make below this entry.

  You can enter a range of numbers by placing a hyphen between the start and end times, as follows:

      08:00AM - 10:00 PM

  You can also enter specific time(s) by separating the entries with commas, as follows:

      08:00 AM, 01:00 PM, 05:00 PM

- **Repeat every**—Specify how often you want Notes to repeat its replication with the server. For example, if you specify 60 minutes, Notes will try to replicate every 60 minutes during the time frame specified for this location.

- **Days of week**—Specify which days of the week you want Notes to replicate with the server. You may elect to have Notes replicate every day of the week, in which case you would select all seven days. However, if you only work at this location on weekends, you may want to specify Fri, Sat, and Sun, as those are most likely the only days in which you want Notes to try to call.

> **Note**
>
> Notes uses the replication information to replicate databases located on your Replicator tab of your workspace. You learn more about this tab in Chapter 19, "Working Remote."

Advanced Settings. You have two settings available to you if you select the section indicator next to the Advanced section in the locations document:

- **Daylight savings time**—Select Observed Here if you want daylight savings time observed for this location. Notes will automatically change the time stamp it uses to match daylight savings time. Otherwise, select Not Observed Here.

- **Only for user**—If you are using a shared workstation, and this location profile is to be used only by a particular person or group, specify the names of the users in this field exactly as they are named in the Public Name & Address Book. Otherwise, leave the asterisk (*) in this entry to indicate that anyone can use this location setting.

Administration Settings. The Administration section of the location document is used to identify individuals that are allowed to make changes to this document. Make the following entries in this section, if applicable:

- **Owner**—Type the full name of the individual allowed to modify this location document exactly as it is spelled in the Public Name & Address Book. If you leave this field blank, any user can modify this document. If you are the only person using this workstation, you do not need to use this field.

- **Administrators**—Enter the full name of any groups or individuals allowed to edit this document. If you leave this field blank, any user can modify this document. If you are the only person using this workstation, you do not need to use this field.

Switching and Editing Locations

You can easily switch between locations at any time by selecting the Location box in the status bar at the bottom of the Notes window, as shown in figure 18.10. Click once on the Locations box to open the list of defined locations, and then select the location you want to use.

You can edit a current location by selecting Edit Current from the list of options. The current location document will open in edit mode for you to modify. The changes occur when you exit and save the entries. (You can also edit a location by opening its document in your Personal Name & Address book.)

III

Going Mobile

Fig. 18.10

You can switch locations from the status bar.

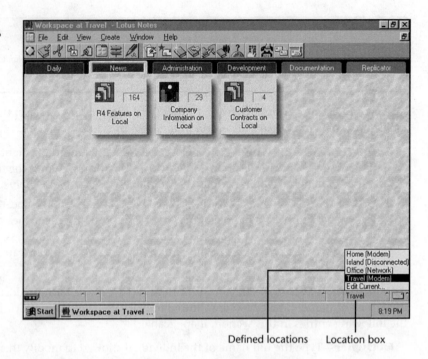

Defined locations   Location box

Setting Up Connections Records

To specify the server(s) you want to use, add their entries to your Personal Address Book as Server Connections.

Note

When your PC was set up initially for remote use, an entry for your Mail server (where your Mail database is located) was created automatically in your Personal Address Book.

To add the server entries to your address book, follow these steps:

1. Open your Personal Address Book. (For information on using Notes address books, see Chapter 5.)

2. Select the indicator next to Servers in the navigator, and then select Connections.

   If you have had a connection previously set up for you, you will see the connections document appear in this view. The view looks similar to the one in figure 18.11. This view indicates that three servers have been set up with connections records: Orlando, Tampa, and Ft. Lauderdale.

   To view the connections record and make edits as necessary, highlight the connections record and press Ctrl+E, or open the document and double-click anywhere within the document to place it in edit mode; then make the necessary changes as described below. If you do not have the server connections document you need, you must create a new one as indicated in step 3.

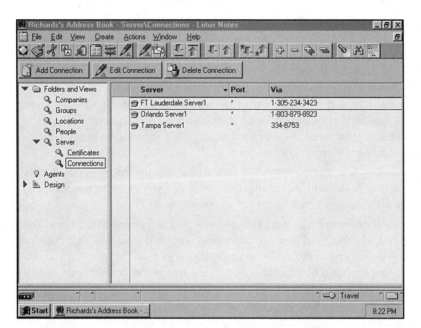

Fig. 18.11

The Server Connections records view lists your defined connections.

3. Choose Create, Server Connection. The Server Connection form opens as shown in figure 18.12.

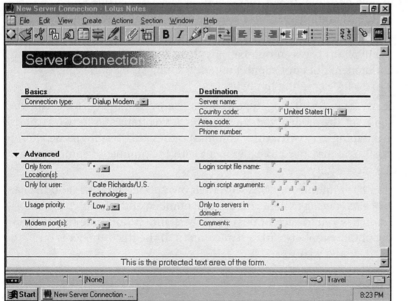

Fig. 18.12

Use this form to create a new connections record.

III

Going Mobile

4. Enter the necessary information. (The list following these steps describes the information needed.)

5. Close the window and choose Yes to save the connections record.

Repeat this process for each remote connection you want to make.

In the Server Connection form, you need to provide the following information:

- **Connection type**—Select Dialup Modem to indicate that you will be accessing this server via a modem.

- **Server name**—Type the exact name of the server you are connecting to. You need to include all hierarchical naming in this entry. You can determine the exact server entry you need to enter by opening the Public Name & Address Book and viewing the server connections.

- **Country code**—Select the country (or type in the country code) in which this server is located. Notes will automatically list the country code for the server if its country location is defined in the list of countries.

- **Area code**—If necessary, enter an area code for this server phone number. You may want to leave this field blank in this document, and enter the area code via the location document as defined previously in the section "Setting Up Locations." Leaving this field blank allows you to use this server connections definition in all of your locations, without having to individually edit the phone number each time you set up a location.

- **Phone number**—Type the unique part of the phone number that must be dialed to connect to the Notes server. The unique part of the phone number is that portion you have to dial no matter where you are calling from. When you dial the server, an entry box enables you to enter a prefix for the server you dial so you can include any numbers that you need to get an outside line. You can also specify the nonunique part of the server phone number when you set up locations, as defined previously in "Setting Up Locations."

  You can use hyphens between numbers; hyphens don't affect the dialing. However, if your modem does not support entering a long string of numbers, you may want to exclude entering hyphens.

  To include pauses in the dialing, type a comma between numbers for each two seconds you want the modem to pause—each comma translates to two seconds. For example, typing 9,,, (with three commas) causes a six-second pause after you dial the 9. You may need to experiment with the number of commas you need to dial successfully.

  If your server has multiple modems with their own phone numbers and they are not set up in a *hunt group* (where you call one number, and a hunt group automatically switches you to each of server numbers until it finds one that is open), separate the phone numbers with a semicolon (;). If the first number is busy, the next one is tried, and so on.

Advanced Connection Settings

To enter advanced settings for a connection record, select the section indicator next to the Advanced section heading in the Remote Connections form. A group of advanced settings will appear. Make entries for any of the following settings as needed:

- **Only From Location(s)**—Select the locations in which you want this connections document to be used. Typing an asterisk (*) in this field allows this connections document to be used for all locations.

- **Only for user**—By default, the document author's name is entered in this field. If you want to enter additional users for this connections record if you are sharing a workstation, enter their full Notes names here.

- **Usage priority**—Select Low priority if you plan to use the priority settings of the database to create a replication schedule for accessing a server based on the importance in which a database must send or receive information, and you don't place an importance on this database replicating on a frequent basis. Select Normal for routine scheduling of database replications with the server. You can also elect to replicate High priority databases through the Replicator tab, as you will learn in Chapter 19. Typically, this setting is made for connections between servers, rather than between remote workstations and servers. However, you can use this option to control the number of times your database replicates with the server during a scheduled replication by using these settings.

- **Modem port(s)**—Select which modem ports can use this connections record. Typing an asterisk (*) in this field allows all modem ports to use this record.

- **Login Script filename**—If applicable, enter the filename for the login script that you need to use to connect to your server. Contact your Notes administrator for information on any script files that may be required.

- **Login Script Arguments**—If you use a login script, and you must pass unique arguments to the script as you connect to the server (for example, passwords, name, and so on), type those arguments in the four fields provided in the order in which they are requested by the login script. Contact your Notes administrator for additional information on these entries.

- **Only to servers in domain**—If you want to connect only to particular remote domain servers, specify their names in this field. This entry is optional for remote users. Typing an asterisk (*) in this field enables this connections record to connect to servers in all domains.

- **Comments**—Specify any additional comments in this field to document the connections record.

Setting Up for Background Replication

Notes enables you to schedule calls to a server to perform background exchanges of information by making setup selections in the location document as defined in the section "Setting Up Locations." A *background exchange* enables you to continue working in Notes remotely as your modem (if it's on) dials and performs an exchange with the server. It also allows you to schedule calls while you are not working so that you can have up-to-date information when you next begin to work.

Meeting the Requirements for Background Replication

You may want to take advantage of the background replication feature if you are traveling and want to have Notes update the information in your databases while you are out of your hotel room. You can set up Notes to call the server at 5:00 PM to exchange information so that you will be working with the latest updates when you return to your room at 6:00 PM.

You can take advantage of the scheduled calling while you are asleep, at meetings, or possibly at times when the calling costs are lower. You may also want to check with your Notes administrator, or check the Phone Calls view in the server's Notes Log database to determine times when the server modems are usually not as busy. Schedule your calls during their slack time, particularly if you are continuously getting busy signals when you call the server during regular work hours.

Keep in mind that you can always force a call to the server outside of the times set in this section when you want to make contact at an unscheduled time.

Lotus Notes performs the background replication if the following conditions are met:

- You have Lotus Notes running.
- You have your modem plugged into an analog jack.
- You have switched to a location that has enabled background replication.

When you start Lotus Notes, Notes checks the replication schedule defined in the location setup and performs the next background replication according to that location's settings. You can follow the progress of the background replication by switching to your Replicator tab. You will learn more about the Replicator in Chapter 19.

Setting Up Windows for *SHARE.EXE*

If you work on a DOS/Windows workstation and you want to take advantage of the background replication option, you must first load the DOS SHARE.EXE program before you try to run a background replication. (SHARE is often already loaded on your system, but if it isn't, you will need to load it.) To load the program, exit Windows and Notes, and then type **SHARE** at the DOS prompt. Restart Notes and Windows and proceed to run a background replication.

To automatically load the SHARE program every time you start your PC, follow these steps at the DOS prompt:

1. Type **EDIT C:\AUTOEXEC.BAT**.

2. Insert the following line in the AUTOEXEC.BAT file—typically about 3–4 lines down:

LOADHIGH C:\DOS\SHARE.EXE

3. Exit and save the modified AUTOEXEC.BAT file.

When you restart your computer, the SHARE program will load automatically.

> **Caution**
>
> When you use the background replication method, Notes will keep trying to call the server within the time parameters you set, which ties up your phone line for any incoming calls that you may receive.
>
> Also, if you begin a database exchange using background exchange with the server, and something happens to terminate the connection, Notes will keep trying to call the server to continue completing the task until the replication is fully completed. If you have a large document, perhaps one that contains several attachments and is over 1 or 2 MB in size, you may continuously be disconnected before the replication successfully completes because large documents often have difficulty making it over phone lines in one piece, particularly if you connect at a low baud rate. Notes will keep trying and will tie up your phone line, as well as the server's, for as long as it takes to be successful, unless you terminate the process manually! Be careful using this feature unsupervised unless you take precautions to not replicate large documents or attachments.

From Here...

If you have followed the instructions in this chapter, your PC and modem should now be configured to successfully use Notes remotely, and you should have at least one location and connection record set up to use when working remote. Often, your Notes administrator has already configured your system for you. It is still wise to scan through this chapter though so that you are familiar with the configuration of your equipment. It will help you if you ever have trouble while working remote. Don't forget to review Appendix F for any troubleshooting you may need to do!

For information on topics that relate to getting set up to work remote, you may want to review some of the following chapters:

- Chapter 5, "Using the Address Books," provides an understanding in how the Name & Address Book works in Notes.
- Chapter 19, "Working Remote," has you learn the procedures to work remote and communicate with the server. You will also learn many tips on how to work smart when you are working remote.
- Chapter 22, "Notes: Under the Hood," provides more information on how Notes servers work, and how you work with them.

III

Going Mobile

Working Remote

If you followed the procedures in Chapter 18, "Setting Up to Go Remote," your PC and connections should all be set up to begin working with Notes remotely. As briefly described at the beginning of the last chapter, working remote involves some different equipment and procedures than when you are working on the network and are directly connected to the server.

This chapter briefly describes the process involved in working remote. It then describes the following:

- Setting up your mail to work remote
- Creating replicas of your databases
- Working interactively
- Replicating information
- Working away from the server
- Techniques for working smart as you work remote

Understanding Remote Access

When you connect to a Notes server through a local area network, you work with the most current database information and have continuous access to databases stored on a server. As you edit documents, create new documents, or delete documents, Notes instantly updates the database on the server. Notes transfers mail instantly, too, so that mail you send is routed immediately through the server to the destination you specify.

Notes works quite differently, however, when you work remote. When you set up Notes on your remote PC, you must create copies of all the databases you want to use on your PC's hard disk (unless you are working strictly via Interactive Connection—discussed later in this chapter). When you first begin to work with Notes remote, the database copies on your PC match the databases on the server. They don't match for long, however. As you travel, you edit, delete, and create new documents in the databases stored on your hard disk. Back at the office, other users are doing the same to the original databases. Soon you have documents on your PC that aren't on the server, and vice-versa.

Every so often you connect your PC to a phone line and tell Notes to perform a replication. Notes calls one or more of your servers, and your PC and the server determine what changes have taken place since the last time you exchanged information. If you have created new documents, Notes transfers them to the server; if you have deleted documents, Notes deletes them from the server. Similarly, any changes that other people have made to the server databases are transferred to your PC. If you are working with Notes mail, you may also be transferring e-mail when you call the server.

After the exchange is complete, Notes disconnects the phone line, and again the database copies on your PC match the databases on the server. As a result, the information in these local copies is only as current as the last time you performed an exchange with Notes.

You can work remote in two ways:

- *Replication* means that you work disconnected from the server in replica copies of databases, dial the server, exchange information, hang up, and then continue working disconnected from the server.

- *Interactive* means that you dial the server, and then work connected on the server as if you were on a network.

Each method is discussed in detail in the following sections.

Understanding How Mail Works Remote

How you set up your Notes mail while working remote depends on how you plan to work with the server. You can use replication, work interactively, or use a combination of the two methods. To understand why it is important to prepare your Notes mail, it is necessary to understand how Notes works with Mail both on and off the network.

A mail message is a Notes document that is composed using a special form. This form contains a field titled SendTo (CopyTo and BlindCopyTo also work this way) that tells Notes to send the document to the recipients. Your standard e-mail memo form, reply forms, and so forth all contain this field to alert Notes that the document is to be treated as mail. You can put this field in any form design to create a mail document. An application developer must take a few additional steps to turn the form into mail; if you are interested in learning about form design, check out Chapter 10, "Designing Forms."

When you are working connected to a network and you mail a document with a SendTo field, you send it to a Notes mail router for delivery to the recipients listed in the field. The mail router runs on a Notes server and carries messages from your workstation to the destination (much like the post office handles paper mail) by looking up the names and groups listed in the To, cc, and bcc fields of your message and comparing them to the names and groups listed in the company's Name & Address Book, which is located on every server. The router verifies that each individual name is valid, and if it is not, the router will try to find people with similar names in the address book and will then prompt you to make a selection. Names can be considered invalid if you have misspelled them, the individual listed has been denied access to Notes by the Notes administrator, or you have otherwise gotten the name wrong.

Once the router has reconciled the names in your memo with the names in the address book, it delivers the message to the recipient's mail database anywhere in the network. If the recipient's mail database is located on the same server as yours, the message is delivered immediately. If the recipient is located on another server, the router finds the path to that server based on the information stored along with your recipient's name in the Name & Address Book.

When you are working disconnected from the server, however, you turn on a switch that tells Notes to store any documents to be mailed in a holding database titled Outgoing Mail. This database's filename is MAIL.BOX (which performs the same service as your mailbox outside your home). When you send messages, Notes looks up the names and groups in your Personal Name & Address Book stored on your hard drive. If the message is addressed to any groups, Notes substitutes the names in the group listing for the group name in your memo. Notes also checks to see whether individuals listed in your memo have forwarding addresses associated with their names in the address books stored on your hard drive, and then substitutes the forwarding names for the names listed in the memo. Notes then uses the Outgoing Mail database to store the messages because you have no mail router available to you until you call the server. Notes does not prompt you if you have misspelled a name or otherwise have it incorrect when you are working remote because you are not required to carry the company Name & Address Book, which is the official listing, on your hard drive. It is the Public Name & Address Book listing that tells Notes where to deliver mail—if the name you type does not match the names listed in this book, Notes will not know where to route the mail.

When you call the server and replicate your Mail database, (you learn more about this process later), your workstation transfers all of the messages you have stored in your Outgoing Mail database to the router on the server in one batch. Because all the memos are dumped on the server at one time, the server receiving the memos does not check to see whether the addressees are valid at that time. As a result, remote users are not prompted if any names are wrong. If the names are wrong, remote users receive a Delivery Failure report the next time they call the server to exchange database information.

Once your outgoing mail is transferred to the server, Notes will begin to update your mail database with any incoming mail that has been sent to you. Notes will also update the server copy of your mail database with any mail you saved in your local copy of your mail database. If you selected any other databases to update that have replicas on the server, Notes will update them during the session as well.

Settings for Mail

When you are working remote and plan to use Mail, you must first decide how you are going to communicate with the server. If you are working using the replication method, choose the Local Mail option in the location document you're using in order to signal Notes to hold all of the mail you are sending in the Outgoing Mail database until you call the server. If you plan to use the interactive method, select the On Server Mail option to signal Notes to immediately transfer the mail to the recipients in the memos you send. When you use the replication method, you work in a replica of your Mail database that is stored on your hard drive. When you work interactively, you typically use the network copy of your Mail database stored on the server. (The section "Preparing a Replica of a Database," which comes later in this chapter, discusses how to create a replica of your Mail database.)

Interactive Mail Setup. To set up your workstation to work remote using the interactive method, verify that the On Server option is selected in the location document you are using for this session. To check whether this option is set, select the Locations box in the status bar at the bottom of the Notes window (see fig. 19.1).

Fig. 19.1

Select a location to edit or review settings.

Locations box ──

Select Edit Current from the pop-up list to view the current location document. Check to verify that the setting in the Mail File Location field is set to On Server. If it is not, place the cursor in that field and press the spacebar to change the setting. You learn more about working with the interactive method in the section titled "Using the Interactive Connection Method" towards the end of this chapter.

Note

On Server is the Mail File Location selection that is used when you are working on the network. When On Server mail is selected, your Outgoing Mail database is turned off, and the Public Name & Address Book is referenced first when you send mail. When you send a mail message, the server immediately routes it to the recipient's mailbox. If you select Local as the Mail File Location, your Outgoing Mail database is turned on, and your Personal Name & Address Book is used for addressing messages. If the recipients you enter are not listed in your Personal Name & Address Book, Notes allows you to mail your message, but it doesn't verify the name until the message is sent to the server for routing.

Replication Mail Setup. If you choose to work using the replication method, you must have a replica of your Mail database stored on your hard drive. If you installed Lotus Notes as remote (or network/remote), a replica of your Mail database was created for you at that time. To check whether you have a replica of your Mail database on your workstation, select View, Server Names, and then look at the database icons on your workspace for a database titled *Your Name* Mail on Local (see fig. 19.2).

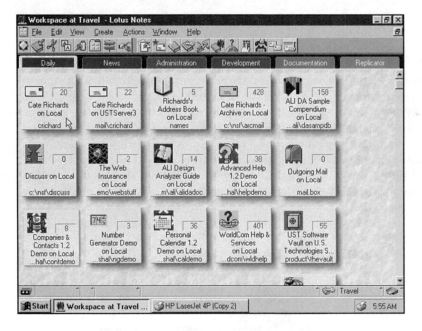

Fig. 19.2

Locating your local Mail database is easy when the icons are not stacked.

If your icons are stacked, select the icon indicator in the upper right corner of the database icon, and check to see whether the Local selection is present, as shown in figure 19.3. If you see this selection, you already have a remote Mail database installed on your workspace. Otherwise, follow the procedures in "Preparing a Replica of a Database" later in this chapter to create a replica of your Mail database on your workspace.

Fig. 19.3

Usually, your local mail database icon will be positioned on top when working at a remote location. However, if you need to switch to the local database, click the small down arrow in the upper right corner of your mail database icon, and then select Local.

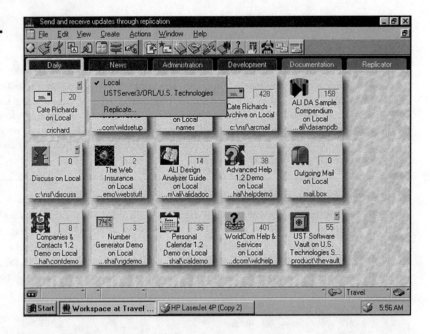

Switching between Local and On Server Mail

If you frequently switch between Local and On Server mail, you should define separate location documents for these options, as described in Chapter 18, "Setting Up To Go Remote." When you first begin a work session, switch to the appropriate location so that the correct mail settings are activated. You can switch locations at the beginning of a work session or any time during a work session by selecting the Locations box in the status bar at the bottom right corner of the Notes window or by selecting File, Mobile, Choose Current Location, as shown in figure 19.4. The Choose Location dialog box appears (see fig. 19.5). Select the location you want to use in this dialog box, and then click OK.

Fig. 19.4

You can use menu commands to switch locations.

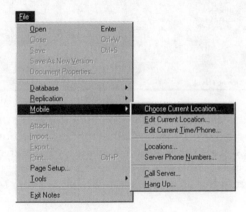

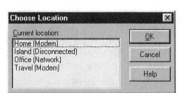

Fig. 19.5

Choose the location you want from the Choose Location dialog box.

Tip

As described in Chapter 18, "Setting Up To Go Remote," make sure you name your location documents so that they are descriptive of the location you are working in. It is highly recommended that you include the type of connection, network or remote, in the name of the location to make choosing locations for work easy. Otherwise, you may have to open and review the location documents frequently to see what type of location setup you are working from.

When You Work Both on and off the Network...

If you frequently work on and off the network, select File, Tools, User Preferences, Prompt for Location to have Notes ask you what location you are working from each time you start Notes. Your location must have the Local option selected for you to work remote, or you will be prompted to call the server each time you send mail. Specifying the Local option turns on the Outgoing Mail database and tells Notes to look only in your Personal Name & Address Book. If your location specifies Local mail while you are working on the server, however, all mail that you send is still held in the Outgoing Mail database until you perform the next replication with the server instead of being routed immediately to the addressees specified in the memo.

If you travel across time zones frequently, check your Date and Time each time you start Notes by selecting the Prompt for Time/Date/Phone option in the location document as described in Chapter 18, "Setting Up To Go Remote." Selecting this option ensures that any scheduled replications that you may have set up in your server locations (see Chapter 18 for further information on scheduled replications) and any timed agents are running at their proper times (see Chapter 15, "Buttons and Agents," for further information on agents).

Replicating a Database

Replication is the process of updating copies, referred to as *replicas*, of a database. After you create a replica of a server database on your hard drive, you work in that copy and then dial the server to exchange new, modified, and deleted documents in the databases.

To work with a replica of a database (one stored on your hard drive), it is helpful to understand how to tell a local copy of a Notes database from a server copy. The icon for a local copy of a database includes the name Local with the database title, whereas a server icon displays the server name. To verify which databases are local and which are on the server, select <u>V</u>iew and make sure that the <u>S</u>how Server Names option is selected. If a server name is present below the title of the database, it is a server copy of the database; otherwise, it is a local database. Double-clicking a server copy's icon when you are working disconnected from the server results in a prompt for you to call a server in order to open the database. Double-clicking a local database icon opens the database from your hard drive when you are working remote. Figure 19.6 shows examples of network and local database icons for the same database.

Fig. 19.6

These are examples of local and network database icons.

If your database icons are stacked (you selected <u>V</u>iew, Stac<u>k</u> Replica Icons), click the icon indicator in the right corner of the database icon to view a list of where each copy of the database is referencing. If Local is one of the options in that list, then you have a local copy of the database stored on your hard drive. You may also see multiple server names listed in the drop-down box if you have added the same network copy of the database icon from multiple servers, as shown in figure 19.7.

Having multiple database icons for the same database that is stored on multiple servers is common for many remote users, and is often convenient for updating purposes. Databases (like the database catalog) that users access frequently may be located on all servers in an organization to facilitate users accessing them—from the network or when calling in from a remote location. Having a popular database stored on many servers often reduces the number of phone calls a remote user needs to make to update all of their databases.

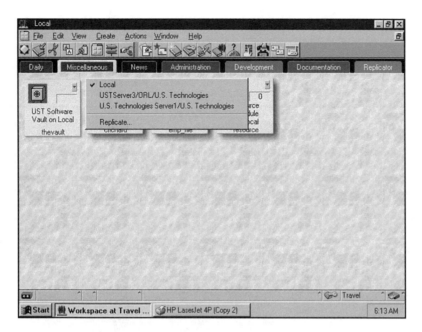

Fig. 19.7

This is an example of stacked icons referencing multiple servers.

To replicate a database, follow these steps:

1. Prepare a first-time replica of a database.
2. Choose appropriate replica options.
3. Verify access levels.
4. Replicate the database.

The following sections discuss these steps in detail.

Preparing a Replica of a Database

Before you use the replication method, you must prepare a replica icon of each database that you plan to use. Replicas of server databases are duplicates of the server databases, including the identification numbers, called *Replica IDs*, that distinguish the database from all others. When you exchange or access a Notes database, Notes looks at the Replica ID, not the name of the database, to determine what database you are trying to access. If the numbers don't match, Notes will not access the server's copy of the database during replication.

Caution

If you do not create replicas of databases when you work remote, your databases will not be able to exchange information with the server! Don't confuse creating replicas (File, Replication, New Replica) of a database with creating copies (File, Database, New Copy). Copies of databases contain all of the database's design and documents, but not the same Replica ID—which

(continues)

(continued)

is what the Notes server looks for when exchanging information with a database. If the Replica ID between your database and the server do not match, you will not be able to replicate the database.

To create a replica of a database, follow these steps:

1. Select the database icon you want to use to create a replica. You may need to connect to the server and add the database icons you want to use to create replicas.

2. Choose File, Replication, New Replica to display the New Replica dialog box (see fig. 19.8).

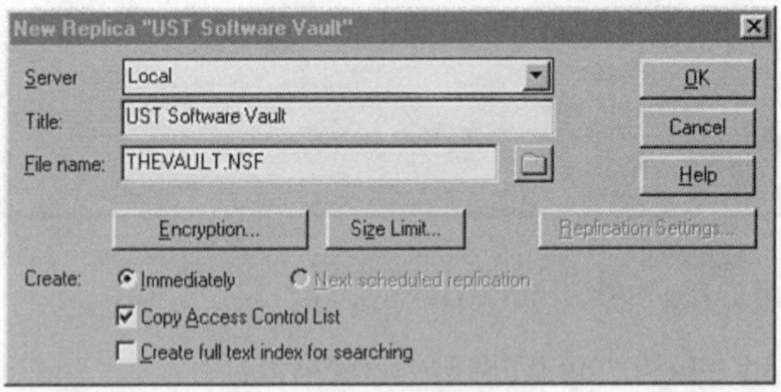

Fig. 19.8

Use this dialog box to create replicas.

3. In the Server list box, select the server where you want to store the replica database—Local in this case.

4. Type the Title of the database as you want it displayed on your replica. By default, Notes enters the network title of the database you selected. You can edit this title if you want to.

5. Type the File name of the database to include its path as you want it stored on your hard drive or floppy disk. By default, Notes enters the filename as it is stored on the network.

> **Note**
>
> Be sure to name replicas of any database the same as they're named on the server. Although this practice isn't mandatory, naming databases this way helps eliminate confusion. If you highlight a copy of a database that you want to make a replica of, Notes automatically fills in the appropriate server and filenames for you when you select File, Replication, New Replica.
>
> If you are making a replica of your Mail database, *always* give the replica the same name as the original database on the server, including any subdirectory names (for example, MAIL\CRICHARD). Otherwise, Notes may not be able to find your Mail database when you switch from On Server mail (on-site) to Local mail (off-site) operations.

6. Select either or both of the following options:

- The Copy Access Control List (recommended) option copies the original database's Access Control List to the new replica. If you do not select this option, you will be listed as the Manager of the database, but servers may not be listed, which will create problems when you try to replicate later.

- The Create full text index for searching option automatically creates a full text index at the time you make the replica of the database so that the Full Text Search option is immediately available. If you do not select this option now, you can always create an index at a later date. Depending on the size of your database, creating an index may take some time—keep this in mind when selecting this option.

7. Choose Immediately to immediately create a replica of the database that is initialized and filled with the contents (or a subset) of the original database, or choose Next scheduled replication to create a shell of the database that will be filled with the contents the first time you perform an exchange.

> ### Tip
>
> Select the First Replication option if you plan to make several replica copies of databases or you expect that the initial replication of the database will be lengthy. You can then replicate with the server once to fill all the database shells at the same time.

8. Make any Encryption, Size Limit, or Replication Settings desired for this replica database. Each of these options is discussed in the following sections.

9. Choose OK to create the replica database.

Setting Database Encryption Options

You can set the security of your local database so that only someone with your Notes ID and password can open it. Follow these steps:

1. Select the Encryption button in the New Replica dialog box. The Encryption dialog box appears (see fig. 19.9).

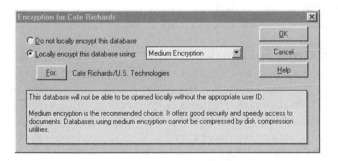

Fig. 19.9

Use this dialog box to encrypt a local database.

2. Select Locally encrypt this database using.

3. Select Simple, Medium, or Strong Encryption from the drop-down list box. Simple Encryption enables you to open the database much quicker than you can with Medium or Strong encryption, so unless you must carry a higher level of security on the database, choose Simple.

4. Click OK to return to the New Replica dialog box.

Notes uses the public portion of your Notes ID encryption key to secure this database from other people accessing it without your Notes ID and password. Keep in mind, however, that if you are sharing a public workstation and encrypt a database locally that others also need to use, they will not be able to access the database with their IDs. For more information on encryption, read Chapter 20, "Security and Encryption."

Identifying a Size Limit

You can specify the maximum size for this database by selecting the Size Limit button in the New Replica dialog box. The Size Limit dialog box appears (see fig. 19.10).

Fig. 19.10

Use this dialog box to set the size limit of a local database.

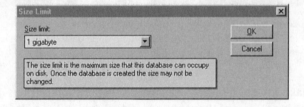

Size limits are set in gigabytes, so you will most likely be able to leave the default (one gigabyte) as your entry. Click OK to exit and save your selection. Chances are your remote PC will not be able to host databases larger than this amount anyway.

> **Note**
>
> You can also set limits on the size of the database (to make limits less than 1 gigabyte) through the Administration pane. You learn more about this option in the "Database Information" section in Chapter 22, "Notes: Under the Hood."

Choosing Replication Settings

To conserve space, speed up replication time, control what is sent to the server, or make any other settings that effect the way a replica database replicates with a server, or servers, you can select the Replication Settings button while creating a new replica of a database. You can also modify replication settings at a later date by highlighting a replica of a database and selecting File, Replication, Settings to display the Replication Settings dialog box shown in figure 19.11.

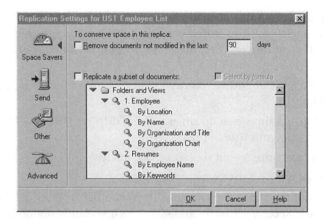

Fig. 19.11

Use the Replication Settings dialog box to control different aspects of the replication process.

To set or change replication settings for a database, perform the following steps:

1. Select the database whose replication settings you want to change.

2. Select the File Replications Settings SmartIcon if you are creating a new replica, or select File, Replication, Settings while highlighting an existing replica database icon to display the Replication Settings dialog box shown in figure 19.11.

3. Choose all options that meet your needs, and then choose OK.

The Replication Settings dialog box offers four panels to facilitate making all of the replication settings for the database; the following sections describe the options available in each panel.

Saving Space. The first panel to appear when you open the Replication Settings dialog box is the Space Savers panel. You may select from any of the following options:

■ **Remove documents not modified in the last ___ days**—This option purges documents that have not been edited within the specified time period. If your database has documents meeting the criteria specified in this option, you will be prompted each time you open the database until you answer Yes to remove the documents, change the number of days, or disable this option. The purging process removes all references to the deletion stub from this replica that can be copied to other replicas of the database. This option is a great way to save space and is discussed in more detail in the section "Working Smart Remotely."

■ **Receive summary and 40K of rich text**—This option only lets you shorten a document by removing bitmaps and other large objects and all attachments from the document copies received from the server. When you select this option, Notes only retrieves the document summary (basic document information, such as author and subject), and the first 40K of information. Notes doesn't remove the large objects and attachments from the documents stored on the server however—just from the copies you receive. This option helps reduce long exchange times and saves valuable disk space by keeping file size low. If you later decide you want to get the information you excluded during replication, you can deselect this option, or work interactively in the server copy of the database to review the entire document.

The following are a few things that you need to keep in mind, however, when selecting this option:

- When you open a shortened document, Notes displays *(TRUNCATED)* as part of the document's title in the title bar.
- You cannot categorize or edit shortened documents.
- Agents do not work on shortened documents.
- Notes does not send shortened documents to another replica unless the replica has the Receive summary and 40K of rich text only option selected.

> **Tip**
>
> If you decide you want to receive the rest of a document that has been shortened using this option, open the document and choose Actions, Retrieve Entire Document. If you want to receive the remainder of more than one document, select the documents in the view and then choose Actions, Retrieve Entire Document, Get documents now via background, and then click OK. If Notes can retrieve the documents from more than one server, it prompts you to choose the server. If the database is located on only one server, Notes will dial that server.

- **Replicate a subset of documents**—This option lets you specify the criteria that will define the specific documents you receive from the server during replication. You can select particular views of documents to replicate, or specify a formula to use to limit the documents you replicate with the server. You will learn more about this feature in the section titled "Selective Replication" later in this chapter.

Limiting What Is Sent to the Server. Just as you can limit what information is received from the server, you can also limit what information is sent to the server by selecting the Send icon in the Replication Settings dialog box. The Send panel of the Replication Settings dialog box appears (see fig. 19.12).

You can make any of the following selections:

- **Do not send deletions made in this replica to other replicas**—When you have this option selected, you can delete documents from your local copy of the database without worrying about passing those deletions on to other replicas on the server. This selection is handy if you can not define a particular selective replication setting (date created, author name, subject matter, etc.) to limit the documents in your local database, and you need to reduce the size of the database you are storing locally. Your deletions will not be passed on to the server. This option is also handy in case you accidentally deleted documents from a local copy and you do not want to risk passing those deletions to the server. If you have the correct access to delete documents from the server copy of the database, you could delete all instances of a particular document if this option is not selected.

- **Do not send changes in database title & catalog info to other replicas**—Select this option if you want to make changes to the title of your local replica of the database and update the catalog information without having the change replicate to the server copy of the database. This setting is primarily used by managers or designers of applications that want to work with them locally. You must have at least Designer level access on the server copy of the database to change database titles on the server copy and catalog information.

- **Do not send changes in local security property to other replicas**— Select this option if you want to change Access Control information for this replica of the database without changing the Access Control information in other replicas. This setting is primarily used by managers of applications that want to work with them locally. You must have Manager level access to change Access Control settings on the server copy of the database.

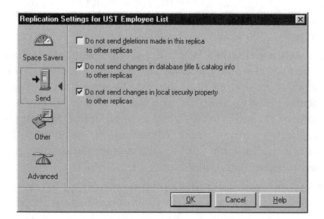

Fig. 19.12

Use the Send panel to limit the information that is sent to the server.

Other Replication Settings. You can temporarily disable replication, assign replication priority, limit documents received during replication according to a specified date, or identify a CD-ROM publishing date. Select the Other icon in the Replication Settings dialog box to display the Other panel shown in figure 19.13.

III

Going Mobile

Fig. 19.13

Use this panel to further control replication.

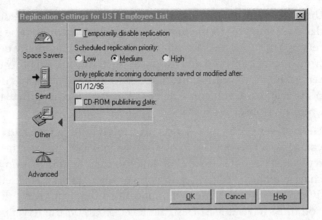

Select from any of these options:

■ **Temporarily disable replication**—When this option is selected, the database will not be included in any replications with other replicas, even if it is selected when you schedule a replication. This option is ideal if you think your application may be corrupted, and you don't want to risk passing on corrupt data to another copy of the database. You can also use this option to disable a database that changes infrequently so that the server won't spend time trying to read it during a scheduled replication. You can later deselect this option when you want to begin replication again.

■ **Scheduled replication priority**—With this option, select Low, Medium, or High to indicate the level at which this database will replicate during scheduled replications. Notes provides options that allow you to opt only to replicate databases with a particular priority setting during a session. The Replicator will let you elect to replicate only High priority databases as an option to limit the number of databases replicated during a scheduled replication. This is particularly useful if you are in a hurry and only want to receive information from databases you have indicated as being highly important.

■ **Only replicate incoming documents saved or modified after**—In this option, enter the cutoff date you want to use to limit the documents you want replicated. This option lets you minimize the number of documents you are replicating to only those created or edited on or before the date specified so that you can reduce the amount of hard disk space that's used and the length of replication time. This setting is ideal if you only want to get the latest information from a database while working remote, particularly if you typically access this database on a frequent basis when you are connected to the network.

Tip

Selecting the Only replicate incoming documents saved or modified after option is a great feature to use if, for some reason, there is a very high volume of documents being added to a database and you go on vacation. This will enable you to replicate only a small subset of the documents rather than everything (which could take a long time).

■ **CD-ROM publishing date**—If you are creating a CD-ROM in which you are publishing a replica of this database, you can tell Notes to specify the publishing date for the replica with this option. The recipient of the CD-ROM copy of the database can then copy the CD-ROM file to his or her local drive (or server), and then replicate with the original database without having to perform a full replication—only the documents created after the publishing date will have to be replicated.

Advanced Replication Options. If you want to get really sophisticated with your replication strategies, select the Advanced icon in the Replication Settings dialog box to open the Advanced panel shown in figure 19.14.

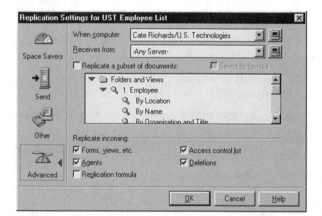

Fig. 19.14

The Advanced panel contains more replication options.

If more than one server contains a replica of a database, you can select the server your replica receives. If you receive from more than one server, you can select different documents and/or different parts of a database's design to receive from each. To select only particular servers to replicate with, do the following:

1. Leave the When computer option at the default, which is your Notes name.

2. Click the server indicator (the computer icon) next to the Receives from box, and then select the server you want to replicate with in the Servers dialog box that appears (see fig. 19.15). Click OK.

Fig. 19.15

You can specify which servers you want to receive from in the Servers dialog box.

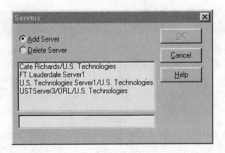

You can also use this dialog box to remove servers that you want to exclude replication with by highlighting their names and selecting the Delete Server option before clicking OK.

3. To receive only selected documents from the server, select the Replicate a subset of documents option, and do one of the following:

   - Select the folders and views you want.
   - Select the Select by formula option and specify a formula.

4. To receive only selected parts of a database's design, do one or more of the following:

   - Select Forms, views, etc., to receive a database's basic design.
   - Select Agents to receive a database's agents.
   - Select Replication formula to receive the formula a database uses to select the documents it receives.
   - Select Access control list to receive a database's Access Control List (ACL).

5. To prevent receiving document deletions from the server copy, deselect Deletions.

6. Click OK to exit the Replication Settings dialog box.

Note

You learn more about using the selective replication sections of the Space Savers and Advanced panels in the "Selective Replication" section later in this chapter.

Verifying Access Levels

When you first make a replica of a server database, you must verify, and possibly modify, the access level for you and for the server(s) you will dial into to perform an exchange. To do so, follow these steps:

1. Select the replica of the database you want to verify.

2. Choose File, Database, Access Control (or select the File Database Access Control SmartIcon). The Database Access Control List dialog box appears (see fig. 19.16).

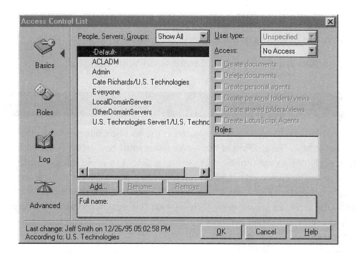

Fig. 19.16

Use this dialog box to verify the Access Control List settings.

3. Select your name in the People, Servers, Groups list box. If your name is not listed, click on the Add button to enter your name—exactly as it is defined in Notes. You may either type your name (including any hierarchical naming conventions), or select the person icon to open the Name & Address Book where you can select your name from the list of users.

4. Choose Person from the User type list box if it is not already selected.

5. Choose Manager from the Access level list box if it is not already selected.

6. Go through the list box to find the Notes server name(s) where the database is located. Select the server name(s) with which you will replicate this database.

7. Choose Server from the User type list box if it is not already selected.

8. Choose Manager in the Access list box for each server to ensure that they can read, write, and modify the databases you replicate.

Tip

You should also have two server entries in your database access list titled LocalDomainServers and OtherDomainServers. If you access the same database on multiple servers in your domain (the more likely case) or across multiple domains (not quite as common), grant one or both of these entries Manager level access as well. If your company maintains only one domain, you can update the access for LocalDomainServers only and feel safe in removing access for the OtherDomainServers setting. Making these updates helps eliminate the possibility of replication problems if the database is moved to another server, and that server's name is not entered in this access list.

III

Going Mobile

9. Repeat steps 6 through 8 for each server you dial to update this database.

10. Choose <u>O</u>K to exit the dialog box and save your changes.

Repeat the preceding process for each replica database on your desktop.

Caution

If the server name isn't present, you must enter the name in the text box directly below the People, Servers, <u>G</u>roups list box. The spelling of the server name must be exactly as the Notes administrator designated; Notes is case-sensitive about this spelling. (To avoid misspellings, select the name of the server by clicking the A<u>d</u>d button, and then select the person icon next to the Person, Server, or Group text entry box to select the server name from the Name & Address Book.) Identify the server as Server in the <u>U</u>ser type list box, assign the server Manager access, and choose <u>A</u>dd User. If the server isn't listed in the ACL, it cannot update your replica of the database after you create it the first time.

Setting Up the Replicator

Notes 4 provides a feature called the Replicator. With Replicator, you can replicate multiple databases with different servers with a single command. You also can do other work while Notes replicates in the background.

To display the Replicator, click the Replicator tab in your workspace. When you switch to the Replicator, the workspace appears as shown in figure 19.17.

Fig. 19.17

The Replicator enables you to manage the replication of your local databases in one place.

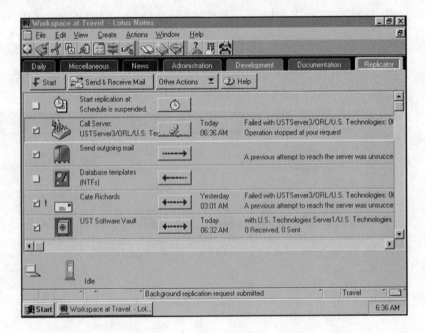

When you use Notes away from the office, you can have Replicator call each server you want to replicate with automatically. If you're using a passthru server or a remote LAN server, you can have Replicator make a single call and replicate all of your local databases at one time, even if they're on different servers. Replicator also lets you customize replication based on the location you are working from. Replicator also provides additional ways to replicate; for example, you can assign High priority to selected databases and replicate only those databases. The following sections describe the Replicator.

Understanding the Replicator Page. Replicator is always the last page on your workspace; you cannot delete it. Replicator automatically contains the following types of entries:

■ **Database**—Replicator contains a database entry for each local replica you have unless you deleted the entry from the Replicator page (see fig. 19.18). When you add replicas of databases to your workstation, they are automatically added to the Replicator. To remove replicas of databases that you do not want on your Replicator, highlight the database entry and press Delete. Select Yes to indicate that you want to remove the entry.

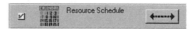

Fig. 19.18

This is an example of a database entry.

■ **Start replication at**—Use this entry to specify a replication schedule and enable scheduled replication. The replication schedule used is dependent on the location you are using and the settings you made in its location document. If you want to modify the time in which you start replication, click the clock icon displayed on the Start replication at entry, and Notes will open your current location document (see fig. 19.19). After you have made any necessary changes, press Esc and select Yes to save your changes.

Fig. 19.19

The Start replication at entry is always first and cannot be deleted.

■ **Database templates**—You can use this entry to refresh the designs of template-based databases (see fig. 19.20).

III

Going Mobile

Fig. 19.20

You cannot delete the Database templates entry.

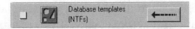

■ **Send outgoing mail**—You can use this entry to send all pending messages from your Outgoing Mail database (MAIL.BOX) (see fig. 19.21).

Fig. 19.21

You cannot delete the Send outgoing mail entry.

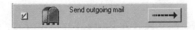

You can also create the following types of entries for mobile locations (such as Home and Travel):

■ **Call**— When you create a Call entry, you specify the server you want to call, and the Replicator uses the information from the Server Connection record, along with any special location prefix and suffix numbers that may have been defined, when it dials (see fig. 19.22).

Fig. 19.22

You can use a Call entry to connect to a server.

■ **Hangup**—You can use a Hangup entry to end a connection with a server (see fig. 19.23).

Fig. 19.23

The Hangup entry tells Notes to end a call with the current server.

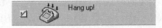

To set up the Replicator, perform any of the tasks described in the following sections.

Moving a Replicator Entry. Except for the Start Replication At entry, which always comes first, you can arrange Replicator entries in any order that you want. For example, you may want to group Replicator entries according to the server on which you want to replicate so that the Replicator only has to call that server one time to exchange all databases in common. To move a Replicator entry, follow these steps:

1. Click and hold the left mouse button over the entry you want to move. Be careful not to drag over the actual button, or you may start the procedure for that button!

2. Drag the entry to its new position.

3. Release the left mouse button.

Creating a Replicator Entry. You can create entries that automatically connect and disconnect from servers when you replicate over a modem. You can create a Call entry or Hangup entry as explained in the following steps.

Note

As previously mentioned, the Replicator automatically adds Database entries when you create replicas of databases. However, if you have deleted a database entry, and you want to add it to the Replicator again, switch to the workpage that has the replica of the database and click the replica's icon. Hold down the left mouse button and drag the icon to the Replicator tab. Release the mouse button when the mouse cursor is positioned over the tab. Notes adds the Database entry to the Replicator again.

To make a Call entry, perform the following steps:

1. If necessary, switch to the location where you use your modem to connect to the Notes servers.

2. On the Replicator tab, click where you want the Call entry to be located. Notes places the Call entry directly above the entry you click.

3. Select Create, Call Entry. Notes automatically creates the entry for your Home server by default.

4. If you want to create a Call entry to a server other than your Home server, double-click the new Call entry's action button (it has a small, yellow phone on its icon). Select the server you want to call, and then click OK.

When creating Call entries, keep the following tips in mind:

- If you have set up a server connection for a passthru server or a remote LAN server, create a single Call entry for this server on the Replicator tab. When you do this, the Replicator can make just one phone call to replicate with all of the servers. You will need to ask your Notes administrator about pass-through and remote LAN server connections particular to your company.

- When Replicator calls a server, it stays connected to the server until it reaches another Call entry or a Hangup entry. You don't need to create a Hangup entry for each Call entry, just the last one.

- If you create two or more Call entries next to each other, Replicator tries each call in turn. When Replicator makes a connection to a server, it then skips to the first entry that is not a Call entry.

III

Going Mobile

- You can replicate over a modem without Call entries. If you don't have Call entries created, Replicator tries to call the last server that the first Database entry replicated with.

You can create a Hangup entry so that the Replicator automatically disconnects from a server when you replicate over a modem. To create a Hangup entry, follow these steps:

1. On the Replicator tab, click where you want the Hangup entry. Notes adds the Hangup entry immediately above the entry you click.

2. Select Create, Hangup Entry. Notes adds a new Hangup entry to the Replicator directly above the entry you clicked.

If you want to make the Hangup entry the last entry in the list, click and hold the left mouse button over the Hangup entry and drag it to the last position. Remember, you only need one Hangup entry, even if you have more than one Call entry. When Replicator reaches a new Call entry, it automatically hangs up the current call!

Specifying Replicator Options. Replicator entries contain action buttons, which you can use to specify Replicator options. The following options are available:

- You can click the clock action button on a Start Replication At entry to specify a replication schedule for the current location. The current location document opens in Edit mode for you to make any changes you want to make. Press Esc and then Yes to save your new settings.

- You can click the arrow action buttons on a Database entry to specify whether you want to send and/or receive documents from a server. If you select the Receive Documents from Server option, you can reduce the length of time it takes for replication by also selecting to receive full documents, document summaries and the first 40 KB of rich text only, or document summaries only.

> ### Tip
>
> If you find errors in your replication with a server and are either not receiving or not sending documents during a session, check to see if the arrow action button is set to send (arrow pointing to the right), receive (arrow pointing to the left), or send and receive (arrow pointing both ways). Make changes as necessary.
>
> If you are still having difficulty, check the access control to make sure both you and the server you are replicating with have the appropriate access level for the database. Finally, check to make sure your database is a replica of the one located on the server, and not just a plain copy.

- You can click any Call entry action button to specify a different server to call. Select the server from the pop-up list that appears when you click this action button. In this list, Notes displays the servers for which you have already defined phone numbers. To add a server to the list or specify a different phone number, refer to the section "Setting Up Connections Records" in Chapter 18.

Deleting a Replicator Entry. You can easily delete Replicator entries by clicking the entry you want to remove and pressing the Delete key. Select Yes to confirm the deletion.

Replicating with the Server

When you are ready to replicate with the server, either to fill the database shells you may have created in the previous section or to exchange information with the server on an ongoing basis, you will need to plug your modem into your PC and connect the modem to the telephone jack. You can either carry your own telephone cable with you when working on the road or unplug the cable from the connection in back of the phone (if possible) and plug it into your modem jack. Make sure the other end of the cable is plugged into the telephone jack in the wall!

It is recommended that you carry a telephone cable with you. In the United States, the telephone jack connector is commonly referred to as an RJ-11; you may need to verify the appropriate cable connector you will need if working internationally as it varies by country. If you need to dial manually (where you must dial through an operator to get an outside line), if the closest phone cable is permanently attached to the phone, or if the phone cable you are trying to use is damaged, you will be thankful you have a spare.

> **Note**
>
> Some phones have data ports located in the back of the phone; in which case, you run a telephone cable from your modem to the back of the phone, rather than directly to the jack. You will need a second cable in this case. When it's possible, running the telephone cable directly from your modem into the wall jack is the preferable option. This setup makes your replications much smoother.

Performing a Replication. You can replicate information between the server and one (or many) of the replica databases located on your workspace. When you perform an exchange (replication), you dial the server, send and receive database information, and hang up. There are two ways to replicate with a server:

- Replicate selected databases in the foreground
- Replicate selected databases with the Replicator

The following sections describe both options.

Replicating in the Foreground. You can replicate one or more databases with the same server in the foreground. Follow these steps:

1. Select the databases you want to replicate.

III

Going Mobile

2. Select File, Replication, Replicate, or select the File Replication Replicate SmartIcon. The Replicate dialog box appears (see fig. 19.24).

Fig. 19.24

The Replicate dialog box appears when you replicate in the foreground.

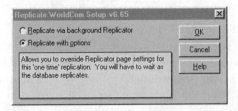

3. Select Replicate with options, and then select OK. The Replicate dialog box displays additional new settings, as shown in figure 19.25.

Fig. 19.25

You can choose additional settings in this Replicate dialog box.

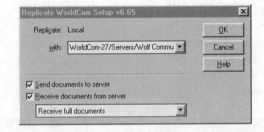

4. Select a different server to replicate with by clicking the down arrow next to the with drop-down list box, if necessary.

5. Select one or both of the following:

- Send documents to server.
- Receive documents from server. If you select this option, you may also specify whether you want to receive full documents, document summaries and the first 40K of rich text only, or document summaries only.

6. Select OK. Notes prompts you for permission to dial the server you selected. Select Yes to begin the replication.

When you use the Replicate with options setting to replicate databases, Notes calls the server and performs the replication in the foreground; you will have to wait until the replication is completed before you can continue working. If you want to continue to work while Notes is replicating, you must use the Replicator as discussed in the following section.

Tip

If you work on-site and off-site, you can decrease the amount of time required to perform remote database exchanges. While you still are connected on-site to the server, perform a database exchange for all your local replicas, as described earlier. You leave the office with the most recent database information and decrease the amount of time needed to perform a remote replication because you don't need to send and receive as many documents. Database replication with the server is also a great deal faster to perform when you do it on the network.

Replicating Databases with the Replicator. You can replicate databases in the background with Replicator. When you replicate in the background, you can continue to do other work while Notes replicates. If your current location is set up for scheduled replication, you don't need to do anything to have Replicator begin background replication when the replication settings criteria is met. If your modem is connected to a phone line, Notes begins calling the first server identified on the Replicator tab and replicates information until it handles the last replication entry. You can also tell Notes to begin a replication sequence whenever you want by clicking the Start button at the top of the Replicator page.

Watch the bottom of the Replicator tab to determine the status of each database as it replicates (see fig. 19.26). Notes communicates each step in the replication progress to you, as well as the estimated time it will take for the replication of each database to be complete. Notice that a hand points to the each entry on the Replicator tab as it becomes active.

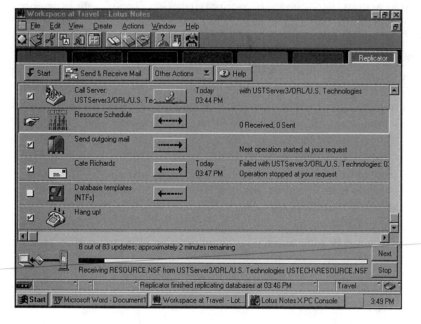

Fig. 19.26

This is how a replication in progress looks when you use the Replicator.

If you select Next, Notes stops replicating the current database and moves to the next entry. Select Stop if you want to completely end the current replication. Notes stops replicating the current database and ignores the remaining entries on the Replicator tab—but does not hang up the connection. If you want to hang up manually, select File, Mobile, Hang Up.

> **Note**
>
> If you work off-site and on a network, keep in mind that any information you have entered into your local replicas doesn't appear on the server copy of the database when you return to the office unless you performed a database exchange after your last entry. To update the server copy of the database, perform a background replication as soon as you connect back on the network.

Using Some Special Actions with Replicator. Often, when working remote, you may want to replicate mail, replicate only one database, replicate only selected databases or with a selected server, or replicate high priority databases only. The Send and Receive Mail Only and the Other Actions buttons enable you to perform the following actions during a replication:

- Select the Send and Receive Mail Only button if you only want to replicate mail during a particular replication. Notes immediately calls your Home/Mail server and exchanges Mail databases. It also transfers all the mail you may have created and stored in your Outgoing Mail database.

- Select Other Actions, Replicate High Priority Databases to begin replicating only those databases whose replication settings indicate high priority (see "Other Replication Settings" earlier in this chapter for information on setting database priorities).

- Select the databases you want to replicate by clicking in the boxes next to their entries. Select Other Actions, Replicate with Server, and then select the server you want to replicate with. Select OK to begin the replication. Notes calls only that server to replicate with. Keep in mind that if the database(s) you select do not have replicas on that particular server, and you are not calling a passthru server, your database(s) will not be updated.

- Select the database you want to replicate by clicking its entry in the Replicator. Select Other Actions, Replicate Selected Database Only. Notes calls the server and replicates only that database.

- Select the databases you want to replicate by clicking the box next to their entries (make sure you deselect those you don't want to replicate as well). Select Other Actions, Replicate Selected Databases Only. Notes calls and replicates only the selected databases.

- To only send your outgoing mail, select Other Actions and then Send Outgoing Mail. Notes will call your server and only transfer your outgoing mail to the server. You will not receive any updates or send any updates to other server databases.

Monitoring Replication History. After you replicate using the Replicator, you see how many documents you sent and received logged directly on each database entry that was selected for replication. However, you may want to see the history of past replications to see who replicated with a particular database and when. You can do so by highlighting the database you are interested in on the regular workpage, and then selecting File, Replication, History. The Replication History dialog box appears (see fig. 19.27).

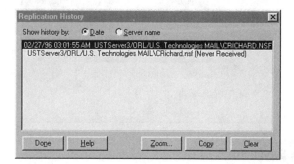

Fig. 19.27

You can view the replication history of a database in this dialog box.

You can Copy the information to the Clipboard to paste into a report, Clear the history, or change the way you view the information (by Server name or by Date). Select Done when you are ready to exit the Replication History dialog box. This technique is ideal for database managers who need to review database activity!

More About Using Mail Remotely

As mentioned in the beginning of this chapter, Notes makes sending and receiving mail documents easy while operating remotely. A few areas about using mail remotely warrant further discussion, however. In the following sections, you learn more about using the Outgoing Mail database (MAIL.BOX) and working remotely with the Notes address books.

Understanding the Outgoing Mail Database

When you use mail remotely, Notes stores all mail that you send (including any return receipt reports for documents you received and opened) in a special Outgoing Mail database named MAIL.BOX. The Outgoing Mail database automatically appears on your workspace if you set up Notes for remote use when you first installed Lotus Notes. If you installed Notes as a network only user and later created a replica of your Mail database, Notes automatically created the Outgoing Mail database at that time.

If you think the Outgoing Mail database is present, but don't see its icon on your workspace, select File, Database, Open and with Local highlighted in the servers list, type **MAIL.BOX** in the Filename text box. Select Add Icon and then select Done. If an error message appears indicating that the file does not exist, create a new one by following these instructions:

1. Select File, Database, New. The New Database dialog box appears (see fig. 19.28).

Fig. 19.28

Use the New Database dialog box to create an Outgoing Mail database.

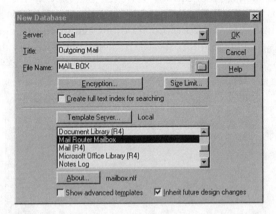

2. Select Local for the Server entry.

3. Type **Outgoing Mail** in the Title box.

4. Edit the File Name to read MAIL.BOX.

Caution

You must name the Outgoing Mail database MAIL.BOX in the File Name field, or Notes will not recognize the filename when trying to store sent mail remotely.

---

5. Select Mail Router Mailbox from the Template list box. If you do not see the Mail Router Mailbox template, enable the Show advanced templates option in the lower left corner of the dialog box to display additional templates to choose from.

6. Select OK. Notes creates the Outgoing Mail database, and adds its icon to your workspace.

If you want to verify whether you sent a mail document from your Mail database (you may not remember whether you chose to mail a document you were working on or you may suspect that your remote mail capabilities are not working correctly), open the Outgoing Mail database. If the mail document title is displayed, the message will transfer to the server the next time you perform a database exchange when you replicate your Mail database. If you decide that you don't want to mail the document, you can delete the document from this database before you perform an exchange.

Likewise, to make sure that all the mail you send is transferred to the server during the last exchange, open the Outgoing Mail database. No documents display in the Mail view if your exchange was performed successfully.

> **Note**
>
> Do not compose memos from the Outgoing Mail database. This database is used only as a holding tank for mail waiting to be transferred to the server! Notes treats this database specially, and you may find that your messages are not being delivered, or otherwise have problems if you try to compose messages from this database.

> **Caution**
>
> Do not open the Outgoing Mail database while you are in the process of transferring mail to the server. This database must be closed during replication for mail to successfully transfer!

Using Address Books Remotely

For mail to be routed properly, the recipients listed in the To, cc, and bcc fields must be spelled exactly as they are in the server's address book. Usually, only users listed in the server's address book can receive Notes mail because the server's address book displays all Notes users set up to receive mail on your network. The exception is if special gateways are installed to work with Notes on your network to route mail to other foreign Notes domains or other types of e-mail systems. (Refer to Chapter 6, "Advanced Mail," for additional information on this exception.)

As previously discussed, Notes looks in your Personal Name & Address Book first to find recipients. If the recipient isn't listed there, Notes transfers the document to the server anyway during a database exchange. The server then looks for the recipient in the Public Name & Address Book. If the server cannot find the name, it sends a non-delivery report to your mail file on the server. You aren't aware of the delivery failure until the next time you perform a database exchange.

If you are a remote-only user, you can use the interactive connection method to connect to your Notes server to update your Personal Name & Address Book with other Notes users' names so that you have their names available to you when you address mail.

To update your Personal Name & Address Book with users' names, follow these steps:

1. Open your Personal Name & Address Book.
2. Choose View, People.
3. Choose Edit, Select All.

> **Caution**
>
> If you follow this procedure, you will delete all of your current entries from the database—including any unique entries (people you have defined that are not in your company). If you use your Personal Name & Address Book to maintain unique entries, then you may want to select only those names that are in your group/company. Be careful when following these procedures so that you do not lose any of your personal, unique names.

4. Delete all the selected documents.

5. Choose File, Mobile, Call Server, and follow the steps in the following section "Using the Interactive Connection Method" to connect to the server.

6. Open the Public Name & Address Book on the server.

7. Choose View, People.

8. Choose Edit, Select All (or you can select each individual name that you want to copy to your Personal Name & Address Book instead). Keep in mind that if you have a large number of users defined in your Public Name & Address Book, your Personal Name & Address Book is going to grow quite large if you copy all user names.

9. Choose Edit, Copy. Notes begins copying all the documents to the Clipboard. (This process can take a while, depending on the number of names that must be copied.)

> **Caution**
>
> If you did not remove all of the names that are in common with the Public Name & Address Book prior to pasting all of the new names into the book, you will have duplicate entries of user names, which will cause Notes to prompt you with error messages when you try to send to the user. Delete all duplicate names from the list.

10. After the copying is complete, exit the Public Name & Address Book.

11. Open your Personal Name & Address Book and choose Edit, Paste. Notes pastes all the names into your Personal Name & Address Book.

12. Choose File, Mobile, Hangup and select the appropriate COM port, and then choose Hangup to end the connection with the server.

Rather than cut and paste documents from the server's address book to your personal one or going without Notes user's names available to you, follow these steps for an alternative method:

Caution

Although the following information works for most Notes users, check with your Notes administrator to make sure that carrying a replica of the Public Name & Address Book for your company does not interfere with any special setup or policy the administrator may have made.

Also, depending on the number of users you have on your network, this database can be quite large, and therefore may be impractical to carry on your hard drive.

Finally, users can make changes to the network copy of this database several times a day, and you may find it too time consuming to replicate this database frequently. Turn off replication or limit replication to a few times a month.

---

1. Make a replica stub of the Public Name & Address Book in your local directory (refer to the section "Preparing a Replica of a Database" earlier in this chapter). Enter any filename other than NAMES.NSF because that is being used by your Personal Name & Address Book. For our example, enter the filename **NAMES2.NSF**.

2. In the Space Savers settings of the Replications Settings dialog box, select the option to Replicate a subset of documents (you will learn more about this feature shortly).

3. Select the people and groups views below the Folders and Views icon, as shown in figure 19.29.

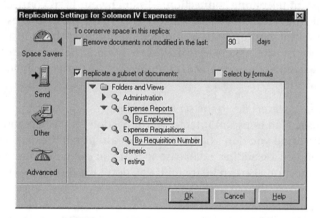

Fig. 19.29

You can set up selective replication for the Public Name & Address Book.

4. Select OK.

When Notes replicates with the Public Name & Address Book, it only replicates group lists and person documents.

> **Note**
>
> If your Notes administrator has added additional views that would be of interest to you, you may select those as well to include in your replication. However, keep in mind that the more views you select, the more you may be adding to the size of the replica Public Name & Address Book on your local drive.

You also need to add a line to your NOTES.INI file to tell Notes that you have another address book to use when addressing mail remotely. For details on updating NOTES.INI, see Chapter 21, "Taking Advantage of Notes Release 4 Features."

After modifying your NOTES.INI file, you should be able to switch between your Personal and Public Name & Address Books while working remote. You can update your replica of the address book by replicating it just like any other database. For more information on using the Address Books, read Chapter 5, "Using the Address Books."

You now have a replica of the Public Name & Address Book to use with the mail address feature when you are working remote. To access the names in the list remotely, follow the instructions in Chapter 5. All of the addressees appear in your Public Name & Address Book.

Using the Interactive Connection Method

An *interactive connection* establishes a direct link between your remote station and the server, requiring a constant telephone connection. Although your PC is connected to the server by telephone lines rather than LAN cables, you can use the databases stored on the server and receive the most up-to-date information in the databases just as though you were working on-site. You receive mail directly from the mail router, and the mail you send is transferred through the mail router directly to the recipient you specify as soon as you send it.

Interactive connections, however, tie up the server for a longer period of time, resulting in higher phone costs. Plan to use an interactive connection only when you work with a very large database and you don't have the resources to install the database on your remote PC or when you are adding a database so that you can create a replica of it. An interactive connection also can be useful if you don't use the database frequently.

> **Caution**
>
> If you use an interactive connection, save documents often. Otherwise, if your connection with the server is discontinued before you complete and save an entry, you may lose the information. If you lose the connection, keep the document you are trying to work with open on your desktop until the connection can be reestablished. Save the file when you are connected back with the server.

To work interactively, you must first call the server. Once you are connected, you can work in the databases on that server as though you were connected on a LAN.

> **Note**
>
> If the databases you want to work in are on different servers, you must repeat this process for each server after you complete the work on one unless you are connecting to a passthru server.

To call the server, follow these steps:

1. Choose File, Mobile, Call Server or press the File Mobile Call Server SmartIcon. The Call Server dialog box shown in figure 19.30 appears.

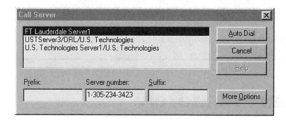

Fig. 19.30

Use this dialog box to call the server directly.

2. Select a server from the server list. The servers listed are the ones for which you have connection documents in your Personal Name & Address Book.

3. Specify any prefix or suffix options you want to use.

4. Choose Auto Dial to have the computer dial the server immediately, or choose Manual Dial if you want Notes to prompt you to pick up the phone to dial manually.

5. Select File, Mobile, Hang up when you are through working with the server.

If you are unsuccessful in connecting to the server, Notes prompts you with the appropriate message. Try to dial the server again. If you still are unsuccessful, refer to Appendix F, "Remote Troubleshooting."

> **Caution**
>
> If you plan to use NotesMail and want to have the memos routed immediately upon sending, make sure you have selected a location that is set up for On Server mail as defined in the section "Setting Up Locations" in Chapter 18, "Setting Up To Go Remote." Use your network copy of your Mail database while working interactively.

III

Going Mobile

You now are connected to the server and can open any database on the server for which you have been granted access. (It's just like a network connection at this point, only slower and less reliable!) If you don't have the server's database icon already on your desktop (it will have the server's name on the icon if you have View, Show Server Names selected), you can add it. If you have stacked your replica icons, click the icon indicator on the database you want to use, and highlight the server name you have just connected with from the drop-down list.

Note

When you use the interactive connection method, you may lose connection with the server on several occasions. An interruption in the phone line causes this problem most often; the problem also may be caused when you don't perform an activity for a long time (for example, if you are reading a long document) and the Hangup if Idle for time expires. If this problem occurs too frequently, refer to the section "Setting Up Your Modem" in Chapter 18, "Setting Up To Go Remote," for details on increasing the Hangup if Idle for setting.

Working Smart Remotely

This section has a wide variety of tips and techniques you can use while working remote to take advantage of Notes capabilities, reduce the amount of hard disk space you are using, minimize the amount of time you are spending on the network, and otherwise work smart!

Transporting Databases on a Floppy Disk

If you work away from the office and use a different remote computer than on the network, you can reduce the cost and time involved in performing an off-site database exchange for the first time by copying a database to a floppy disk while you are on-site, and then copying it to your remote computer off-site. This process takes much less time to perform than setting up a remote replica off-site and then dialing in to perform the first exchange to fill the database with documents.

To copy a database to a floppy disk and then install it on your remote PC, follow these steps:

1. While on-site, make a full replica of the database you want to install on your remote system to your C:\NOTES\DATA directory. (You will want to delete this copy after the procedure, so take note of the icon's location.)

2. Check the database file size by choosing File, Database, Properties, and switching to the Information tab (marked by a small white I). Write this size down for future reference.

3. Using your operating system's commands, copy the database to a floppy disk. Once the database is copied to the floppy disk, delete the copy on your hard drive—unless you have other reasons for keeping it there.

At the remote site, copy the replica of the database on your floppy disk to your remote `C:\NOTES\DATA` directory (or whichever directory you have specified as your Notes data directory) by using your operating systems commands.

> **Caution**
>
> Keep in mind that you must maintain replica copies of databases on your local hard drive if you want to replicate with the server. Using the operating system commands to copy a database to and from a disk will maintain the replica copy status of the database. If you copy the database to or from the floppy disk using Notes' commands, make sure you select File, Replication, New Replica to make the copies—this method is actually slower than using the operating system commands.

4. Launch Lotus Notes.

5. Add the newly copied database to your workspace.

If the replica is too large to fit on a single floppy disk (check the file size you found in the previous step 2), use one of the following methods:

- Make only a partial replica of a database (as discussed in "Preparing a Replica of a Database" earlier in this chapter). Restrict the number of documents in the database replica by selecting the Only Replicate Incoming Documents Saved or Modified After Days option in the Replication Settings dialog box when you create the new replica.

- Use compression programs (such as PKZIP) to reduce a database's size. Your local software dealer can recommend several programs that can help you. PKZIP can often have tremendous returns on compression due to the database structure of Notes. However, should the size of the database when zipped still exceed more than the space available on the disk, you can tell PKZIP to compress onto multiple disks by including the -& command when zipping the file.

- Use your operating system's Backup command to create a backup copy of the replica database in your `C:\NOTES\DATA` directory onto multiple floppy disks. Then use the operating system's Restore command to load the database onto your remote PC. (Refer to your operating system's manual for details on backup and restore procedures.)

- Use any of the other space saving replication settings, such as Subset replication (discussed later in this section), to reduce the size of the database being copied as a new replica.

Maintaining Replica Databases

You can use the options in the Replication Settings dialog box (refer to "Choosing Replication Settings" earlier in this chapter) and a few other techniques to clean out your off-site replica databases from time to time. These options enable you to *purge* (delete) documents automatically from a database replica, delete documents from a database replica manually without copying the deletions back to the network, reduce the size of a database replica through selective replication, compact a database, and delete a database replica from your system. The following sections discuss these techniques in more detail.

Deleting Documents from Replicas. You can remove older documents by deleting them from your database, without deleting them from other replicas. This option is usually used when you cannot automatically remove documents based on the date they were last saved/modified (described in the next section). Follow these steps:

1. Select the database from which you want to remove documents. Display the Replication Settings dialog box by choosing File, Replication, Settings or selecting the File Replication Settings SmartIcon. Select Send to display the Send panel.

2. Choose the <u>D</u>o Not Send Deletions Made in This Replica to Other Replicas option if you don't want to copy any deletions made in this database to the server.

3. Select OK, and then delete any documents that you want from the database without worrying that the documents will also be removed from other replicas. See Chapter 3, "Using Databases" if you need instructions on deleting documents manually.

> **Caution**
>
> If you don't select the <u>D</u>o Not Send Deletions Made in This Replica to Other Replicas option and you have the access on the server copy of the database to delete documents, you will delete all of the documents from the server copy that you delete in your local copy. The server, in turn, will delete all of these same documents from other users replica copies the next time they replicate with the server. Be careful and make sure you have the selection checked.

Automatically Reducing the Number of Documents. You can have Notes automatically reduce the number of documents in a database by filling out the <u>R</u>emove Documents Not Modified in the Last ___ Days option. Notes automatically removes the documents from your replica that were saved/last edited prior to the cutoff date without deleting the documents from the server or leaving deletion identifiers (which take up space!) in your database.

This method is preferable to deleting documents for most databases because you don't have to constantly manage the deletions; however, it is not always feasible. Some databases (such as library databases and the Name & Address Book documents) may contain information that is important because of its topic (or other classification) rather than the date it was created or modified. For these types of databases, you may want to either delete the unwanted documents or set up a selective replication formula (as described later in this section) to limit the database to only those documents you want.

Compacting the Database. Although deleting documents may reduce the number of documents in the database, the document deletion identifiers take up space within the database. Also, after you use a database for a while, your database begins to contain an increasing amount of "white space," just as your hard drive begins to get fragmented over a period of time.

You can remove the white space by highlighting the database icon and selecting File, Database, Properties, and then selecting the Information tab (marked by a small I). Select the Compact button to begin compacting your database. Notes begins to compact the database (squeeze out the white space).

It is usually only necessary to compact a database about once a month or when there is about ten percent to 15 percent unused space in the database. You can find out how much space is used by selecting File, Database, Properties, and then selecting the Information tab (marked by a small I). Select the %Used button to show how much space is being used. Subtract the amount of space used from 100 percent.

Note

Compacting may take awhile if the database is large. When Notes compacts a database, it makes a temporary copy of the active or selected database and copies it over the original file, preserving the original Read/Unread markers while removing unused space. If you try to open the database during the copying process, you see the message `Database is in use by you or another user`.

Caution

If you wait until you have very little free disk space available before you try to compact your databases, you may not have enough free space to perform this function! Be diligent in performing your housekeeping tasks.

If you do find that you do not have enough disk space free to compact a large database, try compacting smaller ones first to see whether you can free up enough space for the larger ones. You may also need to consider deleting databases (or other files) from your hard disk that you no longer use.

Maintaining Special Databases. When working remote, pay special attention to your Mail, Notes Log, and Outgoing Mail databases. The following tips give guidance for maintaining these databases in particular, but they can apply to others as well:

■ Your Mail database will most likely be the most active database while working remote and will therefore require compacting quite frequently. Consider carrying only the last week or two of mail in your database by following the instructions in the "Automatically Reducing the Number of Documents" section previous. (You can always access older mail documents by working interactively

III

Going Mobile

with the server in the network copy of your Mail database, as long as you haven't deleted them.) You may also consider making an Archive Mail database to store documents that you want to carry with you that are older than the specified replication cutoff date. (Refer to Chapter 9, "Creating New Databases," for further information on creating databases.)

■ If you have received and detached attachments in e-mail documents, delete the memo containing the attachments (or if you need to retain the memo, place it in Edit mode and remove the attachments). You may also be able to use the attachments you receive without detaching them (if you only need to read the attachment) from the memo by selecting Launch, which would allow you to read the attachment information without having to save it on your hard drive. For further information on using attachments, refer to Chapter 6, "Advanced Mail."

■ If you selected Log Modem I/O when you set up your modem, Notes creates a document every time you call the server. Even if this selection is not made, your Notes Log database will grow over time and must be cleaned out. You can either set a purge interval as previously discussed in this section; open each view of the Notes Log database, manually delete the documents, and then compact the database; or simply delete the entire database (if you don't need any of the Log history anymore). If you delete the database, you must then recreate it using the Notes Log template available to you. Make sure you name the new database LOG.NSF and store it in your local data directory. (Refer to Chapter 9 for additional information on creating databases from templates.)

■ If you do not have enough disk space available to compact any databases, deleting the Notes Log database and then recreating it after you have compacted all the other databases may be the best way to go. Also, you may get an error message if you try to compact your Log database because Notes may be accessing it for a background process. If you want to reduce your Log file size under this circumstance, you either have to set a purge interval or delete and recreate the database.

■ Over time, your Outgoing Mail database will grow just like other databases, even though documents are only being stored here temporarily. Make it a habit to compact this database whenever you compact your Mail database. You may occasionally receive an error message indicating that your Outgoing Mail file is in use and cannot be compacted. This message is primarily caused if background replication is underway. It is typically easier to find a time to compact this database when you first start Notes.

If you do not have enough space to compact the Outgoing Mail database (or others), you can permanently delete the database and then recreate it.

Deleting a Database Replica. You may want to delete a database replica permanently from your hard disk. (Removing a replica file from your hard disk doesn't affect other replicas of the database on the server.) The steps to delete a replica are the same as deleting any other database:

1. Select the database icon.

2. Choose File, Database, Delete.

3. Select Yes to acknowledge the deletion of this database.

Caution

You will lose all the information stored in any database replica you elect to delete. Make sure that any information you want to keep is replicated with the server or copied and stored in another database before deleting the database.

Selective Replication. Selective replication allows you to control what type of information will transfer from the source database on the server to a replica of a database. You can identify particular folders or views of documents to replicate or use replication formulas to limit the number of documents replicating from the server. Replication settings are a part of the database in which they're created, but they only apply to replication with a particular server. The default is Any Server.

Replication formulas are very similar to the View Selection formulas you may write when designing a view in a database. For example, if you had a Sales Tracking database for all of the regions in which your company does business, and your Western Sales Manager, Lyman James, only wants to receive the documents in his replica of the database that are for the Western region, you can create a replication selection formula in Lyman's replica of the database that tells Notes to receive only the documents that contain the criteria specified in the formula. The selection formula would appear as follows:

```
Select SalesRegion = "Western"
```

Where SalesRegion is the field name used in the database form design to specify the sales regions for this company and Western is the name of Lyman's region. This selection formula limits the data Lyman receives to only those forms in which there is a field titled SalesRegion and the entry in the documents with this field is Western. For more information on writing formulas, refer to Chapter 13, "Working with Formulas."

You automatically have Manager level access for all local replicas of databases, so you have the correct access level to set up selective replication on those databases. You must, however, have Designer or Manager level access to create replication formulas on the server copies of the database because those formulas may affect all database users.

The following information provides you with the steps to follow to set up selective replication for a database. Refer to the chapters on database design for further information on formulas and database design.

III

Going Mobile

> **Note**
>
> Keep in mind that selective replication formulas can only work if the design of the database allows you to select the information in the manner in which you want. For example, if there were no fields distinguishing the Sales Region in Lyman's database, he would not be able to select on that criteria. If you are designing databases that will be replicated to users or other servers, keep this fact in mind as you proceed.

To take advantage of selective replication, follow these steps:

1. Highlight the database you want to set up, and then select <u>F</u>ile, <u>R</u>eplication, <u>S</u>ettings. The Replication Settings dialog box appears (see fig. 19.31).

Fig. 19.31

Use this dialog box to set up selective replication.

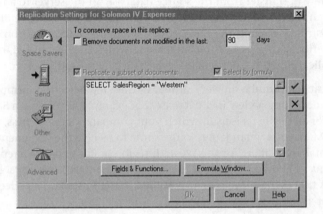

2. In the Space Savers panel, you must first decide whether you want to create a selective replication by highlighting folders and/or views available in the database design or whether you need to write a formula to provide you with the selective replication you need.

3. If you want to replicate based on the folders and/or views available to you in the database design, select Replicate a <u>s</u>ubset of documents by clicking the box next to this option. A checkmark should appear. Then select the folders or views you want to replicate to your hard drive. This method is by far the simplest, particularly for novice users, so if the view or folder definitions will provide you with the subset of information you want, choose this method.

4. If you cannot get the subset of information you require by selecting folders or views to replicate, click the Select by <u>f</u>ormula option. Enter the selective replication formula in the text entry box below this setting. The default formula is SELECT @All, which tells Notes to copy all of the documents from the server. Notes adds the word SELECT to all selection formulas when they are saved, so you don't have to type it. Enter the selection formula just as you would any other Notes formula (refer to Chapter 13 for assistance with formulas).

5. Select <u>O</u>K to save your settings and exit the dialog box.

Notes will now limit the number of documents you replicate from the server based on the criteria you have chosen.

Note

You also can create selective replication formulas in the Advanced panel of the Replication Settings dialog box to have Notes selectively replicate information based on specific servers you replicate with. You could set up replication formulas to replicate all documents with one server, but only documents meeting specific criteria from another server, for example. Follow the preceding instructions for creating the subset replication settings. Refer to the "Choosing Replication Settings" section in this chapter for additional information on the Advanced panel settings.

Replication formulas that the source database Manager writes and applies to a database take precedence over all formulas written and applied to local copies of a database. For example, if the source database Manager creates a selective replication formula telling Notes to replicate only those documents created by the user, the user of a replica cannot use a selective replication formula to replicate all documents— Notes will ignore it. The user can, however, create formulas to further restrict the documents received, as Lyman did in the previous example.

From Here...

The capability to effectively work remote can prove to be a distinct advantage to businesses today as the need to communicate between the home office and the field becomes critical. As you have seen, Lotus Notes makes this capability quite easy whether you always work as a remote user or work on-site part of the time. This chapter has explained what remote communication entails and how to work remote. It has also provided you with many tips for successfully working with Notes remotely.

For more information on the topics discussed in this chapter, refer to the following:

- Chapter 5, "Using The Address Books," provides you with more information on the functions and features of the Name & Address Books, which control how you communicate with Notes.
- Chapter 6, "Advanced Mail," provides further information on working with many of the features in NotesMail that you will use while working remote.
- Chapter 18, "Setting Up To Go Remote," gives you instructions on setting up your system to work from a remote location.

III

Going Mobile

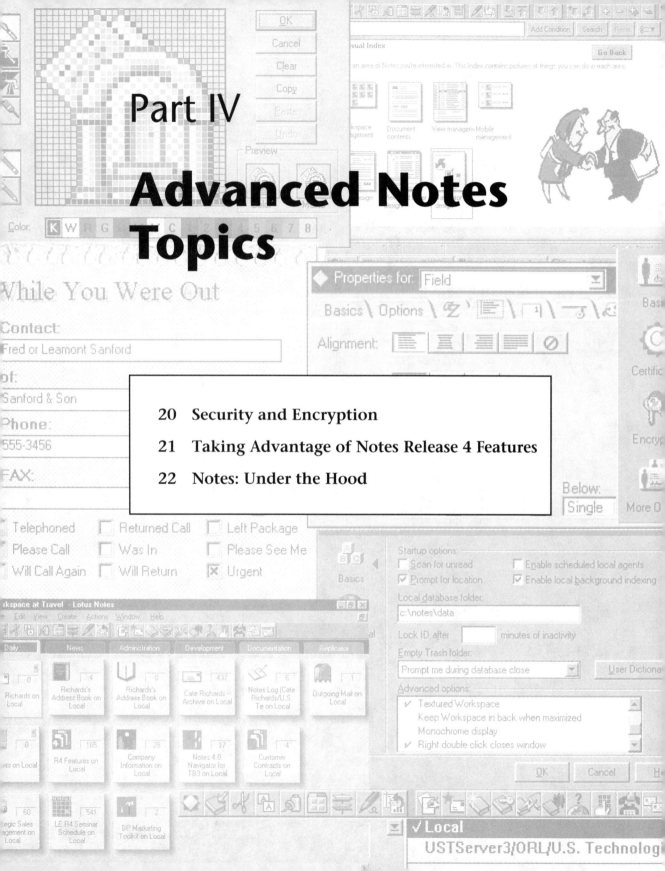

Part IV

Advanced Notes Topics

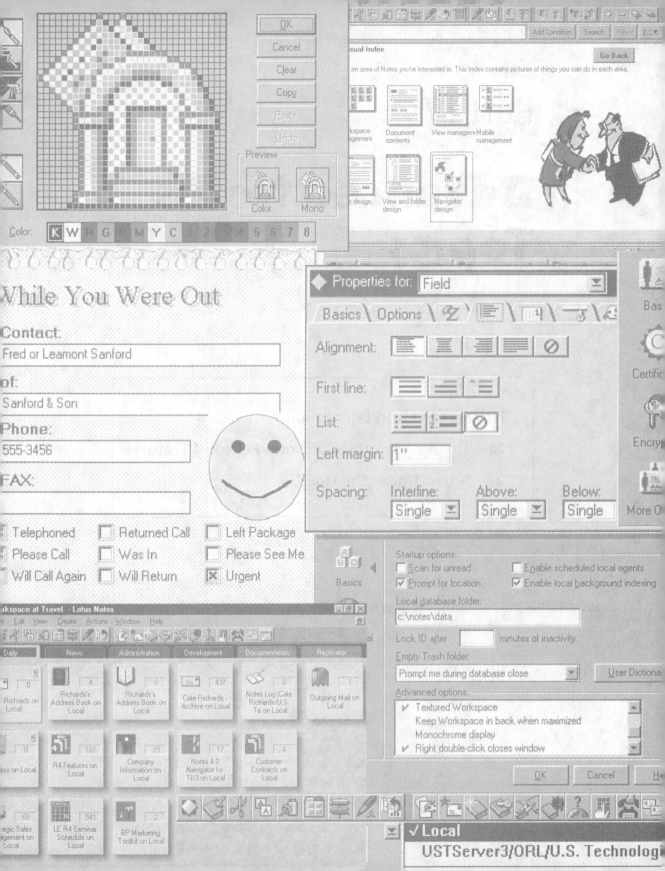

CHAPTER 20

Security and Encryption

Anytime people store and distribute data, there is always the danger that prying eyes will want to intercept or even alter that data. Some data may be subject to simple nosy snooping—perhaps an employee that wants to examine personal records of other employees. Other data may be critical to a project's success, making it attractive to corporate spies.

Whatever the reason, much of the information passed around inside companies is secret from somebody.

The designers of an information system such as Notes must consider the following security issues:

- The system must include security features that can protect information from even knowledgeable snoops. Simple, unsophisticated measures may stop nosy employees or hackers who are just casually curious. However, more sophisticated features are necessary to thwart the corporate spy who may be well-versed in computer security systems and how to defeat them.

- The system must protect data from being altered or forged. For example, when you receive a mail message, you should be confident that the message was sent to you by the person listed in the From field and that the contents of the message were not altered after it was sent.

- Security features must be easy to use, or people won't use them. You never think corporate spies are after *your* information, and it's all too easy in the crush of crucial deadlines to forget about the safety of your data.

Notes provides several features to protect information in various ways, and you learn about these features in this chapter. Specifically, in this chapter you learn how to do the following:

- Understand the varying levels of Notes security
- Request Certificates to allow access to a Notes Server
- Request and send public keys to other Notes users
- Create encryption keys to encrypt fields of a Notes document

Four Levels of Security

Notes offers significant control when it comes to securing your data. By implementing several varying levels of security, Lotus clearly kept the integrity of your databases in mind when developing Notes. There are several security options available to you, ranging from protecting a Notes server from unwanted eyes to verifying the author of a single field of information to prevent forgery. The following list introduces you to the four levels of Notes security available to you:

- **Server-Level Security**—Before users can access a database on a server, they must have access to the server. Server access is controlled by the server administrator through the use of certificates attached to users' ID files and server access lists. This is the first and most general layer of security.

- **Database-Level Security**—Database security for any database on a server is handled by the database *access control list* (*ACL*). The ACL lists users and servers and assigns them rights to the database. Access levels range from Manager—who has total access to the database—to No Access. The database manager creates and controls the ACL. An additional database-level security feature is local encryption, which encrypts local databases so that only specified users can access them.

- **Document-Level Security**—Document security consists of the document's read access list. The read access list is defined by the form's read access list, any reader names fields in the document, and the read access list in the Document Properties InfoBox. The read access list refines the ACL for that document—meaning that if someone has Reader access or better in the ACL but is not listed in any read access list, he or she cannot read the document. If they are not readers in the ACL, they cannot read the document even if they are listed in the document's read access list.

- **Field-Level Security**—Certain fields on a form can be encrypted using encryption keys, so only users with the correct key can read those fields. The database designer specifies that fields are encryptable, and when a key is associated to the document, all encryptable fields are encrypted with the key.

Your Notes ID

The key to protecting your information in Notes is your Notes ID file. All security features in Notes work through the information contained in your ID file. Through your ID file, Notes grants you access to the information you're supposed to see and keeps you out of documents and databases that are off-limits to you.

Your Notes ID file contains the following information:

- Your name
- Your Lotus Notes license, which gives you permission to use Lotus Notes
- Your private and public encryption keys, which Notes uses to encrypt and decrypt messages

▶▶ See "Understanding Encryption," p. 731

- Your password
- Encryption keys and certificates

▶▶ See "Understanding Encryption Keys," p. 732
▶▶ See "Understanding Certificates," p. 725

The name of your Notes ID file usually consists of your first initial and last name with an ID extension. For example, Cathy Morgret's ID file would be CMORGRET.ID. You can usually find your ID file in the Notes Data directory, but some users keep their ID file on a floppy disk as extra security because it can be locked up at night, they can take the file with them when they travel, or they can place it in their home directory on their LAN, so it can be accessed from any workstation on the LAN.

> **Note**
>
> On your computer, Notes may have named your personal ID file USER.ID instead of using your first and last name as described above.

Safeguarding Your Password

If your ID file is your gateway to Notes, then your password is your key to your ID file. Notes will not allow you to use the information stored in your ID file until you have entered your correct password. By requiring you to enter your password, Notes can ensure that only you can use your ID file and the information it contains.

It is crucial that no one but you knows your password. Every security feature found in Notes works under the assumption that no one else knows your password. With your password and access to your ID file, someone else can access your mailbox, read and compose documents in databases that you have access to, send messages with your name, and decrypt messages you receive.

When your system administrator installs Lotus Notes on your PC, he or she creates an ID file that contains your initial password. You should immediately select a new password and store the new password in your ID file. The following sections explain how.

Selecting a New Password. Your choice of passwords plays an important role in determining the security of the information you store in Notes; yet, too many Notes users put more effort into picking this morning's parking space. The privacy of your mailbox and all the databases you have access to depends on the fact that only you know your password, and therefore only you can use your Notes ID file. You must select a password that no one else can discover but that is easy for you to type and remember. Choose your new password carefully, and consider these points when making your decision:

■ Do not pick a password that reflects some aspect of your life that other people might guess. Anyone attempting to guess your password is likely to try the names of your pets, spouse, parents, children, and other relatives, as well as number combinations that represent your birthday, social security number, and anniversary. Similarly, do not pick words that reflect your interests, such as the name of your favorite sports team. People who know you can guess such passwords.

■ Mix letters with other types of characters. A password such as *starshine491* is much harder to guess than simply *starshine*.

■ Mix and match upper- and lowercase characters because Notes is case-sensitive when it comes to typing in your password. Thus *StarsHinE491* is an even more secure password than *starshine491* because it expands the realm of characters used.

■ Longer passwords are harder to guess. Pick a password that is at least eight characters long. Notes will allow you to select passwords as long as 31 characters.

■ One of the best techniques for choosing a password is to select a phrase and construct a password from the first letter of each word in the phrase. For example, you might recall the line "Three rings for the eleven kings under the sky" (from *Lord of the Rings* by J.R.R. Tolkien) and from it construct the password *3r4tekuts*. It is very unlikely that anyone else could guess such a password, and yet you can remember it easily by recalling that famous phrase.

Once you have selected your password, follow these rules to protect it:

■ Never write down your password. Someone may find it.

■ Never tell anyone your password. (Possible exception: a secretary who processes the boss' mail.)

Changing Your Password. Once you have selected a new password, you can use this procedure to change your Notes password:

1. Choose File, Tools, User ID. Notes asks you to type in your current password before you can access any of your user options.

2. Once you've typed your password, click OK to display the User ID dialog box (see fig. 20.1). You'll be working with this screen a lot because this is where many security options can be selected.

3. Click the Set Password button to change your Notes password.

4. Notes prompts you for your *current* password to make sure that it is really you trying to change your password.

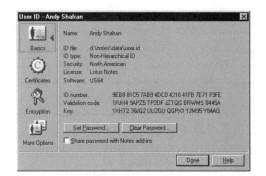

Fig. 20.1

Notes lets you change your password from here.

5. Next, notes displays the Set Password dialog box (see fig. 20.2). The dialog box reminds you that Notes passwords are case-sensitive, which means that if you capitalize any letters in your new password, you must capitalize those same letters each time you use your password in the future. Enter your new password and choose OK.

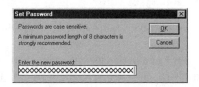

Fig. 20.2

All the Xs hide your password so people can't watch you type it in.

6. Notes displays another Set Password dialog box. Enter your new password again, and choose OK. By making you repeat your password, Notes ensures you didn't mistype your password the first time. If your two attempts to enter your new password don't match, Notes will make you repeat steps 3 and 4.

If You Forget Your Password.... If you can possibly avoid it, try not to forget your password. If you do, ask your system administrator to create a new ID file for you with a new password.

Forgetting your password can cause some difficulty because there is unique encryption information that is stored within each ID file that cannot be re-created. You will lose access to information encrypted by your user ID permanently. Check with your system administrator for his or her recommended ID backup procedures.

Understanding Certificates

One of the crucial components in your ID file is your *certificate*. You can think of your certificate as your company's seal of approval on your Notes ID. The certificate is the electronic equivalent of a notary's seal, telling the Notes servers throughout your company that your ID is was properly created by an authorized administrator within your company. Certificates play a key role in preventing hackers and spies from creating bogus ID files and infiltrating your company's Notes system.

> **Note**
>
> Most users have a single certificate in their ID file, but some people have several. If you regularly access databases that belong to other companies—perhaps you provide technical support for your clients—you might have a certificate in your ID file from each one of those companies. Each server wants to see a certificate that it trusts before you can access that server.

Much like your driver's license, certificates have an expiration date, usually two years from the date they were issued. As the expiration date on your certificate approaches (within 60 days), Notes will display a dialog box warning you that your certificate is about to expire.

When you receive this message, you must have your certificate recertified, just as you must get your driver's license renewed from time to time. To request recertification, you must first mail a "safe copy" of your ID to your system administrator, using the following procedure (a safe copy of your ID is simply a shell of a normal ID file that lets you send, request, and obtain certificates—just think of it like a secure courier system that is protected by your personal password):

1. Before you begin, make sure you know the name of the person in your company who certifies IDs.

2. Choose File, Tools, User ID to bring up the User ID dialog box. Select the Certificate pane, and click Request Certificate. Notes displays the Mail Certificate Request dialog box (see fig. 20.3).

Fig. 20.3

Request a certificate via e-mail through the Mail Certificate Request dialog box.

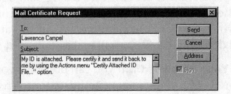

3. Enter the name of the person in your company who certifies IDs in the To text box. If you're unsure of the spelling, you can choose Address to access the company Name & Address Book.

4. Choose Send. Notes sends a mail message to your system administrator with the safe copy of your Notes ID attached and a message requesting that he or she recertify your ID.

Your system administrator will recertify your ID and send it back to you by mail. (You hope he or she accomplishes this task before your certificate expires. Otherwise, you may need to make a few phone calls.)

To accept the new certificate, follow this procedure:

1. Choose File, Tools, User ID to access the User ID dialog box.

2. Notes prompts you first for your Notes password. Enter your password and choose <u>O</u>K.

3. Choose the More Options pane shown in figure 20.4.

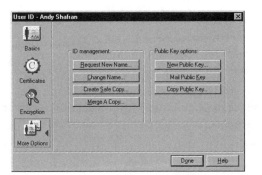

Fig. 20.4

Control your advanced Notes ID options from this pane.

4. Click the <u>M</u>erge a Copy button and select the ID file to merge. Notes copies your new certificate into your Notes ID file, and you're good for another two years.

Tip

Although the process outlined describes how to update a Notes certificate, you follow the same steps to request a new certificate. You've just got to ensure that you are mailing the safe copy of your ID file to the correct individual who can certify you.

Understanding Database Security

Each time you access a database, Notes applies various security features to determine which operations you are allowed to perform. In this section, you come to understand how Notes decides who can perform various database operations and how you can change how people can access databases.

Access Levels

Whenever you attempt to access a Notes database, Notes classifies you into one of several access levels that determines what you are allowed to do while working with that database. Your access level is different for each database you access and is determined by the manager of the database.

The seven possible access levels are the following:

- **No Access**—You cannot access the database in any way.
- **Depositor**—You can create new documents in the database but cannot read any documents stored in the database, even if you created them.

- **Reader**—You can read documents but cannot create new documents or modify documents already stored in the database.

- **Author**—You can create new documents and read existing documents. You can modify documents if you created them.

- **Editor**—Same privileges as Author, except that you can modify documents created by other people as well as by you.

- **Designer**—All the privileges of Editor. In addition, you can modify the design (such as forms and views) of the database.

- **Manager**—You are allowed to perform any operation in the database. Only the Manager can delete the database and can control what others can do to the database. Every database must have at least one Manager.

If you have any permissions other than Manager, your only exposure to database security involves learning what you and your coworkers are allowed to do. However, if you are the Manager of a database, you are responsible for deciding what others can do. In the following section, you learn how to control access to the database.

The Access Control List

Associated with every database is an ACL that specifies who can access a database and what they're allowed to do with the database. Anyone who has access to the database can view the ACL, but only someone with Manager access can modify the ACL.

To display the ACL for a database, select or open the database and choose File, Database, Access Control. Notes displays the Access Control List dialog box (see fig. 20.5).

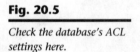

Fig. 20.5

Check the database's ACL settings here.

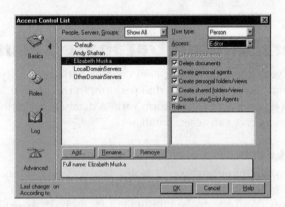

The People, Servers, Groups combo box lists the names all the people, servers, and groups for which the Manager wants to specify access. Whenever the Access Control List dialog box is displayed and one of the names is selected, the remainder of the dialog box shows the access permissions for the name. You can change the selected name just like you change the selected item in any combo box.

In figure 20.5, Elizabeth Muska's name is selected. The Access combo box shows that Elizabeth has Editor privileges for this database, and the User type combo box shows that she is a Person entry in the list. Notice the six checkboxes to the right of the list box; they allow you to further refine the creation and deletion rights of the individual.

If you select a different name from the People, Servers, Groups combo box, the Access combo box, the User type combo box, and the checkboxes change to reflect the permissions for the newly selected name.

The six checkboxes at the right of the dialog box only apply to names with certain privileges. For example, if the selected name has Editor access, Notes grays out the Create documents checkbox so that it is always marked because all Editors can always create documents.

In addition to the names of people, the ACL can contain the names of groups. Every member of that group then receives the same privileges.

The ACL can contain both the name of a group, and the name of one or more people in that group. When deciding what permissions should apply to a specific user, Notes first looks for the person's name. If the person's name is not found, Notes then looks for a group to which that person belongs. This feature enables you to override group permissions for a specific person by making an entry for that person. Remember that using groups to define your ACL requires that your company's Name & Address Book is secure, otherwise individuals could be added to groups and have access to databases they shouldn't.

Every ACL also has an entry for Default. Notes applies these permissions for anyone not listed by name and not a member of any group.

Two predefined names always appear in the ACL:

- **LocalDomainServers**—The access level for this entry determines the access for other servers within your domain, which probably represents your company. For databases that are replicated on other servers within your company, LocalDomainServers must be Reader access or better.

- **OtherDomainServers**—The access level for this entry determines the access for servers outside your domain (probably company). You will probably want to set this entry to No Access unless you are building databases that can be accessed by other companies.

If you have Manager privileges for the database, you will be able to change the permissions for a name in the ACL. Simply select the name you want to change and click the button that represents the access you want that name to have.

Roles

Notes security includes the concept of *roles*, which can help you organize the people who need to access the forms and views in a database. A role is any group of people you define who need to have similar access to the forms and views within a database.

A role is most useful when you can identify a group of people who all need to perform the same operations on a database and will therefore need the same privileges. By creating a role for this group you are simply adding and removing privileges for the entire group.

You can add to the list of roles for a database by selecting the Roles pane from the Access Control List dialog box. Notes displays the list of roles (see fig. 20.6). In this example, three roles—Trainers, Supervisors, and Developers—have been defined.

Fig. 20.6

Set your Notes roles from the Access Control List dialog box.

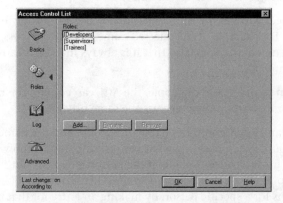

To create a new role, click Add. Notes prompts you for the name of the new role and adds it to the list. To delete a role, select the role from the list and then click Remove. To rename a role, click Rename.

To control which users are included in a role, click the Basics icon to return to the Basics pane and select a name. Any roles that person belongs to are marked in the Roles box. To add another role to the person, click the role in the Roles box. The role will appear with a checkmark next to it. To remove someone from a role, uncheck the role in the Roles box. Figure 20.7 shows Elizabeth Muska assigned with all three roles.

Fig. 20.7

Elizabeth Muska now has three roles assigned to her.

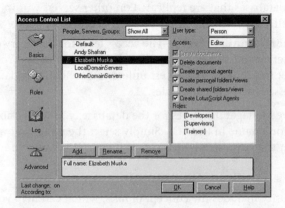

Once you have created a role, you can specify the role in place of a user name in the Read Access Control List dialog box and Compose Access Control List dialog box for forms and views. If you specify that the Supervisor role can access a particular form, all the users you placed in the Supervisor role can access that form. Later, if you decide they no longer have need to access the form, you simply remove the role and none of those users has access.

Understanding Encryption

You may think that since your company is not building nuclear warheads or involved in national security (then again, maybe they are), that you really don't have much need for privacy. However, in even the most mundane of businesses you may encounter sensitive information that you must protect at all costs. Encryption enables you to keep your secrets secret.

If you have no concerns about who sees your data—if you deal exclusively with information that is not particularly private—then Notes' database security is probably all the security you'll ever need, and you can skip the rest of this chapter. But even so, if you want to know how the cloak-and-dagger folks hide their information, read on. This is fascinating stuff!

A Quick History of Encryption

Throughout history people have constantly sought ways to store and convey information in ways that kept it secret from enemies who might try to intercept the information. The oldest technique for sending secret information was *concealment*, in which the sender might simply try to hide the secret information. The sender might send a package that contains a secret compartment or bury a secret message in a letter among otherwise innocent-looking text.

More commonly in recent times, people rely upon *encryption* to conceal information, a process in which the sender scrambles the message in some way to make it unreadable. The receiver then performs a related operation, known as *decryption*, that converts the scrambled message back to its original form. An enemy who intercepts the message along the way sees only the scrambled message.

The earliest forms of encryption relied on keeping the decryption technique secret. The sender encrypted information using a complex technique that they hoped an enemy couldn't figure out. In Roman times, simply substituting one letter for another (A=B, B=C, C=D, and so on) was good enough, but today many newspapers routinely publish such encrypted messages on their puzzles page, and amateur cryptographers crack them in minutes.

Before the 20th century, there was a practical limit to how complex an encryption technique could be. The more complex an encryption system was, the greater the chance that the person encrypting or decrypting the message would make a mistake. Also, quite often encrypted messages are needed in a hurry, such as on a battlefield. If an encryption technique is too complex, people can't use it quickly.

Computers changed everything. They could handle complex encryption and decryption techniques flawlessly and quickly. However, they also enabled code-breakers to crack very complex encrypted messages. The techniques that let you securely encrypt your messages today are very sophisticated, and in the following sections, you'll come to understand the basics of how they work.

Understanding Encryption Keys

Of all the things to learn about Notes, possibly few topics are less understood by users than encryption. Perhaps that's because most users don't feel that their information is sensitive enough to require such secrecy. But like a lot of features, once you know encryption is available, you'll probably find opportunities to use it.

Most encryption schemes today involve some type of scrambling that is controlled by a *key*. The sender selects a secret phrase, word, or number—the key—and uses the key along with some process to encrypt the information. The receiver, who must know the key, applies a reverse process using the same key to decrypt the message and retrieve the original information. If an enemy intercepts the message (and the encryption technique is sophisticated enough), he or she cannot recover the information without the key, even if he or she knows how the technique works for encrypting and decrypting.

This technique is known as *single-key encryption*. Lotus Notes has the ability to encrypt a message using a single key and later decrypt the message back into its original form. In fact, single-key encryption plays an important part in Lotus Notes (see "Using Encryption Keys" later in this chapter).

However, single-key encryption is not well-suited for exchanging e-mail because of an important drawback: both the sender and the receiver must have the same key, but they must manage to keep the key secret from the rest of the world. You must figure out some way to exchange the key ahead of time, and if an enemy should intercept the key, he or she can read your secret messages as easily as the intended receiver.

One of the greatest advances in modern cryptography is the development of a technique that does not require you to exchange keys in secret. This technique is the focus of Notes encryption and of most modern encryption systems.

Understanding Public-Key Encryption. The most recent innovation and the central technique in Lotus Notes is called *public-key encryption*. In this technique, you (and all users) have two keys. Public-key encryption is based on the fact that the keys are related in such a way that a message encrypted with either one of the keys can only be decrypted with the other key.

In any public-key encryption system (including Lotus Notes), you create two keys. (In the case of Notes, Notes performs this operation for you.) You keep one of the keys—known as your *private key*—secret, but the other key—known as your *public key*—can be widely distributed and given to anyone.

If someone wants to send you a secret message, they use your public key, which you have distributed to all your friends and coworkers, to encrypt the message. When you receive the message, you use your private key to decrypt the message. Remember that messages encrypted with one key can only be decrypted with the other key. The crucial feature of public-key encryption is that messages cannot be decrypted with the same key that was used to encrypt them. Thus, an enemy cannot decrypt your message even if he or she knows your public key. Because your public key only lets others encrypt messages for you, you can distribute your public key through normal means without worrying about unfriendlies intercepting it.

How Safe Is Encryption?

Your public and private keys are always related in such a way that messages encrypted with one key can only be decrypted with the other. However, the relationship between the two keys is so complex that the chances of anyone figuring out your private key, even if they know your public key, is virtually nil.

How safe is public-key encryption? Cryptographers widely believed that a good public-key system was virtually uncrackable. In 1977, three leading cryptographers encrypted a short message using a public-key technique, and jokingly offered a $100 prize to anyone who could crack the message. The public-key technique they used was very similar to the technique used by Lotus Notes. They believed that the calculations needed to determine the private key and thus uncover the message would require more time than the lifetime of the universe.

Imagine their surprise when the code was cracked in eight months.

Arjen Lenstra at Bellcore (the research and development outfit jointly owned by the regional Bell telephone companies) couldn't resist the challenge, and organized a team of codebreakers at Iowa State, MIT, and Oxford, along with 600 codebreaker-wannabes on the Internet. After a message effort that required eight months and a lot of mainframe and supercomputer time, Lenstra and his team cracked the code.

For us mere mortals, this exercise probably doesn't mean much. The effort that Lenstra and his team devoted to cracking the message was enormous, and probably no one is willing to devote such an enormous amount of effort and equipment to cracking anything you or I are likely to send through e-mail. And having cracked this one message doesn't lessen the effort Lenstra has to expend to crack a different message encrypted with a different key.

However, it does illustrate that given enough time and money, nothing is ever 100% secure.

Oh, and the message? It turned out to be, "The magic words are squeamish ossifrage."

Lotus Notes creates your private and public keys for you. Both are extremely huge numbers (hundreds of digits each) that Notes selects at random. You do not need to know the specific numbers that Notes selects for your keys; what's important is that they are available for Notes to use when encrypting and decrypting messages and that they have that crucial relationship: message encrypted with one key can only be decrypted with the other key. Your private key is stored in your ID file, and your public key is stored in the Notes Name & Address Book along with your other public information. In this way everyone can access your public key because everyone has access to the Name & Address Book, but only you have access to your private key because only you can access your ID file.

Encrypting Outgoing Mail. If a determined spy really wants to intercept e-mail, he or she can find lots of opportunities. As your electronic message travels from your machine to your recipients, it may pass through numerous machines, miles of network cable, and possibly thousands of miles of public telephone lines. With the proper equipment, your message can be intercepted anywhere along the way.

You can ensure the privacy of an outgoing mail message by encrypting it. Sending encrypted mail is easy with Lotus Notes, and most of the work happens automatically without any action on your part. You can encrypt a message simply by selecting the Delivery Options button at the top of the screen when composing a mail memo. This brings up the Delivery Options dialog box (see fig. 20.8). To encrypt, select the Encrypt option before selecting <u>O</u>K.

Fig. 20.8

Change your delivery options in the Delivery Options dialog box.

Note

If you usually want to encrypt your mail, you can choose <u>F</u>ile, <u>T</u>ools, <u>U</u>ser Preferences to bring up the User Preferences dialog box. Click the Mail pane, and select <u>E</u>ncrypt sent mail. From then on, Notes marks the Encrypt option for you each time you send mail. If you do not want to encrypt a particular message, you can turn the option off for that message by clicking E<u>n</u>crypt when you send the message.

When you tell Lotus Notes to encrypt a message, Notes locates your recipient in the Notes Name & Address Book and retrieves his or her public key. It uses the public key to encrypt the body of the message and then sends the message as it does any other message. When the recipient retrieves the message, Notes recognizes that the message is encrypted, and automatically decrypts the message using the recipient's private key, which is stored in his or her ID file.

If you send an encrypted message to several recipients, Notes encrypts the message in such a way that it can be decrypted using the private key of each of the recipients.

IV

Advanced Notes Topics

Caution

When you encrypt a message, Notes encrypts only the body of the message—not the other fields, such as the subject, date, sender, or recipient's name. You defeat the purpose of encryption if you convey too much information in these fields, especially the subject. For example, if the subject of your message, which is not encrypted, is "Hostile corporate takeover is on for tomorrow," then if your message is intercepted, it won't matter that the body of the message is encrypted—the subject gives it all away!

Obtaining Missing Public Keys. For outgoing mail encryption to work correctly, Notes must know the recipient's public key. As you sit at your desk at work sending mail to your coworkers, you shouldn't have a problem. Notes will retrieve recipients' public keys from your company's Name & Address Book, and you can happily encrypt any mail you want.

However, in the following two situations you may find that Notes doesn't have your recipient's public key:

■ If you send a message to someone outside your company, they won't have an entry in your company's Name & Address Book.

■ If you are using Notes remote and composing mail for later replication (see Chapter 19, "Working Remote"), Notes doesn't have access to your company's Name & Address Book.

If Notes doesn't have access to the public keys it needs, and therefore can't encrypt your message, Notes warns you by displaying the Mail Encryption Failure dialog box (see fig. 20.9). You can select OK to Send to tell Notes to send the message even though it cannot be encrypted. Otherwise, select Cancel Sending if you are not willing to send the note without encryption.

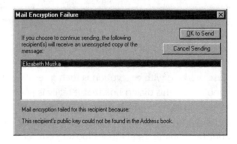

Fig. 20.9

This warning appears when Notes can't properly encrypt a message.

Since Notes can't find the entry it needs in the company Name & Address Book in these situations, you can enable Notes to encrypt messages by placing an entry for the recipient in your personal Name & Address Book along with the public key. The following two sections describe procedures you can use to accomplish this task.

Finding the Public Key for Someone Inside Your Company. You can get the public key for someone inside your company from your company's Name & Address Book. If you are a remote user, you can copy the entry from your company's Name & Address Book into your Personal Address Book by following this procedure (remember, you will not need to perform this procedure if you are not a remote user because Notes will be able to access the Name & Address Book automatically when you send encrypted mail):

1. Dial in to your home server by selecting File, Mobile, Call Server.

2. If your company's Name & Address Book is not already on your workspace, choose File, Database, Add Workspace Icon.

3. Open your company's Name & Address Book database.

4. If the People view is not already showing, choose View, People to display it.

5. Locate the document describing your recipient and select it by clicking it or moving the selection bar to it. (Do not open it by double-clicking it.)

6. Choose Edit, Copy to copy your recipient's entry to your Clipboard.

7. Close your company's Name & Address Book database, and open your personal Name & Address database.

8. Choose Edit, Paste to copy your recipient's entry from your Clipboard into your personal Name & Address database.

Getting the Public Key for Someone Outside Your Company. If you want to be able to send encrypted mail to someone outside your company, you must have the recipient give you his or her public key. Suppose you want to exchange encrypted mail with your friend at another company. She will need to send you her public key, which she can do using this procedure:

1. Choose File, Tools, User ID. Notes prompts for a password, and then displays the User ID dialog box.

> **Note**
>
> Many of the techniques you learn in this chapter involve the User ID dialog box. You will undoubtedly notice that every time you access this dialog box, Notes prompts you for your Notes password. Because working with encryption is such a sensitive activity, Notes needs to ensure whenever you access this dialog box that it really is you typing commands at the keyboard and not someone who happened to sit down at your desk while you were away. You may find it annoying to have to type your password each time you work with this dialog box, but be thankful that Notes is looking out for your security.

2. Choose the More Options icon.

3. Click Mail Public Key. Note displays the Mail Public Key dialog box (see fig. 20.10). Your friend should enter your name in the To field. (If she wants to use the Name & Address Book to help with the addressing, she can select Address.) Notes supplies an appropriate subject for the memo.

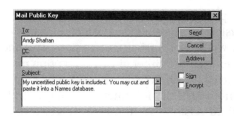

Fig. 20.10

Choose the recipient of your public key from this dialog box.

4. Choose Se_n_d. Notes will send you a mail message containing her public key.

5. Select D_o_ne to close the User ID dialog box.

Recall that you do not need to worry about someone intercepting this message. If an enemy intercepts her message containing her public key, she has only intercepted something that she wants to make public anyway. Remember, having your friend's public key will only enable someone to send encrypted mail to her, but not read her encrypted mail.

When you receive the message containing her public key, the subject of the message will explain what the message contains. The body of the message appears as a huge, seemingly meaningless number.

When you receive your friend's message, follow this procedure to extract the key:

1. Open the message.

2. The body of the message will contain your friend's public key and nothing else. Select the body of the message—all 500 or so digits.

3. Choose _E_dit, _C_opy to copy the key to your Clipboard.

4. Close the message and your mailbox, and open your Personal Address Book.

5. Choose _C_reate, Person to create a document describing your recipient.

6. Complete the first two sections that contain the information about your recipient's name and location.

7. Later in the document, in the section labeled Advanced, there is a field available called Public Key. Place the insertion point there.

8. Choose _E_dit, _P_aste to paste your recipient's public key into the field.

9. Close and save the document by pressing Esc.

Once you complete this procedure, Notes can access your friend's public encryption key, and you can send encrypted mail to your friend. If she wants to send encrypted mail to you, you must perform the first procedure described earlier to send her your public key, and she must perform the second procedure when she receives your message to insert the key into her Name & Address database.

Sending Encrypted Mail Internationally

The U.S. State Department considers encryption technology to be a matter of national security and won't permit the export of the most sophisticated encryption software outside North America. Lotus provides three versions of Notes: one for sale in North America, an international version for sale elsewhere, and a third version which combines security features for the whole world. The three versions work identically, except that the North American version can use either of two encryption methods: a very secure method, which is restricted by the state department, and a different, slightly less secure method, which is not restricted. The international version includes only the less secure method. The third version (North American Worldwide Security) uses a combination of the other two versions of Notes to maintain its security.

Similarly, each Notes user purchases one or both types of licenses: a North American license or an international license. The North American version grants you permission to use the more secure North American encryption scheme, while the international version does not. Your license is included in your ID file. You can tell which type of license you have by displaying the User ID dialog box (choose File, Tools, User ID).

Regardless of which type of license you have, you can use any version of Lotus Notes either within North America or internationally. However, if you send encrypted mail, Notes will only use the more secure North American encryption method if you are using the North American version of Notes and you have a North American license.

Note that if you are using the North American version of Notes and have a North American license, you cannot send encrypted mail to an international user. Your version of Notes will use the robust North American encryption method to encrypt your message, but your international recipient won't be able to decrypt the message with its international version. In this case, you'll want to use the North American–Worldwide Security version of Notes, which is ideal for companies who are international Notes users or require their employees to travel out of the country.

However, an international user can send encrypted mail to a North American user. The North American version of Notes will be able to decrypt the message because it includes the ability to use either decryption method.

Note

With Notes 4.0, Lotus reached a compromise with the United States government so it didn't have to support three versions of security for a single product. Notes now uniformly incorporates the stronger North American security in all versions sold worldwide.

This security uses 64 random bits to ensure that a message is properly encrypted. According to U.S. restrictions, encryption using a maximum of 40 bits (significantly less secure) could be exported. To reach a compromise, Lotus had to give the U.S. a "key" to the last 24 bits of the encryption key. Although this might seem like a security risk, Lotus now offers full 64-bit security (extremely secure) across the world, and the only the U.S. government has the 24-bit key.

Don't worry though, the government would still have to crack the other 40 bits in an encrypted message to break Notes' code. Besides, the government can only use their 24-bit key when investigating criminal activity.

Encrypting Incoming and Saved Mail

In the previous sections, you learned to encrypt mail that you send to others so that it is unreadable as it makes its way to your recipient's mailbox. Another option, encrypting saved mail, enables you to tell Notes that all mail, whether sent in encrypted form or not, should be encrypted when stored in your mailbox. This feature is particularly useful if you store sensitive messages—both sent and received—in your mailbox for long periods of time because it ensures that no one can look through your mailbox.

Note

Your system administrator can configure Notes so that all mail messages arriving in mailboxes on a particular server are encrypted, regardless of the users' settings. This option might be appropriate in a high-security environment, such as a defense contractor or for a server in a company's human resources department, which naturally deals with sensitive issues.

You can encrypt your saved copy of mail that you send to others. Choose File, Tools, User Preferences. Notes displays the Preferences dialog box. Click the Mail icon, and check the Encrypt Saved Mail checkbox. Even when you send mail that is not encrypted, the copy you store in your own mailbox will be encrypted. This feature will also encrypt incoming mail, but only after you have read the mail.

Confidentiality of Personal Mail

If you get along well with the people you work with, it's natural that some of the communication that goes on at work is not strictly business-related. Officially, most companies frown on using the company's e-mail system for personal messages, but realistically everybody knows that some small fraction of any company's e-mail traffic is not about department budgets and sales proposals. As long as everybody keeps the personal messages to a minimum, most companies look the other way.

However, you should understand that your right to privacy on your company's e-mail system is virtually nonexistent. Consider this excerpt from a large company's corporate policy document:

"Electronic mail systems such as Lotus Notes are not public electronic communications services as defined by 28 USC 2510. They are the property of the company who you work for, are restricted to use solely by authorized users for business purposes, and the contents of any such systems are subject to random or periodic monitoring and disclosure by management without notification to users."

People in most western countries have come to expect complete privacy of mail sent through the postal service, but do not be fooled into thinking that this privacy extends to your company's e-mail system. In the U.S., at least, the courts have upheld the right of your company to peruse your mailbox and to insist that you decrypt encrypted mail for their examination. If one of your Lotus Notes messages contains evidence of inappropriate or illegal behavior,

(continues)

(continued)

and a company administrator should happen to see the message in your mailbox, you will not be able to claim that the company illegally searched your personal mail as some employees have tried to do. Unless you work in a country where the rules are different, your mail belongs to your company.

So give a little thought to what you send through Lotus Notes. If you work in a particularly sensitive environment (such as the defense industry), you can bet your company does occasional spot checks in employees' mailboxes. Your plans for a palace coup are best reserved for the U.S. mail.

Encryption and Performance

Should you encrypt all your mail? Is there any disadvantage to encryption? Just one.

Encryption takes time. Every time you encrypt a message, there is a delay of a few seconds while Notes encrypts your message. The larger the message, the longer it takes to encrypt it. Similarly, when your recipient reads your message it takes a few seconds for Notes to decrypt the message. When deciding whether or not to use encryption, you must weigh the extra privacy encryption provides against the slight increase in time it takes Notes to process the encrypted message.

Encrypting Documents

In the preceding sections, you learned how to encrypt mail. However, Notes includes a second type of encryption, unrelated to the public-key encryption technique you saw earlier in this chapter. This second type of encryption lets you encrypt data not only in mail messages, but in other types of documents as well. You can encrypt fields within almost any kind of document if the database designer has enabled this feature. Using encrypted fields, you can ensure that sensitive data stored in databases is as secure as the data you exchange through mail messages.

> **Note**
>
> Many beginning Notes users, struggling to learn about Notes encryption, never realize that Notes contains two separate schemes for encrypting things: public-key encryption and single-key encryption. Although they share some characteristics and can often be used together in some combination, keep in mind as you read this section that you are learning about a completely new technique.

Understanding Single-Key Encryption

Public-key encryption is used almost exclusively to encrypt mail. When using e-mail, one person encrypts the message and sends it to a recipient who decrypts it. But what if you want to encrypt a document that is stored in a database, and you want to make sure only certain people can decrypt it? Single-key encryption is a better choice.

Unlike public-key encryption, which involves a public and private key, the scheme Notes uses for encrypting fields involves only a single key, known simply as an *encryption key*. As with public-key encryption, you use a key to encrypt data, but unlike public-key encryption, you use the same key to decrypt the data.

As a Notes user, you can create any number of encryption keys, which Notes stores in your ID file. You can use these keys to encrypt data so that only you can read it, or you can distribute any of these keys to other users so that they too can decrypt the data.

You can think of your ID file as an electronic version of a key ring. Your key ring can contain keys that you create, as well as copies of keys that other people create and give to you. You can lock (encrypt) data with one of the keys, and other Notes users can unlock (decrypt) the data if they have a copy of the same key. Similarly, they can encrypt data with their keys, which you can read if you have a copy of the same key.

You can have any number of keys on your key ring, and you will probably share different keys with different groups of people. For example, you might have one key that you use to encrypt data that you expect to share with folks in the sales department. Each member of the sales department would have a copy of that key and will thus be able to read any data encrypted with that key. Others outside the sales group cannot read the information because they don't possess the key.

You might create another key and use it to encrypt data that you want to share with people in your Seattle office, and of course you will need to give a copy of that key to everyone in the Seattle office. The sales group and the Seattle group will not be able to read each others' data because members of one group do not possess the key that members of the other group use to encrypt data. You will be able to read both sets of data because you possess both keys. (Obviously, a salesperson in the Seattle office will also possess both keys and will be able to read data from both groups.)

Finally, you might have a key that you use to encrypt data that you do not want to share with anyone and therefore you would not give a copy of the key to anyone.

Thus by knowing who has a copy of a particular key, you can control exactly who can read any data you encrypt.

You learned that one of the characteristics of public-key encryption is that you can freely distribute your public key to anyone because this key can be used only for encrypting data but not decrypting. By contrast, you must carefully control who possesses a particular key in single-key encryption. If the wrong person obtains a key, he or she will be able to read anything that was encrypted with that key.

Table 20.1 summarizes the differences between public-key encryption and single-key encryption.

Table 20.1   Public-Key Encryption versus Single-Key Encryption

Public-Key Encryption	Single-Key Encryption
Each user has only two keys: one public and one private.	Each user can create as many encryption keys as they like.
Your public and private keys are created by Notes when your Notes ID file is created.	You create encryption keys whenever you want, using the procedure described in this chapter.
Notes uses the public key to encrypt messages and the private key to decrypt messages.	Notes uses the same key to encrypt and decrypt messages.
Each user keeps his or her private key secret but can distribute the public key to anyone.	The key's creator must carefully consider who receives a key.
Only the person with the private key can decrypt data.	Anyone with the key can decrypt data that was encrypted with the same key.

Using encryption keys depends on various people performing these procedures:

- Creating encryptable fields
- Creating encryption keys
- Distributing the keys to other users with whom you want to share encrypted data
- Encrypting and decrypting data

In the following sections, you learn how to perform these procedures.

Creating Encryptable Fields

When someone designs a database form (see Chapter 3, "Using Databases," for more information about designing forms), he or she can specify that specific fields are *encryptable*, which means that they can contain encrypted data. (The data in an encryptable field doesn't have to be encrypted; giving a field this attribute simply gives users the option of storing encrypted information in the field.)

You can spot an encryptable field by the corners that surround the field when you compose a document. For most fields the corners are white, but for encryptable fields they are red.

If you are a database designer, you can make a field encryptable with the following procedure:

1. Enter edit mode for the form if you have not already done so. In the database's navigator pane, choose Design and then Forms. In the document selection

window (on the right hand side of the screen), select the form that the field resides on.

2. Double-click the field you want to make encryptable. Notes displays the field's Properties InfoBox (see fig. 20.11).

Fig. 20.11

Enable a field to be encrypted from this InfoBox.

3. Select the Options tab.

4. Click the Security options combo box and choose Enable encryption for this field.

5. Close the Field Properties InfoBox.

Creating Encryption Keys

To encrypt fields within a document, you must use an encryption key, which you or someone else must create. Typically, you create a new key when you identify a group of people that want to be able to share encrypted data. Once you create a key, you distribute that key among the members of that group. For example, when a member of the word processing department realizes that it would be nice for the members of her department to share encrypted data, she creates a key and distributes it to everyone in the word processing department.

To create an encryption key, follow this procedure:

1. Choose File, Tools, User ID.

2. Notes prompts you for your Notes password. Enter your password and choose OK. Notes displays the User ID dialog box (see fig. 20.12).

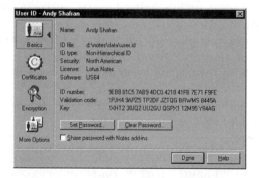

Fig. 20.12

Set your User Preferences in the User ID dialog box.

3. Click the Encryption icon. Notes displays a list showing all the keys currently stored in your ID file (see fig. 20.13). The first key is selected. The Comment box shows a comment for the selected key if there is one. The dialog box also shows the date the selected key was created and restrictions on the key (explained later in this chapter).

Fig. 20.13

The User ID dialog box shows your available encryption keys.

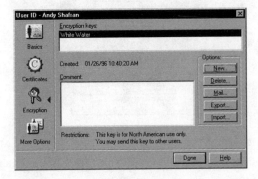

4. Choose New to create a new encryption key. Notes displays the Add Encryption Key dialog box (see fig. 20.14).

Fig. 20.14

Type your new encryption key's name here.

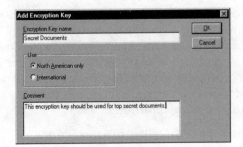

5. Enter a name for your key in the Encryption Key name field. You should select a name that describes who will use the key or what kind of data will be encrypted using the key.

6. Choose either North American or International use. As with public-key encryption, Notes has two schemes for single-key encryption. If you select North American only, Notes uses its more secure encryption method, but you cannot share the key with coworkers outside North America. If you select International, you may share the key with anyone, but Notes uses a less secure encryption method.

 ◀◀ See "Sending Encrypted Mail Internationally," p. 737

7. In the Comment text box, enter any additional information that you may want to keep with the key for your future reference. Your comments can help you remember what a particular encryption key should be used for.

8. Choose OK. Notes returns to the User ID dialog box.

9. If you want to create more keys, repeat this procedure from step 3. Otherwise, select Done to close the User ID dialog box. Notes adds the keys that you created to your ID file.

Caution

Notice that the User ID dialog box contains a Delete button, which you can use to delete keys from your ID file—simply select the key you want to delete, and choose Delete. However, once you delete a key, you will not be able to read any data encrypted with that key without getting another copy from someone. Worse, if *everyone* who has a copy of that key deletes his or her copy, all data encrypted with that key is forever unreadable. Even though someone can create another key with the same name, it is not the same key and cannot be used to decrypt data that was encrypted by the old key. So think twice—or three times—before deleting a key.

Creating an encryption key is only the first step in making it useful. Unless you intend to use the key to encrypt data that you do not want to share, you next must distribute the key to other people. The next two sections tell you how to distribute encryption keys.

Distributing Encryption Keys by E-Mail

Most often you will distribute encryption keys to other users through Notes mail. To mail one of your encryption keys to another user, follow this procedure:

1. Display the User ID dialog box by choosing File, Tools, User ID. Notes prompts you for your password.

2. Click the Encryption icon. Notes displays the list of encryption keys in the Encryption pane (see fig. 20.15).

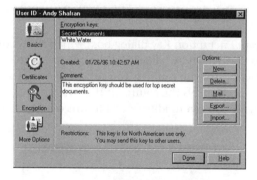

Fig. 20.15

Here are your encryption options again.

3. Click Mail. Notes displays the Mail Address Encryption Key dialog box (see fig. 20.16).

Fig. 20.16

Send your encryption keys to the users indicated on the Mail Address Encryption Key dialog box.

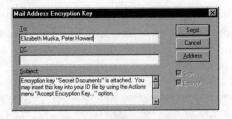

4. Enter the names of the people that you want to mail the key to. You can access the Name & Address Book to help with the addressing, just as with any mail message, by choosing Address. Note that this dialog box doesn't allow you to deselect the Sign and Encrypt checkboxes. All mail messages containing encryption keys must be signed and encrypted.

5. When you have entered all the names, select Send.

6. Notes displays a dialog box asking if you want your recipient to be able to send the encryption key to other people. If you want to be sure that no one has the key other than the people you send it to, choose No. If you choose Yes, people who receive the key from you may pass it on to other users. After you choose Yes or No, Notes sends a message containing the encryption key to the people you specified.

Now consider the recipient of a mail message containing an encryption key. Fortunately, when someone sends you an encryption key, the subject of the mail messages explains what the message contains and tells you what to do.

The encryption key itself appears as an attachment with a strange-looking filename. However, do *not* use the usual technique (described in Chapter 5, "Using the Address Books") to extract this attachment. Instead, follow this procedure:

1. Choose Action, Accept Encryption Key. The second item is new to this menu.

2. Notes prompts you for your Notes password. Enter your password and choose OK.

3. Notes displays the Accept Encryption Key dialog box, which shows the name of the key, the date it was created, and what restrictions the key carries (where it can be used and whether or not you can pass the key on to others) (see fig. 20.17). The dialog box also displays the comment that was entered (if any) when the key was created. You can modify or add to this comment if you want.

Fig. 20.17

Accept encryption keys while reading e-mail.

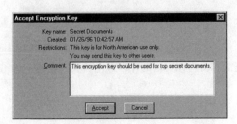

4. To insert the key into your ID file, choose <u>A</u>ccept.

Distributing Encryption Keys by File

Most often you will distribute encryption keys to other users by mail, but occasionally you may need an alternate method. For example, consider these situations:

- Perhaps one of your client companies uses Lotus Notes, but people in that company cannot send or receive mail outside the company. You have made a copy of a database that you want to send them (using the procedure you learned in Chapter 3 for copying a database) onto a floppy disk, but some of the data in the database is encrypted, and you want to send them the encryption key as well.

- As secure as NotesMail is, a floppy disk in your shirt pocket is even more secure. You know your encryption key hasn't been intercepted if you put it on a floppy disk, take it to a coworker, and put it on his or her machine.

Notes enables you to create a file which contains an encryption key. You can write this file onto a floppy disk or onto a network drive, and from there distribute it to other people. You can also make a copy of such a file for safe keeping to ensure that you don't lose an important encryption key.

To create a copy of an encryption key on floppy disk, follow these steps:

1. Display the User ID dialog box by choosing <u>F</u>ile, <u>T</u>ools, <u>U</u>ser ID. Notes prompts you for your password.

2. Click the Encryption icon. Notes displays the list of encryption keys.

3. Select the key you want to write to floppy disk, and select E<u>x</u>port. Notes lets you type in a password to protect this encryption key should it fall in the wrong hands (see fig. 20.18).

Fig. 20.18

Enter a password to protect your encryption key.

4. Notes lets you place restrictions on the encryption key you write to the floppy disk. If you choose <u>R</u>estrict Use, Notes displays the Encryption Key Restrictions dialog box, shown in figure 20.19, and provides you with a text box in which you can specify the name of a single user. Notes will not allow anyone except that user to extract the encryption key stored on the floppy disk. In addition, a checkbox (marked by default) allows that user to pass the encryption key on to other users. If you uncheck the checkbox, the user cannot pass the key on to other users.

Fig. 20.19

Give specific control over who can use this encryption key.

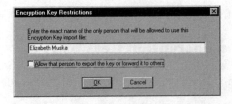

5. After you have entered a user's name and optionally unchecked the checkbox, choose OK and Notes returns to the User ID Encryption Key Export dialog box.

6. The Password and Confirmation text boxes enable you to enter a password to protect your encryption key. No one will be able to read the encryption key from the floppy disk into his or her ID file without this password. This feature provides protection against the floppy disk falling into the wrong hands. Choose a password and enter it in both the Password and Confirmation boxes (the password does not appear on-screen), and choose OK. If you are willing to forego the safety of password-protecting the key (say, if your coworker is just down the hall), you can bypass entering the password by selecting No Password instead of OK.

7. Notes displays a dialog box so that you can enter the name of the file you want to create. To write the file to a floppy disk, enter a filename that begins with A: or B: (depending on which drive you want to access) followed by a name ending in *KEY*. For example, if the key is used by the sales department, you might name the file the following:

    A:SALES.KEY

8. Choose OK and Notes writes the key to the floppy disk.

Instruct your recipient to use the following procedure for importing the key from the floppy disk into his or her ID file, or perform this procedure yourself if you receive a floppy disk containing an encryption key:

1. Display the User ID dialog box by choosing File, Tools, User ID. Notes prompts you for your password.

2. Click the Encryption icon. Notes displays the list of encryption keys.

3. Choose Import. Notes displays a dialog box asking you for the name of the file that contains the key you want to import. Type the name of the file. Alternatively, type **A:** or **B:** to produce a list of all the files on the floppy disk, and select the proper file from the list. Choose OK.

4. If a password was assigned to the encryption key, Notes asks you to type it in. Then, Notes displays the Accept Encryption Key dialog box (refer to fig. 20.17). As before, it displays the name of the key, the date it was created, and what restrictions the key carries (where it can be used and whether or not you can pass the key on to others). To add this key to your ID file, choose Accept.

> **Tip**
>
> When you import an encryption key, the original is not removed from the disk you used. Use Windows Explorer to remove the encryption key from your disk. You may even want to format the disk to ensure that file recovery tools cannot recover the encryption key should the disk used fall in the wrong hands.

Encrypting Data with Encryption Keys

You can use any of your encryption keys—whether you created them yourself or someone else sent them to you—to encrypt data in any document or editing the document:

1. Choose File, Document Properties. Notes displays the Properties InfoBox for the document.
2. Click the tab with the icon key to display the document's security information.
3. Click the Encryption keys combo box. Notes shows all the encryption keys stored in your ID file, any of which you can use to encrypt the document (see fig. 20.20). If the document is currently encrypted, a checkmark appears next to the keys currently in use.

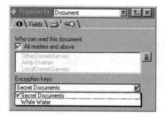

Fig. 20.20

Select the encryption key you want to use here.

4. Select any of your keys from the Encryption keys list. After selecting one or more keys, close the list by clicking the checkmark that you used to open the list.
5. Close the Document Properties InfoBox.

When you encrypt a document, only the encryptable fields—the ones with the red corners—are encrypted. All other fields are still viewable by anyone. As you're entering sensitive information into a document, be sure that you don't enter anything private into a field that is not encryptable (has white corners).

You can remove encryption keys from an encrypted document using the same dialog box. You might want to remove a key if a document is encrypted with several keys, and you later realize that the group that shares a particular key shouldn't be allowed to access the document. Follow the same procedure you used previously to select encryption keys. If you click a key that is currently in use (and has a checkmark next to it), the checkmark disappears and Notes no longer uses the key to encrypt the document. If you deselect all of the encryption keys used to encrypt a document, the document is no longer encrypted.

> **Note**
>
> If you design databases, you sometimes may want all documents within a database to be encrypted. You can specify one or more keys to use by default for encryption. While editing a form in a database's design, choose File, Document Properties. Notes displays a Properties InfoBox similar to the Properties InfoBox you see for individual documents. As before, select the tab with the key icon, and select one or more encryption keys from the Encryption keys combo box. When users create new documents, Notes automatically uses those keys to encrypt the documents. If the users want to specify other keys to use, or if they want to specify that some of the default keys are *not* to be used, they display the Document Properties InfoBox to add or remove any keys they want.

Accessing Encrypted Documents

To access a document that contains encrypted fields, you don't need to do anything out of the ordinary. When you attempt to open an encrypted document, Notes looks in your ID file to see if you have a copy of any of the encryption keys that were used to encrypt the document. As long as you have at least one of the keys, you can read or edit the document as you normally would.

If you do not have a copy of any of the keys, your access to the document is restricted. If you open the document for viewing, you see only the unencrypted fields. If you attempt to edit the document, Notes displays a dialog box explaining that the document is encrypted and that you cannot edit it unless you have a copy of one of the keys.

Understanding Electronic Signatures

In Chapter 4, "Getting Started with Electronic Mail," you learned that you can sign e-mail by marking the Sign checkbox when you send the mail. Now that you have learned how encryption works, you can understand how an electronic signature works.

Encryption enables you to prevent an enemy from intercepting and reading or altering the body of your message. An electronic signature prevents an enemy from forging the other fields in a message. Without electronic signatures, an enemy who is knowledgeable about Notes could produce a message that he or she wrote, but by forging the From field can make the message appear to be from you. Electronic signatures prevent such tampering.

When you sign a message, Notes attaches a hidden electronic code that proves to the receiver that you are the sender of the message and that the message has not been altered along the way. The electronic signature is possible through a curious twist involving public-key encryption.

Earlier in this chapter, in the section "Understanding Public-Key Encryption," you learned that each Notes user has a private encryption key (known only to that user and stored in his or her ID file) and a public encryption key (known to everyone, and stored in the Notes Name & Address Book). You also learned that the key characteristic of public-key encryption is that data encrypted with one key can only be decrypted with the other.

As you've seen, when someone sends you encrypted mail, Notes uses your public key to encrypt the data. When you receive the mail, Notes uses your private key to decrypt the data. At first you would think that for public-key encryption to be useful, the public key is always used to encrypt data and the private key is always used to decrypt data. But recall the definition of public-key encryption: The keys are related in such a way that a message encrypted with either one of the keys can only be decrypted with the other key.

This definition doesn't say that you must use the public key for encryption and the private key for decryption; it says that *either* key can be used to encrypt data, and the other key used to decrypt the data. That is, it's possible to encrypt data with your private key, and decrypt the data with your public key. At first blush that doesn't appear to be a very useful thing to do because the whole world knows your public key, and thus anyone can read the data that's encrypted with your private key. But in the case of electronic signatures, that's exactly what we want.

In constructing an electronic signature, Notes uses your public and private keys in a technique that's backward from the usual encryption scheme. When you send signed mail, Notes builds a 16-byte block of data, called a *fingerprint*, from your message's recipient name, your name, cc field, domain name, and subject. Notes then encrypts the fingerprint with your private key and attaches it to the message.

When your recipient receives your mail, Notes spots the encrypted fingerprint and uses your public key to decrypt the data. Notes then checks the fingerprint against the message's recipient name, sender name, and other fields. If it still matches, Notes can be sure that the message has not been altered along the way because only you (with your private key) could have encrypted the fingerprint in such a way that it could be decrypted correctly with your public key. As your recipient opens your message, Notes displays a message on the status line that reassures your recipient that all is well:

```
Signed by Janet Eriksen on 5/23/96 10:13:51, according to US Technologies
```

Cases can arise where Notes cannot verify the validity of a signature, even though the message was properly signed. Most often, problems in verifying a signature occur when you receive mail from outside your company. Depending on how your system administrator has set up the connection with the other company, Notes may not be able to ensure the validity of the sender's public key. In such a case, Notes displays a message telling you that it cannot verify the signature. This message does *not* mean that Notes has detected anything wrong with the message—merely that Notes doesn't have the information it needs to ensure a proper signature.

Encryption Hazards

Using encryption to secure your data seems like a good idea, and something you would want to always do. But there are hazards to using encryption:

■ **Risk of losing a key**—If you lose an encryption key, your data is lost. This seems like an unlikely occurrence, but all it takes is a disk to go bad, and you could lose the key.

■ **Risk of losing your ID**—If you lose your ID, you lose your private key, meaning that you cannot read your encrypted mail. Also if you forget your password, it's as good as losing your ID.

■ **Difficulty in administering keys**—If you are using encryption keys, you have to make sure you distribute them to all users who need the data. This can become difficult once you get past a few users.

For these reasons, use encryption with care. If an application absolutely requires encryption, use it; but, otherwise, use it sparingly.

From Here...

If you have an interest in learning more about encryption, you'll find no shortage of books in your public library that describe the rich history of the art. Books and magazine articles that discuss public-key encryption will help increase your understanding of Notes encryption (even if they don't mention Notes specifically).

For more information in the topics discussed in this chapter, refer to the following:

■ Chapter 9, "Creating New Databases," teaches you the basics of designing a Lotus Notes database.

■ Chapter 11, "Designing Views," teaches you how to design views, and more about creating folders within the design of a database.

■ Chapter 22, "Notes: Under the Hood," continues your study of Notes advanced topics and shows you how replication works and describes the various Notes platforms.

CHAPTER 21

Taking Advantage of Notes Release 4 Features

So far, you have reviewed many new features for the application development in Lotus Notes 4. These features enable you to develop richer applications that offer more functionality to your users. This enhanced functionality improves ease of use of your applications. R4 takes the next step toward making Lotus Notes a full-featured application development environment.

In this chapter, you learn how to take the next steps to upgrade your Notes R3 application to utilize R4 features. You will watch and learn as an R3 application is converted to R4. The R3 to R4 conversion uses a real-life application that is currently in production with over 1,000 users worldwide. In each example, you see the application design in R3 and the corresponding enhanced design in R4 via actual screen shots of the design.

You will learn how to take advantage of these new features in your application:

- Form and View Action Buttons
- The NOTES.INI file
- Using Hide When in forms design
- Inserting collapsible sections in your documents
- Creating user folders to organize your documents
- Using subforms to simplify the design
- Creating navigators to help users move around the application

The application example is a Data Integration application, called the Sentinel.

What Does the Sentinel Application Do?

Composing Notes forms allows users to bulk import and export data to and from Notes databases. The Sentinel Data Integrator uses a Notes form from the Sentinel Notes Database to initiate, organize, document, and schedule data loading tasks. The Sentinel Engine performs the actual data loading.

The Sentinel Data Integrator is a comprehensive utility tool that enables Notes Developers, administrators, and data warehouse managers to initialize, organize, and schedule data transport and extract tasks in the convenient and easy-to-use Notes interface.

The Sentinel Data Integrator automatically transports and updates legacy or warehouse data into Notes applications without the use of script language or the Notes API toolkit.

Sentinel is useful for Notes application developers and designers who need to initialize and update Notes applications quickly and easily with data from any ASCII or ODBC data source.

The CD-ROM in the back of this book includes an evaluation copy of the Sentinel Data Integrator. The Sentinel application has 21 forms and 15 views. This is a complex application that is typical of the kinds of applications you can deploy using R4.

Note

R3 designs are fully compatible with R4. No work is required to make them run under R4. This chapter covers how to exploit new R4 features for better, more exciting R4 applications.

Adding the Example Databases to Your Notes Workspace

Both the original R3 Sentinel Database and the final R4 design, with the changes outlined in the rest of this chapter, exist on the CD-ROM attached to this book. You may follow along with these examples to actually perform these changes on the R3 databases. Check your work with the completed R4 design. Do not worry if your changes do not exactly match the R4 design. The goal of the exercise is to demonstrate features that you can use immediately on your R3 applications.

To follow along electronically with the provided NSF files on the CD-ROM, copy these files to your Notes working directory (usually C:\NOTES or C:\NOTES\DATA). Files copied from CD-ROMs generally remain read-only on your hard drive. Use the Explorer in Windows 95, or File Manager in Windows 3.1 to copy the files. Select each file and choose File, Properties. In the Attributes section, deselect the Read-only flag. To add these databases to your workspace, use File, Database, Open, and select one of the following databases:

- Integration Tasks 3.5 (R3TASKS.NSF): The R3 Sentinel Database.
- Integration Tasks 4.0 (R4TASKS.NSF): The R4 Sentinel Database with the changes from this chapter.

> **Note**
>
> Even if you do not choose to follow along electronically, the examples in this chapter contain numerous screen pictures that demonstrate each new design feature, and allow you to follow the progression of the application changes from R3 to R4.

Overview of the R3 to R4 Conversion

The Sentinel database has 13 main forms, many of which have portions in common. Some initial analysis work allows you to select the options that will make your R4 design functional for the intended business purpose, as well as aesthetically appealing. There is no right answer or way to perform this conversion. As mentioned earlier, R4 does not require any additional work to make an application run. R3 is completely compatible with R4. That being said, if you do not take advantage of the new features available, your application designs will not be working as hard for you and the end user as you want them to work.

Maintainability. R4 has added some features to make your applications more maintainable. Maintenance of an application can cost as much or more than the original design work. R4 offers new shared design features like subforms that enable you to completely reuse entire portions of a subform across many forms. Just as shared fields enabled R3 designers to reuse a field across all forms, subforms are a common design element that allow all forms to immediately reflect any changes made to inserted subforms. This reduces the maintenance effort substantially, while producing more consistent applications designs.

Layout. Deciding on the layout of the conversion is the hardest part of the task. R3 to R4 conversions require some trial and error to verify which features best utilize the R4 technology while also satisfying the business purpose of the Notes database. Specific rules do not exist to walk you through the process. You must experiment with different styles and design features until you complete a design that fulfills the business objectives of the database with a maintainable application design.

Using Subforms To Standardize Design

Take a minute to review a standard Sentinel form, shown in figure 21.1.

Of the Sentinel's 21 database forms, 13 perform similar functionality. These 13 specify to the Sentinel Engine parameters of data movement. All 13 forms have many sections, or design elements, in common.

Fig. 21.1

A sample R3 Sentinel form before conversion to Notes R4.

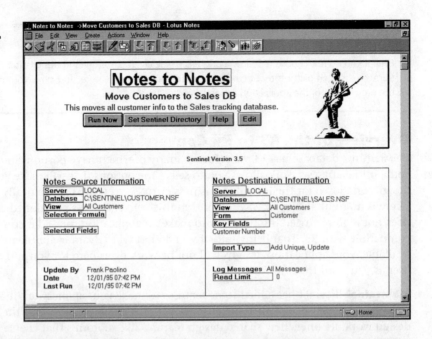

Note

Design Elements contain portions of a form. A design element can contain any of the following items:

- A literal (text describing a field) and a field
- Many literals and many fields
- A table containing fields
- A graphic
- Combinations of the preceding items

Design Analysis of Common Design Elements

In the Sentinel R3 database, each form contains a design element listing information about the data source, as well as a design element listing information about the data destination. Sources and destination databases can be ASCII, ODBC, or Notes. Performing an analysis of forms that have common design elements reveals that ten forms contain identical design elements whenever Notes is listed as the destination database.

Further analysis of the R3 Sentinel database reveals that 11 of the 13 forms have design elements in common. The first major simplification of this R3 to R4 database conversion is to eliminate duplicate elements of the form. The resulting R4 database requires very little maintenance. Table 21.1 shows the results of the analysis of design elements.

Table 21.1 Common Design Elements	
Type	**Number of Occurrences**
Form Heading	13
Notes Source	7
Notes Destination	10
ASCII Source	2
ASCII Destination	1
ODBC Source	1
ODBC Destination	1
Run Now Button	13
Edit Button	13
Save Button	13
Set Sentinel Directory Button	13
Help Button	13
Log Messages	13
Notes Formula	13
User Comments	13

This table shows that changes to one design element in a Notes source impact seven different forms. Changes in one design element in a Notes destination impact ten different forms. ASCII and ODBC sources and destinations are not significant, as they occur in only one or two forms. The Form Heading, listing Task Name and Task Description, appears in all 13 forms. Therefore, the first design change to the Sentinel database is to create a subform for the Task Heading. This immediately reduces maintenance of these 13 forms.

For this example, you will use the Notes to Notes form. See figure 21.2 to review the R3 design of the form.

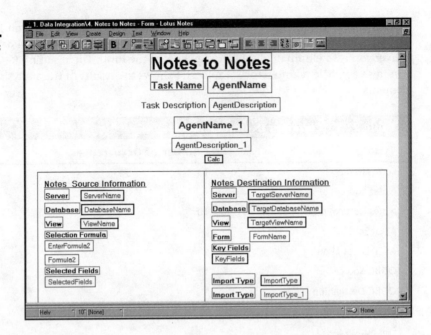

Open the Integration Tasks 3.5 (R3TASKS.NSF) file by double-clicking the icon.

The first task is to select Design Forms from the view pane and click the form "1. Data Integration\4. Notes to Notes" in the forms pane (right-hand pane). Your screen should look similar to figure 21.2.

Note

Figure 21.2 has the programmer pane minimized to show more of the form. When appropriate, the figures in this chapter show the programmer pane. You do not have to change your default design settings to follow these examples.

Creating a Subform TaskHeading

This section of the chapter shows you how to create your first subform and insert it into the main form.

Note

The use of subforms means the elimination of some of the tables in the form, as subforms are not allowed within tables. This is not as bad as it first seems, as collapsible sections, discussed later in this chapter, replace some of the need for tables.

You must now cut and paste the design elements from the main form to the Clipboard. All 13 forms require a unique Task Name and Task Description. This is an obvious place to create a subform across all documents. Start by copying the Notes to Notes pop-up to the very top of the screen, above the table from which you cut it.

Next, cut the design elements starting from the green literal Task Name until the Run Now button. Create a subform and paste these design elements into the new subform. Select Create, Design, Subform, and paste the selection into the subform. Choose File, Save and save this subform as TaskHeading.

Tip

Make sure to check the Include in Insert Subform dialog checkbox. If you do not, the Insert Subform menu choice will not show this subform.

Move to the top of the form, underneath the Notes to Notes pop-up, and select Create, Insert Subform from the menu. Select TaskHeading from the Insert Subform picklist that appears. The entire subform TaskHeading appears in the subform box (see fig. 21.3). Notice the box around the subform area.

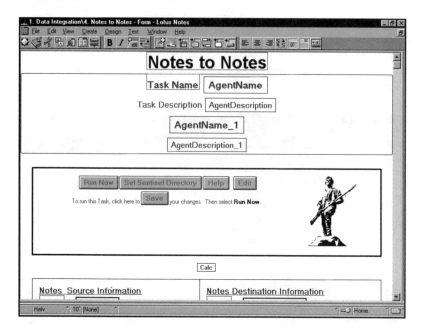

Fig. 21.3

Form redesign by attaching the first subform.

You have now created your first reusable design element. You can insert this into any form in this database. Whenever you change the subform, all documents into which that subform is inserted immediately reflect that change. If you decided to change the color of the Task Name from green to blue, all 13 forms that use this subform would immediately show the newly changed blue field.

Creating Form Action Buttons

Notice the buttons in figure 21.3. Buttons "float" in the window, meaning they may or may not appear on the visible portion of the screen.

You can place Action Buttons on the always visible Action Bar (located below the Search Bar and spanning the entire top of the screen, just like the Search Bar). In R3, buttons are placed on the form wherever is most convenient for the application design. These form buttons still work in R4, of course. The problem with the buttons being placed on the form is that they may not be on the part of the form displayed on the screen. R4 lets you put the buttons always at the top, in the Action Bar.

You can convert R3 applications to R4 by moving the button logic to new Action Buttons on the Action Bar. You must do this form by form. Each form has its own Action Bar. This allows the Action Bar to change as you move from one document to a different document.

Moving a Form Button to the Action Bar

The Sentinel for R3 has a Run Now button that starts the data importing. This button may or may not be on the part of the form displayed when the user wants to execute the Run Now command. Moving this button to the action bar solves that problem.

Select Create, Action to create a new Action, with the Title initially provided by Notes in the Properties InfoBox as (Untitled). The Sentinel needs to call this action button Run Now, which you can type into the Title bar in the Properties InfoBox. Select a Button Icon from the same window. You can select Blank for a text-only button. Pick the icon of a person running (see fig. 21.4).

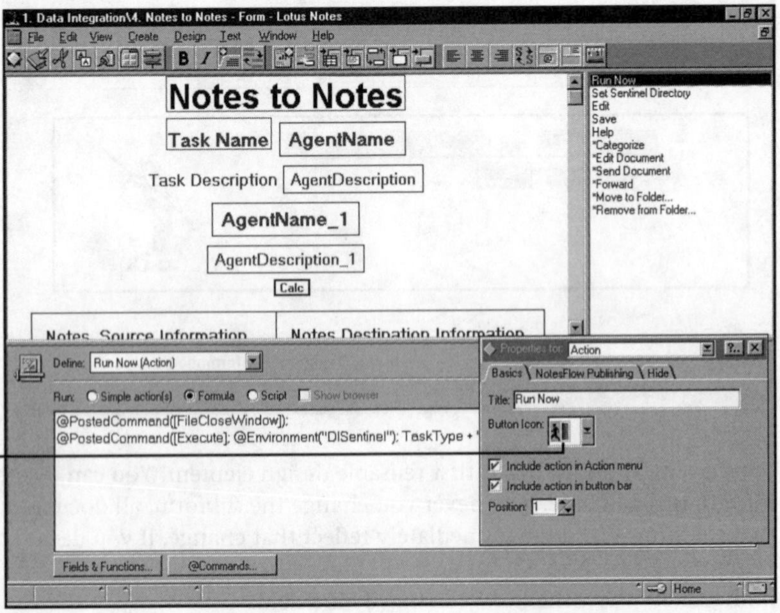

Fig. 21.4

The design of the first action button, Run Now.

Icon—

Next, select the formula from the on-form button. Move to the on-screen form button Run Now and copy the formula that appears in the programmer pane to the Clipboard. Select the Run Now action from the Action pane, and paste the formula into the formula section of the programmer pane.

Hiding the Action Button in Edit Mode

To perform Run Now, the Sentinel wants the document to be open in display mode. An unsaved document may not have passed all the edit checks that are necessary to properly import data. Therefore, on the Properties InfoBox, under the tab Hide, select Previewed for editing and Opened for editing to disable the button during edit mode.

Tip

Once the Action is created, you can copy it to the Clipboard for later reuse in other forms. For the Sentinel, this button needs to be copied and pasted 13 times, once for each form in the database.

Creating Edit and Save Buttons

Four other buttons need to be created, to remove them from the form and place them in the Action Bar.

Two common buttons are the Edit and Save buttons (see figs. 21.5 and 21.6). You can use edit buttons and save buttons during read mode and edit mode, respectively. Make sure to check Hide when editing in the Action Properties InfoBox.

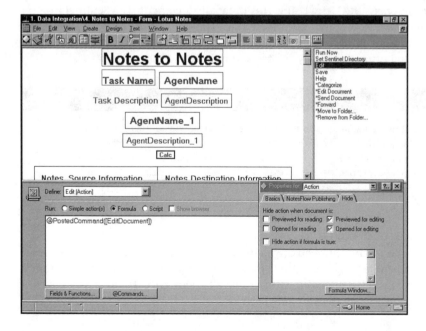

Fig. 21.5

Edit button parameters.

Fig. 21.6

Save button parameters.

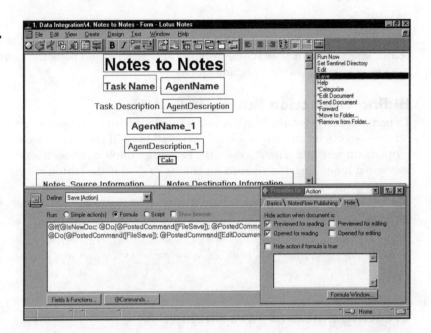

Notice that the Edit button, in the top right pane, can be modified simultaneously with modifying the Notes form. This can be initially confusing. With practice, the ability to "jump around" the various design elements becomes a great time-saver.

Creating a Help Button

The Help button opens the Help, Using This Database document. The Sentinel includes a separate database of user documentation. The Help, Using This Database document contains doclinks to this database. On your own, copy the formula from the on-form help button to a newly created action button.

> **Tip**
>
> If you have built user documentation, create a table of doclinks in your Help, Using This Database document to guide users to more advanced topics. This lets the user quickly doclink to a pertinent subject in much greater detail than available in form pop-ups. You can also store information about your organization's policies and procedures. This helps maintain uniform usage of the database across the organization.

Cleaning Up the Form

Finally, let's eliminate the entire box (which is actually a Notes table of just one row and one column) containing the buttons that are no longer needed, and the Sentinel logo, simplifying and cleaning up the form's overall appearance. Figure 21.7 shows a document composed using the Simplified form.

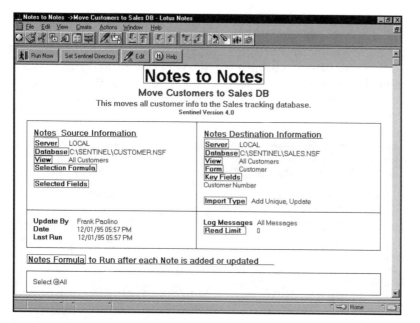

Fig. 21.7

*A document composed
with the R4 Simplified
Sentinel form, using a
subform and form action
buttons.*

Summary of Changes

Save this form by selecting File, Save. Switch to the default view, "1. Task \1. Destination Notes Database Name." Double-click the task Move Customers to Sales DB. Your
form should look similar to figure 21.7.

The following is the summary of changes so far:

- Created a subform comprised of the Task Name and Task Description design
  elements. This subform is inserted into the main form.
- Created the following five action buttons:
  - Run Now
  - Set Sentinel Directory
  - Edit (hidden when editing)
  - Save (hidden when reading)
  - Help
- Performed hide when on two of the buttons, edit and save. Edit is hidden when
  editing and save is hidden when reading.
- Deleted on-form buttons.
- Deleted Table holding all these design elements.

Making Four More Subforms

In the Sentinel, as referenced in Table 21.1, there are seven forms that use Notes as a source to move data. There are ten forms that use Notes as a destination. This section covers creating four more subforms, which will eventually be enhanced to collapsible sections (covered later in this chapter). Figure 21.8 shows four parts of the form that must be converted to sections.

Fig. 21.8

Create four subforms from these four areas.

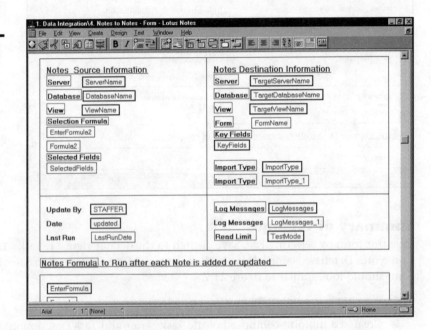

You must move all four of the areas of this form out of the table. Remember, you cannot create subforms within a table.

Creating the Subform NotesSource

From the top left area of the form (Notes Source Information), highlight the common design elements, which is the entire contents of that cell of the table, and copy these design elements to the Clipboard. Select Create, Design, Subform to create a new subform. Paste the design elements into the subform. Name the subform NotesSource in the Properties InfoBox. Make sure to check the Include in Insert Subform dialog checkbox. If you do not, the Insert Subform menu choice will not show this subform. Select File, Save to save this new subform. Select File, Close to close this subform design window. Figure 21.9 shows the subform NotesSource, after pasting in the design elements from the top left area of the form.

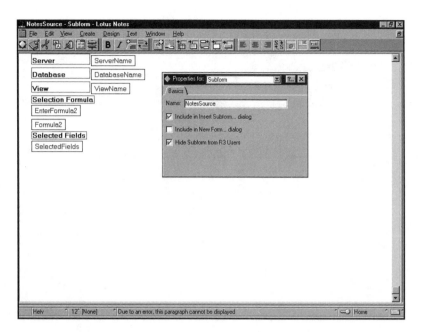

Fig. 21.9

*The design of the Subform
NotesSource.*

Creating the Subform NotesDestination

From the top right area of the form (Notes Source Destination), highlight the common design elements, which is the entire contents of that cell of the table, and copy these design elements to the Clipboard. Select Create, Design, Subform to create a new subform. Paste the design elements into the subform. Name the subform NotesDestination in the Properties InfoBox. Make sure to check the Include in Insert Subform dialog checkbox. Select File, Save to save this new subform. Select File, Close to close this subform design window. Figure 21.10 shows the design of the Subform NotesDestination.

Creating the Subform LogMessages

From the bottom right area of the form (Log Messages), highlight the common design elements, which is the entire contents of that cell of the table, and copy these design elements to the Clipboard. Select Create, Design, Subform to create a new subform. Paste the design elements into the subform. Name the subform LogMessages in the Properties InfoBox. Make sure to check the Include in Insert Subform dialog checkbox. Select File, Save to save this new subform. Select File, Close to close this subform design window. Figure 21.11 shows the design of the Subform LogMessages.

Fig. 21.10

The design of the Subform NotesDestination.

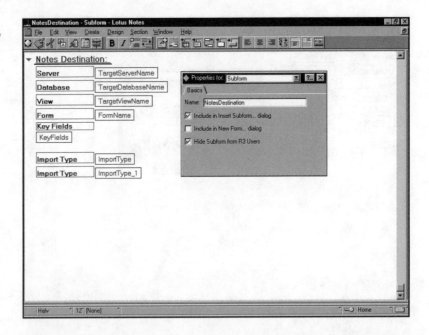

Fig. 21.11

The design of the Subform LogMessages.

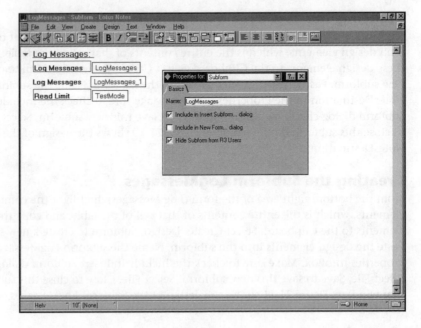

Creating the Subform UpdateInformation

From the bottom left area of the form (UpdateInformation), highlight the common design elements, which is the entire contents of that cell of the table, and copy these design elements to the Clipboard. Select Create, Design, Subform to create a new subform. Paste the design elements into the subform. Name the subform UpdateInformation in the Properties InfoBox. Make sure to check the Include in Insert Subform dialog checkbox. Select File, Save to save this new subform. Select File, Close to close this subform design window. Figure 21.11 shows the design of the Subform UpdateInformation.

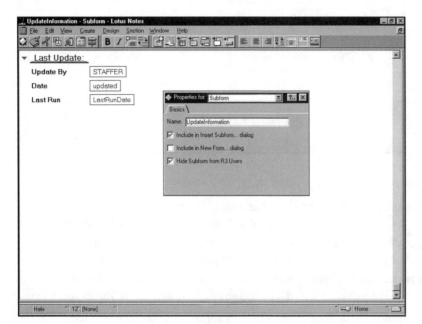

Fig. 21.12

The design of the Subform UpdateInformation.

Inserting the New Subforms into the Notes to Notes Form

If you have not closed the Notes to Notes design window, switch to it using the Window menu choice. If it is not one of the choices, open it for design using the view pane.

Because we have made four new subforms, the table with four areas is no longer necessary. Delete the entire table, and the fields contained within it.

Now you can insert the first subform. Select Create, Insert Subform from the menu. Select NotesSource from the picklist. The entire subform NotesSource appears in the subform box (see fig. 21.13).

Fig. 21.13

Notes to Notes with Inserted NotesSource subform NotesSource.

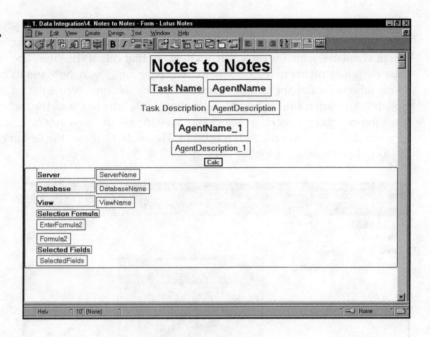

Repeat this process for each of the other three subforms:

1. Select Create, Insert Subform from the menu. Select NotesDestination from the picklist. The entire subform NotesDestination appears in the subform box.

2. Select Create, Insert Subform from the menu. Select LogMessages from the picklist. The entire subform LogMessages appears in the subform box.

3. Select Create, Insert Subform from the menu. Select UpdateInformation from the picklist. The entire subform UpdateInformation appears in the subform box.

To review our progress, you have created five subforms. They are the following:

- TaskHeading
- NotesSource
- NotesDestination
- LogMessages
- UpdateInformation

Building Collapsible Sections

Now that the tables are removed from this form, there needs to be a way to look at summary information on the form without being overwhelmed with multiple pages of fields and data. Sections are a very nice feature that make Notes forms work harder.

R4 of Notes allows sections to collapse into a single title, marked with solid arrows (or twisties) that point right if collapsed, or point down if expanded. Users click the twisties to expand and collapse the section, just as they already know how to do in R3 Notes to expand and collapse a section of a view.

In the Sentinel form, you can collapse the Notes source section into one line on the form that appears as NotesSource. In this way, you can put a whole lot more on every form, without it appearing too crowded.

The NotesSource section is a subform, meaning it is a shared design feature across the database. You can make the section collapsible by making the changes on the subform, not the main form. In changing the subform to make the NotesSource section collapse into one line, all current and future forms that use this subform will automatically reflect this change.

Edit the NotesSource subform by selecting Design Subforms from the view pane. The first task is to create a new section on this form. Move the cursor to the top of the form, where you want to create the new section. Select Create, Section, Standard from the menu. This puts a new section with the name Untitled Section on the top of the form. The fields below are not automatically inserted into the section. You must cut and paste them into the section.

Tip

Sometimes it is difficult to know where the section ends. Type **END** into the section. Click the twisty, and make sure END disappears when collapsed. You now know the boundaries of the section. Paste your fields or text from the Clipboard between the Section Title and the END mark. Either delete the word END when completed, or hide it when reading and editing (so only form designers can see it). This makes your updates easier in the future.

Expand/Collapse Options

Select the Expand/Collapse tab on the Section Properties InfoBox. The database designer must decide whether to show these sections as expanded or collapsed. In this case, there is quite a lot of data. Initially collapsing the sections makes the form easier to read in one glance. Figure 21.14 sets the Expand and Collapse rules to Auto-collapse in both read modes.

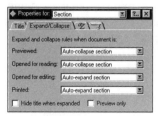

Fig. 21.14

Section Properties InfoBox for Expand/Collapse.

> **Tip**
>
> As a general rule, select Auto-expand when Printed. Otherwise, users of a printed form cannot see the underlying data.

Using Text as a Section Title

You can title sections as either Text or Formula. You could use the simple section title: NotesSource Information. The user would know by this title to expand this section to see more information about the Notes source.

> **Tip**
>
> Spending a few minutes to carefully select this section title can save hours of training and questions later, and result in a more usable application.

Using a Formula as a Section Title

If a section is collapsed when opened for reading, users want to know some of the basic elements in that section without expanding the entire section. A formula for a section title helps users to "peek" beneath the section. Selecting one or two critical fields for display in the section title accomplishes the goal of a more informational title without expanding the section. In the Sentinel, the formula is the following:

```
"Notes Source: " + DatabaseName
```

Figure 21.15 shows the Section Properties InfoBox with the title formula.

Fig. 21.15

*Making a Title formula in
a collapsible section.*

This displays the literals "Notes Source:" plus the database name. This makes the form easy to read when opened for reading. The user can see pertinent information without expanding the section. This "at-a-glance" approach is excellent for previewing forms because the entire form can be summarized in six to eight lines.

Finishing Up the Sections

Now, the remaining task is to create collapsible sections on the other three subforms: NotesDestination, LogMessages, and UpdateInformation. The objective is to make the overall form readable, without overwhelming the users with multiple pages of data when opening the form. Figure 21.16 shows the new Notes to Notes form, after modifying the NotesDestination, LogMessages, and UpdateInformation forms.

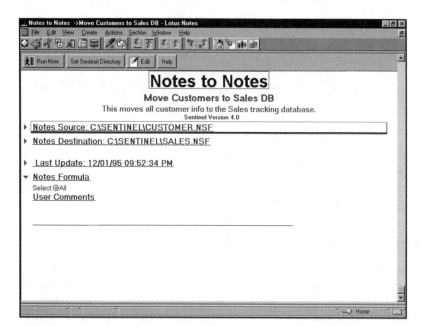

Fig. 21.16

Sample document created with the enhanced Notes to Notes form with sections.

The form has a clean, crisp appearance while presenting summary information to the user. Compare this R4 enhanced design to the original R3 Notes to Notes form shown in figure 21.1.

These collapsed sections also work well with the preview pane. Figure 21.17 shows Move Customers to Sales DB in a preview pane. Notice how the user can see the most significant document information from the following four newly added subforms:

- TaskHeading
- NotesSource
- NotesDestination
- LastUpdate

You can, of course, decide what significant document information to display in your collapsed sections of forms that you design using Notes R4.

Fig. 21.17

Notes to Notes form using the preview pane.

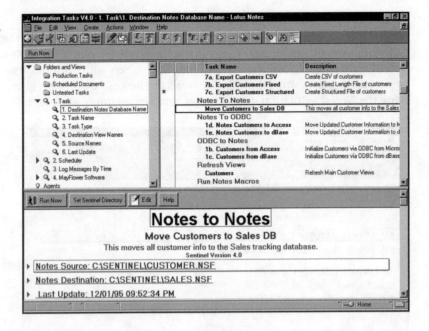

Using the Hide When Feature

Of all the new features in Notes R4, the Hide When feature has the most utility for applications development. The reason is that there is always a need for forms to serve multiple purposes for multiple users in multiple situations. In other programming languages, a simple if statement allows a new section or window to appear to allow additional data to be entered if certain conditions are true. Notes R4 allows similar functionality. In Notes R3, the application designer had to swap forms and shuffle fields around trying to please everyone under all circumstances. R4 has greatly expanded Hide When functionality beyond the R3 Hide When. Instead of just Reading and Editing, you can Hide When based on an evaluation of a formula.

A simple way of thinking of this is to look at an example. When a Hide When formula such as @Username = "Frank Paolino is evaluated, a section of the form could disappear. In addition to the obvious practical jokes that could be played using this feature (such as fields not appearing on the screen for certain users), Hide When is extremely useful for dynamic forms that transform themselves based on dynamically changing conditions.

Let's apply this feature to the Sentinel database. Looking at the Notes Destination Subform, there is a field PKeyFields that is only necessary if the user is importing response documents. It confuses users if it appears unnecessarily, as they assume they must fill it in. In Notes R3, you had to use field help and pop-up boxes to train the users. Now, you can hide the field PKeyFields if the field DocType is Document. Figure 21.18 shows the design of the form. Notice that Hide paragraph if formula is true is checked, and the formula in the formula window.

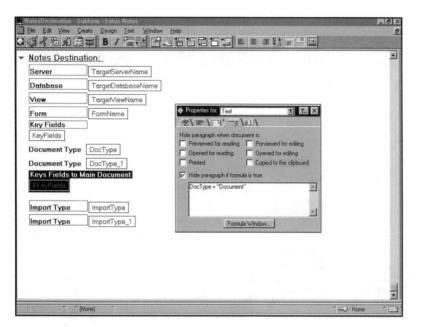

Fig. 21.18

A Notes form using the feature Hide when a condition is true.

It is important to understand that the field PKeyFields will not appear or disappear until the document fields are refreshed. A simple way to accomplish this without refreshing all fields after each field edit is to select the DocType field. Switch to the Properties InfoBox. Select the second tab. Put a checkmark next to the item Refresh fields on keyword change. This will cause the field PKeyFields to appear or disappear properly, without slowing the overall form performance due to unnecessary field refreshes.

Tip

Make all "triggers" to Hide When fields or sections based on fields of Field Type Keywords. This will make the Hide When fields appear and disappear on cue.

Testing the Form

The next job is testing the form. Select Design, Test Form, and Notes lets you simulate actual use of the form. This saves the cycle time of saving the form, switching views, and creating another form, only to discard it, switch view, and return to design mode.

Figure 21.19 shows that the literal Key Fields to Main Document and the field PKeyFields do not appear when the Document Type is Document.

Fig. 21.19

Form Notes to Notes with hidden literal key fields to main document.

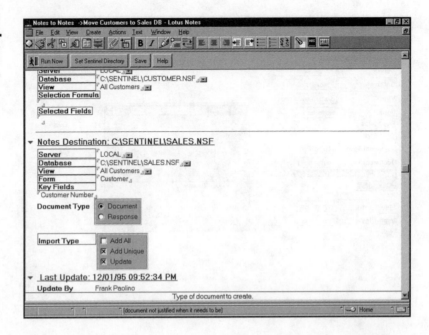

Clicking the field Document Type to change the value from Document to Response makes the literal Key Fields to Main Document and the field PKeyFields appear immediately on the form. Figure 21.20 shows that exact same form after selecting Response.

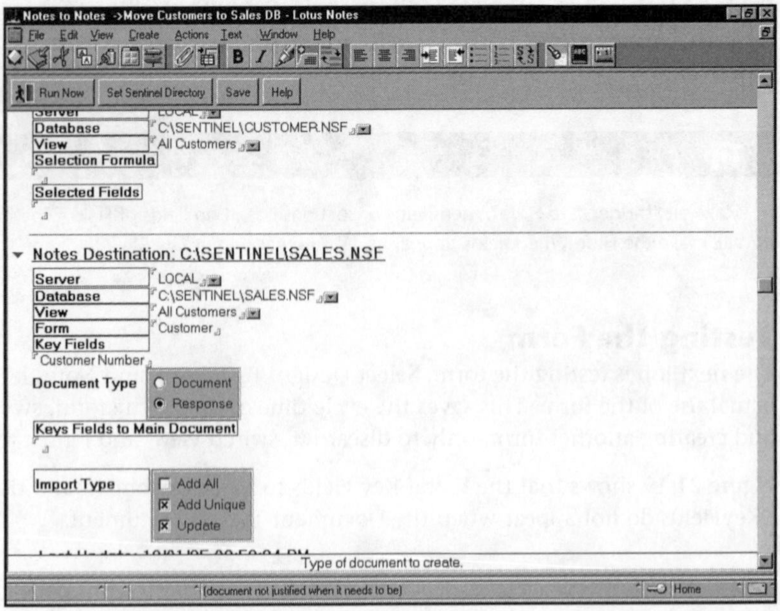

Fig. 21.20

Form Notes to Notes with displayed literal key fields to main document.

Now the form dynamically presents information and fields to the user. This feature represents a major step forward in application design ability in Lotus Notes.

Applying the Subforms to the Other Forms

The last job is modifying the other seven forms that contain the exact same Notes Source design elements. This is simply a cut and paste operation, repeated seven times. The long-term time-saving benefit is that you only need to perform maintenance on one subform. All other forms into which you have inserted subforms do not need to be updated after you have made changes to the subform.

Adding Action Buttons to the View

A very similar feature to Action Buttons is placed at the top of the view. They are similar to the Form Action Buttons. Each view can have its own set of Action Buttons. These are handy to Add, Edit, or Delete documents in a view, as well as to move them among folders.

To place the Run Now button on the View Action Bar, you create it in the same manner as for the Form Action Buttons. Switch to the view pane. Select Design Views. Double-click the default view "1. Task\1. Destination Notes Database Name."

Select Create Action to create a new Action, with the Title initially provided by Notes in the Properties InfoBox as (Untitled). The Sentinel needs to call this Action Button Run Now, which you can type into the Title bar in the Properties InfoBox. Select a Button Icon from the same window. Pick the icon of a person running.

View buttons can interrogate the document and behave differently depending on the values of certain fields. In the Sentinel database, users who upgrade must edit and save the document to recalculate new form fields. This also interrogates a field called VersionNumber, which is calculated in a shared field. If that value is not 4.0, the form prompts the user to edit and save the document before the action is completed. This is the essence of good programming: To check if an operation will be successful before attempting to proceed. The formula is as follows:

```
@If(VersionNumber != "4.0";
@Prompt([OK];"Error";"This document created with a previous version of the
➥Sentinel. Please Edit and Save before Run Now.");
@PostedCommand([Execute]; @Environment("DISentinel"); TaskType + "-" +
➥AgentName))
```

Figure 21.21 shows the design of the view with the formula of the action button Run Now.

Fig. 21.21

Creating a button with a user prompt from View Action Bar.

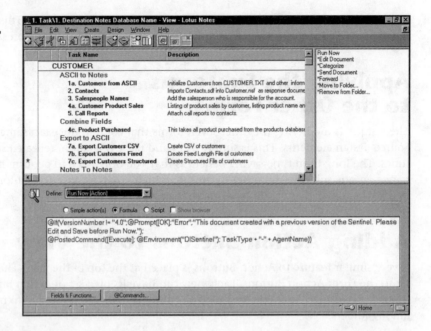

This ability to interrogate a document before attempting an operation is essential to better management of creating response documents. In the Sentinel R3 database, users could mistakenly attempt to compose a response document against a parent or main document that made no sense whatsoever. As R3 allowed you to compose any of the available forms, you had to know which form was the correct form to compose in any situation. This invariably leads to increased training and user frustration.

In R4 View Action Buttons, each button can first check that the form is correct under the circumstances. For example, in a customer tracking database, there are certain business facts that are fundamental:

- Companies have contacts.
- Contacts have call reports.
- Call reports have follow-ups.

In Notes, that means that Company is a main document, Contact is a response document, and Call Reports and Follow-up items are response-to-response documents. In R3, it was possible to mistakenly compose a call report against a customer. This invariably confuses users, while frustrating them. R4 View Action Buttons lets you put four buttons on the View Action Bar:

- Company (Main Document)
- Contact Person (response)
- Call Report (response)
- Follow-Up Item (response)

Each button, when clicked, interrogates the database to determine which form (Note) that the cursor is highlighting. If the cursor is pointing to a valid document, the operation can proceed. If it is not pointing to the appropriate form, the user receives an error message. For example, the Contact button first asks if the document form name is Customer. If not, it prompts the user with a message, and aborts the attempted document creation. Call reports can only be created against contacts in the same way. This guarantees proper field inheritance from main document to response document.

Organizing Views and Folders

In designing applications, have you ever wondered when the number of views that the customer requires will ever end? If you design Notes applications long enough, you know that the requests for more views never end. The biggest request is for special purpose views. If you've tried categories, you know that they help, but do not close the gap to what the user wants. Enter folders. It may take you a couple of minutes to understand the difference between folders and views, but when it hits you, you will be impressed. At first glance, folders appear to be renamed views, and in some ways they are. However, folders are basically ad hoc views, allowing the user to drag documents into another view (actually into a folder) based on some user opinion of the document's importance.

In R3 Sentinel, we put numerous status fields on the form. This allows the user to categorize certain task documents as one of the following categories:

- Production Tasks
- Scheduled Documents
- Untested Tasks

Different users can work on different tasks. Like all software endeavors, Sentinel tasks must be tested to ensure that the user set all the parameters correctly. During testing, the user may want these documents to appear in the Untested Tasks view, for quick reference. These documents are always a subset of all documents in the database. Most importantly, they are individually selected by the user, based on personal criteria that does not have to be set jointly by committee. Figure 21.22 shows the new folder, Untested Tasks, containing two documents.

You can create a new folder by selecting Create, Folders from the view pane. The initial Folder name is Untitled. Type **Untested Tasks** as the Folder name. Selecting the Options button lets you choose a view or folder from which to inherit the design of this folder. This is a private folder, which means only you can place documents into it. Checking the Shared box allows other users to place documents into this folder. The Untested Tasks folder is a private folder for your personal Sentinel tasks.

Fig. 21.22

Creating user folder for Untested Tasks.

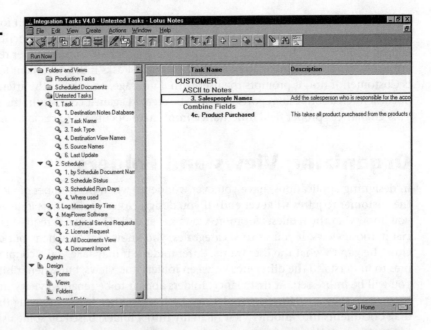

Sales Management's Use of Hot Follow-Ups

In the sales force application, there is a view of Hot Follow-Up items. What makes an item "hot?" No one could decide even after interminable meetings. In reality, a follow-up is hot if the user thinks it is, based on interpretation. With folders, the user simply drags a document from a view into a folder. That document is, in a sense, "categorized" by the user. Now, a hot follow-up is hot if a user says it is, without a view committee meeting. This saves hours of view programming that users may not perceive as valuable. This will slow view proliferation.

Adding Navigators

As discussed in Chapter 3, "Using Databases," navigators are an interesting new feature of Notes R4. They offer the possibility of guided tours through databases by clicking on "hot" sections of a graphical form. The common example of this feature is a geographical map, showing sales territories. Clicking on specific areas of the map moves the user to sales information concerning that territory. This makes navigation through the Notes databases more visually oriented.

Certain databases lend themselves to navigators better than others. Generally, databases where the material is static (that is, where the material changes infrequently) better utilize navigators. Databases where creation of new documents occurs frequently offer more difficult design challenges in utilizing navigators for the application designer.

Good Database Candidates for Navigators

Following is a list of databases that take better advantage of navigators:

- **Help databases**—These databases change infrequently. You can build doclinks from a navigator to already existing documents. Usually one person or department controls database content. This enables that department to fix some hotspots to other documents.

- **Training and How-To databases**—These databases also have fixed content, controlled by one person or department. These are excellent candidates for navigators, as there can be multiple navigator screens moving from basic techniques to more advanced techniques. These databases generally do not have Create options, as users do not participate in their content. All of the content is already established, so the navigators do not have to contemplate additional information, or changes to current information.

- **Bulletin Board databases**—As with Help and Training databases, the content is generally static. An example of a bulletin board database is a list of company policies concerning employees, such as vacation time, sick time, benefits plans, and family leave. Again, all of the content is controlled and managed by one department, so the navigators can be assigned in advance.

The underlying criteria for good to excellent candidates for navigators is a static database controlled by one person or department.

Other Uses for Navigators

In dynamically changing databases, navigators cannot point to specific documents, as that document may not exist, or may not be created yet. Therefore, navigators must primarily point to views that the user might want to visit. However, if this were their only purpose, they would not be adding much value over the view pane to a developer. You can, however, put other buttons on a navigator that point to static information that a user might like. Following is a list of uses for a navigator in a dynamically changing database:

- **Help text**—As in help databases, specific navigators can point to more detailed help information.

- **Another navigator**—Here is where the navigators become powerful. One navigator hotspot can point to another navigator. In this example, that second navigator could be a table of contents of help topics. At this point, you are dealing with static text, and you can place many links within the navigator.

- **User instructions**—This allows simple user instructions to appear in the navigator. R3 is very light on functions that let the application developer guide the user through the application. Pop-ups and the Help Using document are the main facilities. R4 Navigators allow more detailed guidance throughout the application.

- **Create Form buttons**—Using nested navigators and compose buttons, you can guide a user around the database, and offer form creation (R3 compose) buttons at the correct locations. This generally involves hiding all Create form choices from the user and hiding the menu choices for each of the forms from the user. This enables the developer to fully control the user's navigation of the database, allowing form creation via action buttons only, while offering direction and help throughout.

- **View pane replacement**—Navigators can replace the view pane with more graphical representations of folders.

Designing Navigators into the Sentinel

From a designer's perspective, navigators force some difficult decisions. Do you hide the view pane completely? Which views should be in the navigator? How do you let users create private folders and then access them?

The Sentinel database is a dynamic database with some static help information. Earlier in this chapter, we built a View Action Button pointing to the Help Using screen, which pointed to the help database. In this section, you will learn how to upgrade an R3 database design to incorporate a navigator for a dynamically changing database. The navigator will contain hotspots for views, as well as a hotspot to switch back to folders.

From the menu, select Create, Design Navigator. A blank screen appears. You should name this navigator first. As this is the Sentinel database's first navigator, call it Home. Set the background color to red, and select Auto adjust panes at runtime. This allows all navigator buttons to be seen on the screen.

Using Graphics in Navigators. Navigators take excellent advantage of graphics. The Sentinel uses a "Swiss Army Knife" to demonstrate its versatility in moving data from source to destination. To insert graphics into a navigator, you must first copy it to the Clipboard. Once that is done, select Create, Graphic Background. Notes automatically pastes the graphic background onto the screen. Figure 21.23 shows the beginning of the Sentinel's first navigator.

Creating Text To Be Used as Navigation Hotspots. The next task is to create text to be used as navigation hotspots. From the menu, select Create, Text. Using the mouse, click and hold the left button. Drag the rectangle to a size sufficient to hold two or three words.

The next task is to create four hotspot text buttons, one for each major view. Although the Sentinel has 15 views, only one button per major view is necessary.

Create four text box rectangles, one for each view. You can copy and paste these rectangles once you set the properties on the first text rectangle to your liking. Each text caption should be as follows:

- By Destination Name
- Schedule Tasks
- Log Messages
- License Forms

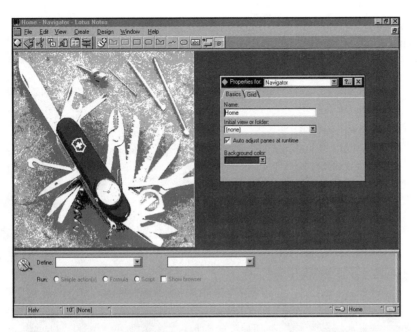

Fig. 21.23

Home Navigator with graphic.

Tip

To align the text boxes properly, select Navigator from the Properties InfoBox. Select the Grid tab, and select Snap to Grid. Make the grid size five pixels or more. This will enable you to drag the text boxes into alignment with one another, for an aesthetically attractive navigator form.

Figure 21.24 shows the Navigator with four action text boxes.

Creating a Way Back to the View Pane via Hotspot Rectangles. Now that we have a navigator, we need a way to get back to the view pane. Once in the navigator, there is no way back to the view pane unless programmed by you, the developer. In the Sentinel example, you can create a text box and a graphic of a folder. Wrapping all of that in a hotspot rectangle makes a hotspot to the view pane.

To do this, first create another text box, as before. Make the Text caption *view pane*. The Action in the programmer pane should be (none). Copy a graphic of a file folder (or whatever you feel represents the view pane window) to the Clipboard. Paste this to the Navigator by selecting Create, Graphic Button. The Action in the programmer pane for the Graphic Button should also be (none). Drag this next to the text that says *view pane*.

You can create a Hotspot Rectangle just as you did to create a Text Rectangle. From the menu, select Create, Hotspot Rectangle. Using the mouse, click and hold the left button. Drag the rectangle to a size approximately the size of the view pane text plus the graphic. A little larger will not cause any problems. Drag this hotspot rectangle on top of the view pane and File Folder graphic. In the programmer pane, type in the formula shown in figure 21.25, which will allow the user to navigate back to the view pane when clicked.

Fig. 21.24

Home Navigator with four action text boxes.

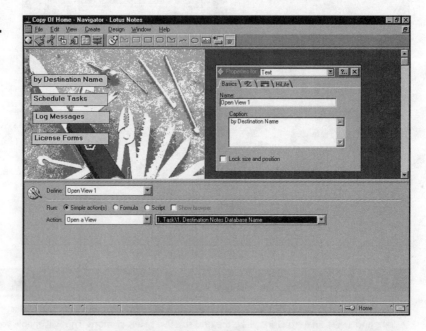

Fig. 21.25

Home Navigator with view pane hotspot rectangle.

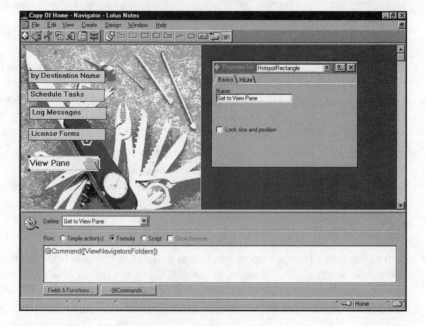

Adding a Navigator Button to the Default View

To enable the user to switch to the navigator, place a button on the default view. This button opens the navigator Home.

Select Design Views from the view pane. Double-click the default view "1. Task \1. Destination Notes Database Name." Select Create, Action. Call this Action Button Navigator in the Properties InfoBox. The formula is as follows:

```
@PostedCommand([OpenNavigator];"Home";"0")
```

Figure 21.26 shows the Navigator with a button using this formula to open the Home Navigator.

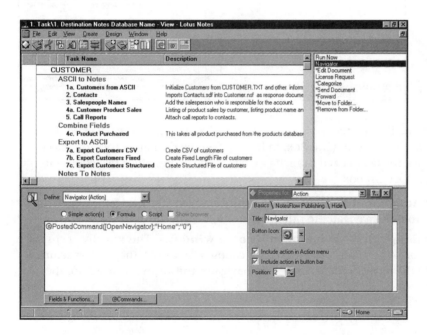

Fig. 21.26

Placing a button on the default view to open the Home Navigator.

When clicked, this button opens the Home Navigator that you created. The parameter 0 means that Home is opened in the view pane (left side of the screen). The parameter 1 opens the navigator in its own window, filling the screen. The second choice is desirable if you want the navigator to be the sole method of moving around the database. This insulates the user from the details of the database design. Figure 21.27 shows the default database view with the Home Navigator appearing in the Action Bar.

Fig. 21.27

Default view with Home Navigator button.

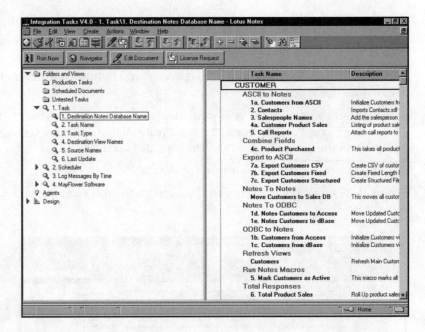

You can optionally open the navigator as soon as the user opens the database. To do this, switch to the Properties InfoBox. In the top field marked Properties for, select Database. Click the tab marked Launch (see fig. 21.28). Notes offers two choices in the On Database Open list box:

- **Open designated Navigator**—This initially opens the navigator. Users can move from the navigator to other views or folders in the database.

- **Open designated Navigator in its own window**—This initially opens the navigator. When users press escape (or choose File, Close), they always return back to the navigator. This makes the navigator truly a "home page" for the database.

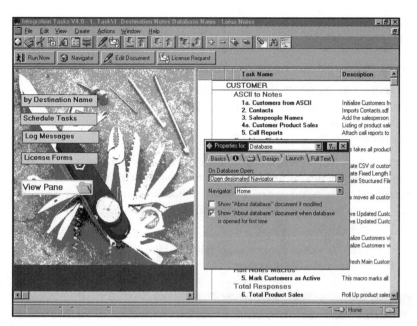

Fig. 21.28

*Setting Launch parameters,
on Database Open, to
reference the Home
Navigator.*

IV

Advanced Notes Topics

The *NOTES.INI* File

The NOTES.INI file (also called the Notes Preference file on the Macintosh) is a settings file that Notes checks when you first start Lotus Notes. The NOTES.INI file resides in the Notes data directory for OS/2 Notes users, and in the Windows directory for most Windows Notes users. If you upgraded from a Release 2 Notes to Release 3, then your NOTES.INI file may be located in the Notes directory instead—as that is where Notes 2 versions placed it.

Information in the file comes from many sources, including installation choices, server console commands, and selections made in the Setup dialog boxes discussed previously in this chapter. Notes uses most of the variables in this file internally, and you can set those through the Notes user interface rather than having to edit the NOTES.INI file using a text editor.

Each time Notes starts, the NOTES.INI file is used to check installation settings, Setup selections (mail, user, and location information—and of course, your DESKTOP.DSK file), and other variables Notes uses.

This section covers a few of the settings that can be made in the NOTES.INI file, that cannot be made through selections in Notes.

Editing *NOTES.INI*

Macintosh users must edit the NOTES.INI file using a resource editor like ResEdit. Other Notes users can do so using any simple text editor—like the Notepad in Windows. Macintosh users should consult their systems documentation before trying to edit the NOTES.INI file.

Before editing NOTES.INI, exit Notes—as the changes you make to the NOTES.INI file will not take effect until the next time you start Notes anyway. Edit the lines of text, insert new lines, or delete lines just as you would text from a Notes document. Make sure, however, that your typing is exact, and that no blank spaces follow any of the lines of text, or you will experience problems.

When you exit the NOTES.INI document you are editing, save your changes. Then restart Notes to have your changes take place.

Caution

Make sure you create a backup copy of your existing NOTES.INI file before you edit it!

Editing the NOTES.INI file can be dangerous to your Notes health if you are not used to editing these types of files—for example, even leaving a blank space after a line of text in the NOTES.INI file can cause trouble when you try to start Notes. If you have a choice, make Notes changes through the Notes selections—or contact your Notes administrator for help.

Changing the New Mail Tune. You can change the tune Notes uses to signal you that new mail has been delivered by editing the NOTES.INI file to reference a new .WAV file—the sound file type used in Notes for the new mail tune. You may already have a few .WAV files available to you in your operating system's directory, in a special sound file directory if you have a sound board; you can also purchase new .WAV files at most software stores, or even find many of them passed along as shareware.

For most users, this is just a fun change, allowing you to have your computer play the theme from "Leave It to Beaver" or to say "bummer" every time you get new mail—if you have these .WAV files available to you.

For those who have computers in which they cannot adjust the sound for the new mail tune, the ability to change the new mail tune, and thus edit the sound volume as well becomes a treat—particularly if you are working close to others.

You must have a sound driver installed to change the new mail tune. If you don't have a sound board installed, and do not have a non-soundboard speaker driver, you will need to consult with your network administrator or local software dealer. Follow your operating system's instructions for installing and changing the volume for sound on your system.

To change the New Mail Tune (for example, to have your computer say "bummer" each time you get new mail), insert the following line in your NOTES.INI file:

```
NewMailTune=drive:\directory\.WAV file name
```

For example:

```
NewMailTune=C:\WINDOWS\BUMMER.WAV
```

This tells Notes to reference the BUMMER.WAV file each time new mail is delivered to you.

You will need to restart Notes to have this edit take effect.

Adding a Second Address Book. If you want to add another Name & Address Book to your workstation that will be searched when Notes verifies recipient names in mail messages, then you will need to modify the NOTES.INI file to tell Notes where to look. The first Name & Address Book to be searched *must* be called NAMES. Subsequent Address Books can have any name up to eight characters in length, followed by the .NSF extension. To have Notes look in more than one Name & Address Book, enter the following line in your NOTES.INI file:

```
Names=Names, Names2
```

Where *Names2* represents the file name for the other Address Book in your data directory.

This entry can come in handy if you have address books for other domains that you are certified to access—like an outside service provider like WorldCom.

When you send a message, Notes will first look in the NAMES.NSF Address Book and then in the NAMES2.NSF Address Book.

For more information on using the Name & Address Book, read Chapter 4, "Getting Started with Electronic Mail."

Eliminating the Design Menu. Though usually used by Notes administrators to keep users from being able to design new databases, you can also use this setting if you have no desire yourself to design database, manage a "public" workstation and want it to be used to get mail only, or simply do not want anyone to be able to design databases from your workstation.

Add this line to your NOTES.INI file:

```
NoDesignMenu=1
```

Where 1 means turn on the No Design Menu function to disallow this feature and remove the menu selection from the menu bar in the Notes window.

Protecting Against Mail-Bomb-Type Viruses. If you want to protect your workstation against "Mail-Bombs"—viruses sent to you via special attachments and features in your mail, then enter the following line:

```
NoExternalApps=1
```

Where 1 turns on the No External Applications command, disallowing the use of any applications outside of Notes.

When you make this setting, you will turn off all external applications that can be accessed while you are working with Notes—however, this means you will not be able to use the following Notes features as long as this selection is made:

- OLE
- DDE
- DIP
- @Command
- @DbLookup (when using non-Notes drivers)
- @DbColumn (when using non-Notes drivers)
- @MailSend
- @DDExxx
- Launching of file attachments
- Subscribe (on Macintosh workstations)

Turning Off the Mail Menu. You may want to turn off the ability for people to use the Mail menu commands—for example, if you are managing a "public" workstation for a group of people, and all they are to access are project databases from that workstation—which would help keep the workstation free more often.

To disable the Mail menu, enter the following line in the NOTES.INI file:

```
NoMailMenu=1
```

Where 1 turns off the Mail menu in Notes. This selection will not only eliminate the Mail menu from the workstation, but will also set the user's mail system to None.

Note

If you are having trouble using Mail, and you are meant to do so, you may want to check the NOTES.INI file of the workstation to make sure this setting has not been made. This setting will override the setting made in the Setup Mail dialog box in Notes to specify which mail package you are using.

Changing the Location of Your ID File. Normally, your ID file is located in your Notes directory, or wherever you specified when you set up Notes. If you want to change where your Notes ID file is located, then you can specify it by entering the following:

```
KeyFilename=<location>
```

Where *location* specifies the drive and directory in which your Notes ID is stored.

This entry is usually used when more than one person is sharing a workstation, and separate NOTES.INI and DESKTOP.DSK files are created and stored in personal subdirectories for each user.

When Something Goes Wrong with *NOTES.INI*

If you have problems with your NOTES.INI file that cannot be resolved—either it is corrupted, you have made mistakes when editing it, or the appropriate default information does not seem to be present, and you cannot seem to correct the problem—then you will need to delete all but the first two lines in the NOTES.INI file, save it, and then restart Notes.

The two lines that you must have in your NOTES.INI file to start Notes are the following:

```
[Notes]

Directory=<Notes data directory>
```

Where *Notes data directory* represents where your data files are located.

For example, the directory line could read:

```
Directory=C:\NOTES\DATA
```

You will need to make your personal Setup selections again, but you will at least be able to start Notes up with all of the default information present.

From Here...

In this chapter, you participated in migrating a complicated Notes application from R3 Notes to R4 Notes. For more information on the topics discussed in this chapter, refer to the following:

- Chapter 10, "Designing Forms," describes how to create and design forms in Notes R4.

- Chapter 22, "Notes: Under the Hood," continues your study of Notes advanced topics and shows you how replication works and describes the various Notes platforms.

- Chapter 25, "Add-On and Third-Party Products," shows you many of the additional products from Lotus and other vendors that can make your Notes installation more effective, such as the Lotus Fax Server and the Lotus Notes Document Imaging module.

CHAPTER 22

Notes: Under the Hood

This chapter will show you how Notes does some of its magic. You will learn the following:

- How replication works
- The role of Notes servers
- Notes network topology
- The Notes Administrator interface
- The new Notes Admin Agent
- The various Notes platforms
- Supporting multiple licenses and Notes servers

Understanding Notes Replication

In today's business environment, as teams become the prevalent work force model and the need to share information across time and geographic boundaries increases, the ability to synchronize databases so that users in disparate locations can share information on a timely basis is becoming more and more critical in order to maintain a competitive advantage. One of the most powerful and complicated features of Notes is its ability to synchronize multiple copies of Notes databases stored on different servers and/or client workstations. This process, known as *replication*, enables users on different networks—even in different time zones or in different countries—to share the same information in a timely and effective manner.

> **Note**
>
> Lotus Notes is the first product on the market to support true client/server replication, and many companies now claim that their products supports replication. This claim must be scrutinized very carefully because most of these products are file system-based in that they must transfer an entire file. As of this writing, Lotus Notes is the only product that supports client/server replication, and Lotus has taken it a step further in Notes 4.0: now replication can be done at the field level. Currently, no other product can make this claim.

The primary reason to use replication is to enable users who do not have direct access to the server where a database resides to work collaboratively with the information it contains. For instance, people who do not have a persistent connection to the LAN, such as salespeople, people who work from home, or people who use a server in a different location, can work with a replica of the database and have their replica synchronized with the original database through the replication process.

A good example of the need for replication is demonstrated by users configured for workstation based mail. When mail messages are delivered to you, they are placed in your mailbox on the server. Workstation based mail dictates that you will have a replica of your mailbox on your workstation. Each time you replicate with your Notes server, the Replicator will synchronize the local copy of your mailbox with the copy on the server.

Replication is not merely a file system-based process where an entire file is copied from one machine to another, but is a true client/server based process that bi-directionally synchronizes each replica of the database with changes from the other copy. In Notes 3.0, this was a document level process. If any changes were made to a document, the entire document was replicated. In Notes 4.0, replication is a field level process. If only one field in a document changes, only the information contained in that field is sent to the other database.

To illustrate the importance of field-based replication, consider this example. Company XYZ has a Marketing Encyclopedia database used to store Microsoft PowerPoint and Freelance Graphics presentations (which can grow quite large) as file attachments in a rich text field. In Notes 3.x, when a user edited a document and changed the Presentation Format field from PowerPoint to Freelance, the entire document—including the large presentation stored as an attachment—was replicated to all replica databases. This can consume a vast amount of time and system resources.

If the same scenario took place in a Notes 4.0 database, only the fields that actually changed—in this case, the Presentation Format field—would be replicated, thus saving a tremendous amount of time and system resources, particularly for dial-up users.

Note

In some cases, field-based replication may not be desirable. It adds overhead on the front end of the process because each database must be searched more thoroughly to determine which fields have changed. If a particular database has frequent changes to large documents, field based replication can be very useful; otherwise, it might actually take more time.

For the replication process to be efficient and effective, Notes must track several pieces of information at the database level, such as the Replica ID and Replication History, and at the document level, such as the Document ID, Created date, Modified date, and Added to file Date.

As you will see in the following sections, replication is a very powerful but very complicated feature of Notes, and I can only scratch the surface in this chapter. In most instances, the Notes Administrator will configure your workstation and you will need not worry about these issues. On the other hand, if you need more information, refer to your Notes manuals and online Help database.

> **Note**
>
> Much of the replication process is controlled by database specific settings accessible through the Replication Settings dialog box. To access this dialog box, right-click the database icon and choose Database Properties to display the Database Property InfoBox. Click the Replication Settings button to display the Replication Settings dialog box. For details on how to use and change these settings, see the section "Choosing Replication Settings" in Chapter 19, "Working Remote."

Replica ID

Each Notes database, when it is first created (when the File, Database, New operation is performed), gets assigned a unique Replica ID. When two or more databases share the same Replica ID, this is the signal to the Notes server that these databases are linked and should be synchronized. Only databases that have identical Replica IDs will be synchronized.

To see the Replica ID of any database, choose File, Database, Properties, right-click the database icon, and choose Properties; or select the database and click the Properties SmartIcon. Either of these actions will display the InfoBox. You can then click the i tab to see the Replica ID of the database. Figure 22.1 displays the i tab of the properties for my mail database.

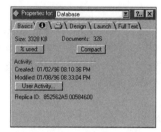

Fig. 22.1

The Replica ID is shown in the Database Properties InfoBox.

When a new replica of a database is created by choosing File, Replication, New Replica, the new database will be assigned the same Replica ID, and replication between the two databases can begin.

> **Caution**
>
> If you have the capability to create replica databases on your server (which can be limited by the Notes administrator), it is very important that you understand the distinction between a replica database and a database copy. A copy of a database, made by choosing File, Database, New Copy, assigns a new Replica ID to the copy. (This is similar to making a copy of the file using your operating system, except that when you use the OS, all of the file information, including the Replica ID, is transferred to the new copy.)
>
> This means that the database will not replicate with the original database. If you want to make a copy of a database that will not replicate with the original, such as a Mail Archive database, this is the method you should use.

Replication History

The first time a database is replicated, a *Replication History* is created that tracks the time, date, username, and actions of that last replication. To access the Replication History of a database, choose File, Replication, History, or right-click the database icon and choose History; the Replication History dialog box shown in figure 22.2 will be displayed.

Fig. 22.2

When a database replicates, the Notes server will examine the Replication History to determine when the database last replicated successfully.

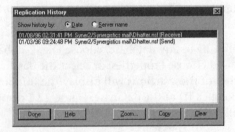

Only successful replications will be logged in the Replication History for a database. For instance, if you are a dial-up user and initiate a replication session while the server's lines are busy, the Replication History will not be updated until the database actually replicates.

Once the Notes server knows the date and time of the last successful replication, it will use special time and date information stored in each document to determine which documents have been added, modified, or deleted since the last successful replication. This is known as *incremental replication* and can drastically reduce the time needed to replicate. If the last successful replication time and date cannot be determined, which could happen if the Replication History was cleared or if the database in question is a brand new replica, a full replication will be performed. This will take much longer and consume more resources because each document in each database must be examined for changes.

> **Tip**
>
> The Replication History can be a valuable troubleshooting tool for experienced Notes administrators because you can quickly determine when a database last replicated, with whom it replicated, and whether information was sent, received, or both. In addition, some replication problems can be solved by clearing the Replication History of a database.
>
> If you have Manager access to a server database or are working with a local copy of a database, you can use the Clear button on the Replication History dialog box shown in figure 22.2 to delete the Replication History of the database and ensure a full replication when the next replication takes place.

Document ID

Much like the Replica ID of a database, each Notes document has a unique *Document ID*. Each document actually has three different IDs that Notes uses to provide varying levels of identification. The value displayed in the Document Properties InfoBox for the ID is all three of the following values concatenated:

- The primary identifier is the Document ID, which can be used to distinguish a document within a database.

- The Universal ID is unique between databases, but is the same for all replicas of the same document.

- The highest level identifier is the Originator ID, which is unique among all documents in all databases.

You can easily view these three dates by selecting any document and choosing File, Document Properties, right-clicking a document in a view or folder, and choosing Document Properties; or selecting a document and clicking the Properties SmartIcon. Figure 22.3 displays the Document Properties InfoBox that shows these three dates and the document's unique ID document.

Fig. 22.3

The Document Properties InfoBox displays pertinent document-level replication information.

The following sections describe the individual dates.

Created Date. Every Notes document will have a Created date associated with it. This is the date document that was originally created (regardless of the replica it was created in) and is database independent. The Created date value will be the same in each copy of the database and will never change.

The dates associated with a document, such as the Created, Modified, and Added to File dates (as well as dates associated with a database), are dependent upon the system date of the workstation or server in use when a document is added, updated, or replicated. If the system date is inaccurate, it can cause replication problems. You should occasionally check your system time and date to ensure that it is correct. To easily check and/or edit the system time and date, choose File, Mobile, Edit Current Time/Phone, which will launch the Time and Phone Information dialog box (see fig. 22.4). You can edit as needed.

Fig. 22.4

Use the Time and Phone Information for Travel dialog box to change your location time, date, and dialing information.

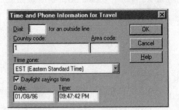

Modified Date. Each time a document is modified after its creation, the Modified date is updated. The Modified date is crucial for replication because Notes uses this date in conjunction with the Replication History to perform incremental replication. The Modified date can vary for replicas of the same document because a user may update a copy of the document in a replica of the original, or vice versa. During replication, Notes views the differences in the dates as a signal that the document has changed and at least one field needs to be replicated. After the databases have replicated, the Modified date should be the same in each copy of the document until the next edit takes place.

Added to File Date. The Added to this file date is database-dependent in that it reflects the date that the document was placed into the copy of the database you are using. For example, if a document originates in the server copy of a database, the Added to this file date will reflect the date the document was saved in that database. When the database next replicates and that document is transferred to the replica, the Added to this file date of the document in the replica will display the date it was placed into the replica. This date will also change to reflect the last modification of the document.

The Replication Process

The ABC Company, for example, maintains a database named Marketing Discussion on Server_A in the Atlanta office. When a new office opens in Chicago, a new replica of the database is made on the Server_B in Chicago, which copies all of the documents in the database from Server_A to Server_B. When the initial replication is completed, the Replication History in the Marketing Discussion database on Server_A should look something like the following:

```
Server_B/ABC Company DATA\MDISCUSS.NSF 10/19/96 08:25:16 PM (Send)
```

From this Replication History, you can see that Server_A sent data from this database to its replica on Server_B on 10/19/96 at 8:25 PM. No data was received from the new database because it contained no data.

The Replication History of the replica database on Server_B should look something like the following:

```
Server_A/ABC Company DATA\MDISCUSS.NSF 10/19/96 08:26:38 PM (Receive)
```

This Replication History tells you that the replica database received data from the Marketing Discussion database on Server_A and took just over a minute to transmit the data. As you have probably guessed, the amount of time required for replication will depend on the size of the data being transmitted and the volume of changes transmitted.

In most instances, if replication is functioning correctly, you will see two distinct entries in the Replication History of each database that replicates with another database. One indicates that data was sent to the other database (Send), and the other indicates that data was received from the other database (Receive).

As users begin to use the new database on Server_B, new documents get added and existing documents get updated or deleted. As an example, follow six documents through the process. Table 22.1 shows the two databases as they exist after the replication on 10/19/96 at 8:25:55 PM.

Table 22.1 Replication Example 1

Doc #	Doc ID*	Created	Modified	Added to File	Server	Deleted
1	ABC234:364VBC	10/20/96 7:22:40 AM	10/20/96 9:31:56 AM	10/21/96 6:22:11 AM	Server_A	
2	AB1X42:BN456X	10/20/96 12:45:32 PM	10/21/96 3:44:11 AM	10/20/96 12:45:32 PM	Server_B	
3	AXV567:CBV768	10/19/96 7:20:45 AM		10/19/96 7:20:45 AM	Server_A	
4	AXV567:CBV768	10/19/96 7:20:45 AM	10/21/96 6:55:11 AM	10/19/96 8:25:55 PM	Server_B	
5	C2SD34:681S45	10/19/96 7:59:08 AM	10/21/96 4:25:22 AM	10/19/96 7:59:08 AM	Server_A	Yes
6	C2SD34:681S45	10/19/96 7:59:08 AM		10/19/96 8:26:57 PM	Server_B	

The document IDs in this example have been shortened in order to save space.

Document 1 was created in another replica (by a remote user perhaps) of the Marketing Discussion database on 10/20/96 and was modified on 10/20/96, but did not get replicated into the copy on Server_A until 10/21/96. (This is a good example of what happens when you have users with local replicas of a database that do not replicate daily).

Document 2 was created in the replica of the Marketing Discussion database on Server_B on 10/20/96 (which is why the Created date and Added to File dates are the same), and it was modified on 10/21/96.

Document 3 was created in the Server_A copy of the Marketing Discussion database on 10/19/96 and has not been modified in this copy.

Document 4 is a replica of Document 3 that was placed into the Marketing Discussion database on Server_B during the initial replication (notice that the Document IDs and Created dates are the same). Document 4 was modified on 10/21/96 at 6:55:11 PM.

Document 5 was created in the Server_A copy of the Marketing Discussion database on 10/19/96 and was deleted from the Server_A database on 10/21/96.

Document 6 is a replica of Document 5 that was placed in the Marketing Discussion replica on Server_B during the initial replication.

Table 22.2 shows the states of the two replica databases after Server_A and Server_B replicate on 10/22/96 at 6:00:00 AM.

Table 22.2   Replication Example 2

Doc #	Doc ID*	Created	Modified	Added to File	Server	Deleted
1	ABC234:364VBC	10/20/96 7:22:40 AM	10/20/96 9:31:56 AM	10/21/96 6:22:11 AM	Server_A	
2	AB1X42:BN456X	10/20/96 12:45:32 PM	10/21/96 3:44:11 PM	10/20/96 12:45:32 PM	Server_B	
3	AXV567:CBV768	10/19/96 7:20:45 AM	10/21/96 6:55:11 PM	10/22/96 6:00:45 AM	Server_A	
4	AXV567:CBV768	10/19/96 7:20:45 AM	10/21/96 6:55:11 PM	10/19/96 8:25:55 PM	Server_B	
5	C2SD34:681S45	10/19/96 7:59:08 AM	10/21/96 4:25:22 PM	10/19/96 7:59:08 AM	Server_A	Yes
6	C2SD34:681S45	10/19/96 7:59:08 AM	10/21/96 4:25:22 PM	10/22/96 6:05:12 AM	Server_B	Yes
7	ABC234:364VBC	10/20/96 7:22:40 AM	10/20/96 9:31:56 PM	10/22/96 6:05:56 AM	Server_B	
8	AB1X42:BN456X	10/20/96 12:45:32 PM	10/21/96 3:44:11 PM	10/22/96 6:01:32 PM	Server_A	

The document IDs in this example have been shortened in order to save space.

After the scheduled replication on 10/22/96 at 6:00:00 AM, the replication history of the Marketing Discussion database on Server_A would look something like this (the actual times will vary based on the size of the documents being replicated):

```
Server_A/ABC Company DATA\MDISCUSS.NSF 10/22/96 06:04:23 AM (Receive)

Server_A/ABC Company DATA\MDISCUSS.NSF 10/22/96 06:01:34 PM (Send)
```

After the scheduled replication on 10/22/96 at 6:00:00 AM, the replication history of the Marketing Discussion database on Server_B would look something like this (the actual times will vary based on the size of the documents being replicated):

```
Server_B/ABC Company DATA\MDISCUSS.NSF 10/22/96 06:00:15 AM (Send)

Server_B/ABC Company DATA\MDISCUSS.NSF 10/22/96 06:05:32 PM (Receive)
```

As you can see in Table 22.2, the databases have been synchronized. The Replicator has created a new instance of Document 1 in Server_B's database (Document 7) because Document 1 was added to Server_A's copy after the first replication with Server_B on 10/19/96.

Likewise, Document 8 in Server_A's copy of the database is a new instance of Document 2 because Document 2 was added to Server_B's copy of the database after the first replication on 10/19/96.

In our example, Document 4 in Server_B's copy was a replica of Document 3 created in Server_B's copy during the initial replication on 10/19/96. On 10/21/96 at 6:55:11 PM, Document 4 was modified in Server_B's copy. During the replication on 10/22/96, the modifications made to Document 4 were made to Document 3 in Server_A's copy. Notice that in Table 22.2, Document 3 and Document 4 now have the same Created and Modified dates; however, the Added to File dates reflect the dates each of these documents were added into their respective databases.

Handling Deleted Documents. Document 5 and Document 6 require some special attention because Document 5 has been deleted. Document 6 in Server_B's database is a replica of Document 5 in Server_A's copy. On 10/21/96 at 4:25:22 PM, Document 5 was deleted from the database on Server_A. If Document 5 was actually physically deleted, then the Replicator process would see that Document 6 exists in Server_B's database and does not exist in Server_A's copy after the next replication. It would then create a new replica of Document 6 in Server_A's database.

To solve this problem, Notes handles deletions in a special way. When a document is deleted, a *deletion stub* is created to act as a flag for the Replicator. During the next replication, the Replicator sees the deletion stubs and knows that the documents that have the same Document IDs should be deleted and deletion stubs should be created in their places (this is necessary so that the deletion stubs are populated throughout all replicas of the database).

In our example, when the replication takes place on 10/22/96, the Replicator will see the deletion stub for Document 5 and will delete Document 6 from Server_B's database. Table 22.2 shows that both documents have been deleted.

Changing the Purge Interval. Deletion stubs are relatively small and contain only enough information for the Replicator task to find the corresponding document in each replica of a database. However, over time, deletion stubs can waste a significant amount of space. Notes enables you to set a *purge interval* so that deletion stubs can be physically removed from the database after a specified period of time.

The purge interval for a database is one-third the number of days specified in the Remove documents not modified in the last X days setting of each database (where X is a numeric value that you supply). The default value for this setting is 90 days. If you do not change this value, then all deletion stubs will be removed from the specified database every 30 days.

To access this setting, choose File, Database, Properties, and click the Replication Settings button on the Database Properties InfoBox that appears, or right-click a database, choose Properties, and click the Replication Settings button on the Database Properties InfoBox. Either of these methods will launch the Replication Settings dialog box shown in figure 22.5.

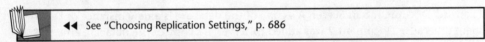

◀◀ See "Choosing Replication Settings," p. 686

Fig. 22.5

Use the Replication Settings dialog box to control replication options for each database.

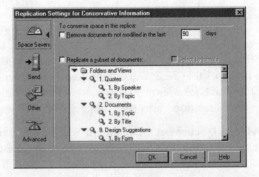

Be aware that if the purge interval for a database is more frequent that the Replication Schedule, then documents that you have deleted will reappear in your copy of the database. This happens because the deletion stubs are removed from your copy of the database before they are sent to the server copy of the database. When the Server copy next replicates with your copy (whether it's local or another server copy), it will re-create each of the deleted documents.

The moral of this story is to ensure that the frequency of replication between replicas of the database is greater than the purge interval for those databases.

> **Tip**
>
> The Do not send deletions made in this replica to other replicas checkbox enables you to delete documents in your database without creating deletion stubs, which means the deletions will not be sent to other replicas. To enable this setting, click the Send icon on the Replication Settings dialog box.

   ◀◀ See "Limiting What Is Sent to the Server," p. 688

Preventing Replication or Save Conflicts. At this point, Server_A and Server_B have identical copies of the Marketing Discussion database. Any other replicas of this database that replicate with Server_A or Server_B will also be synchronized.

If you are familiar with relational databases, by now you are most likely thinking, "But what if you and I edit replicas of the same document in different databases in between scheduled replication?" When this happens—and it inevitably will—a *replication*, or *save conflict*, occurs. Take, for example, a database on Server_A and its replica on Server_B. If you examine Table 22.3 with the knowledge that the two servers last replicated on 10/23/96 at 12:30:01 PM and will next replicate on 10/25/96 at 12:30:00 PM, you can see from the Modified date of the two documents that each was edited in its respective database in between scheduled replications.

Table 22.3   Replication Example 3

Doc #	Doc ID*	Created File	Modified File	Added to File	Server	Deleted
1	C34VB1:98D345	10/23/96 7:22:40 AM	10/24/96 10:37:46 AM	10/23/96 7:22:40 AM	Server_A	
2	C34VB1:98D345	10/23/96 7:22:40 AM	10/24/96 3:24:12 AM	10/23/96 12:30:32 AM	Server_B	

The document IDs in this example have been shortened in order to save space.

By default (and design), the Replicator will not overwrite one user's changes to a replica of a document with the other's changes. Instead, the Replicator will choose a "winner" and make it the *main* or *parent document*. The "loser" will become a *response* or *child document* of the "winner." The document that has been edited and saved most frequently will become the "winner." If both documents have been edited and saved the same number of times, the document that was saved most recently will become the "winner."

> **Note**
>
> Replication or save conflicts can by resolved manually by editing and saving the child docu-
> ment. This will remove the conflict status and elevate the document from a response document
> to a main (parent) document. You can then decide which document has the most correct
> information and delete the others. In addition, replication or save conflicts can be handled
> programmatically. For more information regarding this topic, consult the Lotus Notes Help
> database and Lotus Notes documentation.

How the ACL Affects Replication. Replication is not the all or nothing process it
may appear to be from the prior example. In fact, the replication process is highly
customizable, and the information that's actually replicated will depend on several
factors, such as selective replication settings, database ACLs, and Read Access Lists.

First and foremost, replication is subordinate to the database ACL. For instance, if you
have two servers in your organization, ABC_1 and ABC_2, and ABC_2 has a replica of
a database on ABC_1, the data that replicates between these two servers is wholly
dependent upon the access level each server has been granted to the other's copy of
the database. Table 22.4 briefly demonstrates the effect that various access levels have
on the replication process between servers.

Table 22.4 Database Access Levels

ABC_1 Access ABC_2's Database	ABC_2 Access Level in ABC_1's Database	Effect
Manager	Reader	ABC_1 can send ALL changes (data, design, and ACL) to ABC 2. ABC_1 will accept no changes from ABC_2. Generally speaking, a server should have Manager access to all databases that reside on that server; however, certain security needs may merit lower access levels.
Designer	Author	ABC_1 can send data and design changes to ABC_2. ABC_2 can only send new documents created on ABC_2 and modifications to those documents.
Editor	Editor	ABC_1 can only send new documents and modifications to existing documents. (If the Can Delete Documents option is enabled for Editor access, deletions will also be accepted.) ABC_2 will not accept design or ACL changes from ABC_1. Likewise, ABC_2 can send data changes, but cannot alter the design or ACL of the database ABC_1.

> **Note**
>
> If your changes don't seem to be replicating between replicas of a database, check your Notes Log for messages that indicate that the access level is set in the database in question to disallow replication from the other database. The following is an example of a message you might see:
>
> ```
> Access control is set in DATA\DISCUSS.NSF not to allow
> replication from ABC_1\DATA\DISCUSS.NSF
> ```
>
> This message indicates that server ABC_1 does not have sufficient access rights to replicate with the local database. If this is the case, have your administrator grant you the required access level in the database's ACL.

If you have a local replica of a database, you have Manager access to that database. With Manager access, you not only can create new documents and edit or delete existing documents, you can make changes to the design of the database. However, your access level in the server's copy of the database dictates what changes the server will accept from you. If you make changes to the local copy that you are not authorized to make to the server copy, then the server will overwrite your changes during the next replication.

◄◄ See "Understanding Database Access," p. 335

Limiting Read Access. Another security feature of Notes is the ability to add Read Access Lists to forms, views, folders, and documents. By adding a Read Access List to any of these elements, access is limited exclusively to those users, servers, or groups explicitly named in the list.

What this means in terms of replication is that if a server or user's name is not in the list, that user or server will not have that elements replicated to it. For example, if you work on a local replica of a database and create a document that has a ReaderNames field in it, you must specify the names of all users, servers, and groups who can access this document. If you were to accidentally omit the name of the server where the database is stored, that document would not be replicated to the server and, therefore, would not be accessible to other users. (Normally, if ReaderNames fields are implemented in a form, the database designer will write code to automatically populate the field with the server's name so that the document will replicate with the server.)

◄◄ See "Names Fields," p. 101

> **Note**
>
> Read Access Lists and ReaderNames fields can be very powerful security devices. However, they should not be implemented without a thorough understanding of how replication works and the effect these features have on the replication process. Please see the Lotus Notes Help database and Lotus Notes documentation for more information on ReaderNames fields and Read Access Lists.

Selective Replication. Using the Replicate a subset of documents checkbox in the Replication Settings dialog box enables you to pull only documents that meet criteria you define. This *selective replication* can greatly reduce the amount of data replicated, thereby reducing the amount time and disk space required.

Many people think that selective replication is a security feature because you can limit the documents a workstation or server can replicate. However, as Lotus clearly states in the Notes manuals, this is not a security feature because users with only a rudimentary knowledge of Notes can change the selection formula. If you want to limit the documents that certain users can see, consider using ReaderNames fields in the documents.

▶▶ See "Understanding the Data Types," p. 390
▶▶ See "Selective Replication," p. 715

The Role of Notes Servers

Lotus Notes is a networked application that enables groups of people to collaborate. It consists of two primary components: the Notes server and the Notes workstation. By now, you most likely have worked with the Notes client software extensively and are quite familiar with its functions and features. The Notes server is the glue that holds a Notes installation together because it provides mail routing, replication, authentication, and communication services to users and other servers. Accessing a Notes server requires very little knowledge on the part of the user. (This is by design, because the hard stuff is left to the Notes administrator.) This section explains the role of the Notes server in your Notes installation.

The Notes server is not a file server. A *file server* is a machine that is connected to a network and is running a network operating system (NOS), such as Novell NetWare or Microsoft Windows NTAS, that provides access to shared resources such as applications, printers, disk storage, modems, scanners, and other peripherals.

A *Notes server* on the other hand is application software running on a machine that is connected to a network. Notes servers are built on the client/server model and provide service for Notes users and other Notes servers. Although it is possible to run a Notes server on the same machine that acts as a file server, Lotus recommends that the Notes server software be run on a separate machine.

The Notes server is essential to any Notes installation because it provides the communication mechanism for the workstations. You can think of it as the glue that holds the whole system together. The Notes server provides the following services to Notes clients and other Notes servers:

- Storage and replication of databases
- Directory services
- Mail routing
- Security
- Gateway interface
- Custom server tasks
- Add-ins

The first half of this chapter explored replication; the following sections discuss the other services provided by the server.

Directory Services

If you have read Chapter 5, "Using the Address Books," you are already familiar with the directory services role that the Notes server plays in a Notes installation. All users and servers in a domain (also see Chapter 5 for more information about domains) share a common Public Name & Address Book (N & A Book). The Public N & A Book stores information about all valid Notes users, servers, and groups in the domain and makes this information available to users, servers, and processes.

Mail Routing

As you are probably aware from Chapter 4, "Getting Started with Electronic Mail," and Chapter 6, "Advanced Mail," Notes sports a powerful, integrated, client/server based store and forward mail system built around the cc:Mail interface. The server plays a pivotal role in the mail system for the following reasons:

- It provides a connection point for Notes clients and other servers.
- The *router* is a server task responsible for mail routing and delivery.
- Each mailbox resides on the user's home server.

In most installations, the router runs constantly on each server, continuously checking for new mail messages in the server's MAIL.BOX database. When the router encounters a new mail message, it examines the recipients' addresses to determine whether this server is the home server of any of the recipients. If it is, then a copy of the document will be placed into the mailboxes of the recipients on the server.

If the mailbox of any recipient is on another server or in a different domain, the router task will determine the best route for the mail message and transfer it to MAIL.BOX file on the next server. Once there, the process is repeated until the message has been delivered to all recipients or an error condition is encountered.

Security

From its inception, Lotus Notes was designed as a very secure system that is independent of the platform and operating system. The client/server computing model is, by nature, more secure than file system based setups because access to data is tightly controlled by the server. In addition, Notes utilizes RSA encryption technology, which enables user authentication, certification, encryption, and digital signatures to provide substantial security.

> **Note**
>
> The Rivest, Shamir, and Aldeman (RSA) public key encryption scheme is the leading public key scheme. In this system, each user has two 512-bit keys: one private key, which only the user holds, and one public key, which is made available to other users. Security is then provided by encrypting messages with the recipient's public key, which can only be decrypted with the recipient's private key. This method is extraordinarily secure because it encrypts data in 64-bit blocks. The potential key combinations that would have to be tested to break just one key number is somewhere in the quadrillions.

Notes servers provide essentially four types of security, as follows:

- Authentication
- Access control
- Digital signatures
- Encryption

These features are discussed in the following sections.

Authentication. *Authentication* is a bi-directional verification process that is invoked any time a user and a server or two servers communicate. A good illustration of authentication is the process of logging in to your Notes server.

> **Note**
>
> When the first Notes server in an organization is installed, a special ID known as the *Certifier ID* is created. When a new ID file is created for use in a Notes installation, it must be certified by the Certifier ID. During the certification process, an electronic "stamp" known as a *certificate* is generated based on the private key in the Certifier ID and is placed into each new ID file. The certificate verifies that the public key associated with the new ID file is valid.
>
> For a workstation to communicate with a server, it must have certificates derived from a common or ancestral Certifier ID. For more information on certificates and certification, see the online Help database and the Lotus Notes documentation.

Your server will generate a random number and encrypt it using the public encryption key stored in the Person document (in the Public N & A Book) that corresponds to the user ID in use during the login. Your workstation software will then use the matching private encryption key stored in your user ID to decrypt the number and return it to the server. If your workstation returns the correct number (which can only happen if the matching private encryption key is used), you are authenticated as a valid user on this server. If the correct number is not returned, the server will not grant access. The process is then reversed, and your workstation software attempts to authenticate the server.

Access Control. *Access control* should be a familiar concept by this point. Each database, document, form, view, and folder can employ access control to grant or deny very specific, well-defined user privileges to individual users, servers, and groups. Server access can also be granted or denied to specific users, servers, and groups through the Access server and Not Access server fields in the Server document. For more information on access control and Access Control Lists, see Chapter 9, "Creating New Databases."

Electronic Signatures. *Electronic signatures* are also based on the RSA encryption scheme. They can be used to guarantee that a message is actually from the sender it claims to be from and that the message has not been altered while being transmitted. For more in-depth coverage of this feature, please see Chapter 20, "Security and Encryption."

Encryption. *Encryption* is essentially the scrambling of data by applying an encryption key so that if the data is accessed by unauthorized users, they will not be able to understand it. The data can only be unscrambled with the appropriate key. As mentioned earlier in this section, Notes uses the RSA Public Key encryption scheme. Lotus Notes supports three levels of encryption, as follows:

- First, at the network level, data can be encrypted so that if it is intercepted during transfer, it contains no intelligence without the appropriate key.
- At the message level, mail messages can be encrypted so that only recipients with the appropriate key can decrypt them.
- Finally, Notes supports field level encryption so that information within a document can be encrypted.

Caution

Although encryption is a very powerful security measure, it should be used judiciously and only when absolutely necessary for two reasons. First, encryption and decryption consumes resources and time. The second and more important reason is that all of your encryption keys are stored in your user ID file. If that file became corrupted, got accidentally deleted, or otherwise became unavailable, you would no longer be able to access any of the information that was encrypted using that ID.

There are no "backdoors" to this system; in fact, not even Lotus can help you if you lose your ID. This is especially critical with field and message level encryption. If this is enabled in your system, you should frequently back up your user ID file and keep it protected.

As you can see, Notes provides a security-rich environment that can protect even the most sensitive data from prying eyes. But be aware that many or all of these security features can be circumvented if your user ID or a server ID is compromised. If someone has physical access to an ID file and can crack the password for that ID, then he or she can assume that identity and see and do anything your ID permits.

To prevent unauthorized access, important ID files such as the Certifier ID and server IDs should be physically secured. Further, all passwords should be difficult to guess. (Your wife's name and your son's birthday make poor passwords.) In that regard, long passwords are better than short ones, and a mixture of numeric and text characters in a password makes it even harder to crack. Nonetheless, all passwords should be changed frequently.

Server Programs and Add-in Programs

The Notes server software was designed in a highly modular fashion so that it is easy for the Notes Administrator to configure a server to perform any or all of the tasks shown in Table 22.5. Many of these tasks are automatically loaded on the server by default settings in the NOTES.INI file. Any server program can be loaded or unloaded at any time without shutting down the Notes server. Also, you can create Program documents in the Public N & A Book to launch a server program at a specified time.

To load a server program that is not currently running, at the server console, type the following

```
LOAD <programname> [argument1],[argumentn]
```

where the *<programname>* is the name of the Notes server program to load, and *argument* is the command line parameters this program accepts. Table 22.5 shows the standard Notes server programs.

Table 22.5 Common Server Tasks

Task Name	Program Name To LOAD	Description
Cataloger	CATALOG	Updates the Database Catalog database.
Database Compactor	COMPACT	Compacts all databases on the server, which removes white space and frees disk space.
Database Fixup	FIXUP	Checks databases for corruption, such as truncated documents. Fixes problems when possible.
Designer	DESIGN	Synchronizes the design of any database that has a Design Template with the template.
Indexer	UPDATE	Updates all opened views in a specific database or when other tasks, such as the Replicator, have changes waiting.

Task Name	Program Name To LOAD	Description
Indexer	UPDALL	Updates all changed views and/or full text indexes for all databases on the server. This program accepts several command line parameters.
Login	LOGIN	Listens to enabled ports for requests from users of add-in programs.
Chronos	N/A	Runs background macros and any other time-related tasks. This is always loaded by default; there is no program file to load.
Replicator	REPLICA	Replicates databases with other servers.
Router	ROUTER	Routes mail to other servers.
Statistics	STATLOG	Updates database statistics in the Server's log file.

For more information about Notes server programs, consult the Help database and the Lotus Notes documentation.

If your server is not running the Designer process and you want to load it, then at the server console or by using the Remote Console icon in the Notes Administration dialog box (which can be accessed by choosing File, Tools, Administration), enter the following command:

```
LOAD DESIGN
```

Note

Your ability to interact with the server console and/or load any of these tasks might be limited by your access level.

Notes also enables you to load and run add-in tasks, which are other programs written specifically to run on a Notes server. Your organization, for example, might have a C programmer write an API program to archive Notes databases at 3:00 AM each day. In the next section on gateways, you will see that most of the gateways for Notes are actually Notes add-in tasks. The capacity to create custom programs for the Notes server provides tremendous expansion capabilities.

Gateways

To further expand the capabilities of Lotus Notes and provide easy integration with existing systems, Lotus has developed a wide array of gateways. According to the *LAN Times Encyclopedia of Networking*, a gateway is "a computer system or other device that acts as a translator between two systems that do not use the same communication protocols, data formatting structures, languages, and/or architecture."

Some of the gateways that are currently available for Notes are described in the following sections. As you will see from the large number of gateways, Lotus has made a commitment to connectivity and will continue to provide excellent connectivity with other popular systems.

Incoming/Outgoing Fax Gateway. This is an add-in server task that enables Notes users to send e-mail messages as faxes and receive faxes as e-mail. When faxes are received, the actual fax (which is graphical as opposed to text) is stored as an attachment in the TIFF format. This software comes with the Lotus Image Viewer (LIV) so that the TIFF files can easily be viewed.

Simple Mail Transport Protocol (SMTP) Gateway. The SMTP gateway is an add-in task for OS/2 servers that enables Notes mail users to communicate with Internet mail users. This gateway converts outgoing Notes mail into the Simple Mail Transport Protocol and incoming SMTP mail into the NotesMail format.

Sky-Tel Pager Gateway. The Lotus pager gateway is an OS/2 server add-in task that enables Notes mail messages to be sent to Sky-Tel pagers. This gateway requires a free COM port and modem so that these messages can be sent immediately.

Microsoft Mail Gateway. This gateway requires a dedicated PC and enables your NotesMail users to transparently communicate via e-mail with Microsoft Mail users.

MHS Gateway. The MHS Gateway software is an OS/2 server add-in task that enables NotesMail users to communicate with Novell NetWare messaging services using Novell's Message Handling Server format.

Lotus Connect for X.25 Gateway. This is an OS/2 based add-in task that enables users to connect to an X.25 network.

Lotus Connect for X.400 Gateway. This is an OS/2 based add-in task that enables users to communicate with foreign mail systems using the X.400 protocol.

DEC Message Router. This gateway runs on VAX/VMS and enables NotesMail users to communicate with DEC mail users.

Ca-email+ Gateway. This gateway enables NotesMail users to communicate with Ca-email+ users. It is a CICS based application for IBM host machines.

Dedicating Servers by Task

When planning your Notes network, if you envision multiple servers, consider dedicating each server to a specific task, which can increase performance and greatly simplify the administration of the network. Some suggested dedicated server types to consider are described in the following sections.

Mail Server. Mail servers store users' mail databases and route mail. Some of the benefits of a dedicated mail server are as follows:

■ When the database server is down, users can still access their mail database, and vice-versa.

■ Administration is simplified because all of the mail databases reside on one server, and network traffic is reduced because the vast majority of all messages will not route across the LAN.

■ The amount of mail databases you could reasonably expect to store on one server is dependent upon the number of concurrent users you expect at any given time as well as the server platform you are running.

Database Server. A database server could be used to store only application databases. The following are some of the benefits of setting up a dedicated database server:

■ The administration is easier because databases can be grouped by type, replication, and/or security needs.

■ It's easier for users to find a database when it's only on a limited number of servers.

■ A dedicated server can be "tuned" to achieve optimal performance without considering mail routing, and as the system expands, it's easy to add more database servers.

Dial-Up Server. A dial-up server can be set up to provide a single, secure point of entry into your network for all remote users. Some benefits of a dedicated dial-up server are the following:

■ Security is enhanced because remote users connect with only one server that can provide access to other servers.

■ LAN traffic can be decreased by putting all of the databases that remote users need on the dial-up server.

■ Call tracking and logging is simplified due to the single point of entry.

■ Call costs can be monitored and tuned more easily due to the single entry point.

Passthru Server. A passthru server is a server set up to enable other Notes servers running different LAN protocols to communicate with each other. This, of course, dictates that the passthru server run all of the protocols needed to connect to each network.

After a passthru server has been configured, it can be used as a stepping stone to get to other servers. Users can go through the passthru server to other servers without needing to know all of the routing steps required to make the connection. In addition, dial-up users can call the passthru server and then access other servers on the network from the passthru server.

Some of the benefits of a dedicated passthru server are as follows:

■ Dial-up users can connect to multiple servers with a single phone call.

■ Users on different LANs can communicate with each other through the passthru server.

IV

Advanced Notes Topics

The passthru server feature is new to Notes 4.0. To set up a passthru server, you must create a Passthru Connection document in the Public Name & Address Book. See Chapter 5, "Using the Address Books," for more information on Passthru Connection documents.

Gateway Servers. A dedicated gateway server can reduce the overhead required to run a gateway as an add-in on a production server. For instance, if you wanted to run the Lotus Fax Server software, it may behoove your company to purchase a separate machine to run it on, as this would reduce the overhead on the Notes server and provide faster performance for the Notes server and the Fax gateway.

Hub Server. A hub server is usually set up as the central server that controls replication and mail routing in a hub-and-spoke Notes network. Hub servers are generally not accessed by end users.

Hot-Swap (Backup) Server. A hot-swap server is a server that is fully configured and ready to go in the event that another mission-critical server fails. Users can be redirected to the hot-swap server while the other server is down.

Notes Server Topology Overview

Notes servers can be configured to replicate and route in a variety of ways depending on a number of factors, such as the servers' locations, the number of servers, the frequency with which the servers need to be updated, and the goals of the administrator (to make administration easier or reduce costs).

Based on these factors, there are three common replication topologies: hub-and-spoke, binary tree, and peer-to-peer. The following sections examine the pros and cons of each of these methods.

Hub-and-Spoke Replication

In the hub-and-spoke replication scheme, the hub server initiates all connections, based on scheduled connections (defined in connection documents in the Public N & A Book on the server), and controls replication and mail routing with the spokes (see fig. 22.6). As an example, Table 22.6 displays a subset of four connection documents from the Public N & A Book on the hub.

Table 22.6   An Example of Hub-and-Spoke Connection Documents

From Computer	To Call Computer	Call at Times	Tasks	Use Port
Hub	Spoke A	11:00 PM	Replication, Routing	LAN0
Hub	Spoke B	12:30 AM	Replication, Routing	COM1
Hub	Spoke C	2:00 AM	Replication, Routing	LAN0
Hub	Spoke D	3:30 AM	Replication, Routing	LAN0

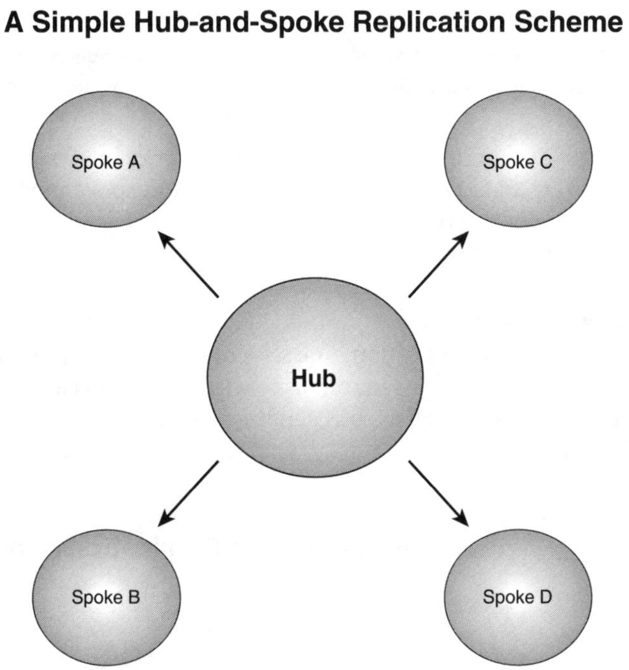

A Simple Hub-and-Spoke Replication Scheme

Fig. 22.6

A graphic representation of a small hub-and-spoke network.

This very simple example assumes that all of the servers are in the same domain, that scheduled calling is enabled in each of these connection documents, and that the hub will only attempt to call each server once a day at the specified time.

Based on the connection documents in Table 22.6, the hub first calls Spoke A for replication and mail routing. Exactly 90 minutes later, the hub calls Spoke B for replication and mail routing. Every 90 minutes, the hub calls the next spoke. When all of the spokes have replicated with the hub, the hub then replicates with other hubs if any exist.

Note

When using the hub-and-spoke replication model, be sure that the connection documents have enough time between scheduled calls to enable the hub to finish replication with one spoke before calling the next. Otherwise, all of the changes may not get transferred correctly.

In this model, all of the necessary connection documents are maintained in the Public N & A Book on the hub server. The following are some of the advantages of this model:

- It enables centralized administration of the Public N & A Book.

- A hub can be used to bridge two LANs running different protocols if the hub supports both protocols.

- Most transactions within the domain are a maximum of two "hops" away, mail routing is peer-to-peer in the same domain, and all mail servers are only one hop away. This helps to drastically reduce the amount of network traffic generated on the LAN.

- The hub-and-spoke model scales well as the installation grows. In other words, as new servers are added to the network, the hub-and-spoke model makes it easy to integrate these new servers into the network because you only need to add a small number of connection documents

Binary Tree Replication

In the binary tree method of replication, one server replicates with two servers at a lower level in the tree, and they in turn replicate with two servers at lower levels until all of the databases have been replicated. Then the servers at the top level replicate with one another. Figure 22.7 shows a diagram of a very simple binary tree replication model.

Fig. 22.7

A Simple Binary Tree Replication Scheme

A graphic representation of a simple binary tree replication model.

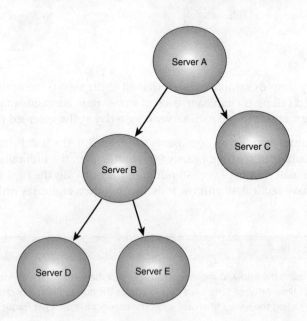

Because it can take a long time for information to move from the top of the tree to the bottom, this method is generally not as efficient as the hub-and-spoke method.

The binary tree method is often used in large international corporations due to the distances between locations and because of political issues.

Peer-to-Peer Replication

The peer-to-peer method of replication dictates that each server in a domain replicate with every other server in the domain (see fig 22.8).

A Simple Peer-to-Peer Replication Scheme

IV

Advanced Notes Topics

Fig. 22.8

The peer-to-peer replication model is too unwieldy for large installations.

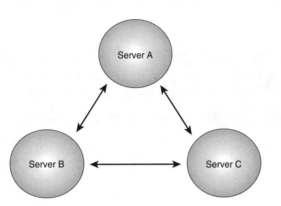

Based on figure 22.8, the Public N & A Book for the domain needs two connection documents for each database because each database must call all other databases. Peer-to-peer replication is highly inefficient and needs additional administration due to the greater number of connection documents required. This method should only be used in installations that have very few servers.

The Admin Agent

The Admin Agent in Notes 4.0 is a great boon to Notes administrators because it helps eliminate the tedious and time-consuming task of cleaning up the Public N & A Book and database ACLs when a user is deleted, recertified, or renamed.

In Notes 3.x, when a user was deleted, recertified, or renamed, the administrator had to try to ferret out all of the groups that the user's or server's name was in, as well as all database ACLs that might have been affected by the change. The Admin Agent will do the searching for you and automatically take the following actions:

- If a user has been deleted, the Admin Agent will remove that user from all Public N & A Book entries and will remove that user from all database ACLs.

- If a user has been recertified or renamed, the Admin Agent will update all documents in the Public N & A Book related to that user and all affected database ACLs so that the user's new information is reflected.

The Notes Administrator Interface

In Notes 3.x, the administrator had to use several different levels of non-intuitive menus to accomplish administrative tasks. The Notes 4.0 workstation software now has a new and vastly improved administrative interface that consolidates most administrative functions in one window. To access this new interface, choose File, Tools, Server Administration, which will launch the Lotus Notes Administration window (see fig. 22.9).

Fig. 22.9

The super-cool new Notes 4.0 System Administrator Interface is easy to use.

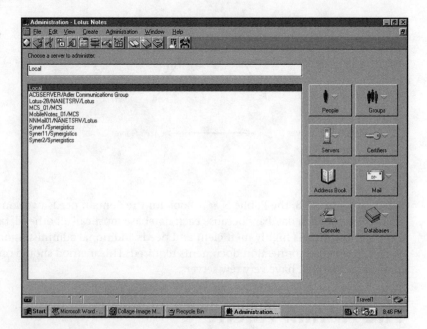

Note

Remember that your ability to use these features will be determined by your server access level.

When the Administration window is displayed, you will see the Choose a server to administer field (and the corresponding list box below it that displays the servers in your Notes named network). You will also see several large buttons that enable you to quickly and easily administer certain key aspects of the server.

Note

Notice that some of the buttons have small down arrows displayed on them. When one of those buttons is pressed, you are presented with a menu that displays additional choices. Buttons that do not have the down arrow launch directly into another screen.

Under the Choose a server to administer field, you will see a list box that should display all of the Notes servers in your Public Name & Address Book. You can select any of the servers from the list, and the name of the server should be displayed in the Choose a server to administer field. When you have selected a server, you can click any of the eight buttons described below to begin administrative tasks.

> **Tip**
>
> If you want to access a server that is not displayed in the list and you know the fully distinguished name, you can simply type the server's name in the Choose a server to administer field.

Each of the eight buttons, People, Groups, Servers, Certifiers, Address Book, Mail, Console and Databases, are covered in detail throughout the remainder of this section.

Changing the List of Users

The People button, when pressed, will present the pop-up menu shown in figure 22.10.

Fig. 22.10

You can use the People button to easily add or maintain Notes users in your installation.

The first option, People View, launches the People view in the Public Name & Address Book.

The second option, Register Person, enables the administrator to register a new Notes user (which creates a new Person document in the Public Name & Address Book and creates a new User ID file).

The last option, Register From File, allows the administrator to automate the registration process by registering new Notes users from a previously created text file.

Changing the Groups

The Groups button presents the pop-up menu shown in figure 22.11.

Fig. 22.11

You can use the Groups button to add or maintain Notes user groups.

The first option, <u>G</u>roups View, launches the Groups view in the Public Name & Address Book.

The second option, <u>C</u>reate Group, enables the administrator to create a new Group document in the Public Name & Address Book.

Changing the Server Settings

The Servers button displays the pop-up menu shown in figure 22.12.

Fig. 22.12

Use the Servers button to configure or analyze your servers.

The first option, <u>S</u>ervers View, launches the Servers view in the Public Name & Address Book.

The second option, <u>C</u>onfigure Servers, opens the Public Name & Address Book and launches the Configuration view.

The third option, Regi<u>s</u>ter Server, enables the administrator to register a new Notes server (which creates a Server document in the Public Name & Address Book and a new Server ID).

The last option, <u>L</u>og Analysis, displays a dialog box that enables the administrator to configure analysis parameters and run an analysis on the Notes Log.

Controlling Certification

The Certifiers button displays the pop-up menu shown in figure 22.13.

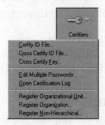

Fig. 22.13

The Certifiers button can be used to perform certification and registra-tion tasks from your workstation.

The Certifiers button pop-up menu has the following options:

- The <u>C</u>ertify ID File option enables the administrator to "stamp" a certificate into an ID file.
- The C<u>r</u>oss Certify ID file option enables the administrator to place a cross-certificate into an ID file.

- Edit Multiple Passwords enables you to perform maintenance on the User ID files that have multiple passwords associated with them.

- The Open Certification Log option opens the Certification Log (CERTLOG.NSF) on the server and launches the view that was last used.

- Register Organizational Unit enables the administrator to certify an organizational unit ID.

- Register Organization enables the administrator to register an Organization ID.

- Register Non-Hierarchical enables the administrator to register a Non-Hierarchical ID.

Accessing Address Book Information

The Address Book button launches the Name and Address Books dialog box that lists all of the Public Name & Address Books on the server along with information, such as each N & A Book's actual filename (see fig. 22.14).

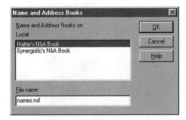

Fig. 22.14

You can generate a list of all the Public N & A Books on the server.

Mail Options

The Mail button displays the pop-up menu shown in figure 22.15.

Fig. 22.15

The Mail button can be used to perform key mail related tasks on the server.

The Open Outgoing Mailbox option opens the server's outgoing mailbox (MAIL.BOX) and launches the view that was opened last

The Send Mail Trace option launches a dialog box that enables you to send a Mail Trace to track a mail message's routing path.

Controlling the Server with the Remote Server Console

The Console button launches the Remote Server Console window shown in figure 22.16.

IV

Advanced Notes Topics

Fig. 22.16

The Remote Server Console window can be used to send commands to a server from your workstation.

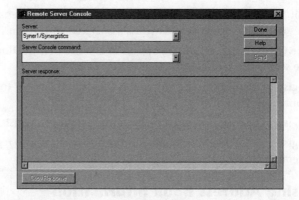

The Remote Server Console window enables the administrator to choose a server and send commands to it remotely. This is a very useful tool because an administrator can troubleshoot and/or "tweak" a server from a remote location.

Database Information

The last button, Databases, displays the pop-up menu shown in figure 22.17.

Fig. 22.17

Database related options are available from the Databases button.

The following options are available from the Databases button menu:

- The first option, Open Log, opens the server's Notes Log database (NOTESLOG.NSF) and launches the view that was last used.

- The Open Catalog option opens the server's Database Catalog (CATALOG.NSF) and launches the view that was last used.

- The Open Statistics option opens the server's Statistics Reporting database (STATSREP.NSF) and launches the last view used.

- The Configure Statistics Reporting option opens the opens Statistics Reporting database (EVENTS4.NSF) and launches the Configuration view.

- The Database Analysis option launches a dialog box that enables the administrator to set various parameters and run a database analysis on a database on the server.

- The Database Compact option launches a dialog box that enables the administrator to choose a database on the server to compact.

- The Database <u>F</u>ull Text option launches a dialog box that enables the administrator to choose a server database to full text index.

- The Database <u>Q</u>uotas option launches a dialog box that enables the administrator to set various parameters that control the size of database on the server.

Notes Server Platforms

Lotus Notes is truly a cross-platform application that is capable of running most popular operating systems. Notes server software is available for Windows 95, Windows NT, OS/2, various flavors of UNIX, and as Novell NetWare servers (NLM). Lotus gives you the flexibility to choose the platform that is the best fit for your organization, depending on the networks and operating systems in use at your company. Notes was originally developed for an OS/2 server, and the OS/2 server software still provides the most functionality and flexibility, although the other server platforms are rapidly catching up.

Supporting Multiple Licenses

Although a Notes installation can quickly provide a high return on investment, a large Notes installation can be costly. Lotus realized that many Notes users did not need to have access to the full Notes workstation functionality, such as the design tools, and therefore could use a subset of the full client to meet their needs at a reduced cost.

Based on the varying need for access to Notes functionality, Lotus responded by developing three types of licenses that provide different degrees of access to Notes features and functionality. The three types of licenses are the following:

- **Full Lotus Notes License**—While being the most costly of the three, it enables each user ID created with this type full access to all of Notes core services. Most users, unless they will be doing database design, will not need the full client.

- **Lotus Notes Desktop License**—This is actually a less costly version of the Full License that has had the database design tools disabled. This license gives users the legal authority to use any Notes database.

- **Lotus Notes Express License**—This supports the least number of features and is the least costly of the three types of licenses. In fact, users who have been given the Express License are legally obliged to use only the five databases that ship with this license.

Notes supports a heterogeneous mixture of different license types within a Notes installation. For instance, you might be using a Notes Desktop License, while your co-worker in the next cube is using an Express License.

To find out what type of license you have been issued, choose File, Tools, User ID. You will then be prompted for your password. After you enter your password and press Enter, you are greeted with the User ID dialog box displayed in figure 22.18.

Fig. 22.18

The License field displays the type of license that you have been granted.

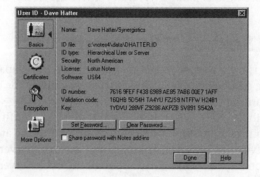

From Here...

This chapter discussed some of the more advanced functionality and features of Notes. After reading this chapter, you might find useful information in the following chapters:

- Chapter 23, "Extending Your Enterprise," explains how you can make Notes even more valuable by connecting to other systems.

- Chapter 25, "Add-On and Third-Party Products," shows you many of the additional products from Lotus and other vendors that can make your Notes installation more effective, such as the Lotus Fax Server and the Lotus Notes Document Imaging module.

Part V

Working with the World of Notes

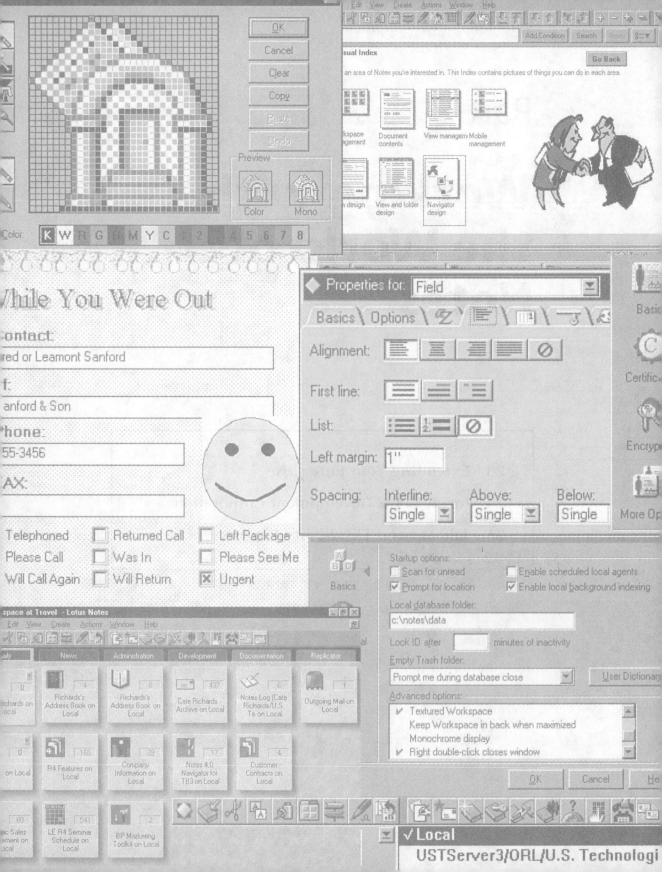

CHAPTER 23

Extending Your Enterprise

In this book, you have been learning how to use Lotus Notes, and about many of the additional products and services that are available to you to tailor Notes to meet your business needs. In this chapter, you learn about some of the possibilities available that let you extend Notes beyond your own enterprise—that is, share applications built for your business needs with other Notes users. This chapter highlights just a few of the companies that provide services and facilities that let you take advantage of Notes as a business tool outside of your company—an extended enterprise.

With extended enterprise applications, Notes users take advantage of the security and versatility of Notes to communicate with vendors, customers, and other business sources. In this chapter, you learn how some of the companies facilitate the communication of those services to you, as well as assist you in communicating with others. You will also see how some companies using Notes have taken advantage of the available resources to communicate outside of their own enterprise.

This chapter provides you information about the following:

- The opportunities available to extend your enterprise through Notes
- AT&T Network Notes
- Pilot groups extending their enterprises through AT&T Network Notes.
- WorldCom and their many services that are available

Why Extend Your Enterprise?

In the past few years, companies have adopted Notes internally to automate many of the business processes. In some companies, Notes applications run virtually all of the internal business communication and workflow tasks. However, as Notes gains in popularity, many users have begun to look for ways to communicate with other Notes users outside of their organizations—thus extending the business communications.

Not all applications are meant for communicating outside of your organization. For example, an application used to track time to a development project is most likely meant for eyes inside of the company—not outside. There are times, however, when you may want to share information with other companies. For example, you may want to share a catalogue of products and services offered by your company with your clients. Notes handles this task easily when you grant other organizations access to the applications on your server. Just a few examples of inter-enterprise applications that may lend themselves to Notes might include the following:

- Client project status
- News services
- Product and marketing information
- Business reference information
- Research reports
- Financial statistics
- Order-entry systems
- New business proposals or applications

> **Note**
>
> Some companies have adopted Lotus Notes as their primary communication platform between their suppliers, distribution, and other vendors. With Notes in place, companies can issue orders directly to their vendors and track the status of the order as it moves through the process; it is ultimately delivered back to their doorstep. This gives the company direct communication with everyone involved in the business and provides a forum for them to ask questions directly. The vendors benefit as well, as their products and services become easier to order—without a lot of paperwork—which is always attractive to companies trying to reduce overhead costs.

Occasionally, the ability to communicate information with outside organizations is desirable, but not practical given your existing hardware infrastructure. If the number of users accessing the information you are sharing via Notes is limited, then your current servers and modems will most likely handle the job. However, if you are planning to communicate to a large number of users, particularly if they are geographically dispersed, you may want to consider using one of the two companies written about in this chapter—AT&T and WorldCom. These companies offer the network infrastructure and security that let you offer applications to a large geographically dispersed audience. Other companies offer similar services, but understanding these two will give you a flavor for how you can extend your Notes enterprise.

AT&T Network Notes

AT&T Network Notes combines Lotus Notes with the sophisticated communications and service capabilities of the AT&T Worldwide Intelligent Network. AT&T Network Notes is the first offering for business customers from AT&T's new public data network platform, and connects a wide range of directory and messaging services, including the Internet.

Lotus and AT&T created AT&T Network Notes in response to feedback from customers and AT&T Business Partners (commonly called co-marketeers) who have been communicating that they need reduced administration and infrastructure costs, and global connectivity. They also need to support remote and mobile users. All of this, of course, is available with Notes running on your server; however, what is often not available is the scalability, reliability, connectivity options, customer service, and support—all of which can be afforded by your company, but at a significant cost. Customers for AT&T Network Notes want to focus on their core business, not on supporting applications that support their business. This is the gap that AT&T Network Notes has focused on filling—managing the services and networks that let you communicate outside of your organization.

What Is AT&T Network Notes?

AT&T Network Notes is a workgroup collaborative service for developing and deploying inter-enterprise applications. Based on Lotus Notes and supporting all current Notes capabilities, AT&T Network Notes enables organizations to communicate and share information with customers, partners, and suppliers over the AT&T Worldwide Intelligent Network. As shown in figure 23.1, AT&T Network Notes provides InterSpan Frame Relay and InterSpan IAS Dial-Up connections that link customers, suppliers, and corporate headquarters together to communicate. This layout is just one of many scenarios that can be put together to facilitate your communication with the outside world.

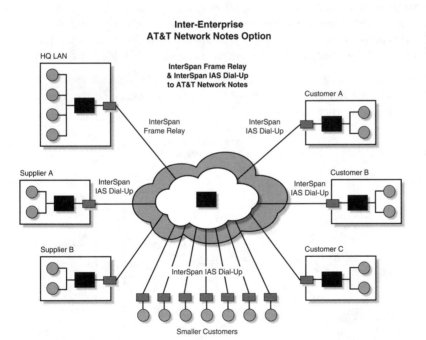

Fig. 23.1

AT&T Network Notes can link you with your coworkers, customers, and suppliers in a variety of ways.

V

The World of Notes

AT&T Network Notes Business Partners, selected by AT&T Network Notes for your area, can assist you in defining your network topology, as well as answer any questions you might have regarding the AT&T Network Notes services. You can contact your Lotus or AT&T representative to get a list of the available Business Partners in your area. Many of these Partners can also help develop the applications you will want to use on the network.

In addition, AT&T provides all the necessary services for installation, system maintenance, and administrative functions for organizations to deploy extended enterprise applications—those that involve more than one company or organization. The service allows companies to communicate beyond their enterprise, regardless of location, via dedicated or dial-up access to AT&T's new public data network.

AT&T Network Notes is not really a "new product." The standard Notes user interfaces, commands, configurations, APIs database formats, security models, network protocols, and replication technology are all present, so existing Notes application developers and users will not need to relearn anything to use the AT&T Network Notes. Typically, AT&T Network Notes applications will be developed for electronic commerce, information and document distributions, and extended workgroup collaboration.

Architectural Overview

From the Notes point of view, each organization involved in an extended enterprise application has its own Notes domain—in other words, a collection of servers and workstations that share a Name & Address Book. Typically, a company using Notes has a single Notes domain. In extended enterprise applications, information is shared among a minimum of two companies or organizations involving at least two Notes domains.

Figure 23.2 illustrates the key elements of the AT&T Network Notes architecture that makes this multi-site communication possible.

Fig. 23.2

The key elements of the AT&T Network Notes architecture make it possible to link with multiple sites.

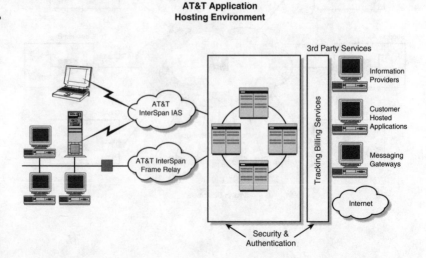

Moving from left to right in the figure, note the following elements: client end-points including workstations and servers are on a LAN, as well as remote (mobile) workstations, all running Notes. These endpoints are then connected to the AT&T applications-hosting environment via a variety of connectivity or network-accessing options. You can have dial-up access via an AT&T service called InterSpan Access Service, or IAS. What this provides is a local phone number which you can use any-where in the States today; and in fact, this connectivity will provide a global number in the near future—where you can dial one number, 950-1ATT. This call is a local call that will connect you right into the AT&T Network Notes server complex—straight into the server hosting your particular application.

You can also elect to set up a dedicated connection via AT&T's InterSpan Frame Relay Service. This gives you T1 speed of 1.5 megabits (which is a lot) to give you much higher bandwidth connection. In the future, there will even be the ability to connect to AT&T Network Notes via wireless communication.

Moving to the right of fig 23.2 is the center of the AT&T Network Notes facility—the hub of the operation. The main application and files that reside here are managed on-site by AT&T personnel. Each AT&T Network Notes customer has a dedicated server (or servers) inside the central facility reserved for communications between the cus-tomer and AT&T. To facilitate communications, each customer is provided with ap-propriate X.25 access scripts, accounts, and passwords.

Note

X.25 refers to a special communications protocol that enables multiple sessions on one line and is available on many systems and network.

The AT&T facility also manages a collection of services for administration, billing, and tracking that are implemented outside the Notes core to provide additional services to AT&T Network Notes and, ultimately, customer applications. One of the most visible applications is the Request database, which automates administrative requests. A des-ignated individual at the customer site can create work requests such as "Create User" or "Modify Group" in this database. All requests are processed automatically and changes are made by AT&T Network Notes.

Finally, there are gateways and bridges to other information providers. These include messaging gateways, such as AT&T EasyLink Services electronic mail (e-mail), which allows you to route mail to other, non-Notes mail recipients like cc:Mail, an outgoing fax, and Internet e-mail.

Application Development with AT&T Network Notes

To successfully develop AT&T Network Notes applications, developers must under-stand the most essential aspect of the AT&T Network Notes architecture—that it is built up from multiple distinct domains. This is a fundamental characteristic of ex-tended enterprise applications, as they involve multiple separate companies.

V

The World of Notes

It is also a result of the way AT&T Network Notes employs domains, as follows:

- Each customer company has its own Notes domain for the servers running at its premises. Customers designate an internal Customer Point of Contact (CPOC) to coordinate their AT&T Network Notes application(s).

- Each customer is then given a second "customer domain" at the AT&T Network Notes facility. The customer does not have full direct access to that domain but can modify it using the Request database built into the system to automatically perform routine administrative tasks upon request. For example, customers have only Reader access to the Name & Address Book and Notes Log database. In order to add or subtract names, or change addresses, they must use the Request database.

- AT&T defines a centralized "intercorporate" domain, which is a safe middle ground through which information flows from every organization involved.

In order to successfully design and implement an application for this multi-domain environment, it is important to test the application in an environment that duplicates the Name & Address Book environment of the deployed application. Customers can do this easily by setting up several Notes servers in separate test domains. AT&T also plans to create a test lab that more fully duplicates its data centers.

Security Considerations

Data security has always been a key feature of Notes, and it takes on a new dimension in extended enterprise applications. In these applications, the concern shifts from one of internal security to one of external security—as many people outside the customer company will be included in the information exchange. Rather than be certain that information sent via Notes is seen only by those people inside a company who really need to see it, companies need to be certain that nobody outside the company will see any proprietary information.

The additional security demanded by the extended enterprise applications requires that customer companies use hierarchical naming conventions. However, there are still sites using a flat naming convention—such as existing Notes users who want to start using AT&T Network Notes. These companies can use one of their existing servers as a bridge between the flat and hierarchical environments by certifying it hierarchically. That way AT&T Network Notes will see a hierarchical server, and the rest of the enterprise can transition to a hierarchical naming convention at its own pace.

Notes Encryption and Digital Signatures are important elements of the overall security model, which is based on "public encryption keys." In Notes, the mechanism used to make keys public is the Name & Address Book. For example, when encrypting a document, Notes knows to look up the public key of the intended recipient in the Name & Address Book.

As previously mentioned, the multiple domains that typically come into play in extended enterprise applications means that there are multiple Name & Address Books for a given application. Since the sender and receiver (or creator and reader) of a message often will not be using the same Name & Address Book, they will not automatically have access to each other's public keys. This will impact their ability to sign and encrypt messages and documents. There are several ways of dealing with this. Users can either use the "encryption key" feature in Notes, exchange safe copies of their user IDs, or use cross-certificates as needed.

As mentioned in the system architecture section, customers have certain limitations to full access to their AT&T servers. This, too, is a security feature, intended to protect the integrity of the information located on the AT&T Server. In particular, changes to the Notes Name & Address Book are restricted and can only be made through the Request database. If a customer has to make a change in a group record in the Name & Address Book, for example, the designated customer contact posts a change request in the Request database. AT&T Network Notes automatically processes all these requests, typically within a few hours.

Another important application design strategy is the use of selective replication to control the flow of information among companies. Replication is the Notes capability that allows a database to be put on more than one server and ensures that the servers remain in sync. As a database replicates within one company, then out to AT&T and on to another company's system, it is important to take steps to make sure that only the information meant to travel between the two organizations does so. Careful use of selective replication formulas, as well as Reader and Author lists, can accomplish this goal.

Communications Considerations

The primary communications consideration for customers in an AT&T Network Notes application is the speed of information transfer. Experience to date has been that typical users connect at dial up speeds of up to 14.4 Kbps (14,400 baud rate). In order to avoid slowing down the system, it is important to minimize communications through careful use of selective replication, maximum use of reader and author Name fields, and, whenever possible, sending several small documents rather than a few large ones.

Provisioning Considerations

There are several steps required to build and install an AT&T Network Notes application, from installing and configuring hardware and software to signing contracts and certifying users. AT&T refers to this process as *provisioning*. In the ongoing trials, AT&T and Lotus have identified some common issues and occasional challenges faced by early users of the service. The following are some important points for customers to consider when building extended enterprise applications for the AT&T Network Notes:

- **Site preparation**—Is the endpoint ready to install the system? Do they have the right hardware, networking software, person capable of serving as the CPOC?

- **Motivation**—Are the prospective users truly motivated to get the new application up and running? Have they asked for it? Do they want it? Will they use it?

- **Customer Notes experience**—Have the customers used Notes? Are they ready to learn it?

- **Integration**—Will the extended enterprise application fit into the customer's existing systems?

- **Flat vs. hierarchical**—Is the site already hierarchical? If not, can it be converted, or can a gateway be put in place?

What AT&T Provides

As described earlier, AT&T maintains the Request database which, at the customer's request, provides automation for many routine administrative tasks such as cross-certification, managing groups, and replicating databases. Changes are logged and can be reviewed to diagnose problems.

AT&T also provides diagnosis of infrastructure problems that includes step-by-step analyses of how far an operation proceeded before it stalled. For example, AT&T can determine whether the call completed, whether the server connected, whether it replicated, or whether there is an error in the Access Control List—all pieces of information that can help identify and resolve problems. Customers can contract for extended service access to support people at AT&T.

All AT&T Servers are monitored for performance and load. On-site experts perform regularly scheduled system backups and troubleshoot for hardware and software problems to ensure a consistently high level of service. AT&T also maintains redundant data centers in different geographical locations to provide disaster recovery, and has staff dedicated to operate each center.

Lotus and the Business Partners

In addition to AT&T's services, AT&T Network Notes brings a lot of other players to the table. Lotus, for example, provides the Notes software (of course). Lotus is also involved in the cataloguing and development of a Business Partner community for Lotus Notes as well as AT&T Network Notes. A select group of Lotus Business Partners have been selected by AT&T and Lotus to work with companies that want to utilize AT&T Network Notes. The Business Partners are available to you for a variety of different things, including the design and implementation of your applications. Some Partners may be information providers, having applications that you can access; while others are available to do training, assist in deployment of your applications, and help maintain support as well. You can contact AT&T directly to find out what AT&T and Lotus Business Partners are available to assist you, or you can ask your current Business Partner to help get you set up to work with AT&T.

The AT&T Network Notes Market Trial

According to the basic extended enterprise model used by Lotus and AT&T, corporate organizations can be segmented into five key enterprise and inter-enterprise areas:

- Functional operations
- Suppliers
- Business, service, and channel partners
- Regulatory bodies
- End customers

AT&T Network Notes is designed to allow corporations to extend beyond their corporate enterprise.

This section, provided by Lotus in an AT&T Network Notes Market Trial brief, briefly describes a few of the current AT&T Network Notes trial customers, and the way in which their enterprise is extended by deploying an important business application electronically. The customers and applications chosen in the trial address three key business solution areas:

- Electronic commerce
- Information/document distribution
- Extended workgroup collaboration

Through these applications, the extended enterprise can include Business Partners, resellers, distributors, suppliers, distant branch offices, clients, and mobile workers. AT&T Network Notes will also provide these businesses the ability to license these applications to other businesses with similar application needs.

As AT&T Network Notes is a new platform to enhance their customer's use of Notes, the best way to begin gaining insight into "what it is," is to look at three of the participants included in the AT&T Network Notes Market Trial Study. The AT&T Network Notes trial includes the following customers, and their applications, for the first two application categories mentioned previously:

- **Egghead Software** (electronic commerce application solution)—Egghead is testing the Electronic Product Catalogue and Ordering System, an electronic ordering status and reporting system for customers and vendors. This application automates the sales process to improve information flow and aid in generating new business—providing a competitive edge to customers using the application.

   Egghead provides a custom AT&T Network Notes-based supplier catalogue for each Egghead customer. The customer can then, within the same application, order the product they want. This enables Egghead customers—regardless of size of company, level of computer sophistication, or geographic location—to search a customized catalogue database to locate product information. These catalogues are customized by product name or category, operating systems, platforms, and price.

Customers using the system select the items to be purchased, state the quantity to be ordered, and provide the relevant shipping instructions. The order is then transacted electronically, and an acknowledgment and/or order is sent by Egghead back to the customer via AT&T Network Notes.

With this application, and the connectivity provided by AT&T Network Notes, customers can receive order status reports that track the progress of an order from the initial receipt through final delivery. Corporate customers and large volume buyers can also obtain customized summary reports of purchases. These reports are itemized by various measurement criteria such as time periods, order numbers, product type, and so forth, providing usage and budget information for customer purchase decisions.

This application uses Notes ViP 1.0 user interface, Notes 3.1.5, and Notes ViP Runtime with Notes Express as the client software.

■ **Compaq Computer Corp.** (information/document distribution application solution)—InfoPaq, a Sales and Marketing document information system for partners, dealers, and other sales channels is being trialed on the new AT&T Notes Network. Compaq has built this application to extend/expand customer bases and improve information flow.

InfoPaq provides an open information distribution platform that lets all users access current product information, marketing collateral, technical information, and many other types of data and support on Compaq's products and marketing programs. This application lets Compaq deliver, replicate, and update documents covering a wide range of marketing programs, service offerings, product specifications, and updates to Compaq's partners, dealers, VARs, and corporate accounts.

Regardless of location, Compaq's marketing partners take advantage of an open, secure, reliable, networked information platform that provides a number of services:

- Enhanced document management for easy navigation and access.
- "Tornado Watch" automatically alerts users to high-priority, newsworthy items and new information.
- Support databases providing views in categories such as products and system specs.
- Integrated feedback tool allowing efficient and interactive, two-way communications between Compaq and the reseller.
- Online document delivery of only the documents that are needed, saving time and disk space.
- Multiple formats including Lotus Notes, Common Ground, and source file, where users can choose how documents are delivered.
- Online catalog and help.
- Benefit of information access—even when disconnected.
- Common Ground viewing technology—allowing original documents to be viewed and printed with graphics and formats intact.

InfoPaq will reside on servers at the AT&T server complex. End users or AT&T Network Notes Access Points dial in to the server via AT&T InterSpan Information Access Service. Documents are downloaded from the server to the AT&T Network Notes Access Points for navigation and viewing. A replication setup utility running on Compaq-based Notes servers prepares documents for replication to the AT&T server complex and the AT&T Network Notes Access Points. Once documents are downloaded, the users can view and work with the information offline.

- **Individual Inc.** (information/document database application solution)—First! For Notes provides customized news/information distribution that is cost effective. For additional information on First!, refer to Chapter 25, "Add-On and Third-Party Products."

Each of these companies has worked with Lotus and AT&T to provide applications that will significantly test the new AT&T Network Notes network infrastructure. The network is being built in phases, so that detailed network infrastructure and support for the platform can be put in place and fully tested in real-world situations before general availability. An insight into the future development of the AT&T network, according to John O'Laughlin of Lotus Development Corporation, includes the following:

- **World-class reliability**—The applications based on AT&T Network Notes will be mission-critical ones, requiring the highest degree of reliability possible.

- **Advanced replication capabilities**—Customers can connect and download selected data, allowing them to work offline in a cost-effective manner. Replication also provides sophisticated data sharing between the AT&T Network Notes servers, local servers, and client endpoints.

- **Confidence-building security**—Confidential corporate information, electronic financial transactions and other sensitive material will be moved, exchanged, and replicated on a continuous basis, using the security already present in Lotus Notes, coupled with a very high security level within the AT&T Network Notes system.

- **Flexible network scalability**—AT&T Network Notes is intended to serve hundreds of thousands of users with a wide variety of applications. The infrastructure being designed and tested is built to ensure that it can be quickly expanded to serve all users efficiently, reliably, and cost effectively.

- **Robust development tools**—The application development tools being incorporated into the AT&T Network Notes system will be accessible and easy-to-use, allowing the rapid creation and use of new applications provided by customers like those participating in the market trial.

- **Rich object store and forward**—The object store capability of AT&T Network Notes will support the transmission of rich text, attachments, sound, video, and other types of multimedia files.

V

The World of Notes

■ **Complete customer care**—During the market trial, AT&T Network Notes is developing, testing, and deploying various customer care services—such as cost tracking/billing and technical assistance. These will form the foundation for additional customer care services like extensive application developer support programs that may offer testing support, training, documentation, and application certification.

AT&T Network Notes will initially be offered in North America, Europe, Australia, and Singapore. Network Notes is currently being used by six large companies in beta tests, but is estimated to be released using a controlled introduction to as many as 300 large companies in the second half of 1995, before a mass roll-out. It is also estimated that dial-up access for the network will be installed in more than 200 cities this year, as it is predicted that as many as 80 percent of the Network Notes customers will be remote users.

The Market Trial provides just a brief insight into the new AT&T Network Notes. Notes users around the world are expected to hear much more on this new Lotus Notes service as 1995 and 1996 progresses.

WorldCom

WorldCom is international network for Lotus Notes and cc:Mail subscribers. Subscribers can communicate with each other, and the world. They can also access public databases and subscription publications. Companies can exchange messages, send files, and replicate databases with ease. This service is ideal for large companies who want to extend what their networks can provide. It is also great for small companies and individual users who do not have access to their own Notes network and servers, and need a company to provide that capability. It's like having your own dial-up Notes network—without having to manage it.

Discussion groups between Notes experts are just one of the benefits of using the WorldCom service. You will read about several of the services provided through WorldCom in the this section.

When you subscribe to WorldCom—using the WorldCom Setup database shown in figure 23.3—one of the databases provided is the WorldCom Help and Services database, which provides you an up-to-date guide on using the services provided, and a detail on those services (see fig. 23.4).

Note

The WorldCom Help and Services database, as well as the WorldCom Setup database, are available on the enclosed CD-ROM. You can review, in detail, a further listing of the services WorldCom provides, as well as sign up as a subscriber if you want to. You should also take a moment to review the screencams provided on the CD-ROM to see examples of many of the databases and services provided.

Fig. 23.3

You can easily sign up for WorldCom services using the WorldCom Setup database included on the enclosed CD-ROM.

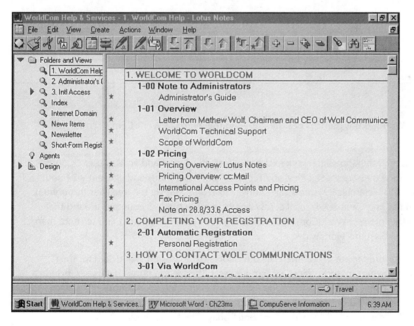

Fig. 23.4

WorldCom provides a Help and Services database to assist you in using their services.

One of the first documents you will see in the database is a letter from Mathew Wolf, Chairman and CEO of Wolf Communications Company welcoming you to WorldCom, as shown in figure 23.5. This letter provides direct doclinks to electronic templates enabling you to send comments directly to the Chief Systems Engineer,

Vice President of Marketing, or Mathew Wolf, himself. Messages and requests for information are responded to—often quite quickly! This is a great service tool for individuals as well as companies who need technical information, want to see a new service, or have feedback about the quality of services given.

Fig. 23.5

Mathew Wolf, President and CEO of WorldCom, takes a personal interest in welcoming newcomers to WorldCom and in receiving feedback directly from WorldCom's customers.

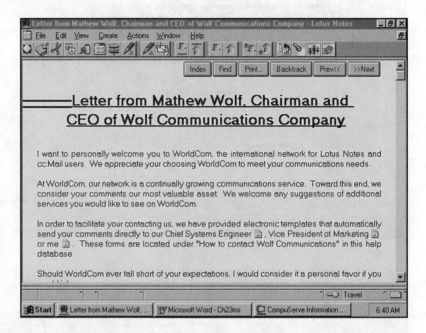

> **Note**
>
> The scope of WorldCom is perhaps best described in the words of WorldCom's Scope documentation:
>
> "WorldCom is an international network exclusively for Lotus Notes and cc:Mail users. Companies can exchange messages, send files, and replicate databases easily and efficiently 24 hours a day. Both flat and hierarchical systems can connect to WorldCom via toll-free lines throughout the United States and Canada, via local access points in more than 93 countries around the world, or via the Internet. WorldCom also provides gateways to the Internet and to more than 100 public e-mail systems worldwide.
>
> Companies can store private or commercial Lotus Notes databases on WorldCom for their clients, trading partners, branch offices, or remote users. WorldCom public databases include a Lotus Notes forum and the LNotes-L mailing list from the Internet. WorldCom's FTP service allows automatic retrieval of large documents and programs from Internet sites around the world. News services include AP Online, Carthage Today, The Notes Report Online, First! by Individual, The Burton Group Information Service, Track-IT, and the UseNet News Groups from Internet."

The following are a few of the databases and services available with WorldCom:

- **WorldCom Help and Services**—This database serves as the initial reference for all of WorldCom's services. It contains separate views for end users and administrators, as well as the international access point list and monthly newsletter, WorldNews. The newsletter includes the principle network developments for that month, Notes administration tips, and client profiles, in addition to monthly guest columns from Notes experts.

  The database also allows clients to look up and request any of the many news services, Internet services, and public discussion forums available on the network.

- **WorldCom Company Directory**—This database is designed to simplify electronic communication between WorldCom clients by listing many of the companies currently connected to WorldCom. This allows you to quickly determine who is out there, and to use the company name when addressing messages to the company to ensure you list the appropriate company domain. Much like a telephone book, listing in this database is optional.

- **WorldCom Master Directory**—This database provides a similar service as the WorldCom Company Directory, but instead provides a directory of all publicly registered WorldCom users. It allows you to send mail to anyone listed in the database—even if you don't know their e-mail address. Duplicate names are differentiated through the use of the users domain name and path to ensure proper routing of messages. (This database is, on a relative scale, less important than the others.)

- **Product and Service Catalog**—This database provides an electronic version of the yellow pages, allowing you to post information about your company and the products and services it offers. It also provides a fast way to provide solutions to other Notes users who need help.

- **Job Openings**—This database provides a focal point for job openings. Individual profiles list the skills desired for filling the position, and you can read about existing openings, or post job descriptions to the database. You can post any job opening—but those with technical abilities definitely tend to dominate. WorldCom also offers a parallel resume database if you are searching for a job.

- **Lotus Notes Discussion**—This database is a forum for the discussion of Notes technical and related issues. You are encouraged to share your expertise in the administration of Notes by posting suggestions and solutions in the database. You may ask any question, or post any problem that you would like other experts to advise you on. This database is a tremendous resource because not only do Business Partners and Lotus employees read the forum, but many Notes administrators of Fortune 500 companies do as well. If you encounter a Notes problem, odds are they already have a solution to save you time.

- **Issues of the Day**—Much like many Internet discussions groups, this database lets WorldCom subscribers share their thoughts and opinions about a variety of topics ranging from the most recent political developments to the "underpinnings of the modern nation-state." As WorldCom's description aptly states: "Discussions are often heated, highly divisive, extremely enlightening, and very funny."

- **Health Care User Group Discussion**—This database is a forum for communication between Notes users in the health care industry, and is intended to provide a venue for the exchange of ideas and information on health care, information services, and related topics. Frequent news items about health care legislation, developments in the health care industry, and Notes implementation at health care sites is also included.

- **Lotus Notes Files**—This database houses large file attachments. Documents in the database hold bitmaps, product demos, and other larger files that may have been referenced in other databases. It is a wealth of information and sample ideas for the Notes developer.

- **AP Online**—This database is a news service compiled and edited from the national and international wires of the Associated Press. Stories are focused and categorized for easier selection. The topics include National/International news, Financial Market highlights, Entertainment, News Analysis, Politics, Weather, Business, Washington, Wall Street, and Sports & Scores. There is no subscription charge for this database.

- **The Burton Group Information Services**—This database is composed of both the Burton Group Report, and the Burton Group Analysis, providing objective analysis of networking technology, market trends, vendor strategies, and networking products. This Burton Group Report provides in-depth research reports on strategic PC networking technologies in which issues appear on a monthly basis. The Burton Group News Analysis provides timely information on key events and announcements in the PC networking industry.

- **TaxBase**—TaxBase is a series of five databases that provide a complete resource on federal and state taxation and related issues. The service reviews a wide array of news and governmental sources (like the Wall Street Journal), as well as Tax Analysts' own writers covering and analysis of the most important news.

- **Commerce Business Daily**—Issued by the U.S. Department of Commerce, this database provides a daily publication of all U.S. Government Requests for Proposals (RFPs) and Award Announcements. Users can find specific project types using Notes full text search capabilities. This database will also allow users to record phone calls, meetings, and other correspondences that take place during the process of soliciting a contract. Finally, the database has a built-in tracking feature that lets users follow a specific RFP through the process.

- **PubWatch**—The LEXIS-NEXIS PubWatch is an electronic way to review many high profile publications quickly. PubWatch encompasses many of the most popular publications in the world, including Industry Week, Fortune, US News and World Report, Time, Information Week, COMPUTERWORLD, American Demographics, Marketing Research, Corporate Legal Times, and more.

- **Carthage Today**—This is a customized news service for Lotus Notes. Scanning more than 10,000 articles per day, from sources including U.S. newspapers, trade magazines, and international news wires including UPI, TASS, and Knight-Ridder, Carthage Today delivers complete global information. Carthage also works with premium information providers such as CMP, Phillips Business, and Dow Jones.

NetFusion, WorldCom's Internet Services

WorldCom has long been a pioneer in integrating the Internet with Lotus Notes. WorldCom subscribers can exchange e-mail with the Internet, read UseNet newsgroups, retrieve files from FTP sites, participate in public mailing lists, and even place their own information on the Internet. With NetFusion, your company can establish an Internet presence as if they had their own dedicated connection to the Internet.

WorldCom's NetFusion is a suite of services designed to give your company a complete Internet presence in the most cost-effective and trouble-free manner possible. Now, instead of maintaining an expensive server, designing multiple documents, and spending thousands of dollars on consultants, your company can create a single Notes database and immediately become a visible and active member of the Internet community.

World Wide Web Publishing. The World Wide Web is the fastest growing means of information distribution in the world today. Using the Web is similar to FTP, in that you can use a local browser to retrieve documents and files from any server on the Internet. However, Web pages are multimedia hypertext links (just like a Notes doclink) to other Web pages anywhere on the Internet. You can jump from document to document with a simple click of your mouse button. Among the hundreds of thousands of Web pages, there are museum exhibits, a tour of the White House, a database of all toll-free 800 numbers, computer spare parts catalogs, and current stock quotes.

Through the World Wide Web component of NetFusion, you can publish any Notes database to the Web. WorldCom converts your databases to Web documents, and your information is immediately available to anyone on the Internet at your very own Web site. When you create your database using the NetFusion Web template, your Web documents will look as good as those created by a trained programmer writing in the complicated HTML language. Your Web pages can even include impressive bitmap graphics and other graphic design features. If your Web page requires an update, it's as simple as replicating your changes to a Notes database. Your information stays current, accessible, and uniform.

WorldCom charges an initial $2,000 setup fee, a $200 monthly maintenance fee for the first 25 MB of data, and $100 for every additional 25 MB of data.

UseNet News Groups. The UseNet newsgroups are interactive forums on the Internet where people discuss a variety of subjects. WorldCom imports these groups into Notes databases, allowing subscribers to receive their own copy of the database by telling WorldCom exactly which databases they want to receive. Users can read and respond to others messages, as well as create their own discussion threads.

Mailing lists are a second type of Internet discussion forum. Mailing lists cover every topic from technical to obscure, from Lotus Notes to Ayn Rand philosophy. To simplify the request process, WorldCom has a catalog of more than 5,900 Internet mailing lists. Each entry contains a list description, as well as a button that allows you to request the mailing list automatically.

Using WorldCom's FTP Server. FTP (file transfer protocol) is the Internet tool that allows users to retrieve very large documents and programs. Users can retrieve both files and directory listings from any Internet site by sending a Notes mail message to **FTPMail @WorldCom**. WorldCom provides a database directory of the Compaq Softpaq and Microsoft FTP sites that allow you to request files and fixes at the touch of a button.

SEC Database. WorldCom provides a listing of 20,000 companies that file documents electronically with the U.S. Securities and Exchange Commission (SEC). You can request anything from annual reports to tax forms merely by pressing buttons. The database is updated by the Edgar Internet site, which is run by the SEC.

There are many more services provided by WorldCom that access the First! database (ideal for smaller companies that want the service, but do not have enough users to make direct subscription viable).

WorldCom pricing is dependent upon the services selected and number of users accessing those services. Pricing this way allows smaller companies and individual users a more affordable method of communicating with the world than some of the more expensive, fixed rate services. For more information on WorldCom, contact them at 1-800-774-2220 or 713-650-6522. E-mail addresses include **info@worldcom.com** or **Info @WorldCom @Notes Net**.

From Here...

These examples of companies that provide services to extend your enterprise beyond its current boundaries has hopefully sparked some creative application development ideas in your mind. There are additional companies providing similar services that you can investigate by contacting your local Lotus representative and Business Partners, or by reviewing the Lotus Notes Guide available through your Lotus representative. Understanding the services will hopefully provide some insight into the rapidly expanding world of Lotus Notes.

For an understanding of the type of assistance you can receive when deploying Lotus Notes and developing applications, refer to the following chapters:

- Chapter 24, "Inside Lotus Development Corporation," talks about the services provided by Lotus in support of your use of Notes.
- Chapter 25, "Add-On and Third-Party Products," provides further descriptions of Lotus products designed to communicate with the Internet, as well as descriptions of other products and services available to Notes users.

Inside Lotus Development Corporation

In other chapters, you have learned a great deal about the capabilities of Lotus Notes—including references to other Companion Products designed to enhance your use of Lotus Notes. In this chapter, you will get a brief overview of some of the services and programs Lotus Development maintains in its support of Lotus Notes and the Notes Companion Products.

As more and more companies join the queue to provide Notes products and services, you may see and hear terms like "Lotus Business Partner" and "Lotus Premium Partner." This section will give you an insight into what these programs mean.

> **Tip**
>
> This chapter can only provide you a "peek" into what is available for Notes users—there is so much more available than what can be listed here. A good place for you to start getting information about the products and services available to you is *The Lotus Notes Guide*, which comes out periodically. Call Lotus at 800-343-5414 for additional information on how to get this guide.

The chapter explores the following topics:

- Where to turn to get assistance when you need it
- Training and certification available for Lotus Notes
- Lotus Business Partner programs

Lotus Notes Support

Lotus' philosophy is to not just supply software, but to solve its clients' problems. Its support services are designed to offer consistent, comprehensive support plans, based on the level of support your company needs. Lotus provides support around the world in a consistent manner by drawing from a worldwide repository of Notes knowledge. Their support is available 24 hours a day, seven days a week, and includes customized services to let you fine-tune your systems.

Lotus also supports a wide range of online technical knowledge support offerings, so you can look up answers for yourself if you want to—which often gives you a much faster response time to solving your problems.

There are a wide variety of support plans, designed to meet various organizational needs—whether your company is large or small, or if you are a new or existing client. Lotus uses a strict worldwide escalation process, which means that your urgent priorities are tackled by the right specialists—regardless of your location. When necessary, they call upon their alliances with other software and hardware manufacturers to help answer your Lotus problems.

The following section briefly describes many of the support services Lotus offers to help your company solve your problems.

Automated Support Services

Lotus provides many ways to get support so that you can get the answers you need 24 hours a day, seven days a week. Complimentary support is provided through the Lotus Automated Support Center to anyone with a touchtone phone or fax machine. You choose one of the following methods:

- Lotus Fax Support.
- World Wide Web.
- Dial-in bulletin boards.
- CompuServe (funded by Lotus, but not officially supported by them. This option typically puts you in touch with several knowledgeable volunteer consultants).

You can dial into any of the services to receive in-depth technical information, which lets you resolve problems quickly without having to wait for a Lotus representative to call you back. These services are fairly comprehensive; if Lotus is aware of the problem, chances are it is defined in one of the references you have available to you through these services. You often can save time in resolving Notes problems by checking the automated services first to see if the problem and resolution are already documented.

Fax on Demand. Through the Lotus Fax service, users have access to thousands of documents on Lotus products that enable them to access technical information (for example, technical references on setting particular platform setup requirements, nuances, and such) and application development tips (like how to build macros, advanced queries, and so on), and troubleshoot potential problems (such as why your new modem is not responding when you try to dial into Notes). Information on Notes education and certification is also available through this service. Users can choose to have the documents faxed to them, or request a catalog of available documents (which will also be faxed). Each catalog contains all of the document titles, brief abstracts, and document order numbers.

> **Note**
>
> The Fax Back Support catalog, as well as some of the support and information documents, can be quite long and can tie up your fax machine for quite some time. You may want to use this service during times in which your fax machine is normally idle!

To order by fax, call 800-346-3508 in the United States, or 800-565-5331 in Canada for 24-hour Fax Back Support.

Bulletin Board Services. Anyone with a modem can access technical information and download sample Lotus Notes applications and modem command files from Lotus directly. Each database is in its own separate zipped file, along with a text file that describes the database. All of the information you received from Fax Back Support is also found on the bulletin board services.

To access the bulletin board services:

- Dial 617-693-7000 in the United States
- Dial 416-364-4941 in Canada

CompuServe. The Lotus forums on CompuServe provide answers to technical questions, allow the exchange of ideas with thousands of other users, and post a wide array of third-party product demos, shareware, and white papers. Users can communicate online with each other on electronic message boards—often receiving in-depth assistance from Lotus consultants and users who volunteer their time. Users can also browse the product libraries or download product information, technical bulletins, product updates, demonstration programs, and application templates.

> **Note**
>
> A few of the application demos located on the CD-ROM accompanying this book have been provided by some of the CompuServe forum members to help provide you with examples of how you can apply Lotus Notes to meet your business needs.

Lotus provides this forum, and occasionally scans through the discussions forum, but does not actively support it—so don't rely on resolving a critical problem solely through this forum. You will get valuable information, like tips on application development, help from other Notes users in resolving server or workstation problems, assistance in working with other Lotus and third-party applications developed to run with Notes, and so on. However, you may have to wait and repost the issue as the members of the forum may not check daily or have the answer readily at hand for some of your issues. If you have a CompuServe account, pop in and check it out—the atmosphere is quite friendly! You can access this forum by typing **GO LOTUSC**.

Go Notes—The CompuServe Lotus Notes Information Service

The CompuServe Lotus Notes Information Service provides global electronic mail connectivity for Lotus Notes users. Supported by CompuServe's communications network, this service lets Notes users communicate and share information with others in over 100 countries—typically through a local phone call. To sign up for this service, simply type **GO NOTES**. The sign-up menu will appear to walk you through the process of cross-certifying your company's mail server with CompuServe so that you can "talk" to each other. (Users that don't have a mail database located on a server can "rent" a private mail database from CompuServe for an extra fee.)

Workgroups in-house, staff on the road, customers, suppliers, and anyone else that joins the service are seamlessly interconnected to one another through the CompuServe Lotus Notes Information Service. This service will let you potentially reach over a million people through other registered Lotus Notes servers, mail hubs, and e-mail gateways, including cc:Mail, CompuServe Mail, MHS Mail, X.400, Internet, MCI Mail, SprintMail, AT&T Mail, Deutsche Bundespost, Infonet, and Advantis.

Pricing for this service is reasonable—between $20–$25 an hour—but there is a $10 a month minimum charge. A private mail database, if needed, incurs an additional per month fee.

To use this service, you need a PC or server running Lotus Notes, a modem, and a CompuServe Lotus Notes Information Service Membership Kit. For immediate expediency, you may download from the sign-up menu when you type **GO NOTES**; or call 800-233-2247 and ask for the CompuServe Lotus Notes Information Service Representative.

The World Wide Web. Lotus hosts a comprehensive array of Lotus product knowledge via the Internet, at the Lotus World Wide Web home page. You can search through Lotus Support's technical solutions, browse the product libraries, and download demonstration programs, application templates, and other resources via their FTP (file transfer protocol) site.

A particular favorite of many is the online interaction with the Knowledge Base, which is a central repository for all of the support documents, technical information, application development tips, and other important communication from Lotus in support of Notes users. While the Knowledge Base is also obtained via CD-ROM on a quarterly basis—and then updated via replication with Lotus' servers—the information is updated almost instantly on the Web using Lotus' InterNotes product and can therefore be considered the most accurate. Lotus' World Wide Web home page is located at **http://www.lotus.com/**.

The Lotus Knowledge Base

The Lotus Knowledge Base is a subscription service, and is a copy of the same Lotus Notes database that the Lotus Notes Support Specialists use to answer technical questions on Lotus Notes and cc:Mail. The database contains a wealth of product knowledge, tech notes, troubleshooting scripts, and other useful information that helps you debug problems you may be having. The views are designed to make it easy to find the necessary information. You can also query against the database, using Lotus Notes' full text search capabilities to find information related to the problems you are having. The Lotus Knowledge Base is delivered each month on CD-ROM to allow you the latest information without the long replication time to receive all of the updates. If you need even more recent information, you can replicate the database with Lotus for a small access charge. A Lotus Notes client is included for those users who want to access the Lotus Knowledge Base but are not licensed for Notes.

Lotus Notes Telephone Support

Lotus offers a wide range of telephone support around the world, allowing your company to call their senior product specialists for assistance. You can purchase a Passport Premium support contract, Working Together Named Caller, or other telephone support service plans.

Passport Premium Phone Support. Available through Lotus' Passport volume purchase plan, Premium support offers comprehensive phone support for all Lotus software. Passport Premium is designed to handle all levels of need for Lotus products within an organization—from the single workgroup need for assistance, to the large Notes deployment problems that may involve multiple platforms, gateways, and applications.

With the Passport, you can customize the support to suit your organization's specific needs. The program offers the following:

- Unlimited calls, or an annual ceiling on calls
- 24-hour support for business days only
- Support for all Lotus software, or for specific products and developer tools
- Support for individual named callers, or support that can be shared by a group of individuals

Passport Premium support can be purchased based on the combination of needs listed above that meet your needs. Contact your local Lotus Authorized Resellers or appropriate Lotus offices worldwide in one of the following ways:

- Dial 800-266-8720 in the United States
- Dial 800-GO-LOTUS in Canada

You can select from either of the following Premium plan options:

- **Unlimited Support**—Designed for organizations that want to be able to call for assistance as often as needed. With this plan, you must specify Named Callers. You will receive a Named Caller ID that must be used by the individual named and cannot be shared. Each Named Caller may call the closest Customer Support Center as often as necessary during normal business hours. These callers may reside anywhere in the world.

  There is also a 7x24 option available with this plan, which extends the basic plan to allow callers the ability to call around the clock. You can also purchase

V

The World of Notes

this plan in "5-incident packs" which allows you to call around the clock as many times as needed to resolve up to five separate problem instances.

- **Limited Support**—This plan is designed for businesses that want to put a cap on the number of support calls for their internal information services or support organizations—and is therefore less expensive. With this plan, you do not have a specified caller, but rather you can share the support calls among a group within your support organization. You purchase this support in "incident packs"—which means that you can have as many calls with the Lotus support group to resolve the number of instances you purchase. There are two packs to choose from—20-incident packs for standard business hours or 5-incident packs for 7x24 round-the-clock support.

With any of the Passport Premium Support plans, you can mix and match the options until you end up with a support plan that meets your needs. The cost of the services depends on the options you select, and can run from fairly inexpensive to a substantial fee. While you have a great number of resources readily available to you that will help answer most of your questions, there are times where you need instantaneous, up-to-the-last minute, detailed, or unique support from a Lotus technician. The support plans, in combination with the other available assistance mentioned in this chapter, will ensure that your support covers your needs.

Working Together Named Caller. A "Working Together" support contract lets your identified callers get support on all of your Lotus products, including NotesSuite during standard business hours only. Users that run Lotus Notes and other Lotus Products may find this support handy—particularly when they are trying to integrate information from one Lotus software package to another.

Other Telephone Support. When you are not working through one of Lotus' Passport volume purchase plans, you can opt to contract for other telephone support—either to get you started or to help supplement your own internal support organizations. The two plans available to you are the following:

- **Annual Support Contracts**—These contracts are put together for businesses starting out with Lotus products and let your callers contact first-line product specialists who answer basic technical questions. Annual support allows calls for up to ten separate incidents, or technical issues, no matter how many calls it takes to resolve each incident or issue.

- **Pay as you go**—If you want to purchase incidental support—support only if/when you need it—Lotus offers Pay Per Incident support. For this plan, Lotus bills your Visa, MasterCard, or American Express for support based on each incident you call in for.

You can contract for other telephone support in one of the following ways:

- Dial 800-437-6391 in the United States
- Dial 416-364-5667 in Canada

On-Site Services

On-Site Services lets companies have Lotus Senior Support Engineers on-site to help in the installation, deployment, and use of Lotus Notes. Some examples of this service include on-site assistance with network configuration, product installation, training for support personnel, educational seminars, and designing prototype databases. Services typically run between a half a day to five days in length. You can elect from one of two programs:

- **Support Account Management Program**—This program assigns you one of Lotus' senior technical engineers for Notes or cc:Mail to analyze calls for support, understand your environment and deployment strategies, help you forecast future problems and needs, and flag your concerns behind the scenes. This service is meant to be a proactive approach to supporting your organization and allows you to stop reacting to problems that arise and start preventing them.

- **Field Support Services**—This service is a typical short-term technical consulting engagement meant to assist your company in the installation, deployment, configuration, and improvement of your Lotus solution. The engineers will help your company ramp up on Notes quickly and learn how to best handle such tasks as optimizing an application, auditing your system security, and piloting Notes. You can think of this service as a mentoring approach to skills transfer of Lotus product knowledge.

Getting Educated

Anyone who has worked with groupware or automation projects gains an appreciation for the strategic role education and training play in the successful implementation of Lotus Notes. Lotus Education focuses on the development and delivery of programs and products to help ensure that a consistent level of competence exists in the technical professionals supporting Notes in their own companies or acting as consultants in the industry. Training is geared for both end users, who need to know what Notes is all about, and professionals, who need to gain and maintain their skill sets through formalized training. Lotus' educational programs and products are designed and developed to provide flexible curriculum schedules for all types of users to best address their needs. Lotus Education core services include:

- Instructor-led training
- Computer-based training
- Curriculum development and customization
- Education needs analysis
- Professional and instructor certification

Lotus maintains a network of over 450 Lotus Authorized Education Centers (LAECs) and 230 Lotus Desktop Training Companies (LDTCs) to assist companies in educating people in Lotus Notes.

Instructor-Led Training

Lotus Education offers a large number of highly skilled professionals who understand both education and technology, and who typically have a wide range of experiences in the industry. These instructors help provide in-class training in a hands-on method to facilitate the participants' learning, with opportunities to address specific questions and needs throughout the course delivery.

Lotus Authorized Education Centers aim at end users, system administrators, and application developers—to include those individuals who are seeking professional certification (discussed later in this chapter). The LAEC network spans across the U.S. and abroad. Each LAEC organization, in partnering with Lotus, demonstrates its commitment to quality education through compliance with the stringent LAEC selection standards. LAECs work closely with Lotus Education representatives to ensure that the needs of the customers are being met and that original Lotus materials are being used. LAEC courses are taught only by Certified Lotus Instructors.

> **Note**
>
> You can receive information regarding LAEC training through most of the support services described in this chapter, like the Fax Back Support services, the Web, and the Lotus Notes User's Guide.

The Lotus Notes LAEC Curriculum consists of the following courses:

- **Basic Notes Concepts**—This course introduces you to Lotus Notes as an information-sharing environment. This hands-on training will help you learn how to navigate within the Notes workspace, compose and view documents in a database, and use NotesMail.

- **Notes Technical User**—This course presents the more technical user features of Notes. Participants learn about Notes database design, automation, and database replication features, as well as a wide variety of advanced user features.

- **Notes Application Development I**—This course provides a solid foundation in Notes database design for application developers. The course is designed for core programming team members, and moves quickly through each fundamental aspect of building Notes applications.

- **Notes Application Development II**—This course provides a more detailed study of Notes application development. This course is meant to facilitate the developer's skill in learning how to develop integrated workflow applications. A thorough knowledge of Notes is required for this course.

- **Notes System Administration I**—This course provides a solid foundation for the Notes system administrator. This course covers every fundamental aspect of setting up, operating, and maintaining Notes servers and client workstations.

■ **Notes System Administration II**—This course provides advanced information for the Notes administrator who is responsible for Notes in large, multi-domain, and multiprotocol environments. This courses extends Notes from the workgroup to the enterprise.

Lotus Desktop Training Companies offer a wide range of training on the Lotus desktop products to include Lotus 1-2-3, Word Pro, Freelance Graphics, Approach, and Organizer.

Computer-Based Training (CBT)

For those users that prefer to pace themselves in training, Lotus offers a wide range of computer-based training software, ranging from Basic Notes Concepts to System Administration II. These courses are designed to let users work on their own desktops at a pace that suits their particular needs. The CBT training courses utilize a simulated environment of highly interactive activities that lets the user engage in a constant dialogue with the course.

Curriculum Development

Lotus Education maintains an in-house staff that is responsible for the development of all course materials for classroom and computer-based training courses. It maintains a close relationship with the Lotus product development teams to ensure timely delivery of new product release courses.

Customized Training/Needs Analysis

Lotus Education offers education needs analysis for clients, working closely with the client to best determine what training solutions will most effectively benefit them. All courses offered by Lotus Education can be tailored to meet an organization's needs, and delivered at the client site if requested. A client can also request a session be customized and then privately delivered at a Lotus or LAEC facility.

Certification

Lotus certification was established to benchmark and qualify individual skill and knowledge levels. Certification is growing as the industry continues to acknowledge its value of qualifying consistent levels of individual skill and knowledge. Lotus Business Partners and other resellers use certification as a way to ensure expert service and support to customers. Non-resellers also use certification as a means to manage resources and quality within their internal support ranks.

The worldwide Certified Lotus Professional (CLP) Program was developed to help provide a quantitative measure of product knowledge among technical professionals using Lotus products. It requires that individuals demonstrate a broad depth of product knowledge and expertise, and ensures that the people and organizations administering and developing Lotus products and applications have met Lotus' strict certification requirements. The CLP candidate is typically, but does not have to be, a

Service Provider within the Lotus product arena, or an Information Technology professional supporting an organization's internal operations.

Lotus Education offers the following professional certification designations (described in the following sections):

- Lotus Certified Notes Application Developer (LCNAD)
- Lotus Certified Notes System Administrator (LCNSA)
- Lotus Certified Notes Consultant (LCNC)
- Lotus Certified Notes Specialist (LCNS)

> **Note**
>
> Certification is Notes release-specific, and as Notes changes, certified individuals will be required to meet new requirements. Certification expires six months following a major product revision. Lotus will notify all certified professionals of recertification requirements as soon as possible. Recertification exams typically focus on the changes between one release and the next—with so many changes in Notes R4, you had better start studying!

Lotus Certified Notes Application Developer (LCNAD)

This certification is for individuals responsible for the design and creation of sophisticated workflow applications. Individuals certifying for LCNAD perform such tasks as application analysis and design, form and view creation, control over database security, writing help and policy documents, and testing the database as part of the rollout.

To qualify for certification as a Lotus Certified Notes Application Developer, you must successfully complete the following three exams:

- Notes Technical User
- Application Development I
- Application Development II

The applicant should also have at least three months' hands-on Notes application development experience.

Lotus Certified Notes System Administrator (LCNSA)

This certification is for individuals responsible for the organization-wide deployment of Notes. Applicants typically applying for LCNSA install and maintain complex Notes networks utilizing multidomain, multi-Notes named networks and multiprotocol environments. Tasks for this individual include interdomain security, replication, mail routing, server monitoring, program document creation, and planning and administering large Notes domains.

To qualify for certification as a Lotus Certified Notes System Administrator you must successfully complete the following three exams:

- Notes Technical User
- System Administration I
- System Administration II

Applicants should also have at least three months' hands-on experience installing and maintaining Notes servers and workstations.

Lotus Certified Notes Consultant (LCNC)

This certification is for individuals responsible for both the installation and rollout of Notes client/server technology and the creation of databases. Typically, candidates for this certification have a mastery of the fundamental aspects of setting up, operating, and maintaining Notes Servers and client workstations *and* a solid foundation in Notes database design.

To qualify for certification as a Lotus Certified Notes Consultant, you must successfully complete the following three exams:

- Notes Technical User
- Application Development I
- System Administration I

The applicant should also have at least three months' hands-on Notes application development and system administration experience.

Lotus Certified Notes Specialist (LCNS)

This certification is for individuals responsible for both the organization-wide deployment of Notes and the design and creation of sophisticated workflow applications. Typically, individuals qualifying for this certification have a mastery in both high level system administration and applications development. Their tasks include the Notes rollout and maintenance in large, multidomain, multi-Notes named networks and multiprotocol environments, and the planning, designing, and implementation of workflow applications.

To qualify for certification as a Lotus Certified Notes Specialist, you must successfully complete the following five exams:

- Notes Technical User
- Application Development I
- Application Development II
- System Administration I
- System Administration II

V

The World of Notes

Applicants should also have at least three months' hands-on experience with Notes between the level I and level II courses.

Obtaining the Certification Guide

You can request a copy of the Lotus Certification Guide, which includes complete requirements for each certification designation, by contacting the Lotus Education Helpline. The Helpline contact numbers are as follows:

North America	800-346-6409
	617-693-4436
Europe	+44 1 784 445692
	+44 1 784 455445
Lotus Education, Central Europe	01 80 5 323220
	+49 89 785 09 398
Lotus Education, Southern Europe	+33 1 41 56 53
Australia/New Zealand	800-627-608
	+61 2 350 7751
Southeast Asia	+65 240 1108
	+65 444 0035
Japan	+81 3 5496 3589

Certification Exams

You may register to take examinations through Drake Authorized Testing Centers by calling Drake at 800-745-6887. All exams for the Lotus Professional Certification program are administered by Drake Testing Centers located worldwide. There are about 200 Drake Testing Centers in North America alone. Drake Testing Centers provide you flexibility in scheduling the exams you want to take, as well as when and where you want to take them. The cost for each exam is US$90.

To register for any of the five exams, perform the following steps:

1. Have the following information ready to provide to the Drake registrar:

    • Your name.

    • Social Security number (to be used as your personal ID number).

    • Mailing address and phone number.

    • Company name.

    • Name and code number of exam you want to take.

    • Date you want to take the exam.

    • Method of payment to Drake (credit card, money order, or check). Payment is due prior to the exam.

2. Call the Drake testing registrar at 800-745-6887, or write:

Drake Prometric
Certification Registration
2601 88th Street West
Bloomington, MN 55431

3. Schedule a time and place to take the exam. (Drake will be able to help you determine a testing location convenient for you.)

You will be given instructions concerning the cancellation policy, location of the testing center, and requirements. Upon confirmation of payment, you will be sent a letter of confirmation from Drake that includes the test time, location, directions to the testing center, and exam procedures.

Exam Content. All exams are closed book, and you may not have any printed material, computers, or calculators with you during the exam. The exams are multiple choice and administered on a computer. Allow an additional 15 minutes before the exam for signing in and getting ready to take the exam. Exams range between one hour and one and a half hours in length. They typically consist of 50 to 90 questions.

Exam Scoring. You will be given an instant on-screen report and printout showing your overall pass/fail and section results as soon as you complete the exam. Your test results will automatically be forwarded to Lotus within five business days. If you do not pass the exam, you may reregister for the exam through Drake. While there is no limit to the number of times you can take a test, each time you take an exam, you must pay the full fee per exam.

Exam Completion. After your successful completion of the necessary exams for each type of certification, Lotus will send you a certificate signifying your accomplishment. It will take about two weeks to process your certificate.

Lotus Business Partners Program

The Lotus Business Partners Program offers a variety of benefits designed to equip, enable, and train the growing community of more than 10,000 partners who offer products and services based on Lotus technologies. Lotus Business Partners include professional application developers, corporate developers, consultants, service providers, education providers, integrators, and resellers. Through the Business Partners Program, Partners of all types can gain access to Lotus software, information, tools, support, and marketing programs to assist them in developing and marketing their products and services. This program has an annual fee (roughly running about $995 a year, but it varies based on the cost of the overall support costs Lotus incurs in providing this service).

Lotus Business Partner Connection

The Lotus Business Partner Connection delivers basic tools to help Business Partners be successful. It is designed for all commercial and corporate developers, service providers, authors, analysts, individual trainers, and education centers with an interest in any Lotus product. The Lotus Business Partner Connection is a "starting point" from which companies can begin a partner relationship with Lotus. Interested parties can call 800-782-7876 (or 800-565-0878 in Canada) to join the Lotus Business Partners Program and subscribe to the Business Partner Connection. The components of the Business Partner Program are available outside of North America—as the Business Partner program is worldwide.

The Lotus Business Partner Connection includes the following:

- **Information**—Technical and marketing information on all Lotus products, sample Notes applications, Lotus strategic messages, and press releases, and the Lotus Information Library CD.

- **Tools**—The Lotus Toolkit Collection CD, an assembly of developer tools and documentation, including the Lotus Notes API Toolkit, the Lotus VIM Developer's Toolkit, the Lotus cc:Mail Import/Export program, the Lotus Forms Designer, SmartText Builder, the Lotus 1-2-3 Add-In Development Kit, Improv Application Development Notes, the Ami Pro Macro Developer's Kit, various DataLens and ODBC drivers (including Notes SQL), and the Lotus ScreenCam Player. Additional tool offerings may be included or excluded as the product changes.

- **Software**—One user license for Notes client, cc:Mail Mobile, and SmartSuite for a period of one year.

- **Support**—30 days of free basic telephone support for Notes client, cc:Mail Mobile, and SmartSuite, and access to the Lotus Knowledge Base, a comprehensive, full-text indexed collection of technical support information for Notes, cc:Mail, and SmartSuite.

- **Training**—Basic Notes Concepts computer-based training.

In addition to the Business Partner Connection, Lotus Business Partners who begin their relationship with Lotus by subscribing to the Business Partner Connection are invited to apply and qualify for four extended offerings by completing the appropriate applications. Applications and additional information may be requested by calling one of the following numbers:

- Dial 800-782-7876 in the United States
- Dial 800-565-0878 in Canada
- Dial +65 339 8348 in the Asian Pacific

- Dial +61 2 350 7777 in Australia
- Dial +44 1784 455 445 in Europe, the Middle East, and Africa
- Dial +81 3 5496 3111 in Japan
- Dial 305-265-7811 in Latin America (HQ Miami)

The following sections discuss extended programs offered by Lotus for Business Partners:

- Lotus Professional Developers Package
- Service Providers Package
- Authorized Education Center Package
- Lotus Premium Partner

Lotus Professional Developers Package. This package is for application developers, product extenders, and other commercial developers building applications that integrate with Lotus products.

The Lotus Professional Developer Package is an extended collection of benefits for qualified professional developers who build applications for commercial sale. This package offers more resources than those included in the Business Partner Connection.

Those who qualify can order software from Lotus at discounted prices, and can consult by phone with technical consultants in the Developer Relations Group when they need information about business and marketing opportunities, integration strategies, and application design and development. Members also have access to Developer Forums, Technology Transfer programs, and a live electronic connection to Lotus.

Service Providers Package. The Service Providers Package is for consultants, integrators, resellers, and other value-added service providers. This package is an extended collection of benefits for qualified service providers—including custom application developers, Value Added Resellers (VAR), consultants, system integrators, and support centers who are looking for additional resources above those offered in the Business Partner Connection.

Authorized Education Center Package. The Authorized Education Center Package is for Lotus-certified companies authorized to provide training for users, administrators, and developers on Lotus products. This package includes an extended collection of benefits for those qualified education centers that have applied and been accepted into the LAEC program. The LAEC Package includes just about all of the benefits of the Lotus Service Provider Package, as well as a LAEC Welcome Aboard kit that contains marketing material and other information on how to successfully run a LAEC.

Selection is based on a number of factors, including proven excellence in training, available facilities and equipment, instructor expertise, and geographic coverage. Instructors are qualified through selection criteria, a comprehensive series of examinations, and Lotus' Train-the-Trainer course.

Lotus Premium Partner. This is the highest level of partnership awarded to Lotus Business Partners. This top tier within the Business Partners Program is awarded only to companies that have demonstrated consistently high performance as Service Providers. These companies enjoy a closer relationship with Lotus field staff, and are recognized in the Business Partner Catalog and the Lotus Notes Guide with a Lotus Premium Partner logo. They also receive extended benefits, such as additional software, support, and training, and access to cooperative marketing funds.

The opportunity to become a Lotus Premium Partner is available to service providers and professional developers. Applicants must be nominated by their field representative, and must meet requirements in three areas—commitment, contribution, and certification. Contact your local Lotus field representative for more information on becoming qualified as a Lotus Premium Partner.

Lotus Product Certification Program

Qualified Professional Developers of commercially available Notes-compatible products may now self-certify their product by completing a detailed application. The application asks a number of specific questions that examine the company's testing of the developer product and ask for verification of the company's relationship with Lotus. Once the application is submitted and approved by Lotus, the product is awarded a "Runs with Lotus Notes" logo for its package. Developers with self-certified products also are eligible for a self-certification designation in the Lotus Partner Catalog and the Lotus Notes Guide.

Beacon Awards

Each year, Lotus takes nominations from Lotus Business Partners and others for their annual Lotus Business Partner Beacon Awards. This award is designed to honor outstanding achievements among Lotus Business Partners. These awards recognize Notes leaders who have provided a "Note-worthy" solution to their customers and to the global groupware industry built by Lotus and the Business Partners.

The judges for these awards include representatives from the press, industry experts, and Lotus. The finalists are announced during the Lotusphere festivities (see "Gearing Up for Lotusphere" in this chapter for more information).

Business Partners may nominate their own company or other Lotus Business Partners for any of the awards. However, only one self-nomination per company will be considered. Details on the submission requirements for each Beacon Award nomination are sent out to all Business Partners each fall.

Award classification descriptions for Beacon Awards are as follows:

- **Greatest Impact on a Customer's Business**—This award recognizes creative solutions that significantly and measurably improved a customer's core business processes. Key measurements are improved productivity, reduced time to market, measurable ROI, and/or increased revenue.

- **Best Cross-Industry Solution**—This is awarded for creative solutions implemented in multiple customer sites that target specific horizontal solutions such as salesforce automation, human resources, or customer service. It is quantified by improved productivity and/or proven ROI.

- **Best Industry-Specific Solution**—For creative solutions targeting specific vertical industries such as healthcare, financial services, pharmaceutical, or manufacturing; it is quantified by improved productivity and/or proven ROI.

- **Most Effective Inter-Enterprise Solution**—This award is for the Notes-based solution that most effectively extends a business process across corporate boundaries to customers, suppliers, and/or partners; it is quantified by improved productivity, proven competitive advantage, and/or measurable cost savings.

- **Most Effective Business Solution Integrating Notes and SmartSuite**—This award recongizes effectiveness in both solving business problems and demonstrating innovative and creative uses of SmartSuite/Notes integration technologies such as Notes/FX, Notes SQL, OLE, and Notes Mail.

- **Most Sophisticated Implementation of a Messaging Solution**—In recognition of complex, enterprise-wide mail-enabled applications that integrate multiple mail environments, this award highlights the best Notes, cc:Mail, and/or Soft*Switch messaging solution.

- **Most Effective Use of Lotus Companion Products**—This award recognizes solutions that use Lotus Companion Products—video, imaging, or telephony—to deliver maximum and measurable business benefits to customers.

- **Best System Administration Tool or Utility**—This award goes to the system administration tool or utility vendor whose product brought measurable market benefits.

- **Best Application Development Tool**—This award recognizes an application development tool vendor whose product brought measurable market benefits.

- **Best Partnering**—This award recongizes the group of partners who were most effective in working together to deliver a total customer solution.

- **Excellence in Customer Support**—This award is for the partner who consistently provides superior customer support for Lotus-based products or technologies.

- **Excellence in Education**—This award recognizes the Lotus Authorized Education Center that demonstrates superior educational programs.

- **Best Philanthropic Solution**—This award is given in recognition of the partner who has developed the most beneficial solution for a not-for-profit, environmental, or humanitarian effort.

■ **Innovation in Sales or Marketing**—Given in recognition of inventive sales or marketing strategy or programs, this award spotlights partners who accelerate sales cycles, open markets, or leverage marketing partnerships.

Gearing Up for Lotusphere

In January, Lotus holds its premier conference, called Lotusphere, in Orlando, Florida. This conference—sold out in both 1995 and 1996—is the highlight of the year, kicking off new products, announcing Lotus Beacon award winners, hosting Lotus Notes Business Partner applications and displays from around the year, and providing conference sessions over four days. Lotusphere '96 sponsored over 200 conference sessions in three different hotels at Walt Disney World Resort. These sessions spanned a wide array of topics, from vertical industry solutions to understanding the new features of Notes Release 4 (R4).

Lotus used Lotusphere '95 to announce the kickoff of the Lotus Notes R4 beta testing—highlighting many of the new R4 features in a demonstration that brought rounds of applause from the audience. Lotusphere '96 was used to formally announce the arrival of the much-awaited Lotus Notes R4. Satellite broadcasts of many of the Lotusphere '96 happenings were provided to multiple sites around the world, so that those who could not make the conference could take part in the celebrations and education.

If you have never been to a Lotusphere conference, but have a desire to learn and see what Notes is all about, this is the function you want to attend. But, you will need to purchase your tickets early or you may be left reading about it in the morning news!

From Here...

In this chapter, you read about many of the services and programs offered by Lotus in support of Lotus Notes. For more information on the topics discussed in this chapter, refer to the following:

■ Chapter 25, "Add-On and Third-Party Products," discusses many of the products provided by Lotus and other third-party vendors that let you maximize your use of Lotus Notes.

■ Chapter 26, "U.S. Technologies," provides you with more information on the types of services available to you for support, training, and custom application design.

■ Chapter 27, "Synergistics, Inc.," also provides you with more information on available training and support—with a focus on sales automation.

■ Chapter 28, "NEXGEN Solutions," discusses how Notes users gain support from their organization, as well as from many of the other services provided.

CHAPTER 25

Add-On and Third-Party Products

Throughout this book, you have been learning about Lotus Notes. In this chapter, you learn about add-on and third-party products that work with Lotus Notes to provide you even more flexibility in meeting your business needs. This chapter is divided into two major sections:

■ Lotus add-on products

■ Third-party products

Note

The products listed in this book are by no means all of the products available today that are designed to work with Lotus Notes. This chapter merely provides you with a sampling of a wide variety of products available to you. For additional information on products and services that work with Notes, consult *The Lotus Notes & cc:Mail Guide*. This guide is free, and provides you with a detailed listing of products, services, and service providers that can help you work with Lotus Notes. To get a copy of the guide, contact your local Lotus representative, or call 1-800-343-5414.

Lotus Add-On Products, Management, and Development Tools

There are a great number of products available from Lotus to enhance your work with Lotus Notes. This section briefly defines those products for you, and discusses some of the benefits you might obtain from using these products. Screencams, product information, and demo applications are available to you on the enclosed CD-ROM if you would like further details on many of these products. This section will take a high-level look at many of the products from Lotus that you may find beneficial to incorporate in your Lotus Notes communication strategy.

Lotus Notes Document Imaging (LN:DI)

Even though there has been widespread deployment of local area networks (LANs), with LAN-connected desktop workstations running a host of applications meant to make life easier for the average working person, most information that workers rely on to get their job done continues to remain on paper. This often creates inconsistency, redundancy, and a disconnection between the information workers are tracking online, and what they receive on paper. Document imaging lets workers get the paper-based information they receive on a daily basis into an electronic format that can be incorporated into their electronic information systems as images, that may also be converted into machine searchable and readable text.

Lotus provides a family of products that assist Lotus Notes users in incorporating paper-based information into their network-based communications—Notes database, for example. The LN:DI (Lotus Notes Document Imaging) family of products capture, process, and manage paper-based information as images. LN:DI (often pronounced *Lindy*) consists of the components described in the following sections.

> **Note**
>
> For additional information on LN:DI and its uses, read Chapter 26, "U.S. Technologies." It provides a discussion on Launch for LN:DI.

The Professional Edition. The LN:DI Professional Edition is designed to process paper through scanners, fax systems, and Optical Character Recognition (OCR) systems. The Professional Edition also gives the user increased flexibility and control over the storage of their imaged files. With the LN:DI Professional Edition, users can quickly and efficiently create and share compound documents using images from a wide range of sources—scanned paper documents, fax transmissions, and files created in other applications.

The Professional Edition lets organizations add desktop document image processing to the capabilities of Notes at a relatively low cost. Incorporating images electronically from a wide range of documents lets users at the workgroup level create high-impact documents at a fraction of the time. By distributing documents electronically, companies can significantly increase their efficiency and effectiveness, while decreasing their cost of copying and distributing paper-based documents.

The Mass Storage System (MSS). The Mass Storage System provides advanced storage management for image-enabled Notes applications. The LN:DI MSS gives organizations a scaleable alternative to storing large images directly in a Notes database by storing them in devices such as hard drives, standalone optical drives, and optical jukeboxes. Using preconfigured storage profiles that describe how the image object is to be stored, the MSS lets the image documents be moved automatically over time to the most cost-efficient storage medium, while remaining accessible to the user.

The LN:DI MSS allows significant performance and cost benefits for companies that manage a large number of image-based documents. Large images can easily fill a Notes database, resulting in a performance decrease as the database grows very large. Storing the objects in the LN:DI MSS reduces the storage demand in the individual databases, while ensuring that they are accessible on demand. Companies can also take advantage of the MSS to move less frequently accessed image documents off of production servers, which are typically high-speed, high-cost machines, to slower, lower-cost storage media.

Finally, companies can take advantage of the MSS to centrally store imaged objects, while creating multiple links to them from Notes documents—without making multiple copies of the imaged object. This helps reduce the amount of valuable storage space required to store images, while still making those images available to all documents referencing them. One thing to keep in mind is that the MSS requires its own physical server, and can be costly. You should weigh the benefits (i.e., do you have an imaging volume that justifies the expenditure) provided by the MSS against the cost to use it.

The Image Processing Server (IPS). The Image Processing Server provides a single point of administration and setup for workgroup image processing. It receives requests from LN:DI clients, NotesMail, and other third-party gateways; distributes the work to the appropriate imaging option; and updates the appropriate Lotus Notes databases when the request is complete. The IPS is the foundation for LN:DI imaging components.

The IPS is the central administrative component, performing the following tasks:

- Receives all user requests
- Preprocesses requests by performing common operations—such as image conversion and audit trail processing
- Routes the requests to the appropriate service engine; some requests may be processed by more than one service
- Balances the load if multiple service engines are available
- Routes all results of the processing to their proper destination

The IPS also provides databases that let you configure all imaging options, monitor the status of all imaging jobs, track any image-processing errors, and view a log of all imaging operations.

The IPS eases the administration of imaging by providing a central point from which all other LN:DI services are performed—such as image import/export and Workgroup OCR. The IPS is easily scaleable, running on any Notes Windows client. An organization can deploy as many IPSes as needed to meet user demand. The IPS also lets you use any previous images you may have created by utilizing its import/export capabilities—saving you time and money while making the document images available to all Notes users via LN:DI.

The Workgroup OCR Option. The Workgroup OCR lets Notes users send TIFF and PCX image files for OCR processing. The Workgroup OCR Option converts the images to editable text and returns the text to the user in a NotesMail message, or inserts it in a Notes document. OCR eliminates the time, expense, and error of rekeying important documents. This option gives Notes the capability of using the full text search engine—letting users easily search and retrieve information stored on imaged documents.

The Workgroup OCR Option lets Notes users use NotesMail to send an image for processing, and convert the image to editable text. The text is then sent back to the user via NotesMail, or placed into a specified field in a Notes document in an application database. Once a document has been processed by the Workgroup OCR Option and added to a Notes document, it can be searched upon using the Notes full text search capability. This is a rather powerful tool in Lotus Notes that lets users define how they want to search a database for relevant information. By using the Workgroup OCR Option in LN:DI, companies can significantly reduce the cost of manually inputting text from documents.

The Lotus Fax Server (LFS). The Lotus Fax Server combines outgoing and incoming fax capabilities for Lotus Notes. The LFS also provides additional features including automatic routing, and print-to-fax driver software that extends the fax capabilities to any Windows-based mail client. The LFS supports a wide variety of fax modems, fax cards, and fax file formats. The Lotus Image Viewer, which shipped separately in Release 3.x of Notes, is now built in to Lotus Notes 4, and provides the user the capability of displaying, manipulating, printing, faxing, and OCR processing incoming faxes. You can read more about using the Lotus Notes 4 viewer in Chapter 6, "Advanced Mail."

The LFS replaces the Notes Outgoing Fax Gateway and Notes Incoming Fax Gateway companion products for Notes. The LFS helps to expand workgroup productivity in a corporation by providing an electronic e-mail-based fax service that lets individuals include fax information along with the rest of their electronic mail—creating a centralized storage facility for all of an individual's communication. The LFS is easy for users to learn as users send a fax version of an e-mail message or attachment in the same way they send NotesMail—simply adjusting the mail address to include the fax number and fax server name.

Tip

With the LFS, users can send attachments to fax recipients as easily as they do to NotesMail users. When an attachment is mailed through the fax gateway in a fax message, the LFS reads the attached file and coverts the information to a fax format. Support file formats include TIFF, PCX, and DCX image file formats. You can also fax Lotus Ami Pro, Lotus Word Pro, Microsoft Word for Windows, WordPerfect, Microsoft Rich Text Format (RTF), and ASCII file format attachments.

> **Note**
>
> When planning your imaging system, you need to take into account what hardware end users are working with in your company. The LN:DI family of products is designed to run with Windows-based clients. Client platforms other than Windows (and in Windows running under OS/2) will have to take this limitation into account when planning your imaging strategy. For example, if you want to use LN:DI products in an environment in which there are some users working with the Macintosh Notes client, you must store the imaged file as an attachment in a Notes database, and then provide a viewer for the Macintosh that can read that imaged attachment.

ImagePlus

As the dust begins to settle from IBM's acquisition of Lotus, it is becoming clear that the Cambridge company's impact will go far beyond securing IBM's place in the world of desktop applications. In fact, the addition of Notes will catalyze the transformation of IBM's core business in production systems and software, allowing it to break out of the confines of the back office to reach tens of thousands of new users and incorporate ad hoc exception processing in a radically new way.

A case in point is ImagePlus, now set to embark on a new strategy that promises to leapfrog the competition by combining production transaction processing with Notes' ability to reach every corner of the enterprise—or across company boundaries—and integrate ad hoc activity into the business process.

ImagePlus is a production document repository and structured workflow application for document-intensive business processes. ImagePlus uses Notes imaging and workflow components to extend the boundaries of an ImagePlus business process to every corner of the enterprise, and to the world outside. In essence, anyone with a Notes mailbox can become an ImagePlus user.

ImagePlus' scaleable repository can be used as a centrally managed archive for Notes documents and attachments, including images. Users concerned about reaching the limits of the Notes database—approximately 4 MB in Notes R4—will be able to archive less active documents to ImagePlus. This relieves user departments from the burden of managing huge volumes of data and documents on the LAN. With ImagePlus as a back-end, users can offload this mass storage problem to a proven production component. The Notes/ImagePlus combination enables a brand new kind of hierarchical storage management for office documents, with Notes as the first tier, and ImagePlus providing an enterprise-scaleable archive. The result of the Notes/ImagePlus integration is a new kind of imaging and workflow platform that breaks the traditional barriers to document-intensive business computing and, at the same time, provides a bottomless managed repository for Notes documents.

V

The World of Notes

RealTime Notes

Lotus RealTime Notes introduces integrated real-time desktop conferencing for Lotus Notes. Real-time conferencing lets users connect to other users' desktop live—sharing data and applications in real time. Notes users can now communicate with others, sharing their information, perspective, and expertise, regardless of location. The real-time desktop conferencing functionality is based on Intel Corporation's ProShare desktop conferencing product. RealTime Notes also provides Notes-based applications and tools to integrate the powerful groupware and messaging functionality of Lotus Notes with the innovative real-time data sharing and desktop videoconferencing of Intel ProShare.

RealTime Notes includes the following features:

- **Free ProShare Premier Conferencing**—RealTime Notes includes a free copy of Intel Corporation's ProShare Premier version 1.6 desktop conferencing software. ProShare Premier delivers full data and application sharing to the Notes desktop, and requires no additional hardware beyond that required for local area network or modem connectivity.

- **Optional Desktop Videoconferencing**—RealTime Notes will support full ProShare desktop videoconferencing in addition to the data and application sharing provided through ProShare Premier. Notes users can incorporate live desktop videoconferencing through the additional purchase of Intel's ProShare Personal Conferencing Video System 200.

- **Notes Real-time Supporting Applications**—RealTime Notes delivers Notes-based applications and tools that facilitate the transition between groupware and messaging, and real-time activities. The quality and effectiveness of real-time conferencing sessions is enhanced by integrating the power of Notes' groupware and messaging environment with ProShare's real-time conferencing technology. RealTime Notes provides the following new features for more powerful and productive team computing:

  - **RealTime Notes Conference Address Book**—Organizes conference connection information and provides automated call initiation directly from Notes.

  - **Conference Journal Database**—Facilitates the tracking and summarization of real-time conference sessions.

  - **Notes Conference Audit Log Database**—Provides system administrators and management with an audit trail of conference activity by account code, person, date, and connection method.

  - **Conference-Enabled Notes Mail Form**—Contains a Return Conference Call button to automatically establish a return real-time conference with the composer of the message.

  - **Conference-Enabled SmartIcon Palette**—Includes a customized conference-enabled SmartIcon palette, providing integrated access to ProShare's desktop conferencing facilities directly from within the Notes environment.

- **Conference Dynamic Link Library (DLL)**—RealTime Notes includes a Conference API which is provided via a dynamic link library (DLL) and a Notes database driver. The API is a custom Notes @DbCommand function designed to facilitate management of ProShare DDE conversations. Third-party business partners and in-house developers can use the Conference DLL to add ProShare desktop conferencing to their new or existing custom Notes applications.

■ **Intel ProShare Desktop Conferencing**—provides the following three fundamental levels of real-time desktop conferencing:

  - **Data Sharing**—Provides a common whiteboard for sharing text, drawing, or posting images from other desktop sources. Data sharing provides an ideal environment for ad hoc brainstorming, review, or process synchronization.

  - **Application Sharing**—Enables conference participants to share desktop applications live, in real time. Both participants work on one version of the data, utilizing the full power of the application and eliminating multiple copies of the information.

  - **Videoconferencing**—Brings full motion, live video to data and application sharing sessions. Video adds audio and visual impact to real-time sessions, enhancing communication.

System Requirements. To use RealTime Notes, you must have the following:

■ Microsoft Windows

■ Lotus Notes desktop or full client Release 3.15 or higher

■ Intel ProShare Premier version 1.6 (included)

■ Intel ProShare Personal Conferencing Video System

■ Lotus VideoNotes Release 1.1

■ 486/33 or faster CPU

■ 8 MB or more of memory

■ 14 MB of storage

■ VGA Display

NotesView

NotesView is a graphical management software tool that gives users control over an enterprise-wide Notes environment. From a single management station, you can monitor and control Notes servers using industry-standard management tools and gain real-time access to Notes network information. With NotesView, complete, up-to-the-minute status of any server is at your fingertips.

NotesView automatically creates multiple map views of your Notes network topology. For example, you can create maps of the replication paths to and from a server, or of your mail routing topology. The color-coded graphical display lets you know of changes in the state of a Notes server. NotesView can also notify you via NotesMail or pager whenever there is a change in the status of the network. This lets you be proactive in managing the servers by providing you critical data—before the server actually goes down!

With NotesView, you can collect data as well as chart the health of servers over time and under different uses. This lets you easily troubleshoot, analyze performance trends, and plan for enhancements to optimize your Notes environment.

NotesView provides real-time monitoring of a distributed Lotus Notes environment by building on the capabilities of SNMP (Simple Network Management Protocol) and Hewlett-Packard OpenView management software. NotesView is tightly integrated with Lotus Notes—providing Notes network protocol support and leveraging existing events and the alarm system—and utilizes the Notes security model.

With NotesView, you can set up a single management station to oversee your entire Notes environment. You can also establish multiple management stations and then delegate Notes management tasks. You can also use NotesView to restart a server, even if Notes is not running.

The NotesView agent currently supports the OS/2, NT, and NLM servers; but by the first quarter of 1996, it should also support Solaris 2.3, HP-UX, AIX, and SCO.

NotesView provides control over the following areas:

- Notes servers
- Replication
- Mail routing
- Notes databases

NotesView contains the following features:

- **NotesView Management Station**—This is a Windows-based management interface for Notes environments that extends the functionality of HP OpenView for Windows. Each management station supports up to 150 Notes servers.

- **NotesView Agent**—The NotesView Agent software resides on Notes servers to collect vital server information. The NotesView Agent enables you to monitor and control Notes servers using industry-standard Simple Network Management Protocols (SNMPs).

NotesView Maps. You can set thresholds for factors like server disk space, mail volume, and user volume. Whenever a threshold is crossed, NotesView will notify you automatically via a color-coded alarm system. Color changes are propagated to all maps. You can quickly reduce the scale of any NotesView map to display more servers. Or pan to focus in on specific areas. The following maps are provided with NotesView:

- **Network topology map**—Displays all networks to which each server is connected, including the status of each connection.
- **Replication maps**—Four replication map types provide instant insight into how information is distributed in your Notes network:
  - **Replication topology maps**—Show all the replication paths between servers in a domain. They also indicate paths to other domains.
  - **Replication maps to/from a selected server**—Show all the servers that replicate to the selected server and all the servers it replicates to.
  - **Replication maps between selected servers**—Allow you to determine the shortest or quickest path for replication between any two servers.
  - **Database replica maps**—Show all servers within a domain that have replicas of a specified Notes database.
- **Mail routing maps**—Three types of mail maps include mail routing topology map, mail routing to/from a selected server, and the monitored mail map which displays servers that are running the NotesView mail reflector agent.
- **Isolation maps**—Lets you devise a map view that meets your needs according to criteria you set. For example, you can create views that correspond to company divisions, physical sites, etc.

Monitoring and Statistics. In addition to the maps provided, NotesView provides the following monitoring and statistical capabilities:

- **InfoBox information resource**—Click a server icon and obtain immediate access to up-to-date status. View and act on information quickly.
- **Servers statistics**—The Server tab in the InfoBox provides up-to-the minute statistics on current tasks, disk space, and users. Or choose to bring up a console window.
- **Mail monitoring**—Select the Mail tab for information on mail volume, pending mail, dead mail, and more. You can also force mail delivery, perform mailbox fixes, shut down, and restart the mail router.
- **Mail probe**—Monitor and control mail probes which provide a continual assessment of the health and performance of your Notes mail routing environment.
- **Replication**—Call up statistics on replication time trends. NotesView also provides replicator status, controls for shutting down and starting the replicator, and the ability to force replication between servers in your environment.
- **Database**—View information on any Notes database in the system, including which servers it resides on. Run utilities like Compact.
- **Network**—Select the Network tab to collect information, such as which protocols are configured on each server and the number of packets transmitted and received.

V

The World of Notes

- **Notes MIB**—NotesView includes an MIB that contains selected entries from the Notes statistics structure and information required to control the Notes server.

Charting Capabilities. NotesView's push-button controls let you quickly chart data collected from individual servers or from the entire network. View and report trends in server, mail replication, and network statistics. Create charts of network-wide trends for capacity planning including replication traffic, network traffic, and network error rate.

NotesView Poller. There are two key features in working with the NotesView Poller:

- **Server status**—Start the Poller, and the status of Notes servers is reported to you automatically at intervals you specify. Configure the Poller to collect information, including number of users, replication traffic, document changes during replication, available disk space, and mailbox size.

- **Server tests**—Use the Poller to monitor the performance of your servers. Configure the Poller to run a series of diagnostic tests on servers to check connections, ports, and so on.

HiTest Tools for Visual Basic and C

With Lotus Notes HiTest Tools, developers can access Notes' robust, distributed, replicated object store, integral messaging, advanced security, and global directory using a high-level, object-based C or Visual Basic (VB) applications programming interface (API). This lets developers create a "dialogue" between applications they write in Visual Basic or C and Lotus Notes. HiTest acts as the bridge across which these two applications communicate with Lotus Notes.

A Link for Delphi Users

Now programmers creating Delphi applications can integrate their applications with Lotus Notes. Delphi/Link is a set of VBXs that allows you to integrate the unique functionality of Lotus Notes into your custom Delphi applications. Delphi/Link consists of three controls:

- **NOTESDATA control**—This control is used for creating connections to Notes databases, creating results of queries to Notes, and performing other Notes-related functions.

- **RICHTEXT control**—This control is used for displaying Notes Rich Text fields on the screen, and contains properties that allow the application to programmatically modify rich text objects in Lotus Notes documents.

- **HLIST control**—The HLIST control displays Lotus Notes views in a hierarchical list box consistent with the NotesView.

These three controls can be used in conjunction with one another to create an unlimited number of applications that integrate with Lotus Notes.

The types of Delphi applications that can be created using Delphi/Link are endless, but the following list contains a few ideas:

- Import/Export/Data Transport from other relational databases and external files

- Custom user interfaces to Notes data

- End-user applications to interface Notes and relational data

- Agents to monitor Notes databases

- Mail-enabled Delphi applications

- Applications where Notes views need to be created "on-the-fly"

Using HiTest, developers can create sophisticated applications in VB or C to enhance the capabilities provided in Notes. For example, developers who need a much faster and robust mathematical processing application can develop it in Visual Basic (as Notes does not easily handle sophisticated mathematical calculations). The Visual Basic code can then pass the calculated information to Lotus Notes for workflow and storage.

Note

Also available to you is the Lotus Notes Application Programming Interface (API) Toolkit, which is a C language subroutine library that provides you with programmatic access to Lotus Notes functions and applications. You can perform a lot of the same types of functions through the use of the API, as you can using VB and C—but it is not a full programming language. A benefit to using the API is that the programs or enhancements you program run on all of the platforms available with Notes—while using Visual Basic can be somewhat limiting if you are running Notes on multiple platforms that don't support programs developed in VB. As with the selection of all programming tools, you should first look at the functions you need to perform and the environment in which your application runs—and then pick the right application for the job!

Lotus Phone Notes

Phone Notes applications let callers access Lotus Notes data from any Touch-Tone telephone. Typical Phone Notes applications include customer support help desks, information fax back systems, and job application status, or information hotlines and project status reporting applications. Phone Notes can also be integrated with the Lotus Notes Fax Server, so that users can fax information to the caller's local fax machine. It can also be redirected to an alphanumeric pager using the Lotus Notes Pager Gateway.

With Phone Notes, the telephone becomes an extremely useful remote client for Notes, allowing users to participate in Notes applications. Using a telephone, users can do the following:

V

The World of Notes

- Access, create, enter data into, and forward Notes documents
- Embed voice messages into Notes documents
- Play and record voice messages
- Read text information from Notes documents (such as e-mail messages) through text-to-speech technology

Phone Notes lets you use Notes as an Interactive Voice Response (IVR) platform. With Phone Notes, a developer can create a simple Touch-Tone menu as a "front-end" to any Notes database using special Phone Notes forms. For example, you can turn your Notes-based Help Desk application (see the following sidebar) into an IVR system. Customers can call in with questions, and Phone Notes will be able to record the message, page a support technician, log the trouble ticket, and provide a status for the client should they dial back into the system to see where the trouble report sits in the queue.

Phone Notes is also capable of creating applications that make outbound calls for applications like seminar evaluations, status reporting, customer surveys, or data collection.

Sample Applications. The Phone Notes Application Kit comes with several sample applications to get developers started:

- **Customer Support Help Desk**—Lets a customer support department track problems and provide service to its customers.

- **Notes Document FaxBack**—Lets callers request information from a library of product literature. The application uses Notes Fax Server to fax requested information to the caller's local fax machine. Lotus support uses FaxBack in their support program when you call into their FaxBack Support program as described in the "Lotus Notes Support" section of Chapter 24.

- **Human Resources Benefits Selection**—Is used by employees to understand, select, and change their healthcare benefits.

- **User Validation**—Adds additional levels of password security to any Phone Notes application.

- **Auto Attendant**—Takes incoming calls into a workgroup or small business and transfers the caller to a live representative, or records a message.

Help Desk and Phone Notes at Work at U.S. Technologies

Chapter 26, "U.S. Technologies," discusses a company that utilizes Notes in all of its functions; in reality, they "Run With Notes." U.S. Technologies utilizes Phone Notes as part of its client support hotline. Clients who subscribe to its 7x24 support program are given a password that they use when they call for help. When they dial into the U.S. Technologies Help Desk, they are prompted through a series of menus to enter their password, and then leave a verbal message of their problem.

Phone Notes looks up the employee assigned to support the client in a Notes database, and dispatches a page to the primary contact. If the primary support representative does not call into the system within 15 minutes and leave a voice response indicating that the help problem is being addressed, the secondary contact is immediately paged. If the secondary contact does not call in, then the company president is called. "Trust me, that has never happened," claims Chuck Berkau of U.S. Technologies.

With a little creativity, companies can incorporate Phone Notes into their Notes systems to really enhance their support and communication offerings.

Notes Reporter

Lotus Notes Reporter is a read-only report writing tool designed specifically for Lotus Notes users to take data from Notes databases to analyze and report. Notes Reporter can access Notes data transparently from files on a local drive or from Notes server-based databases. With Notes Reporter, users can create reports, crosstabs, worksheets, charts, mailing labels on Notes data, and users can distribute any of the data views mentioned here via NotesMail.

Notes Reporter uses the capabilities of the Notes Normalizer, which enables users to organize Notes information in a relational database model. The Normalizer copies information stored in Notes multi-value fields into a separate database, which is automatically joined to the original Notes data. Users can then perform analysis and create grouped reports quickly and easily (see fig. 25.1). The original Notes database remains unchanged.

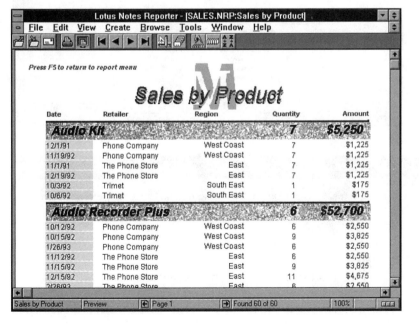

Fig. 25.1

Notes Reporter makes it easy to perform analysis and reporting of Notes data.

V

The World of Notes

Notes Reporter 1.0 provides *WYSIWYG* (what-you-see-is-what-you-get) report designs that let users view data, layout, and calculations through every step of designing and printing of a report. Built-in "assistants" guide users through report creation without requiring them to follow predefined steps—steps can be skipped or users can back-track to make new choices. SmartMaster styles provide professionally designed layouts to enhance report appearance, often through a simple click on some SmartIcons.

Lotus Notes Reporter's worksheet view, complete with powerful crosstab and charting capabilities, further enhances analysis options (see fig. 25.2). Reporter's worksheet view acts like a spreadsheet, but can be transformed into a dynamic crosstab by simply dragging-and-dropping fields. Notes Reporter 1.0 also features the Lotus common chart engine, letting users analyze and present information in a graphical format.

Notes Reporter works directly on Notes data—no importing or translation is required.

Fig. 25.2

Notes Reporter lets you easily chart the data you collect in Notes databases.

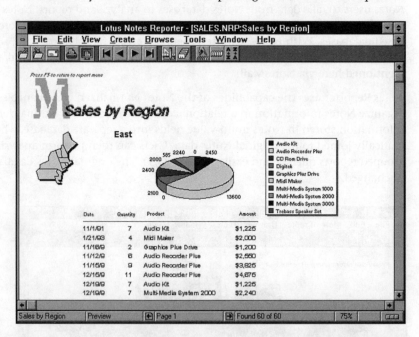

Pager Gateways

The Notes Pager Gateway is software which, when executed as a server task on an OS/2-based Notes server, enables people who use Notes e-mail to send pages to people who subscribe to paging services that utilize the TAP serial data transfer protocol. The

Notes user can compose an e-mail message and address it to a particular individual via the Notes Pager Gateway; another user, if in possession of an alphanumeric pager, can then receive the NotesMail message on the pager—rather than just a simple phone number that requires a call to discover the message.

The Notes Pager Gateway sends pages by dialing a TAP-compliant paging service's main number. Then, the gateway submits faxes which are addressed to individuals via their Personal Identification Numbers (PINs).

You can greatly facilitate your benefit of Notes with a pager gateway, if you are in possession of an alphanumeric pager. For example, you can run an agent against your NotesMail to automatically forward all messages from your boss to your pager—your boss will never know if you are in the office or not! IS support personnel can easily design agents that will send a message directly to their pager if a server begins to reach critical status—thus allowing the Information Systems department to intervene and solve the problem before the server crashes. With a little imagination, this gateway product can greatly simplify communication within a group.

Lotus Video for Notes

Lotus Video for Notes lets any size workgroup capture, record, play, edit, and distribute full-motion video in Notes applications using on-screen, easy to use buttons similar to a VCR. With Video for Notes, stored video can be accessed, distributed, and managed as another data object within Notes.

Using Video for Notes, a user can embed video clips in Notes to assist in the communication of information between workgroup members so that everyone is hearing and seeing a consistent message. This multimedia interaction helps ensure that a project meets business objectives by accurately communicating all of the information on the project. Using Video for Notes lets all members of a project collaborate more efficiently and effectively, no matter where they are located.

Users can view video even when disconnected from the network. For example, an insurance appraiser could download a video of a building site that was taken during the prior field inspection, and then play the video prior to visiting the site to refresh the appraiser's memory of a previous inspection—prior to the next inspection.

Video for Notes has a secure, flexible replication and distribution model that lets administrators easily balance user demands. The Lotus Video for Notes site manager distributes video to Notes users by generating a single copy of the video at each location regardless of how many times the video appears in mail messages or other documents. This distribution mechanism minimizes long-term storage problems.

Video for Notes provides direct and immediate playback from video servers for high-capacity local area networks. When a local area network does not permit continuous playback, staged playback is available. Staged playback lets video be downloaded automatically from a server to the desktop and then viewed. For workgroup members that do not have wide area networks, Video for Notes applications can be distributed through CD-ROM.

Lotus ScreenCam

Similar to the basic operation of a VCR or cassette deck, ScreenCam records and plays back a customer's voice and synchronizes it with every screen movement as thoughts are explained, both visually and verbally. In addition, ScreenCam movies can be played and distributed to anyone, without charge, even if ScreenCam is not available to them (as you will see on the CD-ROM accompanying this book!).

What you need to run ScreenCam is the following:

- Any IBM-compatible 80386 or 80486 processor.
- Microsoft Windows 3.1, 3.11, or Win95.

> **Note**
>
> You can run screencams created in Windows 3.1 using ScreenCam 2.0 or ScreenCam 1.x under Win95, but you will need ScreenCam 2.1 to record movies under Win95.

- A sound card or portable sound device. A sound card is not required to play movies; however, it is required to play sound.
- Less than one additional megabyte of RAM above the "captured" application (the application you are making a movie of) memory requirement is recommended.
- A 3.5-inch disk drive in order to install. ScreenCam also comes free on many Lotus CDs of other products, and you can load it from there as well.

Adding Power to the Learning Environment. Using screencams can significantly enhance your company's ability to educate its users on a wide range of topics. Companies can do the following:

- Create customized learning tools and embed them in any OLE-enabled Windows application
- Share application expertise through brief, informal demonstrations
- Train new employees on any Windows-based systems
- Develop quick access help systems by embedding ScreenCam icons within applications

A company can also utilize screencams to do the following:

- Respond to drafts, spreadsheets, memos, and more
- Communicate thoughts and comments clearly with colleagues
- Edit and provide feedback to proposals and plans
- Clarify and point out potential opportunities and issues
- Review sales, budgets, forecasts, or other financial documents quickly
- Document details and share assumptions

ScreenCam is an interactive tool for creating ad hoc and formal audio/visual presentations. Users can capture screen activity, cursor movements, and sound into an integrated file that can be saved and distributed across local and wide area networks as well as the Internet. Addressing a wide range of business needs, ScreenCam is as easy to use as a VCR and provides a practical way for users to show and say exactly what they mean.

ScreenCam includes captioning, sound compression, editing, and Notes/FX integration. Additionally, ScreenCam sound compression can reduce the space a file's size takes up on a hard drive by as much as 50 percent. Soundless movies with ScreenCam captions can reduce file size by as much as 90 percent.

The captioning capability of ScreenCam offers users the option of creating either sound or captioned movies. The captions allow users to store up to 15 minutes of screen movies on a floppy disk. (In the past, users were limited to sound movies that averaged 1 MB per minute.)

ScreenCam also features timesaving editing capabilities. Users can revise their screen movies without having to re-record the whole segment! Additionally, users will find that the sound compression capabilities can significantly reduce the file size of both sound and captioned movies, optimizing them for distribution via online networks and floppy disk storage.

ScreenCam features new Notes/FX integration, which provides seamless Notes interoperability and the ability to build, archive, and manage libraries of screen movies. The movies can be saved and distributed either as stand-alone executable files or as embedded OLE objects in any Notes document, and can be sent to anyone on the network via Lotus Notes, Lotus cc:Mail, Microsoft Mail, or Novell GroupWise. They can also be posted on e-mail bulletin boards, the Internet, online services, or in a Notes database for central access.

InterNotes Product Family

With the increasing popularity of the Internet services, Lotus has announced the addition of three products to their new InterNotes product family. These products are the following:

- InterNotes Web Publisher
- InterNotes News Groups
- InterNotes Navigator

This section introduces you to the first two products, the InterNotes Web Publisher (now available free on the Lotus Web site), and the InterNotes News Groups. The third product in the InterNotes family is actually incorporated into Lotus Notes R4, and you read about this feature in Chapter 21, "Taking Advantage of Notes Release 4 Features."

V

The World of Notes

InterNotes Web Publisher. The InterNotes Web Publisher lets users publish Notes information to the millions of users on the World Wide Web (WWW), one of today's most popular Internet services. By translating Notes documents and databases into HyperText Markup Language (HTML)—the format used by standard Web browsers— the InterNotes Web Publisher provides the best process for creating and managing enterprise Web sites.

The InterNotes Web Publisher is a Notes server application that runs in conjunction with a standard Web (HTTP) server. The InterNotes Web Publisher performs the following functions:

- Automatically converts Notes documents and views into a series of HTML documents that live on a Web server. By converting Notes views, the InterNotes Web Publisher provides a navigable structure for the Web site.
- Converts Notes doclinks into hypertext links.
- Preserves attachments to Notes documents and allows them to be downloaded from a Web browser.
- Converts Notes tables into HTML tables.
- Converts bitmaps in Notes documents into inline GIF files.
- Provides a Notes database that controls translation parameters such as font mapping and selecting views to translate, consolidates logging and report generation, and handles other processes.

The InterNotes Web Publisher initially supports the Windows NT operating system and will require a Notes server and a standard HTTP server.

InterNotes News. InterNotes News is a Notes server application that exchanges UseNet news articles between Notes and news servers using the Network News Transfer Protocol (NNTP). This offers Notes users a secure and easy way to access and participate in UseNet newsgroups from their familiar Notes environment. By reading news articles from Notes, users can take advantage of hierarchical views in discussion threads, full text search, and multiple indexed views of the news articles.

InterNotes News offers users the following:

- Access to UseNet newsgroups without a personal Internet connection.
- Use of Notes macros, full text search, and mail forwarding to manage UseNet newsgroup articles.
- The ability to participate in newsgroups by writing and posting a response from Notes, or replying directly to the author using NotesMail (with a Simple Mail Transport Protocol (SMTP) gateway).

InterNotes News offers administrators the following:

- The ability to make Internet newsgroups accessible to the organization without putting TCP/IP on every desktop.

- A centralized Notes configuration database that simplifies configuration and administration of the News service. It allows administrators to subscribe to individual UseNet newsgroups, create customized Notes News databases, and control News replication.
- Replication for easy distribution of News databases throughout the organization.
- Notes Access Control Lists (ACLs) to provide selective access to News databases.

A Peek into Third-Party Applications

In addition to the wealth of products available from Lotus Development Corporation, there is a host of third-party providers who have significantly enhanced the value and use of Lotus Notes through the development of products that run with Notes. Applications available in the market for Lotus Notes can range from simple applications that track information, to sophisticated, shrink-wrapped products that enhance the abilities of Lotus Notes in working in your computing environment.

There is no way all products that are available to work with Lotus Notes can be mentioned in this chapter. However, several product highlights have been included to give you a look into what is available. The CD-ROM that is included with this book will also provide you with demos, screencams, and/or white papers and product literature provided by the companies mentioned in this section to provide even greater detail into the offerings they provide.

A Fresh Approach to Notes Training

Corporations have understood the power of collaboration, teamwork, and team-based working for years. Lotus Notes from Lotus Development Corporation makes it possible to realize the power of teams. Lotus Notes provides organizations with the ability to design business systems that combine the strengths of human power and IT and "involve" people. Lotus Notes enables you to communicate with colleagues, collaborate in teams, and coordinate strategic business processes, reducing project cycle time and eliminating the need for paper-based systems.

However, implementing Lotus Notes successfully requires a mental shift and reexamination of current work practices by individuals and managers. The training model used in most corporations is inadequate in bringing the required mental shift. Lotus Notes training today focuses only on the mechanics of using Notes. Trainees leave the classroom without understanding the true nature of group-based working. Their typical response is "So, how is this different from e-mail?" or "I can do this using the Web for one-tenth of the cost."

Business Evolution, Inc. certainly understands that a different method of training is certainly required before organizations can realize the benefit of deploying Notes. No method of training can guarantee creating change in human behavior or group behavioral patterns. But the values of teamwork, collaboration, and strong group focus on system goals will not happen by just teaching the concepts to individuals. It requires the individuals to learn as a group and lots of

(continues)

V

The World of Notes

(continued)

practice to strengthen the learning. Ultimately, the learning is successful and will last only if the group perceives that the new method of working is truly a better model and perceives that the organization demands and reinforces the required values by rewarding such behavior.

GroupFocus, a team-based learning program, uses the Experiential Learning Model for training groups in new work models. Participants learn how to use Notes and learn the concepts of collaborative approach to working, information sharing, and improved decision-making techniques by working on real-life problems or using structured experiences.

The Experiential Learning Model, with its strong emphasis on group participation, exploration, and realization, appears to be most suitable for training people on Lotus Notes and its concepts. GroupFocus is used to help members of an organization create a unified mental model and perspective on the organization and the nature of work. GroupFocus sessions are designed to address the unique learning requirements for the given workgroup.

For more information on GroupFocus, contact them at Business Evolution, Inc., Princeton, New Jersey. Call them at 609-951-0216, or surf them at **http://www.bsns_evolution.com**.

Replic-Action

Replic-Action, developed by Casahl Technology, Inc., is a client/server-based data replication and migration tool to access, transform, migrate, and synchronize data between Lotus Notes and multiple external databases. Replic-Action data transfer applications can be scheduled or can begin on an ad hoc basis. The applications can tie together and control interactions between multiple databases, providing workflow triggers, notifications, and automated actions.

The Replic-Action Composer—the application design user interface—is a Lotus Notes application. Users do not need to learn any new complex scripting or programming languages. With Replic-Action, low-level DBMS APIs are no longer a concern. The Replic-Action system catalog, log file, and help files are all Notes databases as well. Creating a very sophisticated application is as simple as filling out Notes documents!

Generalized Replication. Replic-Action extends the powerful replication facility in Notes to non-Notes databases, enabling external databases to be replicated with Notes databases. Updates can be propagated bi-directionally on a scheduled basis.

This generalized replication between disparate data sources includes the following options:

- One-way update
- Two-way updates
- Selective replication, including replication of selected fields only
- Automatic detection of unique keys and TIMESTAMP fields
- Incremental updates

Replicate Dissimilar Notes Databases. Replic-Action's Notes-to-Notes replication enhances standard Notes replication in two ways. First, Replica-Action allows a Notes database to replicate with another Notes database with a different Notes replica ID and form design. Second, fields can be selectively replicated.

Multi-Source Distributed Query Optimizer. Replic-Action offers a sophisticated query optimizer that allows the following:

- A single SQL query to reference multiple data sources as if their tables were local
- Access to Notes databases through SQL statements

Replic-Action also supports data transfer requests that are heterogeneous. A Notes database can be populated with data coming from multiple databases managed by different DBMSes, which are specified in a single SQL query. This support includes the following:

- Optimization of distributed queries
- Full ODBC SQL syntax and semantics support for multi-source queries
- Asynchronous database processing if supported by the database back end

Triggered Workflow. Because of its triggered actions and stored requests, Replic-Action is an excellent workflow triggering and integration mechanism. Replic-Action itself contains many powerful workflow primitives invoked automatically by the event of transferring data. Triggers are based on insert, update, or delete operations. Actions can include the following operations: Mail Send, Stored Procedures, SQL commands, DDE link construction, and DocLink construction within Notes documents, and so on.

Data Transformation Facility. Replic-Action for Lotus Notes allows you to transform data in the following ways:

- Bi-directional data value transformations
- Full utilization of Notes formulae
- String manipulation
- Date/time value mapping

Replic-Action's data transformation can be employed both when data is inserted into a source, as well as when data is read from a source. Replic-Action applications are configured to act on specific data sets on a regular schedule. Tasks can be run between certain hours, repeated at certain intervals, and on specific days. However, Replic-Action also includes several simple utilities to quickly import and export data on a "one time" basis as well.

Replic-Action Components. Replic-Action has three main components:

- **ODBC Admin Utility**—This configures data sources.
- **Replic-Action Composer**—This is a Notes-based developer's tool.
- **Replic-Action Server**—This is an engine that services assigned applications.

V

The World of Notes

The Replic-Action Server is available in two forms:

- **Production**—This is used to run debugged, tested applications with production databases on a scheduled basis.

- **Development**—This is used for developing applications in a test environment.

The Development Server differs from the Production Server in the following ways:

- Development Servers allow developers to maintain a functioning test environment without disrupting Production Servers.

- Development Servers are limited to only five Replicas, and five Stored Request applications. (Replicas and Stored Requests are two types of applications created with the Replic-Action Composer developer tool.)

- Development Servers cannot execute scheduled applications. Only manual execution is supported.

Functions of the Major Components. The major components of Replic-Action and their relationship to each other are displayed in figure 25.3. The following sections define the components and describe their major functions. The descriptions of each component will also help you understand the process in which Replic-Action works with your data from start to finish.

Fig. 25.3

The major components of the Replic-Action system work together to handle your data transaction.

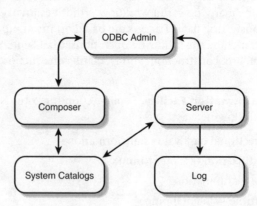

Composer. The Composer is a Notes database used to create a Replic-Action application. The Composer forms define the following:

- The databases to be accessed
- The tables/columns of interest in each database
- Any formatting changes to make data compatible between the two data sources
- Automatic actions started such as mail, docLinks, file attachments, and so on
- The data transfer type (replication, one-way, two-way, etc.), and the schedule

System Catalog. When Composer forms are saved, the application's definition is written to the System Catalog in a format usable by the Server. Multiple Servers and Composers can share the same system Catalog. By doing so, a developer working from a single Composer database can assign individual jobs to different Servers. Data transfer loads can thereby be easily balanced across multiple Servers.

Replic-Action Server. The Server executes stored applications, contains configuration and database test facilities, and offers simple ad hoc data transfer utilities.

ODBC Admin Utility. The ODBC Admin utility allows you to name a ODBC connection, choose its database driver, and configure database specific options.

Log File. The Replic-Action Server records system events and statistics, such as number of records inserted, updated, and deleted during data transfers. Administrators use the Events and Statistics Log database for troubleshooting and maintenance purposes.

Note

For more information on Replic-Action, write Casahl Technology, Inc., 3441 Quail Walk Court, Danville, CA 94506. Or call them at 510-736-7704.

ALI Design Analyzer

ALI Design Analyzer is a utility for Lotus Notes that provides developers, project managers, and database administrators comprehensive application design information necessary to effectively evaluate, customize, standardize, support, and document Lotus Notes databases. It is certified as a Runs With Notes product, and comes from ALI Technologies, Inc.

ALI Design Analyzer profiles the design elements from a Lotus Notes database and writes them into a separate Lotus Notes *Compendium database* making them readily accessible for interpretation. The Compendium database contains one profile document for every design element. Included are all attributes of the following:

- Views
- Columns
- Forms
- Fields
- Buttons
- Pop-ups
- Macros
- ACLs
- Stored queries
- Shared fields
- Selective replication formulas

To fully understand ALI Design Analyzer, you need to see it. On the enclosed CD-ROM, you will find a file containing a sample Compendium database created with ALI Design Analyzer v1.15 from ALI Technologies, Inc. This Compendium database is an actual Lotus Notes database that was created by running ALI Design Analyzer on the Wholesale customer tracking template that comes standard with Lotus Notes.

Tip

Before you convert your Notes R3 applications to Notes R4, you can use the ALI Design Analyzer to record and store your current design in a database for future reference and safekeeping. If you need to refer back to features in the old design, you will have it documented in an easy to read database format!

Another file provided for you is a ScreenCam demo of ALI Design Analyzer v1.15. The three-minute ScreenCam demo shows how easy it is to create and use a Compendium database. It shows how a Compendium database is created, including what options can be selected. The demo then switches to a Compendium database and displays an overview of all the design elements in the application. It will scroll through the View menu to show the 24 views that ship with the product. A few representative forms and views are shown. It also shows how an end user would create customized views, forms, and macros.

Note

The ALI Design Analyzer product is US$149.95, plus shipping and handling. For additional information or to place an order, contact ALI Technologies, Inc. at 617-455-6910, call toll-free within the U.S. at 800-268-8124, or e-mail **alida@ali.com** or **ALIDA @ ALI @ Notes Net**.

CleverWatch

Managing and monitoring Lotus Notes is far from a trivial task. Keeping track of system resources, supporting remote locations, and responding to server problems all take a significant amount of time out of each day. CleverWatch has helped many Notes administrators get control over their Notes environment—whether they have two servers, or 2,000 servers. CleverWatch scales to deliver a flexible management solution. You can centrally manage your servers from any Simple Network Management Protocol (SNMP) network management console, or you can manage directly from a Notes client workstation running on any Notes platform. Using an SNMP console, you can restart failed servers, issue server console commands, and launch programs or batch files.

CleverWatch is an intelligent management agent, which means that it not only detects impending problems, but also automatically takes actions specified by administrators to resolve them. These actions may include launching a program or a batch file, rebooting the server, issuing console commands, and many other tasks. CleverWatch will keep you informed about important activities taking place on the Notes server—wherever you happen to be. It comes with built-in alphanumeric paging, e-mail, and SNMP message notification capabilities.

As happens, servers crash. With CleverWatch, you can even reboot your servers from home, saving you a trip to the office! CleverWatch can also detect when a server has crashed, and if you choose, it will automatically restart it for you.

CleverWatch stores all monitoring and management information in a regular Notes database, which means that it is easy to customize to your specific management needs. You can simply modify existing documents and create new ones in the Notes management database. There are no scripts to write or programming languages to learn.

CleverWatch allows you to monitor just about all aspects of Notes servers. As all activities taking place on the server are recorded in the Notes log database as text messages, CleverWatch lets you specify which messages you want to intercept so that you can take immediate action. For example, you may want to know if a database corruption message appeared in the log and launch a fixup command to remove the corruption and prevent a server crash.

CleverWatch lets you monitor all Notes server tasks, API programs, gateways, and essentially any process running on the server. If the process stops running, CleverWatch will notify you through alphanumeric paging, SNMP traps, or electronic mail. You can also monitor tasks by their activity. If a fax gateway reports an error, you can intercept that message as it enters the Notes log.

> **Note**
>
> For more information on CleverWatch, contact CleverSoft at 207-883-3550 (fax 207-883-3369). You will also find additional documentation about CleverWatch on the enclosed CD-ROM.

PLATINUM InfoPump Integrates Lotus Notes with Relational Databases

PLATINUM InfoPump is a client/server application development tool that provides a new level for bi-directional data movement, data replication, and data warehousing in heterogeneous environments, enabling organizations to get any data, anytime, anywhere.

InfoPump enables you to seamlessly connect all of your databases, without ever writing custom data movement programs or learning database specific APIs. With InfoPump's point-and-click interface, scheduling capabilities, data manipulation capabilities, and automatic data type transformation, InfoPump provides the missing layer in your data infrastructure.

InfoPump is currently being used by over 500 companies for implementing data replication, data movement, workflow computing, and data warehousing applications. PLATIMUM's InfoPump was designed from the ground up to address the problems created by distributed

(continues)

V

The World of Notes

(continued)

data, distributed processing, workflow computing, and warehousing applications. In particular, companies use InfoPump to extend the power of Lotus Notes by integrating Lotus Notes with relational databases.

A major utility company maintains all contract administration with Lotus Notes. Each night, InfoPump scans the Notes database for contacts that have closed. It then extracts data from these contracts and enters it into an application that is used for dispatch and inventory control.

A major telecommunications firm is using InfoPump as the cornerstone of its data warehousing strategy. While Lotus Notes is the corporate standard, InfoPump is used to seamlessly move data from an assortment of mainframes and midrange systems into a Lotus Notes database that serves as the front end to the data warehouse. Instead of forcing users to query multiple systems, InfoPump makes it easy to see exactly the information needed from within a Notes form.

A major brokerage firm found critical client requests for financial transactions and account information were falling between the cracks. By integrating Lotus Notes and InfoPump, the firm found a solution to its problem. All client inquiries are logged into a Notes database and automatically routed by subject classification to the appropriate employee. If the client is not sent a response within a specified time period, InfoPump escalates the request to the next person until the matter is resolved.

A major pharmaceutical company rolled out a Lotus Notes/InfoPump-enabled order management system that serves as the backbone for sales force dialogue and ensures the timely delivery of information. InfoPump replicates order data from Notes files that are dialed in from the sales rep's laptop and delivers them to an Oracle database for receipt by the company's distribution center.

To learn more about PLATINUM's InfoPump, contact PLATINUM technology at 950 Warrenville Road, Lisle, IL 60532. Or call 708-620-5000 (fax 708-241-8206).

JetForm

Though Lotus Notes allows for the creation of many electronic forms through its programming interface, there are times when you may need to create an electronic form that exactly matches the one currently available in paper form—for example, an insurance application. You want the form to look just like the standard paper copy, but you want to be able to populate the form with information stored in Lotus Notes database—or you want to populate a Lotus Notes database from information entered into the form. JetForm is one forms package that will let you do this.

JetForm, from JetForm Corp., is one of the strongest enterprisewide forms solutions on the market. Its crossplatform support, server-based architecture, and honed features are critical in bringing forms automation to companies that have heterogeneous networks. The JetForm solution comprises several programs, including JetForm Design, JetForm Server, Print Director, Fax Director, and Distribution Directory. These programs are intended to help the forms administrator maintain version control and distribute forms across networks.

Interoperability. JetForm provides enterprisewide forms automation. The company is currently shipping different modules for Windows, Windows NT, OS/2, RS/6000, DOS, Macintosh, UNIX (SCO), VAX/VMS, Sun, NCR Corp. Series 3000, and Hewlett Packard minicomputers.

All of JetForm's database linking is accomplished through Open Database Connectivity (ODBC) links. JetForm Design includes many ODBC-compliant drivers which lets it link to dBASE, Paradox, Oracle, Btrieve, NetWare SQL, Microsoft's SQL Server, Excel, DB2, SQL/400, OS/2 DBM, Sybase's SQL Server, Ingres Server, Informix, SDB Enterprise Server, Progress, and Gupta SQL Base. Forms routing is also available for Microsoft Mail, cc:Mail, Banyan IM, Beyond Mail, GroupWise, HP OpenMail, and, of course, Lotus Notes.

JetForm Design comes with a unique Forms Dictionary that is unlike most of the other programs' object libraries and object databases. The Forms Dictionary lets form designers catalog entire forms as well as frequently used form elements into a dictionary. This dictionary is based on several criteria, including the name of the form, date created, author's name, and so on. This information helps a form designer quickly sort and retrieve forms for use in other projects.

JetForm Features. JetForm Design lets you create electronic forms or exact replicas of existing paper forms on your PC. Running under Microsoft Windows, JetForm Design has all of the needed tools to create simple to complex forms. With JetForm's Design, you can save time by reusing form objects stored in an object library. If you change that object later, JetForm updates all the forms using that object.

After you have designed a form, you can use JetForm Design's features to set the form up for being filled in. Extensive validations and calculations, choice lists, checkboxes, and radio buttons provide ways to guarantee efficient and error-free data entry. In addition, the form can be merged with existing data from other client applications— like Lotus Notes—and output via JetForm Server.

Once you've set up the form for fill-in, you can further automate your forms processing by adding links to your existing databases. With support for most industry-standard databases, you can link forms to different databases with full relational capabilities. You can also integrate JetForm with your e-mail system, as mentioned previously, to further enhance your workflow with automated approval processing.

JetForm supports the FX (field exchange) capability also shared by Lotus Notes. This lets you seamlessly pass data between JetForm and Lotus Notes. Using a JetForm template embedded in a Notes document, users can pass information gathered in Lotus Notes to the form for printing. Users can also use the JetForm form as the data input mechanism—where users key information into the fields of the form just as if they were writing out the information—and upon saving the form, the information is passed to a Lotus Notes database for storage. With JetForm, the possibilities are wide open for companies that want to digitize and automate their forms processing.

V

The World of Notes

To learn more about JetForm, call 1-800-JetForm, or 1-703-448-9544 (fax 703-448-9543), or surf their home page at **http://www.jetform.com**. Or you can write to them at U.S. Sales & Marketing, 7600-E Leesburg Pike, Falls Church, VA 22043.

OpenInsight for Workgroups

OpenInsight for Lotus Notes, by RevelationTechnologies, is a collaborative application development tool that lets you develop, share, and reuse application components when building programs for Notes users. This application provides full native access to Notes data, can create new application components with minimal coding, and can manage group development efforts to prevent conflicting actions by group members.

Developers' Tools. You can begin developing quickly in OpenInsight's Form Designer window. From there, you can create a form based on a registered Notes form or view, an OpenInsight table, or the No-Table option, which is useful for creating simple data-entry dialog windows.

To get the parts you need for your form, you can browse through all of the components in a Notes application—including its forms, views, and macros. It is simple to create a basic application interface without writing any code. Objects on the Form Designer toolbar can be dragged-and-dropped onto the form you are creating. Double-clicking any of the objects brings up a Properties screen that can be used for configuring the object.

The QuickEvent Builder tool allows predefined common events, such as Launch Form or Close Window, to be assigned to buttons and menu items. In the Properties window, you can easily view and edit the source code behind the application components; and when you are ready to test what you have, the Test Run button lets you test basic functions while you are working on a form.

Group Development Support. OpenInsight's hierarchical repository of application components is especially helpful for workgroups by making it easy for developers to collaborate in creating and refining components that they can then use again and again. Using the Check Out Entity command, a developer can lock out other developers from a component while working on it. The developer can also check a component out to another drive or even to a floppy disk, which makes it possible for the developer to take a component home to work on without fear of another developer making changes.

From the Application Manager window, you can quickly see which components have been checked out. The Impact Analysis feature shows how modifications that were made to a component would affect various other components that were linked to it. You can also assign access rights and privileges to the applications created—allowing you to give other developers as much or as little access as you want.

OpenInsight, which runs only under a Windows client, is priced at $1,995 per seat—and it runs with Lotus Notes R4. For more information on this product, check out the screencam on the CD-ROM, or contact RevelationTechnologies at 181 Harbor Drive, Stamford, CT 06902. You can call them at 800-262-4747 or 203-975-8755.

Report Designer for Lotus Notes

Report Designer creates impressive presentation-quality reports instantly and easily by drawing on native Lotus Notes data. It lets users natively generate reports using Notes' characteristic variable-length data. With Report Designer, there is no pumping, exporting, or normalizing data—it provides simple, native multi-value access. Report Designer also supports many important Notes features, like rich text format, agents, and full text manipulation. Report Designer hosts the following features:

- WYSIWYG (what-you-see-is-what-you-get) design of your reports as you create them with drag-and-drop tools.
- Object Linking and Embedding (OLE), which lets you include components from other Windows applications in your reports.
- Banding, which lets you group information in different layers for complex breakdowns of data. For example, you can create a report that groups sales by month, sales person, and/or product.
- Two-pass reporting, which lets you perform two series of calculations on a single report. For example, you can display a percentage value of a cumulative total.

Working with QuickReport. For most reports, you can probably take advantage of Report Designer's QuickReport feature, which includes built-in templates to instantly generate three different types of reports. The types of templates available for reporting Notes information include the following:

- **Columnar**—Creates horizontally placed headings with columns of data.
- **Row**—Creates vertically placed headings with rows of data.
- **Labels**—Prints any Avery laser, dot-matrix, or custom-designed label sheets.

Additionally, you can customize forms such as invoices or itineraries, and create professional-looking mailings using Report Designer.

Design Reporter runs on Microsoft Windows 3.1 (there is also a DOS version available). A single license of Report Designer sells for $129. You will need Lotus Notes R3 or greater to work with Design Reporter. For more information on this product, check out the screencam on the CD-ROM, or contact RevelationTechnologies at 181 Harbor Drive, Stamford, CT 06902. You can call them at 800-262-4747 or 203-975-8755.

ViP for Lotus Notes

ViP is an application programming environment which combines the sophisticated advances in visual programming with tight links to the Lotus Notes environment. This combination speeds up the response time of development organizations creating new applications. ViP lets developers do the following:

- Create customized, event-driven front ends to Lotus Notes applications
- Integrate data from Notes and corporate data sources
- Analyze data through sophisticated reports and charts

Harnessing the Power of Notes

ViP capitalizes on Notes' strengths. It provides important features that many Notes developers have grown accustomed to using. These features include the following:

- Full use of all Notes rich text features, including browse, launch, update, and edit.

- Easy access to Notes data, including full text queries through the Notes search engine, as well as access to Notes document hierarchies.

- The ability to mail-enable ViP applications through any Vendor Independent Messaging (VIM) and Mail Application Programming Interface (MAPI) compliant systems.

- Use of Notes validation formulas, document encryption, field formulas, calculated filed updates, and document versioning within ViP applications.

- Full use of Notes transport and automatic replication features.

- The ability to share link behavior libraries and designer tools through Notes.

- The quick results provided by View Paging and the ability to browse subsets of data at a time.

ViP for Lotus Notes requires Windows 3.1 or above, and sells for about $1,295 per developer license. For more information on this product, check out the screencam on the CD-ROM, or contact RevelationTechnologies at 181 Harbor Drive, Stamford, CT 06902. You can call them at 800-262-4747 or 203-975-8755.

From Here...

In this chapter, you learned about many of the Lotus Companion Products, as well as about several products available from third-party providers that further enhance your use of Lotus Notes. For additional information on third-party products and services, check out the files on the CD-ROM. You will find additional information in the following chapters as well:

- Chapter 26, "U.S. Technologies," provides you with more information on the types of services available to you for support, training, and custom application design, as well as a glimpse into some of their Notes products.

- Chapter 27, "Synergistics, Inc.," also provides you with more information on available training and support with a focus on sales automation.

- Chapter 28, "NEXGEN Solutions," discusses how Notes users gain support from their organization, as well as many of the other services they provide their users. You will also learn about some new ventures into the agricultural world of Notes.

Part VI

Achieving Success with Business Partners

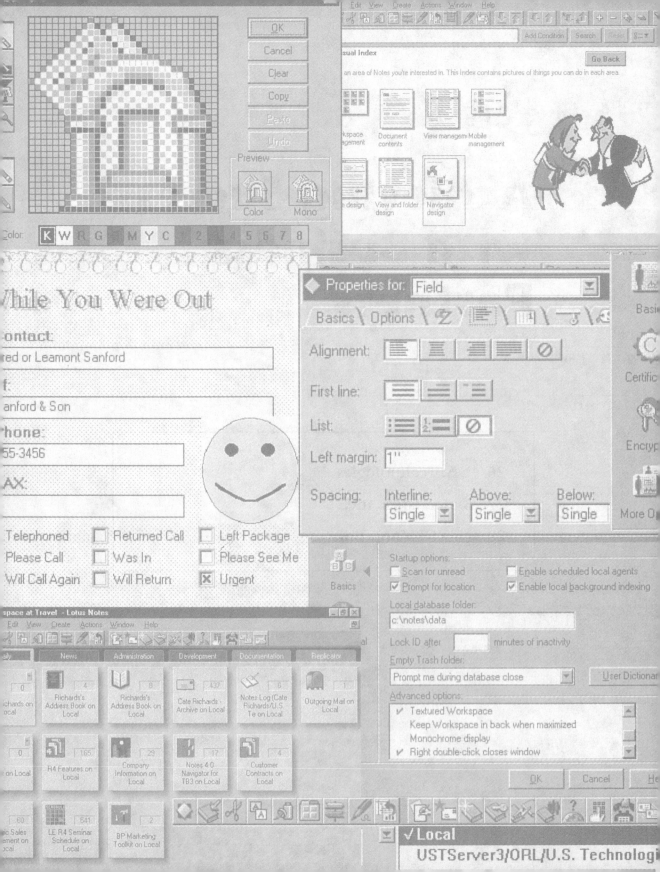

CHAPTER 26

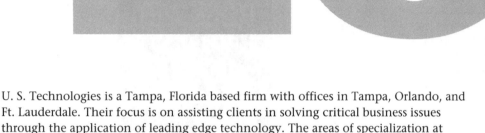

U.S. Technologies

U. S. Technologies is a Tampa, Florida based firm with offices in Tampa, Orlando, and Ft. Lauderdale. Their focus is on assisting clients in solving critical business issues through the application of leading edge technology. The areas of specialization at U.S. Technologies include:

- Groupware
- Workflow
- Document management
- Voice/video integration
- Data integration

The application of these technologies results in changing demands on clients' business processes and network topology. U. S. Technologies also addresses changing requirements in these areas.

This focus on technology and resulting business process re-engineering has resulted in areas of specialization. Unfortunately, these specialized skills are not centrally located. U.S. Technologies needed a vehicle to assist in making this information and expertise available through the internal (employees) and external (clients/Business Partners) enterprise. After careful deliberation and research, Lotus Notes was selected as the workgroup platform most able to support their communication requirements.

The application of Lotus Notes and its companion products (LN:DI, Fax Gateways, Phone Notes) at U.S. Technologies is very widespread. As their business continues to grow, new applications built upon Lotus Notes continue to be developed. The application of Lotus Notes at U.S. Technologies has broken the barrier of sharing information and has enhanced their business relationships with their clients.

The Use of Lotus Notes at U.S. Technologies

U.S. Technologies runs their business on Lotus Notes, and in fact, often displays a copy of the Lotus "Runs With Notes" emblem beside their company logo during presentations (see fig. 26.1).

Fig. 26.1

When you have a product that is certified by Lotus to run with Notes, you will see this graphic on the package!

> **Note**
>
> We began working with Notes several years back—not as a tool to market externally to our clients, but as a system we could create internally that would let us function quickly to meet our clients' needs without the internal overhead costs of a highly staffed administrative group. Once we learned the power of Notes for our internal use, we then decided to market our Notes skills to our clients as well. Any of our clients can visit U.S. Technologies and see Notes, as well as the companion products, up-and-running at any time.
>
> –Peter Steele, President, U.S. Technologies

The following sections illustrate just a few of the applications U.S. Technologies has developed to run their own internal operations.

The Front Desk

The use of Lotus Notes starts with the receptionist. All messages from calls made to U.S. Technologies' facility are entered into a Notes database and mailed to the employee. No matter which office they are working in, they will get the message. U.S. Technologies is in the process of implementing a Lotus Phone Notes application which will give the caller the option to leave a voice message. This voice message will show up in the employees' Notes mail view and can be played back from their desktops. With the assistance of a voice server that has already been installed at U.S. Technologies, an individual's desktop phone is used to record and listen to any voice object embedded in a Notes message.

A Lotus Notes-based Resource Scheduler is also utilized. With the Resource Scheduler, they know where their personnel are at any given time. The Notes-based Resource Scheduler is used to schedule people, facilities, and special equipment. The Resource Scheduler also allows the user to schedule multiple people for a single event. In these instances, the other parties involved are notified of the scheduled event through mail and can then reply as to their availability for the meeting.

Prospecting

All U. S. Technologies account executives utilize Lotus Notes to facilitate the generation of new clients. This process starts in the Prospect database. The Prospect database grows daily when the account executives add new prospects or imports external prospect lists. All information about the prospect and the business solutions they are working on are recorded and tracked in this database. Under any given prospect is a series of Notes documents. These documents may contain scanned images, incoming faxes, WordPro documents, 1-2-3 spreadsheets, or voice objects.

 ◀◀ See "Lotus Notes Document Imaging (LN:DI)," p. 862

The Lotus Notes Document Imaging (LN:DI) system and Notes Fax Gateways enable U.S. Technologies' account executives to be very responsive by putting all of the information they need to help answer their prospect's questions at their fingertips. In addition to maintaining a complete history of all contact with their clients in the Sales Strategy database, information received through glossy advertisement brochures, technical bulletins, white papers, and other communication received in paper format is scanned into Notes databases, and categorized with other technical information received online.

While on the phone with a prospect, the account executive can query these databases, and upon locating the appropriate information, he or she can automatically fax the information to the prospect directly from the database. These tools equip the account executives with all that is required to answer most of their clients' questions—without having to contact one of the technical staff to assist with the sales call.

As the prospect's business objectives unfold, the account executive is building a model of the project in the Prospect database. This database is shared with the U.S. Technologies consulting group. The consulting group utilizes additional Notes research and reference databases to begin defining a right-fit solution. This prospect/project model is automatically routed to different departments to develop the specifications and detail design which will be used in the final sales proposal. Examples of workgroup routing include engineering to verify design and components, pricing to gather current product pricing, management to approve the transaction, and purchasing to order the products.

When the solution is fully developed and ready for the proposal to the client, the account executive selects the appropriate proposal template. These templates are a part of both the Client and Prospect databases. Basic product solutions are laid out in a consistent format using a Word Pro document which is launched from the Notes Compose menu. The account executive clips the specifications developed during the consulting and design phase into the appropriate sections of the document. The proposal is automatically filed below the company profile and available to everyone in the enterprise for reference on future accounts.

Client Projects

When the client approves the proposed solution, the information from the Prospect database is moved into the Client database. This information includes company profiles, contact information, call and meeting records, proposals, and quotations. Background correspondence, statement of work information, solution design documents, and project plans are moved in to a Project database for the client.

The client has access to their Project database via Notes replication. This database contains all information associated with the project. Both the client and U.S. Technologies update the Project database. This database includes everything from project timelines to voice objects covering change orders. As the relationship expands, the client's Project database catalogs all of the business solutions in which U.S. Technology is partnered with their company.

The U.S. Technologies professionals servicing the account record their time in the Time Entry database. By using a Lotus Notes-based timesheet system, all time associated with the project is linked to the project. This facilitates both billing and historical review of the project time estimates. This database also maintains utilization rates for their billable personnel.

The Client database workgroup routing features are used during the project cycle. Routing occurs for invoicing, engineering, and management approvals, and the acknowledgment of receipt of cash against an invoice.

Client Support

During and after a project, the support center is used by their clients needing technical services. The support center database works as follows. Each client is assigned a Client Identification Number. When support is needed, they call the special support hotline. The hotline is answered by a Lotus Phone Notes application on the first ring. The client enters their personal ID, assigns a priority, and leaves a voice message describing the problem. The support center automatically assigns a trouble ticket number which is read back to the client.

When the client hangs up, the support center automatically pages the assigned support contact and sends the trouble ticket number to the pager. When the support contact receives the page, they have 15 minutes to dial into the support center, listen to the problem, and leave a voice message to the problem. If the support individual does not return the page, the call is escalated to the secondary support contact (and if that person does not respond, the President of the company is contacted!). The client can call back at any time, enter their ticket number, and listen to the response left by the support contact. This system is used to track all activity associated with resolving the call.

The Support Center completely eliminates the possibility of phone tag on initial problem discussions and facilitates problem resolution. When the support contact calls the client back, he or she knows exactly what the client reported, not an interpretation of the problem. This prepares the support contact and reduces client frustration often caused by having to repeat detailed messages.

Note

"We had an interesting situation with this system one time," remembers Peter Steele, "in which a client called into the support center on a Saturday in need of a special cable for their system. The client stressed that the call was not an emergency, but would like the support contact to ship a custom cable to them on Monday so that they could complete the installation of their network. The support contact, Vince Collie, received the call. Vince just happened to be in the vicinity of the client's office and had the cable with him. He showed up on their doorstep in less than 15 minutes—with the cable in hand—and knocked the socks off the client!"

Enhancing U.S. Technologies' Competitive Position with Lotus Notes Companion Products

U.S. Technologies is a rapidly expanding systems integrator with offices in Tampa, Orlando, and Ft. Lauderdale, Florida. Like most companies, they were faced with the challenge of coordinating remote facilities to effectively work as a team. To facilitate teamwork, U.S. Technologies made the decision early on to utilize Lotus Notes as the foundation to support their collaborative efforts.

During the design and development of their Lotus Notes-based systems, U.S. Technologies integrated the Lotus Notes Companion Products as part of their internal solution. Currently, U.S. Technologies uses Lotus Notes' Document Imaging, Fax Gateway, and Phone Notes. Very soon, U.S. Technologies will be announcing the integration of Video Notes into their internal Notes applications.

It should be no surprise that the Lotus Notes infrastructure has supported significant revenue growth at U.S. Technologies while minimizing the need to staff additional overhead positions.

The Lotus Notes Document Imaging (LN:DI) product has played a major role in the positive dynamics of U.S. Technologies. LN:DI is a comprehensive suite of Lotus Notes Companion

(continues)

(continued)

Products that helps users incorporate paper-based information into their network based communications. To illustrate this, let's review how LN:DI has solved critical business issues at U.S. Technologies, increasing their competitive edge.

Business challenge:

Keeping product literature current.

LN:DI and Lotus Notes Fax solution:

A collateral database.

Technology is changing. Products continue to get smaller, faster, and less expensive. In the course of planning and completing projects, many various software and hardware components must be selected and reviewed with a client. It is next-to-impossible to keep a paper supply of current product specification sheets, and make it available to all personnel in the company.

Each day, U.S. Technologies receives many new vendor collateral pieces. These items are imaged and stored in a Notes/LN:DI Collateral database. This process ensures that each time a vendor releases new or revised product information, it is on file. An additional benefit is that everyone at U.S. Technologies has access to this available information, not only the individual to whom it was sent.

With the addition of the Lotus Notes Fax Gateway, anyone at U.S. Technologies can be on the phone and during the course of the conversation, search for, locate, and fax product information directly to the client.

"LN:DI effectively compresses the time required to communicate accurate product information to our clients," states Larry Miller, U.S. Technologies' Vice President of Marketing.

Business challenge:

Sharing externally generated documents containing prospect information collected during the sales cycle.

LN:DI solution:

A supporting LN:DI database leveraging U.S. Technologies' Notes Prospect database.

Most project opportunities at U.S. Technologies require the collaboration of individuals from their remote offices in one fashion or another. The implementation of a Notes Prospect database addressed the basic issue of teamwork. While this Notes application facilitated the sharing of information, it contained one area for improvement—the ability to share individual handwritten notes and client-provided supporting documentation. LN:DI resolved this business requirement for them.

LN:DI enhances the Notes Prospect database by facilitating the imaging of external documents generated during the sales cycle. Instead of making numerous copies of client correspondence and supporting information, it is now digitized and shared by the pre-sales team. Handwritten notes of conversations too lengthy to be entered into a Notes activity report are now scanned and made available for review. LN:DI has effectively closed the loop on managing the sales cycle.

U.S. Technologies Products

In addition to the customized and vault applications developed by U.S. Technologies for their clients, U.S. Technologies has also developed two products that have been granted the Runs With Notes approval from Lotus Development Corporation—and they are getting ready to apply for a third certification. These two products are Launch for LN:DI, and the Lotus Notes Integration ToolKit for Solomon IV Software.

Launch for LN:DI

Launch for LN:DI is a document capture, indexing, and quality control subsystem. Launch expands LN:DI's capabilities by providing a structured environment capable of processing large numbers of documents. From core business applications to the occasional ad hoc document, Launch will save your business time in the scanning and indexing of documents.

To facilitate scalability, Launch operates independently of LN:DI and Lotus Notes. Launch only communicates with LN:DI to import documents into Notes databases. Launch utilizes LN:DI's Image Processing Server (IPS) to manage the importing of documents. The IPS import processing is completely transparent to the end user.

Launch processes documents in batches. A batch may consist of a single document or multiple documents. Within a batch, further options are available to categorize and process differing document types uniquely. Launch's architecture provides end users the ability to customize document processing based upon the type of document or Notes database. As shown in figure 26.2, Launch uses a Visual Basic front-end to facilitate the processing of documents with the click of the mouse. The user interface is user-friendly, and walks users through the steps of processing documents, based on the type of scan they want to run.

Fig 26.2

Launch makes processing documents as easy as clicking a mouse button.

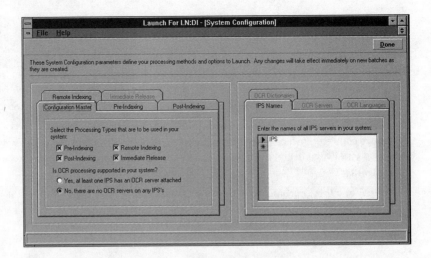

Launch document scanning supports both high-speed production and casual use scanners. This enables a scanner to be selected to match your business requirements.

Launch operates in a variety of document imaging environments ranging from full production to ad hoc systems. Each of these environments brings with it its own set of requirements. To accommodate these differences, Launch supports a variety of document indexing types including those described in the following sections.

Immediate Release. For ad hoc capture requirements, Launch provides an immediate release feature. This approach enables a document to be scanned, indexed, and released to LN:DI in an abbreviated single step. Immediate release is a less structured indexing approach but provides instantaneous importing of documents by the IPS server into a Notes database.

Remote Indexing. This Launch option takes full advantage of your Lotus Notes environment. It utilizes a centralized scanning department serviced by distributed departmental indexing stations. This approach enables those individuals closest to the document to apply the index information. Remote indexing delivers a mail message to the departmental index station indicating that a document is available for indexing. This mail routing can be selected manually or determined automatically using bar codes.

Post Indexing. This is the traditional method of scanning documents with applying index information as a second step. Launch allows indexes to be applied at the scanning station or at a separated designated indexing station. To facilitate the building and indexing of documents, a drag-and-drop document assembly is provided by Launch.

Pre Indexing. Pre Indexing enables document index information to be defined prior to scanning. As the index information is defined, Launch generates an associated bar code. Bar codes can be generated as separator pages or individual labels. Further document options allow for one bar code per document or a bar code for each page of the document.

Automatic Indexing. All Launch document options support automatic document indexing which provides the ability for index information lookup to occur from any ODBC compliant database, including host-based systems. When invoked, Launch's automatic indexing capability reduces manual data entry thus increasing document indexing throughput and accuracy.

Launch also contains option image enhancement facilitates. These include cropping, deskew, despeckle, debump, and despur—which essentially let you "cut out" the portion of the image you want to keep, realign it if it became skewed during the scanning process, and clean up any areas where the image may not have scanned in cleanly. The result is reduced document storage requirements and a crisper image when viewed.

According to U.S. Technologies, Launch provides the following benefits:

- Automates the processing and indexing of user defined document types.
- Enhances users' productivity and improves document indexing accuracy.
- Provides tools to monitor user and task performance by capturing key metrics, thus enabling management to optimize capture and indexing throughput.
- Provides the framework to image-enable document intensive Lotus Notes applications.
- Removes the resource intensive image processing workload from your production Notes environment.
- Is compatible with all LN:DI companion products.

The Lotus Notes Integration ToolKit for Solomon IV Software

The Lotus Notes Integration ToolKit for Solomon IV Software is a utility program providing two-way data migration between Lotus Notes applications and Solomon IV applications. In addition, by utilizing Lotus Notes as a foundation, workflow applications can now be built around Solomon Software.

> **Note**
>
> Solomon IV Software is a Windows-based accounting software package. The ToolKit does not replace any of the functions provided through the Solomon IV software; rather, it enhances the software by providing a tie between Notes' workflow applications and the Solomon IV software.

The Integration ToolKit utilizes Lotus Notes and Lotus Notes ViP. All Integration ToolKit operations are invoked seamlessly from Lotus Notes applications.

The Integration ToolKit consists of three components, described in the following sections.

Data Migration Module. As illustrated in figure 26.3, the Data Migration Module controls the movement of data between Notes and Solomon. Data migration is a background job which is scheduled to run periodically or on-demand. Upon finding data to be processed, the data migration module coordinates the data exchange.

Fig. 26.3

The Data Migration Module controls the movement between Lotus Notes and Solomon IV's accounting system.

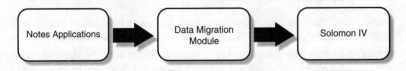

Design Templates. The design templates provide the Lotus Notes forms and views required for experienced Notes developers to design and implement custom applications. A Notes application design template is provided with the Integration ToolKit for each application licensed (such as Accounts Payable, General Ledge, Purchase Order, etc.).

According to U.S. Technologies, the following benefits are realized when using the ToolKit:

- Integration of Lotus Notes workflow processes into the Solomon applications.
- Elimination of tedious re-keying of information.
- Reduction of the probability of error.
- Improvement of the productivity by shortening the work process cycle times.

Sample Applications. The Integration ToolKit ships with a sample Notes workflow application appropriate for the Solomon application selected. These applications can be used as-is or modified to suit your particular needs. The example applications included with the kit are the following:

- **Employee Expense Reporting**—This Notes application lets employees enter expense report information into a Notes database that it is then routed through an approval process. Upon final approval, the expense report is migrated to Solomon IV where an accounts payable voucher is created in Solomon IV.

- **Requisition for Non-Stock Items**—This lets employees enter requisition information into the Integration ToolKit Notes database where it is then routed through an approval process. Upon final approval, the Requisition is converted into a purchase order in Notes. When the product arrives, the receiving information is captured in Notes and an accounts payable voucher is created in Solomon IV.

Additional Products and Services Experience

In addition to their certified Runs With Lotus Notes products, U.S. Technologies offers a wide range of products, services, and platform specialization to their clients. A few, but not all, of their most requested focus areas are described in this section giving you insight into the diversity of skills a Lotus Premium Partner can offer their clients.

Note

"We are always learning, and continue to add to the diversity of our skills every day," says Bob Hamilton, CFO. "Our ongoing objective is to provide our clients with the skills required to support Notes—on all of its platforms. Our employees are continuously training to learn new platforms, applications, and methods to meet our clients' needs."

Consulting. U.S. Technologies consulting services group provides their clients with cooperative team leadership to develop a structured framework for delivering defined business objectives. Their consulting services group is focused on jointly creating business solutions with their clients and partners. In their role as consultants and project managers, the clients' goals will be handled through support of workgroup communications, ensuring solution flexibility for future objectives and focusing attention on integrated processes and innovations which empower organizations to try new ideas, quickly, and with limited risk. U.S. Technologies has adopted Lotus' Accelerated Value Method (AVM) for delivery of all client services. AVM provides a consistent approach and technique that enables U.S. Technologies' team of skilled consultants to provide rapid, value-rich solutions to clients. (You will learn more about AVM in Chapter 24, "Inside Lotus Development Corporation.")

Systems Integration. U.S. Technologies provides objective, thorough analysis of platform and product strategies as they apply to specific requirements within each company. They then help implement these plans to meet the dynamic challenges of the marketplace. If you already have an infrastructure in place, U.S. Technologies can sustain your momentum by supporting your efforts. Specifically, U.S. Technologies' services include strategic planning assistance, network analysis and design, software applications planning and development, multi-vendor product integration, cabling system evaluation and design, equipment procurement, and ongoing systems and user support and training.

Cabling. U.S. Technologies is vertically integrated, which gives them the capability of providing all aspects of computer and telephone connectivity. They offer many products and services for complete cable management solutions. U.S. Technologies designs physical layer infrastructure, provides installation services, and performs project management. They also offer physical layer certification and analyzation, which confirms specifications and proper design.

Phone Notes. Phone Notes is an innovative development environment that allows users to participate in Lotus Notes applications from any touch-tone telephone. Phone Notes makes it possible to extend Notes applications to non-Notes users, and allows Notes users who do not have convenient access to a PC to connect to Notes from a ubiquitous client. Moreover, information captured over the telephone can be stored in a Notes document, which then uses the same integral Notes services as any other document. That is, voice messages can be replicated across a distributed workgroup and can become essential components of workflow applications. U.S. Technologies offers full consulting services in the installation of Phone Notes at client companies.

LN:DI Professional Edition (Client). The Lotus Notes Document Imaging (LN:DI) Professional Client Edition allows users to quickly and efficiently create and share compound documents using images from a variety of sources like scanned paper documents, fax transmissions, and files created in other applications. The Professional Edition enables organizations to increase their productivity, enhance communications, and increase overall efficiency. Adding desktop document image processing to the capabilities of Notes results in significant time savings, since images can be retrieved, processed, and placed in documents electronically, rather than physically located and then recreated in electronic form.

Incorporating images electronically from a wide range of documents allows users at the workgroup level to create high-impact documents. Once created, Notes documents and the image files they contain can be efficiently distributed and stored electronically, significantly reducing the cost of copying and distributing paper-based documents. As described in the "Enhancing U.S. Technologies' Competitive Position with Lotus Notes Companion Products" sidebar, U.S. Technologies has advanced skills in the application of LN:DI and its companion products, and offers these services to their clients.

Workgroup OCR. The Workgroup OCR Option allows Notes users to send TIFF and PCX image files for OCR processing. The Workgroup OCR Option converts the image to editable text and returns the text to the user in a NotesMail message or inserts it in a Notes document. OCR eliminates the time, expense, and error of re-keying important documents. This option provides usage of the full text search engine within Lotus Notes, allowing for easy search and retrieval of information stored on image documents. As with the LN:DI client, U.S. Technologies provides consulting services for the incorporation of the Workgroup OCR Option within their client projects.

Imaging Processing Server (IPS). As with the LN:DI client, U.S. Technologies provides consulting services for the incorporation of Imaging Processing Server within their client projects. The Imaging Processing Server (IPS) provides a single point of administration and setup for workgroup image processing. It receives requests from LN:DI clients, NotesMail, and third-party gateways; distributes the work to the appropriate imaging option; and, updates the appropriate Lotus Notes databases when the request is complete. Although the IPS is a powerful tool in and of itself, it also serves as a foundation for optional imaging components.

Lotus Fax Server (LFS). Not only does U.S. Technologies extensively utilize the Lotus Fax Server within their own operation, but they specialize in the implementation of the Fax Server at their client sites. The Lotus Fax Server combines outgoing and incoming fax capabilities in a single product. This includes automatic routing and print-to-fax driver software that extends fax capabilities to any Windows-based mail client. LFS supports a wide variety of fax modems, fax cards, and fax file formats. The Lotus Image Viewer is included for display, manipulation, printing, faxing, and OCR processing of the incoming fax document.

InterNotes. New to the Lotus Notes product family, and U.S. Technologies skills focus, is InterNotes. InterNotes is a product line that integrates Lotus Notes with popular Internet applications such as the World Wide Web (WWW) and UseNet News. InterNotes enables Notes users to publish Notes applications to the Internet and to access Internet information directly from within Notes. The first two Inter-Notes products are InterNotes Web Publisher and InterNotes News. The InterNotes Web Publisher enables users to publish public information created in Notes on the Web for access by NCSA Mosaic, Netscape, or other WWW browsers. InterNotes News provides Notes users with seamless, bi-directional access to the Internet UseNet News from Notes databases.

AT&T Network Notes. As discussed in Chapter 23, "Extending Your Enterprise," AT&T Network Notes allows businesses access to a cost-effective, secure, and reliable client/server computing platform over the AT&T network without incurring the associated costs of supporting and staffing their own private networks. AT&T Network Notes enables users to communicate, work together, and obtain information better than before by extending their electronic relationships beyond traditional boundaries. AT&T Network Notes is an open platform that connects to a wide range of directory and messaging services, including access to AT&T EasyLink Services and the Internet. U.S. Technologies is one of two co-marketers for AT&T Network Notes in the state of Florida. If you are interested in learning about AT&T Network Notes, or want to incorporate its services in your Notes plan, U.S. Technologies can assist you in this undertaking.

Applied Voice Technologies. Applied Voice Technologies (AVT) offers a broad line of computer telephony solutions designed to solve today's business communication needs. AVT's product offering falls into the following three basic categories:

- Unified messaging and computer telephony integration
- Sophisticated messaging and telephone call processing
- Basic messaging and telephone call routing

All AVT systems share a standard user interface and a cost-effective migration path; so as communication needs grow, you can simply upgrade your AVT system software, without replacing hardware and without retraining users.

I-Link. The I-Link New Business application is a reliable tool that provides for the input and routing of New Business applications between the Producer/Agency, Insurance Carrier, and the Carrier's policy writing system. I-Link is designed to meet the Worker's Compensation New Business needs, but is flexible enough to be customized for other lines of business as well. The package was developed using Lotus Notes, Visual Basic, Lotus Forms, and Hi-Test, and is an excellent example of how Lotus Notes can work with other development languages to meet the needs of the business. As illustrated in figure 26.4, information gathering for the new insurance application takes place in a Visual Basic front-end program that is launched from a button in a Lotus Notes document. The data entry for this application was developed using Visual Basic to take advantage of the speed in which VB can access lookup tables as well as calculate the many sophisticated mathematical formulas used to calculate the insurance premium.

Fig. 26.4

Insurance application information is entered in a Visual Basic front-end program that interfaces with Notes databases to look up and deposit information.

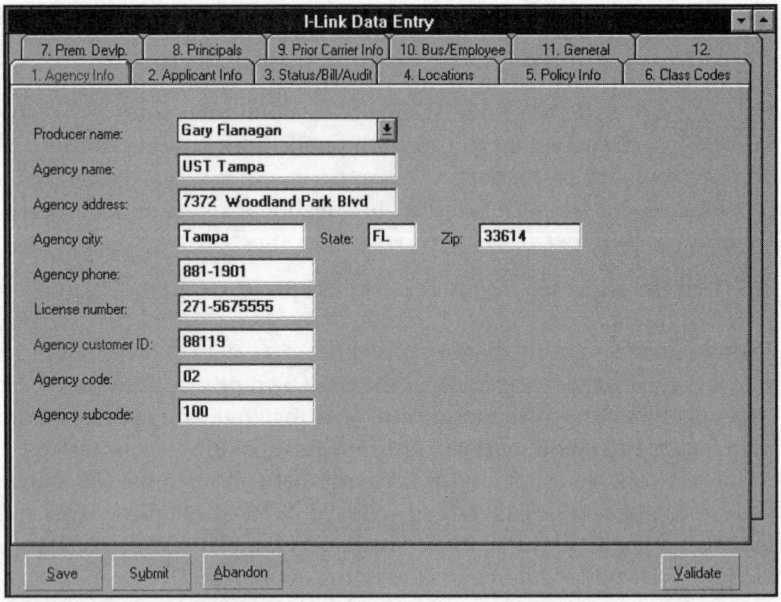

Hi-Test for Visual Basic is used to pass data to and from the Visual Basic interface and a Notes database (see fig. 26.5). The Lotus Notes database is used as the communication hub—workflowing information between the various workgroups, and eventually depositing the completed, approved application in the host system repository (typically a mainframe database system).

Fig. 26.5

Information created in a Visual Basic front-end application is deposited in a Notes database for workflow routing in the company.

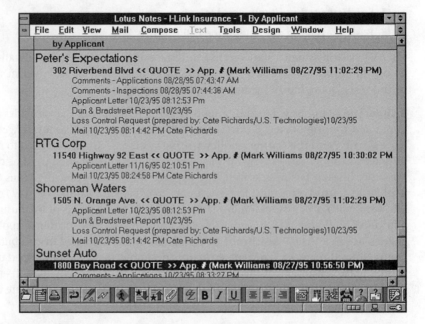

All of the configuration and administration of I-Link is accomplished using Lotus Notes databases, and no Visual Basic development experience is required to maintain the application.

Remark!. Big Sky's family of Remark! Software enhances workgroup communications by extending computer-telephony integration to the full range of workgroup members. These include those who use the telephone as their primary means of communicating with the workgroup, members who use portable PCs with wired or wireless connections, and users whose PCs are not sound-enabled, as well as users with sound-capable PCs. Big Sky's patented architecture enables businesses to use their existing PBX, LAN, personal computers, and telephone handsets to integrate voice and telephony into workgroup applications. U.S. Technologies specializes in bring this technology to their clients.

Novell NetWare. U.S. Technologies is a certified Novell shop, and provides networking consulting to their Novell customers to ensure the success of not only Lotus Notes, but the integration of Notes into the rest of the client organization's environment. NetWare software is optimized for managing, sharing, translating, and synchronizing information through network computing. The NetWare operating system defines the capabilities of a network server, managing the sharing of communications services, file and print services, database services, and messaging services. It allows these services and applications to be shared among different types of computers on the same network.

Novell has assembled a balanced array of networking products for a wide variety of computing needs—from the smallest workgroup of PCs to departmental systems and the largest business-wide environments. NetWare represents the industry's largest installed base of network operating systems helping small business and departmental managers network their computers.

OS/2. As with the Novell expertise, U.S. Technologies also maintains in-house experts for the OS/2 operating system. OS/2 is the most widely installed multitasking operating system in today's PC marketplace. It provides object oriented functions and user interface plus the ability to run traditional DOS and Windows 3.1 applications (without having to install DOS or Windows separately).

OS/2 is capable of providing high performance on a variety of hardware configuration platforms, with available support for multi-processor configurations, DASD Arrays (RAID), and all of the popular PC Bus standards (ISA, EISA, MCA, PCI, etc.). OS/2's popularity is, in part, due to the fact that the Lotus Notes Server for OS/2 provides the widest multi-protocol support of any of the Notes server platforms, thus making OS/2 the first choice for multi-protocol workgroups computing via Lotus Notes.

Windows NT. U.S. Technologies maintains advanced expertise in the configuration and maintenance of Windows NT servers for Lotus Notes, as well as other client networking needs. Windows NT is a platform-independent, scaleable operating system. It runs on systems with Intel x86, reduced instruction set computing (RISC), and DEC Alpha processors, giving you more freedom in choosing your computer systems. It is

VI

Achieving Success

scaleable to symmetric multiprocessing systems, where you can add extra processors if you need higher performance. It has multiple threads of execution, allowing applications to be more powerful; but memory protection assures stability by providing the operating system and applications with separate memory spaces to prevent data corruption. And its preemptive multitasking lets the operating system allocate processing time to each application efficiently. Windows NT is truly designed for the client/server computing environment.

Replic-Action. Replic-Action is a client/server-based data replication and migration tool to access, transform, migrate, and synchronize data between Lotus Notes and multiple external databases. Replic-Action data transfer applications can be scheduled or can begin on an ad hoc basis. Replic-Action applications can tie together and control interactions between multiple databases, providing workflow triggers, notifications, and automated actions. U.S. Technologies is a Value Added Reseller (VAR) for the Replic-Action products, with all of their consultants attending 16 hours of formal training on installing, using, and supporting this product.

Training and Education at U.S. Technologies

The successful transfer of knowledge to client personnel of all systems and database development is a key component of all U.S. Technologies project offerings. U.S. Technologies uses the following three-method approach for transferring skills necessary for successful deployment of any project; the Requirements Analysis phase includes a look at the skills in the client company. From this analysis, U.S. Technologies builds a skills transfer program that includes:

- Training (both formal and customized)
- Mentoring
- Documentation

Formal Training

During the Requirements Analysis phase of the project, U.S. Technologies will assess the core training needs of the client's system support staff. A formal recommendation will be presented with the Requirements documentation indicating areas in which core training are recommended. Recommendations are presented in the form of a training plan for each designated employee, based on that individual's needs. This training will provide the foundation for the system and database specific skills sets needed for managing the project.

U.S. Technologies offers formal classroom training for the following Lotus Authorized Education Curriculum courses. The following courses are open for enrollment by any client:

- Lotus Notes Basic Concepts
- Lotus Notes Technical User

- Lotus Notes Application Development 1
- Lotus Notes Application Development 2
- Lotus Notes System Administration 1
- Lotus Notes System Administration 2

Customized Training

U.S. Technologies develops and delivers customized training based on the requirements and specifications of the system to their client's support staff. This training will include all system administration, support functions, and database management required to successfully manage the applications developed for the client. Additionally, customized end user training and "train-the-trainer" sessions are developed upon request.

Mentoring

In addition to formal training, U.S. Technologies utilizes a mentoring form of knowledge transfer in which the client's staff works alongside the project team to gain experiential knowledge as the project proceeds. This form of hands-on training has proven successful in maximizing the transfer of knowledge, while minimizing the amount of formal post-development training required.

Documentation

Each client project is fully documented so that the client has a source of information to refer to when necessary. This documentation includes the history of the development plans, system specifications, training requirements, application features, maintenance features, and all other information involved in developing, deploying, and maintaining the application provided to the client. The documentation is provided in a Notes database format, in the form of a "guidebook," unless otherwise requested by their client.

For additional information on U.S. Technologies, contact Larry Miller, Vice President of Sales & Marketing at 813-881-1901. You can also fax information to him at 813-884-3564, or send e-mail to **Larry Miller@ U.S. Technologies@ Notes Net**.

Looking Ahead

Based upon the geographic disbursement of their offices and the specialized skills required to work with leading edge technologies, U.S. Technologies would not be where it is today without Lotus Notes. Lotus Notes has supported their continuing growth and assists in keeping overhead down.

Lotus Notes has had a dramatic impact on the personal productivity of their employees. They have been able to capture their most important asset, the knowledge of their people. The distribution of this knowledge through Lotus Notes benefits their clients daily.

VI

Achieving Success

CHAPTER 27

Synergistics, Inc.

Certified Lotus Partner logo.

In today's hectic workplace, people want to work with companies that make doing business easier. Cincinnati-based Synergistics has responded with a comprehensive solution to the complex business of automation: to simplify sales force processes and to maximize their client's investment in Lotus Notes R4.

As a Premium Business Partner and R4 beta test site, Synergistics focuses on developing and implementing Sales Force Automation systems into Lotus Notes. Synergistics has further concentrated on incorporating the new features of Notes R4 into the standard interface of the products they offer during the beta testing period, enabling them to introduce some exclusive products available at the introduction of R4. Always on the cutting edge of technology, their specialties include automation of sales, marketing, and customer service functions.

A sampling of the wide range of services and solutions that Synergistics provides includes the following:

- Educating organizations on sales force automation and its impact.
- Solidifying a firm's vision of a total selling system.
- Creating a project scope.
- Demonstrating products.
- Evaluating and customizing products for the best fit.
- Assisting in product acquisitions, including negotiating hardware, software, and service purchases.
- Helping clients capitalize on a Lotus Notes investment.
- Developing custom software and procedures.
- Modifying and improving existing software and procedures.
- Outlining cost savings and ROI measurements.
- Developing and managing a solid implementation plan.

Focusing on Sales and Marketing Solutions

More than selling a single product or service, Synergistics provides complete business solutions. They take the time to assess and evaluate customer needs and problems. They then develop a solution that is tailor-made for the client.

For example, a leading midwest-based packaging company knew they weren't packing as much punch into their sales presentations as they could. Numerous forms, outdated customer databases, and lack of tracked sales activity crippled the sales force from packaging their sales approach for positive results.

Synergistics worked side-by-side with the packaging company to develop a comprehensive sales and marketing system using Lotus Notes. All customer and project information would ultimately be tracked in Lotus Notes databases. For this solution, Synergistics designed the following:

- A master form from which additional forms for other tasks could be created. This minimized the number of forms, decreased the time sales representatives spent filling them out, and provided a means of tracking feedback to the sales force.
- Online communication for quick, easy contact between the outside sales force and internal departments. Status of sampling or other requests could now be tracked more efficiently electronically.

■ Sales and marketing tools to help the sales force automation run more efficiently. These progressive tools included the following:

- A company Rolodex with office, home, and car phone numbers that offers one-stop, easy access to this critical information.

- A unique marketing encyclopedia that shares presentations, spreadsheets, and product information among sales representatives.

- A competitive information database that tracks information on the competition, their abilities, and their action plans in the market.

- A plant information database, complete with plant contacts, equipment, and processes, which helps the sales representatives decide where to assign jobs.

According to Steven Osborn, Principal of Synergistics, "The manufacturer reports that sales productivity has measurably improved with their new system and use of Lotus Notes. Sales representatives estimate saving one and a half to two hours daily in administrative detail. Representatives find product information easier to access and use. Client files are a cinch to maintain and therefore more accurate."

Sales representatives also found more time to do their job—selling. Their requests are turned around quickly and sales groups now share information. Forms and faxes are no longer incomplete or lost, making it easier to do business both internally and externally. Now the packaging company is poised to penetrate the industry with a customized, automated sales process.

The Heart of Synergistics' Business

The culmination of expertise in Lotus Notes (to include R4), experience in sales and marketing, and foresight into the future of technology has moved Synergistics, a relative newcomer, to a front-running position in their field. Synergistics' solid combination of products, training, and application development, among other professional services, has helped organizations realize their full sales and marketing potential.

To understand the products and services Synergistics provides, a glimpse into their core offering is warranted.

Introducing Prevail

Prevail, Synergistics' premiere product, lets sales forces get down to the business of doing business. This comprehensive sales force automation program, recently upgraded to incorporate Lotus Notes R4 features, helps businesses minimize administrative detail and eliminate duplicative sales and marketing efforts. Prevail is designed to enable a sales force to be better informed, more responsive, and more resourceful. It also gives salespeople the tools to develop compelling and consistent client presentations.

VI

Achieving Success

Designed specifically for the mid- to large-sized firm, Prevail gives customers the competitive advantage by maximizing their use of Lotus Notes capabilities, including the following:

- Contact Manager
- Action Item To-do List
- Electronic notification
- Sales Opportunity Tracking
- Marketing Encyclopedia
- Basic group calendar and scheduler
- E-mail
- Full workflow automation
- Easy integration with other Lotus Notes applications
- Cross-platform, cross-network ability
- Support of forms routing
- Interface with Legacy (mainframe) systems via middleware products
- Flexibility in adapting features to mirror specific business, market, or selling methods
- Integration with other systems

Prevail's System Features

This customized and comprehensive solution is designed specifically to meet sales force automation needs. Implemented one module at a time, Synergistics' Prevail package includes the following:

- **Opportunity Manager & Sales Forecasting**—Opportunity Manager & Sales Forecasting efficiently manages complete sales cycle and forecasting. The application monitors prospecting, lead tracking, and disposition as it develops a win/loss analysis and closure ratio. Deployed in Notes, this module utilizes "near" relational technology to provide a comprehensive view of pending business opportunities.

- **Marketing Encyclopedia**—The Marketing Encyclopedia provides access to a multitude of timely, valuable corporate information, including marketing resources, tools, success stories, and promotions. The Marketing Encyclopedia enables sales representatives to share presentations and selling tools and methods. Technical and product specialists can use the online link to rapidly distribute product and industry information to the field.

- **Prevail Contact Manager**—Contact Manager tracks and maintains all company information from individual contacts and locations to client activity records and correspondence (see fig. 27.1). Contact Manager can create form letters, faxes, and "to-do" lists, and can schedule appointments. The application also assists in the integration of Office Suite, an automated correspondence function.

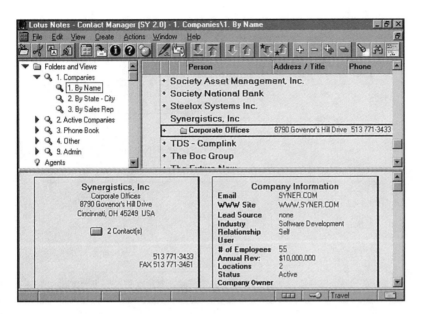

Fig. 27.1

Prevail's Contact Manager lets you see all of your company information at a glance.

- **Prevail Dashboard Option**—Similar to your own pocket calendar, this basic but innovative online time management tool displays daily appointments, action plans, and follow-up schedules. Written in native Notes, the Prevail Dashboard is completely integrated into a selling system, allowing meeting notifications and the like to be automatically updated in every user's calendar, as shown in figure 27.2. Prevail Dashboard also provides week-at-a-glance for travel planning.

- **Competition Tracking and Infobase**—The Competition Tracking and Infobase maintains competitors' profiles, products, and territories. Sales managers use the Infobase to alert their sales force to changes in the field.

- **Actions Manager Database**—This database tracks day-to-day events, meetings, and activities of all system users. Automated notification of new and past due assignments and invitations are automatically generated to other users. Action Items, Meetings, and Activities can be associated with client information, opportunities, and projects. Daily, weekly, monthly, and other periodic activity reports are automatically generated to free users of administrative time and effort.

- **Prevail Control Panel**—The Prevail Control Panel allows the operator to maintain system configuration information, keywords, and information on system users, such as phone and fax numbers. Maintenance of the Prevail Control Panel does not require Lotus Notes application development expertise, yet it can substantially change the way Prevail works for you in your company.

Fig. 27.2

The Prevail Dashboard option let's you keep track of all of your appointments.

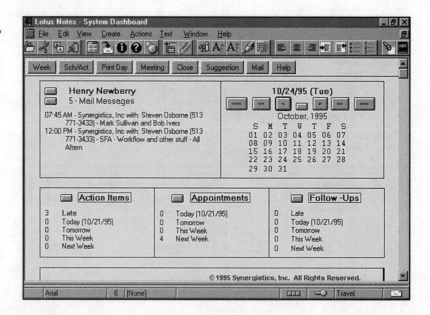

■ **News Wire Feeds Option**—In this rapidly changing business environment, it's critical to keep up with timely issues from around the globe. News Wire Feeds can be integrated with most Windows-based proposal generators to give a sales force easy access to newsworthy events as they happen.

Additional benefits offered by the Prevail application include:

■ **Pre-populated Data Fields**—Prevail lets users pre-populate data fields on-screen. This central design element requires minimal data input tasks.

■ **Pop-up Tables**—Prevail maintains pop-up tables. This central design element requires no Lotus Notes Application Development expertise. The contents of pop-up table lists are highly configurable by administrators without substantial Notes application development experience.

■ **Help Facilities**—Synergistics' system includes comprehensive application-specific help as well as a launch into Lotus Notes Help.

■ **Consistent User Interface**—Consistent use of color, typefaces, screens, reports, and similar functions are found throughout the entire Prevail system. This central design element creates a user-friendly environment that substantially reduces training time.

■ **Design Suggestions**—Prevail rapidly becomes a part of the continuous process improvement within an organization. The Design Suggestion process, included with all Prevail Modules, enables users to take ownership of the system and the business process it automates for them. The users can define and redefine the way the system works, providing continuous feedback to the development and support teams.

■ **Security and Access Control**—Access control techniques have been implemented throughout Prevail to assure that critical corporate information is accessed and utilized by those with the appropriate need-to-know. Security also substantially reduces the amount of data that is replicated to end user systems. Users can control the way in which access control is defined at the client company profile level or at the individual document level.

Mobilizing for Smaller Businesses

MobileNotes!, another Synergistics' exclusive, is the find for younger, smaller businesses looking for a less expensive alternative to automation, as well as large organizations looking to pilot-test a Notes Sales Force Solution. MobileNotes! is a turn-key service that provides all the behind-the-scenes support for a mobile sales force.

A toll-free, dial-in Notes service provides all of the advantages and capabilities of a large sales force automation system without the huge commitment in equipment, computing infrastructure, or capital expenditure. Synergistics eases a small group of users' workload by deploying a high quality application, managing and maintaining the central computing resource, giving businesses more time to concentrate on growing. In addition to the customized Prevail application, MobileNotes! includes options for 7x24 Help Desk support, provisioning and configuration services, and user recovery services.

Looking at the Whole Picture

Synergistics' focuses on ensuring that a customer's system is delivered in a timely fashion. Their project team utilizes Rapid Application Development (RAD) and Joint Application Development (JAD) techniques based on the Accelerated Value Method (AVM) from Lotus Consulting, as they execute each project. Synergistics works side-by-side with clients to thoroughly examine every issue as it relates to the full development of each client's project. This not only helps ensure that no surprises delay a project in the future; but it also brings to light those areas of the system that may have been forgotten, but if addressed will provide an even greater payback for the client. Some of these issues include the following:

■ **System Architecture**—Synergistics analyzes the current Information Systems infrastructure (all of that hardware, software, and cabling that makes up a client's network), and business environment and finds the best technical solution for overall system network architecture. In their goal to provide a robust system that will increase the data flow and reduce data conflicts, Synergistics considers the number of current Notes servers, the Notes server operating system, and the number of Notes servers needed for the project. Depending on the needs of the organization, they may recommend a single, centrally located server with lower initial cost and simplified administration. Or they may recommend a second hierarchical server network that requires a heavier investment in hardware and administration.

- **System Development and Customization**—To accurately deliver a functional system, both the client and the developer must have a clear understanding of the scope of the project, including the following:

  - The business processes that are to be automated
  - The functionality that will be provided
  - All interactions with other business and information systems
  - The persons and organizations being affected
  - The costs involved

Synergistics utilizes Notes databases to store the results of the intensive interviews of several organizational levels within the customers' organization. A final document of the analysis is presented in a Functional Requirement Specification (FRS) report that serves as a road-map to development and implementation.

Customization itself begins with baseline applications. On-going review with the customer spawns ideas that further narrow and define the scope of the project. All the while, the project team meets, tests, reviews, and suggests changes to the system for a custom fit. The team is continuously examining the following areas as the project takes form:

- **Connectivity Issues**—The majority of customers require access to information from non-Notes databases. The Synergistics' project team will evaluate and resolve any connectivity issues to these databases. Specifically, Synergistics defines each client's database needs and recommends any necessary tools and application changes to ensure full implementation.

- **Replication Scheme**—A major component to the success of each client's project is the development of a replication scheme. This replication scheme will facilitate data communication from users to server. Synergistics' project team addresses important technical issues including bandwidth, implementation, and maintenance of reader fields, organizational hierarchy, and information "fire walls." Synergistics implements reader name fields in all forms to facilitate replication scheme, evaluates and plans for corporate replication and its possible limitations and, finally, defines the data flow—or start and end point—for all data classes.

- **Implementation and Configuration**—Before a system can be implemented, Synergistics evaluates a client's site to determine that workstations are compatible and to explore any issues of data migration. Specifically, they study each site in hierarchical order beginning with the corporate office, branch sites, and individual workstations. Upon this evaluation, Synergistics can identify a Prevail server site and implement access control and security as required.

- **Documentation**—Synergistics realizes that thorough documentation is essential for successful implementation of Prevail. Therefore, they develop a prototype and reproduce and distribute documentation for end users, training participants, technical support personnel, as well as corporate, branch, sales management, and other personnel involved with Prevail.

Systems Life Cycle Management

Synergistics offers a range of services throughout the entire system's life cycle. Their specialty in sales and marketing systems, as well as workflow automation, lets them work with clients to provide top professional services—maximizing their investment in Lotus Notes. Synergistics' business and development partnership with Lotus allows them to provide top-of-the-line products and services centered on all aspects of the client's collaborative computing needs. A full line of professional services helps clients improve internal processes and increase sales capabilities.

Throughout the life cycle of the client's systems, Synergistics provides the following types of services:

- **Systems Planning and Design**—Synergistics works with their clients to define the overall system architecture and scope of each project. Specifically, Synergistics assembles the architecture plan based on needs, growth, resources, and time frames; defines the connectivity needs of the sales force; and creates a functionality list for all modules.

- **Pilot Programs and Implementation**—Synergistics develops and implements pilot programs to give a sales staff the opportunity to test the system and make improvements before it is fully integrated.

> **Note**
>
> "Since the best suggestions usually come from the 'lab' environment, we use this opportunity to further sharpen the focus of the software or distribution mechanism to further integrate the solution in our client's business."
>
> –Henry Newberry

- **Systems Performance Consultation**—Lotus Notes has several potential performance pitfalls that can hinder the successful deployment of an application. Synergistics provides consulting on techniques that help avoid these pitfalls. With a large staff of experienced Notes development personnel, Synergistics can draw on experience having already encountered and resolved most Notes performance problems. Nothing is more frustrating than knowing you aren't getting all you can out of a system. Synergistics also evaluates systems and makes recommendations that maximize performance.

- **Customization Support**—Synergistics works independently or jointly with internal development organizations of their clients to customize base Prevail applications and/or other Notes modules into the client's environment.

- **Technical Support**—Synergistics offers three areas of technical support: first-tier end user support, second-tier end user support, and on-site technical support. This support is provided for Notes as well as other components of the clients' environment.

VI

Achieving Success

- **Installation Support**—Synergistics offers complete installation support for the main server and each workstation or laptop configuration. Synergistics' configuration services group specializes in the deployment of portable computing system for the mobile user.

- **Electronic Mail**—Synergistics has expertise in integrating e-mail into a client's applications, or integrating an existing one into their new Prevail system. The Notes e-mail system included in the base Prevail package lets users capture any information on display and send it to the account team, sales manager, client, or other contact on the e-mail system. Prevail integrates easily into existing infrastructures for organizations that may already have an e-mail system.

- **System Enhancements and Upgrades**—All new releases, enhancements, and maintenance upgrades are distributed via Lotus Notes replication. Synergistics has developed internal processes that assure that new enhancements are available to all clients for rapid deployment on their version of Prevail.

- **Support**—Synergistics' level of support is adaptable to each company's specific support needs. Their 24-hour/7-day-a-week Help Desk ensures that they are always available for full support should the need arise.

All-Around Training Keeps Clients Fit

What good is a new system or process if no one knows how to utilize it? Synergistics understands the need for a comprehensive training program that educates their users on sales force automation and its impact. To solidify a company's vision of a total selling system, Synergistics offers Prevail System Training. It's flexible enough to meet a client's needs for face-to-face, intensive learning or for hands-on refresher courses. And Synergistics' team of experts is always available for follow-up questions that may arise after training. All training is customized to the client's application environment so that the experience is maximized for the participants. Their full line of training is discussed in the following sections.

End User Application Training

Participants learn the basics of Lotus Notes as well as specific applications. They also learn local and remote usage of the system.

Technical Administrator Training

Participants from the technical staff learn the basics of administration, replication, and overall system approach of Lotus Notes.

Train-the-Trainer

Synergistics provides instruction for trainers on both the everyday operation and technical aspects of Lotus Notes and the Prevail modules implemented at their company. The trainer is then prepared to teach all users at that site.

Sales Force Automation (SFA) Executive Training

The SFA Executive Training workshop offers a solid understanding of the challenges facing a company that is considering automation of the sales process. Through a formal presentation and break-out sessions, clients develop a more thorough understanding of their sales processes and the roadblocks to selling and account management. Participants also learn how collaborative computing and process automation can transform an organization into a responsive entity, as they answer the following questions:

- What is sales force automation?
- How can it help my organization?
- What technologies are used in SFA?
- What are the common mistakes made in SFA and how do I avoid them?
- What tools or products are available?
- Where do I begin the path to automation?

Specialty Training

Synergistics is currently expanding to offer LAEC training in Lotus Notes Application Development and Lotus Notes System Administration Training as well as Microsoft and Novell.

Addressing Client Business Needs Head-on

In today's aggressive and competitive market, firms face a variety of challenging business problems. How can one company like Synergistics meet the range of sales and marketing issues?

> **Note**
>
> "By applying our expertise in Lotus Notes, Synergistics responded to these critical business issues with an innovative, effective sales force automation system. We realized that these issues are important to a sales force's ability to effectively contact clients and quickly provide them with the information they need to grow the business and increase sales."
>
> –Steven Osborn, Principal, Synergistics

A Case in Point

A world leader in the manufacture of printing blankets realized they were sacrificing quality, accuracy and, ultimately, sales. The internationally dispersed sales staff of 50 direct representatives and 200 dealers had little or no client information on which to pursue leads and finalize sales calls.

VI

Achieving Success

Synergistics worked with the manufacturer to analyze the issues they faced, including late or no reports on calls made to clients, no forecasting, unmonitored quality issues, no national account coordination, and unknown customer usage of the product line.

Synergistics consulted with the manufacturer's sales and MIS departments to document the work and information flow. They developed a system that tracked client company, contact, activity, and printing press information. This system automatically fed a database that provides quality and usage information to the sales representatives. Additional e-mailing capabilities enhanced communications.

The international manufacturer reported that customer information accuracy had improved five-fold. Representatives and dealers now turn to complete account information when they pursue a sale. Call reporting is greatly simplified. Quality departments are more responsive than ever before. Additionally, the system monitors dates and other variables and generates "quality alerts" when anomalies are identified. These alerts are distributed in the same day they are identified. National accounts are now coordinated electronically and up-to-date sales forecasts are automatically transmitted.

Sales Automation Issues

Just as for the international manufacturer discussed here, Synergistics works to resolve issues that a wide range of organizations face. The following sections discuss some of these issues.

Reducing the Cost of Sales. Sales operations are expensive to run. They're even more expensive when they're not efficient. One way to reduce the cost of sales is to enable each salesperson to handle a higher volume of business, to give them the tools to close a higher percentage of their opportunities, and to increase the amount of time they spend in front of customers. A truly effective sales force automation solution must address more than tracking accounts. It must be a vehicle by which salespeople are empowered to do more business faster.

Lotus Notes and Prevail from Synergistics provide these capabilities. Effective information distribution and flow assure that the sales organization is more efficiently addressing their sales opportunities.

Shortening the Sales Cycle. In today's business environment, the decision process can become long and complex. Selling to a corporate account may involve selling to a team of individuals from a variety of functional disciplines. It may involve outside consultants. And it may involve multiple salespeople, both from within a company and from alliance partners. The key to handling all of this complexity and moving the sales process forward quickly is information management.

Notes applications are very powerful in addressing this problem. Using Notes, information is easily and rapidly replicated to the various individuals within an organization that need to participate in decisions. Prevail provides for "virtual" teams that can be assembled to address client support on an as-needed basis.

Managing Account Data Efficiently. It's crucial to reduce data duplication and ensure that all sales representatives are working from the same base of account information. Providing your sales field with up-to-date contact information saves them from an unfortunate situation of using outdated information and potentially losing a sale.

The replication and distribution features of Prevail assure that all the individuals involved with an account have the latest up-to-date information about the activities on the account. Integration with news services, pager gateways, and other Notes technologies can further increase the timeliness and effectiveness of the team selling approach to an account.

Improving Accessibility of Data. To meet the increasing expectations of customers, organizations must sell in a consultative manner. That is, the focus is on providing solutions to customers' business problems. But selling solutions is more difficult than merely selling products. It requires an in-depth knowledge of products and services, a thorough familiarity with a prospect's business and the key issues facing it, and an understanding of how a company interacts with their key customers. The key to success is giving salespeople the ability to manage and access all of that information quickly, easily, and accurately.

The Prevail modules enable a sales organization to accumulate "corporate knowledge" of a client's organization and business practices. Competitive information is also accumulated to assure that sales representatives are well versed in what their clients are hearing from other sources. This guarantees that opportunities are not missed because the client failed to get complete information.

Increasing Sales Force Productivity. One way to define sales force productivity is in terms of the ratio of selling time to non-selling time. If you can decrease the amount of time salespeople spent on non-selling time (such as handling paperwork, looking up information, or trying to communicate with others within the company), the total selling time (that is, the time spent interacting with a client or prospect) will increase. By automating the labor-intensive, non-selling aspects of the job, you can dramatically improve sales force productivity.

This is the area of greatest success of the Prevail system. Several organizations have reported an increase in selling time of over 50 percent after the deployment of Prevail. The automation of administrative tasks has allowed their sales representatives to spend a greater portion of their time doing what they do best—selling.

Maximizing the Value of Notes. An investment in Lotus Notes, both in dollars and in hours, is sizable. Synergistics believes that building a sales force automation system on Notes will help an organization maximize the value of that investment and shorten the learning curve for the individual salesperson and for the corporation. Prevail is a "native" Notes application that does not require tools other than Notes for deployment. It can run on any Notes platform (Windows, OS/2, Mac, and UNIX) or across platforms within the same organization. Other solutions depend on Windows or other environments because they use non-Notes front-ends to their systems.

Leveraging the Value of Sales Training and Methodology. Companies invest large sums in sales training to increase sales force professionalism. When a company has developed a methodology that delivers results, it makes sense to buy a software system for automation that capitalizes on that training and methodology. Investing in an SFA system that mirrors the training and that incorporates a company's methodology will avoid imposing a rigid structure onto a sales force.

Prevail provides the ability to integrate to your company's methodology. Since it is highly customizable, it can be deployed to support a variety of sales methodologies. Synergistics has clients using several of the common methodologies as well as home-grown methodologies.

Speeding Response Time. Potential customers are favorably impressed when a sales-person can respond quickly. Whether it's an answer to a technical question, a price estimate, or a meeting schedule, fast answers translate into an impression of credibility and responsiveness. The secret to quick response is providing salespeople with a tool that simplifies access to the information they need. That means the sales force automation system cannot be an isolated system, but must integrate effectively with other business critical information sources.

Maximizing the Value of Existing Data. Many companies conclude too quickly that existing databases in historical MIS are out-of-date or unusable. A good business partner will work with you to utilize this information and minimize any need for you to start from scratch. Prevail modules are designed to accept data from, and provide data to existing systems.

Benefiting from a Business Partnership

Business partners can help you address specific business needs or problems. By partnering, organizations stand to gain a number of important benefits and positive outcomes. For example, Synergistics' specialists helped a market-leading personal computer company recover from a rut in lagging opportunity tracking, poor forecasting, outdated pricing, and missing account information.

Synergistics "renovated" the company's sales management system and integrated Prevail, including Contact Manager, Activities, calendaring, and scheduling tools. They made the system e-mail- and agent-enabled. Custom development included opportunity tracking and forecasting, field inventory and tracking, pricing and availability, and market development and co-op funds tracking.

Now the innovative company has recaptured its market status. Account information is shared and tracked effectively; the cycle time for special pricing, forecasting, and requests has been reduced; and the organization communicates better and is more responsive.

According to Henry Newberry, Synergistics' sets out to help organizations improve performance and resolve issues such as the following:

- **Closing more business**—An effective system of sales support and automation can enable salespeople to close a higher percentage of the opportunities they handle. Closing more business means that the sales process is more productive; for the same investment of time and energy, your yield is now much higher.

- **Managing more accounts**—One way to measure positive results is to look at the volume of work your people are able to handle. A successful sales automation system will give salespeople the tools to handle more accounts without sacrificing quality. The key is a just-in-time approach to information management. By giving them the information they need, when they need it, the system enables sales professionals to manage a larger number of accounts.

- **Increasing profitability**—By eliminating obstacles and increasing the salesperson's access to information, you can increase the profitability of the sales operation. Wasted effort will be reduced. Mistakes in the sales process will be nearly eliminated.

- **Improving quality of sales process**—One way to improve the quality of the sales process is to make sure that every contact with a prospect adds value to the relationship and moves the sales process closer to closure. By having key information readily available, the sales professional is better prepared to answer questions, provide solutions, suggest alternatives, and solve problems.

- **Penetrating new markets**—To enter new markets, a sales force needs new knowledge. By providing easy access to key information and by allowing a sales force to work together in a collaborative way, organizations can speed penetration of new markets.

- **Selling at higher margins**—Superior knowledge and responsiveness are the keys to adding value to the customer's processes. And adding value is the key to selling at higher margins than competitors.

- **Improving professional image**—Consistency, accuracy, and responsiveness are the characteristics of a highly professional organization. A technologically advanced organization exudes with progress and competency. Those are the qualities that become inherent in an organization when it provides a shared information platform and effective automation tools.

Synergistics: A Personal Profile

Synergistics has been called "Notescentric" in the business, making Lotus Notes expertise their claim to fame. Their relationship with Lotus Development as a Business Partner and Developer has given them a leading edge in the marketplace.

Though relatively new to the market, Synergistics has evolved quickly into a powerhouse provider of sales and marketing solutions. Lotus, Synergistics clients, and industry analysts who've seen the competition, agree that Synergistics provides an innovative, superior product. Their collaborative approach to executing sales and marketing systems has helped small, mid-size, and large firms simplify the complex process of sales force automation.

Synergistics team members culminate 50 years of experience in sales, engineering, programming, and project management. Since May of 1994, this blend of expertise in a multitude of technologies and numerous disciplines has allowed them to success-fully implement programs that are tailored to each individual client.

Backed by Mobile Computing Systems (MCS), Synergistics' financial strength has allowed them to emerge as new leaders in the field. Heavy investing in new technolo-gies lets them develop robust sales force automation systems. Consequently, their technical staff grows rapidly to provide for growth in systems integration, application development, and end user support systems as they apply to collaborative computing.

CHAPTER 28

NEXGEN Solutions

NEXGEN SOLUTIONS, INC.

Your Pathway to Emerging Technologies...™

As mid-1995 approached, there were more than 9,000 Lotus Notes Business Partners, more than 1,500,000 users of Lotus Notes, a burgeoning development community, and a lively marketplace where companies and contractors place their skills on the table and usually have them snatched up by hungry Notes patrons. Companies of all sizes and shapes participate in the frenzy to get the fastest Notes application with the mostest. Large enterprises such as Anderson Consulting are hawking their talent and skills to other like-sized corporations such as General Motors or Marriott Corp. Individual consultants who have only themselves to present are caught up in this whirlwind of Notes marketing, hoping to someday be another Anderson Consulting or Price Waterhouse in the client/server world or at least to work for these corporate giants on projects to make their resumes glow.

Added to this increasingly large and complex melange is the purchase of Lotus by IBM for $3.5 billion, the largest acquisition in software company history, giving Notes muscle that would force Arnold Schwarzenegger (and Bill Gates) to look twice.

Ascending this craggy, wind-driven, yet accessible, mountain is a small, growing enterprise called NEXGEN Solutions, Inc. (NGS), a Washington D.C.-based Lotus Notes Business Partner with unique skills and a unique business profile.

Looking Inside NEXGEN Solutions

In many regards, NGS (formerly known as Personal Computer Consultants, Inc.) embodies a typical entrepreneurial company that caught the Notes wave. There are roughly 20 employees and several contractors that work for them. They pay salaries to their developers and administrators above the industry standard and they provide a full health benefits program. Their primary revenue stream is garnered from professional services. They have a 90s-style staff who is generally technologically savvy, not just Notes aware, and a corporate structure complete with overhead.

One of the areas that makes NEXGEN unique is their employee selection philosophy. Corporate structure doesn't mean corporate culture and the dominant NGS professional direction provides a Notes staff that is "intellectually restless." In the words of Paul Greenberg, Director of Marketing and Communications at NGS:

> "Creative solutions providers are the core of our recruiting policy. It's easy to recruit based on Notes skill sets. You can always find the person who knows the Notes API or Notes administration or development. What you can't find so easily is that extraordinary person who has the combination of healthy ambition and the ability to think on-the-fly. These people are the reason for our success. Our perspective on Lotus Notes is that the flexibility and extendibility of Lotus Notes is a tool for the flexibility and creativity of our staff."

Because staff members have an intellectual curiosity that goes beyond their life at work, they are active in pursuing many outside interests including music, writing, and politics. One employee won the Maryland State Championship with his skills in classical trumpet several years ago!

Note

"The pursuit of outside interests only enhances the quality of work internally," said Steve Chrysostom, one of NGS's chief Notes architects, "It provides the kind of cerebral activities that make the job more significant because problems become challenges to solve, not obstacles to solutions. The solutions are often far more significant and groundbreaking because they emerge from what is perceived as a work-related intellectual puzzle, not a hair-tearing obstacle to progress."

NGS Notes projects have ranged from enterprise-wide Notes services to the design and development of single complex applications. This small company, which began as a marketing enterprise for a hardware security key, became a Notes Business Partner and Developer in 1992. This was the basis for its transformation into one of Washington D.C.'s most rapidly growing minority enterprises.

Note

"When I started the company in 1988, I didn't have any idea that I would become a Lotus Notes Business Partner, nor did I suspect subsequently in any way that it would turn out to be the best business decision I've made to date," says Edward L. Howlette, Jr., President and founder of NGS. "Notes has been the focus and foundation of our business model and a major reason that we are seen as an entrepreneurial success. I think that other aspiring Notes Business Partners would do well to get into the Notes world now, because it is just beginning to grow. I would advise them to make sure that they do two things. First, they hire senior staff who have at least two to three years in developing Lotus Notes; second, I would, if at all possible, begin a program to 'grow your own,' developing in-house Notes capabilities. The competition for excellence is fierce in the Notes world and many Notes developers and administrators stay independent because at this juncture they think they can write their own ticket. So begin in-house development now and it will pay in the long run."

As a result of Lotus Notes contracts, NGS revenues increased by 1800 percent from 1992 to 1993 and 300 percent from 1993 to 1994. Their revenues for 1995 have more than doubled their total revenues for 1994 by a wide margin and are expected to accelerate even more rapidly in 1996.

In addition to its innovative staff recruitment policy, another feature of the NGS business model is its pursuit and recent award of 8(a) certification by the Small Business Administration. This government-mandated program is designed to aid small, historically underutilized businesses in gaining a market advantage until specific financial and size criteria are met. This allows NGS to bring Notes solutions to any government agency and be awarded the business without the usual government bidding process. This has already led to several federal opportunities in the development of Notes architecture for this year.

NEXGEN Clients and Partners

The staff quality has given NGS a growing reputation in the Notes community as a top recruiter. These highly qualified people have been the basis for the NGS client list which combines Fortune 500 companies with government agencies and smaller companies. Coopers & Lybrand, Lockheed Martin, Novell Inc., Marriott Corp., Vantage Technology, Cigna, NYNEX, Ernst & Young, KPMG Peat Marwick, and most interestingly, Lotus Consulting, the Lotus Notes business development group within Lotus, are among the NGS clients.

> **Note**
>
> A more complete list includes the commercial companies Johnson & Johnson, Ernst & Young, GEIS, Interamerican Development Bank, NASD, Novell, Lotus Consulting Group, Fannie Mae, Chase Manhattan Bank, Lever Brothers, Colgate Palmolive, Compucon Corp., Mindbank, Vantage Technologies, Marriott Corp., American Stock Exchange, Coopers & Lybrand, Lockheed Martin, NYNEX, and AT&T. Also included are the U.S. Marines, Environmental Protection Agency, Department of Labor, Internal Revenue Service, U.S. Marshall's Service, and U.S. Army.

The NGS/Lotus Consulting relationship is the most interesting and far more complex than just a typical prime contractor/subcontractor business arrangement. It began in 1994, after a top Lotus Consulting Group official was impressed with the work done by NGS at NYNEX. This has led to what has been called an "extraordinary" association, one that prompted a Lotus Consulting official to nominate NGS for a Lotus Beacon award in the category "Best Partnering with another Business Partner." The partnering relationship? NEXGEN Solutions, Inc. and Lotus Consulting!

More recently, NGS has expanded its relationship with Lotus Consulting to the entire country, working on projects in Cincinnati, Detroit, Denver, and Chicago. This includes the planning of the Avantis Notes Global Communication Project which is a Notes-based service with monthly rates run by IBM subsidiary Avantis. This will involve the largest roll-out of Notes workstations in history, according to Lotus Consulting Midwest Managing Director Mike Harnisch, with 200,000 workstations completed the first year and up to one million subsequently!

NEXGEN's Development Process Philosophy

There is a method to the "madness" in the creation of a product for market and in the successful delivery of an application to a client, says Michael Rose, Director of Consulting Services for NEXGEN Solutions. A tip to keep in mind when you are creating revolves around your ability to rapidly develop value to the client in stages that are clear to the client.

> **Tip**
>
> "We use a process called iterative development. While it resembles prototyping, it is not quite the same. The idea is to have the client heavily involved in the process of creating the application. After the first phase is conceptualized, a working model is delivered to the client and discussed with the client. This phase allows the client to either find the bugs or change the subsequent model or add features that they hadn't thought of until that very day. Then these features are incorporated, and/or the bugs fixed, and/or the model scrapped and changed, and the next iteration is developed and the process begins again. This goes on until the job is successfully accepted by the client," said Rose, "I ran into this recently at one of our Big Six clients. I had completed the application exactly according to the specifications that they had written, but during the meeting after the first iteration of the application, several of the decision makers who had not been involved in the initial technical specifications discussions, decided to change the model that the client had originally developed for us. So iteration number two is now underway."

NEXGEN Provides Problem-Solving Solutions

The core of NGS business still remains commercial. It was a commercial contract in 1993 that provided the breakthrough that catapulted NGS to the level of growth that it currently sustains. They were tasked, initially under a subcontract and later a direct contract by NYNEX, the New York telecommunications giant, to plan, install, develop, and roll out Notes applications for a client/server architecture that was fairly new to NYNEX. Several business areas within the Telesector Resources Group had to be integrated into a workflow that would make sense to the group: sales, pricing, engineering, legal, and contract administration had to be seamlessly joined so that each section was aware of the other's activities. NGS' solution was to develop a highly complex Lotus Notes workflow application that involved Lotus Notes, the Notes API, Lotus 1-2-3, Lotus Freelance, C++, Oracle, REXX, Q&E, OS/2 Presentation Manager, DOS, Windows, UNIX, and a variety of mainframe applications. The savings at NYNEX were considered to be substantial.

Problem-Solving Examples

In addition to helping NYNEX solve their communications problems, NGS has been involved in the solution of several other very challenging projects in the Notes environment.

Problem One. Each day, across every government agency, there are thousands of requests under the Freedom of Information Act that have to be acted upon within government mandated time limits and that are subject to detailed Congressional reporting requirements. Each request for information has to be routed and tracked. The Environmental Protection Agency was subjected to multiple requests in any given day and only a small percentage of what was received could be processed. The processing volume and its tracking had to be increased to meet the requirements.

Solution. Current NGS team members created a national Freedom of Information Request Tracking System using Lotus Notes on a Novell Token Ring Network. The productivity of the EPA increased.

Problem Two. The Department of Labors Office of Microcomputer Support needed a means of tracking all their incoming correspondence and internal correspondence. The difficulty was that each location dealt with tracking in a different way. They needed to address the workflow issues involved and then design the system, since the general approach was considerably more decentralized than the Department of Labor would have liked.

Solution. With Lotus Notes as the engine, a single NGS employee, in a 60-day period, had completed the requirements analysis, produced design documentation, defined the workflow, and developed the prototype national correspondence tracking system.

Problem Three. The American Stock Exchange had large volumes of data that had to be shared between mainframe computer systems and client/server based applications (particularly Lotus Notes). This data had to be placed in commonly utilized word processors and databases.

Solution. NGS wrote a Lotus Notes API (Applications Programming Interface) program to integrate the mainframe and client/server data with the word processors and commonly used databases through Lotus Notes as the interface.

Problem Four. The EPA was getting a large number of requests from the users in their field offices for applications enhancements that had to be reviewed. Several departments had oversight of one part or another of this process, and each of those departments had to approve the actions taken for the part of the process for which they were responsible.

VI

Achieving Success

Solution. NGS designed and installed a Lotus Notes Change Management System. This allowed the various divisions at the EPA to track, monitor, and take action on the application enhancement requests from the various departmental field users.

NEXGEN's Commerce Business Daily (CBD) Connection

NGS's first Notes product, the Commerce Business Daily (CBD) Connection, was released in the early summer as a service on CompuServe's Enterprise Information Link. This venture provides a Lotus Notes interface and engine for Commerce Business Daily subscribers. The product employs the full-text search capabilities of Notes to allow the customer to find the opportunities and awards being issued by the federal government. A variety of views allow the user to find the opportunities and the awards by agency, by date, by dollar amount, and so on.

Working Together with AT&T Network Notes

The NGS business model differs from most Notes Business Partners by its focus on cutting edge technology. This focus, and the innovative approach taken by NGS engineers has led to NGS participation in the "sexy" Lotus Notes projects—those projects that are involved in the creation of new modes or new conventions in Notes, but are very high profile. For example, NGS, initially through its relationship to Lotus Consulting, created the AT&T Network Notes server farm, using its engineers so successfully during the alpha phase in New Jersey, that when the project moved to Missouri, Lotus turned the project over to NGS directly.

Working with Novell's Embedded Systems Technology (NEST)

Additionally, NGS currently is the only small company in the United States that is authorized to develop, train, resell, and support Novell's Embedded Systems Technology (NEST), a cornerstone Novell technology that allows office machines, home appliances, factory floor machine tools, and any other intelligent or potentially intelligent device to connect to the network. This led NGS to devise a creative integration of Lotus Notes with NEST.

Novell tasked NGS to develop a demonstration of their NEST technology at the Networld/Interop conference in Atlanta in September 1994. This was to be a definitive example of NEST that was coupled with Novell Chairman Robert Frankenberg's announcement of the Pervasive Computing strategy designed to take Novell into the twenty-first century. NGS' problem was that they had three weeks to develop a demo that would, at least, stun the conventioneers if not stop them in their tracks. Lotus Notes became a centerpiece of this Novell-sponsored demonstration.

In order to elicit the necessary crowd reactions to support NEST, NGS created a Smart Mailbox, a corporate mail bin that responds to mail placed in the box with a signal that tells Lotus Notes e-mail to send a message that the user's mail is in the mailbox for pickup. The demonstration was a great success.

Currently, NGS is working on creating a Lotus Notes Command Transport Layer that will take devices that are NEST-enabled and use Lotus Notes as the vehicle for delivering instructions to the intelligent devices. For example, a Lotus Notes e-mail could be sent from your office to your VCR at home telling it to record *Star Trek: The Next Generation* at 10:00 o'clock, Tuesday night. This project will be the foundation for the successful marriage of the groupware standard with a cutting edge technology.

Working as a Notes 4.0 Beta Site

The commitment to the cutting edge and their active role with Lotus Consulting led to NGS' selection as part of the 200 plus companies beta testing the first build of Lotus Notes Release 4. The new features of Notes 4.0—such as the robust cc:Mail-like e-mail functions (e.g., intelligent agents) and the use of LotusScript 3.0 rather than the much leaner macro language that has been a Notes focus since its early incarnations—shows the NGS engineers the possibilities to build the kind of full-featured applications with the ease of use that Notes version 3.0 developers could only dream about.

Working on the Cutting Edge

The 1990s has been the decade in which both large and small enterprises and individuals have had their imaginations fired by the possibilities of technologies creating the virtual global village or city (depending on preference) that was only the subject of science fiction up until the 1980s. The incredibly rapid growth of the Internet and the linkage of the human species through cyberspace has not only created new industries (for example, Netscape), but has changed the thinking of humankind.

Passionate arguments and discussions on technologies that were seen as the province of the previous genre of computer professionals, have become the everyday fare of the social marketplace, with intense involvement in the evangelizing for and against particular technologies. It is useful for businesses to be involved in this intense and very public debate and discussion on the use of technology, because the fundamental nature of the form that the global network and universal communications will take is at stake as the millennium approaches. Companies that utilize cutting-edge technologies such as Notes need to be involved in helping to shape this, both for reasons of social responsibility and simple good business sense. There are dozens of opportunities that will be present as the debate continues to be stoked and to burn.

– Michael Rose, Director of Consulting Services for NEXGEN Solutions.

NEXGEN Grows Agriculture

The ability to work on the cutting edge leads to solution areas previously untouched in the Notes community. In the case of NGS, this has led to a unique and interesting niche in the Notes market as 1995 draws to a close. Lotus Notes has been brought to the world of agriculture.

By most standards, rural America doesn't seem to be the place for a product like Lotus Notes. The standard stereotypical perception of the rural resident is the farmer isolated by miles from his neighbor. There is a certain sweet simplicity to this image, capturing America in the 90s—only this image fits the 1890s, not the 1990s. Modern rural agriculture is a high-tech industry that not only applies advanced machinery such as tractors with computerized cabs, but uses such superior methodologies as satellite-based global positioning to determine the state of the crop acreage. Several of the larger organized rural cooperatives (which are multibillion dollar companies) such as Growmark, Inc. have linked themselves via the Internet, running a home page, and have become involved not only in the production and distribution of agricultural products, which was the foundation for their charter, but in the creation and sale of software to enhance that process.

This involvement led the National Council of Farmer Cooperatives (NCFC), a national lobbying and services association representing 4,300 agricultural cooperatives and two million farmers, to seek out NGS to begin the implementation of Lotus Notes at their headquarters in Washington D.C. However, this burgeoned into an increasingly deep alliance as the NCFC realized the possibilities of creating an organized network of two million farmers that could speak with a unified political voice. They also saw the business possibilities of linking suppliers and distributors of disparate cooperatives to make the cycle from commodity production to final buyer more effective. They also saw Lotus Notes as the means to accomplish this. This led to NGS representatives speaking on "Agriculture and Technology" to the CEOs of 32 multibillion dollar cooperatives from the United States and Western Europe at a international conference in Orlando, Florida in May 1995. The subsequent discussion fired the imaginations of the NCFC membership.

At the end of September 1995, a task force was convened to define an "agriculture standard" for technology and communications. The Task Force, hosted by the NCFC, involved the most technologically savvy members of the association and their decision makers including Ocean Spray, Growmark, Southern States Cooperatives, Land O' Lakes, and Sunkist. NGS worked closely with the NCFC on the planning of the conference. Representatives of Lotus Consulting spoke at the conference as did NGS. The result was a ringing endorsement by the NCFC of Lotus Notes as the standard and a public endorsement of NEXGEN Solutions, Inc. as the company to implement it in the agricultural community.

Looking Ahead

NEXGEN Solutions, Inc. is planning a series of new product initiatives in the remainder of 1995 and 1996 that will enhance its presence in the federal government and the government contracting and the quality management markets. They include applications that do the following:

- Use the Electronic Document Interchange (EDI) format mandated by the federal government as the standard for electronic commerce by 1997.

- Bring the entire Code of Federal Regulations (CFR) (86,000 pages) into Notes format and output to the workflow of those corporations involved in regulatory compliance.

- Provide corporations the ability to successfully prepare to be audited to meet the compliance mandated by ISO9000 for certification and include an optional module that will cover the new ISO14000 environmental standard.

- As version 2.0 of the CBD Connection, provide the first phase of automating the request and response processes for bidding on federal contracts. A later incarnation will be EDI-compliant.

NGS is part of the business paradigm that is projected to drive the technology and information markets into the twenty-first century. NGS and Lotus Notes are exciting companions together on the ride.

If you would like more information about NEXGEN, contact Paul Greenberg, Director of Marketing and Communication, NEXGEN Solutions, Inc. Phone - 202-638-7777; Fax - 202-638-6200; Notes Net - Paul Greenberg @NGSINC @NOTES NET. Internet - Paul Greenberg @ngsinc.com.

VI

Achieving Success

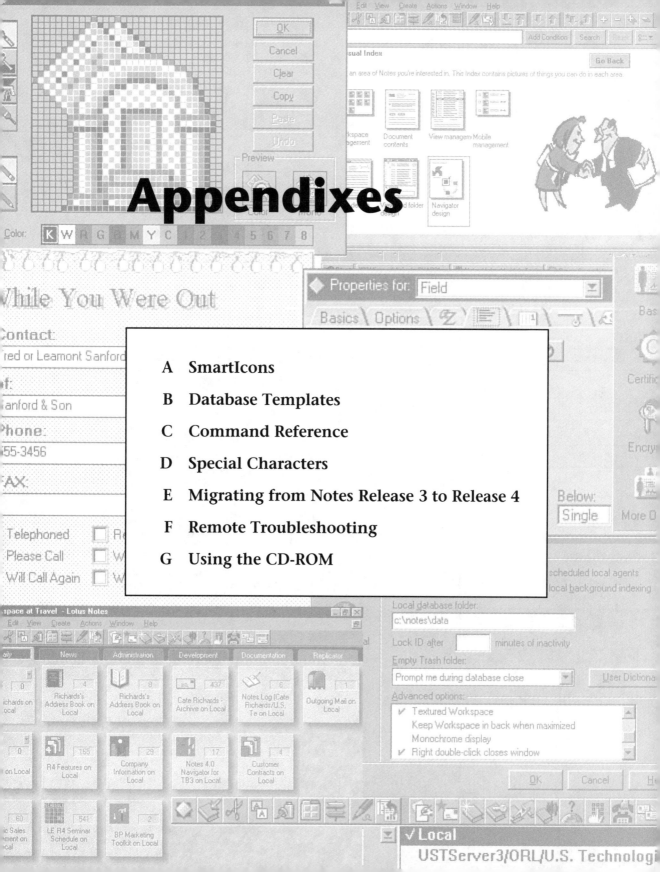

Appendixes

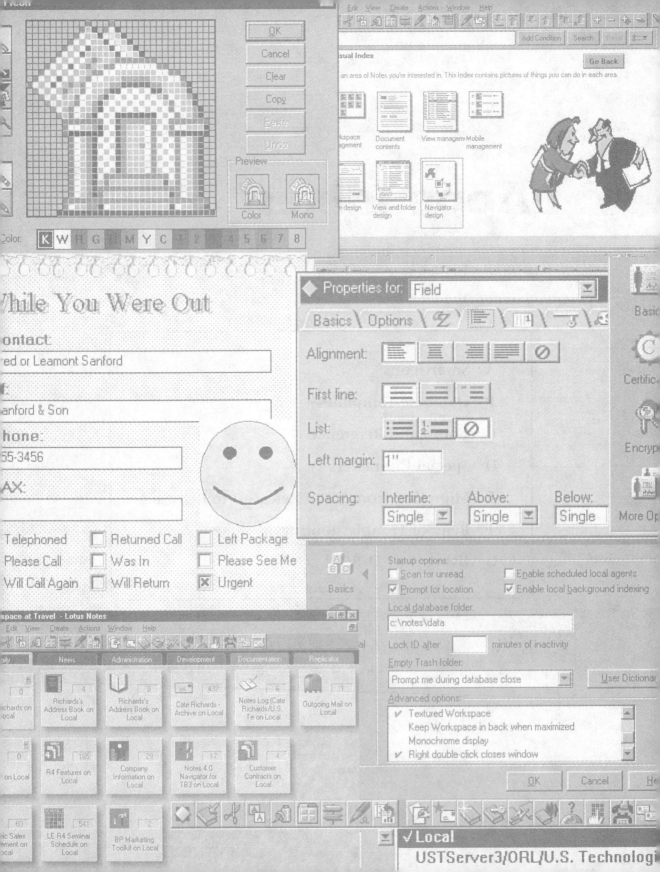

APPENDIX A

SmartIcons

This appendix lists all the SmartIcons available in Notes Release 4, the equivalent menu command, and a brief description.

> **Tip**
>
> If you forget the meaning of any SmartIcon displayed on the SmartIcon bar, click and hold the right mouse button while pointing to the icon. Notes displays the description of the icon at the top of the screen.

SmartIcon	Name
	Actions Categorize
	Actions Edit Document
	Actions Forward
	Create Agent
	Create Button
	Create Ellipse
	Create Field
	Create Folder
	Create Form

(continues)

(continued)

SmartIcon	Name
	Create Graphic Button
	Create Hotspot Text Popup
	Create Hotspot Polygon
	Create Insert New Column
	Create Insert Shared Field
	Create Insert Subform
	Create Layout Region
	Create Mail Memo
	Create Navigator
	Create Object
	Create Page Break
	Create Polygon
	Create Polyline
	Create Rectangle
	Create Shared Field
	Create Subform
	Create Hotspot Rectangle
	Create Rounded Rectangle
	Create Table
abc	Create Textbox
	Create View

SmartIcon	Name
	Design Bring to Front
	Design Send to Back
	Design Column Properties
	Design Field Properties
	Design Form Properties
	Design Icon
	Design View Properties
	Design View Form Formula
	Design View Selection Conditions
	Edit Check Spelling
	Edit Clear
	Edit Copy
	Edit Copy As Link
	Edit Cut
	Edit Find
	Edit Find Next
	Edit Links
	Edit Mark All Read
	Edit Mark All Unread
	Edit Mark Selected Read

(continues)

(continued)

SmartIcon	Name
	Edit Mark Selected Unread
	Edit Paste
	Edit Paste Special
	Edit Scan Choose
	Edit Scan Unread
	Edit Scan Unread Mail
	Edit Select All
	Edit Undo
	File Attach
	File Database Access Control
	File Database Design Synopsis
	File Database Full Text Create
	File Database Full Text Info
	File Database Full Text Update
	File Database Header Footer
	File Database New Copy
	File Database Properties
	File Database Publish
	File Document Properties
	File Exit
	File Export

SmartIcon	Name
	File Import
	File Mobile Call Server
	File Mobile Edit Locations
	File Mobile Hang Up
	File New Database
	File Open Database
	File Page Setup
	File Preferences Mail
	File Preferences Ports
	File Print
	File Print Setup
	File Replication New Replica
	File Replication Replicate
	File Replication Settings
	File Save
	File Switch User ID
	File Tools SmartIcons
	Help Guide Me
	Help Topics
	Logoff

(continues)

(continued)

SmartIcon	Name
	Mail Address
	Mail Open
	Mail Send Document
	Navigate Next
	Navigate Prev
	Navigate Next Main
	Navigate Prev Main
	Navigate Next Selected
	Navigate Prev Selected
	Navigate Next Unread
	Navigate Prev Unread
	Navigate Next Highlight
	Navigate Prev Highlight
	Navigator Properties
	Properties
	Paragraph Properties
	SmartIcons Floating
	SmartIcons Next Set
	Table Delete Selected Row(s)
	Table Delete Row Column
	Table Insert Row Column

SmartIcon	Name
	Table Insert Row
	Table Properties
	Text Align Paragraph Center
	Text Align Paragraph Full
	Text Align Paragraph Left
	Text Align Paragraph Right
	Text Bold
	Text Bullet
	Text Cycle Paragraph Spacing
	Text Enlarge Size
	Text Indent
	Text Indent First Line
	Text Italic
	Text Normal Text
	Text Numbered List
	Text Outdent
	Text Paragraph
	Text Permanent Pen
	Text Properties
	Text Reduce Size

(continues)

(continued)

SmartIcon	Name
	Text Style Cycle Key
	Text Underline
	View Expand
	View Expand All
	View Collapse
	View Collapse All
	View Go Up Level
	View Page Breaks
	View Refresh
	View Ruler
	View Server Names
	View Show/Hide Action Pane
	View Show/Hide Preview Document Links
	View Show/Hide Preview Pane
	View Show/Hide Preview Parent
	View Show/Hide Programming Pane
	View Show/Hide Search Bar
	View Unread Count
	Window Workspace
	Window Cascade
	Window Tile

SmartIcon	Name	Description
		User-customizable icon
		User-customizable icon
		User-customizable icon
		User-customizable icon
		User-customizable icon
		User-customizable icon
		User-customizable icon
		User-customizable icon
		User-customizable icon
		User-customizable icon
		User-customizable icon
		User-customizable icon
		User-customizable icon
		User-customizable icon
		User-customizable icon
		User-customizable icon
		User-customizable icon
		User-customizable icon
		User-customizable icon
		User-customizable icon

Appendixes

(continued)

SmartIcon	Name	Description
		User-customizable icon
		User-customizable icon
		User-customizable icon
		User-customizable icon

Database Templates

Lotus Notes includes several Notes templates that can be used as the foundation for creating new databases. While you may recognize several of these templates if you have previously used other versions of Lotus Notes, many of these database templates are new to Release 4. This appendix provides you a brief description of the database templates that will assist you in designing applications.

◀◀ See "Using Templates," p. 326

You will also see a brief description of those applications used to facilitate the administration of Notes. Listed directly below the template description is the template filename, and the design template name used when creating an application in which you want to control updates to the design through the design template. You can read more about designing applications in Chapter 9, "Creating New Databases."

Application Templates

Here are the application templates that you will most likely use when you begin designing applications in Notes. You can use application templates to speed up your development process by providing a starting point in your application design—for which you can later customize to further meet your business needs:

- **Approval Cycle**—This database provides a place from which organizations can manage their electronic approvals. Using the ApprovalLogic subform, a different form can be designed for each type of approval while all approval forms use the same approval logic. Consequently, when an organization changes its approval policies, only the ApprovalLogic subform will need to be changed, allowing for fast response to changing business needs.

  Template filename: APPROVE4.NTF

  Design template name: StdR4Approval

■ **Discussion**—A workgroup can use this database to share their thoughts and ideas. Almost any group that has information to share among its members can use a discussion database. An engineering group can discuss the products they are designing. An advertising agency can discuss the ad campaigns they are developing. A special interest group can share ideas and opinions on their common interests.

A user can either browse and read documents or take an active role by composing responses to other comments or producing a new main topic for discussion. The history of discussion about issues is preserved in the discussion database.

You can think of a discussion database as an informal meeting place, where the members of a workgroup can share ideas and comments. Like a physical meeting, each member of the workgroup listens to what others have to say and can voice his/her own opinions. However, unlike a physical meeting, the participants do not have to be in the same room at the same time to share information. People can participate when it is convenient for them to do so. And because it is easy for them to share information, they will do so. This database makes it easy for participants to follow the discussions as it maintains a hierarchy of the messages entered.

Template filename: DISCUSS4.NTF

Design template name: StdR4Disc

■ **Document Library**—The Document Library application is an electronic filing cabinet that stores reference documents for access by a workgroup. The database might contain anything from environmental impact statements for a group of engineers to financial statements for a group of loan officers.

Template filename: DOCLIB4.NTF

Design template name: StdR4DocLib

■ **Personal Address Book**—The Personal Address Book is the replacement for the full Name & Address Book from prior versions of Lotus Notes. This address book is tailored to personal use of a Lotus Notes user. Information about a contact's work, home, and e-mail systems is stored in this database. Connection records to other Lotus Notes servers are also stored in this database.

Template filename: PERNAMES.NTF

Design template name: StdR4PersonalAddressBook

■ **Personal Journal**—The Personal Journal database is designed to keep private documents not intended to be shared with others. A personal journal may be used as a diary, a lab notebook, or simply as a holding place to compose documents before they are ready for wider distribution.

Template filename: JOURNAL4.NTF

Design template name: StdR4Journal

- **Project Management (R4)**—This template creates a database that allows workgroups to manage and track their day-to-day activities. The template includes task management and status reporting capabilities.

  Template filename: `PROJECT4.NTF`

  Design template name: StdV4Project

- **Reservation Scheduler**—The Reservation Scheduler is an application designed to allow workgroups to schedule and reserve physical resources such as conference rooms or office equipment. This template uses navigators to display the views in the database.

  Template filename: `RESERVE4.NTF`

  Design template name: StdR4Room

- **Shared Template Components**—This template includes components which are used in many other templates. It is not intended to be used in creating new databases. When design refresh is performed on some of the other templates, elements of this template may be pulled in. For example, the design elements used for archiving are refreshed from this template, into the Discussion template.

  Template filename: `SHARE4.NTF`

  Design template name: StdR4Share

Administration Templates

These are templates used by the Notes Setup program, server software, and Notes administrators. These templates do not appear when users choose File, Database, New unless Show advanced templates is selected.

- **Public Address Book**—This template is used to create a server database that is used by Notes for monitoring users, servers, and groups in a Notes community. It is the full version of the Lotus Notes Name & Address Book, containing all of the forms and views required to successfully administer the Notes Server and its users—where the Personal Name & Address Book contains only forms and views pertaining to the individual user.

  Template filename: `PUBNAMES.NTF`

  Design template name: StdR4PublicAddressBook

- **Administration Requests**—This template is used to create a server database that is used by the Notes Administration Agent to keep track of requests and processes against the server.

  Template filename: `ADMIN4.NTF`

  Design template name: StdR4AdminRequests

■ **Agent Log**—This template is used to create a server log that provides an easy way to review actions and errors that occur during execution of a LotusScript program that uses the NotesLog class.

Template filename: ALOG4.NTF

Design template name: StdR4AgentLog

■ **Certification Log**—This template is used to create a server database that maintains records of certified Notes IDs in a Notes community.

Template filename: CERTLOG.NTF

Design template name: StdNotesCertificationLog

■ **Custom Mail Forms**—This template is used to expand mailing form choices by giving users specialized forms such as fax memos and weekly reports. Designers can add additional forms to this database to roll out customized forms (like purchase order requests, travel approval requisitions, etc.). Typically, custom forms in a company are forms designed for access by the general Notes community of the company—and therefore make sense to have made available to the user. The template is stored on mail servers and is accessed by choosing Create, Custom Forms.

Template filename: FORMS4.NTF

Design template name: StdR4CustomForms

■ **Database Analysis**—You can run an analysis against a single database to determine specifics about its design and other application settings. This template is used to create a server database for storing the results of a single database analysis.

Template filename: DBA4.NTF

Design template name: StdR4DBAnalysis

■ **Database Catalog**—This template is used to create a server reference database that records and stores information about the databases on a Notes server. Information appears in the Database Catalog automatically when a new database is created or copied onto the server—unless the designer elects to not have this database mentioned in the catalog.

Template filename: CATALOG.NTF

Design template name: StdNotesCatalog

■ **Database Library**—Similar to the Database Catalog, this template is used to create a database that contains a list of public databases to which users can request access. The main difference between the two applications is that entries are not automatically placed in the Database Library—the database manager must specify that a particular database be listed. This Database Library is ideal for users who may want to create a library of the databases they have stored on their particular hardware, or which they manage.

Template filename: DBLIB4.NTF

Design template name: StdR4DatabaseLib

- **Mail (R4)**—The Mail template is used to create a database to send and receive electronic mail using Notes. The template can be used to create a mail database either on a local workstation or on a server. The Mail template also contains meeting and task management features which can be used for personal time management or to delegate work to other people. Please select Help, Help Topics for more information on how to use the features of the Mail template.

  Template filename: `MAIL4.NTF`

  Design template name: StdR4Mail

- **Mail Router Mailbox**—This template is used to create a server or local database that stores mail from a user that is en route to another user. This database acts as a holding tank for all mail that is to be transferred to other users.

  Template filename: `MAILBOX.NTF`

  Design template name: StdNotesMailbox

- **Notes Log**—The Notes Log is a special template, used to automatically create a database that records and stores information about all types of Notes server activities, and remote workstation communication activities. The Notes Log (`LOG.NSF`) is automatically created during Notes Setup.

  Server administrators and database managers should look at the Notes Log often to make sure the following are true:

  - Databases are replicating, and how often.
  - Disk space is low.
  - Enough memory is available.
  - Phone communications are working properly.

  Template filename: `LOG.NTF`

  Design template name: StdNotesLog

- **Notes Log Analysis**—This template is used to create a server database for storing the results of a single log analysis.

  Template filename: `LOGA4.NTF`

  Design template name: StdR4LogAnalysis

- **Statistics & Events**—This template is used to create a server database that stores configuration records for statistics reporting and monitoring tools, as well as a listing of server messages.

  Template filename: `EVENTS4.NTF`

  Design template name: StdR4Events

- **Statistics Reporting**—This template is used to create a database that records information about the activity on one or more Notes servers.

  Template filename: `STATREP.NTF`

  Design template name: StdR4StatReport

■ **Web Navigator**—This template is used by the server add-in program WEB.EXE to create the server navigator database that gives Notes users access to the World Wide Web. It also stores Internet documents before they are retrieved by workstations.

Template filename: WEB.NTF

Design template name: StdR4WebNavigator

Command Reference

This appendix lists the menu commands available in Notes. As the different functions in Notes are selected, the menu commands change. In the lists that follow, the available accelerator keys are underlined in the menu and command names. To access these commands, press Alt plus the underlined letter in the menu name, and then press the underlined letter in the command. If a shortcut keystroke that bypasses the menu is available, it is listed in parentheses after the command name.

In some lists, you see some commands indented under other commands. These indented commands comprise a submenu accessed by the command name they follow.

The Actions Menu

The Actions menu enables you to edit documents, move and categorize documents, send or forward mail, run macros, and perform advanced functions. The Actions menu is only active when a database is selected or opened. When a database is selected on the Notes desktop—highlighted but not open—only the macros for that database will be displayed in the Actions menu.

When a database is opened, the following Actions menu items are available:

    Edit Document (Ctrl+E)

    Move to Folder

    Remove from Folder

    Categorize

    Send Document

    Forward

    View Options

        Rename

        Design

        Move

        Delete View

    Retrieve Entire Document

The Agent Menu

The Agent menu enables you to view agent properties and view the agent log. When you click the Agent folder, the following Agent menu commands are available:

> Agent Properties
>
> Log

The Create Menu

The Create menu enables you to select forms from those available in the database you are working in. You can also create folders, views, agents, and design work. Each database can have a unique number of forms, with unique names.

To create a new document, open the database and then pull down the Create menu. Choose the form that you want to create from the drop-down menu. The selected form appears, opened and ready for data entry. With the database open, the following Create menu items are available:

> Mail
>> Memo
>>
>> Reply
>>
>> Replay With History
>>
>> Workflow
>>> Bookmark
>>>
>>> Phone Message
>>>
>>> Task
>>
>> Other
>
> Folder
>
> View
>
> Agent
>
> Design
>> Form
>>
>> Shared Field
>>
>> Subform
>>
>> Navigator

With the database open, you can design new forms. If you select Design, Form, the following Create menu items are available:

> Page Break
>
> Section
>> Standard
>>
>> Controlled Access

Table

Object

Hotspot

    Link Hotspot

    Text Popup

    Button

    Formula Popup

    Action Hotspot

Action

Field

Insert Shared Field

Layout Region

    New Layout Region

    Text

    Graphic

    Graphic Button

Design

    Form

    Shared Field

    Subform

        Navigator

With the database open, you can create new and edit existing views. With the design view open that you are creating or modifying, the following Create menu items are available:

Mail

Memo

    Reply

    Replay With History

    Workflow

        Bookmark

        Phone Message

        Task

    Other

Action

Insert New Column

Append New Column

Design

>   Form
>
>   Shared Field
>
>   Subform
>
>   Navigator

With the database open, you can design new navigators. If you select Design, Navigator, the following Create menu items are available:

Mail

Memo

>   Reply
>
>   Replay With History
>
>   Workflow
>
>   >   Bookmark
>   >
>   >   Phone Message
>   >
>   >   Task
>
>   Other

Graphic Background

Hotspot Rectangle

Hotspot Polygon

Graphic Button

Button

Text

Rectangle

Rounded Rectangle

Ellipse

Polygon

>   Polyline
>
>   Design
>
>   Form
>
>   Shared Field
>
>   Subform
>
>   Navigator

The Design Menu

The Design menu is only displayed when you have clicked the Design folder or have entered design mode for Forms, Views, Shared Fields, Subforms, Navigators, or Other. The following Design commands are available:

Properties

Field Properties

Column Properties

Action Properties

Action Bar Properties

Layout Properties

Object Properties

Bring To Front

Send To Back

Share This Field

Test

The Edit Menu

The Edit menu commands enable you to move (cut), copy, paste, and select text and documents. You also can insert various objects such as attachments, tables, and page breaks. The following commands are available when a document or view is on-screen:

Undo (Ctrl+Z)

Cut (Ctrl+X)

Copy (Ctrl+C)

Copy as Link

Paste (Ctrl+V)

Paste Special

Clear (Del)

Select All (Ctrl+A)

Deselect All

Find/Replace (Ctrl+F)

Find Next (Ctrl+G)

Check Spelling

External Links

Unread Marks

    Mark Selected Read

    Mark All Read

    Mark Selected Unread

    Mark All Unread

    Scan Unread

    Scan Preferred

The File Menu

With File menu commands, you can open and close databases, use Notes import, external file save (export), and attachment capabilities, perform administrative duties, print, and control database and preferences information. The File menu commands are as follows:

> Open (Enter)
>
> Close (Ctrl+W)
>
> Save (Ctrl+S)
>
> Save As New Version
>
> Document Properties
>
> Database
>
> > Properties
> >
> > Access Control
> >
> > Open (Ctrl+O)
> >
> > Open Special
> >
> > New (Ctrl+N)
> >
> > New Copy
> >
> > Publish
> >
> > Delete
> >
> > Refresh Design
> >
> > Replace Design
> >
> > Design Synopsis
>
> Replication
>
> > Replicate
> >
> > Settings
> >
> > New Replica
> >
> > Find Replica
> >
> > Switch Replica
> >
> > History
>
> Mobile
>
> > Choose Current Location
> >
> > Edit Current Location
> >
> > Edit Current Time/Phone
> >
> > Locations
> >
> > Server Phone Numbers
> >
> > Call Server

Hang Up

Attach

Import

Export

Print (Ctrl+P)

Page Setup

Tools

    User Preferences

    SmartIcons

    User ID

    Switch ID

    Lock ID (F5)

    Server Administration

    Debug LotusScript

Exit Notes

The Help Menu

The Help menu enables you to access online help wherever you are working in Lotus Notes. The menu commands for the Help database remain the same regardless of where you are working within Notes. The Help menu contains the following commands:

Help topics

Guide Me(F1)

Release 3 Menu Finder

About This Database

Using This Database

About Notes

The Table Menu

The Table menu commands allow you to modify tables in the Notes design form. The Table menu commands are only available when in design mode and working in a table. The following Table menu commands are available:

Table Properties

Insert Row

Insert Column

Insert Special

Append Row

Append Column

Delete Selected Row(s)

Delete Selected Column(s)

Delete Special

The Text Menu

The Text menu commands allow you to change the properties of the data that is being entered into a form or being edited in a form. The following commands are available:

Text Properties (Ctrl+K)

Permanent Pen

Bullets

Numbers

Normal Text (Ctrl+T)

Italic (Ctrl+I)

Bold (Ctrl+B)

Underline (Ctrl+U)

Enlarge Size (F2)

Reduce Size (Shift+F2)

Color

    Black

    Red

    Blue

    Dark Red

    Dark Green

    Dark Blue

    Dark Magenta

    Dark Yellow

    Dark Cyan

    Other

Align Paragraph

    Left

    Right

    Center

    Full

    No Wrap

Spacing

> Single
>
> One and a Half
>
> Double
>
> Other

Indent (F8)

Outdent (Shift+F8)

Named Styles

The View Menu

With commands on the View menu, you can change the way you look at information on-screen. The View menu changes depending on whether you are working in a database and looking at the view, working in a document in a database, or looking at the database icons with all databases closed. When you have a database open, you see the following commands on the View menu:

Refresh (F9)

Search Bar

Show

> Horizontal Scroll Bar
>
> Design
>
> Unread Only
>
> Selected Only
>
> Categories Only
>
> Search Results Only
>
> Folders
>
> Main Navigator
>
> Views

Document Preview

Arrange Preview

Expand All (Sh+)

Collapse All (Sh-)

Expand/Collapse

> Expand Selected Level (+)
>
> Expand Selected & Children (*)
>
> Collapse Selected Level (-)
>
> Collapse All Folders

Go To

Go To Agents

Go To Design

The following View menu commands are available when you have no databases open, but are looking at the database icons in Notes:

Refresh Unread Count

Arrange Icons

Stack Replica Icons

Show Unread

Show Server Names

The following View menu commands are available when you have a database open and are looking at a view:

Refresh (F9)

Search Bar

Show

Horizontal Scroll Bar

Design

Unread Only

Selected Only

Categorize Only

Search Results Only

Folders

Main Navigator

Views

Document Preview

Arrange Preview

Expand All (Sh +)

Collapse All (Sh -)

Expand Special

Expand Selected Level (+)

Expand Selected & Children (*)

Collapse Selected Level (-)

Collapse All Folders

The following View menu commands are available when you have a database open and are looking at a document in the View, Open document form:

Show

       Horizontal Scroll Bar

       Design

       Unread Only

       Selected Only

       Categorize Only

       Search Results Only

       Folders

       Main Navigator

       Views

Parent Preview

Document Link Preview

Switch Forms

When a document is opened in edit mode, the following View menu commands are available:

Refresh (F9)

Ruler (Ctrl+R)

Show

       Horizontal Scroll Bar

       Design

       Unread Only

       Selected Only

       Categorize Only

       Search Results Only

       Folders

       Main Navigator

       Views

Parent Preview

Document Link Preview

Expand All Sections (Sh+)

Collapse All Sections (Sh-)

Switch Forms

When a you are in the design mode of a database, the following View menu commands are available:

Refresh (F9)

Design Pane

Action Pane

Expand All (Sh+)

Collapse All (Sh-)

Also at the bottom of the View menu is a list of all the views available in the database. Selecting one of these views displays the information for that view.

If a database has been selected, this version of the View menu also lists the titles of all views contained in the selected database. Selecting one of these views opens the database and displays the view selected.

The Window Menu

The Window menu commands enable you to customize the way your windows display on your workspace and to switch between any Notes windows open on your workspace. (Only the list of open windows at the bottom of the Window menu changes while you are working in Notes.) The following commands are available on this menu:

Tile

Cascade

Minimize All

Maximize All

Special Characters

Special characters—usually not found on your keyboard—represent foreign language letters, foreign currency symbols, copyright and trademark characters, and mathematical symbols. By pressing a key combination, you can use special characters in Notes anywhere you can enter text.

Notes uses the keyboard combination Alt+F1 plus special codes to create special characters. For example, to enter the cent symbol (¢), press Alt+F1, then C, then /.

> **Note**
>
> Notes provides several codes for many common characters. You can use whichever seems easiest to type or remember.

Press Alt+F1 Plus...	To Get This Character	Character Description
i	ı	Dotless i
ff	ƒ	Guilder
!!	¡	Inverted exclamation point
cl or c/	¢	Cent sign
l= or l-	£	British pound sterling
y= or y-	¥	Yen
x0 or xo	¤	Universal currency
c0 or co	©	Copyright
a_	ª	Feminine ordinal
o_	º	Masculine ordinal
<<	«	Left quillements (also called left chevron)

(continues)

Press Alt+F1 Plus...	To Get This Character	Character Description
>>	»	Right quillements (also called right chevron)
:-	÷	Division
^0	°	Degrees
+-	±	Plus over minus
^1	^{1}	Superscript 1
^2	^{2}	Superscript 2
^3	^{3}	Superscript 3
/u	μ	Greek letter mu
^.	•	Bullet
14	¼	1/4
12	½	1/2
34	¾	3/4
??	¿	Inverted question mark
A`	À	A with grave accent
A'	Á	A with acute accent
A^	Â	A with circumflex
A~	Ã	A with tilde
A"	Ä	A with umlaut
A*	Å	A with degree
AE	Æ	AE ligature
C,	Ç	C with cedille
E`	È	E with grave accent
E'	É	E with acute accent
E^	Ê	E with circumflex
E"	Ë	E with umlaut
I`	Ì	I with grave accent
I'	Í	I with acute accent
I^	Î	I with circumflex
I"	Ï	I with umlaut
D-	Ð	Capital eth
N~	Ñ	N with tilde
O`	Ò	O with grave accent
O'	Ó	O with acute accent

Press Alt+F1 Plus...	To Get This Character	Character Description
O^	Ô	O with circumflex
O~	Õ	O with tilde
O"	Ö	O with umlaut
O/	Ø	O with a slash through it
U`	Ù	U with grave accent
U'	Ú	U with acute accent
U^	Û	U with circumflex
U"	Ü	U with umlaut
P-	Þ	Capital thorn
ss	ß	S-zed
a`	à	a with grave accent
a'	á	a with acute accent
a^	â	a with circumflex
a~	ã	a with tilde
a"	ä	a with umlaut
a*	å	a with degree
ae	æ	ae ligature
c,	ç	c with cedille
e`	è	e with grave accent
e'	é	e with acute accent
e^	ê	e with circumflex
e"	ë	e with umlaut
i`	ì	i with grave accent
i'	í	i with acute accent
i^	î	i with circumflex
i"	ï	i with umlaut
d-	ð	Lowercase eth
n~	ñ	n with tilde
o`	ò	o with grave accent
o'	ó	o with acute accent
o^	ô	o with circumflex
o~	õ	o with tilde
o"	ö	o with umlaut
o/	ø	o with a slash through it

Appendixes

Press Alt+F1 Plus...	To Get This Character	Character Description
u`	ù	u with grave accent
u'	ú	u with acute accent
u^	û	u with circumflex
u"	ü	u with umlaut
y"	ÿ	y with umlaut
p-	þ	Lowercase thorn
,,	¸	Cedille
-]	¬	End of line
/	¦	Split vertical
_^	‾	Overline
__ or ==	=	Double underline
ro or r0	®	Registered trademark
y'	ý	y with acute accent
Y'	Ý	Y with acute accent
xx	×	Multiplication

Migrating from Notes Release 3 to Release 4

The migration from Lotus Notes Release 3 (R3) to Lotus Notes Release 4 (R4) is a migration that you do not want to rush into. It is a process that needs careful planning and consideration before doing. This appendix will address the key things that needed to be considered and recommended steps to be taken to accomplish the migration from R3 to R4.

Each organization is different and what may be a very large task in one organization may be a not so large task in another. The steps to accomplish the migration will be the same, just the magnitude of the migration will be different.

Migration planning must be done, more in R3 to R4 than in any other upgrade of Lotus Notes. Much was learned from the R2 to R3 migration.

Why Consider Migrating?

You may be asking why you should consider migrating to Lotus Notes R4. The following lists some of the changes:

- New platforms, such as Windows 95 server, Windows 95 workstation, Windows NT workstation, Native PowerMac workstation.
- Extinct platforms, such as Windows 3.1 16-bit server, Solaris 1.x. However, R4 will still communicate with Lotus Notes databases that reside on these servers.
- New protocols, such as AppleTalk on Windows NT 3.51 server, SPX on Windows NT 3.51 server and workstation, NetWare SPX II on NLM 3.x, and NLM 4.x.
- Faster replication of databases because of field level replication.
- Scalability and higher performance, because of fewer servers and more powerful servers.
- Friendlier user interface.
- LotusScript for more programming capability.
- Easier administration by combining administration functions into one area— File, Tools, Server Administration—instead of having disbursed throughout Lotus Notes.

What Do You Need To Do?

Take time to consider what has changed and how those changes will affect your organization. The migration to Notes R4 will depend upon the priorities of your organization. You will want to evaluate the impact of Notes R4 on your users, applications currently running, future applications that you will be building, and the network infrastructure. You may want to answer questions such as the following:

- What will happen to many existing R3 applications when I upgrade?
- How much training will my users, application developers, and administration people need?
- How will my Lotus Notes infrastructure change, will I need fewer servers, will the servers need to be more powerful?
- What benefits can I gain from the migration, i.e., faster replication, fewer servers?
- Do I have to do the migration all at one time, or can I schedule to do sections as needed?

Build a good migration plan covering the following points:

- Identify the team of individuals that are part of the migration plan.
- Identify premigration activities now. Don't wait until you start the migration. For example, what is the test group, who leads the migration, will new hardware be installed and old hardware removed, what servers will be upgraded, will users be upgraded, how will training be structured, dates and timelines for activities, and options for moving back to R3 if problems occur?
- Determine any changes that you may want to make to the Lotus Notes server(s) configuration, (larger, more powerful CPU; fewer servers; more memory; different operating system; more disk storage space; NetWare protocol change).
- Assess the impact of discontinued features, such as Win16 server.
- Create checklists of the servers and applications that will be migrated,
- Have a quality, well-defined training plan in place. Don't do the migration without a comprehensive training plan.
- Test everything and then test it again.
- Make a migration schedule and follow it.
- Prioritize your migration plan.
- Document any changes your organization has made to the standard Lotus Notes templates, such as Name & Address Book, Mail files, Log files.
- Compare your modified R3 templates to the new R4 templates. Some of the modifications that you made in R3 may have been incorporated into R4; therefore, you will not have to make those same modifications.
- Build prototypes.

■ Plan user training on new templates.

■ Plan user training on new and changed features of Lotus Notes R4.

■ If using a R4 Lotus Notes server, have a R4 Name & Address Book. The R4 Lotus Notes server will not run with a R3 Name & Address Book file. However, a R3 Lotus Notes server can and will run with a R4 Name & Address Book.

Sequence of Events

Once you have decided to migrate to R4 and have put together your migration plan, you can start your migration process. Do not try to do a migration without having a migration plan in place. Even if you are only upgrading one Lotus Notes server and a few users, you still need to plan the migration. The migration to R4 should not be taken as a simple upgrade. Following is the sequence of events to do an upgrade:

1. Upgrade any Lotus Notes server hardware.

2. Migrate your selected Lotus Notes servers to R4.

3. Upgrade your user workstations.

4. Upgrade your Lotus Notes applications.

Some of these upgrades may not be performed until some time in the future. For example, you can upgrade your servers and workstations, but not start using R4 application features until some time in the future. This may happen because your applications could be communicating with company external users that have not made the migration to R4, or your company has not trained your application developers on the changes and new features of R4.

> **Tip**
>
> Introduce changes to your existing Lotus Notes structure in a controlled matter. Do not change server hardware, operating system, and Lotus Notes server code at the same time or you may not be able to troubleshoot problems quickly—because you have changed everything all at once. Phase these items in, with Lotus Notes R4 being the last item to implement.

Lotus Notes Servers

Upgrade or replace your existing Lotus Notes servers with new equipment. Well before your upgrade of Lotus Notes R4, make changes to, test, and run production of your new Lotus Notes server hardware and operating systems with Lotus Notes R3. By upgrading your Lotus Notes server first, you will see the following immediately:

■ Fewer Lotus Notes servers.

■ Administrators can be trained faster because they are more technical users.

■ There is less user training since there are fewer administrators.

When upgrading your servers, upgrade by function. When you start to migrate your Lotus Notes servers, it is recommended that you migrate them in the following order:

1. Hub replication servers
2. Hub mail routing servers
3. Hub replication and mail routing servers
4. Mail servers
5. Application servers
6. User mail and application servers
7. Dial-in servers
8. Gateway servers, if at all

Workstations

You will need the client version of R4 to use the new application functionality, such as new mail template and new Name & Address Book template. Once you are ready, follow these steps:

1. Backup the workstation version of Lotus Notes R3. The minimum items to backup and save are DESKTOP.DSK, NOTES.INI, NAMES.NSF.
2. Install R4 software over existing R3.
3. Start the Lotus Notes workstation by clicking the Lotus Notes icon on your computer's desktop. Depending on if you are a Mac, Windows 3.x, Windows 95, or UNIX user, the starting of the applications changes, such as double-clicking, finding the application in the Win95 Start menu, etc.
4. Upgrade the Personal Name & Address Book.
5. Upgrade the Mail database.
6. Compact local databases to make them R4 versions (this is a recommended step) For more information on compacting your databases, refer to Chapter 3, "Using Databases," and Chapter 9, "Creating New Databases."

Applications

Before you begin upgrading any of your existing Lotus Notes R3 applications, you must make certain that all of the intended users of these applications are running on Lotus Notes R4. Remember, any R4 application programming enhancements that you make will only work on an R4 workstation and server.

Why should you upgrade applications? You would want to upgrade your current application to take advantage of the new On Disk Structure which will allow the following:

- Folders and agents
- Re-engineered response hierarchy

- Local security
- Field level replication
- Personal agents and folders that can be stored on the server instead of in the local `DESKTOP.DSK` file

To upgrade an R3 application to R4, do one of the following:

- Run UPDALL and then COMPACT the database.
- Choose <u>F</u>ile, <u>R</u>eplication, <u>N</u>ew Replica and create a new replica copy of the database.
- Choose <u>F</u>ile, <u>D</u>atabase, Ne<u>w</u> Copy and create a new copy of the database.

> **Tip**
>
> Remember that R3 database fields, formulas, views, and macros will still work after you've compacted the database on your R4 server.
>
> The golden rule is "Don't add new R4 features to databases that are being used by R3 workstations."

Steps for Upgrading the Server

After you have developed your migration plan, you are ready to start the process. Migrating to R4 is not a simple and quick process, so make certain that part of your migration plan includes contingency plans should some portion of the migration process not function correctly or causes a problem. You are now ready to start your migration. Use the following steps to perform the migration:

1. Backup all existing files.
2. Upgrade your hardware, operating systems, and any protocols.
3. Install R4 Lotus Notes server software.
4. Put customized templates in data directory.
5. Launch a client.
6. Choose <u>Y</u>es when prompted to upgrade the Name & Address Book design.
7. Run the Roles agent on the Name & Address Book to update all of the users and groups access settings—you only need to perform this on the first server you migrate. Notes will take care of updating the rest of the servers through replication.
8. Run UPDALL to update views and full-text indexes. Even though this is an optional step, it is probably a good idea to perform this function. If you don't, the first user to open the database will force the view(s) to be updated at that time, and depending on the size of the database, the process could take several minutes or more.

9. Run COMPACT to update your database(s) to the new R4 internal Lotus Notes database format. Compacting will not affect the design of the database to add new R4 features, but will change the internal workings of the database to take advantage of the new R4 features like ACL settings, and speed in replicating the database.

10. Start R4 server.

11. Test the new server to make certain that it can communicate with users, other servers, and the network infrastructure; databases are usable; replication works; and remote users can dial in.

Your newly upgraded Lotus Notes databases will work if an R4 notes server is available where the R4 database(s) is stored.

The following table describes the interoperability of R4 and R3 configurations:

Server	Database	Client	Works?
R4	R4	R4	Yes
R4	R4	R3	Yes
R4	R3	R4	Yes
R4	R3	R3	Yes
R3	R4	R4	No
R3	R4	R3	No
R3	R3	R4	Yes
Local	R4	R3	No
Local	R4	R4	Yes
Local	R3	R4	Yes

Replicating an R4 database to an R3 client or server will convert the database from R4 to R3 on the R3 server. The items in the previous table that have No in the far right column will return the error statement ERROR: Invalid NSF format if you try this.

If you want to make certain the R3 servers and users have no problems reading databases on a R4 Notes server, then change the extension of the Lotus Notes file from NSF to NS3 using your operating system commands for renaming a file. NS3 tells R4 that this is a R3 database.

Running R3 and R4 on the Same Workstation

You can run both Lotus Notes R3 and R4 on the same workstation, but not at the same time. However, before you install Notes R4, you need to perform some special functions to prepare for the installation. To work with both versions of Notes, you need to perform the following steps:

1. Copy your NOTES.INI file from the Windows subdirectory into your Lotus Notes R3 directory, and then delete it from the Windows subdirectory. Your Lotus Notes R3 directory is typically C:\NOTES.

2. Rename the NOTES.INI file to a different name, like NOTES.BAK so that Lotus Notes will not reference this older version of the NOTES.INI file when it installs Notes R4 on your workstation.

   If you do not rename this file—or have a copy of it stored anywhere on your workstation—Lotus Notes R4 installation will find it and reference it in the new NOTES.INI file created and stored in the Windows subdirectory. This can cause problems in working with Notes R4, as there are many new settings in Notes R4 NOTES.INI files that may not get referenced correctly. Your data directory and other important files may not be referenced correctly as well.

3. Search and rename any other NOTES.INI files on your system or in your search path.

4. Change your Notes program icon so that the working directory is the location of your Notes data directory and the location of your R3 NOTES.INI file (see Chapter 2, "Customizing Notes," for more information on data directories). It is recommended that you store the NOTES.INI file in the same directory as the rest of your Lotus Notes program files. If you have the NOTES.INI file in your Windows subdirectory, both versions of Notes R3 and R4 will use the same NOTES.INI file because Notes looks there first when it starts up. This will cause problems with the execution of Notes when you run both copies on the same workstation.

5. Install Lotus Notes R4 into a new directory, such as NOTESR4 by typing the new subdirectory when prompted by the Notes installation program. If you do not enter a new subdirectory, Notes will install R4 over R3, and you will lose your ability to run R3.

6. Launch R4 and finish the setup procedure.

7. Copy the NOTES.INI file from your Windows directory to your new R4 directory. The installation process created this file for you and automatically stored it in your Windows directory.

8. Delete the NOTES.INI file from your Windows directory.

9. Change the working directory of your Notes R4 icon to point to the location of the new R4 directory—in this example, NOTESR4.

10. Rename the NOTES.INI file that you modified in step 3 back to NOTES.INI.

You will now be able to run both versions of Notes on the same workstation. When you eventually decide you no longer want to keep your Notes R3 program running on your workstation, you can remove it without risking your Notes R4 files.

Remote Troubleshooting

Although Notes makes working remotely easy, you still may experience some difficulties dialing, making connections with servers, exchanging database information, maintaining connections with a server, and working with NotesMail. This appendix can help you troubleshoot the various common problems that you may have.

Although most often you probably will refer to this appendix only when you are having difficulty with remote usage, take a few moments to scan through the list of problems and solutions. Knowing what problems you may face and why may help you avoid remote problems in your setup and use.

Although most common problems for operating remotely are documented here, you may experience some problems specific to your modem, server setup, work environment, and so on. If you cannot find the explanation to your difficulties in this section, consult the Notes 4 Help database (or Help Lite) for additional error messages, contact your Notes administrator for additional assistance, and consult the respective topics in the other chapters of this book for additional information that may help you work better with Notes.

Tip

The Help Lite (and full Notes 4 Help) database is a fantastic place to start looking when you are experiencing problems with Notes. Open the Help database and switch to the view Messages to see if the error message you are getting is listed. If it is, open and read the document for guidance in resolving the conflict.

You also get to the correct help document most of the time by pressing F1 when an error message is displayed on your screen. You will receive a prompt from Notes if there is no topic corresponding to that particular message.

Before you read through this section, check the following quick checklist for some of the most common reasons for remote connection problems. Also, there are two database files on the CD-ROM that will assist you in locating and fixing many of the problems you might have with working remote—Mobile Survival Kit and SmartForm Modem Doctor.

- Is the modem connected to the phone cable?

- Is the phone line connected to the jack?

- If your modem is external, is the AC adapter plugged in, or is the battery in your modem OK?

- Is the cable working? (If you don't get a dial tone, it might be the cable, rather than the phone line.)

- Is your answering machine on the same line as the modem? If so, and you're listening to your messages, it can cut off your connection to the server.

- Did you disable call waiting before dialing the server?

- Is the server down, or off-line temporarily for updates? Very often, remote users don't get the notices that warn network users that the system will be down for a few minutes.

- Is the phone service down in your area or theirs?

- Did you change modems or locations without changing settings to match?

- Are you using the correct .MDM file for your particular modem?

- Is your modem compatible with the server's modem (ask your Notes administrator)?

Problems Working Off-Site for the First Time

When working off-site for the first time, you may encounter some difficulties, no matter how carefully you set up your PC to work remotely. The most common problems you may encounter include not having a certified ID, not being able to use the online Notes help, and being denied access to the server or particular databases. The following sections discuss these problems and recommend solutions.

Your Certified ID Is Needed

Problem. You receive a message saying that you need a certified ID.

Explanation. Notes verifies that you are authorized to access a server by reading your Notes ID when you dial into the server. Notes verifies that you and the Notes server have a certificate in common. If you don't have a certificate in common, your Notes administrator can "stamp" your user ID with the appropriate certificate to prove its validity. Check with your Notes administrator if you need assistance. You should also keep a safe backup copy of your Notes ID, just in case.

Help Is Unavailable

Problem. When you press F1, a message says that the Help database cannot be located.

Explanation. The Help database wasn't copied to your PC during installation. Reinstall Notes and include the help file in your selection. You can also try to copy it to your system using File, Database, Copy; creating a replica copy; or zipping the file and copying it onto disks. Keep in mind, however, that the Help database is over 21 MB in size, and the Help Lite database exceeds 5 MB. Trying to copy these files may prove more time-consuming than reinstalling them.

Access Is Denied

Problem. A message appears, saying that access to the server or a database is denied.

Explanation. You aren't included in the ACL (Access Control List) as a user or as part of a group with access to the server of the database. Contact your Notes administrator about getting access to a server, and contact the database manager for access to the particular database you want.

Problems with the Modem

Notes makes working with modems very easy; however, sometimes you may experience problems with using the modem, particularly if you are traveling and change the environment you are working in. Some problems that you may face include when the modem isn't detecting a dial tone, dialing the phone number, or responding to Notes; when the call is unsuccessful and connection to the server wasn't made; when the connection is discontinued before you are through working; or when the modem cannot detect a carrier. The following sections discuss these types of problems and describe ways to correct them.

Tip

To help you track down problems with your modem, the following options give you more information:

- Choose the Log Modem I/O option in the Setup Modem dialog box to include modem responses in the Miscellaneous Events view of the log. The Miscellaneous Events view displays log entries of modem activity by date and a period of time. Much of the information you see in this log may not make much sense to you, and is beyond the scope of this book. Your Notes administrator, however, will find the modem activities logged invaluable when helping troubleshoot your modem problems. You can enable the Log Modem I/O option by choosing File, Tools, User Preferences, and selecting the Ports icon. Highlight the COM port in which your modem is connected, and then choose the COM Options button.

- In the Setup Modem dialog box, turn the Speaker Volume on to hear the modem as it dials. Some modems also have physical settings that can be set to hear the modem dialing.

Modem Can't Detect a Dial Tone

Problem. You keep receiving the message Modem cannot detect dial tone.

Explanation. If you cannot hear a dial tone, and you are dialing automatically with the modem's Speaker Volume setting on, the line from the phone jack may be loose or disconnected. Make sure that the phone line is connected to the wall jack and the modem.

Also check the setting of the maximum baud rate in the Setup Modem dialog box. Select File, Tools, User Preferences, and select the Ports icon. Highlight the COM port in which your modem is connected, and then press the COM Options button. Some phone lines cannot handle high-speed baud rates; and even though Notes tries to adjust the rate to meet what the phone line (carrier) can handle, you may want to decrease the baud rate to ensure that it's slow enough for the carrier. Decreasing the baud rate to 2400–4800 baud is usually adequate for most situations in which you have trouble. However, settings this low will dramatically increase the time it takes to replicate, and increase your chance of losing a connection with the server due to the long connect time.

If you hear a dial tone, you are dialing automatically, and you have the modem's Speaker Volume setting on, the phone system may be incompatible and cannot recognize your modem's tones to allow a connection to be made. Check your modem manufacturer's manual for more information about compatible phone systems.

Modem Won't Dial Number

Problem. You set up your modem for the first time, and it does not dial the number.

Explanation. Choose File, Tools, User Preferences, and verify that the correct COM port is enabled in the Communication Ports list box. Check the cable attachments from your computer to the modem and tighten any that are loose or disconnected.

Modem Won't Respond to Notes

Problem. You bought a new modem and cannot get it to respond in Notes.

Explanation. You may have enabled the wrong port. Choose File, Tools, User Preferences, and select the Ports icon and verify that the correct COM port is enabled in the Ports Setup dialog box. Highlight the correct port, choose COM Options, and verify that your modem has been selected from the list. Also, check the cable attachments to and from your computer, modem, and power supply and tighten any that are loose or disconnected. You also may have selected a modem command file (.MDM) that isn't compatible with your modem. Check your modem setup to verify that the information is correct. If you use a battery-operated modem, check to make sure the battery is not dead.

 ◄◄ See "Setting Up Your Modem," p. 651

Call Is Unsuccessful

Problem. The modem cannot complete the call successfully, and the log shows that the modem responded with an error when trying.

Explanation. You may have selected the wrong modem command file when you set up your modem. Choose File, Tools, User Preferences, and select the Ports icon. Highlight the COM port in which your modem is connected, and then choose the COM Options button. If you edited a command file, you may have made typing errors.

You also need to make sure that the phone number you entered is correct. If, for example, you previously dialed 9 at the beginning of a phone number to gain an outside line, and you subsequently change to a location that doesn't require you to dial 9, you cannot connect to the server.

Dial Timeout Expired

Problem. Your modem dials, but you receive a `Dial timeout expired` message before the phone call completes.

Explanation. The Dial Timeout setting in the Additional Setup dialog box may be too short on your PC or on the server. If you want the modem to wait longer for a connection to the server before canceling the attempt, increase the setting.

To reset a default Dial Timeout for your PC, choose File, Tools, User Preferences, and select the Ports icon. Highlight the COM port in which your modem is connected, press the COM Options button, and change the Dial Timeout setting.

You also can override the default setting for a particular session by selecting Tools, Call and typing a length of time for Dial Timeout. Your default setting in the Setup Modem dialog box does not change.

> **Note**
>
> In either situation, the Carrier Detect Timer setting in the modem command file may influence the Dial Timeout setting.

You also may be dialing the wrong number. If you can hear someone answer the phone, you know that you didn't reach the server's modem. Correct the server's phone number by opening your Personal Address Book, opening the Remote Connection form for the server, pressing Ctrl+E to change to edit mode, and correcting the phone number.

Carrier Isn't Detected

Problem. Your modem dials and you can hear a carrier, but the message `Could not detect carrier` appears before the phone call completes. (You hear the carrier when you hear your modem receive a dial tone, ring, or busy tone.)

Explanation. If you can hear a carrier, the Dial Timeout setting may be too low on your PC or the server. Increase the setting temporarily in the Tools Call dialog box when you call the server, or permanently in the Additional Setup dialog box (choose File, Tools, User Preferences, and select the Ports icon. Highlight the COM port in which your modem is connected, and then choose the COM Options button). If changing your setting doesn't work, contact the Notes administrator to increase the setting on the server.

The Carrier Detect Timer setting in the modem command file also may be too short on your PC or on the server. Contact your system administrator.

Also, the cable attachments may be loose. Check the modem cable attachments to your computer and tighten any that are loose or disconnected.

Problems Connecting with the Server

Sometimes connecting to or communicating with the server may be difficult. Occasionally, you may find that the server modem is busy, the remote system no longer responds, your connection is terminated, the server hangs up too early, or a dial tone isn't detected. The following sections provide you with the most common problems that occur when you try to connect to or communicate with the server, along with the solutions to help resolve the problems.

Specified Port(s) in Use

Problem. You get a message that the specified port that you are trying to use is already in use.

Explanation. You may have closed a database while connected to the server, but did not terminate the call. Or your Replicator settings may not include a Hangup entry to end your session with the server. Add a Hangup entry at the end of the Replicator list to ensure that your final server connection is hung up when completed. Finally, you will also get this message if your modem is already busy connecting with another application like fax services or Internet connections.

Server Is Busy

Problem. The server's phone line is busy.

Explanation. The Notes server's modem is connected to another PC or server. Try again later to dial the server. If you get this message often, try connecting at off-peak hours, when fewer people try to connect to the server. You can schedule your PC to call the server at off-peak hours and perform an exchange by enabling the Scheduled Calling option in your server remote connection form. Refer to Chapter 18, "Setting Up To Work Remote," for more information on this topic. Tell your Notes administrator of repeated difficulties.

Remote System No Longer Responds

Problem. You receive a message that the remote system is no longer responding (in OS/2, the message reads Session to server lost while database replication or copy in progress).

Explanation. The Notes server with which you had a session may have been brought down for maintenance or experienced a software or hardware problem that is disturbing communications. As long as you keep your documents open and wait until the server connection is restored, any documents you try to edit can be saved when the Notes server is operating again.

If you must exit Notes, you also can save a document by choosing Edit, Copy to save it temporarily to the Windows or OS/2 Clipboard. Then open a local database or replica, create a new document, and paste the text or graphics into the new document for safekeeping until you can paste them back to the original database.

The Hangup if Idle for setting also may be too short on your PC or at the server. Increase the Hangup if Idle for setting in the Additional Setup dialog box accessed through the Port Settings panel of the User Preferences InfoBox.

Connection Is Cut Off

Problem. Your connection with the server was cut off before you were ready to disconnect.

Explanation. The Hangup if Idle for setting may be too short on your PC or the server. Increase the setting if you need more time. To reset a default Hangup if Idle for time for your PC, choose File, Tools, User Preferences, and select the Ports icon. Highlight the COM port in which your modem is connected, check to make sure it is enabled, and then choose the COM Options button.

You also can override the default setting for a particular session by choosing File, Mobile, Call Server and typing in a length of time. Your default setting in the Additional Setup dialog box will remain unchanged. The server also has a Hangup if Idle setting; the minimum of the two settings is used. You may need to ask the server administrator to lengthen the server's setting if you frequently are cut off too soon.

The phone connection also may have been interrupted. Check to make sure that Call Forwarding, Call Park, and any other special telephone services that can disrupt modem connections are turned off. You may be able to disable the Call Waiting by entering *70 as the dialing prefix on a tone dial phone, or 1170 on a rotary dial phone. Contact your local phone company for assistance in understanding what features can disrupt the modem connections.

Sometimes a disruption in phone service that occurs isn't the fault of any settings on your system, or the server's. Try calling the server again. Occasionally, if you have voicemail from your phone services, or if you have multiple lines into your office or home, you may experience difficulties like this at random times. This is usually due to poor phone line quality. You may need to contact your phone company.

Network Operation Did Not Complete in a Reasonable Period of Time

Problem. You received a message that the network operation did not complete in a reasonable period of time.

Explanation. This message is the same one that LAN users sometimes see, and does not normally signify a problem. Try recalling the server again, or wait until the server is less busy.

You Cannot Connect to the Server

Problem. You cannot connect to the server.

Explanation. The server's number may be incorrect in the Remote Connection form. Open your Personal Address Book, choose View, Server, Connections, and check the number listed in the Phone column. If you need to make changes, select the server's name and double-click to open the Remote Connection form. Double-click anywhere in the document to put it in edit mode, make the necessary changes, and save the revised form.

The server's modem port may be disabled. If you call the server and you continue to hear ringing, check the phone number in your Remote Connection form to verify the number. If the number is correct, call your server administrator to check the server's modem.

The phone number also may be too long for your modem type. Remove any unnecessary commas and hyphens from the phone number and try to make the call again. If you are in a hotel, make sure that you dial the correct number to get an outside line. If you still have difficulties, call your Notes administrator.

Server Hangs Up

Problem. The server hangs up as soon as the number is dialed.

Explanation. The server's number may be correct, but its name is incorrect in the Remote Connection form. Open your Personal Address Book, choose View, Server, Connections, and check that the name is correct. The server name must be spelled exactly as the Notes administrator defined it, including spaces and spelling. Edit if necessary.

No Dial Tone Is Available

Problem. You cannot hear a carrier, and you get a message that your modem cannot detect a dial tone. The log also shows that no dial tone is detected.

Explanation. You possibly are connected to a digital system, not an analog system. (Analog modems work with analog systems.) Your jack also may be turned off. Check with your office telephone representative. The modem file may not be compatible with your modem. If you are working from home, and have only one phone line available, check to make sure that no one else is using the phone.

Problems with Connection Quality

Even if your PC and the server are set up correctly for remote use, you still may experience some difficulties with dialing the server because of the quality of the connection. If the phone connection quality is poor, you may lose connection with the server, or your exchange time may take longer because information may have to be retransmitted. The following sections discuss some of the common problems with the quality of the line and what you should do if you experience these problems.

Unrelated Error Messages

Problem. Error messages that don't seem related to the actual problem appear.

Explanation. Try again. If possible, try picking up another phone and calling the server phone number to see whether the modem on the server is working (you should hear a series of high-pitched sounds in the receiver). This way, you can determine whether the problem is caused by a down server or whether the server's modem is turned off. If the server is down and an alternate modem is available on the server, try dialing its phone number.

If you rule out that the server isn't causing the problem, you may need to have a telephone company representative trace a loose or faulty connection somewhere in the telephone system or lines. Check first to ensure that all the connections to and from your computer, modem, and telephone aren't at fault. Consult your Notes administrator.

Slow Connection

Problem. The connection with the server seems very slow to establish.

Explanation. The phone line quality may be poor, particularly if you are dialing overseas. Try selecting a slower speed for the transmission in the Additional Setup dialog box. Choose File, Tools, User Preferences, and select the Ports icon. Highlight the COM port in which your modem is connected, and then choose the COM Options button. Choose a lower maximum speed.

Slow transmissions also may be due to a large number of CRC (retransmission) errors—see the next section.

CRC Errors

Problem. A large number of CRC errors or retransmission errors appear in the Phone Call Log Entry documents in the Phone Calls view of your Notes log.

Explanation. The Rts/Cts Flow Control setting in the Additional Setup dialog box probably isn't chosen for your PC's modem or the server's. Errors of this type cause impaired performance, especially if you transmit at speeds of 9600 baud or greater. Choose File, Tools, User Preferences, and select the Ports icon. Highlight the COM port in which your modem is connected, and then choose the COM Options button. Choose Hardware flow control if your modem supports this selection.

The phone line quality also may be poor. Try choosing a slower speed for the transmission in the Additional Setup dialog box located in the File, Tools, User Preferences Port Settings panel when you select the COM Options button. Also, if you are using an external modem and are using a desktop machine, a possible solution to this problem may be the UART buffer. Purchasing a UART 16450 COM card may solve the problem, especially for high-speed connections.

Problems in Database Exchange Sessions

You may be able to connect successfully with the server while working remotely, but may experience some difficulties in exchanging information with the server databases. You may experience times when a database file cannot be initialized, a particular database you want to use cannot be found, replication isn't being allowed for a database, no replication occurs during an exchange, or unexpected results occur from a replication. The following sections cover these common problems and provide instructions on how to resolve them.

File Not Initialized

Problem. You choose File, Replication, New Replica to add a new database replica, but a message that the file isn't initialized appears when you try to open the database.

Explanation. Perform a database exchange for this replica "stub." Although you prepared a replica icon, the contents of the database remain empty until you carry out a database exchange with the appropriate server to initialize the replica and copy the documents from the server's database to your replica.

Database Not Found

Problem. You perform a database exchange on a newly created replica database and then see a message that the database cannot be found.

Explanation. The database file you specified when you created the replica icon may not exist on the server you entered as the source server. If you're connected to a server, choose File, Database, Open and scan the available databases. If you aren't connected to the server, use the server's database catalog to verify the database's correct server (assuming that you added the database to your workspace).

Also check the spelling of the filename on the server; it should be the same as the one you specified as the source filename.

The database file also may not be found if any of the following conditions exist:

- The server's database was moved to a different server.
- The server's database was moved to a different directory or subdirectory.
- The server's database was deleted.
- The server's database filename was modified.

When you determine what caused the problem, choose File, Database, Delete to delete the unsuccessful replica permanently from the hard disk. Prepare a new icon using the correct server and filename and carry out the exchange again.

Replication Not Allowed

Problem. When you try to carry out a database exchange, a message that replication isn't allowed for this database keeps appearing.

Explanation. The database may be a "special" database, such as HELP.NSF, which doesn't allow replication. If you need a copy of the help database on your PC, you can copy the database to your Notes data directory (C:\NOTES), or reinstall Notes and include the help files in your selection.

The database manager also may have disabled replication temporarily for the database. Check with the manager for that database to see whether you can replicate it later. You also may not have access granted to replicate a particular database. Contact the manager of the database to make sure you have access to it.

No Replication Occurred

Problem. You included several databases in a database exchange, but the Exchange Statistics dialog box displayed after an exchange shows that the number of databases replicated is one less than expected.

Explanation. One of the databases in your selection didn't replicate successfully. To find out which database didn't replicate, you need to replicate each individually until you find the one that doesn't work. Problems with the Access Control List for the database may prevent you from replicating it. Make sure that the server is granted at least Designer level access on your local replica of the database.

Look for a message in the Replication Events document in your Notes log. The database also may not be a true replica of the database on the server. Choose File, Database, Properties, and Replication settings for your local replica and the server's database; also check to see that the replica IDs in the Replication Settings dialog box match. If they don't, remove the local replica by selecting it and choosing File, Database, Delete; then select Yes to acknowledge the deletion. Create a new replica (choose File, Replication, New Replica) and carry out another database exchange.

Replication Not as Expected

Problem. Databases didn't replicate as expected.

Explanation. Open the entry for the replication in the Replication Events view of the log to find out more about the replications made. If the problem is with Access Control settings, you or the server may not have appropriate access levels to exchange information. You must be assigned at least Editor level access on the server copy of the database, and the server must be assigned at least Manager level access on your local replica.

Contact your system administrator if changing the access levels doesn't relieve the access problem.

Another explanation may be that the database isn't a true replica of the database on the server. Choose File, Database, Properties, and Replication settings for your local replica and the server's database to see whether the replica IDs in the Replication Settings dialog box match. If they don't, select your local replica of the database and then remove the local replica by choosing File, Database, Delete; then choose Yes to acknowledge the deletion. Create a new replica (choose File, Replication, New Replica) and carry out another database exchange.

Problems in Interactive Connection Sessions

If you are trying to work interactively with the server, the following two problems may occasionally occur:

- You get Access Denied messages for database(s) you want to work with.
- You get Access Denied messages when trying to access a server.

The following sections address these problems.

No Access to Database

Problem. You see a message indicating that you don't have access to a particular database.

Explanation. Check with the database manager to see whether you can be assigned appropriate access rights to work on the database.

No Access to Server

Problem. When you try to dial a server, you get a message that you don't have access to it.

Explanation. Check with the server administrator to see whether you can be given access to this server. Make sure that your Notes ID certification hasn't expired—or that you have not been specifically denied access from the server as well.

Problems Sending and Receiving Mail

If you work remote, some special problems that relate directly to using NotesMail may occur. The following sections review the most common problems that occur and provide explanations on how to resolve them.

Name Not Found

Problem. When you send a mail message, you get a message that the recipient's name cannot be found in any address book during an interactive connection session.

Explanation. Notes tried to look up the person specified in the To field of your document, but cannot find an entry for that person. First, check the spelling of the name. If you know the name is valid, notify the Notes administrator.

No Mail File Specified

Problem. You try to send or receive mail and receive a message that no mail file has been specified.

Explanation. You cannot use mail without first specifying a mail file in the Mail Setup dialog box. Choose File, Tools, User Preferences and select the Mail icon. Enter your mail file directory and name. If an entry already is there, make sure that it's spelled correctly. Notes is case-sensitive with this entry.

Outgoing Mail Database Missing

Problem. Your Outgoing Mail database icon (MAIL.BOX) is missing.

Explanation. You may have accidentally removed the icon from your workspace. Try choosing File, Database, Open. Select your Local Notes directory in the Server list box, type **MAIL.BOX** in the Filename text box, choose Add Icon, and then choose Done.

If that doesn't work, the database no longer exists on your hard disk. Follow these instructions in Chapter 18, "Setting Up To Go Remote" to create a new MAIL.BOX file.

APPENDIX G

Using the CD-ROM

The CD-ROM enclosed with this manual has been provided to give you the entire *Special Edition Using Lotus Notes 4* book online, with demo applications, troubleshooting databases, and additional information on Lotus Companion and third-party applications. You will find a host of screencams, applications, technical documents, and more—all stored within a single Notes database on the CD-ROM. You simply have to open the Notes database on the CD-ROM, read through the documents to see what is attached, and then detach and/or launch the file attachments to use them. Each document in the database that contains a file attachment provides instructions on how you might want to work with that file, as well as a brief description of the application.

In addition to this book being provided to you in its entirety, the following table provides you a sneak peek into what is available on the CD-ROM.

Program/File	Contributor
Databases	
Advanced Help 1.2 Demo	Marshall Consulting, Inc.
ALI Design Analyzer	ALI Technologies, Inc.
Companies & Contacts	Marshall Consulting, Inc.
Mobile Survival Kit	Lotus Development Corporation
Notes Reporter Evaluation Guide	Lotus Development Corporation
Number Generator Demo	Marshall Consulting, Inc.
Personal Calendar	Marshall Consulting, Inc.
Project Working Papers	Marshall Consulting, Inc.
Sentinel v.3.5	Mayflower Software
Sentinel v.4	Mayflower Software

(continues)

(continued)

Program/File	Contributor
Databases	
SmartForm Modem Doctor	Lotus Development Corporation
WorldCom's Help & Services	WorldCom
WorldCom's Setup	WorldCom
Demo Programs	
CleverWatch	CleverSoft
OpenInsight	RevelationTechnologies
Sentinel v.3.5	Mayflower Software
Sentinel v.4	Mayflower Software
TLG CoPilot	ENTEX Information Services, Inc.
ViP For Lotus Notes	RevelationTechnologies
Screencams	
ALI Design Analyzer	ALI Technologies, Inc.
EtQ Solutions	EtQ Management Consultants, Inc.
GroupFocus	Business Evolution, Inc.
Launch for LN:DI	U.S Technologies
NotesView	Lotus Development Corporation
Phone Notes	Lotus Development Corporation
TLG CoPilot	ENTEX Information Services, Inc.
WorldCom's Basic Services	WorldCom
Utilities	
Acrobat Reader	Adobe Systems Incorporated
ScreenCam Player 2.0 File	Lotus Development Corporation

All of this is included, plus Lotus screencams, white papers, and more!

Working with the Database

Because all of the files on this CD are located in a single Notes database, accessing these files is as easy as opening any other Notes database. Perform the following steps to access the *Special Edition Using Lotus Notes 4* database:

   1. Select File, Database, Open. The Open Database dialog box appears (see fig. G.1).

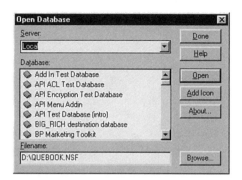

Fig. G.1

Open the database from the CD-ROM to begin exploring the wealth of information contributed from a wide range of sources.

2. Type **D:\QUEBOOK.NSF** in the Filename box as shown in fig. G.1. (Substitute your CD-ROM drive designation for *D:* if necessary to access your CD-ROM drive.)

3. Select Open.

Notes will open the *Special Edition Using Lotus Notes 4* database for you to review its contents. Instructions for using specific files attached to the documents in this database are provided within each document in the "Using This Demo" section. Read through this section to understand how to work with a particular file.

When you exit the database, Notes will leave its icon on your workspace for future use of the database—double-click the icon to open all subsequent accesses to this database. Keep in mind that you will need the CD-ROM accompanying this book in your CD-ROM drive when accessing the database—unless you copied the database to your workspace.

Index

Symbols

A

C

M

X-Y-Z

Complete and Return this Card
for a *FREE* Computer Book Catalo

Thank you for purchasing this book! You have purchased a superior computer book written expressly for your needs. To continue to provide the kind of up-to-date, pertinent coverage you've come to expect from us, we need to hear from you. Please take a minute to complete and return this self-addressed, postage-paid form. In return, we'll send you a free catalog of all our computer books on topics ranging from word processing to programming and the internet.

Mr. ☐   Mrs. ☐   Ms. ☐   Dr. ☐

Name (first) ☐☐☐☐☐☐☐☐☐☐☐☐   (M.I.) ☐   (last) ☐☐☐☐☐☐☐☐☐☐☐☐☐☐☐

Address ☐☐☐☐☐☐☐☐☐☐☐☐☐☐☐☐☐☐☐☐☐☐☐☐☐☐☐☐☐

☐☐☐☐☐☐☐☐☐☐☐☐☐☐☐☐☐☐☐☐☐☐☐☐☐☐☐☐☐

City ☐☐☐☐☐☐☐☐☐☐☐☐   State ☐☐   Zip ☐☐☐☐☐   ☐☐☐☐

Phone ☐☐☐ ☐☐☐ ☐☐☐☐   Fax ☐☐☐ ☐☐☐ ☐☐☐☐

Company Name ☐☐☐☐☐☐☐☐☐☐☐☐☐☐☐☐☐☐☐☐☐☐☐☐☐

E-mail address ☐☐☐☐☐☐☐☐☐☐☐☐☐☐☐☐☐☐☐☐☐☐☐☐☐

1. Please check at least (3) influencing factors for purchasing this book.

Front or back cover information on book .... ☐
Special approach to the content .... ☐
Completeness of content .... ☐
Author's reputation .... ☐
Publisher's reputation .... ☐
Book cover design or layout .... ☐
Index or table of contents of book .... ☐
Price of book .... ☐
Special effects, graphics, illustrations .... ☐
Other (Please specify): _____ ☐

2. How did you first learn about this book?

Saw in Macmillan Computer Publishing catalog .... ☐
Recommended by store personnel .... ☐
Saw the book on bookshelf at store .... ☐
Recommended by a friend .... ☐
Received advertisement in the mail .... ☐
Saw an advertisement in: _____ ☐
Read book review in: _____ ☐
Other (Please specify): _____ ☐

3. How many computer books have you purchased in the last six months?

This book only .... ☐   3 to 5 books .... ☐
2 books .... ☐   More than 5 .... ☐

4. Where did you purchase this book?

Bookstore .... ☐
Computer Store .... ☐
Consumer Electronics Store .... ☐
Department Store .... ☐
Office Club .... ☐
Warehouse Club .... ☐
Mail Order .... ☐
Direct from Publisher .... ☐
Internet site .... ☐
Other (Please specify): _____ ☐

5. How long have you been using a computer?

☐ Less than 6 months   ☐ 6 months to a year
☐ 1 to 3 years   ☐ More than 3 years

6. What is your level of experience with personal computers and with the subject of this book?

	With PCs	With subject of book
New	☐	☐
Casual	☐	☐
Accomplished	☐	☐
Expert	☐	☐

Source Code ISBN: 0-7897-0368-8

Which of the following best describes your job title?

~~~
...ministrative Assistant ............................................ ☐
...oordinator .......................................................... ☐
...anager/Supervisor .............................................. ☐
...rector ............................................................... ☐
...ce President ...................................................... ☐
...esident/CEO/COO .............................................. ☐
...wyer/Doctor/Medical Professional ......................... ☐
...eacher/Educator/Trainer ...................................... ☐
...ngineer/Technician ............................................. ☐
...onsultant ........................................................... ☐
...ot employed/Student/Retired ................................ ☐
...ther (Please specify): _____ ☐
~~~

Which of the following best describes the area of the company your job title falls under?

~~~
...ccounting ......................................................... ☐
...ngineering ........................................................ ☐
...anufacturing ..................................................... ☐
...perations .......................................................... ☐
...arketing ........................................................... ☐
...ales ................................................................. ☐
...ther (Please specify): _____ ☐
~~~

Comments: _____

_____

9. What is your age?

~~~
Under 20 .......................................................... ☐
21-29 ............................................................... ☐
30-39 ............................................................... ☐
40-49 ............................................................... ☐
50-59 ............................................................... ☐
60-over ............................................................. ☐
~~~

10. Are you:

~~~
Male ................................................................ ☐
Female ............................................................. ☐
~~~

11. Which computer publications do you read regularly? (Please list)

_____

_____

_____

_____

_____

_____

_____

_____

Fold here and scotch-tape to mail.

Licensing Agreement

By opening this package, you are agreeing to be bound by the following:

This software product is copyrighted, and all rights are reserved by the publisher and author. You are licensed to use this software on a single computer. You may copy and/or modify the software as needed to facilitate your use of it on a single computer. Making copies of the software for any other purpose is a violation of the United States copyright laws.

This software is sold *as is* without warranty of any kind, either express or implied, including but not limited to the implied warranties of merchantability and fitness for a particular purpose. Neither the publisher nor its dealers or distributors assumes any liability for any alleged or actual damages arising from the use of this program. (Some states do not allow for the exclusion of implied warranties, so the exclusion may not apply to you.)